The 2023-24 NBA Preview Almanac

BY

RICHARD LU

Credits:

Additional Scouting and Editing:
Alan Lu

Stats and Information:
Basketball-Reference.com
Synergy Sports
Spotrac
notradeclause.com
RealGM
prosportstransactions.com/basketball
NBA.com/stats
82games.com
addmorefunds.com/nba/wowy
hoopsrumors.com Two-Way Tracker

Cover:
Hayley Faye, fayefayedesigns on fiverr.com
Cover Photo based on a photo retrieved from:
    https://wallpapercave.com/drazen-petrovic-wallpapers, photo credit unavailable

Back Cover:
Josh Springer
The Candid Crow, joshspringerphotography.com

For all comments, questions, and requests, you can reach the author by email at lurv82@gmail.com, or you can find on the application formerly known as Twitter as @rvlhoops.

If you interested in the author's past work, please go to: www.amazon.com/author/rvlhoops

Table of Contents

Welcome to The 2023-24 NBA Preview Almanac	3
Explaining the Player Projection Pages	5
2022-23 Points Prevented Leaders	8
2023-24 Eastern Conference Preview	23
Boston Celtics	24
Milwaukee Bucks	39
Philadelphia 76ers	56
Cleveland Cavaliers	72
New York Knicks	87
Miami Heat	103
Atlanta Hawks	118
Toronto Raptors	135
Brooklyn Nets	151
Chicago Bulls	168
Washington Wizards	185
Orlando Magic	203
Indiana Pacers	220
Charlotte Hornets	237
Detroit Pistons	254
2023-24 Western Conference Preview	270
Memphis Grizzlies	271
Golden State Warriors	290
New Orleans Pelicans	305
Los Angeles Lakers	321
Dallas Mavericks	336
Los Angeles Clippers	353
Minnesota Timberwolves	371
Denver Nuggets	387
Sacramento Kings	404
Phoenix Suns	421
Oklahoma City Thunder	438
Utah Jazz	459
Houston Rockets	476
San Antonio Spurs	491
Portland Trail Blazers	511
Unsigned Players	525
My 2023-24 NBA Predictions	531
Thank You	536
Alphabetical Player Index	537

Welcome to the 2023-24 NBA Preview Almanac

If this is the first time that you are reading one of my books, then I thank you for giving this a chance. If you have read or picked up one of my previous books, then welcome back and enjoy this preview of the upcoming 2023-24 NBA season. Generally speaking, this version of the season preview almanac will work similarly to the previous versions. Essentially, I will utilize insights that I have gained from years of meticulous research to provide you with loads of worthwhile information to prepare for this new season of NBA basketball. Specifically, I will take data from my own proprietary forecasting system to project and analyze the performance of each team and set of individual players. I will also discuss the results to help you understand the overall expectation levels of each team and get the proper perspective when looking at the performance level of any given player. Usually, this book is less writing intensive than my annual draft almanac because I have sort through a lot of data in a very short time frame. Due to the quick turn-around time, the individual projection pages are explained with short bullet-pointed notes instead of detailed prose to keep things understandable and concise. I also do this to avoid unnecessary re-hashing because this book deals with established NBA players instead of relatively unknown draft prospects. In the past few editions, I have included a review of defensive performance from the season before using a combination of some metrics that I have created and my own analysis. The metrics and the leaderboard from the previous season will still be in this book, but the analysis is now broken down by position and each subgroup will be briefly discussed with a short blurb. This way, the book can go more in-depth on teams than it did in the last few versions. With that being said, if you are already familiar with how my general process works, then you can jump ahead and dive right into the rest of this preview almanac. On the other hand, if you don't quite know how everything works, then the following will help to answer some common questions to give you a clearer idea of what to expect when you read this book.

1. *Who are you and what is your background?*

I have been intensively researching the NBA for almost two decades. Most notably, I provided consulting services to the Phoenix Suns and Chicago Bulls, with the NBA Draft serving as my main area of expertise. Based on this level of knowledge, I put out a draft almanac every year. With the Similarity Based Projection Model that I still use to analyze and evaluate draft prospects, I made a recommendation for the Bulls to use one of their first round picks in the 2011 NBA Draft to select Jimmy Butler out of Marquette University. In the time since that draft, Butler has exceeded all expectations and earned numerous accolades, including MVP of the 2022-23 Eastern Conference Finals, five All-NBA team selections, and six All-Star appearances in his career. Prior to that, I performed advanced lineup analytics to help the Suns in their run to the Western Conference Finals in the 2009-10 season. My primary contribution was that my metrics pointed out a critical defensive switch in the team's first round series against Portland, which swung the momentum back in favor of the Suns. Specifically, the data indicated that the Suns' defense would improve if they used Grant Hill as Andre Miller's primary defender instead of Jason Richardson. Once the switch was made, Miller's effectiveness was largely neutralized, and Richardson thrived offensively due to the fact that he was freed from a difficult defensive responsibility. Richardson averaged over 25 points per game in the final five games, which was a major reason why the Suns got past the first round and made a deep playoff run that season. Based on my past experience and always growing knowledge of the game, I'm able to draw upon my background to give all of my readers a better understanding and a more meaningful insight into the intricacies of the NBA to providing the same type of high-end analysis that I used to assist front office personnel in the league.

2. Please explain your forecasting system. What is it and how does it work?

I had some success with my draft projection model, so I looked to build upon that by utilizing a similar methodology to create this forecasting system that projects the future performance of NBA players and teams. This system has had many different names and acronyms over the years. I eventually settled on calling it the **S**ystematized **C**omparison **H**euristic **R**ationalizing **E**mpirically **M**ethodical **P**erformance **F**orecasts, or **SCHREMPF**. This is named after former Seattle SuperSonics forward and two-time Sixth Man of the Year, Detlef Schrempf. From this point, I'll get into the basics of how this general methodology works. The system takes a weighted average of an established NBA player's stats over the most recent three-year period and uses statistical similarity to compare these numbers against all player seasons from the modern three-point era of the NBA, which covers the 1979-80 season to the present. I also project the performance of incoming rookies and newcomers from overseas by using a combination of forecasted metrics from my draft system and translated stats based on international league strength values that were determined through my research. After the model compares a player's stats against the database, it generates a baseline forecast of future performance based on a set of historical comparables. The bulk of the projected metrics in this book are rate statistics because raw counting stats are dependent on subjective factors like coaching decisions, which are pretty tough to objectively quantify. From here, I use the best estimate of the expected roles of various players and the team's potential playing time distribution to turn the system's forecasted baselines into a base rating of any given team's talent level. At the moment, I haven't found a quantifiable way to account for every variable that comes into play, so I'm not quite able to turn the base rating into a hardline win total projection. Instead, I choose to post each team's base rating and then analyze its legitimacy by taking all of the information at my disposal to estimate that specific team's possible regular season record. This projection system isn't perfect by any means, but the results can be a very helpful tool that gives you a clearer picture of what to expect in the NBA for this coming season.

    In a nutshell, this is basically how everything in this book works. The next section will explain the different metrics and abbreviations that you will see on the projection pages, if you don't already know what they are. If you are familiar with the information on the projection pages, then you can freely skip ahead and jump into all of the projections. As a small disclaimer, I'm not claiming that every projection in this book is going to be perfectly correct. The future is very hard to predict and even the most accurate of projection model can get some things wrong. However, I will assure you that the material in this almanac will provide you with a deeper and more in-depth understanding of the upcoming NBA season by giving you a detailed breakdown of all 30 teams and comprehensive analysis into the projected performance of every current NBA player. If you want the best possible information to get you ready for the new 2023-24 NBA season, or if you just want to gain a greater appreciation of the game of basketball, then read the rest of this book and enjoy The 2023-24 NBA Preview Almanac.

Explaining the Player Projection Pages

If you have read any of my past preview almanacs and you already know how everything works, then you can simply go ahead and dive into all of the different projections in the rest of this book. Otherwise, this section will explain the set of metrics and abbreviations that you will see on the projection page of any given NBA player. To do this, I will walk you through a sample projection to help you understand the different things that you will see on these pages.

Player A [1]

	Height	Weight	Cap #	Years Left
	6'4"	195	$$$$	##

Similar at Age 26

[2]		Season	SIMsc
1	David Thompson*	1980-81	865.0
2	Cedric Ceballos	1995-96	859.1
3	Dennis Johnson*	1980-81	850.1
4	Dan Roundfield	1979-80	844.6
5	Reggie Lewis	1991-92	844.2
6	Darrell Griffith	1984-85	843.6
7	Cuttino Mobley	2001-02	842.9
8	Chris Mullin*	1989-90	842.2
9	Sidney Moncrief*	1983-84	841.4
10	CJ McCollum	2017-18	839.6

Baseline Basic Stats [3]

MPG	PTS	AST	REB	BLK	STL
35.3	19.9	3.2	4.9	0.6	1.3

Advanced Metrics [4]

USG%	3PTA/FGA	FTA/FGA	TS%	eFG%	3PT%
25.1	0.080	0.418	0.574	0.516	0.238

AST%	TOV%	OREB%	DREB%	STL%	BLK%
13.4	9.8	6.7	17.9	1.8	3.1

PER	ORTG	DRTG	WS/48	BPM	VOL
23.57	116.0	100.0	0.261	0.39	0.451

[1] – The top row gives you some basic information like the player's name as well as their listed height and weight. It also displays their current cap number and the number of years that are left on that player's contract after this season. There are several abbreviations that may be listed in the Years Left section and they are as follows:

- PO = Player Option
- TO = Team Option
- ETO = Early Termination Option
- UFA = Unrestricted Free Agent
- RFA = Restricted Free Agent

[2] – This list is the set of the ten most statistically similar players at any given age. The number on the right, abbreviated as SIMsc, is the Similarity Score. This tells you how similar the listed comparable is to the player. The Similarity Scores are taken out of 1000. A score of 900 would represent a 90% degree of similarity. I used 1000 instead of 100 to make the differences between players more distinct. An asterisk indicates that the comparable is currently in the Hall of Fame.

[3] – This row is a weighted average of the player's projected basic per-game stats, based on a composite of the comparables used by the system. The measured composite uses more data points than the ten comparables that are listed on the projection page.

[4] – These three rows show the player's projected advanced stats. Here is what each abbreviation and metric means:

USG%, Usage Percentage – An estimate of the percentage of team plays used by the player while he's on the floor.

3PTA/FGA, Three-Point Attempts per Field Goal Attempt

FTA/FGA, Free Throw Attempts per Field Goal Attempt

TS%, True Shooting Percentage – A measure of shooting efficiency that accounts for field goals, threes, and free throws.

eFG%, Effective Field Goal Percentage – A measure of field goal shooting efficiency that accounts for the additional point value of a three-pointer.

AST%, Assist Percentage – An estimate of the percentage of teammate field goals a player assisted on while he was on the floor.

TOV%, Turnover Percentage – An estimate of turnovers per 100 plays.

OREB%, Offensive Rebound Percentage – An estimate of the percentage of offensive rebounds a player grabbed while he was on the floor.

DREB%, Defensive Rebound Percentage – An estimate of the percentage of defensive rebounds a player grabbed while he was on the floor.

STL%, Steal Percentage – An estimate of the percentage of opponent possessions that ended in a steal by the player while he was on the floor.

BLK%, Block Percentage – An estimate of the percentage of opponent two-point field goal attempts that were blocked by the player while he was on the floor.

PER, Player Efficiency Rating – A linear weights rating developed by John Hollinger that sums up all of a player's positive box score accomplishments and subtracts the negative ones to return a per-minute rating of a player's performance. The built-in average is 15.

ORTG, Offensive Rating – An estimation of points produced per 100 possessions.

DRTG, Defensive Rating – An estimation of points allowed per 100 possessions.

WS/48, Win Shares per 48 Minutes – An estimate of the number of wins contributed by the player per 48 minutes. The league average is approximately 0.100.

BPM, Box Plus-Minus – A box score estimate of the points per 100 possessions that a player contributed above a league-average player, translated to an average team.

VOL, Volatility Rating – My personal metric to measure the level of variability within a given projection. A lower number means that the performance of the comparables is within a reasonable range of the projected metrics. A higher value means that the performance of the comparables varies considerably, and the range is either significantly higher or lower than the projected metrics. A value above 0.400 would be considered volatile.

After you see all of the metrics, there are a series of bullet-pointed notes that will provide you with a brief scouting report on the player. The idea behind this is to give you a better idea of who any given player is and what you can reasonably expect from him this upcoming season. This is basically all that you need to know about these projection pages. From this point, we can move on to the rest of this book. The next section will feature a data set of the two primary defensive metrics that I introduced in the most recent editions of this preview almanac to provide you with some insight into some individual defensive performances from last season. After that, we will move forward with the preview of the 2023-24 season, starting with the Eastern Conference.

2022-23 Points Prevented Leaders

For the past few seasons, I have been tracking individual performance for on-ball defense using a series of created metrics. The first of these metrics is Defensive Degree of Difficulty, **DDD**, which measures the difficulty level of a defender's set of matchups throughout the season. A higher value indicates that the player defended tougher assignments than a player with a lower value. Then, the next metric is **Points Prevented**, which tracks the player's ability to force misses while accounting for the difficulty level of any given matchup. The leaders of this particular stat are listed below. This value is technically, Points Prevented per 100 Partial Possessions, but the name was shortened for the purpose of simplicity. To qualify for this leaderboard, a player had to play 500 or more minutes. This time around, the qualifying players will be sorted by their listed position on Basketball-Reference. If a player was listed at two positions, then they would fall under the category of their most commonly played position. As a final note, a number in parentheses indicates a negative number.

Point Guards

- Defensive Degree of Difficulty ratings above 0.500

	Pos	Team	MP	DDD	PTS Prevented
Jrue Holiday	PG	MIL	2183	0.560	1.924
Dennis Schröder	PG	LAL	1986	0.548	1.206
Alex Caruso	PG	CHI	1575	0.572	0.949
Jevon Carter	PG	MIL	1810	0.512	0.720
Markelle Fultz	PG	ORL	1778	0.523	(0.148)
Marcus Smart	PG	BOS	1957	0.553	(0.733)
Kevin Porter Jr.	PG	HOU	2024	0.511	(0.997)

A few names stand out after looking at this cross-section. First off, Jrue Holiday's presence at the top reaffirms his status as one of the game's best defensive guards. The interesting thing to note is also the inclusion of Jevon Carter in this group of highly productive defensive point guards because Carter and Holiday often played together in smaller lineups for Milwaukee last season. As a result, Holiday spent the bulk of the season as his team's main defensive stopper, which meant that he had to assume a heavier workload by defending elite wings in addition to traditional point guard types. His quality defense at the point of attack has been a lynchpin for Milwaukee's defense in recent years, so his continued proficiency in these metrics confirms this notion considerably. Along those lines, Alex Caruso justified his inclusion to last season's All-Defensive Team. Like Holiday, Caruso became Chicago's primary shutdown defender on the perimeter, and he held up very well to the point where he often held his opponent to a below average level of efficiency. Then, Dennis Schroder had a surprisingly good defensive year because historically, he hasn't been thought of as an elite defender. However, last season, he embraced his new role and reinvented himself as a pest that could make opposing point guards uncomfortable to the point where it would disrupt their performance. This showed in the playoffs because Schroder did an excellent job containing Ja Morant and Stephen Curry in consecutive series. Finally, Marcus Smart's negative Points Prevented value is probably not a major red flag because he's been a good defender in previous seasons. However, this could be a hint that his defense is slipping a bit because he took on fewer high-difficulty assignments in 2021-22 due to the team's switch heavy scheme. Additionally, he wasn't quite the stopper that he was in the past when his matchups got harder last season. It will be interesting to see how he performs in a new environment to possibly counter any slippage on the defensive end of the floor this upcoming season.

- Defensive Degree of Difficulty Ratings between 0.400 and 0.499

	Pos	Team	MP	DDD	PTS Prevented
Dyson Daniels	PG	NOP	1042	0.443	2.257
George Hill	PG	TOT	834	0.436	2.130
Ja Morant	PG	MEM	1948	0.404	1.907
Russell Westbrook	PG	TOT	2126	0.456	1.347
Dennis Smith Jr.	PG	CHH	1390	0.462	1.309
Ben Simmons	PG	BRK	1105	0.493	1.222
Miles McBride	PG	NYK	760	0.417	1.166
Jose Alvarado	PG	NOP	1310	0.442	0.997
James Harden	PG	PHI	2135	0.443	0.867
Shai Gilgeous-Alexander	PG	OKC	2416	0.414	0.795
Kyrie Irving	PG	TOT	2241	0.454	0.785
T.J. McConnell	PG	IND	1526	0.425	0.638
D'Angelo Russell	PG	TOT	2304	0.404	0.590
Cole Anthony	PG	ORL	1552	0.400	0.457
Monte Morris	PG	WAS	1695	0.471	0.314
Kris Dunn	PG	UTA	568	0.463	0.118
Malcolm Brogdon	PG	BOS	1744	0.423	0.117
Davion Mitchell	PG	SAC	1447	0.472	(0.027)
Mike Conley	PG	TOT	2029	0.493	(0.141)
Stephen Curry	PG	GSW	1941	0.418	(0.153)
Collin Sexton	PG	UTA	1145	0.449	(0.214)
Gabe Vincent	PG	MIA	1759	0.454	(0.214)
Darius Garland	PG	CLE	2447	0.419	(0.261)
Reggie Jackson	PG	TOT	1657	0.427	(0.312)
Delon Wright	PG	WAS	1221	0.480	(0.368)
Kyle Lowry	PG	MIA	1718	0.456	(0.401)
Fred VanVleet	PG	TOR	2535	0.496	(0.438)
Tre Jones	PG	SAS	1984	0.472	(0.559)
Damian Lillard	PG	POR	2107	0.418	(0.739)
Jamal Murray	PG	DEN	2133	0.451	(0.766)
De'Aaron Fox	PG	SAC	2435	0.466	(0.834)
Jordan Goodwin	PG	WAS	1106	0.401	(0.873)
Killian Hayes	PG	DET	2154	0.460	(1.314)

The name that jumps out in this group is Dyson Daniels at the top because he excelled in starter level matchups, even though he mostly played in a limited bench role in his rookie season. His defensive performance was impressive enough to allow him to draw some high-end assignments against some of the most potent offensive perimeter players in the league. In a relatively small sample, he flashed the potential to develop into a future stopper because he held Devin Booker, Shai Gilgeous-Alexander, and Jamal Murray to efficiency levels that were below their usual average. He mainly accomplished this because of his excellent combination of length, athleticism, and ball-hawking instincts. He can apply pressure, contest shots, and make a lot of plays on the ball to force turnovers. If he can build on his strong defensive performance from his rookie season, he could emerge as an elite defensive performer in the near future.

- Defensive Degree of Difficulty ratings that are below 0.400

	Pos	Team	MP	DDD	PTS Prevented
Payton Pritchard	PG	BOS	643	0.334	1.677
Ricky Rubio	PG	CLE	566	0.283	1.191
Goran Dragić	PG	TOT	870	0.279	0.777
Luka Dončić	PG	DAL	2391	0.399	0.718
Chris Paul	PG	PHO	1889	0.393	0.012
Tre Mann	PG	OKC	1183	0.271	(0.169)
John Wall	PG	LAC	755	0.390	(0.215)
Trae Young	PG	ATL	2541	0.384	(0.281)
Jordan Poole	PG	GSW	2458	0.375	(0.447)
Aaron Holiday	PG	ATL	845	0.390	(0.488)
Tyus Jones	PG	MEM	1940	0.323	(0.552)
Devonte' Graham	PG	TOT	1338	0.353	(0.554)
Cameron Payne	PG	PHO	968	0.358	(0.637)
LaMelo Ball	PG	CHH	1268	0.386	(0.683)
Tyrese Haliburton	PG	IND	1883	0.394	(0.700)
Bones Hyland	PG	TOT	1085	0.313	(0.831)
Jordan McLaughlin	PG	MIN	678	0.345	(0.865)
Cory Joseph	PG	DET	1227	0.394	(1.051)
Raul Neto	PG	CLE	505	0.313	(1.081)
Daishen Nix	PG	HOU	914	0.377	(1.275)
Malachi Flynn	PG	TOR	691	0.322	(1.277)
Jalen Brunson	PG	NYK	2379	0.393	(1.330)
Théo Maledon	PG	CHH	854	0.371	(1.861)
Patty Mills	PG	BRK	567	0.323	(2.344)

A lot of the point guards that are listed above are rotational backups, but some big names are in this group. The main reason for this is that their team usually hides them in easier matchups to either limit their exposure on defense or allow them to conserve energy to concentrate on offense. It makes sense that there weren't too many guards in this group with positive Points Prevented values. Luka Doncic did play effective on-ball defense in the few matchups where opponents looked to go after him, so he might be able to handle some increased responsibility to broaden his skill set. Aside from him, most of the starting level players in this group played neutral or below average defense to suggest that they could be targets for opponents to exploit. The presence at the bottom of this table is a pretty sizeable red flag for someone like Jalen Brunson because he could end up becoming an obvious weak link that drags down the defensive performance of his team in tight games or critical playoff series in the near future.

Shooting Guards

- Defensive Degree of Difficulty ratings above 0.500

	Pos	Team	MP	DDD	PTS Prevented
RJ Barrett	SG	NYK	2475	0.520	1.245
Josh Okogie	SG	PHO	1350	0.504	1.173
Ayo Dosunmu	SG	CHI	2098	0.504	0.837
Andrew Nembhard	SG	IND	2073	0.565	0.645
Dejounte Murray	SG	ATL	2693	0.522	0.582
Caris LeVert	SG	CLE	2237	0.501	0.308
Gary Harris	SG	ORL	1184	0.533	0.242
Quentin Grimes	SG	NYK	2121	0.610	(0.156)
De'Anthony Melton	SG	PHI	2150	0.592	(0.301)
Patrick Beverley	SG	TOT	1816	0.551	(0.402)
Kentavious Caldwell-Pope	SG	DEN	2381	0.517	(0.787)

For the most part, the two-guards in this section are quality defenders. A few of these players had negative Points Prevented values, but these values were not really indicative of poor performance. Instead, this meant that they were either over-extended by being forced to handle a tougher than normal workload on defense or that they were just unlucky. Out of the names on this list, the two members of the New York Knicks stand out. For starters, Quentin Grimes had the most difficult defensive workload in the league, as he almost exclusively guarded top scorers whenever he was on the floor. He played close to neutral defense in these matchups, so it's impressive enough to suggest that he could warrant consideration for an All-Defensive Team appearance in the future if he can continue to improve his defense against high-end scorers as his career progresses. In addition to Grimes, RJ Barrett wound up as the leader on this list due to his improved ability to defend high difficulty assignments. He continued his ascension into being a shutdown level perimeter defender by improving upon his performance from the season before, so it's very possible that he could garner some All-Defensive consideration as well. From there, Andrew Nembhard had a sneaky good defensive season as a rookie. He showed that he could hold his own against elite scoring guards and wings, so he might be able to build on this to make a bigger impact on defense in his second year. As a final note, Josh Okogie had a good season on defense in a limited rotational role with Phoenix. This is important because he re-signed with the Suns this past off season, and due to their current roster construction, they are lacking depth and quality defensive personnel. This means that Okogie could be a major part of their rotation this upcoming season because he stands to become the Suns' de facto defensive stopper. He had some struggles when he was placed in this role in his early years in Minnesota, but he was very young at the time and still figuring out his game. At this stage, he seems to have matured and embraced his role as an energetic defensive specialist. He could end up playing more important minutes than expected if he continues to defend as effectively as he did last season.

- Defensive Degree of Difficulty ratings between 0.400 and 0.499

	Pos	Team	MP	DDD	PTS Prevented
Derrick White	SG	BOS	2319	0.487	2.657
Zach LaVine	SG	CHI	2768	0.430	1.766
Ochai Agbaji	SG	UTA	1209	0.471	1.756
Nickeil Alexander-Walker	SG	TOT	884	0.465	1.642
Max Christie	SG	LAL	512	0.438	1.616
Austin Reaves	SG	LAL	1843	0.441	1.590
Desmond Bane	SG	MEM	1841	0.450	1.364
Bradley Beal	SG	WAS	1673	0.470	1.152
Bogdan Bogdanović	SG	ATL	1508	0.400	1.040
Jordan Clarkson	SG	UTA	1988	0.448	0.984
Jalen Suggs	SG	ORL	1246	0.456	0.961
Terance Mann	SG	LAC	1872	0.492	0.898
Anfernee Simons	SG	POR	2171	0.458	0.727
Anthony Edwards	SG	MIN	2842	0.475	0.618
Devin Booker	SG	PHO	1835	0.424	0.580
CJ McCollum	SG	NOP	2649	0.431	0.487
Tyler Herro	SG	MIA	2337	0.426	0.455
Talen Horton-Tucker	SG	UTA	1313	0.443	0.370
Grayson Allen	SG	MIL	1972	0.450	0.316
Rodney McGruder	SG	DET	524	0.437	0.149
Jalen Green	SG	HOU	2602	0.460	0.059
Donte DiVincenzo	SG	GSW	1894	0.467	0.021
Eric Gordon	SG	TOT	1965	0.480	(0.012)
Bennedict Mathurin	SG	IND	2222	0.414	(0.064)
Donovan Mitchell	SG	CLE	2432	0.430	(0.109)
Tyrese Maxey	SG	PHI	2016	0.444	(0.239)
Gary Trent Jr.	SG	TOR	2118	0.421	(0.424)
Lonnie Walker IV	SG	LAL	1297	0.466	(0.463)
Devin Vassell	SG	SAS	1178	0.427	(0.691)
Josh Green	SG	DAL	1539	0.427	(0.698)
Victor Oladipo	SG	MIA	1106	0.427	(0.840)
Romeo Langford	SG	SAS	844	0.462	(0.885)
Josh Richardson	SG	TOT	1530	0.452	(1.166)
Jalen Williams	SG	OKC	2276	0.433	(1.166)
Kevin Huerter	SG	SAC	2203	0.411	(1.244)
Jaden Ivey	SG	DET	2304	0.423	(1.307)
Austin Rivers	SG	MIN	1016	0.493	(1.318)
Aaron Wiggins	SG	OKC	1297	0.415	(1.897)
Spencer Dinwiddie	SG	TOT	2725	0.411	(1.977)

Derrick White stands head and shoulders above everyone on this list because he emerged to become one of the best defenders on the Celtics. His performance was so great that Boston felt that they could trade away Marcus Smart in the offseason. White has been a good defender throughout his career, so he is capable of handling the role of being Boston's stopper this upcoming season. As for the other notable names on this list, Ochai Agbaji put in a strong rookie season in a limited role to suggest that he could have a future as a possible defensive stopper. He did a great job in a small sample of possessions against Jayson Tatum, Anthony Edwards, and Ja Morant last season. If he continues to trend upwards on defense, he could become a high-end stopper as soon as next season. In addition to this, Max Christie defended well in a limited number of minutes against starter level competition. There's a chance that he could take a leap forward to becoming a more impactful defender if he continues to develop for the Lakers.

- Defensive Degree of Difficulty ratings below 0.400

	Pos	Team	MP	DDD	PTS Prevented
Immanuel Quickley	SG	NYK	2344	0.389	2.143
Frank Ntilikina	SG	DAL	607	0.386	2.110
James Bouknight	SG	CHH	515	0.324	1.810
Christian Braun	SG	DEN	1181	0.386	1.342
Garrison Mathews	SG	TOT	686	0.283	1.318
Moses Moody	SG	GSW	817	0.352	1.136
Luke Kennard	SG	TOT	1315	0.351	1.086
Cam Thomas	SG	BRK	948	0.336	1.028
Lindy Waters III	SG	OKC	531	0.290	0.839
R.J. Hampton	SG	TOT	750	0.359	0.563
Landry Shamet	SG	PHO	807	0.397	0.238
Malik Beasley	SG	TOT	2093	0.394	0.203
Damion Lee	SG	PHO	1506	0.346	0.028
Isaiah Joe	SG	OKC	1395	0.313	(0.144)
Jaden Hardy	SG	DAL	708	0.305	(0.188)
Malik Monk	SG	SAC	1719	0.322	(0.230)
Alec Burks	SG	DET	1122	0.382	(0.288)
Norman Powell	SG	LAC	1567	0.373	(0.486)
Bryce McGowens	SG	CHH	787	0.337	(0.618)
Seth Curry	SG	BRK	1211	0.350	(0.669)
Coby White	SG	CHI	1730	0.365	(1.005)
Terrence Ross	SG	TOT	1330	0.371	(1.023)
Blake Wesley	SG	SAS	669	0.331	(1.087)
Malaki Branham	SG	SAS	1550	0.377	(1.107)
Shake Milton	SG	PHI	1567	0.354	(1.158)
Josh Christopher	SG	HOU	786	0.337	(1.163)
Ty Jerome	SG	GSW	816	0.341	(1.236)
Jaylen Nowell	SG	MIN	1252	0.342	(1.574)
Shaedon Sharpe	SG	POR	1779	0.377	(1.640)
Terence Davis	SG	SAC	841	0.388	(1.803)
Edmond Sumner	SG	BRK	736	0.390	(2.014)
Will Barton	SG	TOT	993	0.313	(2.019)
Kendrick Nunn	SG	TOT	964	0.355	(2.343)

The bulk of the players in this section are backups or rotational role players, so it's expected that they don't get higher-end defensive assignments. Out of this group, Immanuel Quickley stands out the most because he emerged to become one of the most productive bench players in the league last season, as he finished as the runner-up to Malcolm Brogdon for the Sixth Man of the Year Award. Quickley isn't like most sixth man types because he makes an impact on defense as well as offense. His high Points Prevented value suggests that he might be effective enough to take on more defensive responsibility and play a bigger role for the Knicks in the future. Along these lines, Christian Braun played solid defense in his situational backup role as a rookie. He came in and provided the Nuggets with a valuable injection of energy. He also showed that he could handle tougher assignments on a limited basis. This will be important for him this season because his role is going to be much larger due to the loss of Bruce Brown. If he can build upon his excellent playoff performance to become a reliable defender against higher-end matchups, it could allow the Nuggets to continue on without missing a beat. Otherwise, if his growth stunts in any way, it could force the Nuggets to make some kind of a decision to figure out how to fill Bruce Brown's vacancy as this upcoming season progresses.

Small Forwards

- Defensive Degree of Difficulty ratings above 0.500

	Pos	Team	MP	DDD	PTS Prevented
Gordon Hayward	SF	CHH	1577	0.504	1.369
Tobias Harris	SF	PHI	2436	0.530	1.211
Jaylen Brown	SF	BOS	2405	0.520	1.117
Dillon Brooks	SF	MEM	2214	0.594	1.089
Mikal Bridges	SF	TOT	2963	0.575	0.865
OG Anunoby	SF	TOR	2386	0.568	0.732
Luguentz Dort	SF	OKC	2272	0.592	0.623
Jae'Sean Tate	SF	HOU	677	0.509	0.581
Jaden McDaniels	SF	MIN	2416	0.583	0.556
Matisse Thybulle	SF	TOT	1200	0.556	0.227
Paul George	SF	LAC	1939	0.520	0.088
Deni Avdija	SF	WAS	2020	0.523	0.022
De'Andre Hunter	SF	ATL	2126	0.523	0.010
Reggie Bullock	SF	DAL	2364	0.518	(0.193)
Josh Hart	SF	TOT	2454	0.552	(0.373)
Andrew Wiggins	SF	GSW	1190	0.565	(0.650)
Isaac Okoro	SF	CLE	1652	0.561	(0.716)
Caleb Martin	SF	MIA	2077	0.532	(1.124)
Aaron Nesmith	SF	IND	1816	0.559	(2.530)

To start off, a lot of the league's most reputable defenders like Luguentz Dort, OG Anunoby, and Mikal Bridges appear in the top portion of the list. Also, Tobias Harris had a strong defensive campaign to justify his standing as a plus-level, two-way wing in the league. On top of this, Jaylen Brown improved to play shutdown level defense to go along with being an All-Star scorer. Dillon Brooks validated his All-Defensive Team appearance with effective on-ball defense against some of the most difficult matchups in the league. He has emerged as one of the better defenders in the league. However, it remains to be seen if his defense can offset his inefficiencies on offense and his problematic antics enough to justify his expensive new contract with Houston. Moving on, some younger players like Jaden McDaniels, Deni Avdija, and De'Andre Hunter emerged to play defense at an elite level last season. Also, Matisse Thybulle rebounded after he was buried on Philadelphia's bench by having a solid second half as a member of the Portland Trail Blazers. As for the players that had negative Points Prevented values, nothing really jumped out except for Caleb Martin and Aaron Nesmith. Martin was rather unlucky in the regular season, but his performance improved significantly as the Heat made their run to the Finals because he played solid defense against the likes Jayson Tatum, Jaylen Brown, and Jamal Murray. His playoff performance may be more indicative of his true talent level on defense, so he should be a plus-level defender next season and beyond. As for Nesmith, he was heavily over-extended as the Pacers started to fall out of the playoff hunt late last season. He took on a lot of matchups that were simply too difficult for him to handle, so he will benefit from the addition of Bruce Brown. Brown's presence will allow him to shift to lower leverage matchups that suit his defensive ability, which would help to increase his effectiveness next season. Finally, Gordon Hayward is a name to watch out for as the trade deadline approaches. His skills have diminished, but he still played elite defense last season. He also can space the floor and create offense for himself, so his skill set would be highly valuable to a contender. He's on an expiring contract and playing for a rebuilding team, so there's a chance that he will be moved. If his contract is too large to be traded, then he could be a highly sought-after player if he hits the buyout market, assuming he stays healthy to play in the playoffs.

- Defensive Degree of Difficulty ratings between 0.400 and 0.499

	Pos	Team	MP	DDD	PTS Prevented
John Konchar	SF	MEM	1494	0.438	1.927
Kawhi Leonard	SF	LAC	1748	0.498	1.409
Royce O'Neale	SF	BRK	2409	0.499	1.177
Bruce Brown	SF	DEN	2280	0.460	1.174
Hamidou Diallo	SF	DET	996	0.402	1.129
Buddy Hield	SF	IND	2482	0.461	0.965
Jayson Tatum	SF	BOS	2732	0.471	0.626
Khris Middleton	SF	MIL	801	0.423	0.597
Jalen Johnson	SF	ATL	1042	0.403	0.589
Tim Hardaway Jr.	SF	DAL	2152	0.479	0.380
Brandon Ingram	SF	NOP	1538	0.423	0.301
Michael Porter Jr.	SF	DEN	1798	0.408	0.188
Troy Brown Jr.	SF	LAL	1860	0.477	0.056
Klay Thompson	SF	GSW	2279	0.489	0.005
Jalen McDaniels	SF	TOT	1913	0.450	(0.015)
Wesley Matthews	SF	MIL	820	0.445	(0.020)
Chuma Okeke	SF	ORL	518	0.436	(0.058)
Scottie Barnes	SF	TOR	2678	0.495	(0.283)
Naji Marshall	SF	NOP	1792	0.483	(0.612)
Juan Toscano-Anderson	SF	TOT	700	0.464	(0.684)
Danuel House Jr.	SF	PHI	807	0.451	(0.697)
Franz Wagner	SF	ORL	2609	0.477	(0.746)
Amir Coffey	SF	LAC	625	0.411	(0.909)
Saddiq Bey	SF	TOT	2129	0.451	(0.968)
Keegan Murray	SF	SAC	2382	0.421	(1.095)
Trey Murphy III	SF	NOP	2448	0.425	(1.152)
Keldon Johnson	SF	SAS	2063	0.463	(1.228)
Kelly Oubre Jr.	SF	CHO	1548	0.469	(1.574)
Cam Reddish	SF	TOT	990	0.462	(1.615)

This section is filled with an interesting set of players. Some are stars that occasionally take on tough assignments, but usually take on moderate defensive workloads to ensure that they have enough energy to handle their considerable offensive responsibility. Within this group, players like Kawhi Leonard, Jayson Tatum, and Khris Middleton still rate as players that have the ability to play elite defense whenever it's necessary. However, they don't always need to defend with such a high level of intensity because they have teammates that can handle the hardest assignments on a regular basis. The other item to note is that Klay Thompson's defensive performance slipped last season in his first full year back from his injuries. He was handling a reduced workload in 2021-22 because he was just getting back into the rhythm of playing again after being away from the game for more than two years. Last season, he went back to his usual responsibilities on defense, but it appeared that a combination of age and decline due to injury slowed him down to the point where opposing players had more success whenever he was guarding them. Golden State will have to figure out a way to lighten his defensive workload to increase his on-court effectiveness in the coming years. Another name that stood out was John Konchar at the top. He's not typically seen as a high-end defender because he plays in a reserve role, and he rarely takes on difficult matchups. It's very possible that his performance was inflated because he was playing against other second unit players for a majority of the time. However, he did defend well in a small sample of matchups against quality scorers like Brandon Ingram, CJ McCollum, and Anthony Edwards, so he might be someone to watch out for if he emerges this upcoming season.

- Defensive Degree of Difficulty ratings below 0.400

	Pos	Team	MP	DDD	PTS Prevented
Pat Connaughton	SF	MIL	1443	0.356	2.783
Anthony Lamb	SF	GSW	1195	0.370	1.432
Cedi Osman	SF	CLE	1548	0.340	0.939
Ziaire Williams	SF	MEM	561	0.378	0.904
Sam Hauser	SF	BOS	1290	0.342	0.846
Joe Harris	SF	BRK	1527	0.372	0.538
Jabari Walker	SF	POR	619	0.305	0.523
MarJon Beauchamp	SF	MIL	701	0.365	0.471
Eugene Omoruyi	SF	TOT	645	0.372	0.374
Chris Duarte	SF	IND	897	0.346	0.318
Ish Wainright	SF	PHO	915	0.383	0.212
Kevin Knox	SF	TOT	952	0.358	(0.090)
Yuta Watanabe	SF	BRK	928	0.357	(0.126)
AJ Griffin	SF	ATL	1401	0.367	(0.261)
DeMar DeRozan	SF	CHI	2682	0.389	(0.332)
Caleb Houstan	SF	ORL	812	0.317	(0.366)
Justin Holiday	SF	TOT	706	0.349	(0.474)
Kenyon Martin Jr.	SF	HOU	2292	0.377	(0.729)
Corey Kispert	SF	WAS	2093	0.387	(0.966)
Joe Ingles	SF	MIL	1044	0.366	(1.021)
Nassir Little	SF	POR	976	0.399	(1.169)
Doug McDermott	SF	SAS	1314	0.313	(1.426)
Simone Fontecchio	SF	UTA	766	0.330	(1.458)
Max Strus	SF	MIA	2272	0.396	(2.106)
Jordan Nwora	SF	TOT	1188	0.369	(2.360)
Duncan Robinson	SF	MIA	691	0.331	(3.926)

There isn't much that is noteworthy with this group of players because it mostly consists of lower-end rotational role players that aren't really expected to take on difficult defensive assignments. The only starter level player in this table is DeMar DeRozan. This points out the level to which the Bulls hide him on defense, which may make him less valuable overall. As productive as he still is on offense, he may be giving back some points on the defensive end because opponents can hunt him on switches. Also, his vulnerabilities on defense may force his own team to bring extra help, which will allow opposing teams to get more open shots. These issues will continue to affect the Bulls whenever he's on the floor. If they can get creative to find other ways to cover him up, then they could try to move forward. Otherwise, they may need to rethink their roster construction and direction of their team to find a better pathway to contention. The other noteworthy name in this table is Pat Connaughton because his usage speaks to the inflexibility that was exposed in last season's playoffs. Though he played regularly, he was often shielded away from the important responsibilities because those tasks almost always went to either Jrue Holiday or Jevon Carter. The Bucks rarely switched or changed their looks, so they spent the majority of the time in drop coverages. Sticking to a singular strategy didn't hurt them in the regular season because they were simply playing teams that didn't have the firepower to exploit their inflexibility. However, the playoffs were another story. Specifically, Jimmy Butler broke Milwaukee's first line of defense and the Bucks had no way to adjust their rigid scheme to get back on track. They were ultimately eliminated in the first round, and they made a coaching change to switch things up. Milwaukee is largely depending on the coaching change to get them back into the title hunt, so it will be interesting to see how this affects their defensive tactics and how it impacts role players like Connaughton in the coming season.

Power Forwards

- Defensive Degree of Difficulty ratings above 0.500

	Pos	Team	MP	DDD	PTS Prevented
Torrey Craig	PF	PHO	1948	0.521	1.018
Dorian Finney-Smith	PF	TOT	2009	0.591	0.825
Aaron Gordon	PF	DEN	2055	0.531	0.740
Herbert Jones	PF	NOP	1951	0.606	0.516
Harrison Barnes	PF	SAC	2662	0.508	0.491
P.J. Tucker	PF	PHI	1920	0.599	0.131
Patrick Williams	PF	CHI	2323	0.535	(0.031)
Jimmy Butler	PF	MIA	2138	0.557	(0.280)
Marcus Morris	PF	LAC	1825	0.503	(0.311)
Jerami Grant	PF	POR	2246	0.534	(0.617)
Jeremy Sochan	PF	SAS	1458	0.512	(1.084)
Jarred Vanderbilt	PF	TOT	1879	0.511	(1.333)

For the most part, the players listed in the table above are some of the best defenders in the league. There aren't too many surprising names on this because almost every player in this group is someone that has traditionally been used to guard an elite scorer. Jeremy Sochan is the only rookie that's listed above. He was slightly over-extended in his minutes last season because San Antonio was in a rebuilding situation, and they didn't have too many quality defenders on their roster. He held his own in some matchups and he was over-matched in others. His defensive performance stands to improve because he'll have a year of experience under his belt, and he'll have better rim protection behind him in the presence of Victor Wembanyama. He could take another leap forward in his development to become an elite defender, and he could eventually work his way up to receiving All-Defensive Team consideration if he continues to trend upward in the coming years. The other notable name listed above is Herbert Jones. He took on the second most difficult set of matchups last season and he posted a positive Points Prevented value as well. This was an impressive feat that suggests that he was the most impactful on-ball defender in the NBA last season. His performance against top scorers backs up this idea. In fact, he held an impressive group of All-Star level scorers to a below average level of efficiency. This group included players like: Shai Gilgeous-Alexander, LeBron James, Luka Doncic, Kawhi Leonard, Pascal Siakam, and Ja Morant as well as several others. It was a shock that he wasn't named to either of the All-Defensive Teams, which indicates that there is still a considerable gap in recognizing players for their defensive performance. That being said, he has continued to improve to become one of the most well-rounded defenders in the NBA. As long as he doesn't show any signs of slipping, he should be a fixture on the All-Defensive Team for years to come.

- Defensive Degree of Difficulty ratings between 0.400 and 0.499

	Pos	Team	MP	DDD	PTS Prevented
Draymond Green	PF	GSW	2297	0.473	2.973
Aleksej Pokusevski	PF	OKC	701	0.413	2.690
Giannis Antetokounmpo	PF	MIL	2024	0.420	2.479
Maxi Kleber	PF	DAL	930	0.420	2.132
Kevin Durant	PF	TOT	1672	0.471	2.121
Haywood Highsmith	PF	MIA	969	0.458	1.649
Lauri Markkanen	PF	UTA	2273	0.469	1.518
Kyle Kuzma	PF	WAS	2239	0.485	1.299
Jonathan Kuminga	PF	GSW	1394	0.480	1.264
Evan Mobley	PF	CLE	2715	0.449	1.065
P.J. Washington	PF	CHO	2380	0.464	0.957
Keita Bates-Diop	PF	SAS	1452	0.448	0.692
Cameron Johnson	PF	TOT	1199	0.453	0.573
LeBron James	PF	LAL	1954	0.439	0.316
Paolo Banchero	PF	ORL	2430	0.455	0.270
Isaiah Livers	PF	DET	1199	0.483	0.210
Nicolas Batum	PF	LAC	1709	0.480	(0.127)
Dean Wade	PF	CLE	891	0.429	(0.251)
Justise Winslow	PF	POR	776	0.486	(0.356)
Kyle Anderson	PF	MIN	1957	0.462	(0.411)
Julius Randle	PF	NYK	2737	0.477	(0.805)
Trendon Watford	PF	POR	1182	0.411	(1.015)
John Collins	PF	ATL	2130	0.459	(1.028)
Bojan Bogdanović	PF	DET	1893	0.469	(1.082)
Pascal Siakam	PF	TOR	2652	0.445	(1.092)
Grant Williams	PF	BOS	2045	0.470	(1.100)
Jabari Smith Jr.	PF	HOU	2451	0.481	(1.224)
Kenrich Williams	PF	OKC	1206	0.447	(1.540)
Jeremiah Robinson-Earl	PF	OKC	814	0.448	(1.611)
Anthony Gill	PF	WAS	624	0.406	(1.832)
Tari Eason	PF	HOU	1767	0.403	(1.952)

The names at the top of this particular list consist of some of the most impactful roaming help defenders in the game. It shouldn't be much of a surprise to see Draymond Green's name at the top of this leaderboard because his ability to switch and provide help has been vital to Golden State's success in recent years. Also, Giannis Antetokounmpo and Evan Mobley show up, which indicates that they both are defenders that can make an impact by covering ground to play passing lanes and providing their respective teams with an extra layer of rim protection. Kevin Durant has also adapted his game to make a positive impact in this role. He's very effective at using his considerable length to block shots on the weak side, and he can occasionally take on tougher defensive matchups if his team needs him to guard an elite scorer on the ball. The most interesting name at the top of this list is Aleksej Pokusevski. His season was cut short because he suffered a fracture to his leg, but he was having a very productive year in the games when he was healthy. He improved significantly on both sides of the ball. This improvement really showed up on defense because he turned himself into a very effective help defender. He was especially good at rotating from the weak side to block shots because his Block Percentage nearly doubled. He also used his unique frame to his advantage because he could adequately switch to handle opponents across different positions to disrupt the opposition's rhythm. If he's able to recover from his latest arm injury, his roaming abilities could make Oklahoma City's defense even more stifling because he'll give them another layer of rim protection to go along with the shot blocking skills of Chet Holmgren.

- Defensive Degree of Difficulty ratings below 0.400

	Pos	Team	MP	DDD	PTS Prevented
Derrick Jones Jr.	PF	CHI	893	0.358	2.664
Rui Hachimura	PF	TOT	1466	0.375	2.451
Karl-Anthony Towns	PF	MIN	957	0.375	0.874
Zion Williamson	PF	NOP	956	0.385	0.867
Rudy Gay	PF	UTA	816	0.319	0.588
Santi Aldama	PF	MEM	1682	0.377	0.546
Brandon Clarke	PF	MEM	1090	0.351	0.494
Bobby Portis	PF	MIL	1818	0.376	0.415
Zeke Nnaji	PF	DEN	728	0.332	0.334
Ousmane Dieng	PF	OKC	569	0.229	0.295
JT Thor	PF	CHO	969	0.382	0.159
Bol Bol	PF	ORL	1505	0.368	0.084
David Roddy	PF	MEM	1258	0.370	0.080
Chris Boucher	PF	TOR	1523	0.307	0.015
Robert Covington	PF	LAC	779	0.371	(0.011)
Kevin Love	PF	TOT	1240	0.355	(0.338)
Obi Toppin	PF	NYK	1050	0.328	(0.397)
Dario Šarić	PF	TOT	806	0.336	(0.708)
Georges Niang	PF	PHI	1512	0.351	(0.712)
Josh Giddey	PF	OKC	2367	0.367	(0.932)
Oshae Brissett	PF	IND	1083	0.340	(0.998)
Vlatko Čančar	PF	DEN	889	0.325	(1.005)
Jeff Green	PF	DEN	1091	0.393	(1.063)
Taurean Prince	PF	MIN	1192	0.395	(1.108)
T.J. Warren	PF	TOT	687	0.348	(1.250)
Trey Lyles	PF	SAC	1247	0.309	(1.294)
Chimezie Metu	PF	SAC	689	0.348	(1.352)
Juancho Hernangómez	PF	TOR	614	0.365	(2.033)
JaMychal Green	PF	GSW	797	0.366	(3.450)
Thaddeus Young	PF	TOR	795	0.385	(3.698)

Derrick Jones Jr. and Rui Hachimura stand out because they were far more effective than every other player in this group. Jones has been used in a variety of roles throughout his career, including a few stretches as a defensive stopper. He still possesses elite athleticism and great ball-hawking instincts, so he was an impactful part of Chicago's defense as a roaming help defender with their second unit. Hachimura really found himself after the trade to the Lakers. He became an effective complement to the skills of Anthony Davis because he could make sound rotations inside to help erase mistakes. He also was effective enough in a switching scheme to adequately defend perimeter players for short stretches and defend the interior if it was necessary. From here, the other two interesting names in this table are Karl-Anthony Towns and Zion Williamson. Their respective teams took steps to hide them and reduce their defensive responsibility. This move helped to an extent because both Minnesota and New Orleans had upper-tier defenses. On the other hand, it remains to seen what the impact of hiding stars of this magnitude in lesser defensive roles could have if they have to play in critical playoff series, as they both could wind up being targets that opponents could exploit. To address this possible issue, the Timberwolves and Pelicans may have to find more ways to challenge Towns and Williamson on the defensive end to make them more well-rounded and better equipped to contribute on both ends of the floor on a more consistent basis.

Centers

- Defensive Degree of Difficulty ratings above 0.500

	Pos	Team	MP	DDD	PTS Prevented
Al Horford	C	BOS	1922	0.524	1.841
Mitchell Robinson	C	NYK	1591	0.512	0.939
Jarrett Allen	C	CLE	2220	0.501	0.771
Jusuf Nurkić	C	POR	1391	0.512	0.569
Clint Capela	C	ATL	1730	0.501	(0.100)
Wendell Carter Jr.	C	ORL	1690	0.513	(1.421)

This list is a fairly small one for a few reasons. For starters, there are fewer elite offensive big men in the league for the majority of centers to guard. As a result, the strength of an average center's set of matchups tends to be on the lower side. Also, the bulk of teams like to keep their centers close to the rim to serve as a shot blocking threat or a rebounding presence. Most teams don't employ hard switching schemes that leave their centers on an island against top perimeter scorers. These factors can contribute to a limited number of centers that have higher Defensive Degree of Difficulty ratings. The main player that stands out is Al Horford because he's one of the rare centers that can effectively defend an elite center in the post and adequately handle himself on the perimeter on a switch. His defense against Joel Embiid as well as his continued presence in crucial playoff situations helps to confirm the data that is being presented here. It's interesting that five or the six centers that are listed above are on Eastern Conference teams and only one player plays in the West. An explanation for this is that Eastern Conferences have had to account for the likes of Embiid and the dominant interior scoring of Giannis Antetokounmpo for years, so their lineups have had to skew bigger. On the other hand, the Western Conference may be needing to do some catch-up. After all, those teams have largely been chasing the smaller Golden State Warriors while Denver and Nikola Jokic suddenly emerged to take the top position in the West. A lot of these teams were left ill-equipped to handle a bigger bodied center like Jokic, so there may be a need for centers with the necessary size. Along these lines, Jusuf Nurkic could be a player to watch around the trade deadline. If a trade involving Damian Lillard eventually goes through, it would mean that Portland is heading for a full-scale rebuild. In this scenario, it wouldn't make much sense to keep a veteran like Nurkic around, especially when he could be highly valuable to a contending team. He's always been an effective scorer around the basket and a solid rebounder. Last season, he improved his on-ball defense to the point where he could both hold his own in the post against elite big men and competently handle himself on the perimeter. If his defensive improvement is legitimate, then his skill set could be attractive to any team that is looking to counter somebody like Embiid or Jokic in a future playoff series.

- Defensive Degree of Difficulty ratings between 0.400 and 0.499

	Pos	Team	MP	DDD	PTS Prevented
Brook Lopez	C	MIL	2373	0.476	4.138
Steven Adams	C	MEM	1133	0.497	2.956
Anthony Davis	C	LAL	1904	0.462	2.649
Kristaps Porziņģis	C	WAS	2120	0.427	2.498
Nic Claxton	C	BRK	2271	0.482	2.469
Rudy Gobert	C	MIN	2148	0.457	2.161
Ivica Zubac	C	LAC	2170	0.472	2.040
Bismack Biyombo	C	PHO	874	0.412	1.609
Robert Williams	C	BOS	824	0.406	1.466
Joel Embiid	C	PHI	2284	0.452	1.215
Daniel Gafford	C	WAS	1604	0.407	1.037
Mark Williams	C	CHO	828	0.416	0.854
Jaren Jackson Jr.	C	MEM	1787	0.401	0.766
Onyeka Okongwu	C	ATL	1849	0.404	0.619
Kevon Looney	C	GSW	1958	0.486	0.395
Mike Muscala	C	TOT	945	0.411	0.330
Deandre Ayton	C	PHO	2035	0.461	0.252
Myles Turner	C	IND	1825	0.495	0.229
Drew Eubanks	C	POR	1584	0.436	0.191
Dwight Powell	C	DAL	1458	0.476	0.146
Zach Collins	C	SAS	1441	0.401	0.093
Xavier Tillman Sr.	C	MEM	1180	0.458	0.016
Naz Reid	C	MIN	1251	0.401	0.011
Nikola Jokić	C	DEN	2323	0.433	(0.236)
Darius Bazley	C	TOT	616	0.423	(0.544)
Bam Adebayo	C	MIA	2598	0.489	(0.560)
Jalen Smith	C	IND	1279	0.425	(0.622)
Alperen Şengün	C	HOU	2171	0.449	(0.683)
Mason Plumlee	C	TOT	2054	0.461	(0.698)
Jalen Duren	C	DET	1670	0.403	(0.752)
Jonas Valančiūnas	C	NOP	1968	0.457	(0.880)
Jericho Sims	C	NYK	812	0.432	(1.028)
Jakob Poeltl	C	TOT	1906	0.477	(1.052)
Nikola Vučević	C	CHI	2746	0.473	(1.057)
Marvin Bagley III	C	DET	990	0.437	(1.058)
Blake Griffin	C	BOS	569	0.407	(1.066)
Kelly Olynyk	C	UTA	1942	0.466	(1.185)
Moritz Wagner	C	ORL	1109	0.414	(1.230)
Domantas Sabonis	C	SAC	2736	0.427	(1.702)
Isaiah Stewart	C	DET	1414	0.445	(1.851)
Thomas Bryant	C	TOT	1081	0.458	(2.196)
Precious Achiuwa	C	TOR	1140	0.424	(2.318)
Jaylin Williams	C	OKC	914	0.426	(3.379)
James Wiseman	C	TOT	867	0.414	(3.901)

More or less, this list reads like a list of the league's best and worst rim protectors. The usual set of top rim protectors like Rudy Gobert, Brook Lopez, Jaren Jackson Jr., and Anthony Davis posted positive Points Prevented values while players with lesser reputations finished near the bottom. The most interesting name on the table was Bam Adebayo because he posted a below neutral value. It could be a sign of some slippage because his shot blocking numbers have been declining for a few years. Also, he's relatively short for a center, so he could have some trouble against bigger bodied players like Jokic and Embiid down the line. This could be a warning sign to watch out for this season.

- Defensive Degree of Difficulty ratings below 0.400

	Pos	Team	MP	DDD	PTS Prevented
Charles Bassey	C	SAS	508	0.352	1.690
Walker Kessler	C	UTA	1703	0.393	1.539
Wenyen Gabriel	C	LAL	1024	0.366	1.160
Jock Landale	C	PHO	979	0.351	0.598
Isaiah Hartenstein	C	NYK	1626	0.374	0.329
Montrezl Harrell	C	PHI	681	0.367	0.090
DeAndre Jordan	C	DEN	586	0.363	0.031
Kai Jones	C	CHO	550	0.329	0.017
Luke Kornet	C	BOS	804	0.320	(0.185)
Mo Bamba	C	TOT	769	0.360	(0.246)
Andre Drummond	C	CHI	849	0.340	(0.284)
Isaiah Jackson	C	IND	1042	0.355	(0.450)
Day'Ron Sharpe	C	BRK	552	0.352	(0.579)
Jaxson Hayes	C	NOP	610	0.343	(0.615)
Christian Koloko	C	TOR	802	0.368	(0.692)
Nick Richards	C	CHO	1217	0.379	(0.700)
Christian Wood	C	DAL	1738	0.376	(0.900)
Larry Nance Jr.	C	NOP	1381	0.399	(1.360)
Usman Garuba	C	HOU	970	0.346	(1.589)
Paul Reed	C	PHI	755	0.357	(1.609)
Sandro Mamukelashvili	C	TOT	660	0.319	(2.050)

In general, the names on this list don't really pop because they are mostly backup centers that play limited roles. Walker Kessler is the only one that definitively jumps out because he made the All-Rookie 1st Team last season. He had an excellent rookie year as a shot blocking rim protector, as he ranked second in the NBA in Block Percentage. Utah did a good job of slowly working him into their regular lineup because he initially came off the bench, but later, they stepped him to being their full-time starting center. It will be interesting to see how handles a full starter's workload next season. Based on his performance late last season, he should continue his upward trajectory to becoming one of the better rim protecting centers in the league. Another name to watch out for is Charles Bassey. He was picked up relatively early last season by San Antonio after he was waived by Philadelphia. He spent much of the year on a Two-Way contract, but his solid play as a banging, shot blocker, rebounder, and finisher helped him to land a full-time, multi-year deal with the Spurs. He could emerge to play a larger role because San Antonio could be in need of a bigger bodied center to play alongside Victor Wembanyama to reduce the physical toll that he could be exposed to in the NBA as a rookie. Bassey could fill this important role because he's really the only big man that has the body type and skill set to play this role. As a result, his minutes could increase, and he could help the Spurs by being a center that can provide some physicality while also serving as a rim protector and finisher inside. Essentially, Bassey could wind up becoming something of a breakout player for San Antonio this coming season.

2023-24 Eastern Conference Preview

<u>SCHREMPF Rankings</u>
1. Boston Celtics
2. Milwaukee Bucks
3. Philadelphia 76ers
4. Cleveland Cavaliers
5. New York Knicks
6. Miami Heat
7. Atlanta Hawks
8. Toronto Raptors
9. Brooklyn Nets
10. Chicago Bulls
11. Washington Wizards
12. Orlando Magic
13. Indiana Pacers
14. Charlotte Hornets
15. Detroit Pistons

Rosters are accurate as of August 23, 2023. For my official predictions, turn to page 531.

BOSTON CELTICS

Last Season: 57 - 25, Lost Eastern Conference Finals to Miami (3 - 4)

Offensive Rating: 118.0, 2nd in the NBA   Defensive Rating: 111.5, 5th in the NBA

Primary Executive: Brad Stevens, President of Basketball Operations

Head Coach: Joe Mazzulla

Key Roster Changes

Subtractions
Marcus Smart, trade
Grant Williams, trade
Danilo Gallinari, trade
Mike Muscala, trade
Blake Griffin, free agency

Additions
Jordan Walsh, draft
Kristaps Porziņģis, trade
Oshae Brissett, free agency
Dalano Banton, free agency

Roster

Likely Starting Five
1. *Derrick White*
2. *Jayson Tatum*
3. *Jaylen Brown*
4. *Kristaps Porziņģis*
5. Al Horford

Other Key Rotation Players
Malcolm Brogdon
Robert Williams
Sam Hauser
Oshae Brissett
Payton Pritchard

* Italics denotes that a player is likely to be on the floor to close games

Remaining Roster

- Dalano Banton
- Luke Kornet
- Justin Champagnie
- Jordan Walsh
- JD Davison, 20, 6'3", 195, Alabama (Two-Way)
- Jay Scrubb, 22, 6'5", 220, John A. Logan College (Two-Way)
- D.J. Steward, 22, 6'2", 163, Duke (Exhibit 10)

SCHREMPF Base Rating: 51.5

Season Preview Survey

- *Are the Celtics contending or rebuilding? Where is this team headed?*

The Celtics are clear title contenders this season. After a disappointing loss to Miami in the Conference Finals, Boston shook up their roster to try to find the right mix to get them over the hump. They traded away their defensive stalwart, Marcus Smart in a deal before draft day to acquire former All-Star center, Kristaps Porzingis. Then, they also traded Grant Williams to Dallas in a sign-and-trade, possibly to avoid the new second apron. Even so, they added Oshae Brissett and Dalano Banton to fill out the back-end of their rotation. The primary components of their rotation are still intact, so they should be primed to make a run to win the East and compete for a championship this season.

- *What are the areas of concern for this team heading into this season?*

Boston doesn't have any major concerns, but there are a couple of things that could trip them up if they don't stay focused. In particular, they have to maintain a clear identity as an elite defensive team. Their defense was the primary reason why they were able to reach the Finals in the 2021-22 season because they could use an aggressive switching style to suffocate opponents on a nightly basis. They strayed from that identity and slipped into some bad habits that cost them some critical games in the Miami series. To avoid these mistakes, they will need to lean on their defense to get key stops and maximize their effectiveness in crucial, late-game situations. In addition to this, they haven't had a pure distributor on their roster for a few seasons. At times, their offense stagnates and devolves into a set of trading isolations between their stars. To minimize this weakness, they will have to consistently emphasize ball movement to consistently empower their whole roster and keep their offense flowing. If they address these concerns, they can play to their full potential to become a possible title winner in the coming year.

- *List some possible breakout players for this team.*

Boston has a very veteran heavy team, and their rotation is basically set, so there isn't really much of an opportunity for a young player to break in. The only way that an opportunity could arise is if the team gets hit with some injuries. If this scenario were to occur, then it could provide a pathway for someone to emerge. The only player that qualifies as a breakout candidate would be rookie, Jordan Walsh. He isn't expected to get extended playing time if everything goes as planned. If things go awry and he's pressed into duty, he could play some solid minutes as an energetic three-and-D wing. He had a good Summer League where he made almost 41% of his threes, and he was able to translate his great athleticism into solid defense. He could eventually emerge as a backup wing that could spell Jayson Tatum and Jaylen Brown for stretches as a member of the second unit.

- *What should we expect from them this season?*

The Celtics have an incredibly deep and talented roster, so they are positioned to be one of the favorites to win the Eastern Conference and push for the title this season. Even though they have fallen short in the past few years, they are approaching the breakthrough point in their success cycle. They have almost all of the necessary ingredients to come out on top. They just need to stay healthy and play to their full potential. If they can maintain a high level of defensive intensity and execute efficiently on offense, they should be one of the best teams in the league this upcoming season. It's not a guarantee that they will win the whole thing, but if they play according to their considerable talent level, then they should make another deep playoff run at the very least.

Veterans

Jayson Tatum

	Height	Weight	Cap #	Years Left
	6'8"	210	$32.600M	1 + PO

Similar at Age 24

		Season	SIMsc
1	Tracy McGrady*	2003-04	935.1
2	Gordon Hayward	2014-15	908.5
3	Devin Booker	2020-21	903.7
4	Klay Thompson	2014-15	901.4
5	Kevin Durant	2012-13	900.3
6	Vince Carter	2000-01	897.7
7	Jaylen Brown	2020-21	888.6
8	Carmelo Anthony	2008-09	886.9
9	Danny Granger	2007-08	886.3
10	Brandon Ingram	2021-22	885.7

Baseline Basic Stats

MPG	PTS	AST	REB	BLK	STL
36.7	25.9	4.3	6.5	0.7	1.3

Advanced Metrics

USG%	3PTA/FGA	FTA/FGA	TS%	eFG%	3PT%
31.3	0.407	0.357	0.596	0.537	0.370

AST%	TOV%	OREB%	DREB%	STL%	BLK%
22.1	10.2	2.8	19.6	1.6	1.6

PER	ORTG	DRTG	WS/48	BPM	VOL
23.90	117.1	106.9	0.212	3.97	0.488

- Named to the All-NBA 1st Team for the second consecutive season
- Posted a career best season, excellent in his role as Boston's primary scoring option
- Good pick-and-roll ball handler and isolation player, improved efficiency when posting up smaller players
- Fairly good playmaker that finds open shooters and hits cutters, consistently limits turnovers
- Very good three-point shooter, great spot-up shooter, tends to take difficult shots off the dribble that lower his percentages
- Good at curling off screens to hit mid-range jumpers, explosive finisher in transition
- 2022-23 Defensive Degree of Difficulty: 0.471
- 2022-23 Points Prevented: 0.626
- Occasionally takes on difficult assignments, usually guards starting level players
- Solid on-ball defender, good at staying with perimeter players, has some trouble against stronger players
- Fairly effective pick-and-roll defender, can capably switch, had lapses last season, tended to allow ball handlers to turn the corner
- Will sometimes get caught on screens off the ball, consistently closes out on spot-up shooters
- Good defensive rebounder, can block shots from the weak side, choosing to gamble less, only occasionally gets steals

Jaylen Brown

	Height	Weight	Cap #	Years Left
	6'6"	223	$31.830M	5

Similar at Age 26

		Season	SIMsc
1	Danny Granger	2009-10	916.8
2	Paul George	2016-17	914.2
3	Tracy Murray	1997-98	913.0
4	Jason Richardson	2006-07	909.2
5	Michael Redd	2005-06	909.0
6	Glenn Robinson	1998-99	908.6
7	Stephen Jackson	2004-05	906.3
8	Zach LaVine	2021-22	903.6
9	Isaiah Rider	1997-98	903.5
10	Jim Jackson	1996-97	903.5

Baseline Basic Stats

MPG	PTS	AST	REB	BLK	STL
33.8	19.6	3.4	5.2	0.4	1.1

Advanced Metrics

USG%	3PTA/FGA	FTA/FGA	TS%	eFG%	3PT%
28.0	0.351	0.251	0.566	0.529	0.364

AST%	TOV%	OREB%	DREB%	STL%	BLK%
16.9	11.3	3.3	15.1	1.6	1.0

PER	ORTG	DRTG	WS/48	BPM	VOL
18.27	109.9	109.7	0.113	1.75	0.378

- Made his second All-Star team, named to the All-NBA 2nd Team last season
- Slightly increased his efficiency in his role as a high volume scorer for Boston in 2022-23
- Good at attacking the basket as a pick-and-roll ball handler and isolation player, can struggle against heavy pressure
- Around a league average three-point shooter for his career, slightly above break-even on threes last season
- Most effective as a spot-up shooter, efficiency drops when he shoots off screens or off the dribble
- Solid secondary playmaker that can make simple reads, generally avoids turnovers
- Good cutter off the ball, will opportunistically go the offensive boards to score on put-backs
- 2022-23 Defensive Degree of Difficulty: 0.520
- 2022-23 Points Prevented: 1.117
- Took on a lot of difficult matchups last season, played fairly solid on-ball defense
- Good at limiting three-point attempts in isolation situations, had some trouble defending drives and post-ups, tended to commit a lot of shooting fouls
- Good pick-and-roll defender, can switch to guard ball handlers and screeners
- Sometimes gets caught on screens off the ball, usually closes out in spot-up situations
- Fairly active help defender, gets steals at a moderate rate, occasionally can block a shot, very solid on the defensive glass

Kristaps Porziņģis

	Height	Weight	Cap #	Years Left
	7'3"	240	$36.016M	2

Similar at Age 27

		Season	SIMsc
1	Zydrunas Ilgauskas	2002-03	904.6
2	Rik Smits	1993-94	884.7
3	Patrick Ewing*	1989-90	872.0
4	Brook Lopez	2015-16	865.1
5	Dirk Nowitzki*	2005-06	864.7
6	Ralph Sampson*	1987-88	860.8
7	LaMarcus Aldridge	2012-13	860.1
8	Jermaine O'Neal	2005-06	860.0
9	Nikola Vucevic	2017-18	859.8
10	Randy Breuer	1987-88	858.1

Baseline Basic Stats

MPG	PTS	AST	REB	BLK	STL
31.2	19.3	2.2	8.2	1.6	0.7

Advanced Metrics

USG%	3PTA/FGA	FTA/FGA	TS%	eFG%	3PT%
27.3	0.270	0.337	0.586	0.532	0.385

AST%	TOV%	OREB%	DREB%	STL%	BLK%
12.8	10.2	7.1	22.4	1.1	3.8

PER	ORTG	DRTG	WS/48	BPM	VOL
22.21	115.7	107.9	0.174	2.55	0.411

- Played at an All-Star level in first full season in Washington
- Posted a True Shooting Percentage above 62% in his role as a primary scoring big man
- Solid three-point shooter that made 38.5% of his threes in 2022-23, good pick-and-pop screener and spot-up shooter
- Vertical lob threat due to his height and athleticism, good at rolling to the rim and cutting off the ball
- Runs hard in transition, will selectively go to the offensive boards to score on put-backs
- Good post-up player that shoots over defenders, good passing big man, rarely turns the ball over
- 2022-23 Defensive Degree of Difficulty: 0.427
- 2022-23 Points Prevented: 2.498
- Very good rim protector, uses length to stay vertical, good defensive rebounder and shot blocker
- Generally a solid post defender, can be pushed around by stronger players at time, shows solid mobility when defending in space
- Improved pick-and-roll defender, very good in drop coverages, better when switched onto ball handlers
- Consistently closes out on perimeter shooters, good at defending hand-off plays

Derrick White

	Height	Weight	Cap #	Years Left
	6'4"	190	$18.357M	1

Similar at Age 28

		Season	SIMsc
1	J.J. Redick	2012-13	933.3
2	Rex Chapman	1995-96	924.8
3	Marco Belinelli	2014-15	916.8
4	Randy Foye	2011-12	912.2
5	Derek Anderson	2002-03	912.0
6	Josh Richardson	2021-22	911.2
7	Eldridge Recasner	1995-96	910.6
8	Keyon Dooling	2008-09	910.3
9	Roger Mason	2008-09	908.7
10	Kentavious Caldwell-Pope	2021-22	908.0

Baseline Basic Stats

MPG	PTS	AST	REB	BLK	STL
27.1	11.6	2.5	2.7	0.3	0.8

Advanced Metrics

USG%	3PTA/FGA	FTA/FGA	TS%	eFG%	3PT%
18.8	0.513	0.223	0.561	0.520	0.362

AST%	TOV%	OREB%	DREB%	STL%	BLK%
17.1	10.8	1.9	10.0	1.4	1.7

PER	ORTG	DRTG	WS/48	BPM	VOL
13.68	113.2	110.8	0.109	0.60	0.257

- Named to the All-Defensive 2nd Team last season
- Had his most efficient season in his role as a low usage shooter and secondary ball handler
- Around an average three-point shooter, shot a career best Three-Point Percentage for a whole season
- Most effective as a spot-up shooter or when defenders go under screens on pick-and-rolls
- Effective pick-and-roll ball handler and isolation player that can attack the rim or hit floaters
- Good at cutting off the ball, can curl off screens to knock down mid-range shots
- Solid secondary playmaker and ball control guard, can find open teammates and limit turnovers
- 2022-23 Defensive Degree of Difficulty: 0.487
- 2022-23 Points Prevented: 2.657
- Typically was used as a second unit player but he drew a lot of tough matchups when he was on the floor
- Very good on-ball defender that can defend smaller guards and bigger wings
- Good pick-and-roll defender, effective at switching to guard ball handlers or screeners
- Stays attached to shooters off the ball, good at fighting through screens and closing out in spot-up situations
- Good help defender that picks his spots well, excellent weak side shot blocking guard, fairly solid defensive rebounder
- Gambling less frequently, Steal Percentage is down from his career averages

Al Horford

	Height	Weight	Cap #	Years Left
	6'9"	240	$10.000M	1

Similar at Age 36

		Season	SIMsc
1	Matt Barnes	2016-17	888.3
2	Sam Perkins	1997-98	883.2
3	Mike Dunleavy Jr.	2016-17	872.0
4	P.J. Tucker	2021-22	863.9
5	Juwan Howard	2009-10	860.5
6	Robert Horry	2006-07	858.3
7	Marc Gasol	2020-21	857.9
8	Kurt Thomas	2008-09	857.6
9	Antawn Jamison	2012-13	857.1
10	Carmelo Anthony	2020-21	852.7

Baseline Basic Stats

MPG	PTS	AST	REB	BLK	STL
20.6	6.5	1.4	3.7	0.5	0.5

Advanced Metrics

USG%	3PTA/FGA	FTA/FGA	TS%	eFG%	3PT%
13.3	0.578	0.126	0.576	0.553	0.368

AST%	TOV%	OREB%	DREB%	STL%	BLK%
11.5	9.5	4.3	17.7	1.0	2.7

PER	ORTG	DRTG	WS/48	BPM	VOL
12.55	119.0	109.2	0.119	1.93	0.456

- Regular starting center for Boston, missed a few games due to a lower back injury
- Posted a career best True Shooting Percentage in his role as a very low usage stretch five
- Had a career shooting year where he made almost 45% of his threes
- Mostly used as a spot-up shooter, effective as a pick-and-pop screener, occasionally could make threes off screens
- Rarely plays around the basket, lacks the lift and foot speed to finish around the rim, has a limited ability to post up
- Good passing big man, solid in the hand-off game, can also hit cutters, rarely turns the ball over
- 2022-23 Defensive Degree of Difficulty: 0.524
- 2022-23 Points Prevented: 1.841
- Good rim protector despite declining defensive rebound and block rates, relies more on positioning to defend shots inside
- Good space eater that clogs the lane, stout post defender that can guard elite big men, mobile enough to defend in space on switches
- Pick-and-roll defense slipped, diminishing foot speed made him less effective when making rotations
- Consistently willing to close out on perimeter shooters in spot-up situations

Malcolm Brogdon

	Height	Weight	Cap #	Years Left
	6'5"	229	$22.500M	1

Similar at Age 30

		Season	SIMsc
1	Gordon Hayward	2020-21	941.4
2	Khris Middleton	2021-22	914.0
3	Paul Pierce*	2007-08	912.8
4	Alan Anderson	2012-13	911.4
5	Joe Johnson	2011-12	898.8
6	Mario Elie	1993-94	896.1
7	Marcus Morris	2019-20	894.5
8	Gary Neal	2014-15	894.3
9	Wesley Matthews	2016-17	894.1
10	Mark Aguirre	1989-90	894.1

Baseline Basic Stats

MPG	PTS	AST	REB	BLK	STL
29.9	15.6	4.0	4.4	0.3	0.9

Advanced Metrics

USG%	3PTA/FGA	FTA/FGA	TS%	eFG%	3PT%
22.4	0.373	0.266	0.577	0.531	0.385

AST%	TOV%	OREB%	DREB%	STL%	BLK%
20.9	11.7	2.5	13.9	1.4	0.9

PER	ORTG	DRTG	WS/48	BPM	VOL
16.04	115.2	112.9	0.120	1.52	0.254

- Won the Sixth Man of the Year Award in 2022-23
- Had his most efficient season in a role as a secondary ball handler and moderate usage spot-up shooter
- Good or better in almost every offensive situation, good pick-and-roll ball handler, can attack the rim on isolations
- Made over 44% of his threes last year, great spot-up shooter, will make trail threes in transition
- Can occasionally shoot off screens, less consistent when shooting off the dribble
- Great ball control guard, rarely turns the ball over, good distributor that finds open teammates
- <u>2022-23 Defensive Degree of Difficulty</u>: 0.423
- <u>2022-23 Points Prevented</u>: 0.117
- Used as a defensive stopper in his previous seasons, only occasionally took on tough assignments last year
- Solid on-ball defender that guards multiple positions, had some trouble defending quicker players in 2022-23
- Generally an effective pick-and-roll defender, can functionally switch and contain ball handlers, struggled to defend screeners in a small sample of possessions
- Can get caught on screens off the ball, sometimes was late to close out in spot-up situations
- Stay-at-home defender, does not really post high steals or blocks rates, solid defensive rebounder

Robert Williams

	Height	Weight	Cap #	Years Left
	6'8"	237	$11.571M	2

Similar at Age 25

		Season	SIMsc
1	Clint Capela	2019-20	894.8
2	Josh Boone	2009-10	884.1
3	Brandon Clarke	2021-22	882.7
4	Ben Wallace*	1999-00	878.7
5	Bismack Biyombo	2017-18	875.8
6	Samaki Walker	2001-02	875.6
7	Marcin Gortat	2009-10	875.3
8	Kevon Looney	2021-22	875.2
9	Anthony Avent	1994-95	870.6
10	Ed Davis	2014-15	863.5

Baseline Basic Stats

MPG	PTS	AST	REB	BLK	STL
20.9	7.4	1.1	6.8	1.1	0.5

Advanced Metrics

USG%	3PTA/FGA	FTA/FGA	TS%	eFG%	3PT%
13.7	0.020	0.325	0.675	0.665	0.178

AST%	TOV%	OREB%	DREB%	STL%	BLK%
9.0	14.4	12.8	24.1	1.3	4.7

PER	ORTG	DRTG	WS/48	BPM	VOL
19.20	132.8	106.6	0.189	2.03	0.433

- Missed games while recovering from a torn meniscus in left knee as well as injuries to ankle and hamstring
- Effective in his role as a very low usage rim runner when healthy
- Athletic high motor big man, vertical lob threat, excellent roll man and cutter
- Great offensive rebounder that keeps possessions alive and score off put-backs, runs hard in transition
- Limited offensive skill, rarely attempts a jump shot games, over 95% of his shots were from ten feet and in, has made less than two-thirds of his career free throws
- Flashes some passing skills, can be a bit turnover prone
- 2022-23 Defensive Degree of Difficulty: 0.406
- 2022-23 Points Prevented: 1.466
- Excellent roaming rim protector, great shot blocker and defensive rebounder
- Fairly good at using his length to get steals but Steal Percentage was down last season
- Strong post defender but somewhat lacking in length, had a little bit trouble against much taller post players
- Mobile enough to defend quicker players in space in isolation situations
- Very good pick-and-roll defender, great in drop coverages, can functionally switch to contain ball handlers
- Tends to stay in the paint, does not always come out to contest perimeter shots in spot-up situations

Sam Hauser

	Height	Weight	Cap #	Years Left
	6'8"	215	$1.928M	Team Option

Similar at Age 25

		Season	SIMsc
1	Luke Babbitt	2014-15	896.4
2	Danuel House	2018-19	893.8
3	Steve Novak	2008-09	886.5
4	Duncan Robinson	2019-20	885.5
5	Malcolm Miller	2018-19	885.2
6	Max Strus	2021-22	885.0
7	Haywood Highsmith	2021-22	884.4
8	Okaro White	2017-18	883.6
9	Alfonzo McKinnie	2017-18	883.5
10	Cameron Johnson	2021-22	882.8

Baseline Basic Stats

MPG	PTS	AST	REB	BLK	STL
20.3	8.0	1.1	3.0	0.3	0.5

Advanced Metrics

USG%	3PTA/FGA	FTA/FGA	TS%	eFG%	3PT%
15.6	0.782	0.086	0.592	0.580	0.388

AST%	TOV%	OREB%	DREB%	STL%	BLK%
8.4	7.1	3.2	14.2	1.1	1.2

PER	ORTG	DRTG	WS/48	BPM	VOL
12.28	118.7	112.9	0.111	-0.02	0.497

- Became a regular rotation player for Boston in his second NBA season
- Highly efficient in his role as a low usage shooting specialist
- 85% of his career field goals attempts are threes, has made 42% of his threes over two seasons
- Excellent spot-up shooter, good at shooting off screens, great pick-and-pop screener, knocks down trail threes in transition
- Great at making backdoor cuts if defenders crowd him, limited ability to create his own shot
- Strictly a catch-and-shoot player, not really a dynamic playmaker, rarely turns the ball over
- 2022-23 Defensive Degree of Difficulty: 0.342
- 2022-23 Points Prevented: 0.846
- Very often hidden in favorable matchups against lower leverage players, rarely tested on the ball
- Effective on-ball defender against lower leverage players, adequately stays with his man and holds position in the post
- Fairly solid pick-and-roll defender, gets around the screen to contain ball handlers, had some issues when rotating onto screeners
- Gets caught on screens off the ball, consistently closes out on shooters in spot-up situations
- Mostly a stay-at-home defender, does not really get steals, occasionally can rotate from the weak side to block shots, solid defensive rebounder

Oshae Brissett

	Height	Weight	Cap #	Years Left
	6'7"	210	$2.165M	PO

Similar at Age 24

		Season	SIMsc
1	James Ennis	2014-15	954.1
2	Martell Webster	2010-11	935.9
3	Danuel House	2017-18	928.4
4	Justin Jackson	2019-20	924.6
5	Kenrich Williams	2018-19	924.4
6	PJ Dozier	2020-21	924.3
7	Antoine Wright	2008-09	921.1
8	Rodney Carney	2008-09	918.3
9	Timothé Luwawu-Cabarrot	2019-20	917.2
10	Amir Coffey	2021-22	916.9

Baseline Basic Stats

MPG	PTS	AST	REB	BLK	STL
20.6	8.1	1.2	3.1	0.3	0.6

Advanced Metrics

USG%	3PTA/FGA	FTA/FGA	TS%	eFG%	3PT%
17.1	0.464	0.344	0.554	0.507	0.353

AST%	TOV%	OREB%	DREB%	STL%	BLK%
7.9	9.7	5.2	14.7	1.4	1.2

PER	ORTG	DRTG	WS/48	BPM	VOL
12.65	112.6	114.7	0.079	-1.17	0.360

- Regular rotation player for Indiana in his third season with the team
- Effectiveness slightly declined in his role as a low volume spot-up shooter
- Around a break-even three-point shooter, percentages tend to vary from year-to-year
- Almost exclusively used as a stationary spot-up shooter, Three-Point Percentage was below break-even last season
- Good cutter, athletic finisher in transition, willing to absorb contact to draw fouls
- Not really able to drive to the rim without a screen, very inconsistent when shooting off the dribble
- Strictly a catch-and-shoot player, limited as a playmaker, rarely turns the ball over
- 2022-23 Defensive Degree of Difficulty: 0.340
- 2022-23 Points Prevented: -0.998
- Generally defended second unit level players, played middling on-ball defense
- More effective against stronger players in the post, struggled to stay with perimeter players on isolation plays
- Effective pick-and-roll defender, can functionally switch, good at funneling his man into help
- Sometimes will get caught on screens off the ball, consistently closes out on spot-up shooters
- More of a stay-at-home defender last season, Block Rate dipped significantly, gets steals at a moderate rate, good defensive rebounding wing

Payton Pritchard

	Height	Weight	Cap #	Years Left
	6'1"	195	$4.037M	RFA

Similar at Age 25

		Season	SIMsc
1	Quinn Cook	2018-19	923.1
2	Shawn Respert	1997-98	921.3
3	Seth Curry	2015-16	919.3
4	Langston Galloway	2016-17	916.7
5	Jevon Carter	2020-21	913.3
6	Shammond Williams	2000-01	913.3
7	Devonte' Graham	2020-21	913.0
8	Ryan Arcidiacono	2019-20	912.7
9	Chris Quinn	2008-09	907.8
10	Luther Head	2007-08	906.3

Baseline Basic Stats

MPG	PTS	AST	REB	BLK	STL
18.0	7.3	1.9	1.8	0.1	0.6

Advanced Metrics

USG%	3PTA/FGA	FTA/FGA	TS%	eFG%	3PT%
18.5	0.628	0.106	0.552	0.534	0.383

AST%	TOV%	OREB%	DREB%	STL%	BLK%
15.8	11.2	2.8	9.8	1.4	0.4

PER	ORTG	DRTG	WS/48	BPM	VOL
12.23	110.9	112.0	0.095	-0.88	0.312

- Fell out of the rotation last season, played fringe rotation minutes in his third NBA season
- Efficiency decreased with fewer minutes, used as a lower volume ball handler and spot-up shooter
- Good three-point shooter despite lower Three-Point Percentage last season, has made 40% of his career threes
- Good spot-up shooter, can run off screens and make pull-up jumpers if defenders back off
- Lacks the quickness to consistently create shots in isolation situations, better as a pick-and-roll ball handler
- Solid secondary playmaker that can make simple reads, good at avoiding turnovers, good cutter off the ball
- 2022-23 Defensive Degree of Difficulty: 0.334
- 2022-23 Points Prevented: 1.677
- Usually hidden in lower leverage assignments against second unit players
- Rarely tested on the ball, effective on-ball defender in a small sample of possessions, quick enough to stay with opposing guards
- Effective pick-and-roll defender, good at funneling his man into help
- Fights through screens off the ball, good at defending hand-off plays, will close out but lacks the ideal length to effectively contest shots
- Stay-at-home defender, steal rate is declining, fairly decent defensive rebounding guard

Dalano Banton

	Height	Weight	Cap #	Years Left
	6'9"	204	$2.020M	TO

Similar at Age 23

		Season	SIMsc
1	PJ Dozier	2019-20	916.7
2	Jalen McDaniels	2020-21	911.2
3	DerMarr Johnson	2003-04	907.4
4	Austin Daye	2011-12	905.0
5	Josh Jackson	2020-21	898.4
6	Wenyen Gabriel	2020-21	897.2
7	Darius Miles	2004-05	896.4
8	Cleanthony Early	2014-15	895.7
9	Rodney Carney	2007-08	894.4
10	Sean Higgins	1991-92	893.7

Baseline Basic Stats

MPG	PTS	AST	REB	BLK	STL
19.2	7.8	1.2	3.5	0.5	0.6

Advanced Metrics

USG%	3PTA/FGA	FTA/FGA	TS%	eFG%	3PT%
19.8	0.357	0.226	0.517	0.492	0.299

AST%	TOV%	OREB%	DREB%	STL%	BLK%
14.1	13.0	4.2	15.1	1.9	2.6

PER	ORTG	DRTG	WS/48	BPM	VOL
13.05	104.5	110.5	0.067	-1.26	0.579

- Minutes decreased significantly, played sparingly for Toronto in his second NBA season
- Increased his efficiency in a role as a moderate volume energy wing and spot-up shooter off the bench
- Explosive finisher, great at running the floor and attacking the rim in transition, excellent cutter off the ball
- Slightly improved his outside shot but still makes less than 30% of his threes
- Below break-even when shooting spot-up threes, percentages dramatically drop in other situations
- Lacks the ability to create his own shot, good playmaking wing that finds open teammates, cut his turnover rate significantly last season
- 2022-23 Defensive Degree of Difficulty: 0.316
- 2022-23 Points Prevented: 2.140
- Largely used as a roamer against second unit caliber players, rarely tested as an on-ball defender
- Played solid on-ball defense in a small sample of possessions, flashes ability to guard multiple positions
- Below average pick-and-roll defense, not effective at taking away any specific action due to indecisiveness
- Will stay attached to shooters off the ball, fights through screens and closes out on spot-up shooters
- Very active help defender, jumps passing lanes to get steals, good weak side shot blocker, solid defensive rebounder

Luke Kornet

	Height	Weight	Cap #	Years Left
	7'2"	250	$2.413M	UFA

Similar at Age 27

		Season	SIMsc
1	Tyler Zeller	2016-17	886.8
2	Willie Cauley-Stein	2020-21	879.0
3	Miles Plumlee	2015-16	874.1
4	Alex Len	2020-21	873.0
5	Primoz Brezec	2006-07	863.2
6	Sam Bowie	1988-89	861.6
7	Luc Longley	1995-96	858.2
8	Dewayne Dedmon	2016-17	856.8
9	Robin Lopez	2015-16	856.0
10	Timofey Mozgov	2013-14	854.6

Baseline Basic Stats

MPG	PTS	AST	REB	BLK	STL
20.1	7.5	1.1	5.6	1.1	0.4

Advanced Metrics

USG%	3PTA/FGA	FTA/FGA	TS%	eFG%	3PT%
14.8	0.122	0.251	0.593	0.566	0.244

AST%	TOV%	OREB%	DREB%	STL%	BLK%
9.6	11.0	10.7	18.2	0.9	4.0

PER	ORTG	DRTG	WS/48	BPM	VOL
16.13	124.9	109.3	0.151	-0.17	0.507

- Fringe rotation player for Boston in his first full season with the team
- Had a career best season, mainly filled a role as a very low usage rim runner
- Posted a True Shooting Percentage of almost 70%, efficient finisher despite having around average athleticism
- Excellent at rolling to the rim and cutting off the ball, active offensive rebounder, runs hard in transition
- Used as a stretch big in previous seasons, below break-even three-point shooter for his career
- Not really a post-up threat, fairly good passing big man, good at avoiding turnovers
- 2022-23 Defensive Degree of Difficulty: 0.320
- 2022-23 Points Prevented: -0.185
- Largely plays against second unit players, effective rim protector last season, great shot blocker
- Below average defensive rebounder, looks to block his man out to allow others to grab the rebound
- Played solid on-ball defense, good at defending in the post, mobile enough to defend in space
- Decent pick-and-roll defender, more effective at switching onto ball handlers, had lapses when covering screeners
- Good at contesting spot-up jumpers with a special technique where he jumps high with both hands raised to block the shooter's view

Newcomers

Jordan Walsh

	Height	Weight	Cap #	Years Left
	6'7"	205	$1.120M	2 + TO

Baseline Basic Stats

MPG	PTS	AST	REB	BLK	STL
14.5	5.0	0.8	2.3	0.2	0.5

Advanced Metrics

USG%	3PTA/FGA	FTA/FGA	TS%	eFG%	3PT%
15.3	0.355	0.224	0.501	0.469	0.306

AST%	TOV%	OREB%	DREB%	STL%	BLK%
8.5	10.9	4.2	11.7	1.6	1.1

PER	ORTG	DRTG	WS/48	BPM	VOL
10.22	101.6	106.0	0.055	-1.61	N/A

- Drafted by Sacramento with the 38th overall pick in 2023, traded to Boston
- Played very well at the Las Vegas Summer League
- Solidly effective in his role as a moderate volume scoring wing, will likely play a lower usage role in the NBA
- Struggled to shoot efficiently in college, showed improvement with his outside shot at Summer League
- Shot 11-for-27 (40.7%) on threes in Las Vegas, almost strictly a spot-up shooter at this stage
- Good athlete that explosively finish at the rim with emphatic dunks
- Will attack the basket in transition, draws fouls at a solid rate, selectively goes to the offensive glass to score on put-backs
- Needs to improve his ball handling skills, not really able to create his own shot on a consistent basis
- Played a catch-and-shoot style at Summer League, can make simple passes, good at avoiding turnovers
- Athletic wing defender with great length and good quickness, can potentially guard multiple positions
- Solid pick-and-roll defender, can switch, makes good second effort plays to recover if he's initially beaten
- Needs to improve positioning to maximize his effectiveness against higher quality opponents
- Stays attached to shooters, fights through screens and closes out in spot-up situations
- Fairly active help defender, actively uses length, will jump passing lanes to get steals, solid defensive rebounder at Summer League
- May need some additional seasoning in the G-League to polish his skills on both ends

MILWAUKEE BUCKS

Last Season: 58 - 24, Lost 1st Round to Miami (1 – 4)

Offensive Rating: 115.4, 12th in the NBA

Defensive Rating: 111.9, 4th in the NBA

Primary Executive: Jon Horst, General Manager

Head Coach: Adrian Griffin

Key Roster Changes

Subtractions
Joe Ingles, free agency
Jevon Carter, free agency
Wesley Matthews, free agency
Goran Dragić, free agency
Meyers Leonard, free agency

Additions
Andre Jackson Jr., draft
Chris Livingston, draft
Malik Beasley, free agency
Robin Lopez, free agency

Roster

Likely Starting Five
1. *Jrue Holiday*
2. *Grayson Allen*
3. *Khris Middleton*
4. *Giannis Antetokounmpo*
5. *Brook Lopez*

Other Key Rotation Players
Bobby Portis
Pat Connaughton
Jae Crowder
Malik Beasley
Robin Lopez

* Italics denotes that a player is likely to be on the floor to close games

Remaining Roster

- MarJon Beauchamp
- Thanasis Antetokounmpo
- Andre Jackson Jr.
- AJ Green
- Chris Livingston
- Lindell Wigginton, 25, 6'2", 189, Iowa State (Two-Way)
- Omari Moore, 23, 6'6", 195, San Jose State (Two-Way)
- Jazian Gortman, 20, 6'2", 170, Overtime Elite (Exhibit 10)
- Drew Timme, 23, 6'10", 235, Gonzaga (Exhibit 10)

SCHREMPF Base Rating: 48.8

Season Preview Survey

- *Are the Bucks contending or rebuilding? Where is this team headed?*

The Bucks are looking to bounce back and make another title run after suffering a tough early exit in last year's playoffs. They are hoping that a shift in leadership on the bench will make the difference because they largely kept last season's team intact while they replaced head coach, Mike Budenholzer with former Raptors assistant, Adrian Griffin. Griffin is an unproven, first year coach, so it's uncertain as to how they will change things up this season. Even so, they still have the talent to be a leading contender in the East. However, the clock might be ticking on them because they are now getting a bit older, which could make them more vulnerable than they used to be.

- *What are the areas of concern for this team heading into this season?*

The main concern with Milwaukee is their adaptability because they were very resistant to adjust to different styles in Budenholzer's coaching tenure. It's not clear if Griffin can make the necessary adjustments in a big series because this is his first year as a full-time head coach. However, he has worked under Nick Nurse for several years, so he has experience working with someone that frequently switches tactics. It's possible that some of this influence will rub off and help the Bucks this season. Moving on, the team's increasing age could be an issue because their key players have played a lot of minutes over the years, so they could be more susceptible to injury or age-related decline. This could increase Giannis Antetokounmpo's workload even more to the point where he might not be able to carry them far enough this season. They will need to careful with everyone's minutes to allow them to manage the long season and get everyone to their peak in the playoffs.

- *List some possible breakout players for this team.*

Milwaukee is a very veteran heavy, contending team, so they don't have a lot of minutes available for a young player to step up. They also haven't been a team that builds from within, so they are more likely to make a trade or sign a street free agent if they need help. It's possible that one of the few young players that they have will be buried on the bench. If a breakout player emerges, it's likely to be either MarJon Beauchamp or A.J. Green. Beauchamp has the higher pedigree because he was their first round pick in 2022. He's flashed potential as an athletic, three-and-D wing in limited bursts of playing time. However, he still hasn't proven that he can defend high level players or shoot consistently from outside. If he improves in these areas, he could crack the rotation and give them another wing option to play alongside Khris Middleton. Green is more of a one-dimensional specialist in the sense that he's a designated shooter. That being said, he made almost 42% of his threes last season. If he maintains this level of efficiency, he could fill a role as a valuable floor spacer that draws attention and helps to pull defenders away from the paint.

- *What should we expect from them this season?*

The Bucks still are one of the most talented teams in the league, so they should put up a high regular season win total to earn one of the top seeds in the East. The big issue with them is their ability to match up and adjust to their opponents in critical playoff series. They have been too inflexible to switch up their style under Budenholzer, but it's uncertain if things will change with a new head coach. If they show a greater willingness to experiment with new tactics, then they will increase their chances of success in the playoffs and they could wind up being a much more formidable title contender this season. Otherwise, if things stay the same, they could be susceptible to another early playoff exit in the coming year.

Veterans

Giannis Antetokounmpo

	Height	Weight	Cap #	Years Left
	6'11"	242	$45.640M	1 + PO

Similar at Age 28

		Season	SIMsc
1	Nikola Vucevic	2018-19	863.9
2	Tim Duncan*	2004-05	849.0
3	Patrick Ewing*	1990-91	847.7
4	Amare Stoudemire	2010-11	845.8
5	Chris Webber*	2001-02	845.6
6	LaMarcus Aldridge	2013-14	844.8
7	Dwight Howard	2013-14	843.3
8	Dirk Nowitzki*	2006-07	840.9
9	Brad Miller	2004-05	838.6
10	Blake Griffin	2017-18	836.9

Baseline Basic Stats

MPG	PTS	AST	REB	BLK	STL
33.8	23.5	3.9	10.7	1.4	1.0

Advanced Metrics

USG%	3PTA/FGA	FTA/FGA	TS%	eFG%	3PT%
32.5	0.170	0.504	0.600	0.557	0.318

AST%	TOV%	OREB%	DREB%	STL%	BLK%
26.0	12.7	7.1	28.3	1.4	3.1

PER	ORTG	DRTG	WS/48	BPM	VOL
26.46	116.6	105.1	0.209	8.61	0.442

- Named to the All-NBA 1st Team for the fifth consecutive season, missed some games due to various minor injuries
- Led the NBA in Usage Percentage, excelled as Milwaukee's primary scoring option
- Dynamic downhill driver, excellent at attacking the rim in transition, draws a lot of fouls, good at driving to the rim as a pick-and-roll ball handler and isolation player
- Vertical lob threat, explosive rim runner, great cutter and roll man, active offensive rebounder
- Excellent playmaker that finds open teammates, good at avoiding turnovers
- Shooting has regressed, below average mid-range shooter, made less than 30% of his career threes
- 2022-23 Defensive Degree of Difficulty: 0.420
- 2022-23 Points Prevented: 2.479
- Used as a roamer, excellent defensive rebounder, minor injuries hurt his ability to protect the rim
- Normally gets steals and blocks at a high rate, Steal and Block Percentages dipped significantly in 2022-23
- Solid on-ball defender against starting level players, can defend in the post and on the perimeter
- Decent pick-and-roll defender, good in drop coverages, tends to go too far under screens
- Can gamble too much, tends to get caught on off-ball screens, good at closing out on spot-up shooters

Jrue Holiday

	Height	Weight	Cap #	Years Left
	6'3"	205	$36.862M	PO

Similar at Age 32

		Season	SIMsc
1	Deron Williams	2016-17	917.8
2	Terry Porter	1995-96	911.7
3	Derrick Rose	2020-21	909.7
4	Beno Udrih	2014-15	909.4
5	Chauncey Billups	2008-09	909.0
6	Manu Ginobili*	2009-10	903.6
7	Jarrett Jack	2015-16	892.4
8	Dwyane Wade*	2013-14	892.1
9	Blue Edwards	1997-98	891.2
10	Dell Curry	1996-97	891.2

Baseline Basic Stats

MPG	PTS	AST	REB	BLK	STL
29.8	14.6	5.6	3.3	0.3	1.1

Advanced Metrics

USG%	3PTA/FGA	FTA/FGA	TS%	eFG%	3PT%
22.7	0.422	0.224	0.569	0.530	0.373

AST%	TOV%	OREB%	DREB%	STL%	BLK%
31.2	15.6	2.8	11.1	1.7	0.9

PER	ORTG	DRTG	WS/48	BPM	VOL
17.21	114.0	111.6	0.131	2.15	0.397

- Made his second All-Star team, Named to the All-Defensive 1st Team in 2022-23
- Thrived in his role as Milwaukee's primary ball handler, maintained his usual level of production
- Excellent distributor that consistently finds open teammates, slightly turnover prone
- Good pick-and-roll ball handler, good at making pull-up jumpers from mid-range, needs a screen to get to the rim, less effective as an isolation player
- Reliable three-point shooter, has made 39.5% of his threes in three seasons with Milwaukee
- Good spot-up shooter, effective at making pull-up threes if defenders go under screens
- 2022-23 Defensive Degree of Difficulty: 0.560, had the 15th most difficult set of matchups in the NBA
- 2022-23 Points Prevented: 1.924
- Mainly used as Milwaukee's primary defensive stopper, one of the best point of attack defenders in the NBA
- Great on-ball defender that guards multiple positions, slightly over-extended against bigger wings
- Good pick-and-roll defender, effective at switching on ball handlers and screeners
- Fights through screens off the ball, sometimes would be late to close out in spot-up situations
- May be slowing down due to age, still gets steals at a solid rate, steal and block rates declined, solid defensive rebounder

Khris Middleton

	Height	Weight	Cap #	Years Left
	6'7"	222	$29.321M	1 + PO

Similar at Age 31

		Season	SIMsc
1	Glenn Robinson	2003-04	928.5
2	Gordon Hayward	2021-22	919.9
3	Manu Ginobili*	2008-09	910.1
4	Jerry Stackhouse	2005-06	909.5
5	Lance Stephenson	2021-22	908.3
6	Vince Carter	2007-08	907.1
7	Glen Rice	1998-99	902.6
8	Paul George	2021-22	901.8
9	DeMar DeRozan	2020-21	896.5
10	Eddie A. Johnson	1990-91	895.0

Baseline Basic Stats

MPG	PTS	AST	REB	BLK	STL
29.2	15.9	3.7	4.2	0.3	0.9

Advanced Metrics

USG%	3PTA/FGA	FTA/FGA	TS%	eFG%	3PT%
25.0	0.383	0.281	0.562	0.508	0.366

AST%	TOV%	OREB%	DREB%	STL%	BLK%
23.7	13.0	2.9	13.3	1.5	0.7

PER	ORTG	DRTG	WS/48	BPM	VOL
16.76	112.4	111.3	0.118	0.91	0.354

- Missed most of last season while recovering from wrist surgery, also missed games due to a sore knee
- Effective as Milwaukee's main, high usage perimeter scorer when healthy
- Solid three-level scorer, effectiveness limited due to injury, can post up smaller guards, good mid-range shooter and pick-and-roll ball handler
- Less effective when driving by defenders on isolations, may be slowed due to injury and advancing age
- Had a down shooting year, made threes at a below break-even rate
- Struggled to make threes on the move, most effective when his body was square to the rim
- Percentages bounced back in the playoffs, has made almost 39% of his career threes
- 2022-23 Defensive Degree of Difficulty: 0.423
- 2022-23 Points Prevented: 0.597
- Drew tougher assignments in previous seasons, guarded lower leverage starters last season
- Solid on-ball defender in the past, had some trouble staying with opposing players in one-on-one situations
- Average pick-and-roll defender, good at switching and cutting off penetration, tends to go too far under screens
- Stays attached to shooters off the ball, fights through screens and closes out in spot-up situations
- Steal and Block Percentage declined, less active on the weak side, slowed due to injuries, fairly good defensive rebounder

Brook Lopez

	Height	Weight	Cap #	Years Left
	7'0"	282	$25.000M	1

Similar at Age 34

		Season	SIMsc
1	LaMarcus Aldridge	2019-20	875.6
2	JaVale McGee	2021-22	844.4
3	Marc Gasol	2018-19	823.4
4	Aron Baynes	2020-21	822.2
5	Arvydas Sabonis*	1998-99	817.5
6	Elton Brand	2013-14	815.2
7	James Donaldson	1991-92	804.3
8	Channing Frye	2017-18	803.0
9	Rudy Gay	2020-21	802.1
10	Tim Duncan*	2010-11	799.7

Baseline Basic Stats

MPG	PTS	AST	REB	BLK	STL
20.8	8.8	1.1	4.6	1.1	0.4

Advanced Metrics

USG%	3PTA/FGA	FTA/FGA	TS%	eFG%	3PT%
17.4	0.356	0.215	0.600	0.573	0.347

AST%	TOV%	OREB%	DREB%	STL%	BLK%
5.5	10.7	7.1	16.8	0.9	6.2

PER	ORTG	DRTG	WS/48	BPM	VOL
15.94	116.7	108.2	0.133	0.09	0.452

- Named to the All-Defensive 1st Team, runner-up in the Defensive Player of the Year voting in 2022-23
- Had an excellent bounce back season, highly effective in his role as a low usage stretch big
- Had his best shooting year, made threes at an above average rate last season
- Solid spot-up shooter, good pick-and-pop screener, makes trail threes in transition
- Effective, high motor run runner, good cutter and roll man, active offensive rebounder
- Can punish smaller players on switches in the post, only makes safe passes, rarely turns the ball over
- 2022-23 Defensive Degree of Difficulty: 0.476
- 2022-23 Points Prevented: 4.138
- Fairly solid rim protector, excellent shot blocker, sacrifices position to go for blocks
- Good at boxing out to keep opposing big men off the glass, middling defensive rebounder by himself
- Drew tough assignments against top big men, solid post defender, tends to commit shooting fouls, has trouble defending in space
- Decent pick-and-roll defender, good in drop coverages, tends to back off, gives up open jumpers
- Consistently will come out to contest perimeter shots in spot-up situations

Grayson Allen

	Height	Weight	Cap #	Years Left
	6'4"	198	$8.925M	UFA

Similar at Age 27

		Season	SIMsc
1	Kentavious Caldwell-Pope	2020-21	943.1
2	Gary Harris	2021-22	943.1
3	Austin Rivers	2019-20	942.0
4	Roger Mason	2007-08	929.9
5	Reggie Bullock	2018-19	928.3
6	Rodney McGruder	2018-19	926.4
7	Jerryd Bayless	2015-16	926.4
8	Langston Galloway	2018-19	921.4
9	Keith Bogans	2007-08	921.2
10	Marco Belinelli	2013-14	920.5

Baseline Basic Stats

MPG	PTS	AST	REB	BLK	STL
23.7	9.5	1.6	2.4	0.2	0.7

Advanced Metrics

USG%	3PTA/FGA	FTA/FGA	TS%	eFG%	3PT%
16.1	0.660	0.181	0.587	0.555	0.400

AST%	TOV%	OREB%	DREB%	STL%	BLK%
10.2	9.7	2.3	9.7	1.5	0.6

PER	ORTG	DRTG	WS/48	BPM	VOL
12.10	116.7	113.3	0.099	-0.32	0.319

- Regular starter for Milwaukee in his second season with the team
- Maintained his usual level of effectiveness in a role as a low usage, off-ball shooter
- Reliable outside shooter that has made almost 40% of his career threes, excellent in the corners
- Predominantly a stand-still spot-up shooter, needs to have his feet set, less efficient when shooting on the move
- Lacks the quickness to effectively drive to the rim, less effective in ball handling situations
- Solid cutter off the ball, flashes some secondary playmaking skills, rarely turns the ball over
- 2022-23 Defensive Degree of Difficulty: 0.450
- 2022-23 Points Prevented: 0.316
- Usually guarded starter level players, drew tougher assignments than he did in previous seasons
- Decent on-ball defender, competently stays with opposing guards, struggled to guard taller wings
- Decent pick-and-roll defender, can functionally switch, cuts off penetrations, goes too far under screens
- Tends to get caught on screens off the ball, good at closing out on spot-up shooters
- Slightly more active as a help defender, increased his steal rate last season, decent defensive rebounder

Bobby Portis

	Height	Weight	Cap #	Years Left
	6'10"	250	$11.711M	1 + PO

Similar at Age 27

		Season	SIMsc
1	Kevin Love	2015-16	912.8
2	Mehmet Okur	2006-07	911.9
3	Troy Murphy	2007-08	911.1
4	Ryan Anderson	2015-16	910.2
5	Markieff Morris	2016-17	903.6
6	Jordan Hill	2014-15	903.1
7	Ersan Ilyasova	2014-15	901.8
8	Jon Leuer	2016-17	901.3
9	Mike Gminski	1986-87	900.1
10	Bill Laimbeer	1984-85	898.8

Baseline Basic Stats

MPG	PTS	AST	REB	BLK	STL
28.1	13.5	1.6	7.8	0.5	0.7

Advanced Metrics

USG%	3PTA/FGA	FTA/FGA	TS%	eFG%	3PT%
20.5	0.386	0.191	0.575	0.546	0.392

AST%	TOV%	OREB%	DREB%	STL%	BLK%
8.2	9.8	8.5	26.0	1.1	1.3

PER	ORTG	DRTG	WS/48	BPM	VOL
17.22	115.8	108.8	0.138	0.50	0.387

- Played near starter level minutes for Milwaukee in his third season with the team
- Finished 3rd in the Sixth Man of the Year voting in 2022-23, good in his role as a moderate usage stretch big
- Good three-point shooter throughout his career, better when shooting above the break
- Solid at making spot-up threes, good pick-and-pop screener
- Good at posting up smaller players last season, most effective on the left block
- High effort rim runner, good cutter and roll man, solid offensive rebounder that keeps possessions alive
- Mainly a catch-and-shoot player, only makes safe passes, rarely turns the ball over
- 2022-23 Defensive Degree of Difficulty: 0.376
- 2022-23 Points Prevented: 0.415
- Largely used as a taller perimeter player, usually hidden in lower leverage assignments
- Not really suited to protect the rim, does not really block shots, struggles to contest shots vertically, good defensive rebounder
- Middling on-ball defender, effective when defending in the post, struggles to stay with quicker players
- Below average pick-and-roll defender, late to recognize pick-and-pops, not effective at containing ball handlers
- Consistently will come out to contest perimeter shots in spot-up situations

Pat Connaughton

	Height	Weight	Cap #	Years Left
	6'5"	209	$9.424M	1 + PO

Similar at Age 30

		Season	SIMsc
1	Reggie Bullock	2021-22	947.7
2	Keith Bogans	2010-11	943.3
3	Rodney McGruder	2021-22	930.7
4	Brandon Rush	2015-16	929.8
5	Jud Buechler	1998-99	922.9
6	Anthony Morrow	2015-16	919.5
7	Maurice Evans	2008-09	916.8
8	Wayne Ellington	2017-18	915.5
9	Kyle Korver	2011-12	912.9
10	DeShawn Stevenson	2011-12	912.8

Baseline Basic Stats

MPG	PTS	AST	REB	BLK	STL
21.9	7.0	1.2	2.8	0.2	0.6

Advanced Metrics

USG%	3PTA/FGA	FTA/FGA	TS%	eFG%	3PT%
13.6	0.695	0.119	0.545	0.530	0.353

AST%	TOV%	OREB%	DREB%	STL%	BLK%
7.1	8.5	2.8	14.1	1.4	0.7

PER	ORTG	DRTG	WS/48	BPM	VOL
9.96	111.1	111.3	0.082	-1.22	0.251

- Regular rotation player for Milwaukee, started over half of his games, missed a month due to a calf injury
- Production declined last season, mainly used as a very low usage spot-up shooter
- League average career three-point shooter, percentages tend to vary from year-to-year
- Predominantly a spot-up shooter, flashed an ability to shoot off screens and make pick-and-pop jumpers
- Effective at curling towards the rim on hand-offs, less effective as a finisher around the basket
- Not really used in ball handling situations, catch-and-shoot player, makes safe passes, rarely turns the ball over
- 2022-23 Defensive Degree of Difficulty: 0.356
- 2022-23 Points Prevented: 2.783
- Usually defends second unit players or is hidden in favorable matchups against lower leverage starters
- Played solid on-ball defense, capably held position inside against bigger wings, had some trouble staying with quicker guards
- Below average pick-and-roll defender, goes way too far under screens, struggled to contain ball handlers
- Sometimes gets caught on screens off the ball, good at closing out on spot-up shooters
- Stay-at-home defender last season, did not really get steals or blocks, good defensive rebounder

Jae Crowder

	Height	Weight	Cap #	Years Left
	6'6"	235	$2.020M	UFA

Similar at Age 32

		Season	SIMsc
1	Mike Scott	2020-21	921.5
2	Nicolas Batum	2020-21	914.6
3	Wilson Chandler	2019-20	912.0
4	Dan Majerle	1997-98	906.0
5	Jud Buechler	2000-01	903.5
6	Danny Green	2019-20	902.2
7	Jason Richardson	2012-13	901.4
8	Alan Anderson	2014-15	899.6
9	Devean George	2009-10	897.5
10	Matt Barnes	2012-13	893.2

Baseline Basic Stats

MPG	PTS	AST	REB	BLK	STL
21.9	6.7	1.4	3.4	0.4	0.7

Advanced Metrics

USG%	3PTA/FGA	FTA/FGA	TS%	eFG%	3PT%
12.9	0.736	0.141	0.576	0.558	0.380

AST%	TOV%	OREB%	DREB%	STL%	BLK%
9.4	9.0	3.3	15.1	1.7	1.6

PER	ORTG	DRTG	WS/48	BPM	VOL
11.74	117.5	108.5	0.120	1.06	0.494

- Missed most of the season due to a trade holdout, used as a rotational player after a trade to Milwaukee
- Mainly played a role as a very low usage spot-up shooter
- Shot extremely efficiently in limited minutes, made almost 44% of his threes, usually an above break-even three-point shooters
- Almost exclusively a stationary spot-up shooter, occasionally make shots as a pick-and-pop screener
- Limited as a ball handler or shot creator, does not consistently create his own shot
- Usually a catch-and-shoot player, willing to make the extra pass, rarely turns the ball over
- 2022-23 Defensive Degree of Difficulty: 0.391
- 2022-23 Points Prevented: -0.965
- Drew tough assignments in previous seasons, usually guarded second unit level players last season
- Solid on-ball defender that guards multiple positions, has some trouble defending taller players on post-ups
- Solid pick-and-roll defender, good at switching and contain ball handlers, sometimes is late to recognize pick-and-pop plays
- Sometimes gets caught on screens, not always in position to contest shots in spot-up situations
- Gets steals at a fairly solid rate, occasionally blocks shots on the weak side, fairly good defensive rebounder

Malik Beasley

	Height	Weight	Cap #	Years Left
	6'4"	187	$2.020M	UFA

Similar at Age 26

		Season	SIMsc
1	Grayson Allen	2021-22	929.4
2	Bryn Forbes	2019-20	920.2
3	Matt Thomas	2020-21	918.1
4	Marcus Thornton	2013-14	913.3
5	J.J. Redick	2010-11	911.2
6	Gary Neal	2010-11	907.3
7	Troy Daniels	2017-18	906.0
8	Tyler Johnson	2018-19	905.5
9	Ben McLemore	2019-20	904.5
10	Rex Chapman	1993-94	903.6

Baseline Basic Stats

MPG	PTS	AST	REB	BLK	STL
24.5	10.9	1.7	2.5	0.2	0.7

Advanced Metrics

USG%	3PTA/FGA	FTA/FGA	TS%	eFG%	3PT%
20.0	0.649	0.120	0.546	0.525	0.376

AST%	TOV%	OREB%	DREB%	STL%	BLK%
9.8	8.3	1.7	10.7	1.4	0.5

PER	ORTG	DRTG	WS/48	BPM	VOL
11.94	108.5	114.0	0.064	-1.22	0.308

- Traded from Utah to the L.A. Lakers at the trade deadline, played starter level minutes for both teams
- Played off the bench as a moderate volume shooting specialist
- Fairly reliable three-point shooter, has made over 41% of his career corner threes
- More effective when shooting off screens in 2022-23, solid spot-up shooter historically, inconsistent in these situations last season
- Generally needs a screen to get to the rim, more effective in ball handling situations in Utah, not really efficient when shooting off the dribble
- Strictly a catch-and-shoot at this stage, playmaking skills are limited, rarely turns the ball over
- 2022-23 Defensive Degree of Difficulty: 0.394
- 2022-23 Points Prevented: 0.203
- Usually was hidden in favorable matchups against lower leverage players
- Below average on-ball defender, struggled to stay with opposing guards, had difficulty against bigger wings
- Played decent pick-and-roll defense, limited ability to switch, good at funneling his man into help
- Sometimes gets caught on screens off the ball, consistently closes out on spot-up shooters
- More active as a help defender, Steal Percentage increased a bit, fairly solid defensive rebounder

Robin Lopez

	Height	Weight	Cap #	Years Left
	7'0"	281	$2.020M	UFA

Similar at Age 34

		Season	SIMsc
1	James Donaldson	1991-92	870.2
2	Marcin Gortat	2018-19	866.4
3	Nene	2016-17	845.8
4	Erick Dampier	2009-10	843.6
5	Mikki Moore	2009-10	839.5
6	Joe Kleine	1995-96	839.1
7	Bill Wennington	1997-98	838.2
8	JaVale McGee	2021-22	835.5
9	Aron Baynes	2020-21	835.3
10	Greg Foster	2002-03	830.9

Baseline Basic Stats

MPG	PTS	AST	REB	BLK	STL
13.5	4.7	0.6	2.8	0.4	0.2

Advanced Metrics

USG%	3PTA/FGA	FTA/FGA	TS%	eFG%	3PT%
15.2	0.054	0.290	0.603	0.580	0.381

AST%	TOV%	OREB%	DREB%	STL%	BLK%
8.3	18.1	9.9	12.6	0.5	2.8

PER	ORTG	DRTG	WS/48	BPM	VOL
11.78	111.7	111.4	0.091	-2.54	0.350

- Played sparingly for Cleveland in his first season with the team
- Production steeply declined, primarily used as a very low usage rim runner
- Posted a 67.5% True Shooting Percentage, effective rim runner, relies on his motor, athleticism has diminished
- Good cutter off the ball, solid at rolling to the rim, active offensive rebounder
- Takes most of his shots from between three to ten feet, can make hook shots when he posts up
- Rarely takes outside jumpers, decent passing big man, has become more turnover prone in recent years
- 2022-23 Defensive Degree of Difficulty: 0.339
- 2022-23 Points Prevented: -0.407
- Below average rim protector, shot blocking rates have continued to decline, highly foul prone
- Willing to box out to allow others to grab rebounds, below average defensive rebounder on his own
- Usually guards second unit big men, stout post defender, lacks ideal mobility to effectively defend in space
- Solid pick-and-roll defender, good in drop coverages, effective at hedging out on ball handlers
- Consistently comes out to the perimeter to contest shots in spot-up situations

MarJon Beauchamp

	Height	Weight	Cap #	Years Left
	6'6"	199	$2.609M	2 TO

Similar at Age 22

		Season	SIMsc
1	Timothe Luwawu-Cabarrot	2017-18	934.0
2	Kyle Korver	2003-04	929.1
3	Kevin Brooks	1991-92	927.6
4	Aaron Nesmith	2021-22	926.2
5	Tony Snell	2013-14	924.3
6	Donte DiVincenzo	2018-19	924.2
7	Terrence Ross	2013-14	923.1
8	Nik Stauskas	2015-16	921.8
9	C.J. McCollum	2013-14	921.8
10	Ben McLemore	2015-16	921.5

Baseline Basic Stats

MPG	PTS	AST	REB	BLK	STL
20.2	7.9	1.3	2.6	0.2	0.6

Advanced Metrics

USG%	3PTA/FGA	FTA/FGA	TS%	eFG%	3PT%
18.1	0.518	0.171	0.540	0.515	0.357

AST%	TOV%	OREB%	DREB%	STL%	BLK%
9.0	12.6	4.0	11.0	1.5	0.8

PER	ORTG	DRTG	WS/48	BPM	VOL
10.64	105.2	111.7	0.057	-2.46	0.400

- Fringe rotation player for Milwaukee in his rookie season
- Had an up and down year in a role as a low volume spot-up shooter
- Made threes at a below break-even rate overall, shot an above break-even percentage in the corners
- Strictly a stationary spot-up shooter right now, inefficient when shooting in other situations
- Ineffective pick-and-roll ball handler and isolation player, struggles to create his own shot
- Tends to play too wildly, prone to missing easy shots at the rim, still learning how to move off the ball
- Catch-and-shoot player at this stage, limited passing skills, solid at avoiding turnovers
- 2022-23 Defensive Degree of Difficulty: 0.365
- 2022-23 Points Prevented: 0.471
- Usually guarded second unit players, played solid on-ball defense in these matchups
- Athletic wing, capable of guarding multiple positions
- Decent pick-and-roll defender, can switch and cut off penetration, went too far under screens
- Sometimes gets caught on screens off the ball, good at closing out on spot-up shooters
- Generally a stay-at-home defender, occasionally can get steals, fairly solid defensive rebounder

Thanasis Antetokounmpo

	Height	Weight	Cap #	Years Left
	6'6"	219	$2.020M	UFA

Similar at Age 30

		Season	SIMsc
1	Darvin Ham	2003-04	916.1
2	Vincent Askew	1996-97	909.4
3	Kenny Gattison	1994-95	906.8
4	Billy Owens	1999-00	906.3
5	Major Jones	1983-84	906.2
6	Kermit Washington	1981-82	901.2
7	Sam Mitchell	1993-94	900.1
8	Awvee Storey	2007-08	898.3
9	Charles Davis	1988-89	894.7
10	Marc Iavaroni	1986-87	894.1

Baseline Basic Stats

MPG	PTS	AST	REB	BLK	STL
12.1	3.6	0.6	2.5	0.2	0.4

Advanced Metrics

USG%	3PTA/FGA	FTA/FGA	TS%	eFG%	3PT%
15.0	0.096	0.431	0.501	0.473	0.095

AST%	TOV%	OREB%	DREB%	STL%	BLK%
6.9	16.9	9.2	14.5	1.4	1.5

PER	ORTG	DRTG	WS/48	BPM	VOL
9.84	101.5	108.3	0.063	-4.97	0.332

- Played sparingly for Milwaukee in his fourth season with the team
- Primarily was used as a very low volume energy player off the bench
- Posted a True Shooting Percentage below 50% last season, struggled to make shots in all parts of the floor
- Not really an outside shooting threat, has made less than 55% of his career free throws
- Struggled to finish efficiently at the rim, tends to rush a lot of shots at the rim, plays out of control
- Lacks the ball handling skills to create his own offense, flashed some passing skills in the past, highly turnover prone
- 2022-23 Defensive Degree of Difficulty: 0.240
- 2022-23 Points Prevented: -3.432
- Played mostly in garbage time, has rarely seen action in meaningful portions of games
- Undisciplined on-ball defender, takes bad angles, has trouble staying with opposing players, fairly foul prone
- Below average pick-and-roll defender, indecisive, not effective at taking away any specific action
- Gambles too much, out of position a lot, gets caught on off-ball screens, usually is late to close out on spot-up shooters
- Steal Percentage is declining, somewhat effective as a weak side shot blocker, solid defensive rebounder

A.J. Green

	Height	Weight	Cap #	Years Left
	6'4"	200	$1.902M	2

Similar at Age 23

		Season	SIMsc
1	Daequan Cook	2010-11	936.2
2	Troy Daniels	2014-15	930.6
3	Armoni Brooks	2021-22	908.1
4	John Jenkins	2014-15	897.6
5	Landry Shamet	2020-21	897.4
6	Frank Ntilikina	2021-22	895.8
7	Rodney Purvis	2017-18	895.4
8	Andrew Goudelock	2011-12	889.6
9	Bryn Forbes	2016-17	885.7
10	Travis Diener	2005-06	882.3

Baseline Basic Stats

MPG	PTS	AST	REB	BLK	STL
18.1	7.4	1.2	2.1	0.1	0.5

Advanced Metrics

USG%	3PTA/FGA	FTA/FGA	TS%	eFG%	3PT%
17.1	0.803	0.087	0.583	0.568	0.405

AST%	TOV%	OREB%	DREB%	STL%	BLK%
9.6	7.6	1.8	11.2	1.0	0.4

PER	ORTG	DRTG	WS/48	BPM	VOL
11.67	116.0	113.8	0.100	-0.94	0.422

- Played on a Two-Way contract with Milwaukee, spent time in the G-League with the Wisconsin Herd
- Received limited playing time as a rookie, mainly used as a low volume spot-up shooter
- Great three-point shooter, made almost 42% of his threes at the NBA level
- Almost exclusively a stationary spot-up shooter right now, not really effective when shooting in other situations
- Not really used in other offensive situations in the NBA, played in an offense with minimal movement
- Catch-and-shoot player in the NBA, solid secondary playmaker in the G-League, rarely turns the ball over
- 2022-23 Defensive Degree of Difficulty: 0.268
- 2022-23 Points Prevented: -0.235
- Typically played against lower leverage second unit players or in garbage time
- Rarely tested on the ball, struggled to play effective on-ball defense in a small sample possessions
- Below average pick-and-roll defender, not especially effective at taking away any specific action
- Tends to get caught on screens off the ball, consistently closes out on spot-up shooters
- Stay-at-home defender in the NBA, occasionally got steals in the G-League, fairly solid defensive rebounder

Newcomers

Andre Jackson Jr.

	Height	Weight	Cap #	Years Left
	6'6"	210	$1.120M	2 + TO

Baseline Basic Stats

MPG	PTS	AST	REB	BLK	STL
17.3	5.1	1.2	2.4	0.3	0.7

Advanced Metrics

USG%	3PTA/FGA	FTA/FGA	TS%	eFG%	3PT%
12.9	0.317	0.231	0.503	0.474	0.321

AST%	TOV%	OREB%	DREB%	STL%	BLK%
12.7	15.3	4.5	11.3	2.0	1.4

PER	ORTG	DRTG	WS/48	BPM	VOL
9.99	102.5	101.8	0.058	-1.73	N/A

- Drafted by Orlando with the 36th overall pick in 2023, traded to Milwaukee
- Struggled to play efficiently at the Las Vegas Summer League
- Mainly used as a lower volume playmaker and energy player
- Tended to rush and play out of control, extremely turnover prone, struggled to convert on easy shots
- Posted a True Shooting Percentage below 45%, only made one-third of his field goals and 20% of his threes
- Jump shot is still a work-in-progress, most effective at using his athleticism to attack the rim in transition at the college level
- Solid secondary playmaker with good court vision, tends to force passes into tight windows
- Active offensive rebounder that keeps possessions alive
- Long defender with explosive athleticism, potentially can be a plus-level defender in the future
- Plays out of control on defense, prone to committing cheap fouls to bail opponents out
- Solid on-ball defender on the perimeter, has trouble guarding bigger players in the post
- Fairly good pick-and-roll defender, can effectively switch to guard screeners or ball handlers
- Gambles too much, out of position quite a bit, tends to get caught on off-ball screens, does not always close out on spot-up shooters
- Very active as a help defender, post high steal and block rates at Summer League, good defensive rebounder
- Needs to spend some time in the G-League to improve his discipline and skill level on both ends of the floor

Chris Livingston

	Height	Weight	Cap #	Years Left
	6'6"	220	$1.120M	2 + TO

Baseline Basic Stats

MPG	PTS	AST	REB	BLK	STL
13.6	4.5	0.8	2.0	0.2	0.4

Advanced Metrics

USG%	3PTA/FGA	FTA/FGA	TS%	eFG%	3PT%
15.0	0.391	0.208	0.492	0.465	0.325

AST%	TOV%	OREB%	DREB%	STL%	BLK%
8.0	10.9	4.0	12.7	1.4	1.1

PER	ORTG	DRTG	WS/48	BPM	VOL
9.46	100.4	106.8	0.032	-2.90	N/A

- Drafted by Milwaukee with the 58th overall pick in 2023
- Had a solid performance at the Las Vegas Summer League
- Fairly effective in his role as a low usage energy wing
- Posted a True Shooting Percentage above 56%, drew fouls at a solid rate
- Explosive finisher in transition, good cutter off the ball, will go to the offensive boards to score on put-backs
- Shooting is still a work-in-progress, below break-even three-point shooter in college
- Made less than 30% of his threes and 60% of his free throws at Summer League
- Very rarely was used in ball handling situations in college, lacks the ability to create his own shot
- Decent secondary playmaker in Summer League, tended to play rather wildly, fairly turnover prone
- Great athlete with outstanding length, may potentially be able to become a versatile, plus-level defender in the future
- Good on-ball defender, defends multiple positions on the floor
- Decent pick-and-roll defender, capable of switching, tends to have lapses when making rotations, prone to committing cheap fouls
- Stays attached to shooters off the ball, fights through screens and closes out in spot-up situations
- Good at playing passing lanes to get steals, did not block a shot at Summer League, solid weak side shot blocker in college, fairly good defensive rebounding wing
- Will need to spend time in the G-League to improve his shooting and polish his all-around game

PHILADELPHIA 76ERS

Last Season: 54 - 28, Lost 2nd Round to Boston (3 – 4)

Offensive Rating: 117.7, 4th in the NBA   Defensive Rating: 113.3, 8th in the NBA

Primary Executive: Daryl Morey, President of Basketball Operations

Head Coach: Nick Nurse

Key Roster Changes

Subtractions
Georges Niang, free agency
Shake Milton, free agency
Jalen McDaniels, free agency
Dewayne Dedmon, free agency

Additions
Patrick Beverley, free agency
Mo Bamba, free agency
Filip Petrušev, free agency

Roster

Likely Starting Five
1. James Harden
2. Tyrese Maxey
3. P.J. Tucker
4. Tobias Harris
5. Joel Embiid

Other Key Rotation Players
De'Anthony Melton
Patrick Beverley
Paul Reed
Mo Bamba
Danuel House Jr.

* Italics denotes that a player is likely to be on the floor to close games

Remaining Roster

- Montrezl Harrell
- Furkan Korkmaz
- Jaden Springer
- Filip Petrušev
- Terquavion Smith, 21, 6'4", 165, NC State (Two-Way)
- Ricky Council IV, 22, 6'6", 205, Arkansas (Two-Way)
- Ažuolas Tubelis, 21, 6'11", 245, Arizona (Two-Way)
- Marcus Bagley, 22, 6'8", 215, Arizona State (Exhibit 10)
- Javonte Smart, 24, 6'4", 205, LSU (Exhibit 10)

SCHREMPF Base Rating: 48.6

Season Preview Survey

- *Are the Sixers contending or rebuilding? Where is this team headed?*

The Sixers are one of the better teams in the league and they have the talent to make a deep title run, but they are currently in a fragile position. They haven't been able to really break through to reach the Conference Finals because they have suffered a string of disappointing playoff losses. Also, they may have to retool their roster because James Harden requested a trade in the offseason. They will have to thread the needle of honoring his request and finding the right package to keep them in contention. It will be tough act to pull off because their team has significant flaws even if Harden reconciles with the franchise and comes back to play. Essentially, they have the ability to contend, but there's a considerable risk that things could go off the rails and they could slip into mediocrity if they don't make the right decisions.

- *What are the areas of concern for this team heading into this season?*

Aside from their general roster situation and Harden's trade request, the Sixers still have some issues that they have to address. In particular, their team is overly dependent on the individual talent of Joel Embiid because they have surrounded him with a lot of one-dimensional role players that aren't able to take on additional usage. Those players don't really have the ability to pick up the slack if Embiid is having an off night, so this puts a lot of additional pressure on him to maintain an exceedingly high level of performance. In addition to this, their style is a bit too simplistic and predictable. As a result, they haven't been able to effectively adjust to the tactics and lineups of their opponents, which has put them at a disadvantage in past playoff series. There's a chance that the coaching change to Nick Nurse could improve things incrementally, but they may have to seriously take a hard look at their team to figure the next step to turn them into legitimate title contenders.

- *List some possible breakout players for this team.*

The Sixers don't have a lot of breakout candidates on their team because they are mostly an established, veteran heavy group. Filip Petrusev is the only younger player that could emerge as an unexpected contributor. The Sixers haven't been able to find a reliable backup center to spell Embiid, so Petrusev could possibly fill that spot if he gets an opportunity to play extended minutes. He potentially gives them a different look by being more of a skilled, finesse center that can space the floor with his outside shot and add a passing dimension. He's also different from other international free agents because he was an accomplished college player at Gonzaga before he elected to play in the Adriatic League. He should have no major issues with adjusting to handling NBA level athleticism, so he has a chance to be an impactful bench player if he gets a chance to showcase his talent.

- *What should we expect from them this season?*

The expectations are slightly unclear because their roster situation is in flux due to the possibility of losing James Harden in a trade. If they deal him in a way that allows them to acquire equivalent but more versatile talent, they could make a deeper playoff run if they can quickly sort any possible chemistry issues. Otherwise, their season might end in a similar way to it did in the past couple years with an exit in the second round range. The only way to effectively move away from this fate is for them to alter their system to utilize different concepts like movement on offense and more versatile lineups that can counter the opposition more effectively. This way, they can empower the other players around Embiid to build a much more well-rounded team. If that winds up happening, then they might be able to compete for a championship as soon as this season.

Veterans

Joel Embiid

	Height	Weight	Cap #	Years Left
	7'0"	280	$47.607M	2 + PO

Similar at Age 28

		Season	SIMsc
1	Brook Lopez	2016-17	854.9
2	DeMarcus Cousins	2018-19	834.3
3	Patrick Ewing*	1990-91	831.6
4	Tim Duncan*	2004-05	825.6
5	Marc Gasol	2012-13	824.5
6	Nikola Vucevic	2018-19	813.3
7	Dirk Nowitzki*	2006-07	812.5
8	Amare Stoudemire	2010-11	811.1
9	David Robinson*	1993-94	810.6
10	Chris Kaman	2010-11	809.3

Baseline Basic Stats

MPG	PTS	AST	REB	BLK	STL
32.4	23.4	3.9	10.3	1.5	1.0

Advanced Metrics

USG%	3PTA/FGA	FTA/FGA	TS%	eFG%	3PT%
32.8	0.187	0.514	0.615	0.547	0.376

AST%	TOV%	OREB%	DREB%	STL%	BLK%
21.4	12.2	6.6	28.0	1.5	4.1

PER	ORTG	DRTG	WS/48	BPM	VOL
27.15	117.8	106.1	0.212	8.37	0.423

- 2022-23 MVP, named to the All-NBA 1st Team, led the NBA in scoring for the second straight season
- Had a career best season in his role as Philadelphia's primary scoring option
- Elite post-up player, can score with a variety of moves, does most of his damage from the left block
- Excellent on isolations, can drive by slower big men, draws a lot of fouls, can hit pull-up mid-range jumpers
- Great rim runner, solid cutter and roll man, effective offensive rebounder that scores on put-backs
- Break-even three-point shooter, better on pick-and-pops, less effective as a stationary spot-up shooter
- Good passing big man, finds open shooters out of double teams, good at limiting turnovers
- 2022-23 Defensive Degree of Difficulty: 0.452
- 2022-23 Points Prevented: 1.215
- Great defensive rebounder and shot blocker, solid rim protector, can be a step slow to contest layups
- Usually guarded starting level big men, stout post defender, showed enough mobility to defend in space
- Decent pick-and-roll defender, good in drop coverages, had trouble containing ball handlers on switches
- Tended to stay anchored in the paint, did not always come out to contest perimeter shots in spot-up situations
- Fairly good at using his length to play passing lanes and get steals

James Harden

	Height	Weight	Cap #	Years Left
	6'5"	220	$35.640M	UFA

Similar at Age 33

		Season	SIMsc
1	Manu Ginobili*	2010-11	896.0
2	Paul Pierce*	2010-11	880.4
3	Chauncey Billups	2009-10	867.1
4	Mitch Richmond*	1998-99	862.2
5	Jason Kidd*	2006-07	861.8
6	Vince Carter	2009-10	858.9
7	Clyde Drexler*	1995-96	857.9
8	Goran Dragić	2019-20	856.8
9	Jim Jackson	2003-04	849.7
10	Russell Westbrook	2021-22	848.9

Baseline Basic Stats

MPG	PTS	AST	REB	BLK	STL
32.0	18.4	5.2	4.8	0.4	1.2

Advanced Metrics

USG%	3PTA/FGA	FTA/FGA	TS%	eFG%	3PT%
25.7	0.437	0.409	0.580	0.509	0.364

AST%	TOV%	OREB%	DREB%	STL%	BLK%
32.7	15.8	2.2	16.7	1.8	1.2

PER	ORTG	DRTG	WS/48	BPM	VOL
19.85	114.7	109.4	0.157	3.89	0.342

- Missed games due to an assortment on minor injuries, still played at an All-Star in his first full season in Philadelphia
- Largely operated as Philadelphia's primary playmaker and ball handler
- Great isolation player and pick-and-roll ball handler, still draws fouls at a high rate, not getting to the rim as frequently, taking more floaters
- League average three-point shooter, made 38.5% of his threes last season
- Most effective as a spot-up shooter, solid shoot off the dribble but can be streaky
- Dynamic playmaker with great court vision, slightly turnover prone, rarely moves off the ball
- 2022-23 Defensive Degree of Difficulty: 0.443
- 2022-23 Points Prevented: 0.867
- Usually guards starting level players, decent on-ball defender, effort level is not always high
- Thick frame allows him to be effective against bigger players, has trouble staying with quicker guards
- Below average pick-and-roll defender, not effective at taking away any specific action
- Tends to get caught on screens off the ball, consistently closes out on spot-up shooters
- Gets steals at a moderate rate, Block Percentage is still consistent with his career average, solid defensive rebounder

Tyrese Maxey

	Height	Weight	Cap #	Years Left
	6'2"	200	$4.344M	RFA

Similar at Age 22

		Season	SIMsc
1	Bradley Beal	2015-16	927.4
2	Jamal Murray	2019-20	926.9
3	Ben Gordon	2005-06	924.4
4	Malik Monk	2020-21	923.8
5	Jaylen Nowell	2021-22	921.6
6	Marcus Thornton	2009-10	918.7
7	Jimmer Fredette	2011-12	914.3
8	Damian Lillard	2012-13	910.2
9	Jalen Brunson	2018-19	909.7
10	Lonnie Walker	2020-21	907.8

Baseline Basic Stats

MPG	PTS	AST	REB	BLK	STL
28.4	15.1	3.2	3.0	0.2	0.8

Advanced Metrics

USG%	3PTA/FGA	FTA/FGA	TS%	eFG%	3PT%
23.1	0.369	0.238	0.583	0.543	0.403

AST%	TOV%	OREB%	DREB%	STL%	BLK%
18.4	9.2	1.7	9.3	1.3	0.7

PER	ORTG	DRTG	WS/48	BPM	VOL
16.43	116.1	113.8	0.124	0.47	0.343

- Missed a month with a left foot injury, regular starting guard for Philadelphia when healthy
- Production continued to increase, highly effective as a higher usage scoring guard
- Great pick-and-roll ball handler and isolation player, effective at scoring at all three levels
- Excellent three-point shooter, has made over 43% of his threes over the last two seasons
- Highly efficient spot-up shooter, good shooter off the dribble, less effective when shooting off screens
- Has great speed, excellent at pushing the ball in transition, good at scoring on hand-offs
- Solid secondary playmaker that makes simple reads, rarely turns the ball over
- 2022-23 Defensive Degree of Difficulty: 0.444
- 2022-23 Points Prevented: -0.239
- Usually defends starting level guards, on-ball defense improved slightly
- Effectively stays in front of opposing guards, struggles against bigger perimeter players
- Below average pick-and-roll defender, has trouble containing ball handlers, tends to go too far under screens
- Stays attached to shooters off the ball, fights through off-ball screens and closes out in spot-up situations
- Stay-at-home defender, does not really get steals, block rate decreased significantly, below average defensive rebounder

Tobias Harris

	Height	Weight	Cap #	Years Left
	6'8"	226	$39.270M	UFA

Similar at Age 30

		Season	SIMsc
1	Wilson Chandler	2017-18	933.9
2	Luol Deng	2015-16	933.4
3	Antawn Jamison	2006-07	931.9
4	Marcus Morris	2019-20	927.3
5	Joe Johnson	2011-12	926.0
6	Marvin Williams	2016-17	922.5
7	Danny Ferry	1996-97	919.9
8	Mike Dunleavy Jr.	2010-11	917.7
9	Michael Finley	2003-04	917.6
10	Danilo Gallinari	2018-19	911.8

Baseline Basic Stats

MPG	PTS	AST	REB	BLK	STL
28.6	12.6	2.0	4.6	0.3	0.7

Advanced Metrics

USG%	3PTA/FGA	FTA/FGA	TS%	eFG%	3PT%
19.1	0.377	0.189	0.565	0.533	0.375

AST%	TOV%	OREB%	DREB%	STL%	BLK%
11.5	9.6	3.2	16.3	1.2	1.2

PER	ORTG	DRTG	WS/48	BPM	VOL
13.91	112.1	111.2	0.101	-0.15	0.342

- Regular starting wing for Philadelphia in his fourth full season with the team
- Efficiency increased, shifted to a new role as a low usage spot-up shooter
- Fairly reliable three-point shooter, made almost 39% of his threes last season
- Almost exclusively a stationary spot-up shooter, does not run off screens or shoot off the dribble
- Effective at posting up smaller players, solid isolation player against slower defenders
- Average pick-and-roll ball handler, good cutter, fairly solid secondary playmaker, rarely turns the ball over
- <u>2022-23 Defensive Degree of Difficulty</u>: 0.530
- <u>2022-23 Points Prevented</u>: 1.211
- Routinely drew tough assignments against elite perimeter scorers, generally a solid on-ball defender
- Capable of defending multiple positions, had some trouble staying with quicker players or holding position against stronger fours
- Good pick-and-roll defender, effective at switching to guard ball handlers or screeners
- Stays attached to shooters off the ball, fights through screens, good at closing out in spot-up situations
- Stay-at-home defender, steal and block rates increased slightly, solid defensive rebounder

P.J. Tucker

	Height	Weight	Cap #	Years Left
	6'5"	245	$11.015M	PO

Similar at Age 37

		Season	SIMsc
1	Paul Pierce*	2014-15	873.4
2	Carmelo Anthony	2021-22	870.1
3	Mario Elie	2000-01	857.2
4	Sam Perkins	1998-99	847.5
5	Ray Allen*	2012-13	841.5
6	Andre Iguodala	2020-21	832.0
7	Kyle Korver	2018-19	830.0
8	Bruce Bowen	2008-09	828.5
9	Vince Carter	2013-14	820.1
10	Juwan Howard	2010-11	813.3

Baseline Basic Stats

MPG	PTS	AST	REB	BLK	STL
23.5	6.2	1.3	3.6	0.3	0.7

Advanced Metrics

USG%	3PTA/FGA	FTA/FGA	TS%	eFG%	3PT%
10.5	0.530	0.139	0.540	0.515	0.384

AST%	TOV%	OREB%	DREB%	STL%	BLK%
8.2	13.6	4.7	14.0	1.5	1.0

PER	ORTG	DRTG	WS/48	BPM	VOL
8.45	111.8	112.7	0.080	-2.43	0.625

- Regular starter for Philadelphia in his first season with the team
- Effectiveness declined in a role as an extremely low usage spot-up shooter
- Around a league average career three-point shooter, made over 39% of his threes last season
- Strictly a stationary spot-up shooter, over 91% of his threes came from the corners in 2022-23
- Rarely shoots the ball, often hesitates before shooting, struggled to finish around the rim due to waning athleticism
- Not used in other offensive situations, limited passing skills, slightly turnover prone
- 2022-23 Defensive Degree of Difficulty: 0.599, had the 3rd most difficult set of matchups in the NBA
- 2022-23 Points Prevented: 0.131
- Mainly utilized as Philadelphia's primary defensive stopper, fairly good on-ball defender, plays very physical
- Effectively holds position inside against bigger players, had some trouble staying with quicker scorers
- Played below average pick-and-roll defense, solid in drop coverages, usually went too far under screens, could allow ball handlers to turn the corner
- Stays attached to shooters off the ball, fights through screens and closes out in spot-up situations
- Stay-at-home defender, rarely gets steals or blocks, solid defensive rebounder

De'Anthony Melton

	Height	Weight	Cap #	Years Left
	6'2"	200	$8.000M	UFA

Similar at Age 24

		Season	SIMsc
1	Toney Douglas	2010-11	919.2
2	Donte DiVincenzo	2020-21	916.2
3	Terry Rozier	2018-19	914.6
4	Langston Galloway	2015-16	913.2
5	Jevon Carter	2019-20	908.4
6	Luther Head	2006-07	897.4
7	Mario Chalmers	2010-11	894.0
8	Daniel Gibson	2010-11	891.9
9	Danny Green	2011-12	890.7
10	Iman Shumpert	2014-15	889.8

Baseline Basic Stats

MPG	PTS	AST	REB	BLK	STL
23.3	9.6	2.5	3.3	0.2	1.0

Advanced Metrics

USG%	3PTA/FGA	FTA/FGA	TS%	eFG%	3PT%
18.9	0.603	0.164	0.550	0.521	0.383

AST%	TOV%	OREB%	DREB%	STL%	BLK%
15.3	12.2	3.4	13.1	2.4	1.3

PER	ORTG	DRTG	WS/48	BPM	VOL
13.15	110.0	112.1	0.083	0.05	0.364

- Regular starter for most of his first season with Philadelphia
- Solidly effective in his role as a low volume spot-up shooter and secondary ball handler
- Fairly reliable three-point shooter, made 39% of his threes last season
- Mostly a stand-still spot-up shooter, improved his ability to make threes off pick-and-rolls
- Lacks ideal ball handling skills, struggles to drive as a pick-and-roll ball handler and isolation player
- Played in a static offense, rarely was asked to move off the ball
- Solid secondary playmaker that makes simple reads, good at limiting turnovers
- 2022-23 Defensive Degree of Difficulty: 0.592, had the 5th most difficult set of matchups in the NBA
- 2022-23 Points Prevented: -0.301
- Routinely drew tough assignments against elite scoring guards, may have been over-extended in this role
- Quick enough to stay with opposing guards, had trouble contesting shots against bigger perimeter players
- Played below average pick-and-roll defense, not especially effective at taking away any specific action
- Stays attached to shooters off the ball, fights through screens and closes out in spot-up situations
- Very active help defender, great at playing passing lanes to get steals, effective weak side shot blocker, good defensive rebounder

Patrick Beverley

	Height	Weight	Cap #	Years Left
	6'1"	180	$2.020M	UFA

Similar at Age 34

		Season	SIMsc
1	Bobby Jackson	2007-08	895.7
2	Sedale Threatt	1995-96	882.3
3	Mike Conley	2021-22	881.9
4	Kirk Hinrich	2014-15	881.8
5	Jason Williams	2009-10	880.4
6	Devin Harris	2017-18	879.6
7	Brent Barry	2005-06	876.4
8	Danny Ainge	1993-94	875.9
9	Doc Rivers	1995-96	875.8
10	Garrett Temple	2020-21	873.7

Baseline Basic Stats

MPG	PTS	AST	REB	BLK	STL
21.0	7.2	2.7	2.4	0.3	0.8

Advanced Metrics

USG%	3PTA/FGA	FTA/FGA	TS%	eFG%	3PT%
13.2	0.610	0.230	0.550	0.518	0.349

AST%	TOV%	OREB%	DREB%	STL%	BLK%
17.6	13.1	3.1	11.6	1.8	1.9

PER	ORTG	DRTG	WS/48	BPM	VOL
11.68	115.4	112.1	0.102	-0.21	0.586

- Traded by the L.A. Lakers at the trade deadline, signed with Chicago after he was waived by Orlando
- Regular starting guard for both teams, used as a low usage spot-up shooter and secondary playmaker
- Above average career three-point shooter, Three-Point Percentage has fallen to just above break-even
- May be slowing down due to age, strictly a stationary spot-up shooter right now
- Mostly ineffective in ball handling situations, does not really move off the ball either
- Can push the ball in transition a little bit, solid secondary playmaker, good at limiting turnovers
- 2022-23 Defensive Degree of Difficulty: 0.551
- 2022-23 Points Prevented: -0.402
- Used as a defensive stopper by both teams, still a good on-ball defender that guards multiple positions
- Aggressive guard that can pressure ball handlers on the perimeter, fairly good at handling taller wings
- Played around average pick-and-roll defense last season, good at switching, had lapses when making rotations
- Tended to get caught on screens off the ball, generally was late when closing out on spot-up shooters
- Still an active help defender, gets steals at a high rate, effective weak side shot blocking guard, solid defensive rebounder

Paul Reed

	Height	Weight	Cap #	Years Left
	6'9"	210	$7.723M	2

Similar at Age 23

		Season	SIMsc
1	Larry Micheaux	1983-84	866.8
2	Skal Labissière	2019-20	865.4
3	Pervis Ellison	1990-91	865.0
4	Anthony Randolph	2012-13	864.9
5	Kenny Williams	1992-93	864.6
6	Jordan Bell	2017-18	863.3
7	Tyrus Thomas	2009-10	862.2
8	Earl Cureton	1980-81	861.7
9	Brandan Wright	2010-11	860.7
10	Sam Williams	1982-83	858.3

Baseline Basic Stats

MPG	PTS	AST	REB	BLK	STL
16.2	6.5	0.7	4.1	0.9	0.6

Advanced Metrics

USG%	3PTA/FGA	FTA/FGA	TS%	eFG%	3PT%
18.0	0.042	0.269	0.583	0.555	0.209

AST%	TOV%	OREB%	DREB%	STL%	BLK%
6.9	13.2	13.2	19.3	2.6	4.5

PER	ORTG	DRTG	WS/48	BPM	VOL
18.53	117.0	104.7	0.164	0.07	0.484

- Fringe rotation player for Philadelphia in the regular season, used as the primary backup center in the playoffs
- Highly effective per-minute player, mainly utilized as a low volume rim runner
- High motor rim runner with good athleticism, good roll man and cutter, runs hard in transition
- Great offensive rebounder, sometimes will rush his put-back attempts
- Lacks reliable shooting range outside of three feet, greatly improved his free throw shooting
- Occasionally can flash to the middle on post-ups, limited passing skills, slightly turnover prone
- 2022-23 Defensive Degree of Difficulty: 0.357
- 2022-23 Points Prevented: -1.609
- Good shot blocker and defensive rebounder, middling rim protector, undisciplined with his positioning
- Guards second unit big men, below average on-ball defender
- Can be overpowered by stronger centers, tends to commit shooting fouls in the post, better when defending in space
- Below average pick-and-roll defender, not effective at taking away any specific action
- Tends to sag into the paint, does not always come out to contest outside shots
- Has good anticipation skills, uses length well to jump passing lanes, gets steals at a very high rate

Mo Bamba

	Height	Weight	Cap #	Years Left
	7'0"	231	$2.020M	UFA

Similar at Age 24

		Season	SIMsc
1	D.J. Wilson	2020-21	892.3
2	Sam Bowie	1985-86	887.7
3	Raef LaFrentz	2000-01	886.2
4	Mike Muscala	2015-16	882.5
5	Tony Battie	2000-01	881.3
6	Luke Kornet	2019-20	879.7
7	Larry Sanders	2012-13	872.8
8	Marcin Gortat	2008-09	872.5
9	Trey Lyles	2019-20	871.4
10	Kelly Olynyk	2015-16	870.6

Baseline Basic Stats

MPG	PTS	AST	REB	BLK	STL
21.4	8.2	1.0	5.5	1.4	0.5

Advanced Metrics

USG%	3PTA/FGA	FTA/FGA	TS%	eFG%	3PT%
16.7	0.384	0.239	0.588	0.566	0.367

AST%	TOV%	OREB%	DREB%	STL%	BLK%
8.2	10.4	8.1	21.9	0.9	5.0

PER	ORTG	DRTG	WS/48	BPM	VOL
16.13	117.4	108.6	0.136	0.23	0.407

- Traded from Orlando to the L.A. Lakers, regular rotation player for Orlando, missed the bulk of his games with the Lakers due to a high ankle sprain
- Solidly effective in his role as a low volume stretch big and rim runner
- League average three-point shooter, has made over 38% of his threes over the past two seasons
- Mostly a spot-up shooter, fairly good as a pick-and-pop screener
- Effective rim runner, vertical lob threat, good roll man and cutter, runs the floor in transition, active offensive rebounder
- Not really a post-up threat, catch-and-finish player, limited passing skills, rarely turns the ball over
- 2022-23 Defensive Degree of Difficulty: 0.360
- 2022-23 Points Prevented: -0.246
- Great shot blocker and defensive rebounder, average rim protector, undisciplined position defender, highly foul prone
- Usually guards second unit big men, stout post defender, has trouble defending in space
- Middling pick-and-roll defender, solid in drop coverages, struggles to effectively contain ball handlers on switches
- Generally stays anchored in the paint, does not always come out to contest outside shots

Danuel House Jr.

	Height	Weight	Cap #	Years Left
	6'6"	220	$4.310M	UFA

Similar at Age 29

		Season	SIMsc
1	Cartier Martin	2013-14	950.3
2	Mickael Pietrus	2011-12	927.8
3	James Ennis	2019-20	925.8
4	Alan Anderson	2011-12	917.1
5	Morris Peterson	2006-07	913.7
6	Quentin Richardson	2009-10	912.7
7	Matt Bullard	1996-97	910.4
8	Jud Buechler	1997-98	909.4
9	Alec Burks	2020-21	909.3
10	Damion Lee	2021-22	909.3

Baseline Basic Stats

MPG	PTS	AST	REB	BLK	STL
19.3	6.3	1.0	2.5	0.2	0.5

Advanced Metrics

USG%	3PTA/FGA	FTA/FGA	TS%	eFG%	3PT%
14.4	0.568	0.232	0.557	0.526	0.359

AST%	TOV%	OREB%	DREB%	STL%	BLK%
8.0	10.6	2.0	12.6	1.3	1.1

PER	ORTG	DRTG	WS/48	BPM	VOL
9.72	109.3	112.8	0.068	-2.06	0.376

- Fringe rotation player for Philadelphia in his first season with the team
- Primarily utilized as a low volume spot-up shooter off the bench
- Around a league average career three-point shooter, percentages tend to vary from year-to-year
- Almost exclusively a stationary spot-up shooter, break-even three-point shooter last season
- Limited ball handling skills, unable to create his own shot, solid cutter off the ball
- Strictly a catch-and-shoot player, only makes safe passes, good at avoiding turnovers
- 2022-23 Defensive Degree of Difficulty: 0.451
- 2022-23 Points Prevented: -0.697
- Drew some tough assignments off the bench, played fairly solid on-ball defense
- Good at guarding perimeter players, had trouble guarding bigger wings inside
- More effective pick-and-roll defender, could functionally switch, generally made sound rotations
- Tended to get caught on screens off the ball, good at closing out on spot-up shooters
- Stay-at-home defender, rarely gets steals or blocks, solid defensive rebounder

Montrezl Harrell

	Height	Weight	Cap #	Years Left
	6'7"	240	$2.020M	UFA

Similar at Age 29

		Season	SIMsc
1	Kenneth Faried	2018-19	912.2
2	Clarence Weatherspoon	1999-00	909.7
3	LaPhonso Ellis	1999-00	906.2
4	Brandon Bass	2014-15	902.0
5	Lawrence Funderburke	1999-00	900.9
6	Taj Gibson	2014-15	897.3
7	Carl Landry	2012-13	895.7
8	Daniel Theis	2021-22	894.2
9	Armen Gilliam	1993-94	892.8
10	Matt Harpring	2005-06	891.9

Baseline Basic Stats

MPG	PTS	AST	REB	BLK	STL
20.9	8.5	1.0	5.2	0.6	0.6

Advanced Metrics

USG%	3PTA/FGA	FTA/FGA	TS%	eFG%	3PT%
18.1	0.034	0.426	0.604	0.565	0.163

AST%	TOV%	OREB%	DREB%	STL%	BLK%
8.5	11.5	10.4	17.9	1.2	2.6

PER	ORTG	DRTG	WS/48	BPM	VOL
17.62	120.0	108.6	0.135	0.38	0.442

- Fringe rotation player for Philadelphia in his first season with the team
- Effective in his role as a low volume rim runner off the bench
- Energetic rim runner, good roll man and cutter, good offensive rebounder, great at running the floor in transition
- Good at bullying smaller defenders in the post, lacks reliable shooting range outside of ten feet
- Largely a catch-and-finish player, shows decent passing skills, good at avoiding turnovers
- 2022-23 Defensive Degree of Difficulty: 0.367
- 2022-23 Points Prevented: 0.090
- Effective rim protector despite being undersized, good shot blocker, decent defensive rebounder
- Guarded second unit big men, below average defender
- Can be overpowered by stronger centers, tends to commit shooting fouls, struggles to defend in space
- Average pick-and-roll defender, decent at hedging out on ball handlers, has lapses when covering screeners
- Consistently comes out to contest perimeter shots in spot-up situations
- Likely will miss the entire 2023-24 season due to a torn ACL and meniscus in his right knee

Furkan Korkmaz

	Height	Weight	Cap #	Years Left
	6'7"	202	$5.370M	UFA

Similar at Age 25

		Season	SIMsc
1	Nik Stauskas	2018-19	944.4
2	Reggie Williams	2011-12	936.1
3	Eric Piatkowski	1995-96	936.1
4	Rodney Carney	2009-10	932.9
5	Wesley Johnson	2012-13	932.8
6	Scott Burrell	1995-96	926.1
7	Oscar Torres	2001-02	925.9
8	Sam Mack	1995-96	924.8
9	Damyean Dotson	2019-20	924.4
10	Martell Webster	2011-12	923.9

Baseline Basic Stats

MPG	PTS	AST	REB	BLK	STL
21.0	8.8	1.4	2.6	0.2	0.6

Advanced Metrics

USG%	3PTA/FGA	FTA/FGA	TS%	eFG%	3PT%
19.4	0.457	0.248	0.547	0.511	0.369

AST%	TOV%	OREB%	DREB%	STL%	BLK%
11.3	12.3	2.3	11.2	1.5	0.8

PER	ORTG	DRTG	WS/48	BPM	VOL
11.67	105.2	112.7	0.056	-1.81	0.392

- Fell out of Philadelphia's rotation, played sparingly last season
- Efficiency increased, mainly used as a low volume spot-up shooter
- Bounced back to have a solid shooting year, made over 39% of his threes
- Around a league average career three-point shooter, percentages vary quite a bit
- Mostly a stand-still spot-up shooter last season, effective at shooting on the move in previous seasons
- Lacks the ball handling skills to create his own offense, good cutter off the ball
- Primarily a catch-and-shoot player, shows some passing skills, slightly turnover prone last season
- 2022-23 Defensive Degree of Difficulty: 0.258
- 2022-23 Points Prevented: 0.689
- Mostly guarded second unit players or played in garbage time
- Did not play many meaningful minutes, rarely tested on the ball
- Effective on-ball defender in a small sample of possessions against lower leverage players
- Played solid pick-and-roll defense, could functionally switch, good at funneling his man into help
- Tended to get caught on screens off the ball, good at closing out on spot-up shooters
- Now more of a stay-at-home defender, occasionally gets steals, fairly solid defensive rebounder

Jaden Springer

	Height	Weight	Cap #	Years Left
	6'4"	204	$2.226M	TO

Similar at Age 20

		Season	SIMsc
1	Isaiah Jackson	2021-22	754.9
2	Martin Lewis	1995-96	751.6
3	Amir Johnson	2007-08	741.0
4	Markelle Fultz	2018-19	735.6
5	Wade Baldwin	2016-17	728.9
6	Keldon Johnson	2019-20	725.7
7	Hamidou Diallo	2018-19	725.0
8	Gerald Wallace	2002-03	719.6
9	Travis Outlaw	2004-05	719.3
10	Alen Smailagić	2020-21	718.9

Baseline Basic Stats

MPG	PTS	AST	REB	BLK	STL
17.3	6.5	1.3	3.5	0.6	0.6

Advanced Metrics

USG%	3PTA/FGA	FTA/FGA	TS%	eFG%	3PT%
18.2	0.157	0.191	0.640	0.617	0.280

AST%	TOV%	OREB%	DREB%	STL%	BLK%
11.4	17.2	8.9	14.1	1.9	6.9

PER	ORTG	DRTG	WS/48	BPM	VOL
17.68	112.4	106.5	0.130	2.92	0.626

- Has only played 95 NBA minutes in two seasons, mostly played in the G-League for Delaware
- Used as a moderate volume scoring guard in the G-League
- Below break-even three-point shooter in the G-League, better shooter from mid-range
- Can attack the rim and hit pull-up jumpers as a pick-and-roll ball handler, consistently able to draw fouls at both levels
- Fairly solid secondary playmaker that can make simple reads, rarely turns the ball over
- 2022-23 Defensive Degree of Difficulty: 0.504
- 2022-23 Points Prevented: -7.885
- Data heavily skewed, spent a majority of his minutes guarding Trae Young
- Struggled to defend on the ball, had trouble staying in front of Young in heavy minutes against Atlanta
- Played below average pick-and-roll defense, not able to cut off penetration, also tended to go too far under screens
- Did not have to defend a lot of off-ball motion, generally was late when contesting perimeter shots
- Very active help defender, consistently gets steals and blocks at a high rate, solid defensive rebounder

Newcomers

Filip Petrusev

	Height	Weight	Cap #	Years Left
	6'11"	234	$1.120M	1

Baseline Basic Stats

MPG	PTS	AST	REB	BLK	STL
19.2	7.9	1.1	5.1	0.9	0.5

Advanced Metrics

USG%	3PTA/FGA	FTA/FGA	TS%	eFG%	3PT%
18.0	0.225	0.253	0.583	0.556	0.347

AST%	TOV%	OREB%	DREB%	STL%	BLK%
8.0	12.7	8.4	22.0	1.3	3.8

PER	ORTG	DRTG	WS/48	BPM	VOL
14.40	115.0	114.7	0.104	0.06	0.302

- Drafted by Philadelphia with the 50th overall pick in 2021
- Previously played college basketball at Gonzaga, played last season in the Adriatic League and EuroLeague with KK Crvena Zvezda
- Projection uses translated EuroLeague stats
- Had a solid performance at the Salt Lake City and Las Vegas Summer Leagues
- Used at Summer League as a low volume rim runner, played more of stretch five role in Europe
- High motor rim runner, lacks ideal vertical lift, good finisher around the rim
- Posted a True Shooting Percentage above 60%, good cutter and roll man, runs hard in transition, solid offensive rebounder
- Fairly good three-point shooter in Europe, made 43% of his threes last season
- Primarily a stand-still spot-up shooter, effective at posting up smaller players, flashes some passing skills, slightly turnover prone at Summer League
- Lacks ideal athleticism, high effort defender, good defensive rebounder and shot blocker
- Still undisciplined with his positioning, highly foul prone
- Middling on-ball defender, has trouble defending in the post, limited mobility may hurt his ability to defend in space
- Fairly effective pick-and-roll defender, solid in drop coverages, effective at hedging out on ball handlers
- Will come out to contest perimeter shots in spot-up situations
- Offensive skills may allow him to earn minutes in the NBA, could stand to play in the G-League for a few games to prove himself on defense

CLEVELAND CAVALIERS

Last Season: 51 - 31, Lost 1st Round to New York (1 – 4)

Offensive Rating: 116.1, 9th in the NBA   Defensive Rating: 110.6, 1st in the NBA

Primary Executive: Koby Altman, General Manager

Head Coach: J.B. Bickerstaff

Key Roster Changes

Subtractions
Cedi Osman, trade
Lamar Stevens, trade
Danny Green, free agency
Robin Lopez, free agency
Raul Neto, free agency
Dylan Windler, free agency

Additions
Max Strus, sign-and-trade
Damian Jones, trade
Georges Niang, free agency
Ty Jerome, free agency

Roster

Likely Starting Five
1. *Darius Garland*
2. *Donovan Mitchell*
3. Caris LeVert
4. *Evan Mobley*
5. *Jarrett Allen*

Other Key Rotation Players
Max Strus
Isaac Okoro
Georges Niang
Dean Wade
Ricky Rubio

* Italics denotes that a player is likely to be on the floor to close games

Remaining Roster

- Damian Jones
- Ty Jerome
- Sam Merrill
- Isaiah Mobley, 23, 6'10", 240, USC (Two-Way)
- Emoni Bates, 20, 6'10", 170, Eastern Michigan (Two-Way)
- Craig Porter Jr., 22, 6'2", 186, Wichita State (Two-Way)
- Pete Nance, 23, 6'11", 230, North Carolina (Exhibit 10)

SCHREMPF Base Rating: 47.7

Season Preview Survey

- *Are the Cavaliers contending or rebuilding? Where is this team headed?*

Cleveland is firmly in contention because they have four All-Star caliber players in their starting lineup. They are well-positioned to put up a big regular season win total because they have the necessary star power and enough depth to navigate the long schedule. However, they are still behind the top teams like Boston, Milwaukee, and Philadelphia because they aren't quite built for the playoffs. They don't really match up well with either of those three teams due to a lack of versatility and an imbalanced roster. They will need to find some way to counter the other contenders in a future playoff series. Otherwise, they could suffer another early playoff exit this season.

- *What are the areas of concern for this team heading into this season?*

As it was alluded to earlier, the big area of concern is connected to the quirky makeup of their roster. In particular, their team is built around two smaller guards and two non-shooting big men. This main lineup works in the regular season because they can lean on their elite rim protection to get stops and their guards can generate enough offense to out-score opponents. However, teams are better at attacking obvious weaknesses in the playoffs. The Cavs are going to be vulnerable to opponents that can play five-out lineups to spread them out or use matchup hunting tactics to attack their smaller back-court. Also, the alignment with two big men often leaves without the necessary shooting to generate efficient half-court offense against quality defenses. Therefore, opponents can overload their coverages to stop Mitchell and Garland. They did add Max Strus and Georges Niang to address this problem, but they can't play both of these players without benching one of their two main big men. They will have some issues to deal with on both ends. The fix isn't easy because they may have to make some trade-offs to turn their team into a better performing playoff unit. If they can get creative, they might be able to find a solution that works for them.

- *List some possible breakout players for this team.*

Cleveland doesn't really have many young players on their active roster, so there aren't a lot of breakout candidates to pick from. The few that they do have are largely established in their roles and it's improbable that they will make a major leap in their development. If there is a breakout candidate on this team, it could be someone like Isaiah Mobley, who is currently on a Two-Way contract. He was named MVP of the Summer League Championship Game. If he's able to crack the rotation, he could be useful as a backup big man that can pass, block shots, and provide energy in a limited capacity.

- *What should we expect from them this season?*

Cleveland is a pretty talented team with considerable star power. Also, they have enough depth to get through the 82-game schedule, so they should at the very least be one of the better regular season teams in the league. The big question that they have to answer is if they can take the next step to being a legitimate playoff contender. Right now, they still have some issues to resolve because they have to find a way to match up with their competitors while still maintaining the strengths that they have established with their unique roster construction. They will have to explore different lineup combinations or tactics to try to make their situation work. Otherwise, they may have to consider a shake-up move to make their team better equipped to handle the rigors of playoff basketball. They will at least need to make the second round to show that their current team concept works, or else, they will need to make bigger changes in the future.

Veterans

Donovan Mitchell

	Height	Weight	Cap #	Years Left
	6'1"	215	$33.162M	1 + PO

Similar at Age 26

		Season	SIMsc
1	Bradley Beal	2019-20	918.6
2	Ray Allen*	2001-02	893.8
3	Fred VanVleet	2020-21	893.1
4	Terry Rozier	2020-21	892.8
5	Chauncey Billups	2002-03	888.0
6	Damian Lillard	2016-17	887.3
7	Norman Powell	2019-20	886.4
8	Kemba Walker	2016-17	883.2
9	Kyrie Irving	2018-19	881.6
10	Buddy Hield	2018-19	876.3

Baseline Basic Stats

MPG	PTS	AST	REB	BLK	STL
35.1	23.4	5.3	4.2	0.4	1.3

Advanced Metrics

USG%	3PTA/FGA	FTA/FGA	TS%	eFG%	3PT%
30.4	0.444	0.266	0.584	0.535	0.374

AST%	TOV%	OREB%	DREB%	STL%	BLK%
25.0	10.6	2.7	10.7	1.9	0.9

PER	ORTG	DRTG	WS/48	BPM	VOL
21.20	116.0	112.0	0.155	4.80	0.290

- Named to the All-NBA 2nd Team, made his fourth consecutive All-Star team
- Had a career best season in his role as Cleveland's primary scorer
- Dynamic three-level scorer, excellent as a pick-and-roll ball handler and isolation player, explosive finisher in transition
- Reliable and consistent three-point shooter, has made almost 40% of his career corner threes
- Great spot-up shooter, solid shooter off the dribble, inefficient when shooting off screens
- Solid playmaker that can make simple reads, avoids turnovers, rarely moves off the ball
- 2022-23 Defensive Degree of Difficulty: 0.430
- 2022-23 Points Prevented: -0.109
- Guards starting level players, hidden in favorable matchups in previous seasons
- Average on-ball defender, struggles to stay with quicker players, more effective against bigger perimeter players
- Average pick-and-roll defender, more effective at funneling his man into help, tended to go too far under screens
- Fights through screens off the ball, tended to be late when closing out on spot-up shooters
- More active off the ball, gets steals at a fairly high rate, decent defensive rebounder

Darius Garland

	Height	Weight	Cap #	Years Left
	6'1"	192	$34.005M	4

Similar at Age 23

		Season	SIMsc
1	Dennis Schroder	2016-17	928.2
2	Brandon Knight	2014-15	924.7
3	Jameer Nelson	2005-06	922.4
4	Raymond Felton	2007-08	915.2
5	Mo Williams	2005-06	913.0
6	Stephon Marbury	2000-01	912.9
7	Kemba Walker	2013-14	910.7
8	Tony Parker*	2005-06	910.7
9	Nick Van Exel	1994-95	909.9
10	Brandon Jennings	2012-13	908.6

Baseline Basic Stats

MPG	PTS	AST	REB	BLK	STL
33.0	17.6	5.9	3.2	0.2	1.1

Advanced Metrics

USG%	3PTA/FGA	FTA/FGA	TS%	eFG%	3PT%
26.2	0.368	0.270	0.571	0.522	0.387

AST%	TOV%	OREB%	DREB%	STL%	BLK%
32.7	13.6	1.7	8.5	1.7	0.4

PER	ORTG	DRTG	WS/48	BPM	VOL
18.78	114.2	111.0	0.133	1.73	0.268

- Played at an All-Star level in his fourth NBA season
- Increased his efficiency in a role as a high usage playmaker and scoring guard for Cleveland
- Great distributor with outstanding court vision to find open teammates, cut his turnover rate significantly
- Great three-point shooter throughout his career, made 41% of his threes in 2022-23
- Generally good at shooting in all situations, makes spot-up jumpers, can run off screens, solid shooter off the dribble
- Good at attacking the rim on pick-and-rolls, can hit floaters, willing to draw more fouls, slightly less effective on isolations
- 2022-23 Defensive Degree of Difficulty: 0.419
- 2022-23 Points Prevented: -0.261
- Usually is hidden in favorable matchups against lower leverage players, average on-ball defender
- Taller players can shoot over him, quick enough to stay with perimeter players on drives
- Average pick-and-roll defender, limited ability to switch, effective at funneling his man into help
- Tends to get caught on screens, usually is late to close out on spot-up shooters
- Can be a pesky defender, can pressure ball handlers or play passing lanes to get steals, below average defensive rebounder

Jarrett Allen

	Height	Weight	Cap #	Years Left
	6'11"	243	$20.000M	2

Similar at Age 24

		Season	SIMsc
1	Clint Capela	2018-19	945.5
2	Ivica Zubac	2021-22	944.7
3	Joakim Noah	2009-10	923.0
4	DeAndre Jordan	2012-13	920.8
5	Bill Laimbeer	1981-82	914.7
6	Dave Corzine	1980-81	913.2
7	LaSalle Thompson	1985-86	912.8
8	Mike Gminski	1983-84	912.6
9	Dale Davis	1993-94	912.5
10	Jonas Valanciunas	2016-17	910.9

Baseline Basic Stats

MPG	PTS	AST	REB	BLK	STL
28.9	11.9	1.5	8.9	1.2	0.7

Advanced Metrics

USG%	3PTA/FGA	FTA/FGA	TS%	eFG%	3PT%
17.5	0.020	0.384	0.630	0.600	0.213

AST%	TOV%	OREB%	DREB%	STL%	BLK%
8.7	12.6	11.0	24.4	1.2	3.3

PER	ORTG	DRTG	WS/48	BPM	VOL
19.73	124.1	106.9	0.182	1.26	0.263

- Regular starting center for Cleveland in his second full season with the team
- Production was more in line with his career averages, effective as a low usage rim runner
- Very athletic big man that plays with high energy, vertical lob threat
- Great cutter and roll man, very active offensive rebounder, runs hard in transition
- Can flash to the middle on post-ups, effective at shooting from 16 feet and in
- Not likely to be a high volume scorer, lacks ball handling and shooting skills to perform this role
- Mainly a catch-and-finish player that makes safe passes, good at avoiding turnovers
- 2022-23 Defensive Degree of Difficulty: 0.501
- 2022-23 Points Prevented: 0.771
- Great rim protector, very good shot blocker and defensive rebounder
- Draws tough assignments against top big men, good post defender, mobile enough to defend in space, tends to back off to allow open jumpers
- Decent pick-and-roll defender, better at switching onto ball handlers last season, had some trouble making rotations in drop coverages
- Tends to stay anchored in the paint, does not always come out to contest shots in spot-up situations

Evan Mobley

	Height	Weight	Cap #	Years Left
	7'0"	215	$8.883M	Team Option

Similar at Age 21

		Season	SIMsc
1	Pau Gasol*	2001-02	914.9
2	Kevin Garnett*	1997-98	897.6
3	Skal Labissiere	2017-18	895.4
4	Giannis Antetokounmpo	2015-16	889.4
5	Antonio McDyess	1995-96	887.9
6	Andrew Bogut	2005-06	883.2
7	Spencer Hawes	2009-10	883.2
8	Donyell Marshall	1994-95	881.5
9	Dirk Nowitzki*	1999-00	880.0
10	Rashard Lewis	2000-01	879.5

Baseline Basic Stats

MPG	PTS	AST	REB	BLK	STL
32.8	16.7	2.4	8.1	1.7	0.9

Advanced Metrics

USG%	3PTA/FGA	FTA/FGA	TS%	eFG%	3PT%
21.5	0.058	0.344	0.558	0.522	0.244

AST%	TOV%	OREB%	DREB%	STL%	BLK%
13.4	12.8	8.2	19.5	1.3	3.3

PER	ORTG	DRTG	WS/48	BPM	VOL
17.60	111.5	106.5	0.135	2.23	0.401

- Named to the All-Defensive 1st Team in 2022-23
- Increased his efficiency in his role as a moderate volume rim runner for Cleveland
- Vertical spacing threat, athletic big man with great leaping ability and length
- Excellent rim runner, great at rolling to the rim and cutting off the ball, highly explosive finisher in transition, active offensive rebounder that scores off put-backs
- Less effective in half-court situations, below average effectiveness as a post-up or isolation player
- Three-Point Percentage fell to below 25%, much better at making spot-up long twos
- Solid passing big man that hit cutters out of the high post, good at avoiding turnovers
- 2022-23 Defensive Degree of Difficulty: 0.449
- 2022-23 Points Prevented: 1.065
- Primarily used as a roaming help defender off the ball, very rangy, great weak side shot blocker and defensive rebounder
- Guarded starting level players, did not really draw tougher assignments
- Solid on-ball defender against low leverage starters, good post defender, great mobility to defend in space
- Mobile pick-and-roll defender, can effectively switch, has lapses when making rotations, tends to back off to allow open jumpers
- Stays attached to shooters off the ball, fights through screens and closes out in spot-up situations

Caris LeVert

	Height	Weight	Cap #	Years Left
	6'6"	205	$15.385M	1

Similar at Age 28

		Season	SIMsc
1	Alec Burks	2019-20	941.9
2	Rodney Stuckey	2014-15	940.1
3	Jonathon Simmons	2017-18	939.6
4	Greivis Vasquez	2014-15	936.3
5	George McCloud	1995-96	935.8
6	Gordon Hayward	2018-19	934.2
7	Evan Fournier	2020-21	933.1
8	Marquis Daniels	2008-09	932.8
9	Spencer Dinwiddie	2021-22	931.3
10	Terrence Ross	2019-20	931.3

Baseline Basic Stats

MPG	PTS	AST	REB	BLK	STL
28.8	12.9	2.7	3.4	0.3	1.0

Advanced Metrics

USG%	3PTA/FGA	FTA/FGA	TS%	eFG%	3PT%
20.1	0.456	0.223	0.540	0.507	0.369

AST%	TOV%	OREB%	DREB%	STL%	BLK%
16.6	11.4	2.4	11.2	1.7	1.0

PER	ORTG	DRTG	WS/48	BPM	VOL
13.11	108.6	111.3	0.083	-0.54	0.280

- Played starter level minutes for Cleveland in his first full season with the team
- Mainly used as a low volume spot-up shooter and occasional ball handler off the bench
- Above break-even career three-point shooter, made over 39% of his threes last season
- Mostly effective as a stand-still spot-up shooter, can make threes off the dribble if defenders back off him
- Above average ability to score in ball handling situations, can draw fouls and finish at the rim, sometimes can be out of control
- Solid secondary playmaker, usually limits turnovers, good cutter off the ball
- 2022-23 Defensive Degree of Difficulty: 0.501
- 2022-23 Points Prevented: 0.308
- Drew a lot of difficult assignments against elite perimeter scorers
- Played good on-ball defense, effective at guarding multiple positions
- Decent pick-and-roll defender, good at containing ball handlers, had some trouble when switched onto a screener
- Fights through screens off the ball, sometimes will be late when closing out on spot-up shooters
- Picks his spots to play the ball on the weak side, Steal Percentage increased slightly, fairly solid defensive rebounder

Max Strus

	Height	Weight	Cap #	Years Left
	6'5"	215	$14.488M	3

Similar at Age 26

		Season	SIMsc
1	Joe Harris	2017-18	934.7
2	Duncan Robinson	2020-21	929.4
3	Danuel House	2019-20	926.3
4	Troy Daniels	2017-18	926.2
5	Gary Neal	2010-11	925.5
6	Grayson Allen	2021-22	923.1
7	Allen Crabbe	2018-19	921.3
8	Iman Shumpert	2016-17	920.4
9	Kentavious Caldwell-Pope	2019-20	919.1
10	Malcolm Brogdon	2018-19	919.0

Baseline Basic Stats

MPG	PTS	AST	REB	BLK	STL
24.8	10.4	1.7	2.9	0.2	0.6

Advanced Metrics

USG%	3PTA/FGA	FTA/FGA	TS%	eFG%	3PT%
18.0	0.662	0.140	0.567	0.542	0.376

AST%	TOV%	OREB%	DREB%	STL%	BLK%
10.4	8.7	2.0	11.2	1.0	0.6

PER	ORTG	DRTG	WS/48	BPM	VOL
11.57	112.1	113.6	0.086	-1.18	0.414

- Played starter level minutes in his third season with Miami
- Started some games, mainly used as a low usage shooting specialist
- Three-Point Percentage fell to around the league average, has made 47.5% of his career corner threes
- Most consistent as a spot-up shooter, effectiveness dropped when shooting on the move, can make quick pull-up threes on pick-and-rolls
- Not really able to create his own shot, rarely looks to drive to the rim, primarily a catch-and-shoot player
- Passing improved, can functionally make plays to set up others, rarely turns the ball over
- 2022-23 Defensive Degree of Difficulty: 0.396
- 2022-23 Points Prevented: -2.106
- Tended to be hidden in favorable matchups against lower leverage players or played in zone defenses
- Rarely tested on the ball, could play angles to cut off penetration, had trouble against stronger wing players
- Below average pick-and-roll defender, not effective at taking away any specific action
- Fights through screens off the ball, tends to be late when closing out on spot-up shooters
- Stay-at-home defender, rarely gets steals or blocks, fairly solid defensive rebounder

Isaac Okoro

	Height	Weight	Cap #	Years Left
	6'5"	225	$8.921M	RFA

Similar at Age 22

		Season	SIMsc
1	Casey Jacobsen	2003-04	931.8
2	Josh Hart	2017-18	925.9
3	Desmond Bane	2020-21	914.5
4	Josh Okogie	2020-21	912.5
5	Sterling Brown	2017-18	911.3
6	Jaylen Brown	2018-19	907.3
7	Josh Richardson	2015-16	905.3
8	Quincy Pondexter	2010-11	905.2
9	Dillon Brooks	2017-18	904.4
10	Derrick Jones Jr.	2019-20	904.0

Baseline Basic Stats

MPG	PTS	AST	REB	BLK	STL
25.1	9.7	1.5	3.5	0.3	0.8

Advanced Metrics

USG%	3PTA/FGA	FTA/FGA	TS%	eFG%	3PT%
15.3	0.438	0.285	0.591	0.554	0.373

AST%	TOV%	OREB%	DREB%	STL%	BLK%
9.0	10.0	3.5	10.2	1.6	1.3

PER	ORTG	DRTG	WS/48	BPM	VOL
12.24	118.3	111.9	0.115	-0.36	0.360

- Regular rotation player for Cleveland in his third NBA season, started over half of his games
- Increased his efficiency in a role as a very low volume spot-up shooter
- Improving three-point shooter, made over 36% of his threes last season
- Over 85% of his threes were from the corners, almost exclusively a stationary spot-up shooter
- Good cutter off the ball, attacks the rim in transition, draws fouls at a solid rate
- Generally limited as a shot creator, rarely used as a ball handler
- Catch-and-shoot player, only makes safe passes, rarely turns the ball over
- <u>2022-23 Defensive Degree of Difficulty</u>: 0.561, had the 14th most difficult set of matchups in the NBA
- <u>2022-23 Points Prevented</u>: -0.716
- Mainly used as Cleveland's primary defensive stopper, fairly good on-ball defender that guards multiple positions
- Slightly over-extended, less effective when guarding elite scorers in one-on-one situations
- Fairly good pick-and-roll defender, good at containing ball handlers or funneling them into help
- Tends to get on screens off the ball, does not always close out on spot-up shooters
- Increased his activity level on the weak side, posted a career high Steal Percentage, became an effective weak side shot blocker, improved to become a fairly decent defensive rebounder

Georges Niang

	Height	Weight	Cap #	Years Left
	6'7"	230	$8.800M	2

Similar at Age 29

		Season	SIMsc
1	Anthony Tolliver	2014-15	931.7
2	Kyle Korver	2010-11	920.8
3	Doug McDermott	2020-21	913.6
4	Joe Harris	2020-21	913.1
5	Cartier Martin	2013-14	911.0
6	Mickael Pietrus	2011-12	910.0
7	C.J. Miles	2016-17	909.9
8	Eric Piatkowski	1999-00	906.7
9	Morris Peterson	2006-07	906.3
10	Quentin Richardson	2009-10	906.0

Baseline Basic Stats

MPG	PTS	AST	REB	BLK	STL
20.0	7.4	1.1	2.8	0.2	0.5

Advanced Metrics

USG%	3PTA/FGA	FTA/FGA	TS%	eFG%	3PT%
16.2	0.662	0.122	0.577	0.556	0.384

AST%	TOV%	OREB%	DREB%	STL%	BLK%
7.8	9.5	2.2	12.7	1.1	0.9

PER	ORTG	DRTG	WS/48	BPM	VOL
10.70	111.4	112.5	0.081	-1.42	0.353

- Regular rotation player for Philadelphia in his second season with the team
- Production was consistent with his career averages, mainly used as a low usage spot-up shooter
- Very reliable three-point shooter, has made over 40% of his career threes
- Excellent spot-up shooter and pick-and-pop screener, less effective when shooting off screens
- Rarely goes to the basket, non-dribbling plays accounted for 97.6% of his offense according to Synergy
- Catch-and-shoot player, willing to make the extra pass, rarely turns the ball over
- 2022-23 Defensive Degree of Difficulty: 0.351
- 2022-23 Points Prevented: -0.712
- Usually defended second unit players or was hidden in favorable matchups against lower leverage players
- Average on-ball defender, played angles well to stay with perimeter players, had trouble guarding stronger post players inside
- Solidly effective pick-and-roll defender, can functionally switch, generally makes sound rotations
- Can get caught on screens off the ball, consistently closed out on spot-up shooters
- Stay-at-home defender, rarely gets steals or blocks, fairly solid defensive rebounder

Dean Wade

	Height	Weight	Cap #	Years Left
	6'9"	228	$5.710M	2

Similar at Age 26

		Season	SIMsc
1	Yuta Watanabe	2020-21	915.4
2	Patrick Patterson	2015-16	910.2
3	Kyle Singler	2014-15	908.5
4	Juancho Hernangómez	2021-22	904.7
5	Georges Niang	2019-20	899.2
6	Maxi Kleber	2017-18	897.6
7	Marvin Williams	2012-13	894.9
8	Davis Bertans	2018-19	894.8
9	Timothé Luwawu-Cabarrot	2021-22	894.4
10	Yakhouba Diawara	2008-09	894.3

Baseline Basic Stats

MPG	PTS	AST	REB	BLK	STL
19.1	5.7	0.9	3.4	0.3	0.5

Advanced Metrics

USG%	3PTA/FGA	FTA/FGA	TS%	eFG%	3PT%
12.3	0.650	0.158	0.545	0.527	0.358

AST%	TOV%	OREB%	DREB%	STL%	BLK%
6.6	8.5	3.5	15.6	1.4	1.5

PER	ORTG	DRTG	WS/48	BPM	VOL
9.88	112.1	109.2	0.090	-1.00	0.300

- Missed games due to injuries to his right knee and left shoulder, regular rotation player for Cleveland when healthy
- Effectiveness declined last season, mostly used as a very low usage stretch big
- Around a league average three-point shooter, Three-Point Percentage has been declining for the past three seasons
- Almost exclusively a stationary spot-up shooter, much less effective when shooting on the move
- Effective at cutting off the ball, can finish at the rim, very rarely plays around the basket
- Not really a post-up threat, strictly a catch-and-shoot player, limited passing skills, rarely turns the ball over
- <u>2022-23 Defensive Degree of Difficulty</u>: 0.429
- <u>2022-23 Points Prevented</u>: -0.251
- Drew tough assignments off the bench, solid on-ball defender despite his athletic limitations
- Effectively defends post players and will play angles to stay with perimeter players
- Average pick-and-roll defender, can functionally switch, tends to drop back too far or go too far under screens
- Stays attached to shooters off the ball, fights through screens and closes out in spot-up situations
- Good rim protector despite low shot blocking numbers, stays vertical to contest shots, gets steals at a solid rate, solid defensive rebounder

Ricky Rubio

	Height	Weight	Cap #	Years Left
	6'3"	190	$6.146M	1

Similar at Age 32

		Season	SIMsc
1	Kirk Hinrich	2012-13	917.3
2	Devin Harris	2015-16	915.5
3	Jarrett Jack	2015-16	914.7
4	Ray Williams	1986-87	913.9
5	Goran Dragic	2018-19	909.0
6	Terry Porter	1995-96	908.6
7	Doc Rivers	1993-94	908.0
8	Charlie Ward	2002-03	904.9
9	Gary Grant	1997-98	904.4
10	Anthony Johnson	2006-07	903.5

Baseline Basic Stats

MPG	PTS	AST	REB	BLK	STL
21.2	7.3	3.3	2.1	0.2	0.8

Advanced Metrics

USG%	3PTA/FGA	FTA/FGA	TS%	eFG%	3PT%
18.0	0.456	0.216	0.489	0.448	0.313

AST%	TOV%	OREB%	DREB%	STL%	BLK%
26.5	15.7	1.7	11.5	2.1	0.7

PER	ORTG	DRTG	WS/48	BPM	VOL
11.61	103.4	109.4	0.064	-1.67	0.465

- Missed the first half of last season while recovering from an ACL injury, fringe rotation player for Cleveland when healthy
- Had his least effective season, mainly used as a low usage, pass-first backup point guard
- Great playmaker throughout his career, outstanding court vision, cut his turnover rate significantly
- Struggled to score efficiently, rated as average or worse in every offensive situation according to Synergy
- Below break-even career three-point shooter, made less than 30% of his threes last season
- Better at spotting up and hitting pull-up jumpers from mid-range, more effective when shooting long twos
- Inconsistent shot and diminishing quickness limit his ability to attack the rim off the dribble
- <u>2022-23 Defensive Degree of Difficulty</u>: 0.283
- <u>2022-23 Points Prevented</u>: 1.191
- Strategically used as a roamer, usually guarded lower leverage second unit players
- Uses length and anticipation to post high steals, posted the highest Block Percentage of his career, solid defensive rebounder
- Fairly effective on-ball defender, plays angles well to stay with perimeter players, struggled against bigger players inside
- Solid pick-and-roll defender, can get around screens to contain ball handlers
- Stays attached to shooters off the ball, fights through screens, consistently closes out in spot-up situations

Damian Jones

	Height	Weight	Cap #	Years Left
	6'11"	245	$2.587M	UFA

Similar at Age 27

		Season	SIMsc
1	Willie Cauley-Stein	2020-21	921.8
2	Alex Len	2020-21	908.9
3	Chris Engler	1986-87	901.1
4	Dewayne Dedmon	2016-17	893.7
5	Cherokee Parks	1999-00	893.6
6	Ronny Turiaf	2009-10	892.2
7	Dwight Powell	2018-19	891.2
8	Miles Plumlee	2015-16	890.3
9	Jake Voskuhl	2004-05	889.2
10	Andrew Lang	1993-94	889.0

Baseline Basic Stats

MPG	PTS	AST	REB	BLK	STL
17.1	5.4	0.8	4.2	0.8	0.4

Advanced Metrics

USG%	3PTA/FGA	FTA/FGA	TS%	eFG%	3PT%
13.8	0.128	0.356	0.635	0.605	0.490

AST%	TOV%	OREB%	DREB%	STL%	BLK%
6.7	15.6	8.7	18.6	1.0	3.4

PER	ORTG	DRTG	WS/48	BPM	VOL
14.05	120.4	111.6	0.116	-1.07	0.333

- Played sparingly for the L.A. Lakers, traded to Utah, used as a rotational backup center after the trade
- Primarily used by both teams as a very low usage rim runner
- Athletic big man that can be a vertical spacing threat, had a True Shooting Percentage of almost 72% last season
- Good cutter and roll man, active offensive rebounder, runs hard in transition, draws fouls at a solid rate
- Has continued to experiment with shooting threes, went 10-for-14 (71.4%) in Utah on mostly spot-up jumpers
- Not really a post-up threat, fairly limited passing skills, a bit turnover prone
- 2022-23 Defensive Degree of Difficulty: 0.332
- 2022-23 Points Prevented: 1.292
- Fairly solid rim protector, good shot blocker, decent defensive rebounder, can be undisciplined with positioning at times
- Usually guarded second unit level big men, average on-ball defender
- Stout post defender with solid mobility, tends to commit unnecessary fouls
- Below average pick-and-roll defender, not effective at taking away any specific action
- Consistently comes out to contest perimeter shots in spot-up situations

Ty Jerome

	Height	Weight	Cap #	Years Left
	6'5"	195	$2.439M	1

Similar at Age 25

		Season	SIMsc
1	Von Wafer	2010-11	929.8
2	Shake Milton	2021-22	929.3
3	Damyean Dotson	2019-20	927.8
4	Chris Quinn	2008-09	927.5
5	Lucious Harris	1995-96	925.9
6	Wayne Ellington	2012-13	925.8
7	Nando De Colo	2012-13	922.2
8	Malcolm Brogdon	2017-18	920.3
9	Sasha Danilovic	1995-96	920.0
10	Matthew Dellavedova	2015-16	918.9

Baseline Basic Stats

MPG	PTS	AST	REB	BLK	STL
22.0	8.8	2.4	2.3	0.1	0.7

Advanced Metrics

USG%	3PTA/FGA	FTA/FGA	TS%	eFG%	3PT%
17.9	0.442	0.175	0.553	0.522	0.364

AST%	TOV%	OREB%	DREB%	STL%	BLK%
19.7	11.1	1.6	9.6	1.5	0.5

PER	ORTG	DRTG	WS/48	BPM	VOL
12.68	113.3	113.2	0.091	-0.91	0.431

- Played all of last season on a Two-Way contract with Golden State, used as a fringe rotation player
- Greatly increased his efficiency in a role as a low volume shooter and playmaker
- Made almost 39% of his threes last season, league average career three-point shooter, percentages vary from year-to-year
- Mainly a stationary spot-up shooter, can make quick pull-up threes if defenders go under screens
- Crafty pick-and-roll ball handler that leverages the threat of his shot to occasionally get to the rim, not really quick enough to create his own shot on isolation plays
- Solid playmaker with good court vision, controls the ball well, rarely turns the ball over
- 2022-23 Defensive Degree of Difficulty: 0.341
- 2022-23 Points Prevented: -1.236
- Typically defends lower leverage second unit players, rarely tested on the ball
- Effective on-ball defender in a small sample of possessions, can functionally guards ones and twos
- Fairly solid pick-and-roll defender, generally makes sound rotations, good at funneling his man into help
- Will get caught on screens off the ball, tends to be late to close out on spot-up shooters
- More of a stay-at-home defender last season, steals rate was down, below average defensive rebounder

Sam Merrill

	Height	Weight	Cap #	Years Left
	6'4"	205	$1.997M	1

Similar at Age 26

		Season	SIMsc
1	Wayne Ellington	2013-14	911.9
2	Langston Galloway	2017-18	904.9
3	Matt Thomas	2020-21	898.1
4	Richie Frahm	2003-04	897.8
5	Damion Lee	2018-19	895.7
6	Theo Pinson	2021-22	892.6
7	Dakota Mathias	2021-22	886.5
8	Troy Daniels	2017-18	886.1
9	Denzel Valentine	2019-20	885.4
10	Keljin Blevins	2021-22	884.5

Baseline Basic Stats

MPG	PTS	AST	REB	BLK	STL
19.2	7.8	1.4	2.4	0.1	0.6

Advanced Metrics

USG%	3PTA/FGA	FTA/FGA	TS%	eFG%	3PT%
17.5	0.700	0.140	0.546	0.524	0.339

AST%	TOV%	OREB%	DREB%	STL%	BLK%
11.6	6.2	1.6	13.1	1.6	0.2

PER	ORTG	DRTG	WS/48	BPM	VOL
12.36	114.2	113.1	0.093	-1.41	0.427

- Spent most of last season in the G-League with the Cleveland Charge, signed to a standard contract with Cleveland late in 2022-23
- Mainly used throughout his NBA career as a low volume shooting specialist
- Solid three-point shooter in the NBA in a limited number of attempts, made over 43% of his threes in the G-League
- Mostly a spot-up shooter in the NBA, flashed some ability to make shots off screens
- Not really able to create his own shot, decent secondary playmaker, rarely turns the ball over
- 2022-23 Defensive Degree of Difficulty: 0.067
- 2022-23 Points Prevented: 4.032
- Only used in garbage time last season, rarely tested on defense throughout his career
- Played decent on-ball defense in a small sample of NBA possessions, plays angles well to compensate for lack of ideal athleticism
- Fairly effective pick-and-roll defender in limited action, shows a functional ability to switch and make rotations
- Tends to get caught on screens off the ball, not always in position to close out on spot-up shooters
- Capable of getting steals at a solid rate, fairly solid defensive rebounder

NEW YORK KNICKS

Last Season: 47 - 35, Lost 2nd Round to Miami (2 – 4)

Offensive Rating: 117.8, 3rd in the NBA

Defensive Rating: 114.8, 19th in the NBA

Primary Executive: Leon Rose, President

Head Coach: Tom Thibodeau

Key Roster Changes

Subtractions
Obi Toppin, trade
Derrick Rose, free agency

Additions
Donte DiVincenzo, free agency

Roster

Likely Starting Five
1. Jalen Brunson
2. Quentin Grimes
3. R.J. Barrett
4. Julius Randle
5. Mitchell Robinson

Other Key Rotation Players
Immanuel Quickley
Josh Hart
Donte DiVincenzo
Isaiah Hartenstein
Jericho Sims

* Italics denotes that a player is likely to be on the floor to close games

Remaining Roster

- Miles McBride
- Evan Fournier
- Isaiah Roby
- DaQuan Jeffries
- Jaylen Martin, 20, 6'6", 216, Overtime Elite (Two-Way)
- Nathan Knight, 26, 6'10", 253, William & Mary (Two-Way)
- Dylan Windler, 27, 6'6", 196, Belmont (Two-Way)
- Jacob Toppin, 23, 6'9", 200, Kentucky (Exhibit 10)
- Duane Washington Jr., 23, 6'3", 210, Ohio State (Exhibit 10)
- Obadiah Noel, 24, 6'4", 196, UMass-Lowell (Exhibit 10)
- Dmytro Skapintsev, 25, 7'1", 260, Cal State Northridge (Exhibit 10)

SCHREMPF Base Rating: 47.4

Season Preview Survey

- *Are the Knicks contending or rebuilding? Where is this team headed?*

The Knicks bounced back to reach the second round of the playoffs after finishing in the lottery the season before. They are looking to build on their success from last season to take the next step, but they are exercising some patience to find the right deal to level up. They have enough pieces to make a major move, but there isn't a needle moving piece that's available right now. As of now, they are looking to grow internally to maintain their progress and continue to build a sustainable winning team. They have the talent to get a guaranteed playoff berth, but they don't quite have enough to be true title contenders this season.

- *What are the areas of concern for this team heading into this season?*

The Knicks have some issues that they will need to address to become a more well-rounded team. In particular, they have some vulnerabilities on the defensive end. Namely, they have to consistently hide Jalen Brunson because he consistently has trouble keeping opponents in front of him. As a result, he's often a target that opponents will seek out to get favorable match-ups. This is also compounded by the fact that they tend to stick to very big lineups that keep a traditional center in the paint. They often send help to account for Brunson's deficiencies and they overload the paint, so they give up a lot of open outside shots. They will need to experiment with zones or different coverages to defend the three-point line and hide Brunson, or else they will not go far in the playoffs. Also, they will need to speed up their tempo to make them better equipped to play against teams that push the pace to get them out of their methodical comfort zone.

- *List some possible breakout players for this team.*

The Knicks don't have many breakout candidates on their roster because a lot of their young players have already graduated to becoming reliable contributors to their team. It is possible that one of these players could develop even more to raise their game to another level. If that happens, it's likely that a big breakthrough would come from either R.J. Barrett or Immanuel Quickley because both have shown strong two-way skills in the past couple years, and they have the kind of physical ability to become high-impact players. Either of them could mature and tap into more of their talent to reach a much higher level if things break right. As for a more unheralded type, the best candidate is someone like Miles McBride because he could develop to emerge as a pesky defensive, backup point guard similar to Jevon Carter, if he's able to shoot consistently enough to stay on the floor.

- *What should we expect from them this season?*

The Knicks aren't going to take anyone by surprise this coming season because opponents will have a better idea of what to expect from them. Even so, they have a solid enough base of talent to consistently win games in the regular season and earn a playoff spot. The next step for them is figuring out a way to translate their talent and regular season success into better playoff performance. They will need to open themselves up to new ideas to find more lineups to counter different styles and diversify their tactics to minimize their weaknesses. If they can figure out some more ways to stretch their talent to reach a higher level, then they could become a viable challenger to the elite contenders in the East. Otherwise, they may need to keep exploring ways to make the right deal to give themselves the necessary talent to legitimately push for a championship in the coming years.

Veterans

Julius Randle

	Height	Weight	Cap #	Years Left
	6'8"	250	$28.227M	1 + PO

Similar at Age 28

		Season	SIMsc
1	Blake Griffin	2017-18	925.0
2	David Lee	2011-12	906.3
3	Jamal Mashburn	2000-01	901.4
4	Paul Millsap	2013-14	894.9
5	Karl Malone*	1991-92	893.5
6	Carmelo Anthony	2012-13	893.4
7	Carlos Boozer	2009-10	885.0
8	Zach Randolph	2009-10	883.3
9	Chris Webber*	2001-02	881.6
10	Kevin Love	2016-17	881.0

Baseline Basic Stats

MPG	PTS	AST	REB	BLK	STL
35.6	21.6	3.7	8.8	0.5	1.0

Advanced Metrics

USG%	3PTA/FGA	FTA/FGA	TS%	eFG%	3PT%
27.5	0.340	0.345	0.556	0.508	0.340

AST%	TOV%	OREB%	DREB%	STL%	BLK%
19.3	12.2	5.5	23.6	1.2	1.0

PER	ORTG	DRTG	WS/48	BPM	VOL
18.96	111.2	108.9	0.129	3.27	0.334

- Named to the All-NBA 3rd Team, made his second All-Star team in 2022-23
- Had a bounce back season, highly effective in his role as New York's primary scoring option
- Good isolation player and pick-and-roll ball handler, can barrel to the rim to finish or draw fouls, good at making pull-up jumpers from mid-range
- Above break-even three-point shooter, percentages tend to vary from year-to-year
- Mostly a spot-up shooter, situational consistency constantly varies
- Effective rim runner that plays high a motor, good cutter and roll man, decent offensive rebounder
- Good playmaking big man, effective in the short roll game, good at avoiding turnovers
- 2022-23 Defensive Degree of Difficulty: 0.477
- 2022-23 Points Prevented: -0.805
- Drew tougher assignments last season, usually guards starting level players
- Improved to become a solid on-ball defender, capable of guarding big men and wing players
- Average pick-and-roll defender, solid in drop coverages, tends to go too far under screens
- Fights through screens off the ball, tends to late when closing out on spot-up shooters
- Stay-at-home defender, rarely gets steals or blocks, not really a rim protector, good defensive rebounder

Jalen Brunson

	Height	Weight	Cap #	Years Left
	6'1"	190	$26.347M	1 + PO

Similar at Age 26

		Season	SIMsc
1	Mike Conley	2013-14	941.7
2	Mo Williams	2008-09	939.4
3	Mike Bibby	2004-05	938.8
4	Terry Rozier	2020-21	934.7
5	Dennis Schröder	2019-20	927.9
6	Trey Burke	2018-19	927.4
7	Dan Dickau	2004-05	918.7
8	Troy Hudson	2002-03	918.2
9	Eric Murdock	1994-95	917.6
10	Kemba Walker	2016-17	916.1

Baseline Basic Stats

MPG	PTS	AST	REB	BLK	STL
31.7	15.9	5.1	3.2	0.2	1.1

Advanced Metrics

USG%	3PTA/FGA	FTA/FGA	TS%	eFG%	3PT%
24.0	0.331	0.265	0.570	0.526	0.388

AST%	TOV%	OREB%	DREB%	STL%	BLK%
26.8	11.3	1.7	9.8	1.5	0.5

PER	ORTG	DRTG	WS/48	BPM	VOL
17.91	116.5	112.6	0.136	2.03	0.282

- Produced at an All-Star level in his first season with New York
- Had a breakout season in a role as a high usage, primary ball handler for New York
- Good pick-and-roll ball handler and isolation player, effective at scoring at all three levels
- Reliable three-point shooter, made almost 42% of his threes last season
- Excellent spot-up shooter, good shooter off the dribble, less effective when running off screens
- Great at pushing the ball in transition, very ball dominant in New York, rarely moved off the ball
- Good playmaker that makes sound decisions, can find open teammates, good at avoiding turnovers
- 2022-23 Defensive Degree of Difficulty: 0.393
- 2022-23 Points Prevented: -1.330
- Usually hidden in favorable matchups against lower leverage players, rarely tested on the ball
- Played competent on-ball defense in these lower leverage assignments, may not be able to guard higher-end players
- Decent when guarding pick-and-rolls, limited ability to switch, funnels his man into help but sometimes allows ball handlers to turn the corner
- Tends to get caught on screens off the ball, tends to be late when closing out on spot-up shooters
- Stay-at-home defender, does not really get steals or blocks, fairly decent defensive rebounder

RJ Barrett

	Height	Weight	Cap #	Years Left
	6'6"	214	$23.884M	3

Similar at Age 22

		Season	SIMsc
1	Jason Richardson	2002-03	927.7
2	Isaiah Rider	1993-94	925.9
3	Tim Hardaway Jr.	2014-15	920.0
4	Brandon Roy	2006-07	919.8
5	Mike Miller	2002-03	919.5
6	DeMar DeRozan	2011-12	918.4
7	Victor Oladipo	2014-15	917.8
8	Keldon Johnson	2021-22	913.1
9	Saddiq Bey	2021-22	911.6
10	Dillon Brooks	2017-18	909.9

Baseline Basic Stats

MPG	PTS	AST	REB	BLK	STL
32.9	17.7	2.9	4.4	0.3	1.0

Advanced Metrics

USG%	3PTA/FGA	FTA/FGA	TS%	eFG%	3PT%
25.5	0.295	0.325	0.539	0.490	0.345

AST%	TOV%	OREB%	DREB%	STL%	BLK%
14.7	10.7	3.0	12.9	1.3	0.7

PER	ORTG	DRTG	WS/48	BPM	VOL
15.38	107.8	112.2	0.082	-0.58	0.344

- Regular starter for New York in his fourth NBA season
- Scoring efficiency increased a bit, largely used as a high usage scoring wing
- Above break-even career three-point shooter, had a down shooting season in 2022-23
- Really struggled to make shots off the dribble, better as a stand-still spot-up shooter
- Shooting struggles affected him in ball handling situations, defenders could back off him to limit his effectiveness
- Fairly solid secondary playmaker that makes simple reads, generally avoids committing turnovers
- 2022-23 Defensive Degree of Difficulty: 0.520
- 2022-23 Points Prevented: 1.245
- Usually drew tough assignments against elite perimeter scorers, fairly solid on-ball defender
- Capable of guarding multiple positions, tends to back off his man, gives up relatively open jumpers
- Decent pick-and-roll defender, can functionally switch, good at cutting off penetration, goes too far under screens
- Tends to get caught on screens off the ball, good at closing out in spot-up situations
- Stay-at-home defender, rarely gets steals or blocks, fairly good defensive rebounder

Mitchell Robinson

	Height	Weight	Cap #	Years Left
	7'0"	240	$15.682M	2

Similar at Age 24

		Season	SIMsc
1	Jakob Poeltl	2019-20	893.9
2	JaVale McGee	2011-12	893.3
3	Tree Rollins	1979-80	885.8
4	Cody Zeller	2016-17	884.9
5	Duane Causwell	1992-93	884.8
6	Robert Williams	2021-22	882.1
7	DeAndre Jordan	2012-13	881.9
8	Lucas Nogueira	2016-17	881.4
9	Marcus Camby	1998-99	878.7
10	Dan Gadzuric	2002-03	878.7

Baseline Basic Stats

MPG	PTS	AST	REB	BLK	STL
23.0	7.7	0.9	7.2	1.6	0.7

Advanced Metrics

USG%	3PTA/FGA	FTA/FGA	TS%	eFG%	3PT%
13.0	0.003	0.444	0.629	0.636	0.210

AST%	TOV%	OREB%	DREB%	STL%	BLK%
5.4	12.5	15.4	21.5	1.5	5.6

PER	ORTG	DRTG	WS/48	BPM	VOL
18.83	130.4	106.0	0.193	1.36	0.293

- Missed games due to a fractured thumb, regular starting center for New York when healthy
- Highly effective in his role as an extremely low volume rim runner
- Vertical lob threat, over 69% of his made field goals were dunks
- Great cutter and roll man, led the NBA in Offensive Rebound Percentage, runs the floor hard in transition
- Limited offensive skill, below average post player, lacks reliable shooting range outside of three feet
- Career Free Throw Percentage is below 55%, not really a passer, solid at avoiding turnovers
- 2022-23 Defensive Degree of Difficulty: 0.512
- 2022-23 Points Prevented: 0.939
- Great rim protector, excellent shot blocker, very solid defensive rebounder
- Drew tough assignments against top scoring big men, stout post defender, has some trouble defending in space
- Good pick-and-roll defender, good in drop coverages, solid at hedging out on ball handlers
- Tends to stay anchored in the paint, does not always come out to contest perimeter shots in spot-up situations
- Good at using his length to play passing lanes, gets steals at a fairly high rate

Quentin Grimes

	Height	Weight	Cap #	Years Left
	6'5"	205	$2.386M	TO

Similar at Age 22

		Season	SIMsc
1	Desmond Bane	2020-21	941.7
2	Josh Hart	2017-18	940.1
3	Donte DiVincenzo	2018-19	927.6
4	Svi Mykhailiuk	2019-20	924.0
5	Ayo Dosunmu	2021-22	922.0
6	Malik Beasley	2018-19	921.7
7	Nik Stauskas	2015-16	920.5
8	Tony Snell	2013-14	918.3
9	Josh Richardson	2015-16	915.6
10	Miye Oni	2019-20	914.4

Baseline Basic Stats

MPG	PTS	AST	REB	BLK	STL
25.6	10.1	1.8	3.2	0.3	0.7

Advanced Metrics

USG%	3PTA/FGA	FTA/FGA	TS%	eFG%	3PT%
16.2	0.603	0.153	0.579	0.555	0.382

AST%	TOV%	OREB%	DREB%	STL%	BLK%
10.2	9.7	2.3	10.7	1.4	1.1

PER	ORTG	DRTG	WS/48	BPM	VOL
11.83	115.4	113.4	0.098	-0.51	0.247

- Became a regular starter for New York in his second NBA season
- Increased his productivity in his role as a low usage spot-up shooter
- Has made over 38% of his threes in his two seasons, also has made over 47% of his career corner threes
- Predominantly a stand-still spot-up shooter, needs to have his feet set, not really effective when shooting in other situations
- Good cutter off the ball, can effectively knock down jumpers or get to the rim on hand-offs
- Very rarely used in ball handling situations, not able to create his own shot
- Catch-and-shoot player, improving slightly as a passer, rarely turns the ball over
- 2022-23 Defensive Degree of Difficulty: 0.610, had the most difficult set of matchups in the NBA
- 2022-23 Points Prevented: -0.156
- Emerged to become New York's primary defensive stopper, almost exclusively guarded elite scorers
- Great on-ball defender that effectively guards multiple positions on the floor
- Fairly solid pick-and-roll defender, can switch to guard ball handlers and screens, tends to take bad angles that hurt his effectiveness
- Tends to get caught on screens off the ball, sometimes is late to close out on spot-up shooters
- More of a stay-at-home defender last season, getting fewer steals, occasionally blocks shots on the weak side, below average defensive rebounder

Immanuel Quickley

	Height	Weight	Cap #	Years Left
	6'3"	190	$4.172M	RFA

Similar at Age 23

		Season	SIMsc
1	Terry Rozier	2017-18	946.3
2	Malik Monk	2021-22	929.6
3	Rex Chapman	1990-91	926.6
4	Malik Beasley	2019-20	926.5
5	Luther Head	2005-06	923.5
6	Brandon Knight	2014-15	923.2
7	Damian Lillard	2013-14	920.2
8	Steve Nash*	1997-98	919.7
9	Byron Scott	1984-85	916.4
10	Leandro Barbosa	2005-06	916.0

Baseline Basic Stats

MPG	PTS	AST	REB	BLK	STL
28.3	14.1	3.4	3.1	0.2	0.9

Advanced Metrics

USG%	3PTA/FGA	FTA/FGA	TS%	eFG%	3PT%
22.5	0.486	0.254	0.565	0.519	0.373

AST%	TOV%	OREB%	DREB%	STL%	BLK%
19.9	10.2	2.2	11.7	1.6	0.6

PER	ORTG	DRTG	WS/48	BPM	VOL
16.27	115.8	112.1	0.128	0.77	0.335

- Runner-up for the Sixth Man of the Year Award, played starter level minutes for New York
- Had his most productive season in a role as a moderate volume ball handler off the bench
- Good pick-and-roll ball handler and isolation player, changes speeds well, gets to the rim and hits mid-range pull-up jumpers, took fewer long twos
- Solid three-point shooter in his career, percentages have varied slightly during his three years in the NBA
- Mostly a stand-still spot-up shooter, better when he's square to the rim, a bit inconsistent when shooting threes off the dribble
- Solid secondary playmaker, rarely turns the ball over, great at pushing the ball in transition
- 2022-23 Defensive Degree of Difficulty: 0.389
- 2022-23 Points Prevented: 2.143
- Usually guards second unit players or lower leverage starters, middling on-ball defender
- More effective when defending bigger wing players, struggled to stay with opposing guards on the perimeter
- Solid pick-and-roll defender, good at funneling his man into help, has some functional ability to switch
- Tends to get caught on screens off the ball, consistently closes out on spot-up shooters
- More active on the weak side, posted his highest Steal Percentage, fairly solid defensive rebounding guard

Josh Hart

	Height	Weight	Cap #	Years Left
	6'5"	215	$12.960M	4

Similar at Age 27

		Season	SIMsc
1	Shandon Anderson	2000-01	920.5
2	Tomas Satoransky	2018-19	917.6
3	John Salmons	2006-07	913.2
4	Lance Stephenson	2017-18	907.6
5	Damion Lee	2019-20	903.8
6	P.J. Tucker	2012-13	903.6
7	Gene Banks	1986-87	901.7
8	Keith Bogans	2007-08	899.4
9	DeMarre Carroll	2013-14	898.6
10	James Ennis	2017-18	898.3

Baseline Basic Stats

MPG	PTS	AST	REB	BLK	STL
25.3	8.4	2.3	4.1	0.2	0.9

Advanced Metrics

USG%	3PTA/FGA	FTA/FGA	TS%	eFG%	3PT%
15.0	0.404	0.301	0.578	0.541	0.358

AST%	TOV%	OREB%	DREB%	STL%	BLK%
15.1	15.2	4.9	17.7	1.8	0.7

PER	ORTG	DRTG	WS/48	BPM	VOL
13.27	115.1	111.8	0.104	0.13	0.297

- Traded from Portland to New York, regular starter for Portland, played off the bench for New York
- Played starter level minutes overall, effective in his role as a low volume spot-up shooter and energy player for both teams
- Around a league average three-point shooter, Three-Point Percentage spiked after the trade to New York
- Almost exclusively a stand-still spot-up shooter, has made 41.5% of his career corner threes
- Attacks the rim in transition, draws fouls at a solid rate, good cutter, solid offensive rebounding wing
- Inconsistent in ball handling situations, more effective before the trade in Portland
- Fairly solid secondary playmaker that makes simple reads, can be a bit turnover prone
- 2022-23 Defensive Degree of Difficulty: 0.552, had the 20th most difficult set of matchups
- 2022-23 Points Prevented: -0.373
- Used as a defensive stopper in Portland, took on slightly easier matchups in New York
- Good on-ball defender that can effectively guard multiple positions
- Decent pick-and-roll defender, can switch to defend screeners, has some trouble containing ball handlers
- Sometimes gets caught on screens off the ball, occasionally will be late to close out on spot-up shooters
- Active help defender that gets steals at a solid rate, good defensive rebounder

Donte DiVincenzo

	Height	Weight	Cap #	Years Left
	6'4"	203	$10.900M	3

Similar at Age 26

		Season	SIMsc
1	Marcus Thornton	2013-14	916.1
2	Jon Barry	1995-96	911.0
3	Rex Walters	1996-97	910.1
4	Kent Bazemore	2015-16	908.9
5	Jerian Grant	2018-19	908.7
6	Anthony Peeler	1995-96	908.1
7	Grayson Allen	2021-22	908.1
8	Charlie Bell	2005-06	908.0
9	Alex Caruso	2020-21	905.7
10	Danny Green	2013-14	905.6

Baseline Basic Stats

MPG	PTS	AST	REB	BLK	STL
24.5	9.1	2.1	2.9	0.2	1.0

Advanced Metrics

USG%	3PTA/FGA	FTA/FGA	TS%	eFG%	3PT%
16.6	0.594	0.182	0.556	0.524	0.377

AST%	TOV%	OREB%	DREB%	STL%	BLK%
14.9	13.4	3.5	12.2	2.1	0.7

PER	ORTG	DRTG	WS/48	BPM	VOL
12.43	111.6	112.9	0.080	-0.58	0.391

- Played close to starter level minutes in his first season with Golden State
- Maintained his usual effectiveness in a role as a low volume spot-up and secondary ball handler
- League average career three-point shooter, made almost 40% of his threes last season
- Primarily a stationary spot-up shooter, good at making shots off screens in a small sample of attempts
- Lacks dynamic ball handling ability and quickness, not really effective at creating his own offense off the dribble
- Fairly good secondary playmaker, slightly turnover prone, effective cutter off the ball
- 2022-23 Defensive Degree of Difficulty: 0.467
- 2022-23 Points Prevented: 0.021
- Typically guarded starting level players, drew some high-end assignments against top scorers
- Played solid on-ball defense last season, could capably defend both guard spots
- Solid pick-and-roll defender, funnels his man into help, effective at switching onto screeners or ball handlers
- Tends to get caught on screens off the ball, not always in position to effectively contest shots in spot-up situations
- Very active help defender that play passing lanes, consistently get steals at a high rate, fairly good defensive rebounder

Isaiah Hartenstein

	Height	Weight	Cap #	Years Left
	7'0"	250	$9.245M	UFA

Similar at Age 24

		Season	SIMsc
1	Gorgui Dieng	2013-14	910.0
2	Tyler Zeller	2013-14	909.1
3	Duane Causwell	1992-93	908.4
4	Rasho Nesterovic	2000-01	906.3
5	Clifford Rozier	1996-97	906.2
6	Darko Milicic	2009-10	905.6
7	Andrew Bogut	2008-09	905.1
8	Cody Zeller	2016-17	904.8
9	Kosta Koufos	2013-14	901.9
10	Ivica Zubac	2021-22	901.3

Baseline Basic Stats

MPG	PTS	AST	REB	BLK	STL
21.0	7.3	1.0	6.0	1.2	0.5

Advanced Metrics

USG%	3PTA/FGA	FTA/FGA	TS%	eFG%	3PT%
14.9	0.058	0.298	0.584	0.559	0.206

AST%	TOV%	OREB%	DREB%	STL%	BLK%
10.1	15.4	11.4	21.7	1.4	4.7

PER	ORTG	DRTG	WS/48	BPM	VOL
16.43	119.2	107.9	0.145	0.19	0.367

- Regular rotation player for New York in his first season with the team
- Production level regressed a bit, still effective in a role as a very low usage rim runner
- Physical, high motor big man, does not always get enough lift to finish shots at the rim
- Decent rim runner, solid cutter and roll man, good offensive rebounder, did not really run the floor in New York
- Shot more threes last season, percentages crashed, usually a below break-even three-point shooter
- Limited as a post player, fairly solid passing big man, slightly turnover prone
- 2022-23 Defensive Degree of Difficulty: 0.374
- 2022-23 Points Prevented: 0.329
- Great rim protector, good shot blocker and defensive rebounder
- Usually guards second unit big men, below average post defender, tends to commit a lot of shooting fouls, slightly better when defending in space
- Decent pick-and-roll defender, has to compensate for lumbering foot speed, solid at hedging onto ball handlers, tended to be late when rotating to guard screeners
- Consistently comes out to contest perimeter shots in spot-up situations, uses length well to get steals

Jericho Sims

	Height	Weight	Cap #	Years Left
	6'10"	245	$1.928M	TO

Similar at Age 24

		Season	SIMsc
1	Tony Bradley	2021-22	908.0
2	Eric Mobley	1994-95	895.3
3	Josh McRoberts	2011-12	892.5
4	Cole Aldrich	2012-13	888.6
5	Damian Jones	2019-20	887.0
6	Josh Boone	2008-09	881.4
7	Jordan Hill	2011-12	879.8
8	Marcin Gortat	2008-09	874.8
9	Greg Smith	2014-15	874.4
10	Richaun Holmes	2017-18	873.8

Baseline Basic Stats

MPG	PTS	AST	REB	BLK	STL
16.1	5.2	0.7	4.6	0.7	0.4

Advanced Metrics

USG%	3PTA/FGA	FTA/FGA	TS%	eFG%	3PT%
11.6	0.024	0.353	0.664	0.657	0.094

AST%	TOV%	OREB%	DREB%	STL%	BLK%
6.3	17.1	11.6	21.4	1.2	3.4

PER	ORTG	DRTG	WS/48	BPM	VOL
15.08	128.1	110.2	0.138	-0.51	0.385

- Fringe rotation player for New York in his second NBA season
- Production level increased in his role as an extremely low usage rim runner
- Vertical lob threat, over 73% of his made field goals were dunks last season
- Great cutter and roll man, very good offensive rebounder that scores on tip dunks, runs hard in transition
- Lacks reliable shooting range outside of ten feet, has made less than 55% of his career free throws
- Not really a post-up threat, very limited passing skills, highly turnover prone
- 2022-23 Defensive Degree of Difficulty: 0.432
- 2022-23 Points Prevented: -1.028
- Improved to become a good rim protector, good shot blocker, solid defensive rebounder
- Drew some tough assignments off the bench, stout post defender, had trouble defending in space, prone to committing unnecessary shooting fouls
- Decent pick-and-roll defender, mobile enough to hedge out on ball handlers, tends to have lapses when rotating to guard screeners
- Consistently comes out to the perimeter to contest shots in spot-up situations

Miles McBride

	Height	Weight	Cap #	Years Left
	6'2"	200	$1.836M	RFA

Similar at Age 22

		Season	SIMsc
1	Chris Robinson	1996-97	912.1
2	Daniel Gibson	2008-09	905.6
3	Jaylen Adams	2018-19	905.5
4	Donte DiVincenzo	2018-19	902.9
5	Frank Ntilikina	2020-21	901.6
6	Terry Rozier	2016-17	901.3
7	Khyri Thomas	2018-19	897.7
8	Keyon Dooling	2002-03	896.1
9	Daniel Ewing	2005-06	895.6
10	Ty Jerome	2019-20	892.2

Baseline Basic Stats

MPG	PTS	AST	REB	BLK	STL
19.1	7.7	2.3	2.5	0.2	0.7

Advanced Metrics

USG%	3PTA/FGA	FTA/FGA	TS%	eFG%	3PT%
17.8	0.574	0.173	0.522	0.498	0.359

AST%	TOV%	OREB%	DREB%	STL%	BLK%
17.7	10.1	2.1	9.3	2.1	0.8

PER	ORTG	DRTG	WS/48	BPM	VOL
12.12	109.8	111.4	0.091	-0.22	0.465

- Fringe rotation player for New York in his second NBA season
- Productivity increased, still inefficient in his role as a low usage spot-up shooter
- Posted a True Shooting Percentage below 50%, has made less than 30% of his career threes
- Mostly used as a stand-still spot-up shooter, has not been able to regularly make shots in any specific situation
- Defenders can back off him to limit his effectiveness as a pick-and-roll ball handler and isolation player
- Good cutter off the ball, solid secondary playmaker that makes sound decisions, rarely turns the ball over
- 2022-23 Defensive Degree of Difficulty: 0.417
- 2022-23 Points Prevented: 1.166
- Usually defended second unit level players, occasionally drew tough assignments off the bench
- Decent on-ball defender, capable of defending bigger guards or wings, had some trouble staying with quicker perimeter players
- Middling pick-and-roll defender, limited ability to switch, can cut off penetration, goes too far under screens
- Stays attached to shooters off the ball, fights through screens, closes out in spot-up situations
- Active help defender, gets steals at a high rate, can block shots on the weak side, below average defensive rebounder

Evan Fournier

	Height	Weight	Cap #	Years Left
	6'7"	205	$18.857M	TO

Similar at Age 30

		Season	SIMsc
1	George McCloud	1997-98	934.9
2	Kyle Korver	2011-12	934.3
3	Terrence Ross	2021-22	926.0
4	Nick Young	2015-16	925.0
5	Gerald Green	2015-16	923.4
6	Gordan Giricek	2007-08	922.0
7	C.J. Miles	2017-18	921.7
8	Chandler Parsons	2018-19	914.0
9	James White	2012-13	912.6
10	Alan Anderson	2012-13	908.2

Baseline Basic Stats

MPG	PTS	AST	REB	BLK	STL
22.1	8.6	1.3	2.6	0.2	0.6

Advanced Metrics

USG%	3PTA/FGA	FTA/FGA	TS%	eFG%	3PT%
17.4	0.590	0.151	0.528	0.502	0.360

AST%	TOV%	OREB%	DREB%	STL%	BLK%
9.8	10.0	1.6	10.6	1.5	0.8

PER	ORTG	DRTG	WS/48	BPM	VOL
10.05	105.9	112.1	0.059	-2.18	0.433

- Fell out of New York's rotation, playing time dropped significantly in his second season with the team
- Effectiveness dramatically declined in his role as a low usage shooting specialist
- Normally a reliable three-point shooter in his career, Three-Point Percentage cratered to below break-even
- Usually a player that makes spot-up jumpers and runs off screens, decent spot-up shooter last season
- Effective on hand-offs and pick-and-rolls in the past, shooting struggles greatly limited his performance last season
- Solid secondary playmaker that makes simple reads, consistently avoids committing turnovers
- 2022-23 Defensive Degree of Difficulty: 0.385
- 2022-23 Points Prevented: -0.823
- Generally defended second unit players, guarded starter level players in the past
- Played fairly solid on-ball defense last season, solid at staying with perimeter players, had some trouble against stronger wings inside
- Middling pick-and-roll defender, can functionally switch, tends to go too far under screens
- Fights through off-ball screens, tends to late when closing out on spot-up shooters
- Fairly active help defender, still gets steals at a solid rate, below average defensive rebounder

Isaiah Roby

	Height	Weight	Cap #	Years Left
	6'8"	230	$2.067M	UFA

Similar at Age 24

		Season	SIMsc
1	Qyntel Woods	2005-06	928.4
2	Omri Casspi	2012-13	919.4
3	Chris Singleton	2013-14	918.6
4	Patrick Patterson	2013-14	918.4
5	Brian Evans	1997-98	916.2
6	Anthony Tolliver	2009-10	915.2
7	Devean George	2001-02	913.9
8	Lamar Stevens	2021-22	912.1
9	Luke Walton	2004-05	911.5
10	Jumaine Jones	2003-04	910.1

Baseline Basic Stats

MPG	PTS	AST	REB	BLK	STL
20.3	7.8	1.3	3.9	0.4	0.6

Advanced Metrics

USG%	3PTA/FGA	FTA/FGA	TS%	eFG%	3PT%
17.8	0.374	0.286	0.555	0.526	0.346

AST%	TOV%	OREB%	DREB%	STL%	BLK%
10.8	12.5	5.6	17.7	1.5	1.5

PER	ORTG	DRTG	WS/48	BPM	VOL
13.24	109.8	112.9	0.076	-1.16	0.393

- Played limited minutes for San Antonio in 2022-23, waived near the end of the season
- Struggled to play efficiently in a new role as a low volume spot-up shooter
- Around a league average career three-point shooter, percentages vary significantly from year-to-year
- Almost exclusively a stationary spot-up shooter, much more effective when shooting from the corners
- More effective as a high energy rim runner, athletic finisher around the rim, will go to the offensive boards
- Limited as a shot creator, shows fairly solid secondary playmaking skills, slightly turnover prone
- <u>2022-23 Defensive Degree of Difficulty</u>: 0.349
- <u>2022-23 Points Prevented</u>: -2.642
- Usually guarded second unit players, average on-ball defender
- Effective when defending perimeter players, struggled to guard bigger players in the post
- Played below average pick-and-roll defense, showed some ability to switch in previous seasons, not effective at taking away any specific action in 2022-23
- Tends to get caught on screens off the ball, usually was late to close out on spot-up shooters, takes some bad gambles
- Active help defender, gets steals at a high rate, good weak side shot blocker in the past, good defensive rebounder

DaQuan Jeffries

	Height	Weight	Cap #	Years Left
	6'5"	230	$2.067M	UFA

Similar at Age 25

		Season	SIMsc
1	Abdel Nader	2018-19	878.6
2	Yakhouba Diawara	2007-08	875.5
3	Haywood Highsmith	2021-22	874.7
4	Treveon Graham	2018-19	870.1
5	Semi Ojeleye	2019-20	868.1
6	Dante Exum	2020-21	863.7
7	Jamel Artis	2017-18	861.0
8	Jaron Blossomgame	2018-19	858.9
9	Joe Harris	2016-17	857.8
10	Georges Niang	2018-19	857.2

Baseline Basic Stats

MPG	PTS	AST	REB	BLK	STL
14.8	4.6	0.8	2.5	0.2	0.4

Advanced Metrics

USG%	3PTA/FGA	FTA/FGA	TS%	eFG%	3PT%
12.5	0.567	0.100	0.518	0.505	0.233

AST%	TOV%	OREB%	DREB%	STL%	BLK%
8.9	8.3	3.1	16.5	1.1	0.8

PER	ORTG	DRTG	WS/48	BPM	VOL
8.71	110.5	114.9	0.055	-3.58	0.460

- Spent most of last season in the G-League with Westchester, signed to multiple ten-day contracts with New York
- Mainly used in the G-League as a moderate volume complementary shooter
- Above break-even three-point shooter in the G-League, percentages vary quite a bit
- Primarily a stand-still spot-up shooter at this stage
- Energetic player that attacks the rim in transition, ball handling skills are limited, not really able to create his own shot at the NBA level
- Mainly a catch-and-shoot player, passing skills improved a bit last season, rarely turns the ball over
- 2021-22 Defensive Degree of Difficulty: 0.179
- 2021-22 Points Prevented: -6.155
- Only played 9 minutes in the NBA in 2021-22, most significant playing time came in the 2020-21 season
- Mostly guarded second unit players in 2020-21, played decent on-ball defense, could capably guard multiple positions
- Struggled to defend pick-and-rolls, largely ineffective when making rotations
- Tended to get caught on screens off the ball, good at closing out on spot-up shooters
- Very active help defender in the G-League, posts high steal and block rates, solid defensive rebounder

MIAMI HEAT

Last Season: 44 - 38, Lost NBA Finals to Denver (1 – 4)

Offensive Rating: 113.0, 25th in the NBA

Defensive Rating: 113.3, 9th in the NBA

Primary Executive: Pat Riley, President

Head Coach: Erik Spoelstra

Key Roster Changes

Subtractions
Max Strus, sign-and-trade
Victor Oladipo, trade
Gabe Vincent, free agency
Cody Zeller, free agency
Omer Yurtseven, free agency
Udonis Harlem, free agency

Additions
Jaime Jaquez Jr., draft
Josh Richardson, free agency
Thomas Bryant, free agency

Roster

Likely Starting Five
1. Kyle Lowry
2. Tyler Herro
3. Jimmy Butler
4. Caleb Martin
5. Bam Adebayo

Other Key Rotation Players
Duncan Robinson
Kevin Love
Josh Richardson
Thomas Bryant
Jaime Jaquez Jr.

* Italics denotes that a player is likely to be on the floor to close games

Remaining Roster

- Haywood Highsmith
- Orlando Robinson
- Nikola Jović
- Jamaree Bouyea, 24, 6'2", 180, San Francisco (Two-Way)
- Dru Smith, 26, 6'3", 203, Missouri (Two-Way)
- Jamal Cain, 24, 6'7", 191, Oakland (Two-Way)
- Drew Peterson, 24, 6'8", 195, USC (Exhibit 10)
- Caleb Daniels, 24, 6'4", 210, Villanova (Exhibit 10)
- Cole Swider, 24, 6'9", 220, Syracuse (Exhibit 10)
- Alondes Williams, 24, 6'5", 210, Wake Forest (Exhibit 10)
- Justin Champagnie, 22, 6'6", 200, Pittsburgh (Exhibit 10)

SCHREMPF Base Rating: 46.5

Season Preview Survey

- *Are the Heat contending or rebuilding? Where is this team headed?*

After last season's impressive Finals run, the Heat are primed to make another push to go for a championship. They lost a couple of key rotation players, as Max Strus and Gabe Vincent left to sign with other teams in free agency. However, they have consistently been able to develop new contributors from within their system. It's very possible that they could find a few suitable replacements to allow them to maintain their place in the Eastern Conference. There's also the possibility that they could level up their front-end talent by trading for Damian Lillard. If that happens, they would be a bit depleted from a depth perspective, but they would have increased firepower to give them a better chance to reach the Finals again and making a title run this coming season.

- *What are the areas of concern for this team heading into this season?*

If Miami's roster remains as it is, then their offense is going to be an issue because they don't have a lot of high-end scoring options outside of Jimmy Butler. They also lost a couple of their supplementary floor spacing threats, so it may be more of a grind for them to score on a consistent basis. If they are able to pull off a trade to acquire Lillard, it could resolve a lot of the issues related to their offense because he would allow them to have one of the best shot creating lead guards in the game. However, the possible addition of Lillard isn't going to address another potential problem, which would be their depth. A deal for Lillard would make this issue more pronounced because they would lose more valuable rotation players. At the moment, they don't have a lot of proven bench players. There's a chance that they could have some struggles in managing the schedule. On the flip side, they have been able to find unheralded contributors in past seasons, so they could draw from their developmental system to cobble together a workable bench to allow them to keep pace with the top teams in the East.

- *List some possible breakout players for this team.*

There will be minutes available for an unheralded player to get an opportunity and possibly break out. Out of the players that are currently on the roster, they have a couple of guys that could make an impact in their rotation. Haywood Highsmith played well in short bursts in the playoffs, so he could play a bigger role as an energetic defensive specialist. He just needs to show that he can credibly knock down threes to make himself a viable offensive threat. The other candidate is Orlando Robinson. He played on a Two-Way contract last season, and he had a pretty strong showing at Summer League this year. He has the ability to do a little bit of everything because he can finish inside, occasionally knock down a three, block shots, and rebound. He also gives them a different look because he's a long, big body center that could be useful against someone Joel Embiid. He could step up to fill their vacant backup center slot. Finally, Jamal Cain could emerge out of the Two-Way ranks to give them another solid complementary wing that provide depth by giving them some additional defense and floor spacing.

- *What should we expect from them this season?*

After a down regular season, the Heat rebounded to make a deep playoff run last season. They still have their main core players in place, and they have sound system in place to fall back on. They should be one of the better teams in the Eastern Conference, even if they don't wind up with Lillard. Either way, their ability to maximize talent and make tactical adjustments will make them a very tough out in the playoffs. Even though they have an unheralded group around the likes of Jimmy Butler and Bam Adebayo, they have a solid chance of pushing for another Finals berth this coming season.

Veterans

Jimmy Butler

	Height	Weight	Cap #	Years Left
	6'7"	230	$45.184M	1 + PO

Similar at Age 33

		Season	SIMsc
1	Clyde Drexler*	1995-96	900.3
2	Manu Ginobili*	2010-11	881.3
3	Dan Issel*	1981-82	874.8
4	Paul Pierce*	2010-11	874.6
5	Steve Mix	1980-81	873.2
6	Grant Hill*	2005-06	866.2
7	Vince Carter	2009-10	861.7
8	Armen Gilliam	1997-98	861.3
9	Larry Bird*	1989-90	857.7
10	Frank Brickowski	1992-93	857.1

Baseline Basic Stats

MPG	PTS	AST	REB	BLK	STL
32.0	18.4	4.3	5.4	0.5	1.4

Advanced Metrics

USG%	3PTA/FGA	FTA/FGA	TS%	eFG%	3PT%
25.1	0.182	0.489	0.597	0.522	0.314

AST%	TOV%	OREB%	DREB%	STL%	BLK%
23.8	10.3	5.9	14.1	2.5	1.2

PER	ORTG	DRTG	WS/48	BPM	VOL
23.12	122.5	108.0	0.216	5.76	0.383

- Named to the All-NBA 2nd Team, also named Eastern Conference Finals MVP in 2022-23
- Had a career best season, thrived in his role as Miami's primary scorer and ball handler
- Attacks the rim aggressively as a pick-and-roll ball handler and isolation player, draws fouls at a high rate
- Great playmaker that makes sound decisions and finds open teammates, rarely turns the ball over
- Below break-even career three-point shooter, above break-even three-point shooter last season
- Most effective as a stand-still spot-up shooter on threes, great at making pull-up jumpers from mid-range
- Moves well without the ball, excellent cutter, solid offensive rebounder that scores on put-backs
- 2022-23 Defensive Degree of Difficulty: 0.557, had the 17th most difficult set of matchups in the NBA
- 2022-23 Points Prevented: -0.280
- Routinely guards top scorers, primarily served as Miami's defensive stopper
- Good on-ball defender, stays with most perimeter players, had some trouble against bigger players inside
- Good pick-and-roll defender in previous seasons, can effectively switch, tended to take bad angles that hurt his effectiveness last season
- Sometimes gets caught on screens off the ball, great at closing out on spot-up shooters
- Great help defender, consistently gets steals at a high rate, occasional weak shot blocker, solid defensive rebounder

Bam Adebayo

	Height	Weight	Cap #	Years Left
	6'9"	255	$32.600M	2

Similar at Age 25

		Season	SIMsc
1	Greg Monroe	2015-16	932.9
2	Carlos Boozer	2006-07	928.5
3	Paul Millsap	2010-11	921.7
4	Chris Webber*	1998-99	919.2
5	Al Jefferson	2009-10	914.9
6	Kenyon Martin	2002-03	913.3
7	Juwan Howard	1998-99	909.5
8	Derrick Coleman	1992-93	908.2
9	Julius Randle	2019-20	907.4
10	Blake Griffin	2014-15	906.9

Baseline Basic Stats

MPG	PTS	AST	REB	BLK	STL
33.3	18.4	3.0	9.0	0.8	1.0

Advanced Metrics

USG%	3PTA/FGA	FTA/FGA	TS%	eFG%	3PT%
25.5	0.040	0.351	0.572	0.525	0.192

AST%	TOV%	OREB%	DREB%	STL%	BLK%
16.9	12.6	7.9	23.1	1.7	2.1

PER	ORTG	DRTG	WS/48	BPM	VOL
20.40	112.4	106.7	0.148	1.88	0.287

- Made his 2nd All-Star team, named to the All-Defensive 2nd Team for the fourth straight season
- Solidly effective in his role as a primary interior scorer and playmaking big man
- Good at driving by slower centers, can effectively face up from the post or isolate from further away
- Energetic rim runner, scores on a high volume of cuts and rolls to the rim, active offensive rebounder
- Draws fouls at a solid rate, runs hard in transition, tends to settle for less efficient floaters instead going all the way to the rim
- Great passing big man that finds cutters and open shooters, cut his turnover rate significantly
- Not really a three-point shooting threat, more effective when shooting from 10 to 16 feet
- 2022-23 Defensive Degree of Difficulty: 0.489
- 2022-23 Points Prevented: -0.560
- Rim protection skills seem to be declining, has trouble contesting shots vertically, blocks rate decreased
- Plays more like a tall perimeter players, better as a weak side shot blocker, good at using length to get steals, good defensive rebounder
- Good on-ball defender that draws tough assignments, stout post defender, mobile enough to defend in space
- Solid pick-and-roll ball handler, good at switching out onto ball handlers, fairly decent in drop coverages
- Tends to sag into the paint, does not always come out to contest perimeter shots in spot-up situations

Tyler Herro

	Height	Weight	Cap #	Years Left
	6'5"	195	$27.000M	3

Similar at Age 23

		Season	SIMsc
1	Damian Lillard	2013-14	915.2
2	Allan Houston	1994-95	914.2
3	Jordan Crawford	2011-12	913.6
4	Brandon Ingram	2020-21	908.8
5	Zach LaVine	2018-19	908.0
6	Jordan Clarkson	2015-16	907.4
7	Ray Allen*	1998-99	905.9
8	Lonnie Walker IV	2021-22	901.9
9	Desmond Bane	2021-22	901.7
10	Rashad McCants	2007-08	899.8

Baseline Basic Stats

MPG	PTS	AST	REB	BLK	STL
31.1	18.3	3.6	3.8	0.2	0.9

Advanced Metrics

USG%	3PTA/FGA	FTA/FGA	TS%	eFG%	3PT%
26.4	0.450	0.208	0.570	0.530	0.380

AST%	TOV%	OREB%	DREB%	STL%	BLK%
20.0	11.3	1.8	14.2	1.2	0.7

PER	ORTG	DRTG	WS/48	BPM	VOL
16.77	110.5	112.9	0.100	0.69	0.225

- Played as Miami's starting two-guard in the regular season, missed most of the playoffs due to a fractured right hand
- Maintained his efficiency level in his role as a high volume scoring guard
- Reliable three-point shooter, has made over 43% of his career corner threes
- Great spot-up shooter, makes pull-up threes if defenders go under screens, less effective when running off screens
- Better as a pick-and-roll ball handler, needs a screen to consistently get to the rim
- Good cutter off the ball, solid playmaker that can make sound decisions, good at limiting turnovers
- 2022-23 Defensive Degree of Difficulty: 0.426
- 2022-23 Points Prevented: 0.455
- Hidden in favorable matchups in previous seasons, took on tougher assignments last season
- Decent on-ball defender, competently guards perimeter players, has some trouble against quicker guards
- Solid pick-and-roll defender, good at funneling his man into help, can functionally switch to make sound rotations
- Stays attached to shooters off the ball, fights through screens, good at closing out on spot-up shooters
- Stay-at-home defender, rarely gets steals or blocks, good defensive rebounder

Kyle Lowry

	Height	Weight	Cap #	Years Left
	6'0"	196	$29.683M	UFA

Similar at Age 36

		Season	SIMsc
1	Terry Porter	1999-00	907.9
2	Andre Miller	2012-13	891.2
3	Chris Paul	2021-22	873.7
4	Mark Jackson	2001-02	872.5
5	Darrell Armstrong	2004-05	871.8
6	David Wesley	2006-07	869.5
7	Jeff Hornacek	1999-00	865.0
8	Chauncey Billups	2012-13	861.7
9	Anthony Carter	2011-12	860.4
10	Derek Fisher	2010-11	854.4

Baseline Basic Stats

MPG	PTS	AST	REB	BLK	STL
24.0	8.6	4.0	2.7	0.2	0.8

Advanced Metrics

USG%	3PTA/FGA	FTA/FGA	TS%	eFG%	3PT%
17.1	0.582	0.277	0.563	0.514	0.357

AST%	TOV%	OREB%	DREB%	STL%	BLK%
24.2	17.5	2.0	12.4	1.6	0.8

PER	ORTG	DRTG	WS/48	BPM	VOL
12.61	110.3	110.8	0.095	0.30	0.583

- Missed games due to injuries to his left knee, regular starting point guard for Miami when healthy
- Production is steadily declining due to age, now used as a low volume playmaker and spot-up shooter
- Great playmaker, effectively runs a team, makes sound decisions with the ball, slightly turnover prone
- Had a down shooting year, generally a reliable three-point shooter throughout his career
- Good stand-still spot-up shooter, can make threes if defenders go under screens on pick-and-rolls
- Diminishing speed, occasionally drives to the rim as a pick-and-roll ball handler and isolation player as a change-of-pace
- 2022-23 Defensive Degree of Difficulty: 0.456
- 2022-23 Points Prevented: -0.401
- Usually defends starting level guards, played good on-ball defense last season
- Plays angles well to stop drives on the perimeter, has great strength that allows him to defend bigger players
- Good pick-and-roll defender, can functionally switch despite a lack of ideal height, good at funneling ball handlers into help
- Tends to get caught on screens off the ball, good at closing out on spot-up shooters
- More active as a help defender, could play passing lanes to get steals, occasional will block shots from the weak side, solid defensive rebounder

Caleb Martin

	Height	Weight	Cap #	Years Left
	6'5"	205	$6.803M	PO

Similar at Age 27

		Season	SIMsc
1	Kentavious Caldwell-Pope	2020-21	938.4
2	Rodney McGruder	2018-19	932.0
3	Josh Richardson	2020-21	931.0
4	Wesley Johnson	2014-15	927.5
5	James Ennis	2017-18	926.7
6	Courtney Lee	2012-13	924.6
7	Damion Lee	2019-20	922.7
8	Pat Connaughton	2019-20	922.3
9	DeMarre Carroll	2013-14	920.3
10	Kyle Korver	2008-09	918.7

Baseline Basic Stats

MPG	PTS	AST	REB	BLK	STL
24.7	9.2	1.6	3.3	0.4	0.9

Advanced Metrics

USG%	3PTA/FGA	FTA/FGA	TS%	eFG%	3PT%
15.8	0.503	0.204	0.571	0.542	0.385

AST%	TOV%	OREB%	DREB%	STL%	BLK%
9.2	10.8	3.8	13.1	1.8	1.4

PER	ORTG	DRTG	WS/48	BPM	VOL
12.41	112.7	111.0	0.097	-0.29	0.282

- Ascended to a regular starting role in his second season with Miami
- Mainly used as a low volume spot-up shooter
- League average three-point shooter, has developed into an effective mid-range shooter
- Almost exclusively takes spot-up jumpers, flashed some ability to shoot off the dribble
- Effective cutter off the ball, explosive finisher in transition, selectively crashes the offensive glass
- Can handle the ball on a limited basis, effective in a small sample of possessions as a pick-and-roll ball handler and isolation player
- Catch-and-shoot player, may have some passing skills, good at limiting turnovers
- 2022-23 Defensive Degree of Difficulty: 0.532
- 2022-23 Points Prevented: -1.124
- Drew a lot of difficult matchups in his first season as a starter, may have been over-extended
- Solid on-ball defender, good against perimeter players, struggled to guard stronger players in the post
- Good pick-and-roll defender, solid at switching to guard ball handlers or screeners
- Stays attached to shooters off the ball, fights through screens, good at closing out in spot-up situations
- Fairly active help defender, gets steals at a fairly good rate, weak side shot blocking threat, fairly good defensive rebounder

Duncan Robinson

	Height	Weight	Cap #	Years Left
	6'7"	215	$18.154M	1 + ETO

Similar at Age 28

		Season	SIMsc
1	Georges Niang	2021-22	938.4
2	Sam Mack	1998-99	931.4
3	Mickael Pietrus	2010-11	927.7
4	Jarvis Hayes	2009-10	925.8
5	Ryan Broekhoff	2018-19	919.5
6	Doug McDermott	2019-20	917.1
7	Jason Kapono	2009-10	911.9
8	Cartier Martin	2012-13	911.0
9	Bojan Bogdanovic	2017-18	910.0
10	Bobby Simmons	2008-09	908.8

Baseline Basic Stats

MPG	PTS	AST	REB	BLK	STL
20.9	8.2	1.2	2.5	0.2	0.5

Advanced Metrics

USG%	3PTA/FGA	FTA/FGA	TS%	eFG%	3PT%
16.7	0.772	0.140	0.554	0.529	0.359

AST%	TOV%	OREB%	DREB%	STL%	BLK%
9.1	9.6	1.7	11.0	1.2	0.5

PER	ORTG	DRTG	WS/48	BPM	VOL
9.73	108.2	112.9	0.064	-2.90	0.420

- Missed a month due to a finger injury that required surgery, fringe rotation player for Miami when healthy
- Had a down regular season, bounced back to his previous levels in the playoffs, low volume shooting specialist throughout his career
- Shooting percentages took a dive last season, has made around 40% of his career threes
- Reliable spot-up shooters, good movement shooter that runs off screens in previous seasons
- Good at making threes off hand-offs, makes pull-up threes as a pick-and-roll ball handler
- Limited ability to create his own shot, gradually improving as a passer, rarely turns the ball over
- 2022-23 Defensive Degree of Difficulty: 0.331
- 2022-23 Points Prevented: -3.926
- Usually hidden in favorable matchups against lower leverage players or plays in zone defenses
- Below average on-ball defender, struggles to guard quicker players, more effective at guarding bigger players inside
- Decent pick-and-roll defender, good at funneling his man into help, less effective at switching onto screeners
- Fights through off-ball screens, not always in position to contest shots in spot-up situations
- Stay-at-home defender, rarely gets steals, did not block a shot last season, fairly solid defensive rebounder

Kevin Love

	Height	Weight	Cap #	Years Left
	6'8"	251	$3.836M	PO

Similar at Age 34

		Season	SIMsc
1	Rudy Gay	2020-21	892.4
2	Paul Millsap	2019-20	865.5
3	Zach Randolph	2015-16	861.5
4	Al Horford	2020-21	860.1
5	Anthony Tolliver	2019-20	859.7
6	Luis Scola	2014-15	851.0
7	Brad Miller	2010-11	850.2
8	Jeff Green	2020-21	849.0
9	Chuck Person	1998-99	848.6
10	Carmelo Anthony	2018-19	846.7

Baseline Basic Stats

MPG	PTS	AST	REB	BLK	STL
20.4	8.8	1.5	4.7	0.4	0.5

Advanced Metrics

USG%	3PTA/FGA	FTA/FGA	TS%	eFG%	3PT%
18.8	0.598	0.220	0.558	0.523	0.355

AST%	TOV%	OREB%	DREB%	STL%	BLK%
12.0	10.6	6.0	27.1	0.9	1.5

PER	ORTG	DRTG	WS/48	BPM	VOL
14.52	114.1	109.6	0.114	0.57	0.389

- Regular rotation player for Cleveland, bought out, then signed with Miami and started most of his games
- Mainly used by both teams in a role as a low volume stretch big
- Solid three-point shooter throughout his career, had an uncharacteristic slump in the regular season in Miami
- Consistently good at hitting threes in transition, solid spot-up shooter, less efficient on pick-and-pops
- Average post-up player, has trouble finishing over length, effective rim runner despite waning athleticism
- Very good passing big man, excellent outlet passer, consistently avoid turnovers
- <u>2022-23 Defensive Degree of Difficulty</u>: 0.355
- <u>2022-23 Points Prevented</u>: -0.338
- Below average rim protector, not really a shot blocking threat, excellent defensive rebounder
- Usually guards second unit big men or is hidden in favorable matchups
- More effective overall on-ball defender in Cleveland, struggled to defend in the post and in space with Miami
- Decent pick-and-roll defender, can functionally switch, solid in drop coverages, tended to have lapses when making rotations in Cleveland
- Not always in position to contest perimeter shots in spot-up situations, sometimes stays anchored in the paint

Josh Richardson

	Height	Weight	Cap #	Years Left
	6'5"	200	$2.891M	PO

Similar at Age 29

		Season	SIMsc
1	Roger Mason	2009-10	940.3
2	George McCloud	1996-97	935.3
3	Charlie Bell	2008-09	930.0
4	Cory Joseph	2020-21	928.8
5	Anthony Peeler	1998-99	926.1
6	Francisco Garcia	2010-11	925.1
7	Damion Lee	2021-22	925.0
8	Mario Elie	1992-93	925.0
9	Terrence Ross	2020-21	924.5
10	Courtney Lee	2014-15	924.5

Baseline Basic Stats

MPG	PTS	AST	REB	BLK	STL
25.0	9.1	1.9	2.6	0.2	0.8

Advanced Metrics

USG%	3PTA/FGA	FTA/FGA	TS%	eFG%	3PT%
16.9	0.486	0.174	0.548	0.515	0.376

AST%	TOV%	OREB%	DREB%	STL%	BLK%
12.1	11.3	2.5	9.5	1.8	1.0

PER	ORTG	DRTG	WS/48	BPM	VOL
11.45	108.9	111.9	0.078	-0.98	0.206

- Traded from San Antonio to New Orleans at the trade deadline, regular rotation player for both teams
- Mostly used as a lower usage spot-up shooter, took on more usage with San Antonio
- Solid three-point shooter, better in the corners, has made over 40% of his career corner threes
- Almost exclusively a stationary spot-up shooter, not consistent when shooting in other situations
- Efficient mid-range shooter, fairly effective in a small sample of pick-and-roll possessions, needs a screen to get to the rim
- Good secondary playmaker that makes simple reads, good at avoiding turnovers
- 2022-23 Defensive Degree of Difficulty: 0.452
- 2022-23 Points Prevented: -1.166
- Drew a lot of tough assignments off the bench, used as a defensive stopper in previous seasons
- Fairly solid on-ball defender, good against perimeter players, struggles against stronger players inside due to a relatively thin frame
- Played below average pick-and-roll defense, not effective at taking away any specific action last season
- Fights through screens off the ball, sometimes can be late when closing out on spot-up shooters
- Great at playing passing lanes to get steals, occasional weak side shot blocker, below average defensive rebounder

Thomas Bryant

	Height	Weight	Cap #	Years Left
	6'10"	248	$2.528M	PO

Similar at Age 25

		Season	SIMsc
1	Jabari Parker	2020-21	915.3
2	Al Horford	2011-12	912.5
3	Jelani McCoy	2002-03	910.3
4	Dwight Powell	2016-17	900.9
5	Chris Hunter	2009-10	900.8
6	Bobby Portis	2020-21	900.2
7	Darryl Dawkins	1981-82	900.1
8	Carl Landry	2008-09	899.4
9	Derrick Favors	2016-17	897.3
10	Malik Allen	2003-04	894.4

Baseline Basic Stats

MPG	PTS	AST	REB	BLK	STL
21.5	9.7	1.2	5.8	0.9	0.6

Advanced Metrics

USG%	3PTA/FGA	FTA/FGA	TS%	eFG%	3PT%
18.4	0.172	0.299	0.635	0.613	0.434

AST%	TOV%	OREB%	DREB%	STL%	BLK%
7.6	11.3	8.3	21.9	1.1	3.3

PER	ORTG	DRTG	WS/48	BPM	VOL
18.07	121.7	110.0	0.147	0.20	0.519

- Started most of his games for the L.A. Lakers, traded to Denver then sparingly played
- Used by both teams as a low usage rim runner and stretch big
- Effective rim runner that plays with high energy, great cutter and roll man, fairly active offensive rebounder
- Struggled to finish efficiently and did not run the floor in transition as often in Denver
- Fairly good three-point shooting big man, percentages have varied from year-to-year
- Solid spot-up shooter, effective as a pick-and-pop screener
- Can bully weaker defenders around the rim on post-ups, decent passing big man, rarely turns the ball over
- 2022-23 Defensive Degree of Difficulty: 0.458
- 2022-23 Points Prevented: -2.196
- Good defensive rebounder, decent shot blocker, below average rim protector, undisciplined with his positioning
- Defended starting level big men, below average on-ball defender, tends to commit a lot of shooting fouls
- Struggles to defend opposing centers in the post, lacks the mobility to defend in space
- Below average pick-and-roll defenders, usually has lapses when making rotations
- Tends to stay anchored in the paint, does not always come out to contest perimeter shots

Haywood Highsmith

	Height	Weight	Cap #	Years Left
	6'7"	220	$1.902M	UFA

Similar at Age 26

		Season	SIMsc
1	Cartier Martin	2010-11	922.7
2	Sam Mack	1996-97	917.2
3	Timothé Luwawu-Cabarrot	2021-22	914.4
4	Juancho Hernangómez	2021-22	914.1
5	James Anderson	2015-16	913.4
6	Yakhouba Diawara	2008-09	912.9
7	Dorian Finney-Smith	2019-20	911.9
8	Sterling Brown	2021-22	908.6
9	Solomon Hill	2017-18	905.4
10	Maurice Harkless	2019-20	904.4

Baseline Basic Stats

MPG	PTS	AST	REB	BLK	STL
17.8	5.7	1.0	2.8	0.3	0.6

Advanced Metrics

USG%	3PTA/FGA	FTA/FGA	TS%	eFG%	3PT%
14.0	0.523	0.138	0.530	0.520	0.360

AST%	TOV%	OREB%	DREB%	STL%	BLK%
7.0	11.7	5.5	13.3	1.6	1.6

PER	ORTG	DRTG	WS/48	BPM	VOL
9.87	106.5	111.9	0.065	-2.57	0.358

- Fringe rotation player for Miami in his first full season with the team
- Had his most effective season, utilized as a very low volume spot-up shooter and energy wing
- Around a break-even career three-point shooter, better when shooting above the break
- Strictly a stationary spot-up shooter at this stage, not really effective when shooting in other situations
- Shooting stroke is still inconsistent, has made less than 50% of his career free throws
- Athletic finisher that plays with high energy, decent cutter, active offensive rebounding wing
- Limited ability to create his own shot, not really a passer, somewhat turnover prone
- 2022-23 Defensive Degree of Difficulty: 0.458
- 2022-23 Points Prevented: 1.649
- Drew a lot of tough assignments off the bench, usually guarded starting level players
- Solid on-ball defender that can guard multiple positions, can be over-aggressive, prone to committing cheap fouls or taking bad angles
- Good pick-and-roll defender, can switch to defend ball handlers or screeners in different coverages
- Sometimes gets caught on screens off the ball, consistently closes out on spot-up shooters
- Active help defender, posted high steal and block rates last season, solid defensive rebounder

Orlando Robinson

	Height	Weight	Cap #	Years Left
	7'0"	235	$1.802M	1

Similar at Age 22

		Season	SIMsc
1	Travis Knight	1996-97	938.9
2	Nick Fazekas	2007-08	930.3
3	Hilton Armstrong	2006-07	914.0
4	Willie Cauley-Stein	2015-16	913.3
5	Jordan Hill	2009-10	911.4
6	Bill Wennington	1985-86	910.1
7	Olivier Sarr	2021-22	906.9
8	Scott Williams	1990-91	904.4
9	Cody Zeller	2014-15	904.0
10	Dale Davis	1991-92	901.6

Baseline Basic Stats

MPG	PTS	AST	REB	BLK	STL
18.3	6.2	0.9	4.9	0.9	0.5

Advanced Metrics

USG%	3PTA/FGA	FTA/FGA	TS%	eFG%	3PT%
14.5	0.050	0.353	0.559	0.524	0.040

AST%	TOV%	OREB%	DREB%	STL%	BLK%
8.9	14.2	10.7	20.7	1.5	3.1

PER	ORTG	DRTG	WS/48	BPM	VOL
13.98	115.6	108.0	0.123	-1.31	0.434

- Played on a Two-Way contract with Miami, spent some time with Sioux Falls in the G-League
- Had a solidly effective rookie season, used in the NBA as a low usage rim runner
- Effective rim runner, relies more on energy, lacks the ideal vertical lift, has some trouble finishing against athletic big men
- Good at rolling to the rim, good offensive rebounder, plays physical, willing to absorb contact to draw fouls
- Not really used as a post-up option in the NBA, shot some threes in the G-League, made them at a below break-even rate
- Flashes some ability to pass and hit cutters, good at avoiding turnovers
- 2022-23 Defensive Degree of Difficulty: 0.358
- 2022-23 Points Prevented: -3.419
- Effective rim protector in limited NBA minutes, good defensive rebounder, solid shot blocker
- Usually guarded second unit level big men, played below average on-ball defense
- Committed a lot of shooting fouls in the post, struggles to effectively hold position
- Rarely tested on the perimeter, ability to defend in space is uncertain
- Decent pick-and-roll defender, effective at hedging out onto ball handlers, had lapses when covering screeners
- Tended to stay anchored in the paint, did not always come out to contest perimeter shots

Nikola Jović

	Height	Weight	Cap #	Years Left
	6'10"	209	$2.352M	2 TO

Similar at Age 19

		Season	SIMsc
1	Martell Webster	2005-06	908.6
2	Sekou Doumbouya	2019-20	904.9
3	JT Thor	2021-22	894.8
4	Alen Smailagić	2019-20	888.6
5	Tobias Harris	2011-12	879.3
6	Ersan Ilyasova	2006-07	878.1
7	Kevin Knox	2018-19	876.0
8	Troy Brown	2018-19	873.1
9	Aaron Gordon	2014-15	868.1
10	Jonathan Kuminga	2021-22	863.7

Baseline Basic Stats

MPG	PTS	AST	REB	BLK	STL
21.6	8.6	1.0	3.3	0.4	0.7

Advanced Metrics

USG%	3PTA/FGA	FTA/FGA	TS%	eFG%	3PT%
19.4	0.412	0.282	0.567	0.516	0.329

AST%	TOV%	OREB%	DREB%	STL%	BLK%
8.5	11.4	4.3	14.5	1.9	1.3

PER	ORTG	DRTG	WS/48	BPM	VOL
13.40	109.7	112.1	0.086	-1.79	0.450

- Played very sparingly for Miami in his rookie season
- Mainly used as a low usage spot-up shooter in limited minutes
- Made less than 30% of his threes, slightly better at shooting from mid-range, went 18-for-19 (94.7%) from the free throw line
- Generally used as a stand-still spot-up shooter, struggled to make shots as a pick-and-pop screener
- Energetic player that runs hard in transition, efficient finisher that made almost 85% of his shots at the rim
- Not really a shot creator at this stage, catch-and-shoot player right now, good at avoiding turnovers
- <u>2022-23 Defensive Degree of Difficulty</u>: 0.410
- <u>2022-23 Points Prevented</u>: -4.764
- Usually played in garbage time, drew some tough assignments during a four-game stretch where he played extended minutes
- Average on-ball defender, competently stays with opposing players, tends to bail out his man by committing cheap fouls
- Decent pick-and-roll defender, can functionally switch, tends to make sound rotations
- Tends to get caught on screens, sometimes can be late to close out on spot-up shooters
- Posted a moderately high Steal Percentage, fairly solid defensive rebounder

Newcomers

Jaime Jaquez Jr

	Height	Weight	Cap #	Years Left
	6'7"	225	$3.511M	1 + 2 TO

Baseline Basic Stats

MPG	PTS	AST	REB	BLK	STL
20.4	7.4	1.5	3.5	0.4	0.7

Advanced Metrics

USG%	3PTA/FGA	FTA/FGA	TS%	eFG%	3PT%
17.5	0.229	0.234	0.500	0.469	0.335

AST%	TOV%	OREB%	DREB%	STL%	BLK%
11.2	11.9	5.4	13.5	1.8	1.3

PER	ORTG	DRTG	WS/48	BPM	VOL
12.64	101.6	100.6	0.082	-0.50	N/A

- Drafted by Miami with the 18th overall pick in 2023
- Had a very solid showing at the Sacramento Summer League
- Slightly over-extended, effective as a high usage scorer, likely will be a lower volume player in the NBA
- Shot well in Sacramento, posted a 56% True Shooting Percentage, made 4 of his 9 threes (44.4%)
- Below break-even three-point shooter in college, mostly a stand-still spot-up shooter, solid at making mid-range pull-up jumpers
- Scores on hustle plays around the rim, crafty with the ball in his hands, could get to his spots in college
- Lacks explosive quickness or dynamic ball handling ability, not likely to be a shot creator in the NBA
- Solid secondary playmaker that can make simple reads, slightly turnover prone with higher usage at Summer League
- Lacks ideal physical tools but plays with a high motor and a physical edge
- Decent on-ball defender, plays bigger than his size, has some trouble staying with quicker players on the perimeter
- Solidly effective pick-and-roll defender, good at containing ball handlers, tended to be late when making rotations against screeners
- Tended to get caught on off-ball screens, consistently would close out on spot-up shooters
- Stay-at-home defender at Summer League, only recorded one steal, did not block a shot, decent defensive rebounder

ATLANTA HAWKS

Last Season: 41 - 41, Lost 1st Round to Boston (2 - 4)

Offensive Rating: 116.6, 7th in the NBA   Defensive Rating: 116.3, 22nd in the NBA

Primary Executive: Landry Fields, General Manager

Head Coach: Quin Snyder

Key Roster Changes

Subtractions
John Collins, trade
Aaron Holiday, free agency
Tyrese Martin, waived
Vit Krejci, waived

Additions
Kobe Bufkin, draft
Mouhamed Gueye, draft
Patty Mills, trade

Roster

Likely Starting Five
1. Trae Young
2. Dejounte Murray
3. Saddiq Bey
4. De'Andre Hunter
5. Clint Capela

Other Key Rotation Players
Bogdan Bogdanović
Onyeka Okongwu
A.J. Griffin
Jalen Johnson
Kobe Bufkin

* Italics denotes that a player is likely to be on the floor to close games

Remaining Roster

- Patty Mills
- Wesley Matthews
- Bruno Fernando
- Garrison Mathews
- Mouhamed Gueye
- Seth Lundy, 23, 6'6", 220, Penn State (Two-Way)
- Miles Norris, 23, 6'10", 220, UC Santa Barbara (Two-Way)
- Jarkel Joiner, 24, 6'1", 180, NC State (Exhibit 10)
- David Singleton, 24, 6'4", 210, UCLA (Exhibit 10)

SCHREMPF Base Rating: 44.9

Season Preview Survey

- *Are the Hawks contending or rebuilding? Where is this team headed?*

The Hawks are trying to contend, but they appear to be stuck in place as a lower tier playoff team. They didn't really improve because they had limited assets and they got little in return in the John Collins trade. They will need some significant internal growth to exceed expectations. Otherwise, they will remain in their current position unless they drastically reverse course and deal one of their two stars.

- *What are the areas of concern for this team heading into this season?*

There are several areas of concerns for the Hawks coming into the season. For starters, their team appears to be overly dependent on their star guards to generate offense. They have had trouble incorporating movement into their offense because Trae Young has been unwilling to actively move off the ball. In order to unlock another level of efficiency, head coach, Quin Snyder needs to bridge the divide between the coaching staff and Young. This way, he can get Young to sacrifice some usage to empower the others. Also, the Hawks don't have a lot of lineup flexibility because they consistently play two smaller guards and a traditional center. They could be vulnerable on the defensive end, especially if opponents try to spread them out. In addition to this, their group of wings is very inexperienced, so it could be tough for them to find reliable production from this set of players throughout the year.

- *List some possible breakout players for this team.*

The inexperience of their set of wings could create an opening for a young player to emerge. The best candidates to become impact rotational players could be A.J. Griffin and Jalen Johnson. Griffin had his moments as a rookie because he shot the ball very efficiently from long range. With increased playing time, he could emerge as a valuable floor spacer for the Hawks. Also, Johnson took a leap forward in his development by being effective as a defender and energy player on the second unit. If he proves that he can handle tough defensive assignments and becomes a more reliable shooter, then he could make a greater impact for Atlanta this upcoming season. Additionally, the Hawks have a small void that needs to be filled in their backup point guard slot. Kobe Bufkin could slot into that role because he flashed some potential as a scoring guard at Summer League. If he demonstrates that he's a more effective option than veteran, Patty Mills, then he could become another valuable rotational player for the Hawks this season.

- *What should we expect from them this season?*

Unless something changes in a major way, the Hawks are expected to finish around where they did last season. They didn't make any major additions to their roster this offseason, so it's not likely that they will gain any ground on the other contenders, based on their personnel. If they take any kind of positive stride, it will probably the result of internal growth. They have some interesting young players, but they don't really have any major high upside prospects that can really raise their ceiling. Most likely, they will participate in the play-in tournament and earn one of the two lower playoff seeds. If they can be competitive in their first round series, they will meet expectations. Otherwise, they may need to re-examine their situation and consider changing their core to better clarify the direction of their franchise.

Veterans

Trae Young

	Height	Weight	Cap #	Years Left
	6'1"	180	$40.064M	2 + PO

Similar at Age 24

		Season	SIMsc
1	Kyrie Irving	2016-17	917.7
2	Dennis Schroder	2017-18	905.5
3	Devonte' Graham	2019-20	903.5
4	Stephon Marbury	2001-02	901.7
5	Kenny Anderson	1994-95	895.1
6	Kevin Johnson	1990-91	894.8
7	Tony Parker*	2006-07	893.4
8	Nick Van Exel	1995-96	889.3
9	D.J. Augustin	2011-12	888.7
10	Isiah Thomas*	1985-86	888.6

Baseline Basic Stats

MPG	PTS	AST	REB	BLK	STL
33.9	21.1	7.6	3.2	0.2	1.1

Advanced Metrics

USG%	3PTA/FGA	FTA/FGA	TS%	eFG%	3PT%
30.0	0.333	0.394	0.577	0.503	0.355

AST%	TOV%	OREB%	DREB%	STL%	BLK%
39.9	14.2	2.0	8.4	1.6	0.4

PER	ORTG	DRTG	WS/48	BPM	VOL
21.67	116.3	114.3	0.156	2.27	0.335

- Overall production level dropped slightly, still played at an All-Star level
- Dynamic playmaker that excelled as Atlanta's primary ball handler, led the NBA in Total Assists last season
- Plays a ball dominant style, good pick-and-ball handler and isolation player
- Solid three-point shooter with deep range, prefers to take difficult shots that lower his percentages
- Made almost 38% of his spot-up threes, below break-even in almost every other situation
- Has the ability to make shots off screens, seems to be unwilling to cut or move off the ball
- 2022-23 Defensive Degree of Difficulty: 0.384
- 2022-23 Points Prevented: -0.281
- Often hidden in favorable matchups against lower leverage assignments
- Played average on-ball defense but can be targeted by opponents on switches due to his smallish size
- Fairly effective pick-and-roll handler that could funnel his man into help, has limited ability to switch
- Can get caught on screens off the ball, does not always close out on spot-up shooters, lacks the ideal length to effectively contest shots
- Posted a career best Steal Percentage, not an especially active help defender, effort level not always on high, below average defensive rebounder

Dejounte Murray

	Height	Weight	Cap #	Years Left
	6'4"	180	$18.214M	3 + PO

Similar at Age 26

		Season	SIMsc
1	Vernon Maxwell	1991-92	932.5
2	Mike Conley	2013-14	929.3
3	Monta Ellis	2011-12	922.4
4	Jrue Holiday	2016-17	920.9
5	Goran Dragic	2012-13	920.0
6	Cuttino Mobley	2001-02	916.1
7	John Starks	1991-92	913.5
8	Gary Payton*	1994-95	913.3
9	Jason Terry	2003-04	913.0
10	Derek Harper	1987-88	912.6

Baseline Basic Stats

MPG	PTS	AST	REB	BLK	STL
32.6	16.3	5.2	3.6	0.3	1.4

Advanced Metrics

USG%	3PTA/FGA	FTA/FGA	TS%	eFG%	3PT%
24.0	0.289	0.203	0.537	0.502	0.348

AST%	TOV%	OREB%	DREB%	STL%	BLK%
27.4	11.9	2.4	13.3	2.2	0.7

PER	ORTG	DRTG	WS/48	BPM	VOL
17.51	110.3	110.2	0.106	2.08	0.240

- Production level regressed back toward his career averages, posted the second best season of his career in 2022-23
- Improved his efficiency in his role as a higher usage, secondary ball handler
- Good pick-and-roll ball handler that can slash to the rim or make pull-up jumpers from mid-range
- Great at using his speed to attack defenders in transition, solid playmaker that avoid turnovers
- Around a break-even three-point shooter for his career, mainly a spot-up shooter
- Percentages have varied a bit from year-to-year, made almost 44% of his corner threes last season
- Effective at moving off the ball, good cutter, can curl off screens to hit mid-range shots
- 2022-23 Defensive Degree of Difficulty: 0.522
- 2022-23 Points Prevented: 0.582
- Fairly good on-ball defender that draws difficult assignments against elite guards and wings
- Slightly over-matched against bigger wings, better at defending players that are his own size
- Played average pick-and-roll defense, can contain ball handlers, had trouble against bigger players on switches, tended to go too far under screens
- Stays attached to shooters off the ball, will fight through screens and close out in spot-up situations
- Usually an active help defender, posts high steals rate, very good defensive rebounding guard, rates were down in his first year in Atlanta

Clint Capela

	Height	Weight	Cap #	Years Left
	6'10"	240	$20.616M	1

Similar at Age 28

		Season	SIMsc
1	Enes Freedom	2020-21	921.8
2	Marcin Gortat	2012-13	918.0
3	Emeka Okafor	2010-11	903.0
4	Tristan Thompson	2019-20	899.8
5	Samuel Dalembert	2009-10	896.2
6	Richaun Holmes	2021-22	894.1
7	Dale Davis	1997-98	893.4
8	Derrick Favors	2019-20	891.9
9	Ed Davis	2017-18	887.3
10	Kris Humphries	2013-14	883.4

Baseline Basic Stats

MPG	PTS	AST	REB	BLK	STL
25.0	10.1	0.9	8.9	1.2	0.5

Advanced Metrics

USG%	3PTA/FGA	FTA/FGA	TS%	eFG%	3PT%
15.9	0.003	0.281	0.619	0.616	0.263

AST%	TOV%	OREB%	DREB%	STL%	BLK%
5.4	9.5	14.1	28.5	1.1	4.1

PER	ORTG	DRTG	WS/48	BPM	VOL
19.83	127.2	107.8	0.181	1.62	0.446

- Starting center for Atlanta in his third healthy season with the team, minutes slightly down
- Thrives as a low usage rim runner, posted a True Shooting Percentage of almost 66% last season
- Vertical spacing threat that can catch high lobs, good roll man and cutter, runs hard in transition
- Excellent offensive rebounder, score on a high volume of put-backs, prone to rushing his attempts inside
- Offensive skill is limited, over 99% of his shots are from ten feet and in, rarely attempts a jump shot
- Typically a poor free throw shooter, Free Throw Percentage did improve to above 60% last season
- Strictly a catch-and-finish player, has limited passing skills but good at avoiding turnovers
- 2022-23 Defensive Degree of Difficulty: 0.501
- 2022-23 Points Prevented: -0.100
- Excellent rebounder, solid shot blocker, average rim protector because his Block Percentage is declining
- Draws tough assignments against top interior players, struggled to play effective post defense, can bite fakes, prone to committing cheap shooting fouls inside
- Fairly effective at defending in space on isolations, can play angles to stop drives to the rim
- Mostly used in drop coverages on pick-and-rolls, can wall off the rim to stop roll men, has some trouble containing ball handlers
- Consistently will close out on perimeter shooters in spot-up situations

De'Andre Hunter

	Height	Weight	Cap #	Years Left
	6'8"	225	$20.089M	3

Similar at Age 25

		Season	SIMsc
1	James Jones	2005-06	944.9
2	Tracy Murray	1996-97	939.1
3	Doug McDermott	2016-17	935.3
4	Jarvis Hayes	2006-07	933.5
5	Tobias Harris	2017-18	927.3
6	Bojan Bogdanovic	2014-15	926.9
7	Kyle Singler	2013-14	926.1
8	Jason Kapono	2006-07	925.9
9	Jerami Grant	2019-20	925.6
10	Dennis Scott	1993-94	925.1

Baseline Basic Stats

MPG	PTS	AST	REB	BLK	STL
26.5	11.8	1.6	3.9	0.3	0.7

Advanced Metrics

USG%	3PTA/FGA	FTA/FGA	TS%	eFG%	3PT%
19.6	0.391	0.230	0.557	0.520	0.371

AST%	TOV%	OREB%	DREB%	STL%	BLK%
8.4	9.1	2.6	12.7	1.1	0.9

PER	ORTG	DRTG	WS/48	BPM	VOL
12.57	110.5	114.4	0.072	-1.52	0.350

- Full-time starter for Atlanta in his fourth season with the team
- Efficiency increased in his role as a low volume spot-up shooter
- Almost exclusively a catch-and-shoot player, around a league average three-point shooter
- Primarily a spot-up shooter, better at shooting in transition and in the corners last season
- Lacks the ball handling skills to consistently drive to the rim, not really a reliable one-on-one player right now
- Improved his effectiveness as a pick-and-roll ball handler and isolation player by making a higher percentage of his pull-up jumpers from mid-range
- Effective cutter, has limited playmaking skills but rarely turns the ball over
- 2022-23 Defensive Degree of Difficulty: 0.523
- 2022-23 Points Prevented: 0.010
- Used as Atlanta's primary stopper on the wing, played decent on-ball defense against top scorers
- Good at limiting three-point attempts on isolation plays, tended to commit shooting foul when defending drives
- Played around average pick-and-roll defense, good at defending the jump shot, tended to allow ball handlers or screeners to get to the rim
- Tended to get caught on screens off the ball, good at closing out in spot-up situations
- Stay-at-home defender, rarely gets blocks or steals, fairly solid defensive rebounder

Saddiq Bey

	Height	Weight	Cap #	Years Left
	6'7"	215	$4.557M	RFA

Similar at Age 23

		Season	SIMsc
1	Martell Webster	2009-10	942.1
2	Rodney Hood	2015-16	941.9
3	Chase Budinger	2011-12	940.3
4	Cedi Osman	2018-19	932.5
5	Khris Middleton	2014-15	932.4
6	Michael Finley	1996-97	932.3
7	Michael Redd	2002-03	932.0
8	Calbert Cheaney	1994-95	925.6
9	Glen Rice	1990-91	923.2
10	Solomon Hill	2014-15	921.5

Baseline Basic Stats

MPG	PTS	AST	REB	BLK	STL
29.8	14.0	2.1	4.0	0.3	1.0

Advanced Metrics

USG%	3PTA/FGA	FTA/FGA	TS%	eFG%	3PT%
21.2	0.475	0.252	0.557	0.512	0.364

AST%	TOV%	OREB%	DREB%	STL%	BLK%
11.2	8.3	3.6	13.0	1.6	0.6

PER	ORTG	DRTG	WS/48	BPM	VOL
15.22	113.3	113.8	0.100	0.05	0.414

- Regular starter for Detroit, then was used as a rotational bench player after a trade to Atlanta
- Mainly used as a lower volume spot-up shooter in Atlanta, played a higher usage role in Detroit
- Around a league average three-point shooter for his career, made 40% of his threes after the trade to Atlanta
- Mostly a stationary spot-up shooter, has made over 40% of his career corner threes
- Lacks the ball handling skills to score consistently on isolation plays
- More effective at attacking the rim in transition or as a pick-and-roll ball handler
- Largely a catch-and-shoot, flashed some passing ability in 2021-22, rarely turns the ball over
- 2022-23 Defensive Degree of Difficulty: 0.451
- 2022-23 Points Prevented: -0.968
- Typically guarded starting level players, defensive performance declined, showed the ability to defend multiple positions in previous seasons
- Capable of staying with perimeter players in isolation situations, can be overpowered by stronger players in the post, sometimes will commit cheap shooting fouls inside
- Decent pick-and-roll defender, can effectively switch, struggled to make sound rotations last season
- Can get caught on screens off the ball, tends to be late when closing out on perimeter shooters
- Solid defensive rebounder, increased his Steal Percentage to a career best last season

Bogdan Bogdanović

	Height	Weight	Cap #	Years Left
	6'6"	220	$18.700M	2 + TO

Similar at Age 30

		Season	SIMsc
1	Carlos Delfino	2012-13	940.5
2	Wesley Matthews	2016-17	939.3
3	Jason Richardson	2010-11	934.2
4	Alan Anderson	2012-13	931.6
5	Jud Buechler	1998-99	929.0
6	J.R. Smith	2015-16	928.2
7	Terrence Ross	2021-22	923.9
8	Morris Peterson	2007-08	923.8
9	Dan Majerle	1995-96	923.5
10	Kyle Korver	2011-12	922.1

Baseline Basic Stats

MPG	PTS	AST	REB	BLK	STL
25.6	10.5	1.8	3.2	0.2	0.8

Advanced Metrics

USG%	3PTA/FGA	FTA/FGA	TS%	eFG%	3PT%
18.5	0.571	0.146	0.565	0.542	0.383

AST%	TOV%	OREB%	DREB%	STL%	BLK%
12.1	8.9	1.9	11.8	1.5	0.8

PER	ORTG	DRTG	WS/48	BPM	VOL
13.20	113.0	113.0	0.092	0.36	0.308

- Missed the first 22 games of last season while recovering from surgery on his right knee
- Primarily used as a shooting specialist and sixth man, usage and overall production level declined slightly
- Reliable three-point shooter, has made almost 39% of his career threes
- Knocks down threes in all situations, good spot-up shooter, can run off screens and make shots off the dribble
- Can leverage the threat of his shot to score off the dribble as a change of pace
- Good pick-and-roll ball handler, can score on hand-offs, can drive by defenders if they crowd him
- Solid secondary playmaker, Assist Percentage was slightly down, rarely turns the ball over
- <u>2022-23 Defensive Degree of Difficulty</u>: 0.400
- <u>2022-23 Points Prevented</u>: 1.040
- Typically defends second unit level players, tends to be hidden in favorable matchups against starters
- Below average on-ball defender, struggled to stay with his man on drives to the rim
- Decent pick-and-roll defender, can functionally switch and funnel his man into help, tends to go too far under screens
- Stays attached to shooters off the ball, will close out and fight through screens
- More of a stay-at-home defender last season, Steal Percentage was down, around an average defensive rebounder for his size

Onyeka Okongwu

	Height	Weight	Cap #	Years Left
	6'8"	235	$8.109M	RFA

Similar at Age 22

		Season	SIMsc
1	Kenneth Faried	2011-12	910.3
2	Amir Johnson	2009-10	909.5
3	Paul Millsap	2007-08	907.2
4	Daniel Gafford	2020-21	904.1
5	Drew Eubanks	2019-20	902.6
6	Marquese Chriss	2019-20	902.3
7	Kevon Looney	2018-19	899.0
8	Travis Knight	1996-97	897.8
9	Quincy Acy	2012-13	897.2
10	Tony Battie	1998-99	896.7

Baseline Basic Stats

MPG	PTS	AST	REB	BLK	STL
22.9	9.6	1.1	6.6	1.1	0.7

Advanced Metrics

USG%	3PTA/FGA	FTA/FGA	TS%	eFG%	3PT%
15.7	0.012	0.394	0.665	0.634	0.252

AST%	TOV%	OREB%	DREB%	STL%	BLK%
7.2	13.0	11.7	19.9	1.4	4.1

PER	ORTG	DRTG	WS/48	BPM	VOL
19.02	130.1	110.6	0.181	0.56	0.332

- Only missed two games in 2022-23, played heavy rotation minutes in his third NBA season
- Highly effective in his role as a low usage rim runner, athletic big man that plays with high energy
- Good cutter and roll man, runs hard in transition, active offensive rebounder that scores on put-backs, draws fouls at a fairly high rate
- Flashes some offensive skill, can bully smaller defenders and flash to the middle on post-ups, occasionally can step out to knock down a mid-range jumper
- Mainly a catch-and-finish player, occasionally can hit cutters, good at avoiding turnovers
- 2022-23 Defensive Degree of Difficulty: 0.404
- 2022-23 Points Prevented: 0.619
- Used as a roaming rim protector, good at defending shots around the basket, posts high shot blocking rates, solid defensive rebounder
- Still highly foul prone but his foul rate has dropped slightly
- Fairly good on-ball defender, good against bigger post players, can guard perimeter players in space
- Above average pick-and-roll defender, good at switching out onto ball handlers
- Has trouble guarding screeners in drop coverages, can be late to recognize pick-and-pops, tends to let screeners slip by him
- Usually comes out to the perimeter to close out in spot-up situations

AJ Griffin

	Height	Weight	Cap #	Years Left
	6'6"	222	$3.713M	2 TO

Similar at Age 19

		Season	SIMsc
1	Martell Webster	2005-06	916.5
2	J.R. Smith	2004-05	897.3
3	Moses Moody	2021-22	892.1
4	Jamal Murray	2016-17	891.2
5	Rashad Vaughn	2015-16	891.1
6	James Young	2014-15	884.1
7	Troy Brown	2018-19	878.0
8	Xavier Henry	2010-11	875.1
9	Patrick Williams	2020-21	872.0
10	Sekou Doumbouya	2019-20	870.7

Baseline Basic Stats

MPG	PTS	AST	REB	BLK	STL
21.9	9.5	1.4	2.7	0.2	0.6

Advanced Metrics

USG%	3PTA/FGA	FTA/FGA	TS%	eFG%	3PT%
19.4	0.458	0.158	0.581	0.561	0.405

AST%	TOV%	OREB%	DREB%	STL%	BLK%
9.8	9.2	2.6	11.6	1.5	0.6

PER	ORTG	DRTG	WS/48	BPM	VOL
13.19	113.4	116.6	0.073	-0.66	0.200

- Regular rotation player for Atlanta in his rookie season
- Solidly effective in his role as a lower volume spot-up shooter
- Posted a Three-Point Percentage of 39% last season, made almost 41% of his corner threes
- Mainly a stationary spot-up shooter at this stage, was less efficient when he was shooting off screens
- Mostly played off the ball, flashed some ability to leverage the threat of shot to drive to the rim
- Good cutter, can score on hand-offs, used as a catch-and-shoot player as a rookie, can functionally pass, rarely turns the ball over
- 2022-23 Defensive Degree of Difficulty: 0.367
- 2022-23 Points Prevented: -0.261
- Primarily defended second unit players or lower leverage starters
- Average on-ball defender, can functionally defend multiple positions, tends to commit unnecessary shooting fouls
- Struggled to effectively defend pick-and-rolls, indecisive when making rotations, tended to allow ball handlers to turn the corner
- Will fight through screens off the ball, tends to late on his close-outs in spot-up situations
- Generally a stay-at-home defender, occasionally gets steals, below average defensive rebounder

Jalen Johnson

	Height	Weight	Cap #	Years Left
	6'9"	220	$2.925M	Team Option

Similar at Age 21

		Season	SIMsc
1	Quincy Miller	2013-14	928.3
2	JaKarr Sampson	2014-15	919.8
3	Ivan Rabb	2018-19	919.4
4	Michael Porter Jr.	2019-20	916.4
5	Jumaine Jones	2000-01	915.0
6	Shawne Williams	2007-08	914.6
7	Deni Avdija	2021-22	914.0
8	Luka Šamanić	2020-21	913.5
9	Darrell Arthur	2009-10	911.2
10	Travis Outlaw	2005-06	909.4

Baseline Basic Stats

MPG	PTS	AST	REB	BLK	STL
20.6	8.3	1.2	4.2	0.5	0.6

Advanced Metrics

USG%	3PTA/FGA	FTA/FGA	TS%	eFG%	3PT%
17.6	0.251	0.223	0.554	0.531	0.295

AST%	TOV%	OREB%	DREB%	STL%	BLK%
9.3	12.5	4.7	19.4	1.5	1.7

PER	ORTG	DRTG	WS/48	BPM	VOL
12.96	108.4	112.0	0.077	-1.03	0.411

- Became a regular rotation player for Atlanta in his second NBA season
- Fairly effective in his role as a low usage energy wing and spot-up shooter
- Athletic wing that plays with high energy, made almost 72% of his shots from three feet and in
- Explosive finisher in transition, decent cutter, will go to offensive boards to score on put-backs
- Outside shot is still a work-in-progress, career Three-Point Percentage is below 30%
- Stroke is still inconsistent, has made less than 65% of his career free throws, stationary spot-up shooter if his shot is falling
- Lacks the ability to create his own shot, decent secondary playmaker that avoid turnovers
- 2022-23 Defensive Degree of Difficulty: 0.403
- 2022-23 Points Prevented: 0.589
- Mainly defends second unit players, occasionally will defend a higher leverage starter
- Played solid on-ball defense, effectively guarded multiple positions as a second unit player
- Average pick-and-roll defender, good at dropping back or switching onto screeners, has trouble preventing ball handlers from turning the corner
- Fights through screens off the ball, usually will be late to close out on spot-up shooters
- Active help defender, gets steals and blocks at a high rate, very good defensive rebounding wing

Patty Mills

	Height	Weight	Cap #	Years Left
	6'1"	180	$6.803M	UFA

Similar at Age 34

		Season	SIMsc
1	Bobby Jackson	2007-08	925.9
2	Nick Van Exel	2005-06	911.0
3	D.J. Augustin	2021-22	902.0
4	Leandro Barbosa	2016-17	900.9
5	Jason Williams	2009-10	898.0
6	Danny Ainge	1993-94	896.0
7	Joe Dumars*	1997-98	895.5
8	Mike Conley	2021-22	892.8
9	Raymond Felton	2018-19	891.9
10	Steve Kerr	1999-00	890.1

Baseline Basic Stats

MPG	PTS	AST	REB	BLK	STL
20.7	7.8	2.1	1.8	0.1	0.6

Advanced Metrics

USG%	3PTA/FGA	FTA/FGA	TS%	eFG%	3PT%
16.7	0.647	0.138	0.564	0.542	0.384

AST%	TOV%	OREB%	DREB%	STL%	BLK%
14.2	11.0	1.5	7.8	1.3	0.5

PER	ORTG	DRTG	WS/48	BPM	VOL
11.11	110.5	115.6	0.056	-1.64	0.473

- Played sparingly for Brooklyn in his second season with the team, fell out of the rotation
- Maintained his effective from the season before when he played, used as a low volume shooting specialist
- Good three-point shooter, has made almost 39% of his career threes
- Mainly a spot-up shooter due to his declining quickness, can run off screens and make shots off the dribble in a limited capacity
- Lacks the quickness to effectively attack the rim, pick-and-roll abilities have declined as a result
- Can functionally make plays for others, will make the right pass, good at limiting turnovers
- 2022-23 Defensive Degree of Difficulty: 0.323
- 2022-23 Points Prevented: -2.344
- Usually hidden in favorable matchups against second unit level players
- Rarely tested as an on-ball defender, can be targeted on switches due to his smallish size, taller players can routinely shoot over him
- Below average pick-and-roll defender, limited ability to switch, struggles to contain ball handlers
- Stays attached to off-ball shooters, fights through screens and closes out, lacks length to adequately contest shots
- Generally a stay-at-home defender at his age, occasionally gets steals, below average defensive rebounder

Wesley Matthews

	Height	Weight	Cap #	Years Left
	6'4"	220	$2.020M	UFA

Similar at Age 36

		Season	SIMsc
1	Dan Majerle	2001-02	894.1
2	Jose Calderon	2017-18	886.0
3	Trevor Ariza	2021-22	880.9
4	Mike Dunleavy Jr.	2016-17	879.9
5	Richard Jefferson	2016-17	874.1
6	Kyle Korver	2017-18	871.8
7	J.J. Redick	2020-21	869.5
8	Eddie Jones	2007-08	868.4
9	Shawn Marion	2014-15	866.1
10	James Jones	2016-17	864.5

Baseline Basic Stats

MPG	PTS	AST	REB	BLK	STL
17.6	4.8	1.1	2.2	0.2	0.5

Advanced Metrics

USG%	3PTA/FGA	FTA/FGA	TS%	eFG%	3PT%
11.7	0.698	0.147	0.520	0.494	0.322

AST%	TOV%	OREB%	DREB%	STL%	BLK%
6.8	9.4	3.5	10.6	1.3	1.0

PER	ORTG	DRTG	WS/48	BPM	VOL
7.79	108.9	112.4	0.064	-2.52	0.678

- Fringe rotation player for Milwaukee in 2022-23, missed some games due to a strained calf and hamstring
- Has been utilized by multiple teams over the past four seasons as an extremely low volume spot-up shooter
- Good three-point shooter in his career, was a below break-even three-point shooter last year
- Shooting efficiency has declined, almost strictly a stationary spot-up shooter, not really able to shoot in other situations
- Strictly a catch-and-shoot player, not used in ball handling situations at all, makes safe passes, rarely turns the ball over, good cutter off the ball
- 2022-23 Defensive Degree of Difficulty: 0.445
- 2022-23 Points Prevented: -0.020
- Generally defended second unit players, drew some tough assignments against top scorers off the bench
- Defensive stopper in years past, on-ball defense declined
- Solid against bigger players in the post, lacks quickness to stay with perimeter players in his advanced age
- Played below average pick-and-roll defense, had trouble getting around the screen to stay with ball handlers
- Usually stayed attached to shooters off the ball, occasionally got caught on screens, consistently closed out in spot-up situations
- Stay-at-home defender, rarely gets steals or blocks, below average defensive rebounder

Bruno Fernando

	Height	Weight	Cap #	Years Left
	6'9"	240	$2.582M	1 + TO

Similar at Age 24

		Season	SIMsc
1	Ronny Turiaf	2006-07	898.0
2	Tony Bradley	2021-22	891.9
3	Freddie Gillespie	2021-22	891.0
4	Samaki Walker	2000-01	890.7
5	Josh Powell	2006-07	886.5
6	Bison Dele	1993-94	885.0
7	Jerome Moiso	2002-03	884.3
8	Jordan Hill	2011-12	882.9
9	Marlon Maxey	1993-94	882.9
10	Gorgui Dieng	2013-14	882.1

Baseline Basic Stats

MPG	PTS	AST	REB	BLK	STL
18.2	6.5	1.1	5.2	1.0	0.5

Advanced Metrics

USG%	3PTA/FGA	FTA/FGA	TS%	eFG%	3PT%
16.6	0.037	0.430	0.589	0.546	0.107

AST%	TOV%	OREB%	DREB%	STL%	BLK%
9.7	16.3	11.5	22.8	1.0	5.0

PER	ORTG	DRTG	WS/48	BPM	VOL
16.53	115.2	110.3	0.116	-0.81	0.426

- Played sparingly for Houston before he was traded to Atlanta, mainly used in garbage time after the trade
- Mainly used as a low volume rim runner, usage spiked in Atlanta's final regular season game
- Effective finisher inside, has made over 68% of his shots from inside three feet in his career
- Good at rolling to the rim, active offensive rebounder, decent at cutting to the rim off the ball
- Limited offensive skills, not really a post-up threat, has not developed a reliable jump shot
- Has flashed some passing ability, Assist Percentage rose significantly, can be a bit turnover prone
- <u>2022-23 Defensive Degree of Difficulty</u>: 0.368
- <u>2022-23 Points Prevented</u>: -0.951
- Good shot blocker, solid defensive rebounder, below average rim protector, undisciplined with his positioning, highly foul prone
- Effective at guarding second unit level big men in the post, struggled to defend quicker players in space
- Below average pick-and-roll defender, indecisive when making rotations, had trouble defending ball handlers and screeners
- Tends to stay anchored in the paint, does not always come out to contest perimeter shots in spot-up situations

Garrison Mathews

Height	**Weight**	**Cap #**	**Years Left**
6'5"	215	$2.000M	Team Option

Similar at Age 26

		Season	SIMsc
1	Keith Bogans	2006-07	932.0
2	Richie Frahm	2003-04	924.0
3	Timothé Luwawu-Cabarrot	2021-22	918.5
4	Theo Pinson	2021-22	916.3
5	Iman Shumpert	2016-17	913.2
6	Allen Crabbe	2018-19	913.2
7	Danuel House	2019-20	912.7
8	Malcolm Hill	2021-22	906.5
9	Abdel Nader	2019-20	902.5
10	Mickael Pietrus	2008-09	899.1

Baseline Basic Stats

MPG	PTS	AST	REB	BLK	STL
18.4	5.9	1.0	2.5	0.2	0.5

Advanced Metrics

USG%	3PTA/FGA	FTA/FGA	TS%	eFG%	3PT%
14.3	0.777	0.250	0.554	0.512	0.344

AST%	TOV%	OREB%	DREB%	STL%	BLK%
6.6	8.6	2.1	12.0	1.5	0.8

PER	ORTG	DRTG	WS/48	BPM	VOL
9.60	113.0	115.6	0.068	-2.50	0.312

- Used as a fringe rotation for Houston, played very little after being traded to Atlanta
- Has been used as a low volume shooting specialist throughout his career, efficiency declined slightly in last season
- Around a league average three-point shooter, has made 39.5% of his career corner threes
- Primarily a stationary spot-up shooter, can make threes off hand-offs, inconsistent when shooting off screens
- Effective cutter off the ball, doesn't do this often because he's played in static offenses in his career
- Rarely handles the ball, unable to create his own shot, limited as a passer, rarely turns the ball over
- 2022-23 Defensive Degree of Difficulty: 0.283
- 2022-23 Points Prevented: 1.318
- Has been hidden in favorable matchups against lower leverage players throughout his career
- Rarely tested on the ball last season, middling on-ball defender at best, usually struggles to stay with quicker players on the perimeter
- Below average pick-and-roll defender, not really effective at taking away any specific action
- Plays with high effort, stays attached to shooters off the ball, will fight through screens and close out in spot-up situations
- Activity increased when playing help defense, got steals at a higher rate, fairly decent defensive rebounder

Newcomers

Kobe Bufkin

	Height	Weight	Cap #	Years Left
	6'4"	195	$4.094M	1 + 2 TO

Baseline Basic Stats

MPG	PTS	AST	REB	BLK	STL
19.9	8.5	2.2	2.4	0.2	0.7

Advanced Metrics

USG%	3PTA/FGA	FTA/FGA	TS%	eFG%	3PT%
19.9	0.367	0.208	0.515	0.483	0.338

AST%	TOV%	OREB%	DREB%	STL%	BLK%
17.4	12.8	2.5	10.4	1.8	1.0

PER	ORTG	DRTG	WS/48	BPM	VOL
12.42	100.1	106.0	0.051	-1.88	N/A

- Drafted by Atlanta with the 15th overall pick in 2023
- Performed inconsistently at this year's Las Vegas Summer League
- Struggled to score efficiently in his role as a ball dominant, high usage ball handler
- Posted a True Shooting Percentage below 45%, made only 33.3% of his field and less than 20% of his threes, will likely have to play a lower volume role in the NBA
- Better at attacking the rim, drew fouls at a decent rate at Summer League
- More effective as a spot-up shooter in college, made almost 37% of his spot-up threes last season
- Good cutter off the ball, showed fairly solid playmaking skills, tended to play wild and out of control, much more turnover prone at Summer League
- Has solid athleticism and length but lacks the versatility to guard bigger players due to his slight frame
- Fairly good on-ball defender against players that are his own size in college, shows good quickness to stop opposing guards from penetrating
- Good pick-and-roll defender, effective at fighting over screens to contain ball handlers
- Tends to gamble too much off the ball, can allow shooters to get free for open looks
- Very active help defender at Summer League, could block shots from the weak side, could occasionally get steals, fairly solid defensive rebounder

Mouhamed Gueye

	Height	Weight	Cap #	Years Left
	6'11"	210	$1.120M	2 + TO

Baseline Basic Stats

MPG	PTS	AST	REB	BLK	STL
14.2	5.3	0.7	3.1	0.5	0.4

Advanced Metrics

USG%	3PTA/FGA	FTA/FGA	TS%	eFG%	3PT%
17.9	0.135	0.257	0.483	0.451	0.271

AST%	TOV%	OREB%	DREB%	STL%	BLK%
7.7	12.7	9.2	14.4	1.5	2.2

PER	ORTG	DRTG	WS/48	BPM	VOL
12.43	99.7	103.4	0.055	-1.69	N/A

- Drafted by Charlotte with the 39th overall pick, traded to Boston, then traded again to Atlanta
- Had a strong showing at the Las Vegas Summer League
- Played effectively in his role as a low volume rim runner and stretch big
- High motor big man that has decent vertical athleticism, solid roll man and cutter, active on the offensive boards, runs hard in transition
- Frame is very slight, has some trouble finishing against stronger defenders
- Flashed some stretch potential, went 6-for-16 (37.5%) on threes at Summer League
- Lacks the advanced post moves to play on the block on a regular basis, not really a ball handling threat
- Shows some ability to pass, can hit cutters or find open shooters, a bit turnover prone at Summer League
- Long and mobile big man that blocks shots at a high rate
- Below average defensive rebounder for his size, can be undisciplined with his positioning
- Tends to bite on fakes, can be highly foul prone
- Solid post defender in college despite thin frame, could be vulnerable against bigger bodied centers in the NBA
- Has had trouble defending in space, does not really look to take any specific action away
- Solid pick-and-roll defender in drop coverages, rarely asked to switch onto ball handlers in college
- Tends to stay anchored to the paint, does not always come out to contest perimeter shots
- Could benefit from some additional seasoning in the G-League to begin his career

TORONTO RAPTORS

Last Season: 41 - 41, Missed the Playoffs

Offensive Rating: 115.5, 11th in the NBA   Defensive Rating: 114.0, 12th in the NBA

Primary Executive: Masai Ujiri, President/Vice Chairman

Head Coach: Darko Rajakovic

Key Roster Changes

Subtractions	Additions
Fred VanVleet, free agency	Gradey Dick, draft
Dalano Banton, free agency	Dennis Schröder, free agency
Will Barton, free agency	Jalen McDaniels, free agency
Joe Wieskamp, free agency	

Roster

Likely Starting Five
1. *Dennis Schröder*
2. *OG Anunoby*
3. *Scottie Barnes*
4. *Pascal Siakam*
5. Jakob Poeltl

Other Key Rotation Players
Gary Trent Jr.
Chris Boucher
Precious Achiuwa
Gradey Dick
Jalen McDaniels

* Italics denotes that a player is likely to be on the floor to close games

Remaining Roster

- Otto Porter Jr.
- Thaddeus Young
- Christian Koloko
- Malachi Flynn
- Ron Harper Jr., 23, 6'6", 245, Rutgers (Two-Way)
- Markquis Nowell, 24, 5'8", 160, Kansas State (Two-Way)
- Javon Freeman-Liberty, 24, 6'4", 180, DePaul (Two-Way)
- Kevin Obanor, 24, 6'8", 235, Texas Tech (Exhibit 10)
- Jeff Dowtin, 26, 6'3", 185, Rhode Island (Exhibit 10)
- Mouhamadou Gueye, 25, 6'9", 210, Pittsburgh (Exhibit 10)

SCHREMPF Base Rating: 44.0

Season Preview Survey

- *Are the Raptors contending or rebuilding? Where is this team headed?*

Toronto appears as if they are trying to win and go for a playoff spot, but it's unclear if that is the right path that their team should take. They don't really have enough talent to earn a guaranteed playoff berth, let alone compete for a championship. Also, their top players are nearing the end of their current contracts. This should have been a sign that they should go in a different direction and rebuild, but they chose to stay intact and make another playoff push. It's not certain as if this plan will pan out, so they could wind up as a lower seeded play-in team this coming season.

- *What are the areas of concern for this team heading into this season?*

The Raptors' main concern is that they simply don't have a clearly established strength on either side of the ball. They were above average on offense and defense last season, but they performed in a way that seems unsustainable because they couldn't consistently make shots or force misses. Of the two sides, offense is the biggest potential problem because they took a big hit when Fred VanVleet left to sign with Houston this offseason. They lost an All-Star level initiator for their offense and didn't really get another distributor to replace him. Their offense tended to stall and devolve into stagnant isolations with VanVleet on the roster. There's a strong possibility that things could get worse with him gone. The only hope for them is if Scottie Barnes can make the leap from being a solid supporting player to a high-end, primary weapon on offense. If he capitalizes on his potential, it could allow the Raptors to stay in the playoff hunt. Otherwise, they may need to start over and launch a rebuild immediately.

- *List some possible breakout players for this team.*

Toronto doesn't have a lot of young players on its roster because they largely kept their veteran-laden unit from last season together. They really are counting on Scottie Barnes to step his game up another level to become a star level player. He has the talent to make this sort of transition, but the Raptors will need to adjust their approach to play more to his strengths. They need to find some way to open up the floor to allow him to thrive as a slashing playmaker that gives the offense a threat to score at the rim or set up others. If the team adjusts their style to fit around Barnes, he could reach his ceiling to become an extremely impactful player that affects the game in numerous ways. Aside from Barnes, they could get rotational contributions from their lottery pick, Gradey Dick because he projects to be an outside shooting threat that can improve their spacing. Also, Christian Koloko could produce as another rim protecting option and a possible lob threat on the offensive end this season.

- *What should we expect from them this season?*

If their team stays as it is, the results are probably going to be pretty similar to what they were a season ago. There might be some slight differences because they might be less efficient on offense, but better on defense if they switch to a scheme that's more focused on positioning and less reliant on over-aggressive gambling. Essentially, they are likely to be a play-in team that might land a back-end playoff seed if things break right. On the other hand, if they get off to a slow start that forces them to rethink their current strategy, then they could possibly change course to sell off veterans like Pascal Siakam and OG Anunoby to launch a full-scale rebuilding effort around the trade deadline. Either way, it's pretty likely that they could miss the playoffs this season.

Veterans

Pascal Siakam

	Height	Weight	Cap #	Years Left
	6'9"	230	$37.893M	UFA

Similar at Age 28

		Season	SIMsc
1	Rudy Gay	2014-15	943.4
2	Al Harrington	2008-09	927.7
3	Rasheed Wallace	2002-03	925.1
4	Jamal Mashburn	2000-01	919.5
5	Clifford Robinson	1994-95	918.4
6	Tobias Harris	2020-21	916.5
7	Larry Bird*	1984-85	915.9
8	David Lee	2011-12	915.5
9	Antoine Walker	2004-05	914.5
10	Danny Granger	2011-12	914.5

Baseline Basic Stats

MPG	PTS	AST	REB	BLK	STL
33.6	18.7	3.0	6.6	0.6	0.9

Advanced Metrics

USG%	3PTA/FGA	FTA/FGA	TS%	eFG%	3PT%
25.0	0.238	0.303	0.553	0.509	0.341

AST%	TOV%	OREB%	DREB%	STL%	BLK%
18.8	10.7	5.1	17.9	1.4	1.4

PER	ORTG	DRTG	WS/48	BPM	VOL
18.37	112.6	109.9	0.130	2.49	0.332

- Made his second All-Star team in 2022-23
- Matched his production level from last season, thrived as Toronto's primary scoring option
- Great downhill driver, effective pick-and-roll ball handler and isolation player, draws fouls at a high rate, great at pushing the ball in transition
- Very good playmaker that can find open shooters and hit cutters, good at avoiding turnovers
- Good at posting up smaller players, solid rim runner that can score off rolls and cuts to the rim
- Below break-even three-point shooter, more efficient when shooting shorter mid-range shots
- 2022-23 Defensive Degree of Difficulty: 0.445
- 2022-23 Points Prevented: -1.092
- Good at challenging shots around the basket despite low shot blocking rates, does not really get steals either, solid defensive rebounder
- Guards starting level players, used more as an off-ball help defender
- Played solid on-ball defense, can defend in the post and on the perimeter
- Played below average pick-and-roll defense, not especially effective at taking away any specific action
- Tends to get caught on screens off the ball, consistently closes out on spot-up shooters

OG Anunoby

	Height	Weight	Cap #	Years Left
	6'7"	232	$18.643M	PO

Similar at Age 25

		Season	SIMsc
1	Jae Crowder	2015-16	945.0
2	Tracy Murray	1996-97	938.7
3	Jared Dudley	2010-11	928.5
4	Cedi Osman	2020-21	922.4
5	Dennis Scott	1993-94	920.1
6	Carlos Delfino	2007-08	919.6
7	Harold Pressley	1988-89	917.0
8	Lamond Murray	1998-99	915.3
9	Taurean Prince	2019-20	909.2
10	J.R. Smith	2010-11	908.4

Baseline Basic Stats

MPG	PTS	AST	REB	BLK	STL
27.7	11.9	2.0	4.4	0.4	1.0

Advanced Metrics

USG%	3PTA/FGA	FTA/FGA	TS%	eFG%	3PT%
19.9	0.423	0.225	0.560	0.526	0.371

AST%	TOV%	OREB%	DREB%	STL%	BLK%
10.6	11.2	4.1	13.0	2.1	1.5

PER	ORTG	DRTG	WS/48	BPM	VOL
14.55	111.0	110.1	0.093	0.40	0.316

- Made the All-Defensive 2nd Team in 2022-23
- Slightly raised his efficiency, mainly used as a complementary, lower usage spot-up shooter
- Reliable three-point shooter, has made over 46% of his corner threes in each of the last two seasons
- Almost exclusively a stationary spot-up shooter, needs to set his feet to knock down shots
- Athletic finisher in transition, good cutter off the ball, good at scoring on hand-offs
- Limited as a ball handler, struggles to create his own offense
- Mostly a catch-and-shoot player that makes safe passes, rarely turns the ball over
- 2022-23 Defensive Degree of Difficulty: 0.568, had the 11th most difficult set of matchups in the NBA
- 2022-23 Points Prevented: 0.732
- Primarily used as Toronto's defensive stopper
- Great on-ball defender that guards multiple positions on the floor
- Good pick-and-roll defender, effectively can switch to guard screeners or ball handlers, makes sound rotations
- Fights through screens off the ball, tends to late when closing out on spot-up shooters
- Very active help defender, posted very high steal and block rates, fairly solid defensive rebounder

Scottie Barnes

	Height	Weight	Cap #	Years Left
	6'9"	227	$8.009M	TO

Similar at Age 21

		Season	SIMsc
1	Aaron Gordon	2016-17	945.9
2	Wilson Chandler	2008-09	930.1
3	Omri Casspi	2009-10	928.1
4	Rudy Gay	2007-08	923.9
5	Joe Johnson	2002-03	918.2
6	Marvin Williams	2007-08	916.9
7	Rashard Lewis	2000-01	913.2
8	Donyell Marshall	1994-95	911.1
9	Jeff Green	2007-08	910.6
10	Danilo Gallinari	2009-10	909.9

Baseline Basic Stats

MPG	PTS	AST	REB	BLK	STL
32.7	15.2	2.3	5.8	0.6	1.0

Advanced Metrics

USG%	3PTA/FGA	FTA/FGA	TS%	eFG%	3PT%
19.9	0.166	0.261	0.537	0.499	0.313

AST%	TOV%	OREB%	DREB%	STL%	BLK%
15.3	11.8	6.2	14.3	1.6	1.5

PER	ORTG	DRTG	WS/48	BPM	VOL
15.17	112.0	110.9	0.107	0.99	0.218

- Regular starting forward for Toronto in his second NBA season
- Usage slightly increased, efficiency declined, mainly used as an energy player and secondary playmaker
- Good secondary playmaker, makes good reads in the short roll game, good at avoiding turnovers
- Better as a rim runner, good as the roll man on pick-and-rolls, fairly effective cutter, active offensive rebounder
- Below break-even three-point shooter, inconsistent stand-still spot-up shooter
- Defenders can back off him to limit his effectiveness as a pick-and-roll ball handler and isolation player, only around average in these situations
- <u>2022-23 Defensive Degree of Difficulty</u>: 0.495
- <u>2022-23 Points Prevented</u>: -0.283
- Drew tougher assignments in his second season, solid on-ball defender that guards multiple positions
- Good perimeter defender with great quickness, has trouble defending stronger power forwards in the post
- Fairly solid pick-and-roll defender, good at containing ball handlers, has lapses when he rotates onto screeners
- Tends to get caught on screens off the ball, sometimes is late when closing out on spot-up shooters
- Posted a decent Steal Percentage, effective as a weak side shot blocker, solid defensive rebounder

Jakob Poeltl

	Height	Weight	Cap #	Years Left
	7'1"	245	$19.500M	2 + PO

Similar at Age 27

		Season	SIMsc
1	Vlade Divac*	1995-96	922.9
2	Alton Lister	1985-86	916.5
3	Derrick Favors	2018-19	909.1
4	Timofey Mozgov	2013-14	906.0
5	Rasho Nesterovic	2003-04	905.5
6	Rudy Gobert	2019-20	899.5
7	Richaun Holmes	2020-21	897.6
8	Robin Lopez	2015-16	895.7
9	Benoit Benjamin	1991-92	895.0
10	Emeka Okafor	2009-10	893.0

Baseline Basic Stats

MPG	PTS	AST	REB	BLK	STL
27.0	10.4	2.0	8.1	1.5	0.7

Advanced Metrics

USG%	3PTA/FGA	FTA/FGA	TS%	eFG%	3PT%
17.1	0.011	0.298	0.595	0.582	0.278

AST%	TOV%	OREB%	DREB%	STL%	BLK%
13.3	14.8	12.2	23.2	1.3	3.8

PER	ORTG	DRTG	WS/48	BPM	VOL
18.71	118.2	109.4	0.139	0.87	0.198

- Traded from San Antonio to Toronto at the trade deadline, regular starting center for both teams
- Had his best NBA season in a role as a low volume rim runner
- Physical big man that plays with a high motor, made over 76% of his shots from three feet and in
- Great offensive rebounder, solid cutter and roll man, draws fouls at a solid rate
- Effective at flashing to the middle on post-ups, can hit short mid-range jumpers, shooting range is limited to 16 feet and in
- Has become a good passing man, can hit cutters and find open shooters, slightly turnover prone
- 2022-23 Defensive Degree of Difficulty: 0.477
- 2022-23 Points Prevented: -1.052
- Fairly solid rim protector, good shot blocker and defensive rebounder, quicker players can exploit his limited lateral mobility
- Guarded a lot of high-end big men, stout post defender, plays angles well to compensate for his slower foot speed
- Average pick-and-roll defender, usually in the right spot but tended to be late when making rotations
- Sometimes sagged too far into paint, not always able to close out to contest outside shots
- Effective at using his length to post a high Steal Percentage last season

Dennis Schröder

	Height	Weight	Cap #	Years Left
	6'3"	172	$12.405M	1

Similar at Age 29

		Season	SIMsc
1	Stephon Marbury	2006-07	933.9
2	B.J. Armstrong	1996-97	929.5
3	Danny Ainge	1988-89	926.2
4	Kenny Smith	1994-95	923.4
5	Tyronn Lue	2006-07	922.0
6	Sleepy Floyd	1989-90	921.9
7	Ramon Sessions	2015-16	921.1
8	Jeff Teague	2017-18	920.7
9	Johnny Davis	1984-85	919.3
10	Vernon Maxwell	1994-95	919.0

Baseline Basic Stats

MPG	PTS	AST	REB	BLK	STL
24.4	10.4	3.7	2.1	0.1	0.8

Advanced Metrics

USG%	3PTA/FGA	FTA/FGA	TS%	eFG%	3PT%
20.2	0.320	0.301	0.527	0.471	0.341

AST%	TOV%	OREB%	DREB%	STL%	BLK%
22.1	14.1	1.6	8.3	1.5	0.4

PER	ORTG	DRTG	WS/48	BPM	VOL
12.51	106.9	112.2	0.068	-1.79	0.373

- Became a starting guard for the L.A. Lakers in his second stint with the team
- Solidly effective in a different role as a low usage spot-up shooter and secondary ball handler
- Around a break-even career three-point shooter, percentages tend to vary from year-to-year
- Most effective as a stand-still spot-up shooter, inconsistent shooter off the dribble
- Average scorer in ball handling situations, can use change-of-pace moves to get to the rim and draw fouls
- Solid playmaker that can make simple reads, better at limiting turnovers as a complementary player
- 2022-23 Defensive Degree of Difficulty: 0.548
- 2022-23 Points Prevented: 1.206
- Drew a lot of difficult assignments last season, used as a stopper against elite scoring guards
- Solid on-ball defender, capable of defending bigger guards, can stay with quicker players, sometimes takes bad angles
- Decent pick-and-roll defender, can functionally switch and cut off penetration, can have lapses when making rotations
- Stays attached to shooters off the ball, fights through screens and closes out in spot-up situations
- Stay-at-home defender last season, did not really get steals or blocks, decent defensive rebounder

Gary Trent Jr.

	Height	Weight	Cap #	Years Left
	6'5"	209	$18.560M	UFA

Similar at Age 24

		Season	SIMsc
1	Marcus Thornton	2011-12	939.1
2	Victor Oladipo	2016-17	936.0
3	Kentavious Caldwell-Pope	2017-18	934.4
4	Courtney Lee	2009-10	930.6
5	Tim Hardaway Jr.	2016-17	929.7
6	Anthony Morrow	2009-10	927.7
7	Wesley Matthews	2010-11	923.5
8	Gary Harris	2018-19	920.6
9	Jodie Meeks	2011-12	918.0
10	Marco Belinelli	2010-11	917.6

Baseline Basic Stats

MPG	PTS	AST	REB	BLK	STL
28.8	13.0	2.1	3.1	0.2	1.0

Advanced Metrics

USG%	3PTA/FGA	FTA/FGA	TS%	eFG%	3PT%
20.9	0.482	0.218	0.555	0.515	0.377

AST%	TOV%	OREB%	DREB%	STL%	BLK%
10.4	7.4	1.7	9.0	2.0	0.7

PER	ORTG	DRTG	WS/48	BPM	VOL
14.57	113.2	112.5	0.107	0.04	0.256

- Regular starter for Toronto in his second full season with the team
- Had his most productive NBA season, primarily used as a moderate volume shooting specialist
- Reliable three-point shooter, has made almost 39% of his threes since the 2019-20 season
- Excellent spot-up shooter, better at shooting off screens in previous seasons
- Good at scoring on hand-offs, effective cutter off the ball
- Ball handling skills are limited, not really effective as a pick-and-roll ball handler or isolation player
- Strictly a catch-and-shoot player, only makes safe passes, led the NBA in Turnover Percentage last season
- 2022-23 Defensive Degree of Difficulty: 0.421
- 2022-23 Points Prevented: -0.424
- Generally defended starting level players, around an average on-ball defender
- Solid when defending bigger wings, struggled to stay in front of quicker guards
- Average pick-and-roll defender, effective at switching onto screeners, had trouble containing ball handlers
- Fights through screens off the ball, tends to be late when closing out on spot-up shooters
- Actively plays passing lanes, gets steals at a high rate, below average defensive rebounder

Chris Boucher

	Height	Weight	Cap #	Years Left
	6'9"	200	$11.750M	1

Similar at Age 30

		Season	SIMsc
1	Dean Garrett	1996-97	883.9
2	Larry Nance	1989-90	883.7
3	Brandan Wright	2017-18	880.5
4	Rod Higgins	1989-90	877.0
5	Donyell Marshall	2003-04	876.7
6	Antonio McDyess	2004-05	874.4
7	Gerald Green	2015-16	871.5
8	Aaron Williams	2001-02	870.8
9	Antonio Davis	1998-99	870.6
10	Ersan Ilyasova	2017-18	868.6

Baseline Basic Stats

MPG	PTS	AST	REB	BLK	STL
25.1	10.2	1.3	6.3	1.1	0.6

Advanced Metrics

USG%	3PTA/FGA	FTA/FGA	TS%	eFG%	3PT%
17.5	0.271	0.306	0.563	0.522	0.326

AST%	TOV%	OREB%	DREB%	STL%	BLK%
5.6	8.9	9.5	20.6	1.3	3.7

PER	ORTG	DRTG	WS/48	BPM	VOL
16.46	117.8	108.5	0.132	-0.14	0.387

- Regular rotation player for Toronto in his fifth season with the team
- Solidly effective in his role as a low usage stretch big and rim runner
- Break-even career three-point shooter, has shot an above break-even percentage in only one NBA season
- Better as a stand-still spot-up shooter, less efficient as a pick-and-pop screener
- More effective as a rim runner, good offensive rebounder, effective cutter and roll man
- Has some trouble finishing in traffic due to his thin frame, draws fouls at a solid rate
- Not a post-up threat, very limited as a passer, rarely turns the ball over
- 2022-23 Defensive Degree of Difficulty: 0.307
- 2022-23 Points Prevented: 0.015
- Good shot blocker and defensive rebounder, average rim protector, does not really provide strong resistance at the rim
- Usually guarded second unit big men, played solid on-ball defense
- Strong post defender despite thin build, mobile enough to defend in space, tended to back off his man too much
- Average pick-and-roll defender, good in drop coverages, had trouble containing ball handlers on switches
- Consistently closes out in spot-up situations, occasionally uses his length to get steals

Precious Achiuwa

	Height	Weight	Cap #	Years Left
	6'8"	225	$4.380M	RFA

Similar at Age 23

		Season	SIMsc
1	Chimezie Metu	2020-21	927.0
2	Donyell Marshall	1996-97	924.6
3	David Benoit	1991-92	923.1
4	Isaiah Roby	2021-22	921.0
5	Obi Toppin	2021-22	917.2
6	Kenneth Faried	2012-13	913.5
7	Jordan Mickey	2017-18	913.4
8	Kurt Thomas	1995-96	913.1
9	Brandon Clarke	2019-20	912.3
10	Ed Davis	2012-13	911.5

Baseline Basic Stats

MPG	PTS	AST	REB	BLK	STL
24.5	10.6	1.2	5.7	0.6	0.7

Advanced Metrics

USG%	3PTA/FGA	FTA/FGA	TS%	eFG%	3PT%
19.5	0.257	0.284	0.552	0.522	0.325

AST%	TOV%	OREB%	DREB%	STL%	BLK%
7.1	10.7	8.0	20.7	1.3	2.0

PER	ORTG	DRTG	WS/48	BPM	VOL
15.26	111.3	110.4	0.105	-1.34	0.412

- Missed games due to a torn ligament in his ankle, regular rotation player for Toronto when healthy
- Increased his effectiveness in a role as a low usage stretch big and rim runner
- Below break-even three-point shooter, struggled to shoot efficiently in all jump shooting situations
- More effective as a rim runner, drew more fouls, made over 73% of his shots inside of three feet last season
- Fairly solid roll man and cutter, active offensive rebounder that scores on put-backs, still prone to rushing shots inside
- Limited as a post player or ball handler, not really a passer, catch-and-finish player that avoids turnovers
- 2022-23 Defensive Degree of Difficulty: 0.424
- 2022-23 Points Prevented: -2.318
- Good rim protector despite being undersized, solid shot blocker, good defensive rebounder
- Drew some tough assignments against starting level players, solid on-ball defender
- Effective post defender that holds position against bigger players, good mobility allows him to defend in space
- Good pick-and-roll defender, effective in drop coverages, solid at switching onto ball handlers
- Fights through screens off the ball, tends to sag back into the paint, does not always come out to contest outside shots in spot-up situations

Jalen McDaniels

	Height	Weight	Cap #	Years Left
	6'9"	205	$4.516M	1

Similar at Age 25

		Season	SIMsc
1	Otto Porter	2018-19	938.7
2	DerMarr Johnson	2005-06	930.4
3	Al-Farouq Aminu	2015-16	930.2
4	Devean George	2002-03	928.4
5	Francisco Garcia	2006-07	924.2
6	Maurice Harkless	2018-19	921.2
7	Derrick McKey	1991-92	920.1
8	Rodney Carney	2009-10	919.8
9	Jake Layman	2019-20	919.2
10	Omri Casspi	2013-14	915.4

Baseline Basic Stats

MPG	PTS	AST	REB	BLK	STL
25.3	9.9	1.5	4.3	0.5	0.9

Advanced Metrics

USG%	3PTA/FGA	FTA/FGA	TS%	eFG%	3PT%
17.2	0.412	0.243	0.560	0.526	0.345

AST%	TOV%	OREB%	DREB%	STL%	BLK%
9.4	11.5	4.1	15.1	1.7	1.6

PER	ORTG	DRTG	WS/48	BPM	VOL
12.63	109.9	111.8	0.079	-1.14	0.471

- Traded from Charlotte to Philadelphia at the trade deadline, regular rotation player for both team that played almost starter level minutes
- Primarily used as a low usage spot-up shooter and energy wing for both teams
- Above break-even three-point shooter, percentages tend to vary quite a bit
- Strictly a stationary spot-up shooter, does not really shoot on the move or off the dribble
- Explosive finisher in transition, effective cutter and roll man, has some trouble finishing in traffic
- Limited as a ball handler, catch-and-shoot player that makes safe passes, good at avoiding turnovers
- 2022-23 Defensive Degree of Difficulty: 0.450
- 2022-23 Points Prevented: -0.015
- Drew tougher assignments against elite scorers, fairly solid on-ball defender, more effective with Charlotte
- Solid against bigger interior players despite his thin frame, generally stayed with perimeter players, slight tendency to commit shooting fouls in Philadelphia
- Average pick-and-roll defender, good at switching in Charlotte, struggled to make sound rotations in Philadelphia
- Tended to get caught on screens off the ball, not always in position to contest shots in spot-up situations
- Active help defender, gets steals and blocks at a fairly high rate, fairly good defensive rebounder

Otto Porter Jr.

Height	**Weight**	**Cap #**	**Years Left**	
6'8"	198	$6.300M	UFA	

Similar at Age 29

	Player	Season	SIMsc
1	Dorell Wright	2014-15	899.1
2	Jamario Moon	2009-10	897.2
3	DeMarre Carroll	2015-16	895.4
4	Mickael Gelabale	2012-13	893.9
5	Rodney Hood	2021-22	885.8
6	Trevor Ariza	2014-15	885.3
7	Bobby Simmons	2009-10	882.5
8	Randolph Keys	1995-96	879.3
9	Keith Askins	1996-97	877.2
10	Chandler Parsons	2017-18	870.1

Baseline Basic Stats

MPG	PTS	AST	REB	BLK	STL
25.8	8.7	1.6	4.2	0.3	1.1

Advanced Metrics

USG%	3PTA/FGA	FTA/FGA	TS%	eFG%	3PT%
13.8	0.557	0.208	0.572	0.535	0.347

AST%	TOV%	OREB%	DREB%	STL%	BLK%
8.8	9.7	4.1	15.1	2.5	0.8

PER	ORTG	DRTG	WS/48	BPM	VOL
12.87	116.9	108.3	0.119	0.61	0.656

- Only played 8 games last season, out due to injuries to his hamstring and toe
- Effective in very limited action as a low volume spot-up shooter
- Reliable three-point shooter throughout his career, has made almost 40% of his career threes
- Solid spot-up shooter, effective at shooting on the move in previous seasons
- More effective in motion-oriented offenses, good at cutting and diving to the rim, can go to the offensive boards
- Has been slowed by past injuries, not really able to create his own offense now
- Mainly a catch-and-shoot player, still a good passer, rarely turns the ball over
- 2022-23 Defensive Degree of Difficulty: 0.379
- 2022-23 Points Prevented: 1.208
- Guarded second unit players or was hidden in lower leverage assignments in limited minutes
- Generally an average on-ball defender when healthy, can passably guard multiple positions, struggles in more difficult matchups
- Average pick-and-roll defender, usually is in good position, can be a step slow when making rotations
- Stays attached to shooters off the ball, fights through screens and closes out in spot-up situations
- Still an active help defender, gets steals at a fairly high rate, fairly good defensive rebounder

Thaddeus Young

	Height	Weight	Cap #	Years Left
	6'8"	235	$8.000M	UFA

Similar at Age 34

		Season	SIMsc
1	George Lynch	2004-05	888.5
2	Tom Gugliotta	2003-04	888.0
3	Udonis Haslem	2014-15	886.0
4	Christian Laettner	2003-04	879.7
5	Grant Long	2000-01	874.6
6	Jerome Kersey	1996-97	873.9
7	James Johnson	2021-22	873.4
8	Rick Fox	2003-04	873.2
9	Dave Cowens*	1982-83	872.7
10	Corie Blount	2002-03	870.9

Baseline Basic Stats

MPG	PTS	AST	REB	BLK	STL
18.0	5.1	1.3	3.3	0.3	0.7

Advanced Metrics

USG%	3PTA/FGA	FTA/FGA	TS%	eFG%	3PT%
14.9	0.189	0.164	0.529	0.514	0.233

AST%	TOV%	OREB%	DREB%	STL%	BLK%
12.6	15.7	7.6	14.8	2.4	1.3

PER	ORTG	DRTG	WS/48	BPM	VOL
12.40	106.7	108.8	0.079	-1.14	0.636

- Fringe rotation player for Toronto in his first full season with the team
- Production level is declining, mainly used as a low usage short roll playmaker
- Solid secondary playmaker, can find open teammates in the short roll game, slightly turnover prone
- Does most of his damage around the rim, most effective as a cutter and offensive rebounder
- Below break-even career three-point shooter, percentages vary considerably, not effective as a jump shooter last season
- Rated by Synergy as average or worse in almost every offensive situation last season
- 2022-23 Defensive Degree of Difficulty: 0.385
- 2022-23 Points Prevented: -3.698
- Usually guarded second unit players, used mostly as a roaming help defender
- Played decent on-ball defender, effective against bigger interior players, a step slow when guarding wings
- Average pick-and-roll defense, good in drop coverages, struggled to effectively contain ball handlers
- Fights through screens off the ball, tends to sag back into the paint, usually late when closing out on spot-up shooters
- Posts very high steal rates, Block Percentage dropped significantly, fairly solid defensive rebounder

Christian Koloko

	Height	Weight	Cap #	Years Left
	7'1"	230	$1.720M	1

Similar at Age 22

		Season	SIMsc
1	Jim McIlvaine	1994-95	910.0
2	Travis Knight	1996-97	896.6
3	JaVale McGee	2009-10	891.1
4	Steven Hunter	2003-04	888.9
5	Larry Sanders	2010-11	887.3
6	Sean Williams	2008-09	887.1
7	Duane Causwell	1990-91	885.9
8	John Salley	1986-87	885.3
9	Michael Stewart	1997-98	877.9
10	Elden Campbell	1990-91	877.3

Baseline Basic Stats

MPG	PTS	AST	REB	BLK	STL
18.9	5.7	0.6	4.6	1.6	0.5

Advanced Metrics

USG%	3PTA/FGA	FTA/FGA	TS%	eFG%	3PT%
12.1	0.048	0.409	0.547	0.514	0.150

AST%	TOV%	OREB%	DREB%	STL%	BLK%
5.3	12.2	10.0	15.7	1.3	6.1

PER	ORTG	DRTG	WS/48	BPM	VOL
13.42	116.0	107.8	0.122	-1.37	0.407

- Fringe rotation player for Toronto in his rookie season
- Decently effective in his role as a very low volume rim runner
- Athletic big man with great length, vertical lob threat, struggles to finish in traffic due to his thin frame
- Good offensive rebounder, better as a roll man, great at running the floor in transition, prone to missing some easy shots at the rim
- Rarely used as a post player, lacks reliable shooting range outside of three feet, limited passing skills, good at avoiding turnovers
- 2022-23 Defensive Degree of Difficulty: 0.368
- 2022-23 Points Prevented: -0.692
- Good rim protector, excellent shot blocker, sacrifices position to go for blocks, below average defensive rebounder
- Usually guards second unit big men, stout post defender, has trouble defending in space, highly foul prone
- Below average pick-and-roll defender, not effective at taking away any specific action
- Consistently comes out to contest outside shots in spot-up situations

Malachi Flynn

	Height	Weight	Cap #	Years Left
	6'1"	175	$3.873M	RFA

Similar at Age 24

		Season	SIMsc
1	Shabazz Napier	2015-16	926.7
2	Kyle Guy	2021-22	919.3
3	Charles R. Jones	1999-00	916.8
4	Travis Diener	2006-07	916.0
5	Yogi Ferrell	2017-18	914.4
6	Steve Blake	2004-05	914.3
7	Lionel Chalmers	2004-05	912.9
8	Brandon Goodwin	2019-20	912.4
9	Quincy Douby	2008-09	912.2
10	Aaron Holiday	2020-21	911.1

Baseline Basic Stats

MPG	PTS	AST	REB	BLK	STL
19.4	7.7	2.7	1.9	0.1	0.6

Advanced Metrics

USG%	3PTA/FGA	FTA/FGA	TS%	eFG%	3PT%
18.6	0.509	0.157	0.519	0.492	0.364

AST%	TOV%	OREB%	DREB%	STL%	BLK%
21.0	10.2	1.9	10.3	1.7	0.5

PER	ORTG	DRTG	WS/48	BPM	VOL
12.56	110.3	113.8	0.069	-1.12	0.377

- Fringe rotation player for Toronto in his third NBA season
- Productivity decreased significantly, mainly used as a low volume spot-up shooter
- Career True Shooting Percentage is below 50%, struggled in ball handling situations, defenders could back off him to limit his effectiveness
- Made threes at an above break-even rate last season, around break-even for his career
- Less effective as a spot-up shooter, efficiently made pull-up threes as a pick-and-roll ball handler
- Fairly solid secondary playmaker that can make simple reads, rarely turns the ball over
- 2022-23 Defensive Degree of Difficulty: 0.322
- 2022-23 Points Prevented: -1.277
- Typically defends lower leverage second unit players, middling on-ball defender
- Struggles to stay with quicker guards, more effective when guarding taller players
- Average pick-and-roll defender, limited ability to switch, funnels his man into help, has some trouble stopping his man from turning the corner
- Stays attached to shooters off the ball, fights through screens and closes out in spot-up situations
- Steal Percentage has been steadily declining, fairly solid defensive rebounder

Newcomers

Gradey Dick

	Height	Weight	Cap #	Years Left
	6'8"	205	$4.537M	1 + 2 TO

Baseline Basic Stats

MPG	PTS	AST	REB	BLK	STL
19.0	7.5	1.1	2.6	0.2	0.6

Advanced Metrics

USG%	3PTA/FGA	FTA/FGA	TS%	eFG%	3PT%
16.9	0.452	0.213	0.541	0.509	0.360

AST%	TOV%	OREB%	DREB%	STL%	BLK%
9.0	10.4	3.4	11.8	1.7	0.9

PER	ORTG	DRTG	WS/48	BPM	VOL
11.87	104.7	104.9	0.069	-1.28	N/A

- Drafted by Toronto with the 13th overall pick in 2023
- Had a fairly solid performance at the Las Vegas Summer League
- Over-extended a bit in a role as a high usage scoring wing
- Posted a 50% True Shooting Percentage, made less than 30% of his threes
- Made over 40% of his threes in college, most effective when his body was square to the rim, less effective when shooting off screens
- Not likely to be a shot creator, lacks the ball handling skills to be effective as an isolation player or pick-and-roll ball handler
- Good cutter off the ball, good athlete that can finish above the rim in transition
- Fairly good secondary playmaker at Summer League, effective at making simple reads, good at avoiding turnovers
- Hidden in favorable defensive matchups in college, good athlete, did not appear to be a liability at Summer League
- Rarely tested as an on-ball defender, can passably guard multiple positions
- Struggled to play effective pick-and-roll defense, indecisive, struggles to cut off penetration, also goes too far under screens
- Fights through screens off the ball, tends to be late when closing out on spot-up shooters
- More active as a help defender at Summer League, showed solid anticipation skills, got steals at a good rate, fairly solid defensive rebounder

BROOKLYN NETS

Last Season: 45 - 37, Lost 1st Round to Philadelphia (0 – 4)

Offensive Rating: 115.0, 17th in the NBA   Defensive Rating: 114.1, 13th in the NBA

Primary Executive: Sean Marks, General Manager

Head Coach: Jacque Vaughn

Key Roster Changes

Subtractions
Joe Harris, trade
Patty Mills, trade
Seth Curry, free agency
Yuta Watanabe, free agency
Edmond Sumner, waived

Additions
Dariq Whitehead, draft
Noah Clowney, draft
Lonnie Walker IV, free agency
Darius Bazley, free agency
Dennis Smith Jr., free agency
Trendon Watford, free agency

Roster

Likely Starting Five
1. *Spencer Dinwiddie*
2. *Mikal Bridges*
3. *Cameron Johnson*
4. *Dorian Finney-Smith*
5. *Nic Claxton*

Other Key Rotation Players
Royce O'Neale
Ben Simmons
Lonnie Walker IV
Cam Thomas
Dennis Smith Jr.

* Italics denotes that a player is likely to be on the floor to close games

Remaining Roster

- Darius Bazley
- Day'Ron Sharpe
- Trendon Watford
- Noah Clowney
- Dariq Whitehead
- Jalen Wilson, 22, 6'8", 225, Kansas (Two-Way)
- Armoni Brooks, 25, 6'3", 195, Houston (Two-Way)
- Patrick Gardner, 24, 6'11", 250, Marist (Exhibit 10)

SCHREMPF Base Rating: 43.8

Season Preview Survey

- *Are the Nets contending or rebuilding? Where is this team headed?*

The Nets are trying to win, and they have enough talent to compete for a playoff spot, but they simply don't have the necessary firepower to keep pace with the top contenders. They do have a trove of future first round picks and tradeable contracts to make a deal for an established star, but there really isn't a major impact player that is available for them to pull a trigger on a big trade. In the meantime, Brooklyn has to bide their time to find the right deal to level up their team. They will work with what they have to field a team that will really battle and grind it out on a possession-by-possession basis to push for the playoffs in the East.

- *What are the areas of concern for this team heading into this season?*

The biggest concern with the Nets is that they don't have an established, go-to scorer on their roster. On the plus side, Mikal Bridges showed that he can maintain his efficiency with a higher offensive workload. However, Brooklyn just doesn't have enough quality scorers around him to threaten defenses and allow others to get easier looks, so it will be a challenge for them to score on a consistent basis. They will really need to lean on their defense to stay competitive and carry them through the season. This means that they will have to play at a very high intensity level for the whole season to maximize their performance, which raises some questions about if they can keep the switch on high for all 82 games. They could be in for a drop if they have to deal with some injuries or they start to wear down late in the season.

- *List some possible breakout players for this team.*

Most of their roster is comprised of already established veterans, so there aren't too many breakout candidates on their team. The player that is best positioned to raise his game up another level is Cam Thomas. The Nets are devoid of scoring talent, so Thomas could fill this big void if he puts everything together. He's had some stretches where he's had big scoring outbursts and flashed his talent. However, he hasn't been consistent enough to do this for an entire season. There is a reasonable pathway for him to get an increased opportunity to play, so all he needs to do is improve his efficiency. If he makes this improvement, he could give the Nets some badly needed scoring punch as either a lead guard or a sixth man type off the bench. In addition to him, the Nets don't really have an established backup center on their roster. This could allow either Day'Ron Sharpe or Noah Clowney to emerge and the fill the slot behind Nic Claxton. Finally, Dariq Whitehead has great athleticism and the upside to be an impactful wing in the future, but the team already has a lot of veterans ahead of him. He's blocked for playing time, but if he gets healthy and he taps into the potential that he showed in high school, he could make a push for some minutes.

- *What should we expect from them this season?*

The Nets are interesting because they have an ideal support system to surround a superstar, except that they don't have one right now. It will be an uphill climb for them, and it will not be easy for them to win games this season. Even so, they do have enough talent and reliable veteran character to lean on a solid defense to keep them in games. Their defense should pose some problems for opponents because their main lineup is filled with quality on-ball defenders that can switch across multiple positions. This ability to defend should allow them to beat lesser opponents and post a high enough win total to get into the play-in tournament. From there, they should at least be a tough out, which would make them a probable bet to end up with a back-end playoff seed this season.

Veterans

Mikal Bridges

	Height	Weight	Cap #	Years Left
	6'6"	209	$21.700M	2

Similar at Age 26

		Season	SIMsc
1	Chris Mills	1995-96	940.8
2	Gordan Giricek	2003-04	930.4
3	Dan Majerle	1991-92	929.8
4	Matt Carroll	2006-07	925.5
5	Shandon Anderson	1999-00	925.5
6	Nick Anderson	1993-94	922.7
7	Eddie Jones	1997-98	921.3
8	Klay Thompson	2016-17	921.2
9	Kevin Gamble	1991-92	920.2
10	Arron Afflalo	2011-12	919.3

Baseline Basic Stats

MPG	PTS	AST	REB	BLK	STL
32.0	14.3	2.5	3.9	0.4	1.0

Advanced Metrics

USG%	3PTA/FGA	FTA/FGA	TS%	eFG%	3PT%
19.6	0.388	0.231	0.579	0.540	0.381

AST%	TOV%	OREB%	DREB%	STL%	BLK%
12.5	8.9	2.9	11.0	1.6	1.3

PER	ORTG	DRTG	WS/48	BPM	VOL
15.24	116.0	111.0	0.120	1.30	0.352

- Played in 83 games between Phoenix and Brooklyn, led the NBA in Minutes Played in 2021-22 and 2022-23
- Used as a low volume spot-up shooter in Phoenix, became Brooklyn's primary scoring option after the trade
- Reliable three-point shooter, best used in catch-and-shoot situations, good spot-up shooter, flashes ability to shoot off screens
- Effective pick-and-roll ball handler and isolation player, can make pull-up mid-range jumpers, more willing to attack the rim and draw fouls
- Solid cutter off the ball, improved to become a solid secondary playmaker, rarely turns the ball over
- 2022-23 Defensive Degree of Difficulty: 0.575, had the 9th toughest set of matchups in the NBA
- 2022-23 Points Prevented: 0.865
- Good on-ball defender, routinely draws tough assignments against top scorers, defends multiple positions
- Solid pick-and-roll defender, can switch to guard screeners and ball handlers, tends to go too far under screens
- Tended to get caught on screens, not always on time when closing out on spot-up shooters
- Fairly active help defender, gets steals at a solid rate, can block shots on the weak side, decent defensive rebounder

Cameron Johnson

	Height	Weight	Cap #	Years Left
	6'8"	210	$25.679M	3

Similar at Age 26

		Season	SIMsc
1	Dorell Wright	2011-12	928.5
2	Kyle Korver	2007-08	927.3
3	Wilson Chandler	2013-14	922.2
4	Rodney Hood	2018-19	921.5
5	Dennis Scott	1994-95	919.8
6	Martell Webster	2012-13	919.6
7	Chase Budinger	2014-15	919.0
8	Kelly Oubre Jr.	2021-22	915.2
9	Danny Green	2013-14	914.1
10	Reggie Bullock	2017-18	913.2

Baseline Basic Stats

MPG	PTS	AST	REB	BLK	STL
25.1	10.7	1.5	3.4	0.3	0.8

Advanced Metrics

USG%	3PTA/FGA	FTA/FGA	TS%	eFG%	3PT%
18.7	0.539	0.222	0.587	0.553	0.399

AST%	TOV%	OREB%	DREB%	STL%	BLK%
9.0	8.2	2.8	13.2	1.6	0.9

PER	ORTG	DRTG	WS/48	BPM	VOL
14.41	115.8	111.1	0.115	1.08	0.332

- Missed games due to a knee injury, regular starter for Phoenix and Brooklyn when healthy
- Had the most efficient season of his career, used as a moderate usage spot-up shooter for both teams
- Reliable three-point shooter, has made over 39% of his threes over his four seasons in the NBA
- Primarily a stationary spot-up shooter, occasionally can shoot off screens, has made 43.5% of his career corner threes
- Handled the ball more in Brooklyn, needs a screen to get to the rim, not really effective on isolation plays
- Good cutter, can score on hand-offs, catch-and-shoot player, limited passing skills, rarely turns the ball over
- 2022-23 Defensive Degree of Difficulty: 0.453
- 2022-23 Points Prevented: 0.573
- Generally guarded starting level players, played around average on-ball defense, can adequately guard multiple positions
- Struggled to stay with quicker players in Brooklyn, was overpowered by bigger post players in Phoenix
- Solid pick-and-roll defender, can effectively switch, tended to go too far under screens
- Usually stayed attached to shooters off the ball, good at fighting through screens, sometimes was late to close out on spot-up shooters
- Increased activity as a help defender, posted a career best Steal Percentage, solid defensive rebounder

Nic Claxton

	Height	Weight	Cap #	Years Left
	6'11"	215	$9.625M	UFA

Similar at Age 23

		Season	SIMsc
1	Elden Campbell	1991-92	928.1
2	John Henson	2013-14	914.3
3	Daniel Gafford	2021-22	910.6
4	Ed Davis	2012-13	902.6
5	Dale Davis	1992-93	896.8
6	JaVale McGee	2010-11	896.1
7	Kurt Nimphius	1981-82	887.5
8	Keon Clark	1998-99	886.1
9	Jarrett Allen	2021-22	885.7
10	Clint Capela	2017-18	884.2

Baseline Basic Stats

MPG	PTS	AST	REB	BLK	STL
24.5	9.3	1.0	7.0	1.5	0.7

Advanced Metrics

USG%	3PTA/FGA	FTA/FGA	TS%	eFG%	3PT%
16.0	0.009	0.393	0.637	0.630	0.130

AST%	TOV%	OREB%	DREB%	STL%	BLK%
7.6	11.7	10.3	22.3	1.4	5.2

PER	ORTG	DRTG	WS/48	BPM	VOL
19.30	125.7	105.7	0.184	1.40	0.245

- Became Brooklyn's regular starting center in his fourth NBA season
- Had a career best season in a role as a low volume rim runner
- Led the NBA in Effective Field Goal Percentage in 2022-23, excellent vertical spacing threat
- Athletic big man that plays with high energy, great roll man and cutter, runs hard in transition, active offensive rebounder
- Draws fouls but has made less than 55% of his free throws, improving passer that avoids turnovers
- Flashes some ability to make short mid-range jumpers, went 19-for-29 (65.5%) on spot-up twos last season
- 2022-23 Defensive Degree of Difficulty: 0.482
- 2022-23 Points Prevented: 2.469
- Excellent rim protector, improved his discipline, great shot blocker and defensive rebounder, cut his foul rate
- Good at defending quicker players in space on isolation plays, can be pushed around by stronger post players
- Good pick-and-roll defender, great in drop coverages, very effective at hedging or switching out on ball handlers
- Consistently comes out to contest perimeter shots in spot-up situations
- Steal Percentage increased a bit last season, can occasionally use his length to get deflections

Spencer Dinwiddie

	Height	Weight	Cap #	Years Left
	6'5"	215	$20.357M	UFA

Similar at Age 29

		Season	SIMsc
1	Gerald Henderson	2016-17	925.6
2	Arron Afflalo	2014-15	925.2
3	Bobby Phills	1998-99	922.8
4	Malcolm Brogdon	2021-22	919.9
5	Alec Burks	2020-21	919.8
6	Mitch Richmond*	1994-95	918.5
7	Aaron McKie	2001-02	914.0
8	Buddy Hield	2021-22	911.5
9	Bogdan Bogdanović	2021-22	911.0
10	John Salmons	2008-09	910.5

Baseline Basic Stats

MPG	PTS	AST	REB	BLK	STL
29.3	13.4	3.1	3.4	0.2	0.9

Advanced Metrics

USG%	3PTA/FGA	FTA/FGA	TS%	eFG%	3PT%
20.6	0.422	0.288	0.550	0.500	0.367

AST%	TOV%	OREB%	DREB%	STL%	BLK%
20.6	11.5	1.9	11.1	1.4	0.7

PER	ORTG	DRTG	WS/48	BPM	VOL
14.25	111.7	113.1	0.098	0.36	0.389

- Regular starter for Dallas and Brooklyn, solidly effective overall with both teams
- Used as a secondary ball handler in Dallas, became Brooklyn's primary distributor
- Good playmaker that can set up his teammates, controls the ball well and avoids turnovers
- Solid pick-and-roll ball handler and isolation player, inconsistent when shooting off the dribble
- Break-even career three-point shooter, shot more efficiently in Dallas with more open looks
- Most effective as a stand-still spot-up shooter, not quite as effective when shooting on the move
- Can post up smaller guards, effective cutter off the ball but does not do this very often
- 2022-23 Defensive Degree of Difficulty: 0.411
- 2022-23 Points Prevented: -1.977
- Usually guarded starting level players, overall defense was better after the trade to Brooklyn
- Solid on-ball defender, capable of guarding both backcourt positions
- Solid pick-and-roll defender, good at containing ball handlers, had some trouble defending screeners on switches
- Generally stays attached to shooters off the ball, consistently fights through screens, tended to be late on close-outs in Dallas
- Stay-at-home defender overall, steal rate was higher in Brooklyn, normally doesn't get steals or blocks, fairly decent defensive rebounder

Dorian Finney-Smith

	Height	Weight	Cap #	Years Left
	6'7"	220	$13.932M	1 + PO

Similar at Age 29

		Season	SIMsc
1	Shane Battier	2007-08	944.8
2	Quentin Richardson	2009-10	940.8
3	Ime Udoka	2006-07	930.8
4	Jared Dudley	2014-15	923.5
5	James Posey	2005-06	923.4
6	Joe Harris	2020-21	919.9
7	Solomon Hill	2020-21	919.7
8	Cartier Martin	2013-14	914.1
9	Reggie Bullock	2020-21	913.6
10	Danny Green	2016-17	911.4

Baseline Basic Stats

MPG	PTS	AST	REB	BLK	STL
25.0	7.9	1.5	3.6	0.4	0.7

Advanced Metrics

USG%	3PTA/FGA	FTA/FGA	TS%	eFG%	3PT%
13.6	0.617	0.132	0.550	0.531	0.366

AST%	TOV%	OREB%	DREB%	STL%	BLK%
7.9	10.4	4.8	12.5	1.5	1.5

PER	ORTG	DRTG	WS/48	BPM	VOL
10.68	111.4	111.2	0.083	-0.51	0.345

- Traded from Dallas to Brooklyn at the trade deadline, regular starter throughout last season
- Utilized by both teams as a low usage spot-up shooter, efficiency dropped in Brooklyn with fewer open shots
- League average three-point shooter for his career, Three-Point Percentage fell to below break-even in Brooklyn
- Predominantly a stationary spot-up shooter, historically better in the corners, has made almost 39% of his corner threes
- Good cutter, can go to the offensive boards to score on put-backs
- Not able to create his own shot, catch-and-shoot player with limited passing skills, rarely turns the ball over
- 2022-23 Defensive Degree of Difficulty: 0.591, had the 7th toughest set of matchups in the NBA
- 2022-23 Points Prevented: 0.825
- Utilized as a primary defensive stopper by Dallas and Brooklyn
- Good on-ball defender that guards multiple positions, had some trouble against stronger post players
- Normally a good pick-and-roll defender, can switch to guard screeners and ball handlers, indecision caused him to be ineffective when making rotations
- Sometimes got caught on screens, tended to be late when closing out on spot-up shooters
- Steal and Block Percentages are still consistent with his career averages, fairly solid defensive rebounder

Royce O'Neale

	Height	Weight	Cap #	Years Left
	6'4"	226	$9.500M	UFA

Similar at Age 29

		Season	SIMsc
1	Buddy Hield	2021-22	919.5
2	Keith Bogans	2009-10	910.9
3	Solomon Hill	2020-21	909.9
4	Quentin Richardson	2009-10	909.5
5	Greg Buckner	2005-06	903.8
6	Jae Crowder	2019-20	903.7
7	P.J. Tucker	2014-15	898.7
8	Randy Foye	2012-13	893.7
9	James Posey	2005-06	891.6
10	Wesley Matthews	2015-16	888.5

Baseline Basic Stats

MPG	PTS	AST	REB	BLK	STL
27.0	8.6	2.1	4.3	0.3	0.9

Advanced Metrics

USG%	3PTA/FGA	FTA/FGA	TS%	eFG%	3PT%
13.2	0.667	0.113	0.556	0.540	0.384

AST%	TOV%	OREB%	DREB%	STL%	BLK%
11.9	13.6	3.3	14.0	1.5	1.3

PER	ORTG	DRTG	WS/48	BPM	VOL
9.93	112.1	112.6	0.079	-0.22	0.446

- Played starter level minutes in his first season in Brooklyn, moved to the bench after the trades
- Typically used throughout his career as a very low volume spot-up shooter, usage increased slightly
- Reliable three-point shooter that has made over 38% of his career threes
- Mostly a stand-still spot-up shooter, can make trail threes in transition when his feet are set
- Generally not a player that creates his own shot, used more as a pick-and-roll ball handler, can make pull-up jumpers if defenders back off him
- Decent secondary playmaker, increased his Assist Percentage, turnover rate increased in a more movement-oriented system
- 2022-23 Defensive Degree of Difficulty: 0.499
- 2022-23 Points Produced: 1.177
- Used as a stopper in his years with Utah, still can take on tough assignments when needed
- Good on-ball defender that guards multiple positions on the floor
- Decent pick-and-roll defender, good at dropping back to stop screeners, had some trouble containing ball handlers on the perimeter
- Stays attached to shooters off the ball, will fight through screens and close out in spot-up situations
- Steal Percentage decreased a bit, better at blocking shots on the weak side, solid defensive rebounder

Ben Simmons

	Height	Weight	Cap #	Years Left
	6'10"	240	$37.893M	1

Similar at Age 26

		Season	SIMsc
1	Clemon Johnson	1982-83	894.1
2	Tim Kempton	1989-90	886.2
3	Mason Plumlee	2016-17	885.1
4	Gustavo Ayon	2011-12	880.6
5	Jeff Ruland	1984-85	877.9
6	Larry Nance	2018-19	875.7
7	Kent Benson	1980-81	875.4
8	Dwight Powell	2017-18	873.6
9	Andrew DeClercq	1999-00	870.6
10	Bison Dele	1995-96	869.6

Baseline Basic Stats

MPG	PTS	AST	REB	BLK	STL
23.1	9.0	2.3	5.8	0.8	0.8

Advanced Metrics

USG%	3PTA/FGA	FTA/FGA	TS%	eFG%	3PT%
17.3	0.032	0.338	0.568	0.547	0.213

AST%	TOV%	OREB%	DREB%	STL%	BLK%
22.4	20.6	6.7	20.2	1.9	2.2

PER	ORTG	DRTG	WS/48	BPM	VOL
15.31	110.6	107.2	0.117	0.70	0.547

- Missed games due to knee and back injuries, regular starter for Brooklyn when healthy
- Production declined in a new role as a low usage facilitating playmaker
- Still a dynamic playmaker that displays great court vision, much more turnover prone due increased passing frequency
- Good at driving by slower big men on isolation plays, effective cutter off the ball, pushes the ball in transition
- Below average in other situations, rarely shoots jump shots in games, not comfortable when used as a screener, less effective on post-ups
- 2022-23 Defensive Degree of Difficulty: 0.493
- 2022-23 Points Prevented: 1.222
- Still capable of taking on difficult assignments against top scorers, solid on-ball defender
- Defends multiple positions, better against perimeter players, had some trouble against stronger big men
- Good pick-and-roll defender, effective at switching to guard ball handlers or screeners
- Tends to gamble too much, can be caught out of position, doesn't always close out or get around off-ball screens
- Active roaming help defender, gets steals and blocks at a high rate, very good defensive rebounder

Lonnie Walker IV

	Height	Weight	Cap #	Years Left
	6'4"	204	$2.020M	UFA

Similar at Age 24

		Season	SIMsc
1	Gary Harris	2018-19	948.9
2	Shannon Brown	2009-10	942.9
3	Marco Belinelli	2010-11	934.8
4	Wayne Ellington	2011-12	933.4
5	Voshon Lenard	1997-98	932.5
6	Landry Shamet	2021-22	931.8
7	Marcus Thornton	2011-12	929.7
8	Malik Beasley	2020-21	929.2
9	Austin Rivers	2016-17	928.9
10	Tim Hardaway Jr.	2016-17	924.9

Baseline Basic Stats

MPG	PTS	AST	REB	BLK	STL
24.2	11.0	1.9	2.5	0.2	0.7

Advanced Metrics

USG%	3PTA/FGA	FTA/FGA	TS%	eFG%	3PT%
21.0	0.495	0.194	0.549	0.513	0.362

AST%	TOV%	OREB%	DREB%	STL%	BLK%
11.6	8.6	1.6	9.3	1.4	0.8

PER	ORTG	DRTG	WS/48	BPM	VOL
12.97	108.8	114.3	0.064	-0.89	0.243

- Regular rotation player in his first season with the L.A. Lakers, missed games due to a bruised tailbone
- Had his most efficient season in a role as a moderate volume spot-up shooter
- Around a league average three-point shooter last season, percentages tend to vary from year-to-year
- Mostly effective as a stand-still spot-up shooter, can make pull-up threes if defenders back off him, less effective when shooting off screens
- Can attack the rim as a pick-and-roll ball handler, less effective in isolation situations
- Took better shots with the Lakers, mainly a catch-and-shoot player, has some passing skills, rarely turns the ball over
- 2022-23 Defensive Degree of Difficulty: 0.466
- 2022-23 Points Prevented: -0.463
- Mainly guarded starting level players, occasionally drew tough assignments, may have been over-matched
- Struggled as an on-ball defender, had trouble staying with opposing guards, could be overpowered by bigger players inside
- Good pick-and-roll defender, will funnel his man into help, can functionally switch
- Can get caught on screens off the ball, consistently closes out on spot-up shooters
- Stay-at-home defender, rarely gets steals or blocks, fairly decent defensive rebounding guard

Cam Thomas

	Height	Weight	Cap #	Years Left
	6'4"	210	$2.240M	Team Option

Similar at Age 21

		Season	SIMsc
1	Dion Waiters	2012-13	935.5
2	Duane Washington Jr.	2021-22	928.6
3	Antonio Blakeney	2017-18	925.2
4	Jamal Murray	2018-19	922.4
5	Bracey Wright	2005-06	920.5
6	Jordan Poole	2020-21	920.4
7	John Jenkins	2012-13	920.1
8	Rashad McCants	2005-06	918.1
9	Malik Monk	2019-20	917.6
10	Jaylen Nowell	2020-21	916.5

Baseline Basic Stats

MPG	PTS	AST	REB	BLK	STL
25.3	12.8	2.4	3.0	0.2	0.7

Advanced Metrics

USG%	3PTA/FGA	FTA/FGA	TS%	eFG%	3PT%
22.9	0.268	0.271	0.542	0.496	0.338

AST%	TOV%	OREB%	DREB%	STL%	BLK%
13.4	11.1	1.9	10.1	1.4	0.5

PER	ORTG	DRTG	WS/48	BPM	VOL
12.92	106.8	115.2	0.058	-2.14	0.389

- Fringe rotation player for Brooklyn in his second NBA season
- Increased his efficiency despite fewer minutes, mainly used as a high volume scoring guard off the bench
- Good isolation that can create his own shot, will attack the rim to draw fouls and hit pull-up jumpers, can be streaky with his shot
- Less effective as a pick-and-roll ball handler, limits turnovers but is not really a natural playmaker
- Took better shots last season, Three-Point Percentage increased to above 38%
- Excellent spot-up shooter especially from the corners, flashed an ability to shoot off screens
- Effective cutter, good at scoring on hand-off plays
- <u>2022-23 Defensive Degree of Difficulty</u>: 0.336
- <u>2022-23 Points Prevented</u>: 1.028
- Typically hidden in favorable matchups against lower leverage second unit players
- Below average on-ball defender, struggled to defend on the perimeter and inside last season
- Ineffective pick-and-roll defender, limited ability to switch, tended to allow ball handlers to turn the corner
- Usually fought through screens off the ball, generally was late when closing out on spot-up shooters
- Stay-at-home defender, does not really get blocks or steals, decent defensive rebounder

Dennis Smith Jr.

	Height	**Weight**	**Cap #**	**Years Left**
	6'2"	205	$2.020M	UFA

Similar at Age 25

		Season	SIMsc
1	Ronnie Price	2008-09	915.1
2	Keith McLeod	2004-05	913.1
3	John Starks	1990-91	906.6
4	Vinnie Johnson	1981-82	906.2
5	Shaquille Harrison	2018-19	901.8
6	Kris Dunn	2019-20	901.2
7	Lorenzo Romar	1983-84	899.2
8	Tierre Brown	2004-05	898.6
9	T.J. McConnell	2017-18	898.6
10	Carlos Arroyo	2004-05	898.0

Baseline Basic Stats

MPG	PTS	AST	REB	BLK	STL
21.1	8.4	3.2	2.3	0.3	1.0

Advanced Metrics

USG%	3PTA/FGA	FTA/FGA	TS%	eFG%	3PT%
19.5	0.241	0.273	0.500	0.457	0.274

AST%	TOV%	OREB%	DREB%	STL%	BLK%
25.2	15.2	2.8	9.6	2.4	1.3

PER	ORTG	DRTG	WS/48	BPM	VOL
13.10	104.2	109.9	0.070	-1.10	0.437

- Regular rotation player for Charlotte last season, missed games due to injuries to his ankle and toe
- Used as a low volume distributing point guard, production was on par with his career averages
- Solid playmaker that can run a team and find open teammates, cut his turnover rate last season
- Average or worse in most offensive situations, defenders can back off him to limit his effectiveness
- Not really a shooting threat, below break-even three-point shooter throughout his career
- Good cutter, speedy guard that can push the ball in transition
- 2022-23 Defensive Degree of Difficulty: 0.462
- 2022-23 Points Prevented: 1.309
- Sometimes drew tough assignments off the bench, usually guarded starting level players
- Decent on-ball defender, better against bigger players, struggled to stay with quicker players in isolation situations
- Good pick-and-roll defender, effective at containing ball handlers or funneling them into help
- Can get burned trying shoot the gap, will get caught on screens off the ball, consistently closes out on spot-up shooters
- Very active help defender, gets steals and blocks at a very high rate, fairly solid defensive rebounding guard

Darius Bazley

	Height	Weight	Cap #	Years Left
	6'8"	208	$2.020M	UFA

Similar at Age 22

		Season	SIMsc
1	Maurice Harkless	2015-16	929.0
2	Jerami Grant	2016-17	915.4
3	Taurean Prince	2016-17	905.5
4	Donyell Marshall	1995-96	903.6
5	Dorell Wright	2007-08	901.7
6	Renaldo Balkman	2006-07	900.2
7	Antoine Wright	2006-07	897.0
8	Precious Achiuwa	2021-22	896.5
9	Rodney Carney	2006-07	894.9
10	JaKarr Sampson	2015-16	893.9

Baseline Basic Stats

MPG	PTS	AST	REB	BLK	STL
22.4	8.7	1.1	4.0	0.8	0.7

Advanced Metrics

USG%	3PTA/FGA	FTA/FGA	TS%	eFG%	3PT%
18.0	0.324	0.310	0.540	0.514	0.356

AST%	TOV%	OREB%	DREB%	STL%	BLK%
8.2	10.7	4.6	16.6	1.5	3.4

PER	ORTG	DRTG	WS/48	BPM	VOL
13.26	107.8	111.4	0.080	-1.20	0.344

- Traded from Oklahoma City to Phoenix, regular rotation player for Oklahoma City, barely played for Phoenix
- Mainly used as a low volume energy wing and spot-up shooter
- More effective as a rim running energy player, good at cutting off the ball and rolling to the rim, explosive finisher in transition
- Below break-even career three-point shooter, made almost 38% of his threes in limited attempts last season
- Almost exclusively a stand-still spot-up shooter, not really effective when shooting in other situations
- Limited ability to create his own shot, catch-and-shoot player that makes safe passes, rarely turns the ball over
- 2022-23 Defensive Degree of Difficulty: 0.423
- 2022-23 Points Prevented: -0.544
- Usually guarded starting level players, used as a defensive stopper in previous years with Oklahoma City
- Decent on-ball defender, capable of guarding multiple positions, struggled in one-on-one situations last season
- Solid pick-and-roll defender, good at getting around screens to contain ball handlers, can functionally switch
- Tends to get caught on screens off the ball, good at closing out on spot-up shooters
- Highly active help defender, great weak side shot blocker, set a career high in Steal Percentage, good defensive rebounder

Day'Ron Sharpe

	Height	Weight	Cap #	Years Left
	6'11"	265	$2.210M	Team Option

Similar at Age 21

		Season	SIMsc
1	Kosta Koufos	2010-11	930.6
2	Al Jefferson	2005-06	902.9
3	Ivica Zubac	2018-19	896.6
4	Erick Dampier	1996-97	894.2
5	Greg Oden	2008-09	882.2
6	Chris Mihm	2000-01	882.1
7	Isaiah Hartenstein	2019-20	877.7
8	Jahlil Okafor	2016-17	873.7
9	Dalibor Bagaric	2001-02	870.1
10	Michael Doleac	1998-99	868.4

Baseline Basic Stats

MPG	PTS	AST	REB	BLK	STL
18.9	7.6	0.7	5.8	0.9	0.4

Advanced Metrics

USG%	3PTA/FGA	FTA/FGA	TS%	eFG%	3PT%
18.0	0.025	0.330	0.571	0.547	0.245

AST%	TOV%	OREB%	DREB%	STL%	BLK%
7.6	15.5	16.8	20.6	1.1	3.3

PER	ORTG	DRTG	WS/48	BPM	VOL
16.75	115.3	108.6	0.134	-1.83	0.449

- Minutes increased slightly, mainly a fringe rotation player for Brooklyn in his second NBA season
- Solidly effective with limited playing time as a low volume rim runner
- High motor big body center, does not always get great lift when shooting inside, can miss some easy shots
- Fairly effective cutter and roll man, excellent offensive rebounder, does not always run the floor in transition
- Generally not an outside shooting threat, attempting more jumpers in games, went 6-for-11 (54.5%) on threes last season
- Lacking in offensive skills, not really a reliable post player, somewhat turnover prone, adequate passer
- 2022-23 Defensive Degree of Difficulty: 0.352
- 2022-23 Points Prevented: -0.579
- Good shot blocker, solid defensive rebounder, undisciplined with his positioning, average rim protector, highly foul prone
- Stout post defender with great strength, struggled to stay with quicker players when defending in space
- Understanding of defensive rotations is still unpolished, struggled to make effective rotations when guarding pick-and-rolls
- Tends to stay anchored in the paint, does not always come out to contest perimeter shots in spot-up situations

Trendon Watford

	Height	Weight	Cap #	Years Left
	6'9"	240	$2.020M	UFA

Similar at Age 22

		Season	SIMsc
1	Josh McRoberts	2009-10	919.5
2	Marquese Chriss	2019-20	917.7
3	Kyle Anderson	2015-16	916.8
4	Pat Garrity	1998-99	914.8
5	Isaiah Roby	2020-21	914.8
6	Xavier Tillman Sr.	2020-21	911.4
7	James Johnson	2009-10	904.4
8	Moritz Wagner	2019-20	902.4
9	Thomas Robinson	2013-14	901.9
10	David Lee	2005-06	901.7

Baseline Basic Stats

MPG	PTS	AST	REB	BLK	STL
18.5	7.0	1.3	4.3	0.5	0.6

Advanced Metrics

USG%	3PTA/FGA	FTA/FGA	TS%	eFG%	3PT%
17.3	0.185	0.317	0.587	0.551	0.363

AST%	TOV%	OREB%	DREB%	STL%	BLK%
13.8	14.3	6.2	18.7	1.5	2.0

PER	ORTG	DRTG	WS/48	BPM	VOL
14.90	115.4	112.3	0.101	-0.74	0.332

- Regular rotation player for Portland in his second NBA season
- Solidly effective in his role as a low volume energy player and secondary playmaker
- Plays with a high motor, draws fouls, runs hard down the floor in transition
- Scores on a high volume of cuts and rolls to the rim, lacks the lift to efficiently finish in traffic
- Improved to make over 39% on a limited number of attempts, mainly a stand-still spot-up shooter
- Sometimes can post up smaller players, effective ball handler in a small sample of pick-and-roll possessions
- Good secondary playmaker that finds open teammates, slightly turnover prone
- 2022-23 Defensive Degree of Difficulty: 0.411
- 2022-23 Points Prevented: -1.015
- Drew some tough defensive assignments off the bench, around an average on-ball defender
- More effective in the post against bigger players, struggled to stay with quicker wings on the perimeter
- Middling pick-and-roll defender, good in drop coverages, struggled to contain ball handlers, tended to go too far under screens
- Fights through screens off the ball, usually would be late when closing out on spot-up shooters
- More of a stay-at-home defender last season, Block Percentage declined significantly, occasionally gets steals, fairly good defensive rebounder

Newcomers

Noah Clowney

	Height	Weight	Cap #	Years Left
	6'10"	210	$3.090M	1 + 2 TO

Baseline Basic Stats

MPG	PTS	AST	REB	BLK	STL
20.2	7.4	1.1	4.2	0.6	0.6

Advanced Metrics

USG%	3PTA/FGA	FTA/FGA	TS%	eFG%	3PT%
16.8	0.381	0.288	0.520	0.485	0.290

AST%	TOV%	OREB%	DREB%	STL%	BLK%
8.6	12.7	5.2	16.8	1.3	1.8

PER	ORTG	DRTG	WS/48	BPM	VOL
11.99	101.6	102.8	0.059	-1.65	N/A

- Drafted by Brooklyn with the 21st overall pick
- Struggled to play efficiently at the Las Vegas Summer League
- Primarily used as a low volume rim runner and stretch big
- Posted a True Shooting Percentage below 35%, struggled to finish in traffic against stronger big men
- Athletic finisher with good vertical pop, potentially can be a lob threat if he adds strength
- Went 4-for-17 (23.5%) on threes at Summer League, made below 30% of his college threes
- Shooting stroke still inconsistent, has trouble repeating his shooting motion
- Needs to improve his ball handling, middling effectiveness as a post player in college, decent passer for his size, limits turnovers
- Long and athletic big man, high potential to be an effective rim protector
- Active weak side defender in Summer League, excellent shot blocker, uses length well to get steals, fairly solid defensive rebounder
- Tends to be undisciplined with his positioning, will bite on fakes, highly foul prone
- Thin frame, may get pushed around by stronger post players in the NBA, mobile enough to defend in space
- Needs to improve pick-and-roll defenders, tends to be indecisive, not really effective at taking away any specific action
- Willing to come out to the perimeter to close out in spot-up situations
- Likely will need additional seasoning in the G-League to polish his skills on both ends

Dariq Whitehead

	Height	Weight	Cap #	Years Left
	6'7"	220	$2.966M	1 + 2 TO

Baseline Basic Stats

MPG	PTS	AST	REB	BLK	STL
20.9	8.0	1.4	2.9	0.3	0.7

Advanced Metrics

USG%	3PTA/FGA	FTA/FGA	TS%	eFG%	3PT%
17.9	0.421	0.200	0.520	0.488	0.330

AST%	TOV%	OREB%	DREB%	STL%	BLK%
10.3	12.8	2.8	11.5	1.6	0.8

PER	ORTG	DRTG	WS/48	BPM	VOL
10.73	99.1	107.1	0.052	-1.64	N/A

- Drafted by Brooklyn with the 22nd overall pick
- Missed the Las Vegas Summer League, recovering from foot surgery, expected to be ready for training camp
- Mainly used as an off-ball shooter in a moderate volume role at Duke
- Made almost 43% of his threes, almost exclusively was used as a stand-still shooter
- Most effective when spotting up, good at making trail threes in transition, not really able to shoot on the move right now
- Flashed some ability to make pull-up mid-range jumpers and get to the rim as a pick-and-roll ball handler
- Effects of a prior foot injury limited his explosion, not able to play effectively in isolation situations
- Mostly a catch-and-shoot player, a bit turnover prone, has trouble reading defenses
- Played injured last season, showed good athleticism even in a diminished state
- Long and explosive athlete when healthy, has the potential to defend multiple positions on the ball
- Solid pick-and-roll defender, effective at containing ball handlers, can functionally switch onto screeners
- Stays attached to shooters off the ball, fights through screens and closes out in spot-up situations
- Fairly active help defender, can play passing lanes to post high steal rates, occasionally blocks shots on the weak side, decent defensive rebounder
- Could use a redshirt year to ensure that his foot has healed to recapture his full athleticism level
- May also benefit from some additional seasoning in the G-League to polish his skills on both ends

Chicago Bulls

Last Season: 40 - 42, Missed the Playoffs

Offensive Rating: 113.5, 24th in the NBA   Defensive Rating: 112.2, 5th in the NBA

Primary Executive: Artūras Karnišovas, Executive Vice President of Basketball Operations

Head Coach: Billy Donovan

Key Roster Changes

Subtractions
Patrick Beverley, free agency
Derrick Jones Jr., free agency
Javonte Green, free agency
Marko Simonovic, waived

Additions
Julian Phillips, draft
Torrey Craig, free agency
Jevon Carter, free agency

Roster

Likely Starting Five
1. Jevon Carter
2. *Zach LaVine*
3. *DeMar DeRozan*
4. Patrick Williams
5. *Nikola Vučević*

Other Key Rotation Players
Alex Caruso
Coby White
Ayo Dosunmu
Torrey Craig
Andre Drummond

* Italics denotes that a player is likely to be on the floor to close games

Remaining Roster

- Dalen Terry
- Carlik Jones
- Terry Taylor
- Julian Phillips
- Lonzo Ball
- Adama Sanogo, 21, 6'9", 245, UConn (Two-Way)
- Justin Lewis, 21, 6'7", 245, Marquette (Two-Way)
- Onuralp Bitim, 24, 6'6", 205, Turkey (Two-Way)

SCHREMPF Base Rating: 43.5

Season Preview Survey

- *Are the Bulls contending or rebuilding? Where is this team headed?*

The Bulls are trying to win, but they don't quite have the pieces to truly compete with the elite teams in the Eastern Conference. They appear to be topped out as a lower playoff seed or a play-in team at best because their core group is on the older side and the bulk of their rotation is filled with above average veteran players. They don't have a lot of room to grow unless someone like Patrick Williams makes a huge leap this season. In addition to this, they don't have a lot of tradeable assets or cap flexibility to make a meaningful addition. Most likely, they will remain as they are and fight for a spot in the play-in tournament for this upcoming season.

- *What are the areas of concern for this team heading into this season?*

Even though the Bulls have some individually talented offensive players, they haven't been able to find a way to efficiently score as a cohesive unit. Often times, possessions stall due to a lack of ball movement, which causes the offense to devolve into a turn-based, one-on-one system. Ideally, they would have looked to add a natural playmaker to make up for the fact that they have lost Lonzo Ball for multiple seasons due to injury. However, they went in the other direction to add defensive-minded players that are limited on offense. The onus will be on their stars to draw the attention of defense and keep everyone else involved. If they can add some more movement to their offensive system, they could over-achieve and push for a playoff spot. Otherwise, they could have some rough stretches offensively, which would not allow them to keep pace with the better teams in the Eastern Conference.

- *List some possible breakout players for this team.*

Chicago is a veteran heavy team with a lot of established players, so there aren't too many breakout candidates to choose from. Out of their set of current group of younger players, last year's first round pick, Dalen Terry has a chance to crack the rotation. He's facing some tough odds because the Bulls have a lot of guards and wings in front of him that are blocking him from getting substantial minutes. If he does receive an opportunity to play, he could contribute by giving the Bulls a credible floor spacer, an additional ball mover, and an energetic defender. In addition to Terry, this year's second round pick, Julian Phillips could be sleeper candidate to earn some playing time by giving the team an incredibly athletic, energy wing to finish plays in transition and effectively replace Derrick Jones Jr.

- *What should we expect from them this season?*

The Bulls largely left their team from last year intact and made some minor tweaks. More than likely, they will finish in the same range that they did a season ago, so they will probably be in the mix for a play-in spot. They will be a tough team to play against because they are leaning more into their strengths as a stout defensive unit. The additions of Jevon Carter and Torrey Craig should give them a couple of extra stoppers to go along with Alex Caruso. This should give them more flexibility to switch and utilize different tactics to keep themselves competitive on a night-to-night basis. Even so, their lack of a cohesive offense will hold them back because they will be overly dependent on the individual talents of their stars to carry them. However, Zach LaVine and DeMar DeRozan simply don't have the elite ability to do this as well as the very best superstars in the league. In all probability, Chicago will compete for a back-end seed and participate in the play-in tournament this coming season.

Veterans

Zach LaVine

	Height	Weight	Cap #	Years Left
	6'5"	200	$40.064M	2 + PO

Similar at Age 27

		Season	SIMsc
1	Ray Allen*	2002-03	938.8
2	CJ McCollum	2018-19	927.2
3	Steve Smith	1996-97	922.4
4	Damian Lillard	2017-18	915.7
5	Jordan Clarkson	2019-20	911.6
6	Allan Houston	1998-99	911.5
7	Ricky Davis	2006-07	908.9
8	Bradley Beal	2020-21	906.7
9	Marco Belinelli	2013-14	905.9
10	Evan Fournier	2019-20	905.9

Baseline Basic Stats

MPG	PTS	AST	REB	BLK	STL
33.2	19.1	3.6	3.7	0.2	0.9

Advanced Metrics

USG%	3PTA/FGA	FTA/FGA	TS%	eFG%	3PT%
26.6	0.427	0.275	0.581	0.534	0.385

AST%	TOV%	OREB%	DREB%	STL%	BLK%
19.3	11.0	1.9	11.7	1.2	0.6

PER	ORTG	DRTG	WS/48	BPM	VOL
18.19	113.3	113.2	0.122	1.31	0.395

- Played at a near All-Star level in his sixth season with Chicago
- Generally maintained his usual level of efficiency in a role as a high usage primary scoring option
- Good pick-and-roll ball handler and isolation player, can get to the rim and make pull-up mid-range jumpers
- Reliable three-point shooter, has made almost 47% of his career corner threes
- Most effective off the catch when his feet are set, less consistent when shooting off the dribble or on the move
- Solid playmaker that can make simple reads, good at avoiding turnovers
- 2022-23 Defensive Degree of Difficulty: 0.430
- 2022-23 Points Prevented: 1.766
- Guards starting level players, defended higher-end assignments in the past
- Solid on-ball defender that can guard multiple positions
- Mostly an effective pick-and-roll defender, good at containing ball handlers, had some trouble when switched onto screeners
- Stays attached to shooters off the ball, fights through screens and closes out on spot-up shooters
- Stay-at-home defender, does not really get steals or blocks, fairly solid defensive rebounder

DeMar DeRozan

	Height	Weight	Cap #	Years Left
	6'6"	220	$28.600M	UFA

Similar at Age 33

		Season	SIMsc
1	Paul Pierce*	2010-11	915.2
2	Vince Carter	2009-10	910.8
3	Manu Ginobili*	2010-11	908.3
4	Bernard King*	1989-90	906.9
5	Dominique Wilkins*	1992-93	901.0
6	Kobe Bryant*	2011-12	899.3
7	Larry Bird*	1989-90	894.6
8	Mitch Richmond*	1998-99	892.9
9	Michael Jordan*	1996-97	891.1
10	Walter Davis	1987-88	883.7

Baseline Basic Stats

MPG	PTS	AST	REB	BLK	STL
33.8	20.9	4.2	4.8	0.3	1.0

Advanced Metrics

USG%	3PTA/FGA	FTA/FGA	TS%	eFG%	3PT%
27.8	0.158	0.368	0.568	0.504	0.336

AST%	TOV%	OREB%	DREB%	STL%	BLK%
20.7	10.2	2.2	13.2	1.6	1.0

PER	ORTG	DRTG	WS/48	BPM	VOL
19.70	113.1	110.7	0.136	1.80	0.068

- Named to his sixth All-Star team in his second season with Chicago
- Maintained his usual efficiency level in a role as one of the Bulls' main scoring options
- One of the NBA's best mid-range scorers, makes pull-up jumpers as a pick-and-roll ball handler and isolation player, good at posting up smaller players
- Great finisher in transition, draws fouls at a high rate, good playmaker, rarely turns the ball over
- Normally doesn't take many threes, below break-even three-point shooter, mostly a stationary spot-up three-point shooter
- 2022-23 Defensive Degree of Difficulty: 0.389
- 2022-23 Points Prevented: -0.332
- Often hidden in favorable matchups against lower leverage players, can be targeted on switches
- Rarely tested on the ball, average on-ball defense, better against perimeter players, had trouble against stronger players in the post
- Below average pick-and-roll defender, not effective at taking any specific action
- Stays attached to shooters off the ball, fights through screens and closes out in spot-up situations
- Usually a stay-at-home defender, steal and block rates increased last season, decent defensive rebounder

Nikola Vučević

	Height	Weight	Cap #	Years Left
	6'11"	260	$18.519M	2

Similar at Age 32

		Season	SIMsc
1	Bill Laimbeer	1989-90	899.8
2	Al Horford	2018-19	878.3
3	Marc Gasol	2016-17	873.5
4	Carlos Boozer	2013-14	872.1
5	David West	2012-13	866.5
6	Tim Duncan*	2008-09	865.1
7	Zach Randolph	2013-14	864.2
8	Kevin Garnett*	2008-09	861.7
9	Dirk Nowitzki*	2010-11	859.3
10	LaMarcus Aldridge	2017-18	858.8

Baseline Basic Stats

MPG	PTS	AST	REB	BLK	STL
29.8	14.6	2.7	8.5	0.9	0.7

Advanced Metrics

USG%	3PTA/FGA	FTA/FGA	TS%	eFG%	3PT%
22.1	0.267	0.159	0.552	0.528	0.354

AST%	TOV%	OREB%	DREB%	STL%	BLK%
15.0	10.9	6.6	28.4	1.2	2.2

PER	ORTG	DRTG	WS/48	BPM	VOL
17.48	110.2	107.8	0.119	1.84	0.271

- Started all 82 games at center for Chicago in his second full season with the team
- Maintained his usual level of effectiveness, used as a moderate volume post-up player and stretch big
- Can bully weaker defenders and flash to the middle on post-ups, good passing big man that limits turnovers
- Above break-even three-point shooter, has made over 42% of his career corner threes
- Most effective as a stand-still spot-up shooter, less efficient when used as a pick-and-pop screener
- Effective rim runner despite of ideal vertical lift, good cutter and roll man, selectively goes to the offensive boards to score on put-backs
- 2022-23 Defensive Degree of Difficulty: 0.473
- 2022-23 Points Prevented: -1.057
- Average rim protector, shot blocking rates are slightly declining, excellent defensive rebounder
- Will draw tough assignments against top scoring centers, stout post defender, better at defending in space last season
- Average pick-and-roll defender, effective at switching out on ball handlers, a step slow when rotating to guard screeners
- Tended to stay anchored in the paint, did not always come out to contest perimeter shots in spot-up situations

Patrick Williams

	Height	Weight	Cap #	Years Left
	6'7"	215	$9.836M	RFA

Similar at Age 21

		Season	SIMsc
1	Kenyon Martin Jr.	2021-22	942.8
2	Kawhi Leonard	2012-13	924.1
3	Martell Webster	2007-08	924.1
4	Kessler Edwards	2021-22	920.6
5	Kelly Oubre	2016-17	916.8
6	P.J. Washington	2019-20	912.6
7	Chase Budinger	2009-10	912.5
8	Justise Winslow	2017-18	912.5
9	Kevin Knox	2020-21	911.3
10	Luke Kennard	2017-18	909.1

Baseline Basic Stats

MPG	PTS	AST	REB	BLK	STL
26.4	10.7	1.6	4.2	0.5	0.8

Advanced Metrics

USG%	3PTA/FGA	FTA/FGA	TS%	eFG%	3PT%
16.5	0.291	0.227	0.575	0.546	0.398

AST%	TOV%	OREB%	DREB%	STL%	BLK%
8.2	11.8	3.9	12.4	1.5	1.7

PER	ORTG	DRTG	WS/48	BPM	VOL
12.13	111.1	112.1	0.087	-0.69	0.376

- Regular starter for Chicago in his third NBA season
- Solidly effective in his role as a low volume spot-up shooter and energy wing
- Great three-point shooter that has made over 41% of his career threes
- Almost exclusively a stationary spot-up shooter, break-even three-point shooter in transition
- Good cutter, explosive finisher in transition, flashed some ability to attack the rim on pick-and-rolls
- Lacks ball handling ability to create his own shot in isolation situations
- Mainly a catch-and-shoot player, limited as a passer, good at avoiding turnovers
- 2022-23 Defensive Degree of Difficulty: 0.535
- 2022-23 Points Prevented: -0.031
- Drew a lot of tough assignments against top scoring wings, used as one of Chicago's main defensive stoppers
- Good on-ball defender that can guard opponents on the perimeter and inside
- Fairly solid pick-and-roll defender, good at containing ball handlers, had lapses when switching onto screeners
- Tended to get caught on screens off the ball, consistently closed out on spot-up shooters
- Active help defender, uses length well to get steals, good weak side shot blocker, solid defensive rebounder

Jevon Carter

	Height	Weight	Cap #	Years Left
	6'1"	200	$6.190M	1 + PO

Similar at Age 27

		Season	SIMsc
1	Jerryd Bayless	2015-16	935.3
2	Derek Fisher	2001-02	930.4
3	Austin Rivers	2019-20	920.4
4	Langston Galloway	2018-19	913.8
5	Craig Hodges	1987-88	906.6
6	Chasson Randle	2020-21	904.5
7	Patrick Beverley	2015-16	904.1
8	Patty Mills	2015-16	903.5
9	Troy Daniels	2018-19	903.1
10	Roger Mason	2007-08	902.0

Baseline Basic Stats

MPG	PTS	AST	REB	BLK	STL
22.0	7.9	2.1	2.2	0.1	0.7

Advanced Metrics

USG%	3PTA/FGA	FTA/FGA	TS%	eFG%	3PT%
15.3	0.618	0.104	0.550	0.533	0.402

AST%	TOV%	OREB%	DREB%	STL%	BLK%
14.6	11.1	2.1	9.8	1.6	0.9

PER	ORTG	DRTG	WS/48	BPM	VOL
11.05	112.0	112.1	0.086	-0.70	0.331

- Regular rotation player for Milwaukee in his first full season with the team, started almost half of his games
- Solidly effective in his role as a low volume spot-up shooter and secondary ball handler
- Reliable three-point shooter in his career, made over 42% of his threes last season
- Mostly effective when he's stationary and his feet are set, has made over 43% of his career corner threes
- Not really able to create his own offense, less effective with the ball in his hands
- Fairly solid secondary playmaker that makes simple reads, good at avoiding turnovers
- 2022-23 Defensive Degree of Difficulty: 0.512
- 2022-23 Points Prevented: 0.720
- Routinely drew assignments against top scoring perimeter players
- Good on-ball defender, effective at defending both guard spots
- Fairly solid pick-and-roll defender, can functionally switch despite lack of size, occasionally allows ball handlers to turn the corner
- Stays attached to shooters off the ball, fights through screens and closes out in spot-up situations
- Pesky defender that pressures ball handlers, gets steals at a fairly high rate, decent defensive rebounding guard

Alex Caruso

	Height	Weight	Cap #	Years Left
	6'4"	186	$9.460M	1

Similar at Age 28

		Season	SIMsc
1	Garrett Temple	2014-15	912.2
2	Kirk Hinrich	2008-09	907.6
3	Delon Wright	2020-21	902.3
4	Greg Buckner	2004-05	893.4
5	C.J. Watson	2012-13	893.2
6	Michael Carter-Williams	2019-20	892.8
7	Doc Rivers	1989-90	890.3
8	Morlon Wiley	1994-95	889.1
9	Jon Barry	1997-98	888.1
10	Tony Smith	1996-97	888.0

Baseline Basic Stats

MPG	PTS	AST	REB	BLK	STL
23.1	6.9	2.6	2.7	0.3	1.1

Advanced Metrics

USG%	3PTA/FGA	FTA/FGA	TS%	eFG%	3PT%
12.7	0.536	0.221	0.545	0.511	0.360

AST%	TOV%	OREB%	DREB%	STL%	BLK%
15.8	15.7	2.7	10.5	2.4	1.6

PER	ORTG	DRTG	WS/48	BPM	VOL
10.84	111.0	108.7	0.101	-0.13	0.149

- Named to the All-Defensive 1st Team in 2022-23, regular rotation player for Chicago, started over half of his games
- Had his most efficient season in a role as a very low usage spot-up shooter and secondary playmaker
- League average career three-point shooter, percentages tend to vary from year-to-year
- Predominantly a stand-still spot-up shooter, not really effective when shooting on the move or off the dribble
- Effective cutter, can push the ball in transition, solid pass-first playmaker, good at avoiding turnovers
- Lacks explosive quickness or dynamic ball handling skills, not able to create his own offense
- 2022-23 Defensive Degree of Difficulty: 0.572, had the 10th most difficult set of matchups in the NBA
- 2022-23 Points Prevented: 0.949
- Utilized as Chicago's primary defensive stopper on the perimeter
- Great on-ball defender, can effectively guards ones, two, and threes
- Good pick-and-roll defender, good at switching to defend ball handler and screeners
- Tends to gamble too much, can be caught out of position off the ball, gets caught on screens, sometimes is late to close out on spot-up shooters
- Led the NBA in Steal Percentage, good weak side shot blocker, fairly solid defensive rebounder

Coby White

	Height	Weight	Cap #	Years Left
	6'5"	195	$11.111M	2

Similar at Age 22

		Season	SIMsc
1	Malik Beasley	2018-19	955.4
2	Terrence Ross	2013-14	944.2
3	Luke Kennard	2018-19	936.4
4	Desmond Bane	2020-21	928.7
5	Lonnie Walker	2020-21	928.0
6	Furkan Korkmaz	2019-20	924.2
7	Evan Fournier	2014-15	924.0
8	Nik Stauskas	2015-16	923.1
9	Terence Davis	2019-20	921.6
10	Marco Belinelli	2008-09	920.0

Baseline Basic Stats

MPG	PTS	AST	REB	BLK	STL
26.3	12.3	2.3	2.9	0.2	0.8

Advanced Metrics

USG%	3PTA/FGA	FTA/FGA	TS%	eFG%	3PT%
20.0	0.511	0.166	0.565	0.535	0.382

AST%	TOV%	OREB%	DREB%	STL%	BLK%
15.4	10.2	1.4	11.5	1.4	0.6

PER	ORTG	DRTG	WS/48	BPM	VOL
13.27	111.5	113.3	0.088	-0.75	0.293

- Regular rotation player for Chicago in his fourth NBA season
- Increased his efficiency in his role as a low volume spot-up shooter and secondary ball handler
- Solid overall three-point shooter, has made 44% of his career corner threes
- Excellent stand-still spot-up shooter, much less effective when shooting in other situations
- Average pick-and-roll ball handler and isolation player, can hit floaters and get to the rim, inconsistent when shooting off the dribble
- Solid secondary playmaker, rarely turns the ball over, does not really move off the ball
- 2022-23 Defensive Degree of Difficulty: 0.365
- 2022-23 Points Prevented: -1.005
- Usually defends second unit level players or is hidden in favorable matchups
- Average on-ball defender, can stay with opposing guards on the perimeter, can be overpowered inside by stronger players
- Below average pick-and-roll defender, not effective at taking away any specific action
- Gets caught on screens off the ball, usually is late when closing out on spot-up shooters
- Posted a career high in Steal Percentage, usually more of a stay-at-home defender, solid defensive rebounder

Ayo Dosunmu

	Height	Weight	Cap #	Years Left
	6'5"	200	$6.481M	2

Similar at Age 23

		Season	SIMsc
1	Courtney Lee	2008-09	942.9
2	Malik Monk	2021-22	926.3
3	Wesley Person	1994-95	925.7
4	Voshon Lenard	1996-97	922.8
5	Josh Richardson	2016-17	922.3
6	MarShon Brooks	2011-12	921.9
7	Nik Stauskas	2016-17	921.8
8	Cuttino Mobley	1998-99	921.1
9	Allen Crabbe	2015-16	921.0
10	Aaron Wiggins	2021-22	920.8

Baseline Basic Stats

MPG	PTS	AST	REB	BLK	STL
26.7	10.5	2.1	3.2	0.3	0.8

Advanced Metrics

USG%	3PTA/FGA	FTA/FGA	TS%	eFG%	3PT%
16.8	0.393	0.184	0.573	0.545	0.365

AST%	TOV%	OREB%	DREB%	STL%	BLK%
14.0	12.6	2.3	10.6	1.5	1.1

PER	ORTG	DRTG	WS/48	BPM	VOL
12.46	111.7	112.4	0.090	-1.01	0.240

- Started a majority of his games for Chicago in his second NBA season
- Effectiveness dropped slightly, mainly used as a low volume spot-up shooter and secondary ball handler
- Three-Point Percentage fell to below break-even last season, above break-even three-point shooter in his two-year career
- Almost exclusively a stand-still spot-up shooter, not really able to shoot efficiently in other situations
- Can attack the rim or make mid-range pull-up jumpers on pick-and-rolls, not able to create his own shot on isolation plays
- Solid secondary playmaker, cut his turnover rate last season, effective cutter off the ball
- 2022-23 Defensive Degree of Difficulty: 0.504
- 2022-23 Points Prevented: 0.837
- Drew a lot of tough assignments against elite perimeter scorers
- Good on-ball defender that guards multiple positions
- Good pick-and-roll defender, can effectively switch to defend ball handlers or screeners
- Fights through screens off the ball, tends to late on his close-outs in spot-up situations
- Generally a stay-at-home defender, occasionally gets steals or blocks, slightly below average defensive rebounder

Torrey Craig

	Height	Weight	Cap #	Years Left
	6'7"	221	$2.528M	1

Similar at Age 32

		Season	SIMsc
1	Shane Battier	2010-11	932.3
2	Matt Barnes	2012-13	921.4
3	Alan Anderson	2014-15	912.0
4	Danny Green	2019-20	911.2
5	Jud Buechler	2000-01	911.1
6	Walt Williams	2002-03	910.5
7	Marvin Williams	2018-19	908.9
8	J.R. Smith	2017-18	907.7
9	Dan Majerle	1997-98	901.0
10	Caron Butler	2012-13	900.0

Baseline Basic Stats

MPG	PTS	AST	REB	BLK	STL
22.0	6.7	1.4	3.5	0.5	0.7

Advanced Metrics

USG%	3PTA/FGA	FTA/FGA	TS%	eFG%	3PT%
13.2	0.578	0.121	0.556	0.541	0.353

AST%	TOV%	OREB%	DREB%	STL%	BLK%
8.7	12.9	5.5	14.9	1.5	2.2

PER	ORTG	DRTG	WS/48	BPM	VOL
10.92	111.0	110.3	0.088	-0.80	0.335

- Regular starter for Phoenix in his first full season with the team
- Increased his effectiveness in his role as a low volume spot-up shooter
- Above break-even career three-point shooter, made 39.5% of his threes last season
- Mostly a stationary spot-up shooter, can occasionally make threes as a pick-and-pop screener or in transition
- Good cutter off the ball, will go to the offensive boards to score off put-backs
- Rarely used in ball handling situations, only makes safe passes, rarely turns the ball over
- 2022-23 Defensive Degree of Difficulty: 0.521
- 2022-23 Points Prevented: 1.018
- Mainly served as Phoenix's primary perimeter stopper
- Very good on-ball defender that can guard multiple positions on the floor
- Played below average pick-and-roll defense, not really effective at taking away any specific action, good at switching in previous seasons
- Tends to get caught on screens off the ball, consistently closes out on spot-up shooters
- Good weak side shot blocker, occasionally can get steals, fairly good defensive rebounder

Andre Drummond

	Height	Weight	Cap #	Years Left
	6'10"	279	$3.360M	UFA

Similar at Age 29

		Season	SIMsc
1	Oliver Miller	1999-00	856.4
2	Nene	2011-12	853.6
3	Aron Baynes	2015-16	853.5
4	Dwight Howard	2014-15	837.3
5	Emeka Okafor	2011-12	835.0
6	Erick Dampier	2004-05	834.1
7	Elton Brand	2008-09	833.4
8	Glen Davis	2014-15	831.8
9	Derrick Favors	2020-21	830.2
10	Kendrick Perkins	2013-14	829.3

Baseline Basic Stats

MPG	PTS	AST	REB	BLK	STL
24.2	10.4	1.6	8.8	0.9	0.9

Advanced Metrics

USG%	3PTA/FGA	FTA/FGA	TS%	eFG%	3PT%
20.2	0.034	0.409	0.570	0.550	0.101

AST%	TOV%	OREB%	DREB%	STL%	BLK%
10.1	17.2	15.4	32.6	2.2	3.3

PER	ORTG	DRTG	WS/48	BPM	VOL
18.99	110.8	104.5	0.133	-0.32	0.493

- Fringe rotation player for Chicago in his first season with the team
- Maintained his usual level of effectiveness in his role as a moderate volume rim runner
- Efficient finisher, vertical lob threat, solid cutter and roll man, excellent offensive rebounder, effective at running the floor in transition
- Draws fouls but is a poor free throw shooter, career Free Throw Percentage is below 50%
- Can bully weaker players in the post, no reliable shooting range outside of ten feet
- Flashed passing skills in previous seasons, a bit turnover prone
- 2022-23 Defensive Degree of Difficulty: 0.340
- 2022-23 Points Prevented: -0.284
- Great rim protector, good shot blocker, current career leader in Defensive Rebound Percentage
- Good at using his length and active hands to get steals at a high rate
- Mostly guarded second unit big men, stout post defender, mobile enough to stay with lower leverage perimeter players on switches
- Effective pick-and-roll defender, good in drop coverages, effective at switching onto ball handlers last season
- Usually stays anchored in the paint, does always come out to contest perimeter shots in spot-up situations

Dalen Terry

	Height	Weight	Cap #	Years Left
	6'7"	195	$3.351M	2 TO

Similar at Age 20

		Season	SIMsc
1	CJ Elleby	2020-21	903.9
2	C.J. Miles	2007-08	898.3
3	Jarrett Culver	2019-20	897.2
4	Paul George	2010-11	893.9
5	Kelly Oubre	2015-16	892.6
6	Ricky Davis	1999-00	890.6
7	Hamidou Diallo	2018-19	889.9
8	Gerald Green	2005-06	888.6
9	Greg Brown III	2021-22	888.1
10	Brandon Boston Jr.	2021-22	887.5

Baseline Basic Stats

MPG	PTS	AST	REB	BLK	STL
17.1	6.6	1.1	2.7	0.3	0.6

Advanced Metrics

USG%	3PTA/FGA	FTA/FGA	TS%	eFG%	3PT%
18.8	0.394	0.257	0.528	0.492	0.307

AST%	TOV%	OREB%	DREB%	STL%	BLK%
12.3	10.7	5.3	12.7	2.1	1.5

PER	ORTG	DRTG	WS/48	BPM	VOL
12.79	108.9	110.7	0.083	-1.08	0.291

- Played sparingly for Chicago as a rookie, spent some time in the G-League with the Windy City Bulls
- Mainly used as a low usage spot-up shooter and secondary playmaker
- Made less than 30% of his NBA threes, made 40% of his threes in limited attempts in the G-League
- Primarily a stand-still spot-up shooter, not really effective when shooting in other situations
- Struggled in ball handling situations in the NBA, lacks ball handling skills to consistently get to the rim, not really effective at shooting off the dribble
- Solid secondary playmaker that makes simple reads, rarely turns the ball over
- 2022-23 Defensive Degree of Difficulty: 0.265
- 2022-23 Points Prevented: -1.949
- Mainly defended second unit players or played in garbage minutes
- Rarely tested on the ball, played solid on-ball defense in a small sample of possessions, effectively could stay with opposing perimeter players
- Fairly solid pick-and-roll defender, good at funneling his man into help, had difficulty switching onto screeners in a small sample of possessions
- Tended to get caught on screens off the ball, usually was late to close out on spot-up shooters
- Very active help defender, posted high steal and block rates in limited minutes, solid defensive rebounder

Carlik Jones

	Height	Weight	Cap #	Years Left
	6'1"	185	$1.928M	1

Similar at Age 25

		Season	SIMsc
1	Tierre Brown	2004-05	908.7
2	Jimmer Fredette	2014-15	905.9
3	A.J. Price	2011-12	901.5
4	Vonteego Cummings	2001-02	898.4
5	Dwight Buycks	2014-15	896.3
6	Raul Neto	2017-18	895.4
7	Aaron Holiday	2021-22	894.1
8	Shawn Respert	1997-98	893.0
9	Tony Delk	1998-99	893.0
10	John Crotty	1994-95	891.7

Baseline Basic Stats

MPG	PTS	AST	REB	BLK	STL
17.9	6.6	2.6	1.7	0.1	0.6

Advanced Metrics

USG%	3PTA/FGA	FTA/FGA	TS%	eFG%	3PT%
18.6	0.309	0.337	0.484	0.431	0.339

AST%	TOV%	OREB%	DREB%	STL%	BLK%
20.8	15.4	2.3	8.6	1.8	0.2

PER	ORTG	DRTG	WS/48	BPM	VOL
9.99	100.0	110.9	0.017	-3.52	0.601

- Spent most of last season in the G-League with the Windy City Bulls, signed with Chicago late in 2022-23
- Used as a low volume spot-up shooter in the NBA, was a high usage scoring guard in the G-League
- Above break-even three-point shooter in the G-League, percentages tended to vary, prone to streakiness
- Only played 56 NBA minutes, used almost exclusively as a stand-still spot-up shooter
- Shifty guard that can use hesitation moves and make pull-up mid-range shots on pick-and-rolls
- Lacks explosive quickness to consistently score on isolations or blow by defenders
- Fairly good playmaker with solid court vision to set up teammates, good at avoiding turnovers
- 2022-23 Defensive Degree of Difficulty: 0.150
- 2022-23 Points Prevented: -2.553
- Mostly played against second unit players or in garbage time, only played extended minutes in three games
- Allowed zero points in two isolations possessions, forced one miss and one turnover
- Allowed nine points in seven pick-and-roll possessions, only forced two misses on six shots, forced a turnover
- Allowed nine points in ten spot-up possessions, forced six misses in nine shot attempts
- Allowed a made two-pointer and forced one miss on two hand-off possessions
- Consistently gets steals at a solid rate, decent defensive rebounding guard

Terry Taylor

	Height	Weight	Cap #	Years Left
	6'5"	230	$2.020M	1

Similar at Age 23

		Season	SIMsc
1	Anthony Lamb	2020-21	900.4
2	Dwayne Bacon	2018-19	895.2
3	Sterling Brown	2018-19	894.0
4	Quincy Pondexter	2011-12	892.4
5	DaQuan Jeffries	2020-21	891.6
6	Ignas Brazdeikis	2021-22	891.1
7	Alex Poythress	2016-17	889.9
8	Lamar Stevens	2020-21	887.0
9	Kirk Snyder	2006-07	886.0
10	Orlando Johnson	2012-13	885.1

Baseline Basic Stats

MPG	PTS	AST	REB	BLK	STL
15.5	5.3	0.8	2.5	0.2	0.5

Advanced Metrics

USG%	3PTA/FGA	FTA/FGA	TS%	eFG%	3PT%
15.8	0.290	0.205	0.564	0.542	0.292

AST%	TOV%	OREB%	DREB%	STL%	BLK%
7.4	10.2	8.8	11.7	1.3	1.0

PER	ORTG	DRTG	WS/48	BPM	VOL
13.21	115.3	114.1	0.091	-2.00	0.562

- Waived by Indiana, signed a Two-Way contract with Chicago after the trade deadline
- Played sparingly for both teams, solidly effective in very limited action as a low usage energy player
- Energetic rim runner, has made almost 76% of his shots inside of three feet in two NBA seasons
- Good cutter and roll man, active offensive rebounder that scores on put-backs
- Has made less than 30% of his career threes, takes the majority of his threes in the corner
- Strictly a stationary spot-up shooter, not really able to shoot in other situations
- Lacks the ability to create his own offense, limited as a passer, rarely turns the ball over
- 2022-23 Defensive Degree of Difficulty: 0.331
- 2022-23 Points Prevented: 1.308
- Mostly guarded second unit players, rarely tested on the ball in limited action
- Average on-ball defender, good at closing down air space on the perimeter, tended to commit shooting fouls to bail his man out
- Decent pick-and-roll defender, can effectively switch, tends to go too far under screens
- Sometimes can get caught on screens off the ball, occasionally was late when closing out on spot-up shooters
- Effective weak side shot blocker, does not really get steals, decent defensive rebounder

Lonzo Ball

	Height	Weight	Cap #	Years Left
	6'6"	190	$20.465M	PO

Similar at Age 25

		Season	SIMsc
1	Delon Wright	2017-18	922.4
2	Rudy Fernandez	2010-11	915.7
3	Brent Barry	1996-97	914.7
4	Terrence Ross	2016-17	909.9
5	Danny Green	2012-13	892.9
6	Gabe Vincent	2021-22	892.6
7	Brian Shaw	1991-92	889.8
8	Donte DiVincenzo	2021-22	889.1
9	Willie Anderson	1991-92	884.6
10	Justin Holiday	2014-15	883.4

Baseline Basic Stats

MPG	PTS	AST	REB	BLK	STL
25.0	9.6	2.9	3.3	0.5	1.1

Advanced Metrics

USG%	3PTA/FGA	FTA/FGA	TS%	eFG%	3PT%
18.0	0.602	0.172	0.559	0.532	0.383

AST%	TOV%	OREB%	DREB%	STL%	BLK%
19.9	14.5	3.0	13.1	2.3	1.8

PER	ORTG	DRTG	WS/48	BPM	VOL
14.78	110.8	109.9	0.099	1.49	0.250

- Has not played since January 2022, has not been able to recover from a left knee injury
- Will likely miss the entire 2023-24 season, knee injury may possibly be career-ending
- Effective low volume playmaker and spot-up shooter when healthy
- Dynamic playmaker with plus-level court vision, great at pushing the ball in transition, fairly turnover prone
- Solid three-point shooter, made almost 39% of his threes over his last three healthy seasons
- Mostly a stand-still spot-up shooter, can sometimes make threes if defenders go under screens
- Not really an effective one-on-one scorer, not always able to drive to the rim, solid cutter off the ball
- 2021-22 Defensive Degree of Difficulty: 0.514
- 2021-22 Points Prevented: 0.285
- Used as Chicago's main defensive stopper before the knee injury
- Fairly solid on-ball defender that can guard multiple positions, can be undisciplined with his positioning
- Solid pick-and-roll defender, can functionally switch to guard ball handlers or screeners
- Gambles too much, not always in good position off the ball, does not always get around screens and can be late on his close-outs
- Great roamer off the ball, disruptive presence that consistently posts high steals rate, effective weak side shot blocker, good defensive rebounder

Newcomers

Julian Phillips

	Height	Weight	Cap #	Years Left
	6'8"	198	$1.600M	2 + TO

Baseline Basic Stats

MPG	PTS	AST	REB	BLK	STL
16.0	5.4	1.0	2.7	0.4	0.5

Advanced Metrics

USG%	3PTA/FGA	FTA/FGA	TS%	eFG%	3PT%
15.6	0.294	0.351	0.497	0.448	0.290

AST%	TOV%	OREB%	DREB%	STL%	BLK%
10.3	12.5	5.5	13.0	1.6	2.0

PER	ORTG	DRTG	WS/48	BPM	VOL
11.21	102.3	102.0	0.065	-1.55	N/A

- Drafted by Boston with the 35th overall pick, traded to Washington, traded again to Chicago
- Put together a solidly effective performance at the Las Vegas Summer League
- Efficient in his role as a low usage energy wing
- Posted a True Shooting Percentage of just above 60%, drew fouls at a high rate
- Explosive finisher around the basket, great at running the floor in transition, active offensive rebounder
- Went 4-for-9 (44.4%) on threes, shooting stroke still not consistent, made less than 60% of his free throws
- Generally a stand-still spot-up shooter if his shot is falling
- Needs to improve his ball handling, not able to consistently create his own shot
- Limited playmaking skills, did not record an assist at Summer League, a bit turnover prone
- Long, athletic, very rangy defender, used as a roamer in college, more of a stay-at-home defender at Summer League
- Good weak side shot blocker, can occasionally use his length to get steals, struggled to be an effective presence on the defensive glass
- Fairly solid on-ball defender, good at guarding quicker perimeter players, not as effective against stronger post players
- Solid pick-and-roll defender, effective at getting around screens to contain ball handlers
- Stays attached to shooters off the ball, fights through screens and closes out in spot-up situations
- Likely needs some additional seasoning in the G-League to improve his skills on both ends of the floor

WASHINGTON WIZARDS

Last Season: 35 - 47, Missed the Playoffs

Offensive Rating: 114.4, 22nd in the NBA   Defensive Rating: 115.6, 21st in the NBA

Primary Executive: Michael Winger, President

Head Coach: Wes Unseld Jr.

Key Roster Changes

<u>Subtractions</u>
Bradley Beal, trade
Kristaps Porziņģis, trade
Monte Morris, trade
Jordan Goodwin, trade
Isaiah Todd, trade
Kendrick Nunn, free agency
Taj Gibson, free agency

<u>Additions</u>
Bilal Coulibaly, draft
Tyus Jones, trade
Landry Shamet, trade
Danilo Gallinari, trade
Mike Muscala, trade
Jordan Poole, trade
Patrick Baldwin Jr., trade
Ryan Rollins, trade

Roster

<u>Likely Starting Five</u>
1. *Tyus Jones*
2. *Jordan Poole*
3. *Deni Avdija*
4. *Kyle Kuzma*
5. Daniel Gafford

<u>Other Key Rotation Players</u>
Corey Kispert
Landry Shamet
Danilo Gallinari
Delon Wright
Mike Muscala

* Italics denotes that a player is likely to be on the floor to close games

Remaining Roster

- Bilal Coulibaly
- Anthony Gill
- Patrick Baldwin Jr.
- Johnny Davis
- Ryan Rollins
- Xavier Cooks
- Eugene Omoruyi, 26, 6'7", 244, Oregon (Two-Way)
- Jared Butler, 23, 6'3", 195, Baylor (Two-Way)

SCHREMPF Base Rating: 42.9

Season Preview Survey

- *Are the Wizards contending or rebuilding? Where is this team headed?*

The Wizards traded away Bradley Beal and Kristaps Porzingis in the offseason, so this was a strong signal that they are going back into a rebuilding mode. They are in the early stages of this rebuild because they don't have a definite core player on their current roster. The focus this season will be to accumulate assets and secure a high draft position. They will likely try to flip some of the other veterans that they acquired in their offseason trades, so it's likely that they will bottom out and finish with one of the league's worst records this season.

- *What are the areas of concern for this team heading into this season?*

The Wizards are in the beginning stages of a full scale rebuild, so there aren't too many concerns for the short-term because it's expected that they will be a losing team. The real question that arises is if they were too late to start this process. After all, a generational talent was available in this draft, and they didn't give themselves a real chance to get the top pick. Also, this coming draft doesn't appear to be as strong at the top. Therefore, it's very possible that this rebuilding process could be a long one for Washington. In addition to this, they don't have a lot of players on their roster with great trade value, so they might not get a lot of high-end assets even if they sell off a few veterans near the deadline. In general, their rebuild could be a bigger challenge because of the suspect decision-making of the previous regime.

- *List some possible breakout players for this team.*

Washington shifted a lot of pieces around after they dealt away their star players, but they still kept a few interesting young players that could make significant leaps forward due to an increase in opportunity. In particular, Patrick Baldwin Jr. could a player to watch out for because he flashed an interesting skill set in limited minutes with Golden State. He's a tall combo forward that displayed an ability to knock down threes and make some plays off the ball on defense. With some playing time available, the chance is there for him to tap into some of the potential that he showcased in high school to become a long and versatile wing that contributes on both ends. In addition to Baldwin, their lottery pick, Bilal Coulibaly could emerge as a potential core player if he's able to adjust to the NBA. He didn't have the best showing at Summer League because the event took place right after his season ended in France, so he appeared worn out. If he plays like he did in France, he could give the Wizards a productive complementary player by being an energetic defender, athletic finisher, and occasional floor spacer in a lower usage role.

- *What should we expect from them this season?*

The Wizards are probably going to be one of the worst teams in the NBA this season because they dealt away their two best players in the offseason. They did acquire some productive veterans in those trades, so there is a faint possibility that they could be better than expected if they tap into those players' respective strengths and find a unique style that allows them to punch above their weight. Even so, their focus appears to be on the long-term. This will mean that they will look to sell off some of their more valuable veterans for additional draft capital, and they are likely to prioritize the development of their younger players over winning in the short-term. In all probability, Washington will be looking to secure a high draft position by maintain a spot near the bottom of the standings this season.

Veterans

Kyle Kuzma

	Height	Weight	Cap #	Years Left
	6'10"	221	$25.568M	3

Similar at Age 27

		Season	SIMsc
1	Rashard Lewis	2006-07	926.9
2	Hedo Turkoglu	2006-07	918.7
3	Lamar Odom	2006-07	913.3
4	Keith Van Horn	2002-03	911.4
5	Terry Mills	1994-95	908.5
6	Tobias Harris	2019-20	905.1
7	Mike Miller	2007-08	904.9
8	Rasheed Wallace	2001-02	904.6
9	Pascal Siakam	2021-22	904.1
10	Chris Bosh*	2011-12	902.4

Baseline Basic Stats

MPG	PTS	AST	REB	BLK	STL
32.1	15.7	2.7	6.3	0.6	0.8

Advanced Metrics

USG%	3PTA/FGA	FTA/FGA	TS%	eFG%	3PT%
23.6	0.415	0.245	0.556	0.522	0.355

AST%	TOV%	OREB%	DREB%	STL%	BLK%
15.6	12.8	4.2	18.6	1.0	1.4

PER	ORTG	DRTG	WS/48	BPM	VOL
15.27	107.9	111.6	0.080	0.06	0.206

- Regular starter for Washington in his second season with the team
- Scored at a high volume, moderately efficient as one of Washington's primary scorers
- Break-even career three-point shooter, percentages tend to vary from year-to-year
- Mostly a spot-up shooter, occasionally shoots off screens
- Average pick-and-roll ball handler and isolation player, efficient finisher around the rim, inconsistent shooter off the dribble
- Good cutter off the ball, good secondary playmaker that makes simple reads, good at limiting turnovers
- 2022-23 Defensive Degree of Difficulty: 0.485
- 2022-23 Points Prevented: 1.299
- Drew tougher assignments against top scorers, played middling on-ball defense last season
- Capable multi-position defender in the past, struggled to defend on the perimeter and in the post
- Decent on-ball defender, good at containing ball handler, a step late when rotating onto screeners
- Stays attached to shooters, fights through screens and closes out in spot-up situations
- More of a stay-at-home defender, solid weak side shot blocker in the past, block rate went down last season, good defensive rebounder

Jordan Poole

	Height	Weight	Cap #	Years Left
	6'4"	194	$27.955M	3

Similar at Age 23

		Season	SIMsc
1	Ben Gordon	2006-07	935.0
2	Jordan Crawford	2011-12	932.7
3	Damian Lillard	2013-14	931.0
4	D'Angelo Russell	2019-20	918.4
5	Zach LaVine	2018-19	916.5
6	Rashad McCants	2007-08	913.5
7	Bradley Beal	2016-17	909.7
8	Rex Chapman	1990-91	907.5
9	Randy Foye	2006-07	905.7
10	Isaiah Rider	1994-95	905.5

Baseline Basic Stats

MPG	PTS	AST	REB	BLK	STL
31.3	18.3	3.9	3.6	0.3	0.9

Advanced Metrics

USG%	3PTA/FGA	FTA/FGA	TS%	eFG%	3PT%
26.9	0.485	0.278	0.579	0.528	0.364

AST%	TOV%	OREB%	DREB%	STL%	BLK%
21.0	12.3	1.8	10.4	1.3	0.8

PER	ORTG	DRTG	WS/48	BPM	VOL
16.65	112.1	112.9	0.106	0.20	0.322

- Played starter level minutes for Golden State in his fourth season, appeared in all 82 games
- Effectiveness declined slightly, mainly used as a high usage scoring guard
- Average pick-and-roll ball handler and isolation player, willing to draw fouls, can finish at the rim or hit floaters
- Shot selection is suspect, inconsistent shooter off the dribble, better at spotting up or running off screens
- Break-even three-point shooter, can be rather streaky, percentages vary from year-to-year
- Fairly solid playmaker that makes simple reads, generally avoids turnovers
- 2022-23 Defensive Degree of Difficulty: 0.375
- 2022-23 Points Prevented: -0.447
- Usually hidden in favorable matchups against lower leverage players
- Below average on-ball defender, struggles to stay with opposing guards, can decently hold position against taller players inside
- Below average pick-and-roll defender, effort sometimes was lacking, not effective at taking away any specific action
- Gets caught on screens off the ball, generally closes out on spot-up shooters
- Stay-at-home defender, rarely gets steals or blocks, below average defensive rebounder

Tyus Jones

	Height	Weight	Cap #	Years Left
	6'0"	196	$14.000M	UFA

Similar at Age 26

		Season	SIMsc
1	Earl Watson	2005-06	910.0
2	John Bagley	1986-87	909.9
3	Jameer Nelson	2008-09	909.7
4	Devonte' Graham	2021-22	908.1
5	Dan Dickau	2004-05	906.0
6	Monte Morris	2021-22	903.8
7	Seth Curry	2016-17	903.3
8	Shammond Williams	2001-02	903.2
9	Fred VanVleet	2020-21	896.6
10	D.J. Augustin	2013-14	896.4

Baseline Basic Stats

MPG	PTS	AST	REB	BLK	STL
26.3	10.6	4.5	2.5	0.2	1.0

Advanced Metrics

USG%	3PTA/FGA	FTA/FGA	TS%	eFG%	3PT%
18.4	0.441	0.157	0.532	0.503	0.366

AST%	TOV%	OREB%	DREB%	STL%	BLK%
28.3	10.8	1.5	9.4	2.0	0.4

PER	ORTG	DRTG	WS/48	BPM	VOL
14.94	115.8	111.8	0.117	0.73	0.227

- Played starter level minutes for Memphis, appeared in all but two games last season
- Solidly effective in his role as a low usage, pass-first point guard
- Great ball control guard, rarely turns the ball over, solid playmaker that makes sound decisions
- Around a league average three-point shooter, percentage tend to vary, made 53% of his corner threes last season
- Most effective at making threes in transition, below break-even shooter in half court situations
- Average pick-and-roll ball handler and isolation player, lacks the explosiveness to consistently drive, not really able to create his own shot
- 2022-23 Defensive Degree of Difficulty: 0.323
- 2022-23 Points Prevented: -0.552
- Usually hidden in favorable matchups against lower leverage players or guards second unit players
- Average on-ball defender, can stay with opposing guards, struggles against taller players due to his smallish stature
- Good pick-and-roll defender, funnels his man into help, usually makes sound rotations
- Tends to get caught on screens off the ball, sometimes can be late to close out on spot-up shooters
- Pesky defensive guard that can play passing lanes to get steals, below average defensive rebounder

Daniel Gafford

	Height	Weight	Cap #	Years Left
	6'10"	234	$12.402M	2

Similar at Age 24

		Season	SIMsc
1	Ronny Turiaf	2006-07	915.2
2	Clemon Johnson	1980-81	913.3
3	Ekpe Udoh	2011-12	905.0
4	Ivica Zubac	2021-22	901.9
5	Bison Dele	1993-94	901.2
6	Josh Boone	2008-09	900.9
7	Theo Ratliff	1997-98	900.9
8	Nick Richards	2021-22	898.2
9	Jerome Moiso	2002-03	897.4
10	Duane Causwell	1992-93	896.5

Baseline Basic Stats

MPG	PTS	AST	REB	BLK	STL
22.0	8.4	0.9	6.6	1.3	0.5

Advanced Metrics

USG%	3PTA/FGA	FTA/FGA	TS%	eFG%	3PT%
16.0	0.004	0.431	0.658	0.638	0.111

AST%	TOV%	OREB%	DREB%	STL%	BLK%
6.6	13.4	11.8	20.7	1.1	4.9

PER	ORTG	DRTG	WS/48	BPM	VOL
18.98	126.4	109.9	0.172	0.48	0.231

- Regular rotation player for Washington, started over half of his games
- Maintained his usual level of effectiveness, mainly used as a low volume rim runner
- Athletic big man with great length, vertical lob threat, True Shooting Percentage was almost 74%
- Excellent roll man and cutter, good offensive rebounder, explosive finisher in transition, draws fouls at a high rate
- Good at flashing to the middle on post-ups, not really able to score efficiently with his back to the basket
- Lacks reliable shooting range outside of ten feet, limited as a passer, slightly turnover prone
- 2022-23 Defensive Degree of Difficulty: 0.407
- 2022-23 Points Prevented: 1.037
- Good rim protector, great shot blocker, solid defensive rebounder
- Used as a roamer, below average on-ball defender
- Can be overpowered in the post, tends to commit shooting fouls, struggles to effectively defend in space
- Average pick-and-roll defender, solid at switching out onto ball handlers, has lapses when defending screeners
- Tends to stay anchored in the paint, does not always come out to contest perimeter shots

Deni Avdija

	Height	Weight	Cap #	Years Left
	6'9"	210	$6.263M	RFA

Similar at Age 22

		Season	SIMsc
1	Omri Casspi	2010-11	919.8
2	Hedo Turkoglu	2001-02	917.1
3	Aaron Gordon	2017-18	915.8
4	Mike Dunleavy Jr.	2002-03	915.6
5	Maurice Harkless	2015-16	914.7
6	Jumaine Jones	2001-02	914.1
7	Harrison Barnes	2014-15	911.8
8	Mario Hezonja	2017-18	911.0
9	Otto Porter Jr.	2015-16	910.9
10	Cedi Osman	2017-18	910.4

Baseline Basic Stats

MPG	PTS	AST	REB	BLK	STL
27.1	10.7	1.9	4.7	0.5	0.9

Advanced Metrics

USG%	3PTA/FGA	FTA/FGA	TS%	eFG%	3PT%
17.7	0.392	0.239	0.540	0.506	0.336

AST%	TOV%	OREB%	DREB%	STL%	BLK%
12.3	12.7	3.8	17.8	1.6	1.4

PER	ORTG	DRTG	WS/48	BPM	VOL
12.65	106.9	110.8	0.078	-1.01	0.376

- Regular starter for Washington in his third NBA season
- Production level held steady in his role as a low volume spot-up shooter
- Below break-even three-point shooter, made less than 30% of his threes last season
- Struggled to make outside shots in a half-court set, better when taking threes in transition
- Solid secondary playmaker with improving court vision, slightly turnover prone
- Decent finisher off cuts and transition, defenders can back off him to limit his effectiveness in ball handling situations
- 2022-23 Defensive Degree of Difficulty: 0.523
- 2022-23 Points Prevented: 0.022
- Frequently used by Washington as a defensive stopper, slightly over-matched
- High effort defender, capable of guarding multiple positions, has some struggles due to a lack of quickness and strength
- Average pick-and-roll defender, can functionally switch, tends to back off or go too far under screens
- Fights through screens off the ball, sometimes will be late when closing out on spot-up shooters
- Steal Percentage increased, more of a stay-at-home defender, block rate decreased, good defensive rebounder

Corey Kispert

	Height	Weight	Cap #	Years Left
	6'7"	220	$3.722M	TO

Similar at Age 23

		Season	SIMsc
1	Tony Snell	2014-15	918.1
2	Chase Budinger	2011-12	913.4
3	Justin Jackson	2018-19	911.5
4	Allen Crabbe	2015-16	911.4
5	Cameron Reynolds	2018-19	907.8
6	Martell Webster	2009-10	906.2
7	Glenn Robinson III	2016-17	904.8
8	Harrison Barnes	2015-16	903.4
9	Cameron Johnson	2019-20	903.0
10	Jeff Taylor	2012-13	900.3

Baseline Basic Stats

MPG	PTS	AST	REB	BLK	STL
25.9	10.7	1.5	3.3	0.2	0.6

Advanced Metrics

USG%	3PTA/FGA	FTA/FGA	TS%	eFG%	3PT%
17.0	0.601	0.176	0.596	0.568	0.391

AST%	TOV%	OREB%	DREB%	STL%	BLK%
8.2	8.6	2.3	10.5	1.0	0.7

PER	ORTG	DRTG	WS/48	BPM	VOL
12.16	115.6	116.1	0.083	-1.29	0.443

- Played starter level minutes for Washington in his second NBA season
- Increased his efficiency in a role as a low usage shooting specialist
- Great three-point shooter, made over 42% of his threes last season, excellent in the corners
- Predominantly a stationary spot-up shooter, above average when shooting on the move
- Needs a screen to get to the rim, not really an isolation player, effective as a pick-and-roll ball handler
- Effective cutter, good at scoring on hand-offs and in transition
- Strictly a catch-and-shoot player, only makes safe passes, rarely turns the ball over
- 2022-23 Defensive Degree of Difficulty: 0.387
- 2022-23 Points Prevented: -0.966
- Usually guards second unit player or is hidden in favorable matchups against lower leverage players
- Played decent on-ball defense, solid against lower leverage perimeter players, struggled to guard stronger players inside
- Below average pick-and-roll defender, not especially effective at taking away any specific action
- Tends to get caught on screens, not always in position to contest shots in spot-up situations
- Stay-at-home defender, rarely gets steals or blocks, below average defensive rebounder

Landry Shamet

	Height	Weight	Cap #	Years Left
	6'4"	190	$10.250M	1 + TO

Similar at Age 25

		Season	SIMsc
1	Grayson Allen	2020-21	947.5
2	Troy Daniels	2016-17	935.2
3	J.J. Redick	2009-10	932.7
4	Tyler Johnson	2017-18	931.2
5	Luther Head	2007-08	930.5
6	Wayne Ellington	2012-13	927.9
7	Damon Jones	2001-02	926.5
8	Lucious Harris	1995-96	924.4
9	Malik Beasley	2021-22	924.4
10	Matt Thomas	2019-20	924.1

Baseline Basic Stats

MPG	PTS	AST	REB	BLK	STL
21.1	8.5	1.9	2.1	0.1	0.6

Advanced Metrics

USG%	3PTA/FGA	FTA/FGA	TS%	eFG%	3PT%
17.4	0.647	0.171	0.557	0.527	0.380

AST%	TOV%	OREB%	DREB%	STL%	BLK%
14.1	9.8	1.5	8.5	1.4	0.5

PER	ORTG	DRTG	WS/48	BPM	VOL
11.47	112.3	113.9	0.084	-0.97	0.343

- Out for two months with a foot injury, regular rotation player for Phoenix when healthy
- Production held steady in a role as a low usage shooting specialist
- Solid three-point shooter in his career, has made 43.5% of his career corner threes
- Great spot-up shooter, can knock down threes if defenders go under screens, average at shooting off screens
- Not able to drive by defenders on isolations, better with a screen as a pick-and-roll ball handler
- Catch-and-shoot player for most of his career, Assist Percentage spiked, rarely turns the ball over
- 2022-23 Defensive Degree of Difficulty: 0.397
- 2022-23 Points Prevented: 0.238
- Usually guarded second unit players or lower leverage starters, solid on-ball defender in these matchups
- Capably defends both guard spots, not quite good enough to draw tougher assignments
- Played solid pick-and-roll defense, effectively contained ball handlers or funneled them into help, limited ability to switch
- Fights through screens off the ball, tends to late when closing out on spot-up shooters
- More active as a help defender, Steal Percentage increased to a career high, below average defensive rebounder

Danilo Gallinari

	Height	Weight	Cap #	Years Left
	6'10"	233	$6.803M	UFA

Similar at Age 34

		Season	SIMsc
1	Jeff Green	2020-21	912.5
2	Mike Dunleavy Jr.	2014-15	905.6
3	Sam Perkins	1995-96	904.8
4	Matt Bonner	2014-15	897.7
5	Danny Ferry	2000-01	894.3
6	Derrick Coleman	2001-02	892.9
7	Dirk Nowitzki*	2012-13	890.4
8	Chuck Person	1998-99	889.7
9	Rasheed Wallace	2008-09	886.2
10	Richard Jefferson	2014-15	880.1

Baseline Basic Stats

MPG	PTS	AST	REB	BLK	STL
21.9	9.2	1.2	3.3	0.3	0.5

Advanced Metrics

USG%	3PTA/FGA	FTA/FGA	TS%	eFG%	3PT%
17.1	0.486	0.302	0.593	0.541	0.385

AST%	TOV%	OREB%	DREB%	STL%	BLK%
8.2	7.8	2.5	16.1	1.0	1.1

PER	ORTG	DRTG	WS/48	BPM	VOL
13.90	119.4	113.8	0.117	-0.35	0.398

- Missed the entire 2022-23 season due to a torn ACL in his left knee, did not play for Boston
- Used as a lower volume shooting specialist in his last healthy season
- Reliable three-point shooter, career Three-Point Percentage is just above 38%
- Mostly a spot-up shooter in 2021-22, good screener on pick-and-pops
- Can post up smaller players, effective at driving by slower big men on isolation plays
- Losing a step due to age and his past injury history, not really able to take on higher usage
- Good cutter off the ball, catch-and-shoot player now, willing to make the extra pass, rarely turns the ball over
- 2021-22 Defensive Degree of Difficulty: 0.345
- 2021-22 Points Prevented: -0.598
- Usually guarded second unit players or lower leverage starters, solid on-ball defender in these matchups
- Competently defended both forward positions, could play angles to compensate for diminishing athleticism
- Decent pick-and-roll defender, can functionally switch, sometimes allows ball handlers to penetrate into the lane
- Gets caught on screens off the ball, tends to be late when closing out on spot-up shooters
- Stay-at-home defender, does not really get steals or blocks, solid defensive rebounder

Delon Wright

	Height	Weight	Cap #	Years Left
	6'5"	185	$8.195M	UFA

Similar at Age 30

		Season	SIMsc
1	Garrett Temple	2016-17	906.3
2	Don Buse	1980-81	904.4
3	Larry Hughes	2008-09	900.2
4	Jon Barry	1999-00	898.8
5	Doc Rivers	1991-92	889.8
6	Mike Gale	1980-81	889.3
7	Hubert Davis	2000-01	888.0
8	Derek Anderson	2004-05	887.7
9	Dudley Bradley	1987-88	885.2
10	Trent Tucker	1989-90	884.7

Baseline Basic Stats

MPG	PTS	AST	REB	BLK	STL
24.3	7.7	3.2	2.9	0.3	1.2

Advanced Metrics

USG%	3PTA/FGA	FTA/FGA	TS%	eFG%	3PT%
13.5	0.372	0.215	0.555	0.519	0.339

AST%	TOV%	OREB%	DREB%	STL%	BLK%
19.5	13.1	3.8	11.4	2.9	1.2

PER	ORTG	DRTG	WS/48	BPM	VOL
14.39	118.9	108.3	0.128	2.53	0.312

- Missed games due to a hamstring strain, regular rotation player for Washington when healthy
- Increased his effectiveness in a role as a low usage secondary playmaker and spot-up shooter
- Good playmaker that makes sound reads, good at pushing the ball in transition, generally avoids turnovers
- Above break-even three-point shooter, percentages tend to vary from year-to-year
- Solid spot-up shooter, a bit inconsistent when shooting off the dribble
- Effective pick-and-roll ball handler and isolation player, can change speeds to get to the rim, lacks the quickness to create his own shot regularly
- 2022-23 Defensive Degree of Difficulty: 0.480
- 2022-23 Points Prevented: -0.368
- Drew a lot of tough assignments against elite scoring guards off the bench
- Fairly solid on-ball defender, quick enough to stay with opposing guards, had trouble guarding taller wings
- Solid pick-and-roll defender, effective at switching to guard ball handlers and screeners
- Stays attached to shooters off the ball, fights through screens and closes out in spot-up situations
- Highly active help defender, disruptive in the passing lanes, posts very high steal rates, fairly solid defensive rebounder

Mike Muscala

	Height	Weight	Cap #	Years Left
	6'10"	240	$3.500M	UFA

Similar at Age 31

		Season	SIMsc
1	Jonas Jerebko	2018-19	914.4
2	Matt Bonner	2011-12	907.1
3	Patrick Patterson	2020-21	904.4
4	Markieff Morris	2020-21	903.3
5	Brad Lohaus	1995-96	903.0
6	Vladimir Radmanovic	2011-12	902.5
7	Anthony Tolliver	2016-17	897.6
8	Nemanja Bjelica	2019-20	896.0
9	Mirza Teletovic	2016-17	894.6
10	Ersan Ilyasova	2018-19	889.6

Baseline Basic Stats

MPG	PTS	AST	REB	BLK	STL
17.0	6.2	1.0	3.2	0.4	0.3

Advanced Metrics

USG%	3PTA/FGA	FTA/FGA	TS%	eFG%	3PT%
15.9	0.642	0.172	0.601	0.577	0.398

AST%	TOV%	OREB%	DREB%	STL%	BLK%
7.6	7.6	4.0	17.3	0.9	2.3

PER	ORTG	DRTG	WS/48	BPM	VOL
13.78	120.4	111.7	0.125	0.48	0.385

- Traded from Oklahoma City to Boston, fringe rotation player for both teams
- Production level dropped slightly, mainly used as a low usage stretch big
- Fairly reliable three-point shooter, has made almost 40% of his career corner threes
- Mostly a spot-up shooter with both teams, effective pick-and-pop screener with Oklahoma City
- Rarely shoots around the basket, used less frequently as a rim runner due to declining athleticism
- Strictly a catch-and-shoot big man, not a post-up threat, only makes safe passes, rarely turns the ball over
- 2022-23 Defensive Degree of Difficulty: 0.411
- 2022-23 Points Prevented: 0.330
- Average rim protector, can challenge shots but blocks rate is declining, fairly solid defensive rebounder
- Guarded starting level big men, stout post defender, plays angles well but lacks the quickness to consistently defend in space
- Average pick-and-roll defender, effective when hedging out on ball handlers, a step slow when covering screeners
- Tended to stay anchored in the paint, did not always close out on spot-up shooters

Anthony Gill

	Height	Weight	Cap #	Years Left
	6'7"	230	$1.997M	UFA

Similar at Age 30

		Season	SIMsc
1	David Wood	1994-95	902.4
2	Lance Thomas	2018-19	894.4
3	Kermit Washington	1981-82	892.1
4	Brandon Bass	2015-16	890.1
5	Matt Barnes	2010-11	889.6
6	Kenny Gattison	1994-95	888.0
7	Major Jones	1983-84	885.7
8	Darvin Ham	2003-04	885.4
9	Quincy Pondexter	2018-19	885.3
10	Ed Nealy	1990-91	884.0

Baseline Basic Stats

MPG	PTS	AST	REB	BLK	STL
15.2	4.9	0.8	2.7	0.3	0.4

Advanced Metrics

USG%	3PTA/FGA	FTA/FGA	TS%	eFG%	3PT%
14.4	0.299	0.353	0.579	0.542	0.336

AST%	TOV%	OREB%	DREB%	STL%	BLK%
7.5	10.7	6.3	12.3	0.9	1.3

PER	ORTG	DRTG	WS/48	BPM	VOL
11.62	117.3	114.6	0.091	-3.19	0.516

- Played limited minutes for Washington in his third NBA season
- Slightly less effective in a role as low usage energy player and spot-up shooter
- More effective as an energy player that scores on hustle plays, made 78% of his shots inside of three feet
- Great cutter off the ball, active offensive rebounder, very good at running the floor in transition
- Below break-even three-point shooter but percentages cratered, really struggled to make spot-up jumpers
- Not really able to create his own shot, strictly a catch-and-shoot player, limited passing skills, rarely turns the ball over
- 2022-23 Defensive Degree of Difficulty: 0.406
- 2022-23 Points Prevented: -1.832
- Usually guarded second unit players, drew a few tough assignments off the bench, average on-ball defender
- Plays angles well to compensate for middling athleticism, solid on the perimeter, struggled against bigger post players, prone to committing shooting fouls
- Average pick-and-roll defender, can functionally switch, has some trouble containing ball handlers on the perimeter
- Gets caught on screens off the ball, usually was late when closing out on spot-up shooters
- Does not really get steals, decently effective weak side shot blocker, fairly solid defensive rebounder

Patrick Baldwin Jr.

	Height	Weight	Cap #	Years Left
	6'9"	220	$2.338M	2 TO

Similar at Age 20

		Season	SIMsc
1	Jalen Johnson	2021-22	907.5
2	Ziaire Williams	2021-22	867.6
3	Deni Avdija	2020-21	866.6
4	Džanan Musa	2019-20	865.1
5	Rodions Kurucs	2018-19	863.4
6	Danilo Gallinari	2008-09	860.4
7	Antonis Fotsis	2001-02	859.2
8	Wilson Chandler	2007-08	858.8
9	Zeke Nnaji	2020-21	857.8
10	Tobias Harris	2012-13	855.3

Baseline Basic Stats

MPG	PTS	AST	REB	BLK	STL
21.0	9.0	1.2	3.7	0.4	0.5

Advanced Metrics

USG%	3PTA/FGA	FTA/FGA	TS%	eFG%	3PT%
21.0	0.655	0.151	0.577	0.559	0.390

AST%	TOV%	OREB%	DREB%	STL%	BLK%
8.5	9.1	2.1	16.3	1.3	1.5

PER	ORTG	DRTG	WS/48	BPM	VOL
13.58	110.4	113.2	0.081	-0.52	0.483

- Split time between Golden State and Santa Cruz in the G-League, played sparingly at the NBA level
- Generally used as a moderate to low usage spot-up shooter at both levels
- Made over 38% of his NBA threes, just above break-even three-point shooter in the G-League
- Predominantly a stand-still spot-up shooter, flashed some ability to shoot on the move
- Fairly good athlete, has some trouble finishing in traffic due to his thin frame, middling effectiveness as a rim runner
- Not used in ball handling situations in the NBA, mostly a catch-and-shoot player, rarely turns the ball over
- <u>2022-23 Defensive Degree of Difficulty</u>: 0.275
- <u>2022-23 Points Prevented</u>: -0.944
- Mostly guarded second unit players or played in garbage time, rarely tested on the ball
- Struggled to play effective on-ball defense in a small sample of possessions
- Decent pick-and-roll defender, can functionally switch, solid at cutting off penetration, tends to go too far under screens
- Tends to get caught on screens, good at closing out on spot-up shooters
- Decently effective weak side shot blocker, does not really get steals, fairly good defensive rebounder

Johnny Davis

	Height	Weight	Cap #	Years Left
	6'5"	196	$5.051M	2 TO

Similar at Age 20

		Season	SIMsc
1	CJ Elleby	2020-21	914.5
2	Daequan Cook	2007-08	910.6
3	Jarrett Culver	2019-20	907.1
4	Malik Beasley	2016-17	905.3
5	Rashad Vaughn	2016-17	904.7
6	Gary Trent	2018-19	901.4
7	Frank Ntilikina	2018-19	898.4
8	Hamidou Diallo	2018-19	897.9
9	Markelle Fultz	2018-19	896.9
10	Brandon Boston Jr.	2021-22	896.7

Baseline Basic Stats

MPG	PTS	AST	REB	BLK	STL
18.3	7.5	1.1	2.2	0.2	0.5

Advanced Metrics

USG%	3PTA/FGA	FTA/FGA	TS%	eFG%	3PT%
19.3	0.527	0.144	0.521	0.506	0.345

AST%	TOV%	OREB%	DREB%	STL%	BLK%
8.8	8.5	2.3	11.8	1.4	1.1

PER	ORTG	DRTG	WS/48	BPM	VOL
10.41	104.7	114.7	0.040	-3.31	0.306

- Split time between Washington and Capital City in the G-League, played limited minutes in the NBA
- Struggled with his efficiency in the NBA as a moderate volume spot-up shooter
- Made less than 25% of his NBA threes, below break-even three-point shooter in the G-League
- Mostly a stand-still spot-up shooter, not especially effective when shooting in any situation
- Defenders could back off him to limit his effectiveness as a pick-and-roll ball handler and isolation player
- Showed some ability to curl off screens to make mid-range shots
- Largely a catch-and-shoot player, showed some playmaking skills in the G-League, rarely turns the ball over
- 2022-23 Defensive Degree of Difficulty: 0.339
- 2022-23 Points Prevented: 0.441
- Typically guarded second unit players, rarely tested on the ball in limited minutes
- Fairly effective as a perimeter defender in isolation situations, had some trouble with bigger wings inside
- Below average pick-and-roll defender, not effective at taking away any specific action
- Stays attached to shooters off the ball, fights through screens and closes out in spot-up situations
- Did not really get steals at the NBA level, occasionally blocks shots on the weak side, fairly solid defensive rebounder

Ryan Rollins

	Height	Weight	Cap #	Years Left
	6'4"	180	$1.720M	1

Similar at Age 20

		Season	SIMsc
1	Jeremy Lamb	2012-13	879.4
2	Théo Maledon	2021-22	840.3
3	Dejounte Murray	2016-17	837.8
4	Archie Goodwin	2014-15	825.6
5	Cole Anthony	2020-21	821.7
6	Jaylen Nowell	2019-20	817.4
7	Kevin Porter Jr.	2020-21	814.3
8	R.J. Hampton	2021-22	811.9
9	Jalen Suggs	2021-22	810.2
10	Tre Mann	2021-22	808.8

Baseline Basic Stats

MPG	PTS	AST	REB	BLK	STL
20.8	8.6	2.5	2.9	0.2	0.7

Advanced Metrics

USG%	3PTA/FGA	FTA/FGA	TS%	eFG%	3PT%
22.6	0.444	0.233	0.531	0.479	0.368

AST%	TOV%	OREB%	DREB%	STL%	BLK%
16.0	25.7	3.8	14.4	1.5	1.1

PER	ORTG	DRTG	WS/48	BPM	VOL
7.08	91.1	112.9	-0.064	-6.16	0.654

- Split time between Golden State and Santa Cruz in the G-League, only played 62 NBA minutes
- Used as a high volume ball handler whenever he was on the floor at both levels, over-extended in this role in the NBA
- Break-even three-point shooter, strictly a stand-still spot-up shooter, did not really move off the ball
- Lacks the ball handling skills to drive all the way to the rim, inconsistent shooter off the dribble, struggled to create his own shot at the NBA level
- Decent secondary playmaker, can only make simple reads, highly turnover prone in the NBA
- 2022-23 Defensive Degree of Difficulty: 0.228
- 2022-23 Points Prevented: 1.363
- Tended to play in garbage time or guard second unit players, rarely played meaningful NBA minutes
- Rarely tested on the ball, effective perimeter defender in a very small sample of possessions, had trouble against taller players
- Played below average pick-and-roll defense, had trouble preventing ball handlers from turning the corner
- Tended to get caught on screens, fairly good at closing out on spot-up shooters
- Posted fairly high Steal Percentages in the G-League, occasionally could block shots on the weak side, solid defensive rebounder

Xavier Cooks

	Height	Weight	Cap #	Years Left
	6'8"	183	$1.720M	1 + TO

Similar at Age 27

		Season	SIMsc
1	Jeremy Evans	2014-15	879.9
2	Josh Childress	2010-11	872.3
3	Alvin Scott	1982-83	868.2
4	Ed Pinckney	1990-91	862.3
5	Bo Outlaw	1998-99	859.4
6	Renaldo Balkman	2011-12	857.8
7	Marvin Barnes	1979-80	850.7
8	Charles A. Jones	1988-89	844.4
9	Eric Fernsten	1980-81	844.0
10	Gus Gerard	1980-81	843.3

Baseline Basic Stats

MPG	PTS	AST	REB	BLK	STL
18.5	5.5	1.1	4.6	0.7	0.7

Advanced Metrics

USG%	3PTA/FGA	FTA/FGA	TS%	eFG%	3PT%
13.3	0.032	0.354	0.578	0.566	0.119

AST%	TOV%	OREB%	DREB%	STL%	BLK%
7.6	18.0	12.2	18.5	1.9	2.3

PER	ORTG	DRTG	WS/48	BPM	VOL
13.99	114.0	109.2	0.105	-1.04	0.773

- Played for the Sydney Kings in Australian NBL, signed late in the season by Washington
- Named NBL MVP in 2022-23, used as a low volume energy player in the NBA
- Athletic finisher, very effective at scoring around the rim on hustle plays, made almost 61% of his field goals
- Great roll man and cutter, excellent offensive rebounder, plays with high energy, great in transition
- Not really a threat to make outside shots, made less than 30% of his threes in Australia, struggles to make free throws
- Defenders can back off him to limit his effectiveness in ball handling situations
- Fairly good passer in Australia, somewhat turnover prone in the NBA
- 2022-23 Defensive Degree of Difficulty: 0.308
- 2022-23 Points Prevented: -1.849
- Used as a roamer against second unit players, very rarely tested on the ball
- Not especially effective at guarding perimeter or post players at the NBA level in very limited action
- Solid at guarding pick-and-rolls, effective at switching to guard ball handlers or screeners
- Tended to get caught on screens, good at closing out on spot-up shooters
- Very active help defender, great at using his length to get steals, good weak side shot blocker, fairly good defensive rebounder

Newcomers

Bilal Coulibaly

	Height	Weight	Cap #	Years Left
	6'6"	230	$6.614M	1 + 2 TO

Baseline Basic Stats

MPG	PTS	AST	REB	BLK	STL
15.0	4.8	0.9	2.1	0.2	0.5

Advanced Metrics

USG%	3PTA/FGA	FTA/FGA	TS%	eFG%	3PT%
13.4	0.383	0.255	0.523	0.501	0.308

AST%	TOV%	OREB%	DREB%	STL%	BLK%
9.4	13.9	3.6	10.5	1.6	0.8

PER	ORTG	DRTG	WS/48	BPM	VOL
9.62	99.1	103.7	0.055	-0.27	0.325

- Drafted by Indiana with the 7th overall pick in 2023, traded to Washington
- Struggled to play effectively at the Las Vegas Summer League
- Season with Metropolitans 92 had just ended, fatigue may have negatively impacted his performance
- Inconsistent in his role as a low volume energy player and spot-up shooter
- Posted a True Shooting Percentage under 50%, made less than 20% of his threes
- Able to make wide open spot-up threes in France, stroke still inconsistent, made less than 60% of his free throws
- Excellent athlete, explosive finisher in traffic, vertical lob threat that can finish at the rim on rolls and cuts
- Ball handling still needs improvement, not yet able to consistently create his own shot
- Somewhat turnover prone, willing to make the extra pass
- Has ideal physical tools on defense, great length and athleticism could allow him to be a versatile defender in the future
- Demonstrated an ability to defend multiple positions in France and at Summer League
- Solid pick-and-roll defender, could effectively switch to guard ball handlers and screeners
- Generally stayed attached to shooters off the ball, fought through screens and closed out in spot-up situations
- Had a tendency to make bad gambles, can get caught out of position
- Great at using his length to get steals in France, excellent weak side shot blocker at Summer League, decent defensive rebounder
- Could benefit from some additional seasoning in the G-League to improve his skills on both ends

ORLANDO MAGIC

Last Season: 34 - 48, Missed the Playoffs

Offensive Rating: 111.6, 26th in the NBA   Defensive Rating: 114.2, 16th in the NBA

Primary Executive: Jeff Weltman, President of Basketball Operations

Head Coach: Jamahl Mosley

Key Roster Changes

Subtractions
Admiral Schofield, free agency*
Michael Carter-Williams, free agency
Bol Bol, waived

Additions
Anthony Black, draft
Jett Howard, draft
Joe Ingles, free agency

* Orlando let Schofield go then re-signed him to a Two-Way contract

Roster

Likely Starting Five
1. *Markelle Fultz*
2. *Gary Harris*
3. *Franz Wagner*
4. *Paolo Banchero*
5. *Wendell Carter Jr.*

Other Key Rotation Players
Cole Anthony
Jalen Suggs
Moritz Wagner
Joe Ingles
Anthony Black

* Italics denotes that a player is likely to be on the floor to close games

Remaining Roster

- Jett Howard
- Caleb Houstan
- Chuma Okeke
- Goga Bitadze
- Jonathan Isaac
- Kevon Harris, 26, 6'6", 216, Stephen F. Austin (Two-Way)
- Admiral Schofield, 26, 6'5", 241, Tennessee (Two-Way)
- Trevelin Queen, 26, 6'6", 190 New Mexico State (Exhibit 10)
- Mac McClung, 25, 6'2", 185, Texas Tech (Exhibit 10)

SCHREMPF Base Rating: 40.4

Season Preview Survey

- *Are the Magic contending or rebuilding? Where is this team headed?*

The Magic appear as if they are moving into a different phase because they seem to have a promising core group in place with the forward combination of Paolo Banchero and Franz Wagner. They also have solid young players that they can plug into supporting roles, and they were much more competitive in the second half of last season. The goal this season will be to see if they build on what they did in those finals months to become a much more competitive team. They still aren't really a polished group, so it's not likely that they will be a play-in team. However, they could get themselves within shouting range to become an exciting, young team that has considerable potential to grow in the coming years.

- *What are the areas of concern for this team heading into this season?*

Even though they have an athletic team that plays at a high tempo, they really struggled to score efficiently last season. Banchero showed that he can score in volume, but his shot-making abilities aren't fully developed enough to make him a reliable primary scorer in the league. On top of this, they don't have many consistent outside threats in their rotation, which cramps their spacing. As a result, their half-court offense tends to grind to a halt for long stretches of time. They will need some internal growth from their young players in the shooting department to give themselves better ways to threaten defenses and generate higher quality shots. Otherwise, it will be much tougher for them to keep pace with the more potent offensive teams in the league on a nightly basis.

- *List some possible breakout players for this team.*

Orlando is fielding a very young team with a lot of players that are still in the development phases of their careers. There are plenty of candidates that could break out and improve to reach another level this season. To start off, Paolo Banchero and Franz Wagner could step up their game to emerge as potential All-Star level performers with another year of experience under their belt. Also, Jalen Suggs could take a big step forward and settle into a consistent role, now that the Magic's pecking order is more established. He doesn't quite fit as a primary scoring, lead ball handler. However, he's flashed strong defensive skills as well as the ability to set up others and make stationary spot-up jumpers. If he sticks to his strengths, he could add value to the team as a defender and connecting role player this season. In addition to these players, Orlando has a couple of promising lottery picks in the form of Anthony Black and Jett Howard. Both can come into make positive contributions as rookies. Black has the ability to be an athletic, ball-hawking defender and a tall playmaker while Howard can affect the game in different ways by guarding multiple positions on defense and providing some supplementary scoring on offense.

- *What should we expect from them this season?*

Orlando is in an interesting position because they aren't quite good enough to be a viable playoff contender, but they are further along in their rebuilding process. Their focus should shift from developing individual talent to building a more cohesive unit that can compete and win games. They have the ability to be a plucky team that could surprise opponents if they don't give full effort, so they could increase their win total a bit. However, they still are a work-in-progress, and their team isn't a fully polished product, so there will be some struggles as they transition into being a team that tries to contend in the future. They are close to being a consistently competitive team, but they are not all the way there yet. It's likely that they miss the playoffs once again, but they will be a much more promising and exciting unit this coming season.

Veterans

Paolo Banchero

	Height	Weight	Cap #	Years Left
	6'10"	250	$11.608M	2 TO

Similar at Age 20

		Season	SIMsc
1	Michael Beasley	2008-09	894.4
2	Carmelo Anthony	2004-05	890.0
3	Derrick Williams	2011-12	886.3
4	Shareef Abdur-Rahim	1996-97	882.9
5	Amare Stoudemire	2002-03	880.9
6	Lamar Odom	1999-00	878.7
7	Tim Thomas	1997-98	874.4
8	Chris Bosh*	2004-05	874.3
9	Kevin Durant	2008-09	873.3
10	Franz Wagner	2021-22	872.3

Baseline Basic Stats

MPG	PTS	AST	REB	BLK	STL
33.1	19.5	2.8	7.7	0.7	0.9

Advanced Metrics

USG%	3PTA/FGA	FTA/FGA	TS%	eFG%	3PT%
28.0	0.205	0.415	0.550	0.494	0.334

AST%	TOV%	OREB%	DREB%	STL%	BLK%
16.4	12.0	4.9	18.0	1.2	1.3

PER	ORTG	DRTG	WS/48	BPM	VOL
18.04	108.8	110.5	0.103	0.59	0.316

- Made the All-Rookie 1st Team, named Rookie of the Year in 2022-23
- Had a productive rookie season as Orlando's primary scoring option, scored a lot in volume
- Average efficiency as a pick-and-roll ball handler and isolation player, good at drawing fouls and attacking the rim, inconsistent shooter off the dribble
- Made less than 30% of his threes, above break-even in the corners
- Good at posting up smaller players, explosive finisher in transition, solid cutter off the ball
- Good secondary playmaker that finds open teammates, consistently limits turnovers
- 2022-23 Defensive Degree of Difficulty: 0.455
- 2022-23 Points Prevented: 0.270
- Mostly guarded starting level players, played solid on-ball defense
- Strong enough to hold position in the post, good quickness to stay with opposing perimeter players
- Decent pick-and-roll defender, good at containing ball handlers, struggled to effectively rotate onto screeners
- Tends to get caught on screens off the ball, consistently closes out on spot-up shooters
- Generally a stay-at-home defender, occasionally blocks shots from the weak side, fairly good defensive rebounder

Franz Wagner

	Height	Weight	Cap #	Years Left
	6'9"	225	$5.509M	TO

Similar at Age 21

		Season	SIMsc
1	Aaron Gordon	2016-17	946.7
2	Mike Miller	2001-02	937.9
3	Joe Johnson	2002-03	935.2
4	Omri Casspi	2009-10	935.0
5	Rudy Gay	2007-08	926.4
6	Wilson Chandler	2008-09	923.5
7	Jaylen Brown	2017-18	921.8
8	Danilo Gallinari	2009-10	921.6
9	Rashard Lewis	2000-01	911.5
10	Luol Deng	2006-07	910.0

Baseline Basic Stats

MPG	PTS	AST	REB	BLK	STL
33.2	16.0	2.5	5.4	0.5	1.0

Advanced Metrics

USG%	3PTA/FGA	FTA/FGA	TS%	eFG%	3PT%
21.3	0.222	0.270	0.557	0.513	0.352

AST%	TOV%	OREB%	DREB%	STL%	BLK%
14.8	11.2	3.8	12.0	1.5	0.9

PER	ORTG	DRTG	WS/48	BPM	VOL
14.83	111.0	112.2	0.097	0.25	0.256

- Started all but two games for Orlando in his second NBA season
- Increased his efficiency, took on slightly more usage in his role as a moderate volume scoring wing
- Effective as a pick-and-roll ball handler, can get to the rim and make pull-up jumpers, less effective on isolation plays
- League average three-point shooter, made 48% of his transition threes
- Mainly a spot-up shooter in the half court, inconsistent when shooting threes off the dribble
- Can curl off screens to make mid-range shots, good cutter, athletic finisher in transition
- Great secondary playmaker that makes sound reads, good at avoiding turnovers
- 2022-23 Defensive Degree of Difficulty: 0.477
- 2022-23 Points Prevented: -0.746
- Drew a lot of difficult assignments against starting level players
- Good on-ball defender, effectively guards multiple positions
- Fairly solid pick-and-roll defender, good at containing ball handler, effective at switching, has lapses when defending screeners
- Fights through screens off the ball, sometimes can be late when closing out on spot-up shooters
- Stay-at-home defender, gets steals at a moderate rate, blocks rate declined, fairly solid defensive rebounder

Wendell Carter Jr.

	Height	Weight	Cap #	Years Left
	6'10"	270	$13.050M	2

Similar at Age 23

		Season	SIMsc
1	Victor Alexander	1992-93	914.7
2	Noah Vonleh	2018-19	902.5
3	Mehmet Okur	2002-03	898.1
4	Deandre Ayton	2021-22	896.6
5	Byron Mullens	2012-13	895.1
6	Enes Freedom	2015-16	894.5
7	Jahlil Okafor	2018-19	889.0
8	Jared Sullinger	2015-16	887.4
9	Carlos Boozer	2004-05	886.6
10	Vitaly Potapenko	1998-99	885.3

Baseline Basic Stats

MPG	PTS	AST	REB	BLK	STL
24.1	11.9	1.4	7.4	0.5	0.6

Advanced Metrics

USG%	3PTA/FGA	FTA/FGA	TS%	eFG%	3PT%
21.7	0.271	0.306	0.591	0.557	0.339

AST%	TOV%	OREB%	DREB%	STL%	BLK%
11.4	12.2	9.2	25.4	1.1	1.8

PER	ORTG	DRTG	WS/48	BPM	VOL
18.49	115.9	109.3	0.148	0.63	0.514

- Missed games due to injuries to his foot and hip, regular starting center for Orlando when healthy
- Maintained his effectiveness in a role as a moderate volume stretch big and rim runner
- Around a league average three-point shooter last season, below break-even for his career
- Most effective as a stand-still spot-up shooter, less effective as a pick-and-pop screener
- High energy rim runner, good cutter and roll man, active offensive rebounder
- Slightly below average as a post-up player, good passing big man that hits cutters around the rim, good at avoiding turnovers
- 2022-23 Defensive Degree of Difficulty: 0.513
- 2022-23 Points Prevented: -1.421
- Very good rim protector despite declining block rates, stays vertical to contest shots, good defensive rebounder
- Takes on tough assignments against elite big men, stout post defender, has trouble defending in space
- Below average effectiveness as a pick-and-roll defender, struggled to make sound rotations in general
- Tended to stay anchored in the paint, did not always come out to contest perimeter shots

Markelle Fultz

	Height	Weight	Cap #	Years Left
	6'3"	209	$17.000M	UFA

Similar at Age 24

		Season	SIMsc
1	Kris Dunn	2018-19	929.8
2	Randy Livingston	1999-00	921.7
3	Jrue Holiday	2014-15	921.7
4	Reggie Jackson	2014-15	919.2
5	Carlos Arroyo	2003-04	912.6
6	Anthony Peeler	1993-94	906.8
7	Erick Strickland	1997-98	903.1
8	Jerryd Bayless	2012-13	901.5
9	Marcus Banks	2005-06	899.1
10	Billy Ray Bates	1980-81	898.4

Baseline Basic Stats

MPG	PTS	AST	REB	BLK	STL
27.1	12.4	5.0	2.9	0.2	1.2

Advanced Metrics

USG%	3PTA/FGA	FTA/FGA	TS%	eFG%	3PT%
23.1	0.233	0.223	0.540	0.502	0.326

AST%	TOV%	OREB%	DREB%	STL%	BLK%
33.4	14.2	2.8	10.5	2.3	1.0

PER	ORTG	DRTG	WS/48	BPM	VOL
17.14	110.4	111.3	0.098	0.58	0.365

- Missed a month due to a fractured toe, regular starting point guard for Orlando when healthy
- Had a best season in the NBA, highly effective in his role as a moderate volume distributor and penetrator
- Great playmaker with excellent court vision, finds open teammates, slightly turnover prone
- Effective pick-and-roll ball handler and isolation player, slashes hard to the rim, hits short mid-range pull-ups and floaters
- Made more than 30% of his threes for the first time in his career, normally not a long range threat
- Around a league average spot-up shooter in a small sample of attempts, good cutter off the ball
- 2022-23 Defensive Degree of Difficulty: 0.523
- 2022-23 Points Prevented: -0.148
- Guarded a lot of difficult matchups, may have been over-extended
- Had trouble guarding elite players on the ball, struggled to defend on the perimeter and interior
- Fairly decent pick-and-roll defender, can functionally switch and cut off penetration, goes too far under screens
- Tends to get caught on screens off the ball, good at closing out on spot-up shooters
- Active help defender, consistently gets steals at a high rate, occasionally blocks shots on the weak side, fairly solid defensive rebounder

Gary Harris

	Height	Weight	Cap #	Years Left
	6'4"	210	$13.000M	UFA

Similar at Age 28

		Season	SIMsc
1	Damion Lee	2020-21	947.8
2	Iman Shumpert	2018-19	938.8
3	Keith Bogans	2008-09	931.3
4	Austin Rivers	2020-21	928.4
5	Anthony Morrow	2013-14	927.4
6	Fred Jones	2007-08	921.6
7	Pat Connaughton	2020-21	920.0
8	Randy Foye	2011-12	919.7
9	Wayne Ellington	2015-16	917.4
10	Tony Snell	2019-20	916.6

Baseline Basic Stats

MPG	PTS	AST	REB	BLK	STL
22.6	8.1	1.4	2.4	0.2	0.7

Advanced Metrics

USG%	3PTA/FGA	FTA/FGA	TS%	eFG%	3PT%
14.1	0.682	0.147	0.577	0.552	0.396

AST%	TOV%	OREB%	DREB%	STL%	BLK%
8.4	9.4	1.9	8.3	1.6	0.7

PER	ORTG	DRTG	WS/48	BPM	VOL
10.17	113.6	113.6	0.078	-1.67	0.379

- Missed games due to knee and adductor injuries, regular starter for Orlando when healthy
- Had his most efficient shooting season in a role as a low usage shooting specialist
- Three-Point Percentage spiked to above 43%, solid career three-point shooter, percentages tend to vary
- Good spot-up shooter, can also make shots off screens, great at knocking down threes in transition
- Occasionally can leverage the threat of his shot to score on pick-and-rolls, not really able to drive without a screen, limited as a ball handler or shot creator
- Mainly a catch-and-shoot player, can make the extra pass, rarely turns the ball over
- 2022-23 Defensive Degree of Difficulty: 0.533
- 2022-23 Points Prevented: 0.242
- Used as Orlando's main defensive stopper, slightly over-extended or slowed by injuries
- Solid on-ball defender in the past, can defend multiple positions, had trouble staying with opposing players
- Fairly solid pick-and-roll defender, funnels his man into help, can contain ball handlers, had some lapses when guarding screeners
- Sometimes gets caught on screens off the ball, tended to be late when closing out on spot-up shooters
- Steal and Block Percentages increased, below average defensive rebounder

Cole Anthony

	Height	Weight	Cap #	Years Left
	6'2"	185	$5.540M	RFA

Similar at Age 22

		Season	SIMsc
1	Immanuel Quickley	2021-22	931.5
2	Jalen Brunson	2018-19	912.6
3	Aaron Holiday	2018-19	907.9
4	Brandon Knight	2013-14	905.2
5	Brandon Williams	2021-22	903.7
6	Anfernee Simons	2021-22	902.7
7	Jerryd Bayless	2010-11	901.5
8	Stephen Curry	2010-11	901.3
9	J.R. Bremer	2002-03	899.0
10	Jordan Clarkson	2014-15	896.4

Baseline Basic Stats

MPG	PTS	AST	REB	BLK	STL
27.2	14.1	4.0	3.2	0.2	0.8

Advanced Metrics

USG%	3PTA/FGA	FTA/FGA	TS%	eFG%	3PT%
22.9	0.373	0.257	0.567	0.519	0.384

AST%	TOV%	OREB%	DREB%	STL%	BLK%
24.8	12.4	2.3	14.1	1.4	1.0

PER	ORTG	DRTG	WS/48	BPM	VOL
16.26	113.6	114.1	0.110	0.58	0.443

- Regular rotation player for Orlando in his third NBA season
- Had his most effective season in a role as a moderate volume ball handler off the bench
- Solid playmaking guard that can find open teammates and make solid decisions, good at avoiding turnovers
- Improved to become a solid outside shooter, consistently made threes at above the league average
- Decent as a spot-up shooter, better at making threes in transition and off pick-and-rolls
- More effective pick-and-roll ball handler, can get to the rim and hit pull-up jumpers, less effective as an isolation player
- 2022-23 Defensive Degree of Difficulty: 0.400
- 2022-23 Points Prevented: 0.457
- Usually guarded second unit players or lower leverage starters
- Below average on-ball defender, struggled to stay with opposing perimeter players
- Below average when guarding pick-and-rolls, not effective at taking away any specific action
- Stays attached to shooters off the ball, fights through screens and closes out in spot-up situations
- Mostly a stay-at-home defender, usually does not get steals, Block Percentage spiked to a career high, good defensive rebounding guard

Jalen Suggs

	Height	Weight	Cap #	Years Left
	6'4"	205	$7.252M	TO

Similar at Age 21

		Season	SIMsc
1	De'Anthony Melton	2019-20	923.4
2	Rashad McCants	2005-06	921.6
3	Austin Rivers	2013-14	920.4
4	Frank Ntilikina	2019-20	917.6
5	Smush Parker	2002-03	916.1
6	Emmanuel Mudiay	2017-18	914.9
7	Nickeil Alexander-Walker	2019-20	913.4
8	Shannon Brown	2006-07	911.3
9	Chauncey Billups	1997-98	911.2
10	Rodney Stuckey	2007-08	911.0

Baseline Basic Stats

MPG	PTS	AST	REB	BLK	STL
23.4	10.0	2.9	2.9	0.3	0.9

Advanced Metrics

USG%	3PTA/FGA	FTA/FGA	TS%	eFG%	3PT%
20.5	0.305	0.259	0.516	0.478	0.314

AST%	TOV%	OREB%	DREB%	STL%	BLK%
20.0	15.8	3.5	9.9	2.2	1.2

PER	ORTG	DRTG	WS/48	BPM	VOL
11.65	102.6	112.9	0.041	-1.85	0.288

- Missed games due to a concussion and ankle injury, regular rotation player for Orlando when healthy
- Greatly improved in his second NBA season, decently effective as a moderate volume secondary playmaker
- Solid secondary playmaker that kicks the ball out to open shooters, still turnover prone at this stage
- Improved his shooting percentage, still a below break-even three-point shooter
- Most effective when shooting with an on-ball screen, inconsistent as a spot-up shooter
- Not especially efficient in ball handling situations, defenders can back off him to limit his effectiveness
- Tends to play out of control, prone to missing easy shots at the rim
- 2022-23 Defensive Degree of Difficulty: 0.456
- 2022-23 Points Prevented: 0.961
- Drew a lot of difficulty assignments off the bench, over-extended in these matchups
- Played below average on-ball defense, struggled to stay with opposing players in general
- Solid pick-and-roll defender, effective at switching to guard ball handlers and screeners
- Fights through screens off the ball, sometimes will be late to close out on spot-up shooters
- Increased his activity on the weak side, posted higher Steal and Block Percentages, decent defensive rebounder

Moritz Wagner

	Height	Weight	Cap #	Years Left
	6'11"	245	$8.000M	TO

Similar at Age 25

		Season	SIMsc
1	Frank Kaminsky	2018-19	936.8
2	Kelly Olynyk	2016-17	921.0
3	Joffrey Lauvergne	2016-17	909.9
4	Steve Stipanovich	1985-86	900.7
5	Charlie Villanueva	2009-10	898.9
6	Willy Hernangómez	2019-20	893.5
7	Dario Šarić	2019-20	893.3
8	Mike Muscala	2016-17	893.1
9	Brad Miller	2001-02	891.3
10	Chris Anstey	1999-00	890.8

Baseline Basic Stats

MPG	PTS	AST	REB	BLK	STL
22.3	10.1	1.7	5.7	0.4	0.6

Advanced Metrics

USG%	3PTA/FGA	FTA/FGA	TS%	eFG%	3PT%
19.8	0.432	0.356	0.612	0.561	0.348

AST%	TOV%	OREB%	DREB%	STL%	BLK%
11.7	12.1	6.2	21.6	1.4	1.4

PER	ORTG	DRTG	WS/48	BPM	VOL
16.76	119.2	110.6	0.149	0.75	0.364

- Missed games due to a foot injury and a sprained ankle, regular rotation player for Orlando when healthy
- Solidly effective in his role as a moderate usage spot-up shooter and rim runner
- Below break-even career three-point shooter, slightly better at making long twos
- Most effective as a stand-still spot-up shooter, largely inefficient when shooting in other situations
- High motor rim runner, solid cutter and roll man, physical, draws a lot of fouls by seeking out contact, fairly active offensive rebounder
- Flashed some ability to post up smaller players, good passing big man, good at limiting turnovers
- 2022-23 Defensive Degree of Difficulty: 0.414
- 2022-23 Points Prevented: -1.230
- Below average rim protector, not really a shot blocking threat, fairly foul prone
- Generally guarded second unit big men or lower leverage starters, below average on-ball defender
- Can be overpowered by stronger big men in the post, shows enough mobility to defend in space
- Below average pick-and-roll defender, not effective at taking away any specific action
- Tends to stay anchored in the paint, does not always come out to contest perimeter shots in spot-up situations

Joe Ingles

	Height	Weight	Cap #	Years Left
	6'8"	220	$11.000M	TO

Similar at Age 35

		Season	SIMsc
1	Hedo Turkoglu	2014-15	904.7
2	Kyle Korver	2016-17	903.0
3	Richard Jefferson	2015-16	901.3
4	Mike Dunleavy Jr.	2015-16	896.4
5	Shane Battier	2013-14	891.1
6	James Jones	2015-16	890.6
7	Dan Majerle	2000-01	887.0
8	Glen Rice	2002-03	884.3
9	Joe Johnson	2016-17	882.9
10	Trevor Ariza	2020-21	881.9

Baseline Basic Stats

MPG	PTS	AST	REB	BLK	STL
18.3	5.9	1.3	2.2	0.2	0.4

Advanced Metrics

USG%	3PTA/FGA	FTA/FGA	TS%	eFG%	3PT%
13.4	0.647	0.129	0.582	0.564	0.390

AST%	TOV%	OREB%	DREB%	STL%	BLK%
13.5	14.5	1.7	11.6	1.2	0.7

PER	ORTG	DRTG	WS/48	BPM	VOL
10.05	114.1	113.0	0.096	-0.97	0.422

- Missed most of the first half of the season while recovering from a torn ACL in his left knee
- Efficiency increased, mainly used as a very low volume shooter and secondary ball handler
- Shooting bounced back to his normal levels, has made almost 41% of his career threes
- Excellent spot-up shooter, can make threes off dribble, solid shooter off screens in previous seasons
- Crafty pick-and-roll ball handler, occasionally gets to the rim if he has a screen, not effective in isolation situations
- Good playmaker that consistently finds open teammates, slightly turnover prone
- 2022-23 Defensive Degree of Difficulty: 0.366
- 2022-23 Points Prevented: -1.021
- Guarded second unit players last season, took on tougher assignments in the past
- Played below average on-ball defense, struggled to stay with opposing players, may be losing a step due to age
- Decent pick-and-roll defender, can functionally switch, tends to go too far under screens
- Tended to get caught on screens off the ball, usually was late when closing out on spot-up shooters
- Steal Percentage increased last season, usually a stay-at-home defender, decent defensive rebounder

Caleb Houstan

	Height	Weight	Cap #	Years Left
	6'8"	205	$2.000M	1 + TO

Similar at Age 20

		Season	SIMsc
1	Ziaire Williams	2021-22	916.1
2	Deni Avdija	2020-21	892.0
3	Terrance Ferguson	2018-19	885.2
4	Nicolas Batum	2008-09	881.7
5	Martell Webster	2006-07	878.4
6	Deividas Sirvydis	2020-21	873.1
7	OG Anunoby	2017-18	872.6
8	Mario Hezonja	2015-16	872.1
9	Zeke Nnaji	2020-21	867.0
10	Gordon Hayward	2010-11	865.5

Baseline Basic Stats

MPG	PTS	AST	REB	BLK	STL
20.2	6.9	1.1	2.5	0.2	0.5

Advanced Metrics

USG%	3PTA/FGA	FTA/FGA	TS%	eFG%	3PT%
14.0	0.706	0.143	0.545	0.522	0.366

AST%	TOV%	OREB%	DREB%	STL%	BLK%
7.0	9.6	3.4	9.8	1.1	0.8

PER	ORTG	DRTG	WS/48	BPM	VOL
8.90	110.1	115.8	0.058	-2.49	0.493

- Fringe rotation player for Orlando in his rookie season
- Primarily used in a role as an extremely low volume spot-up shooter
- Almost 75% of his shots were threes, above break-even overall three-point shooter, made almost 48% of his corner threes
- Mainly a spot-up shooter, effective when shooting off screens in a very small sample of possessions
- Very rarely used in ball handling situations, not really able to create his own offense right now
- Strictly a catch-and-shoot player, playmaking skills are limited, rarely turns the ball over
- 2022-23 Defensive Degree of Difficulty: 0.317
- 2022-23 Points Prevented: -0.366
- Mostly guarded lower leverage second unit players, played fairly decent on-ball defense
- Fairly solid when defending perimeter players, had some trouble against stronger players inside
- Below average pick-and-roll defender, not effective at taking away any specific action
- Tends to get caught on screens off the ball, good at closing out on spot-up shooters
- Stay-at-home defender, rarely gets steals or blocks, below average defensive rebounder

Chuma Okeke

	Height	Weight	Cap #	Years Left
	6'6"	229	$5.267M	RFA

Similar at Age 24

		Season	SIMsc
1	Sterling Brown	2019-20	926.4
2	Stanley Johnson	2020-21	923.1
3	Carlos Delfino	2006-07	920.9
4	Solomon Hill	2015-16	919.4
5	Quincy Pondexter	2012-13	915.5
6	Kenrich Williams	2018-19	915.0
7	Henry Walker	2011-12	911.7
8	Dean Wade	2020-21	910.6
9	James Jones	2004-05	905.6
10	Justin Anderson	2017-18	901.9

Baseline Basic Stats

MPG	PTS	AST	REB	BLK	STL
21.8	7.4	1.3	3.5	0.3	0.7

Advanced Metrics

USG%	3PTA/FGA	FTA/FGA	TS%	eFG%	3PT%
14.7	0.623	0.177	0.521	0.492	0.336

AST%	TOV%	OREB%	DREB%	STL%	BLK%
9.5	9.6	4.0	14.9	1.8	1.6

PER	ORTG	DRTG	WS/48	BPM	VOL
10.90	108.2	112.8	0.070	-0.92	0.414

- Fell out of the rotation, played limited minutes for Orlando in his third NBA season
- Effectiveness declined, primarily used as a low volume spot-up shooter
- Below break-even career three-point shooter, far better in the corners, has made over 39% of his career corner threes
- Strictly a stationary spot-up shooter, inefficient when shooting in other situations
- Limited ball handling skills, not really able to create his own shot, solid cutter but doesn't do this very often
- Mainly a catch-and-shoot player, shows some secondary playmaking skills, rarely turns the ball over
- 2022-23 Defensive Degree of Difficulty: 0.436
- 2022-23 Points Prevented: -0.058
- Drew some tough matchups off the bench in limited minutes, played below average on-ball defense
- Struggled to stay with opposing perimeter players, has trouble guarding stronger power forwards
- Middling pick-and-roll defender, shows some ability to switch, has lapses when making rotations
- Tends to get caught on screens off the ball, usually was late to close out on spot-up shooters
- Active help defender, gets steals and blocks at a fairly high rate, fairly good defensive rebounder

Goga Bitadze

	Height	Weight	Cap #	Years Left
	6'11"	250	$2.067M	UFA

Similar at Age 23

		Season	SIMsc
1	Terrence Jones	2014-15	905.9
2	Samuel Dalembert	2004-05	905.6
3	Isaiah Hartenstein	2021-22	904.0
4	Mike Muscala	2014-15	896.8
5	Darko Milicic	2008-09	895.7
6	Richaun Holmes	2016-17	892.0
7	Moritz Wagner	2020-21	891.8
8	Scott Haskin	1993-94	890.1
9	Mehmet Okur	2002-03	889.3
10	Scot Pollard	1998-99	889.2

Baseline Basic Stats

MPG	PTS	AST	REB	BLK	STL
19.3	7.4	1.2	5.2	1.0	0.6

Advanced Metrics

USG%	3PTA/FGA	FTA/FGA	TS%	eFG%	3PT%
16.6	0.203	0.343	0.593	0.565	0.239

AST%	TOV%	OREB%	DREB%	STL%	BLK%
10.9	13.1	11.5	18.3	1.5	4.4

PER	ORTG	DRTG	WS/48	BPM	VOL
17.36	120.6	110.0	0.151	0.18	0.312

- Waived by Indiana at the trade deadline, signed with Orlando afterwards
- Played sparingly for Indiana, became a regular rotation player for Orlando, used as a low usage rim runner and stretch big
- Energetic rim runner, has some trouble finishing shots due to a lack of vertical lift
- Decent cutter and roll man, good offensive rebounder, physical player that will draw fouls
- Takes some threes but has been an inefficient shooter, career Three-Point Percentage is below 30%
- Not really a post-up threat, fairly good passing big man, solid at avoiding turnovers
- 2022-23 Defensive Degree of Difficulty: 0.335
- 2022-23 Points Prevented: 0.430
- Fairly good rim protector, great shot blocker, sacrifices positioning to go for blocks, decent defensive rebounder
- Usually guards second unit big men, tends to commit a lot of shooting fouls in the post, has trouble defending in space
- Effective pick-and-roll defender, good in drop coverages, solid at hedging out on ball handlers
- Tends to sag into the paint, does not always come out to contest perimeter shots in spot-up situations
- Steal Percentage increased to a career high last season

Jonathan Isaac

	Height	Weight	Cap #	Years Left
	6'11"	230	$17.400M	1

Similar at Age 25

		Season	SIMsc
1	Roy Tarpley	1989-90	835.3
2	Andray Blatche	2011-12	820.9
3	Jonas Jerebko	2012-13	818.2
4	Vernon Macklin	2011-12	816.5
5	Nazr Mohammed	2002-03	810.8
6	Adreian Payne	2016-17	809.5
7	Keita Bates-Diop	2020-21	809.3
8	Derrick Favors	2016-17	809.0
9	Willy Hernangómez	2019-20	809.0
10	Ryan Kelly	2016-17	808.5

Baseline Basic Stats

MPG	PTS	AST	REB	BLK	STL
18.9	7.9	0.9	5.1	0.6	0.6

Advanced Metrics

USG%	3PTA/FGA	FTA/FGA	TS%	eFG%	3PT%
19.3	0.242	0.228	0.547	0.527	0.381

AST%	TOV%	OREB%	DREB%	STL%	BLK%
7.5	9.4	11.5	23.6	3.4	2.7

PER	ORTG	DRTG	WS/48	BPM	VOL
19.28	114.5	103.7	0.154	2.43	0.832

- Briefly returned after missing the past two seasons while recovering from an ACL injury, later shut down due to a torn left adductor
- Used as a moderate usage spot-up shooter and energy player in a limited number of healthy minutes
- Break-even three-point shooter in his career, percentages tend to vary from year-to-year
- Predominantly a stationary spot-up shooter, did not shoot in other situations last season
- Athletic rim runner before the injuries, good offensive rebounder, effective cutter and roll man
- Strictly a catch-and-shoot player, limited ability to create his own shot or pass, rarely turns the ball over
- 2022-23 Defensive Degree of Difficulty: 0.533
- 2022-23 Points Prevented: -1.965
- Drew a lot of difficult assignments in very limited minutes when healthy
- Still a good on-ball defender that can guard multiple positions
- Solid pick-and-roll defender, can effectively switch to guard ball handlers or screeners
- Tends to gamble too much, gets caught out of position, does not stay attached to shooters off the ball
- Very active help defender, gets steals and blocks at a very high rate, good defensive rebounder, can provide an extra layer of rim protector from the weak side

Newcomers

Anthony Black

	Height	Weight	Cap #	Years Left
	6'7"	198	$7.245M	1 + 2 TO

Baseline Basic Stats

MPG	PTS	AST	REB	BLK	STL
20.5	7.7	2.5	2.8	0.3	0.9

Advanced Metrics

USG%	3PTA/FGA	FTA/FGA	TS%	eFG%	3PT%
18.6	0.250	0.345	0.511	0.467	0.318

AST%	TOV%	OREB%	DREB%	STL%	BLK%
19.6	16.6	3.9	11.5	2.3	1.0

PER	ORTG	DRTG	WS/48	BPM	VOL
13.23	100.2	102.5	0.061	-1.07	N/A

- Drafted by Orlando with the 6th overall pick in 2023
- Had an up and down performance at the Las Vegas Summer League
- Over-extended in a role as a moderate volume playmaker
- Struggled to shoot efficiently, posted a True Shooting Percentage below 45%, inefficient shooter from all areas of the court
- Below break-even three-point shooter in college, mainly a stand-still spot-up shooter
- Athletic slasher in college, defenders could back off him to limit his effectiveness in ball handling situations
- Good playmaker with solid court vision, tended to play out of control, highly turnover prone at Summer League
- Long and athletic defender with great physical tools, can potentially guard multiple positions in the future
- Good on-ball defender, can pressure opposing guards, holds up well against bigger wings
- Solid pick-and-roll defender, good at funneling ball handlers into help, can effectively switch
- Stays attached to shooters off the ball, fights through screens and closes out in spot-up situations
- Very active help defender at Summer League, great at using his anticipation skills to get steals, effective weak side shot blocker, good defensive rebounder

Jett Howard

	Height	Weight	Cap #	Years Left
	6'8"	215	$5.027M	1 + 2 TO

Baseline Basic Stats

MPG	PTS	AST	REB	BLK	STL
19.3	7.6	1.1	2.6	0.3	0.5

Advanced Metrics

USG%	3PTA/FGA	FTA/FGA	TS%	eFG%	3PT%
17.8	0.516	0.212	0.532	0.502	0.343

AST%	TOV%	OREB%	DREB%	STL%	BLK%
10.0	10.7	2.2	11.3	1.2	1.1

PER	ORTG	DRTG	WS/48	BPM	VOL
11.02	101.4	107.2	0.054	-1.67	N/A

- Drafted by Orlando with the 11th overall pick in 2023
- Had a decent performance at the Las Vegas Summer League
- Put up some counting numbers, slightly struggled with his efficiency in a moderate volume role as a shooter and secondary playmaker
- Posted a True Shooting Percentage below 50%, largely struggled to drive to the rim, made less than 40% of his two-pointers
- Made 40% of his Summer League threes, good shooter off the catch in college, better as a spot-up shooter
- Moves fairly well off the ball, effective cutter, can make shots off screens, good at running the floor in transition
- Fairly good secondary playmaker that can make simple reads, played a bit wildly, slightly turnover prone in Vegas
- Good athlete, not overwhelmingly explosive, fairly sound defender in college
- Effective on-ball defender that could capably defend multiple positions
- Better pick-and-roll defender when used in aggressive coverages, can capably switch to guard screeners or ball handlers
- Stays attached to shooters off the ball, fights through off-ball screens and closes out in spot-up situations
- Fairly active help defender in Vegas, posted fairly high steal and block rates, below average defensive rebounder

Indiana Pacers

Last Season: 35 - 47, Missed the Playoffs

Offensive Rating: 114.6, 19th in the NBA   Defensive Rating: 117.7, 26th in the NBA

Primary Executive: Kevin Pritchard, President of Basketball Operations

Head Coach: Rick Carlisle

Key Roster Changes

Subtractions
Chris Duarte, trade
Oshae Brissett, free agency
George Hill, free agency
James Johnson, free agency

Additions
Jarace Walker, draft
Ben Sheppard, draft
Obi Toppin, trade
Bruce Brown, free agency

Roster

Likely Starting Five
1. *Tyrese Haliburton*
2. Andrew Nembhard
3. Buddy Hield
4. Bruce Brown
5. Myles Turner

Other Key Rotation Players
Bennedict Mathurin
Obi Toppin
Aaron Nesmith
Jarace Walker
Jalen Smith

* Italics denotes that a player is likely to be on the floor to close games

Remaining Roster

- Isaiah Jackson
- T.J. McConnell
- Ben Sheppard
- Jordan Nwora
- Daniel Theis
- Isaiah Wong, 23, 6'4", 184, Miami (FL) (Two-Way)
- Oscar Tshiebwe, 23, 6'9", 260, Kentucky (Two-Way)
- Kendall Brown, 20, 6'8", 205, Baylor (Two-Way)
- Darius McGhee, 24, 5'9", 180, Liberty (Exhibit 10)

SCHREMPF Base Rating: 40.1

Season Preview Survey

- *Are the Pacers contending or rebuilding? Where is this team headed?*

The Pacers are essentially rebuilding on the fly. They are not totally bottoming out, but they are still building their team around a younger core group while still trying to be competitive. The signing of Bruce Brown reflects this strategy because he's the type of player that adds to their support system, so they can allow their young talent to develop to their optimal level. They have shown positive signs of growth because they were pretty competitive for stretches last season. If they can build on this, they might be able to push for a play-in berth this season.

- *What are the areas of concern for this team heading into this season?*

Indiana plays an exciting brand of basketball because they really push the pace and play a wide open style. However, they still haven't really established a clear strength on either side of the ball. They have the potential to be solid on both ends, but they haven't picked a direction yet. Defensively, they have some ability to switch and apply pressure on the perimeter. Aside from Brown, they still don't have many established on-ball defenders to be a plus-level defense right now. On offense, they can spread the floor around Tyrese Haliburton a little bit because they can play a few five-out lineups that could give opponents some trouble, but they don't have a player that can consistently put downhill pressure on defenses to really force into making mistakes. Their offense doesn't quite have the necessary pieces to score efficiently on a consistent basis. Unless they get some considerable internal growth, they will continue to be an exciting but inefficient team next season.

- *List some possible breakout players for this team.*

Indiana has a roster filled with young players that still have some untapped potential. Obi Toppin has been in the league for three years, but he was stuck behind Julius Randle as a member of the Knicks. He didn't really get an extended opportunity to play heavy minutes. In Indiana, there is a slight void at the power forward position because the Pacers don't have a traditional four on their roster other than him. Toppin has a chance to put up bigger scoring numbers if he can become a consistent scoring combo forward this season. As for the other young players, Jarace Walker could make some big contributions on the wing as an energy player and a three-and-D guy. Also, Bennedict Mathurin could take the next step to becoming an impact secondary scoring wing if he increases his efficiency against starting level players. Then, Andrew Nembhard could continue his development to turn himself into a more productive defensive stopper and connector on offense.

- *What should we expect from them this season?*

The Pacers are probably not going to be a playoff contender because they don't quite have enough front-end talent to put up a big regular season win total. It's very likely that they will miss the playoffs this season, but they have an interesting enough mix of players to keep themselves competitive. They could sneak up on teams early and put themselves into the conversation for a play-in berth. However, they might not be able sustain any kind of success for an entire season because they haven't really established a clear identity on either side of the ball. They will have to pinpoint a strength to lean on to get wins and turn themselves into a consistent playoff level team. Otherwise, they will remain in their current position as an entertaining, high-tempo unit that can out-score opponents on a good night but doesn't quite have enough ability to come out on top for an entire 82-game schedule. They will probably be within shouting range of a play-in spot, but they are likely to fall short and be a lottery team once again.

Veterans

Tyrese Haliburton

	Height	Weight	Cap #	Years Left
	6'5"	185	$5.808M	5

Similar at Age 22

		Season	SIMsc
1	Jamal Crawford	2002-03	916.7
2	Elfrid Payton	2016-17	905.9
3	Stephen Curry	2010-11	901.6
4	D'Angelo Russell	2018-19	899.5
5	Delonte West	2005-06	886.6
6	Jamal Murray	2019-20	885.8
7	Jordan Poole	2021-22	881.7
8	Jordan Clarkson	2014-15	881.5
9	Latrell Sprewell	1992-93	880.3
10	Kerry Kittles	1996-97	877.1

Baseline Basic Stats

MPG	PTS	AST	REB	BLK	STL
32.5	16.7	5.3	3.8	0.4	1.3

Advanced Metrics

USG%	3PTA/FGA	FTA/FGA	TS%	eFG%	3PT%
23.1	0.434	0.237	0.585	0.545	0.396

AST%	TOV%	OREB%	DREB%	STL%	BLK%
34.7	14.2	2.1	10.2	2.1	1.0

PER	ORTG	DRTG	WS/48	BPM	VOL
19.45	117.7	114.0	0.135	3.07	0.448

- Named to his first All-Star team in 2022-23, missed games due to an assortment on minor injuries
- Had a breakout season in a role as a moderate usage playmaking ball handler
- Led the NBA in Assist Percentage, dynamic playmaker with excellent court vision, good at limiting turnovers
- Very reliable shooter that has made over 40% of his career threes, displays great shot selection
- Excellent spot-up shooter, can knock down threes if defenders go under screens on pick-and-rolls, less effective when shooting off screens
- Can get to the rim as a pick-and-roll ball handler and isolation player, very efficient mid-range shooter
- 2022-23 Defensive Degree of Difficulty: 0.394
- 2022-23 Points Prevented: -0.700
- Often hidden in favorable matchups against lower leverage players, mainly used as a roamer on defense
- Average on-ball defender, more effective against bigger wings, had trouble staying with quicker guards
- Solid pick-and-roll defender, can effectively switch, generally made sound rotations last season
- Gambles too much, out of position quite a bit, tends to get caught on screens or is late when closing out on spot-up shooters
- Active help defender, consistently posts high steal rates, occasional weak side shot blocker, decent defensive rebounder

Myles Turner

	Height	Weight	Cap #	Years Left
	6'11"	250	$20.975M	1

Similar at Age 26

		Season	SIMsc
1	Alex Len	2019-20	887.0
2	Ronny Turiaf	2008-09	884.8
3	Bobby Portis	2021-22	878.6
4	Troy Murphy	2006-07	876.6
5	Raef LaFrentz	2002-03	871.6
6	Andrew Nicholson	2015-16	870.2
7	Charlie Villanueva	2010-11	869.9
8	Channing Frye	2009-10	868.9
9	Spencer Hawes	2014-15	867.3
10	Marcin Gortat	2010-11	867.0

Baseline Basic Stats

MPG	PTS	AST	REB	BLK	STL
26.4	11.1	1.2	7.0	1.5	0.6

Advanced Metrics

USG%	3PTA/FGA	FTA/FGA	TS%	eFG%	3PT%
18.7	0.362	0.293	0.611	0.581	0.370

AST%	TOV%	OREB%	DREB%	STL%	BLK%
6.8	11.3	6.3	22.5	1.0	5.9

PER	ORTG	DRTG	WS/48	BPM	VOL
17.44	116.5	109.6	0.131	1.30	0.408

- Regular starting center for Indiana, missed a few games due to a back injury and other minor injuries
- Had his best NBA season, greatly increased his efficiency in a role as a moderate volume stretch big and rim runner
- Around a league average career three-point shooter, Three-Point Percentage increased last season
- Good spot-up shooter and pick-and-pop screener, mostly a stationary shooter
- Athletic rim runner, good at rolling to the rim and cutting off the ball, good at running the floor in transition, effective offensive rebounder that scores on put-backs
- Improving as a post-up player, catch-and-shoot or catch-and-finish player, limited as a passer, rarely turns the ball over
- 2022-23 Defensive Degree of Difficulty: 0.495
- 2022-23 Points Prevented: 0.229
- Excellent shot blocker, good defensive rebounder, solid rim protector, sometimes can be undisciplined with his positioning
- Draws tough assignments against top big men, stout post defender, had trouble defending in space
- Good pick-and-roll defender, good in drop coverages, solid at hedging out onto ball handlers
- Consistently will come out to contest perimeter shots in spot-up situations

Bruce Brown

	Height	Weight	Cap #	Years Left
	6'4"	202	$22.000M	TO

Similar at Age 26

		Season	SIMsc
1	Blue Edwards	1991-92	939.2
2	Caleb Martin	2021-22	933.5
3	Cody Martin	2021-22	927.5
4	Kent Bazemore	2015-16	922.5
5	Josh Richardson	2019-20	921.9
6	David Nwaba	2018-19	917.8
7	Felipe Lopez	2000-01	916.3
8	Fred Jones	2005-06	915.9
9	Courtney Lee	2011-12	914.2
10	Erick Strickland	1999-00	911.9

Baseline Basic Stats

MPG	PTS	AST	REB	BLK	STL
25.4	10.0	2.2	3.2	0.4	0.9

Advanced Metrics

USG%	3PTA/FGA	FTA/FGA	TS%	eFG%	3PT%
17.5	0.313	0.229	0.557	0.523	0.365

AST%	TOV%	OREB%	DREB%	STL%	BLK%
13.7	11.9	4.0	12.2	1.8	1.6

PER	ORTG	DRTG	WS/48	BPM	VOL
13.30	111.9	112.0	0.090	-0.67	0.285

- Played starter level minutes for Denver in his first season with the team
- Solidly effective part of a championship rotation, mainly used as a low usage spot-up shooter and secondary playmaker
- Made threes at around the league average last season, percentages tend to vary from year-to-year
- Predominantly a stand-still spot-up shooter, takes most of his threes from the corners
- Good cutter off the rim, effective at making short floaters on rolls to the rim
- Inconsistent scorer in ball handling situations, solid secondary playmaker that limits turnovers
- 2022-23 Defensive Degree of Difficulty: 0.460
- 2022-23 Points Prevented: 1.174
- Drew a lot of tough assignments off the bench, used as a defensive stopper in previous seasons with other teams
- Good on-ball defender that guards multiple positions and pressures opponents
- Solid pick-and-roll defender, can effectively switch to defend ball handlers and screeners, sometimes would go too far under screens
- Stays attached to shooters off the ball, fights through screens and closes out in spot-up situations
- Active weak side defender, gets steals and blocks at a high rate, solid defensive rebounder

Buddy Hield

	Height	Weight	Cap #	Years Left
	6'4"	220	$19.280M	UFA

Similar at Age 30

		Season	SIMsc
1	Wesley Matthews	2016-17	943.7
2	Randy Foye	2013-14	924.8
3	Eric Gordon	2018-19	922.2
4	Jason Richardson	2010-11	917.8
5	Dan Majerle	1995-96	909.1
6	Anthony Peeler	1999-00	906.7
7	Carlos Delfino	2012-13	906.4
8	J.R. Smith	2015-16	906.1
9	Voshon Lenard	2003-04	896.4
10	Alec Burks	2021-22	895.0

Baseline Basic Stats

MPG	PTS	AST	REB	BLK	STL
30.9	13.3	2.5	3.3	0.3	0.9

Advanced Metrics

USG%	3PTA/FGA	FTA/FGA	TS%	eFG%	3PT%
19.7	0.629	0.130	0.564	0.544	0.389

AST%	TOV%	OREB%	DREB%	STL%	BLK%
12.7	10.9	2.3	12.2	1.6	0.9

PER	ORTG	DRTG	WS/48	BPM	VOL
12.86	108.7	114.4	0.067	0.05	0.217

- Regular starter for Indiana in his first full season with the team
- Had a bounce back season in a role as a moderate volume shooting specialist
- Career Three-Point Percentage is just above 40%, has made 47.5% of his career corner threes
- Most effective when spotting up, taking trail threes in transition, and making threes off hand-offs
- Needs a screen to create space with the ball in his hands, better on pick-and-rolls, not really able to score efficiently in isolation situations
- Moves well without the ball, good cutter, could make threes off screens in previous seasons
- Solid secondary playmaker, good at avoiding turnovers
- <u>2022-23 Defensive Degree of Difficulty</u>: 0.461
- <u>2022-23 Points Prevented</u>: 0.965
- Took on tougher defensive assignments, hidden in favorable matchups in previous seasons
- Decent on-ball defender, can stay with quicker guards, struggles to defend taller wing players
- Below average pick-and-roll defender, not really effective at taking away any specific action
- Tends to get caught on screens off the ball, not always in position to effectively close out on spot-up shooters
- More active as a help defender, Steal Percentage increased last season, fairly good defensive rebounder

Andrew Nembhard

	Height	Weight	Cap #	Years Left
	6'5"	193	$2.132M	1 + TO

Similar at Age 23

		Season	SIMsc
1	Courtney Lee	2008-09	934.9
2	E'Twaun Moore	2012-13	931.3
3	Cuttino Mobley	1998-99	927.9
4	Matthew Dellavedova	2013-14	925.8
5	Steve Nash*	1997-98	920.5
6	Ty Jerome	2020-21	918.3
7	Anthony Johnson	1997-98	917.6
8	Terrence Ross	2014-15	916.4
9	Wesley Person	1994-95	916.0
10	Trent Tucker	1982-83	914.7

Baseline Basic Stats

MPG	PTS	AST	REB	BLK	STL
25.6	10.4	2.5	2.6	0.2	0.8

Advanced Metrics

USG%	3PTA/FGA	FTA/FGA	TS%	eFG%	3PT%
18.3	0.412	0.168	0.540	0.512	0.365

AST%	TOV%	OREB%	DREB%	STL%	BLK%
19.1	13.7	2.1	9.4	1.6	0.6

PER	ORTG	DRTG	WS/48	BPM	VOL
12.05	108.5	114.8	0.061	-1.60	0.357

- Regular starting guard for Indiana as a rookie
- Decently effective in his role as a low usage playmaker and spot-up shooter
- Solid playmaker with good court vision, can effectively run a team, slightly turnover prone
- Made threes at just below the league average, slightly better at shooting corner threes
- Predominantly a stationary spot-up shooter, less effective when shooting in other situations
- Can make pull-up mid-range shots on isolation plays, less effective when scoring off the dribble, does not really get to the rim or make threes off the dribble
- 2022-23 Defensive Degree of Difficulty: 0.565, had the 13th most difficult set of matchups in the NBA
- 2022-23 Points Prevented: 0.645
- Mainly used as Indiana's primary perimeter stopper as a rookie
- Effective on-ball defender, can defend ones and twos, has some trouble staying with more explosive guards
- Played below average pick-and-roll defense, not really effective when making rotations, did not take any specific action away
- Usually fights through screens, tends to be late when closing out on spot-up shooters
- Fairly active help defender, gets steals at a solid rate, below average defensive rebounder

Bennedict Mathurin

	Height	Weight	Cap #	Years Left
	6'6"	210	$6.916M	2 TO

Similar at Age 20

		Season	SIMsc
1	RJ Barrett	2020-21	929.1
2	Devin Booker	2016-17	918.7
3	Harrison Barnes	2012-13	910.1
4	Quentin Richardson	2000-01	899.3
5	Cam Thomas	2021-22	898.4
6	Martell Webster	2006-07	898.1
7	Bradley Beal	2013-14	896.5
8	J.R. Smith	2005-06	895.7
9	Jamal Murray	2017-18	895.2
10	Troy Brown Jr.	2019-20	892.3

Baseline Basic Stats

MPG	PTS	AST	REB	BLK	STL
33.2	17.5	3.1	4.7	0.3	0.8

Advanced Metrics

USG%	3PTA/FGA	FTA/FGA	TS%	eFG%	3PT%
25.7	0.316	0.389	0.555	0.486	0.349

AST%	TOV%	OREB%	DREB%	STL%	BLK%
12.7	11.6	3.9	11.6	1.1	0.5

PER	ORTG	DRTG	WS/48	BPM	VOL
14.94	109.0	116.1	0.073	-1.49	0.439

- Named to the All-Rookie 1st Team in 2022-23, played starter level minutes for Indiana
- Primarily used as a high volume scoring sixth man off the bench
- Great athlete, really excels at scoring in transition, attacks the rim to finish around the rim or draw fouls
- Less effective when handling the ball in half-court situations, inconsistent shooter off the dribble, needs a running start to drive to the rim
- Below break-even three-point shooter, most effective at making threes in transition
- Plays with a heavy score-first mindset, not really a passer at this stage, good at avoiding turnovers
- 2022-23 Defensive Degree of Difficulty: 0.414
- 2022-23 Points Prevented: -0.064
- Tended to guard second unit players or lower leverage starters
- Average on-ball defender, effectively stayed with quicker guards, had trouble against taller wing players
- Below average pick-and-roll defender, indecisive, not effective at taking away any specific action
- Fights through screens off the ball, tends to be late when closing out on spot-up shooters
- Stay-at-home defender, does not really get steals or blocks, fairly solid defensive rebounder

Obi Toppin

Height 6'9"	**Weight** 220	**Cap #** $6.803M	**Years Left** RFA

Similar at Age 24

		Season	SIMsc
1	Luke Babbitt	2013-14	935.0
2	Jake Layman	2018-19	934.8
3	Brian Cook	2004-05	934.5
4	Juancho Hernangómez	2019-20	931.7
5	Taurean Prince	2018-19	929.7
6	Dean Wade	2020-21	929.1
7	Bostjan Nachbar	2004-05	928.9
8	Vladimir Radmanovic	2004-05	927.5
9	Kyle Kuzma	2019-20	926.1
10	Chimezie Metu	2021-22	926.0

Baseline Basic Stats

MPG	PTS	AST	REB	BLK	STL
21.8	9.1	1.3	3.9	0.3	0.5

Advanced Metrics

USG%	3PTA/FGA	FTA/FGA	TS%	eFG%	3PT%
19.0	0.498	0.190	0.562	0.534	0.334

AST%	TOV%	OREB%	DREB%	STL%	BLK%
9.5	9.2	3.8	17.0	1.1	1.4

PER	ORTG	DRTG	WS/48	BPM	VOL
13.74	112.8	112.6	0.092	-0.45	0.337

- Regular rotation player for New York in his third NBA season
- Production declined last season, mainly used as a low volume spot-up shooter off the bench
- Improved to make threes at an above break-even percentage, below break-even career three-point shooter
- More efficient when taking threes in transition, below break-even on spot-up threes last season
- More effective as an energetic rim runner, good cutter off the ball, explosive finisher in transition
- Not really a post-up threat or shot creator, flashes some passing skills, rarely turns the ball over
- 2022-23 Defensive Degree of Difficulty: 0.328
- 2022-23 Points Prevented: -0.397
- Usually guards lower leverage second unit players, played solid on-ball defense in these matchups
- Can functionally guard multiple positions, effective in space and on the interior
- Solid pick-and-roll defender, good in drop coverages, effective at switching out onto ball handlers
- Tends to get caught on screens off the ball, sometimes would be late to close out on spot-up shooters
- Less active on the weak side, good shot blocker in previous years, Block Percentage dropped significantly, fairly solid defensive rebounder

Aaron Nesmith

	Height	Weight	Cap #	Years Left
	6'5"	215	$5.634M	RFA

Similar at Age 23

		Season	SIMsc
1	Arron Afflalo	2008-09	952.3
2	Josh Hart	2018-19	934.9
3	Orlando Johnson	2012-13	928.6
4	Henry Walker	2010-11	927.1
5	Elijah Hughes	2021-22	926.6
6	Timothe Luwawu-Cabarrot	2018-19	926.4
7	P.J. Hairston	2015-16	922.3
8	Keith Bogans	2003-04	921.2
9	Sterling Brown	2018-19	919.8
10	Anthony Morrow	2008-09	918.6

Baseline Basic Stats

MPG	PTS	AST	REB	BLK	STL
23.7	9.0	1.6	3.4	0.3	0.7

Advanced Metrics

USG%	3PTA/FGA	FTA/FGA	TS%	eFG%	3PT%
17.2	0.564	0.202	0.563	0.530	0.365

AST%	TOV%	OREB%	DREB%	STL%	BLK%
8.8	11.0	3.1	13.0	1.4	1.1

PER	ORTG	DRTG	WS/48	BPM	VOL
11.20	109.4	113.4	0.072	-1.74	0.351

- Became a regular starter for Indiana in his first season with the team
- Had a career best season in a role as a low usage spot-up shooter
- Made threes at an above league average percentage last season, percentages have varied from year-to-year
- Predominantly a stationary spot-up shooter, flashes some ability to make shots off screens
- Not usually a shot creator, was effective as a pick-and-roll ball handler in a small sample of possessions
- Mainly a catch-and-shoot player, only makes safe passes, good at avoiding turnovers
- 2022-23 Defensive Degree of Difficulty: 0.559, had the 16th toughest set of matchups in the NBA
- 2022-23 Points Prevented: -2.530
- Used as a defensive stopper against elite scoring wings, over-extended in this role
- Decent on-ball defender, effectively stayed with perimeter players, had trouble against stronger players inside
- Played below average pick-and-roll defense, not really effective at taking away any specific action
- Fights through screens off the ball, not always in position to contest perimeter shots in spot-up situations
- Get steals at a decently moderate rate, occasionally can block shots on the weak side, fairly solid defensive rebounder

Jalen Smith

	Height	Weight	Cap #	Years Left
	6'10"	215	$5.044M	PO

Similar at Age 22

		Season	SIMsc
1	Eddie Griffin	2004-05	924.5
2	Donyell Marshall	1995-96	912.6
3	Trey Lyles	2017-18	900.2
4	John Henson	2012-13	898.8
5	John Collins	2019-20	898.4
6	Thomas Bryant	2019-20	895.5
7	Marvin Bagley III	2021-22	893.4
8	Michael Porter Jr.	2020-21	892.3
9	Austin Daye	2010-11	890.2
10	Larry Nance	1981-82	887.7

Baseline Basic Stats

MPG	PTS	AST	REB	BLK	STL
22.2	10.3	1.1	5.6	1.0	0.5

Advanced Metrics

USG%	3PTA/FGA	FTA/FGA	TS%	eFG%	3PT%
20.1	0.299	0.251	0.562	0.534	0.311

AST%	TOV%	OREB%	DREB%	STL%	BLK%
7.6	10.7	8.8	20.6	1.0	3.5

PER	ORTG	DRTG	WS/48	BPM	VOL
16.15	112.1	111.2	0.103	-0.74	0.421

- Regular rotation player for Indiana in his first full season with the team, started some games in 2022-23
- Solidly effective in his role as a moderate volume stretch big and rim runner
- Has made less than 30% of his career threes, slightly better at making long twos
- More effective at making threes in transition, less effective as a spot-up shooter and pick-and-pop screener
- Better as a rim runner, efficient finisher at the rim, good cutter, solid roll man, active offensive rebounder, runs hard in transition, willing to draw fouls
- Below average post player, limited passing skills, does not really turn the ball over
- 2022-23 Defensive Degree of Difficulty: 0.425
- 2022-23 Points Prevented: -0.622
- Good rim protector, good defensive rebounder and shot blocker
- Generally guarded lower leverage starting big men and second unit players
- Average on-ball defender, can be overpowered by stronger big men, tends to commit shooting fouls, shows solid mobility when defending in space
- Solid pick-and-roll defender, good in drop coverages, effective at switching out onto ball handlers
- Tended to sag back into the paint, did not always come out to contest perimeter shots in spot-up situations

Isaiah Jackson

	Height	Weight	Cap #	Years Left
	6'10"	206	$2.696M	TO

Similar at Age 21

		Season	SIMsc
1	Brandan Wright	2008-09	889.0
2	Kenny Williams	1990-91	884.1
3	Nicolas Claxton	2020-21	882.4
4	Sean Williams	2007-08	882.2
5	Kevon Looney	2017-18	878.9
6	Amir Johnson	2008-09	871.4
7	Precious Achiuwa	2020-21	870.2
8	Tyrus Thomas	2007-08	868.8
9	JaVale McGee	2008-09	866.1
10	Mitchell Robinson	2019-20	865.8

Baseline Basic Stats

MPG	PTS	AST	REB	BLK	STL
21.0	8.2	0.9	5.5	1.5	0.5

Advanced Metrics

USG%	3PTA/FGA	FTA/FGA	TS%	eFG%	3PT%
16.9	0.035	0.399	0.581	0.546	0.234

AST%	TOV%	OREB%	DREB%	STL%	BLK%
6.5	12.6	11.3	17.7	1.5	5.3

PER	ORTG	DRTG	WS/48	BPM	VOL
16.73	117.3	110.1	0.126	-0.12	0.385

- Regular rotation player for Indiana in his second NBA season
- Maintained his efficiency level from the previous season, used as a low usage rim runner
- Athletic big man with good length, vertical lob threat, good roll man and cutter, runs hard in transition, draws fouls at a high rate
- Active offensive rebounder, sometimes will rush his put-back attempts, occasionally misses shots at the rim
- Lacks reliable shooting range outside of three feet, has made less than two-thirds of his career free throws
- Not really a reliable post-up player, improving but still limited as a passer, cut his turnover rate
- 2022-23 Defensive Degree of Difficulty: 0.355
- 2022-23 Points Prevented: -0.450
- Good rim protector, excellent shot blocker, fairly solid defensive rebounder, good at using his length to get steals
- Generally used as a roaming help defender, usually guards second unit big men
- Effective post defender, good mobility to defend opponents in space, prone to committing shooting fouls
- Below average pick-and-roll defender, indecisive, struggled to make effective rotations
- Tended to stay anchored in the paint, did not always come out to contest perimeter shots in spot-up situations

T.J. McConnell

	Height	Weight	Cap #	Years Left
	6'1"	190	$8.700M	1

Similar at Age 30

		Season	SIMsc
1	Charlie Ward	2000-01	920.1
2	Eric Murdock	1998-99	918.6
3	Mo Williams	2012-13	916.2
4	Anthony Johnson	2004-05	905.6
5	Will Solomon	2008-09	903.8
6	Bimbo Coles	1998-99	901.0
7	Rajon Rondo	2016-17	900.9
8	Pooh Richardson	1996-97	900.8
9	Brian Taylor	1981-82	898.1
10	Randy Brown	1998-99	897.5

Baseline Basic Stats

MPG	PTS	AST	REB	BLK	STL
22.6	7.7	4.7	2.6	0.2	1.0

Advanced Metrics

USG%	3PTA/FGA	FTA/FGA	TS%	eFG%	3PT%
17.3	0.176	0.134	0.545	0.526	0.349

AST%	TOV%	OREB%	DREB%	STL%	BLK%
32.2	17.8	2.6	11.6	2.4	0.7

PER	ORTG	DRTG	WS/48	BPM	VOL
14.85	112.0	113.9	0.084	-0.24	0.553

- Regular rotation player for Indiana in his fourth season with the team
- Bounced back to his previous levels of effectiveness as a game managing backup point guard
- Excellent distributor, great at setting up teammates for open looks, fairly turnover prone
- Crafty pick-and-roll ball handler, can change speeds to take pull-up mid-range shots or get to the rim
- Very good mid-range shooter overall, above break-even career three-point shooter
- Mostly a stationary spot-up shooter, Three-Point Percentage tends to vary from year-to-year
- 2022-23 Defensive Degree of Difficulty: 0.425
- 2022-23 Points Prevented: 0.638
- Draws some tough assignments off the bench, usually guards second unit players
- Pesky on-ball defender, good at pressuring opposing guards, smallish size makes him vulnerable against taller players
- Good pick-and-roll defender, limited ability to switch, good at funneling his man into help, makes sound rotations
- Stays attached to shooters off the ball, fights through screens and closes out in spot-up situations
- Uses active hands to consistently get steals at a high rate, good defensive rebounding guard

Jordan Nwora

	Height	Weight	Cap #	Years Left
	6'8"	225	$3.000M	UFA

Similar at Age 24

		Season	SIMsc
1	James Jones	2004-05	939.7
2	Taurean Prince	2018-19	939.6
3	Kyle Kuzma	2019-20	938.5
4	De'Andre Hunter	2021-22	937.0
5	Chase Budinger	2012-13	931.7
6	Vladimir Radmanovic	2004-05	929.7
7	Bostjan Nachbar	2004-05	929.0
8	Rodney Hood	2016-17	927.1
9	OG Anunoby	2021-22	926.4
10	Tobias Harris	2016-17	926.2

Baseline Basic Stats

MPG	PTS	AST	REB	BLK	STL
21.4	9.0	1.2	3.5	0.3	0.6

Advanced Metrics

USG%	3PTA/FGA	FTA/FGA	TS%	eFG%	3PT%
19.1	0.478	0.177	0.549	0.522	0.381

AST%	TOV%	OREB%	DREB%	STL%	BLK%
9.0	10.5	3.9	15.5	1.2	1.2

PER	ORTG	DRTG	WS/48	BPM	VOL
12.42	108.1	112.5	0.070	-1.23	0.354

- Regular rotation player for Milwaukee and Indiana, playing time increased after the trade to Indiana
- Used as an off-ball spot-up shooter, usage increased with more minutes in Indiana
- Good three-point shooter overall, made almost 41% of his threes last season
- Predominantly a stationary spot-up shooter, needs to have his feet set, less effective when shooting in other situations
- More effective as a pick-and-roll ball handler in Indiana, flashed some secondary playmaking skills
- Not really used as a shot creator throughout his career, good at avoiding turnovers
- 2022-23 Defensive Degree of Difficulty: 0.369
- 2022-23 Points Prevented: -2.360
- Generally defended second unit players, below average on-ball defender
- Struggled to stay with perimeter players, had trouble holding position against stronger players inside
- Decent pick-and-roll defender, good at funneling his man into help, less effective when switched onto a screener
- Tended to get caught on screens, often was late to close out on spot-up shooters
- Stay-at-home defender, did not really get steals or blocks last season, good defensive rebounder

Daniel Theis

	Height	Weight	Cap #	Years Left
	6'8"	245	$9.108M	TO

Similar at Age 30

		Season	SIMsc
1	Kris Humphries	2015-16	892.8
2	Markieff Morris	2019-20	885.0
3	David Andersen	2010-11	884.3
4	Trevor Booker	2017-18	882.2
5	Brandon Bass	2015-16	881.0
6	Sean Marks	2005-06	881.0
7	Jason Maxiell	2013-14	874.5
8	Mike Muscala	2021-22	872.2
9	Ersan Ilyasova	2017-18	871.4
10	Matt Barnes	2010-11	869.8

Baseline Basic Stats

MPG	PTS	AST	REB	BLK	STL
18.3	6.8	1.1	4.2	0.5	0.5

Advanced Metrics

USG%	3PTA/FGA	FTA/FGA	TS%	eFG%	3PT%
17.6	0.289	0.272	0.534	0.511	0.251

AST%	TOV%	OREB%	DREB%	STL%	BLK%
9.2	10.1	7.7	18.5	1.2	3.2

PER	ORTG	DRTG	WS/48	BPM	VOL
13.57	109.8	109.8	0.098	-1.45	0.589

- Missed most of last season while recovering from right knee surgery, only played in seven games
- Moderate to low usage rim runner and stretch big when healthy
- Knee injury hurt his ability to finish, True Shooting Percentage dropped to below 50%
- Solid high motor rim runner when healthy, effective cutter and roll man, active offensive rebounder, runs hard in transition
- Below break-even three-point shooter, mostly a stationary spot-up shooter
- Very limited as a post player, shows some ability to pass, consistently limits turnovers
- 2022-23 Defensive Degree of Difficulty: 0.422
- 2022-23 Points Prevented: -2.857
- Injury affected his ability to challenge shots at the rim, decent rim protector when healthy, still a good shot blocker, decent defensive rebounder
- Decent on-ball defender, can guard starting level big men, fairly effective post defender, mobile enough to defend in space, somewhat foul prone
- Solid pick-and-roll defender, good in drop coverages, effective at switching out onto ball handlers
- Tends to sag back into the paint or he will over-compensate by closing out too aggressively in spot-up situations

Newcomers

Jarace Walker

	Height	Weight	Cap #	Years Left
	6'8"	240	$6.060M	1 + 2 TO

Baseline Basic Stats

MPG	PTS	AST	REB	BLK	STL
20.1	7.6	1.2	4.0	0.5	0.7

Advanced Metrics

USG%	3PTA/FGA	FTA/FGA	TS%	eFG%	3PT%
17.3	0.256	0.257	0.499	0.469	0.322

AST%	TOV%	OREB%	DREB%	STL%	BLK%
9.4	11.0	6.4	15.4	1.6	2.2

PER	ORTG	DRTG	WS/48	BPM	VOL
13.38	101.2	99.1	0.074	-1.49	N/A

- Drafted by Washington with the 8th overall pick in 2023, traded to Indiana
- Had an up and down performance at the Las Vegas Summer League
- Put up counting stats, struggled with his efficiency when used as a high usage scoring wing
- Posted a True Shooting Percentage below 40%, made less than 20% of his threes
- Solid stationary spot-up shooter in college, not really efficient when shooting in other situations
- Shooting stroke still inconsistent, made less than two-thirds of his college free throws
- Solid secondary playmaker that makes simple reads, good at avoiding turnovers
- Rarely used in ball handling situations in college, projects to be an off-ball player in the NBA
- Energetic wing that can score around the rim, good cutter, attacks the rim in transition, athletic finisher
- Advanced defensive prospect, well-schooled, great athleticism and length
- Potentially can develop into a shutdown level defender, capable of guarding multiple positions on the floor
- Good pick-and-roll defender, effective at switching to guard ball handlers and screeners, makes sound rotations
- Stays attached to shooters off the ball, fights through screens and closes out in spot-up situations
- Active help defender at Summer League, good at using his length to play passing lanes and get steals, good weak side shot blocker and defensive rebounder

Ben Sheppard

	Height	Weight	Cap #	Years Left
	6'6"	190	$2.537M	1 + 2 TO

Baseline Basic Stats

MPG	PTS	AST	REB	BLK	STL
19.1	7.0	1.5	2.2	0.2	0.7

Advanced Metrics

USG%	3PTA/FGA	FTA/FGA	TS%	eFG%	3PT%
16.2	0.397	0.208	0.503	0.477	0.330

AST%	TOV%	OREB%	DREB%	STL%	BLK%
11.4	11.3	2.3	9.6	1.6	0.6

PER	ORTG	DRTG	WS/48	BPM	VOL
10.81	98.3	102.4	0.056	-1.58	N/A

- Drafted by Indiana with the 26th overall pick in 2023
- Had a solid performance at the Las Vegas Summer League
- Decently effective in a limited role as a very low usage spot-up shooter
- Went 12-for-31 (38.7%) on threes, mostly took spot-up jumpers at Summer League
- Very good three-point shooter throughout his college career, good at spotting up and running off screens
- Could make pull-up jumpers if defenders went under screens
- Not really used as an isolation player at Belmont, very rarely looked to drive to the rim at Summer League, not likely to be a shot creator in the NBA
- Used strictly as a catch-and-shoot player, passing skills appeared to be limited, rarely turned the ball over
- Projects to be a neutral defender, has average athleticism, not bad enough on defense to be a liability
- Average on-ball defender, quick enough to stay with perimeter players, thin frame, struggled to guard stronger players inside
- Below average pick-and-roll defender, goes too far under screens, not really effective if asked to switch
- Tends to get caught on screens off the ball, gambles a bit too much, better at closing out on shooters in spot-up situations
- Generally a stay-at-home defender at Summer League, rarely got steals or blocks, slightly below average defensive rebounder
- May need some additional seasoning in the G-League to diversify his overall skill set

CHARLOTTE HORNETS

Last Season: 27 - 55, Missed the Playoffs

Offensive Rating: 109.2, 30th in the NBA   Defensive Rating: 115.3, 20th in the NBA

Primary Executive: Mitch Kupchak, President of Basketball Operations/General Manager

Head Coach: Steve Clifford

Key Roster Changes

Subtractions
P.J. Washington, free agency
Kelly Oubre, free agency
Dennis Smith Jr., free agency
Svi Mykhailiuk, free agency

Additions
Brandon Miller, draft
Nick Smith Jr., draft
Miles Bridges, free agency
Frank Ntilikina, free agency

Roster

Likely Starting Five
1. LaMelo Ball
2. Terry Rozier
3. Gordon Hayward
4. Miles Bridges
5. Mark Williams

Other Key Rotation Players
Brandon Miller
Nick Richards
Cody Martin
JT Thor
Bryce McGowens

* Italics denotes that a player is likely to be on the floor to close games

Remaining Roster

- Kai Jones
- Nick Smith Jr.
- James Bouknight
- Kobi Simmons
- Frank Ntilikina
- Amari Bailey, 19, 6'5", 185, UCLA (Two-Way)
- Leaky Black, 24, 6'8", 200, North Carolina (Two-Way)
- Nathan Mensah, 25, 6'10", 230, San Diego State (Exhibit 10)
- Angelo Allegri, 24, 6'7", 215, Eastern Washington (Exhibit 10)
- R.J. Hunter, 30, 6'5", 185, Georgia State (Exhibit 10)

SCHREMPF Base Rating: 40.0

Season Preview Survey

- *Are the Hornets contending or rebuilding? Where is this team headed?*

The Hornets are putting a younger group around LaMelo Ball, so it appears as if they are rebuilding. However, they are also still committed to their longstanding veterans like Gordon Hayward and Terry Rozier. This is strange considering that they haven't made any major changes in either direction for the past few summers. Essentially, they are a bad team that is stuck in place because they aren't making significant moves to improve their team and they're not trying hard enough to accumulate assets to set up something in the future. It's unclear if they have a coherent plan to move forward, so they could be in a losing situation for this season and the foreseeable future.

- *What are the areas of concern for this team heading into this season?*

The overall direction of the franchise is a major concern for Charlotte because it doesn't seem as if they have a distinct plan to build their team. It really seems as if they are simply content to pin all their hopes on the next lottery pick to elevate the franchise, but they don't have the infrastructure in place to maximize that type of talent. Even though they have some interesting young players on their roster, they might be placing them in an adverse environment, which could stunt their growth and keep them in their current situation. Charlotte is need of a major organizational overhaul to bring in some new voices to shake things up and establish a clear vision for their franchise. Otherwise, if they stay on their current path, they could be mired in futility for years to come.

- *List some possible breakout players for this team.*

There are a lot of young players on the roster and there will be ample opportunities for them to prove themselves at the NBA level. By virtue of being the second overall pick in this past draft, there will be big expectations placed on Brandon Miller. He had some struggles in creating his own offense at Summer League, but if he can stay within himself, he might be able to play off a playmaker like LaMelo Ball to put up some scoring numbers as a rookie. Outside of Miller, Mark Williams is the best bet to have a breakout season. There is a clear pathway for him to play because there's limited competition at the center spot, so he could make an impact as a rim runner and rim protector this season. In addition to him, Bryce McGowens could make some improvements to provide value as an energy player and occasional floor spacer. Then, if either James Bouknight or Nick Smith Jr. can become more efficient and consistent offensive players, they could contribute off the bench to provide the Hornets with some extra scoring punch.

- *What should we expect from them this season?*

Unless they make some unforeseen changes, the Hornets should be expected to remain near the bottom of the standings in the Eastern Conference. They were able to bring back Miles Bridges, so they have their core group from two seasons ago in place. That group was able to land a back-end play-in berth, so there's a chance that they could be somewhat competitive this season. However, they really have not done much to improve their roster since the end of the 2021-22 season, and other teams in the East have taken steps to get better. Even if they try to recapture whatever they had in the 2020-21 and 2021-22 season, they still might finish outside of a play-in berth because they just don't have the talent to win on a consistent basis. In all likelihood, Charlotte will finish as a lottery team for the eighth consecutive season.

Veterans

LaMelo Ball

	Height	Weight	Cap #	Years Left
	6'6"	180	$10.901M	5

Similar at Age 21

		Season	SIMsc
1	D'Angelo Russell	2017-18	908.5
2	Devin Booker	2017-18	877.4
3	Jeremy Lamb	2013-14	874.5
4	Kevin Porter Jr.	2021-22	874.3
5	Tyler Herro	2020-21	871.3
6	Kyrie Irving	2013-14	870.6
7	Cole Anthony	2021-22	869.8
8	Lonzo Ball	2018-19	867.9
9	Zach LaVine	2016-17	867.6
10	Tyrese Haliburton	2021-22	866.0

Baseline Basic Stats

MPG	PTS	AST	REB	BLK	STL
32.9	20.7	5.7	4.3	0.4	1.2

Advanced Metrics

USG%	3PTA/FGA	FTA/FGA	TS%	eFG%	3PT%
27.6	0.322	0.233	0.550	0.509	0.357

AST%	TOV%	OREB%	DREB%	STL%	BLK%
33.8	14.6	3.2	13.4	1.9	0.9

PER	ORTG	DRTG	WS/48	BPM	VOL
17.70	109.5	113.5	0.093	2.99	0.181

- Missed most of last season due to multiple injuries to his ankles
- Efficiency declined slightly, put up increased counting stats as Charlotte's primary scorer and ball handler
- Excellent playing with outstanding court vision, primarily a passer in pick-and-roll situations, cut his turnover rate last season
- Average scorer in isolation and pick-and-roll situations, doesn't always get to the rim, inconsistent shooter off the dribble
- Good three-point shooter, most effective as a stationary spot-up shooter, does not really move off the ball
- 2022-23 Defensive Degree of Difficulty: 0.386
- 2022-23 Points Prevented: -0.683
- Usually hidden in favorable matchups against lower leverage players
- Played better on-ball defense against lesser competition, can functionally guard multiple positions
- Below average pick-and-roll defender, not effective at taking away any specific action
- Willing to fight through screens, tends to late to close out on spot-up shooters
- Ankle injuries limited his mobility, Steal and Block Percentages were down, good defensive rebounder

Gordon Hayward

	Height	Weight	Cap #	Years Left
	6'7"	225	$31.500M	UFA

Similar at Age 32

		Season	SIMsc
1	Caron Butler	2012-13	923.5
2	Eric Piatkowski	2002-03	923.2
3	Jerry Stackhouse	2006-07	922.9
4	Joe Johnson	2013-14	922.2
5	Marcus Morris	2021-22	921.4
6	Chris Mills	2001-02	915.4
7	Bojan Bogdanović	2021-22	914.7
8	Michael Finley	2005-06	914.5
9	Boris Diaw	2014-15	913.5
10	Paul Pierce*	2009-10	909.9

Baseline Basic Stats

MPG	PTS	AST	REB	BLK	STL
25.3	10.6	2.0	3.5	0.2	0.6

Advanced Metrics

USG%	3PTA/FGA	FTA/FGA	TS%	eFG%	3PT%
19.2	0.374	0.230	0.550	0.511	0.347

AST%	TOV%	OREB%	DREB%	STL%	BLK%
15.2	12.1	2.4	13.3	1.3	0.8

PER	ORTG	DRTG	WS/48	BPM	VOL
13.07	107.8	112.0	0.080	-0.92	0.322

- Missed games due to injuries to his shoulder, hamstring, and thumb
- Regular starter when healthy, production declined in his role as a moderate volume complementary scorer
- Three-Point Percentage fell to below break-even, more reliant on his mid-range game last season
- Normally a good spot-up shooter, has made almost 41% of his career corner threes
- Slightly better at shooting threes in transition and on the move last season
- Better at driving to rim on isolations and pick-and-rolls, more efficient finisher at the rim, drew more fouls
- Good cutter off the ball, solid secondary playmaker that finds open teammates, good at limiting turnovers
- 2022-23 Defensive Degree of Difficulty: 0.504
- 2022-23 Points Prevented: 1.369
- Used by Charlotte as their primary wing stopper, played very good on-ball defense last season
- Good at defending multiple positions, athleticism is diminishing, compensates by playing angles
- Average pick-and-roll defender, effective at switching onto screeners, tended to allow ball handlers to turn the corner
- Usually stays attached to shooters off the ball, consistently closes out in spot-up situations, fights through screens
- More of a stay-at-home defender, steal and block rates declined, fairly solid defensive rebounder

Terry Rozier

	Height	Weight	Cap #	Years Left
	6'1"	190	$23.205M	2

Similar at Age 28

		Season	SIMsc
1	Mike Bibby	2006-07	949.6
2	Tony Delk	2001-02	923.9
3	Raymond Felton	2012-13	922.1
4	Bobby Jackson	2001-02	916.9
5	Eric Bledsoe	2017-18	916.8
6	Jameer Nelson	2010-11	916.4
7	CJ McCollum	2019-20	914.6
8	Dell Curry	1992-93	911.6
9	Kemba Walker	2018-19	911.2
10	Mike Conley	2015-16	909.0

Baseline Basic Stats

MPG	PTS	AST	REB	BLK	STL
30.5	15.8	4.5	3.4	0.2	1.0

Advanced Metrics

USG%	3PTA/FGA	FTA/FGA	TS%	eFG%	3PT%
23.8	0.490	0.193	0.544	0.511	0.359

AST%	TOV%	OREB%	DREB%	STL%	BLK%
23.1	10.4	2.3	10.6	1.7	0.8

PER	ORTG	DRTG	WS/48	BPM	VOL
15.89	110.7	113.4	0.087	1.08	0.240

- Regular starter for Charlotte in his fourth season with the team
- Production declined, over-extended in a role as a high usage scorer while LaMelo Ball was out due to injury
- Shooting percentages took a major hit, got fewer open looks due to increased attention from defenses
- Normally a solid three-point shooter, most effective at making stand-still spot-up threes
- Average pick-and-roll ball handler and isolation player, inconsistent shooter off the dribble, does not always get to the rim, good at making mid-range floaters
- Good secondary playmaker that makes simple reads, rarely turns the ball over
- 2022-23 Defensive Degree of Difficulty: 0.499
- 2022-23 Points Prevented: -1.010
- Usually guarded starting level players, drew a lot of tough assignments against elite scoring guards
- Normally a solid on-ball defender in previous seasons, over-matched against top guards, struggled to play effective on-ball defense last season
- Middling pick-and-roll defense, can funnel his man into help, tends to be indecisive when making rotations
- Get caught on screens off the ball, tends to late when closing out on spot-up shooters
- Gets steals at a solid rate, tends to gamble a bit too much, can be caught out of position, fairly solid defensive rebounding guard

Miles Bridges

	Height	Weight	Cap #	Years Left
	6'6"	225	$7.921M	UFA

Similar at Age 24

		Season	SIMsc
1	Tobias Harris	2016-17	921.8
2	Jaylen Brown	2020-21	918.1
3	Danny Granger	2007-08	917.7
4	Tyrone Nesby	1999-00	915.2
5	Tracy Murray	1995-96	912.8
6	Pascal Siakam	2018-19	911.9
7	Danny Green	2011-12	908.6
8	Aaron Gordon	2019-20	908.5
9	Quentin Richardson	2004-05	907.8
10	Mike Miller	2004-05	907.6

Baseline Basic Stats

MPG	PTS	AST	REB	BLK	STL
31.9	16.1	2.7	5.4	0.6	1.0

Advanced Metrics

USG%	3PTA/FGA	FTA/FGA	TS%	eFG%	3PT%
21.9	0.412	0.258	0.590	0.549	0.363

AST%	TOV%	OREB%	DREB%	STL%	BLK%
15.1	11.3	3.4	16.8	1.5	1.9

PER	ORTG	DRTG	WS/48	BPM	VOL
17.16	114.8	111.4	0.116	1.00	0.435

- Missed all last season while dealing with legal ramifications connected to a serious domestic violence incident
- Will miss the first 10 games of the 2023-24 while serving a suspension related to the incident
- Effective as a moderate volume scoring wing in the 2021-22 season
- Strong wing that can attack the rim as a pick-and-roll ball handler and isolation player
- Solid secondary playmaker that limits turnovers, good cutter off the ball, athletic finisher in transition
- Above break-even three-point shooter, most effective as a stationary spot-up shooter
- 2021-22 Defensive Degree of Difficulty: 0.483
- 2021-22 Points Prevented: 0.779
- Generally defended starting level players, drew a lot of tough assignments against top scoring wings
- Solid on-ball defenders, better against stronger post players, had some trouble staying with quicker players
- Average pick-and-roll defender, can functionally switch, has lapses when making rotations
- Tends to get caught on screens, consistently closes out on perimeter shooters in spot-up situations
- Doesn't usually get steals, good weak shot blocking wing, good defensive rebounder

Mark Williams

	Height	Weight	Cap #	Years Left
	7'1"	241	$3.908M	2 TO

Similar at Age 21

		Season	SIMsc
1	Moses Brown	2020-21	935.9
2	JaVale McGee	2008-09	912.1
3	Isaiah Hartenstein	2019-20	908.2
4	Vlade Divac*	1989-90	907.7
5	Andris Biedrins	2007-08	903.2
6	Tyson Chandler	2003-04	901.5
7	Robin Lopez	2009-10	899.2
8	Deyonta Davis	2017-18	898.1
9	Jason Smith	2007-08	894.5
10	Alex Len	2014-15	891.5

Baseline Basic Stats

MPG	PTS	AST	REB	BLK	STL
22.1	8.3	1.0	6.9	1.2	0.6

Advanced Metrics

USG%	3PTA/FGA	FTA/FGA	TS%	eFG%	3PT%
16.3	0.011	0.409	0.617	0.589	0.106

AST%	TOV%	OREB%	DREB%	STL%	BLK%
5.9	14.3	11.5	24.0	1.6	3.9

PER	ORTG	DRTG	WS/48	BPM	VOL
17.39	119.5	108.4	0.148	0.29	0.512

- Spent most of his rookie season in the G-League with Greensboro, became a regular rotation player late in 2022-23
- Solidly effective in his role as a low volume rim runner, posted a True Shooting Percentage of almost 66%
- Athletic big man with great length, vertical lob threat, good cutter and roll man, active offensive rebounder, runs hard in transition
- Not really a polished post player, lacks reliable shooting range outside of ten feet
- Strictly a catch-and-finish player, very limited passing skills, makes safe passes to avoid turnovers
- 2022-23 Defensive Degree of Difficulty: 0.416
- 2022-23 Points Prevented: 0.854
- Good shot blocker and defensive rebounder, still undisciplined with his positioning, only an average rim protector, somewhat foul prone
- Solid on-ball defender, stout post defender, mobile enough to defend quicker players in space
- Good pick-and-roll defender, effective in drop coverages, good at switching onto ball handlers
- Consistently comes out to contest perimeter shots in spot-up situations

Nick Richards

	Height	Weight	Cap #	Years Left
	7'0"	245	$5.000M	2

Similar at Age 25

		Season	SIMsc
1	Cody Zeller	2017-18	937.1
2	Damian Jones	2020-21	931.3
3	Duane Causwell	1993-94	921.2
4	Marcin Gortat	2009-10	919.9
5	Eric Riley	1995-96	914.2
6	Timofey Mozgov	2011-12	912.4
7	Festus Ezeli	2014-15	907.3
8	Will Perdue	1990-91	906.4
9	Jake Voskuhl	2002-03	904.9
10	Kelvin Cato	1999-00	903.4

Baseline Basic Stats

MPG	PTS	AST	REB	BLK	STL
18.8	6.6	0.8	5.4	0.9	0.4

Advanced Metrics

USG%	3PTA/FGA	FTA/FGA	TS%	eFG%	3PT%
15.2	0.020	0.487	0.631	0.594	0.486

AST%	TOV%	OREB%	DREB%	STL%	BLK%
5.9	14.5	10.5	21.1	0.8	3.9

PER	ORTG	DRTG	WS/48	BPM	VOL
15.85	121.0	110.2	0.138	-0.93	0.376

- Became a regular rotation player for Charlotte in his third NBA season
- Had a career best season in a role as a low usage rim runner
- Athletic big man that plays with high energy, efficient finisher at the rim, posted a True Shooting Percentage of almost 68%
- Great roll man and cutter, good offensive rebounder that scores on put-backs, runs hard in transition
- Limited offensive skills, below average post player, limited passing skills
- Cut his turnover rate, experimenting with shooting outside shots but rarely shoots jumpers in games
- 2022-23 Defensive Degree of Difficulty: 0.379
- 2022-23 Points Prevented: -0.700
- Effective rim protector, good shot blocker and defensive rebounder
- Mainly guards second unit players, played below average on-ball defense
- Can be pushed around inside by stronger post players, struggles to stay with quicker players when defending in space, commits fouls at a high rate
- Average pick-and-roll defender, good at switching out on ball handlers, has lapses when defending screeners
- Tends to stay anchored into the paint, does not always come out to contest perimeter shots

Cody Martin

	Height	Weight	Cap #	Years Left
	6'5"	205	$7.560M	2

Similar at Age 27

		Season	SIMsc
1	Laron Profit	2004-05	934.6
2	Kenrich Williams	2021-22	927.5
3	Michael Curry	1995-96	925.8
4	Richie Frahm	2004-05	924.3
5	Iman Shumpert	2017-18	923.8
6	Doug Lee	1991-92	921.0
7	Chase Budinger	2015-16	920.9
8	Greg Buckner	2003-04	916.0
9	Quinton Ross	2008-09	915.3
10	Sam Young	2012-13	914.4

Baseline Basic Stats

MPG	PTS	AST	REB	BLK	STL
19.8	6.9	1.3	2.9	0.2	0.7

Advanced Metrics

USG%	3PTA/FGA	FTA/FGA	TS%	eFG%	3PT%
14.4	0.451	0.210	0.529	0.503	0.330

AST%	TOV%	OREB%	DREB%	STL%	BLK%
10.8	8.8	4.5	12.7	1.7	1.0

PER	ORTG	DRTG	WS/48	BPM	VOL
11.36	113.3	112.9	0.088	-1.28	0.496

- Missed almost of all last season due to a knee injury, only played seven games
- Mainly used as a low usage spot-up shooter and energy wing, injury heavily diminished his production
- Below break-even career three-point shooter, shooting percentages regressed to career averages
- Strictly a stationary spot-up shooter when his shot is falling
- Good athlete when healthy, explosive finisher in transition, good cutter off the ball
- Lacks the ability to create his own shot, solid secondary playmaker, good at avoiding turnovers
- 2022-23 Defensive Degree of Difficulty: 0.445
- 2022-23 Points Prevented: -4.584
- Typically guarded starting level players, injury diminished his effectiveness, average defender when healthy
- Played below average on-ball defense, struggled to stay with opposing wings
- Struggled to defend pick-and-rolls, not effective at taking away any specific action
- Tended to be out of position off the ball, late when closing out on spot-up shooters, could fight through screens
- Typically an active help defender gets steals and blocks shots from the weak side, activity limited due to his knee injury, solid defensive rebounder

JT Thor

	Height	Weight	Cap #	Years Left
	6'10"	205	$1.836M	Team Option

Similar at Age 20

		Season	SIMsc
1	Greg Brown III	2021-22	903.7
2	Deni Avdija	2020-21	899.9
3	Rodions Kurucs	2018-19	896.1
4	Jaden McDaniels	2020-21	890.2
5	Nicolas Batum	2008-09	890.1
6	Jalen Smith	2020-21	888.7
7	Jonathan Isaac	2017-18	888.5
8	Gordon Hayward	2010-11	888.2
9	DerMarr Johnson	2000-01	886.0
10	Kevin Knox	2019-20	885.7

Baseline Basic Stats

MPG	PTS	AST	REB	BLK	STL
22.3	8.3	1.3	4.0	0.6	0.7

Advanced Metrics

USG%	3PTA/FGA	FTA/FGA	TS%	eFG%	3PT%
15.8	0.480	0.243	0.546	0.514	0.317

AST%	TOV%	OREB%	DREB%	STL%	BLK%
8.5	12.3	4.3	13.8	1.4	2.2

PER	ORTG	DRTG	WS/48	BPM	VOL
11.45	107.9	112.9	0.073	-1.77	0.514

- Became a back-end rotation player for Charlotte in his second NBA season
- Efficiency decreased slightly, mainly used as a low volume stretch four and energy wing
- Below break-even three-point shooter, Three-Point Percentage improved by over five percent
- Almost exclusively a stationary spot-up shooter, better in the corners, has made over 39% of his career corner threes
- Explosive finisher, good cutter, selectively goes to the glass to score on put-backs, tends to play wildly, will miss a lot of easy shots in transition
- Not really able to create his own shot, limited passing skills, good at limiting turnovers
- 2022-23 Defensive Degree of Difficulty: 0.382
- 2022-23 Points Prevented: 0.159
- Good roaming rim protector, effective weak side shot blocker, decent defensive rebounder
- Usually guards second unit players, average on-ball defender
- Better against interior players, struggles to stay with quicker perimeter players
- Middling pick-and-roll defender, effective in drop coverages, has trouble containing ball handlers
- Gets caught on screens off the ball, consistently will close out on spot-up shooters

Bryce McGowens

	Height	Weight	Cap #	Years Left
	6'7"	179	$1.720M	1 + TO

Similar at Age 20

		Season	SIMsc
1	Brandon Boston Jr.	2021-22	900.4
2	R.J. Hampton	2021-22	888.8
3	Théo Maledon	2021-22	885.7
4	Kevin Huerter	2018-19	885.1
5	Isaac Bonga	2019-20	883.3
6	Gordon Hayward	2010-11	883.0
7	Anfernee Simons	2019-20	879.6
8	Martell Webster	2006-07	878.9
9	Ben McLemore	2013-14	877.5
10	Jamal Crawford	2000-01	877.2

Baseline Basic Stats

MPG	PTS	AST	REB	BLK	STL
21.2	8.7	1.6	2.5	0.2	0.6

Advanced Metrics

USG%	3PTA/FGA	FTA/FGA	TS%	eFG%	3PT%
17.4	0.458	0.324	0.560	0.508	0.366

AST%	TOV%	OREB%	DREB%	STL%	BLK%
10.9	12.6	2.2	10.1	1.2	0.6

PER	ORTG	DRTG	WS/48	BPM	VOL
11.49	108.5	115.2	0.071	-2.37	0.495

- Began the season on a Two-Way contract with Charlotte then was signed to a standard contract
- Became a regular rotation player in his rookie season, mostly used as a low usage spot-up shooter
- Made threes at a below break-even rate overall, made almost 40% of his spot-up threes, much less effective when shooting in other situations
- Athletic finisher, effective cutter, draws fouls at a high rate, tends to play out of control, struggled to score efficiently in transition
- Inefficient in ball handling situations, not really suited to being a shot creator
- Mainly a catch-and-shoot player, has some passing skills, slightly turnover prone
- <u>2022-23 Defensive Degree of Difficulty</u>: 0.337
- <u>2022-23 Points Prevented</u>: -0.618
- Usually guarded second unit level players, fairly solid on-ball defender against lower leverage players
- Has good quickness, effective against quicker perimeter players, can be overpowered by stronger players inside
- Average pick-and-roll defender, good at switching onto screeners, struggled to effectively guard ball handlers
- Tends to get caught on screens off the ball, not always in position to contest shots in spot-up situations
- Rarely gets steals or blocks, fairly decent defensive rebounder

Kai Jones

	Height	Weight	Cap #	Years Left
	6'11"	218	$3.048M	Team Option

Similar at Age 22

		Season	SIMsc
1	Nic Claxton	2021-22	918.2
2	Skal Labissiere	2018-19	917.4
3	Hilton Armstrong	2006-07	903.8
4	Olivier Sarr	2021-22	896.2
5	Thon Maker	2019-20	896.1
6	Deyonta Davis	2018-19	886.7
7	Nazr Mohammed	1999-00	883.8
8	Viktor Khryapa	2004-05	882.2
9	Sylvester Norris	1979-80	879.7
10	Darren Tillis	1982-83	878.7

Baseline Basic Stats

MPG	PTS	AST	REB	BLK	STL
18.1	6.2	0.8	4.5	1.0	0.5

Advanced Metrics

USG%	3PTA/FGA	FTA/FGA	TS%	eFG%	3PT%
14.8	0.096	0.359	0.596	0.586	0.233

AST%	TOV%	OREB%	DREB%	STL%	BLK%
6.8	17.6	7.9	16.9	1.3	4.1

PER	ORTG	DRTG	WS/48	BPM	VOL
13.00	109.3	110.9	0.085	-2.63	0.515

- Split time between Charlotte and Greensboro in the G-League
- Effectiveness increased slightly in the NBA, mainly used as a low volume rim runner and occasional stretch big
- More effective as a rim runner, athletic big man, made almost 84% of his shots from three feet and in
- Good cutter, can roll to the rim, effective offensive rebounder, runs hard in transition
- Tries to take outside shots but shot is unreliable right now, below break-even three-point shooter
- Best as a stand-still shooter, more comfortable taking shorter mid-range shots
- Not a real post-up threat, not able to create his own offense, limited passing skills, highly turnover prone
- 2022-23 Defensive Degree of Difficulty: 0.329
- 2022-23 Points Prevented: 0.017
- Good roaming rim protector, decent defensive rebounder, good shot blocker, uses length well to get steals
- Generally guarded second unit level big men, played effective post defense
- Had some trouble staying with quicker players in space, committed fouls at a fairly high rate
- Solid pick-and-roll defender, good in drop coverages, can effectively switch out onto ball handlers
- Tends to stay anchored in the paint, does not always come out to contest perimeter shots in spot-up situations

James Bouknight

	Height	Weight	Cap #	Years Left
	6'5"	190	$4.570M	Team Option

Similar at Age 22

		Season	SIMsc
1	Tyler Dorsey	2018-19	939.8
2	Rodney Buford	1999-00	937.3
3	Ty Jerome	2019-20	932.9
4	Jeremy Lamb	2014-15	929.3
5	Jerome Robinson	2019-20	928.3
6	C.J. McCollum	2013-14	926.2
7	Daequan Cook	2009-10	925.4
8	Allan Ray	2006-07	924.5
9	Manny Harris	2011-12	922.7
10	Darrun Hilliard	2015-16	920.4

Baseline Basic Stats

MPG	PTS	AST	REB	BLK	STL
19.6	8.6	1.5	2.2	0.2	0.6

Advanced Metrics

USG%	3PTA/FGA	FTA/FGA	TS%	eFG%	3PT%
20.4	0.409	0.201	0.520	0.488	0.360

AST%	TOV%	OREB%	DREB%	STL%	BLK%
12.0	11.0	3.2	10.9	1.5	0.6

PER	ORTG	DRTG	WS/48	BPM	VOL
11.30	103.0	113.7	0.037	-3.04	0.384

- Split time between Charlotte and Greensboro in the G-League
- Production level declined significantly in the NBA, mainly used as a lower volume spot-up shooter
- Average or worse in almost every offensive situation according to Synergy
- Below break-even three-point shooter in the NBA, percentages have varied in the G-League
- Most effective as a stationary spot-up shooter in the corners
- Really struggled in ball handling situations, shot selection needs improvement, rarely moves off the ball
- Decent secondary playmaker that can make simple reads, effective at limiting turnovers
- 2022-23 Defensive Degree of Difficulty: 0.324
- 2022-23 Points Prevented: 1.810
- Usually defended lower leverage second unit players, played average on-ball defense
- More effective at holding position against bigger players, had trouble staying with quicker players on the perimeter, tended to commit a lot of shooting fouls
- Played solid pick-and-roll defense, can occasionally switch, good at funneling his man into help
- Fights through screens off the ball, tended to be late when closing out on spot-up shooters
- Stay-at-home defender, rarely gets steals or blocks, fairly solid defensive rebounder

Kobi Simmons

	Height	Weight	Cap #	Years Left
	6'5"	166	$2.067M	UFA

Similar at Age 25

		Season	SIMsc
1	Antonius Cleveland	2019-20	775.7
2	Roko Ukic	2009-10	760.8
3	Drew Barry	1998-99	759.7
4	Mychal Mulder	2019-20	756.9
5	Marcus Brown	1999-00	756.4
6	Brodric Thomas	2021-22	753.6
7	Alex Abrines	2018-19	750.4
8	Dylan Windler	2021-22	749.2
9	Kadeem Allen	2017-18	748.1
10	Alexey Shved	2013-14	741.0

Baseline Basic Stats

MPG	PTS	AST	REB	BLK	STL
17.9	6.9	2.1	1.9	0.1	0.5

Advanced Metrics

USG%	3PTA/FGA	FTA/FGA	TS%	eFG%	3PT%
14.6	0.703	0.256	0.521	0.458	0.355

AST%	TOV%	OREB%	DREB%	STL%	BLK%
23.9	11.2	2.4	11.4	1.0	3.3

PER	ORTG	DRTG	WS/48	BPM	VOL
14.34	116.9	115.8	0.095	0.86	0.315

- Only played 28 NBA minutes, spent most of the season with Greensboro in the G-League
- Used as a low usage spot-up shooter in limited NBA action, played a moderate volume role as a secondary ball handler in the G-League
- Made almost 38% of his threes in the G-League last season, below break-even career three-point shooter in the NBA, mostly a spot-up shooter
- Solid secondary playmaker that makes simple reads, slightly turnover prone
- Not really asked to create his own shot in the NBA, not expected to be a high usage scorer
- 2022-23 Defensive Degree of Difficulty: 0.120
- 2022-23 Points Prevented: 1.619
- Mainly played in garbage time, rarely tested on defense in limited action in the NBA
- Defended one isolation play last season, allowed a three-pointer
- Allowed zero points in eight pick-and-roll possessions, forced six misses and two turnovers
- Allowed a made three and forced two misses in three possessions when defending a spot-up shooter
- Allowed a made two-pointer and forced one miss in two hand-off possessions
- Fairly active help defender in the G-League, gets steals at a solid rate, fairly solid defensive rebounder

Frank Ntilikina

	Height	Weight	Cap #	Years Left
	6'4"	200	$2.020M	UFA

Similar at Age 24

		Season	SIMsc
1	Kim English	2012-13	932.6
2	Norman Powell	2017-18	931.0
3	Eric Washington	1998-99	929.1
4	Jerian Grant	2016-17	925.4
5	Trajan Langdon	2000-01	925.1
6	Caleb Martin	2019-20	925.0
7	Walter Bond	1993-94	922.8
8	Wayne Ellington	2011-12	921.6
9	Matthew Dellavedova	2014-15	920.3
10	Gabe Vincent	2020-21	920.1

Baseline Basic Stats

MPG	PTS	AST	REB	BLK	STL
17.5	6.1	1.8	2.0	0.1	0.6

Advanced Metrics

USG%	3PTA/FGA	FTA/FGA	TS%	eFG%	3PT%
15.7	0.496	0.219	0.514	0.483	0.346

AST%	TOV%	OREB%	DREB%	STL%	BLK%
15.8	14.1	1.9	10.6	1.7	0.8

PER	ORTG	DRTG	WS/48	BPM	VOL
9.66	103.9	112.2	0.055	-2.13	0.412

- Missed some games due to knee and ankle injuries, played limited minutes for Dallas last season
- Production declined precipitously, struggled in his role as a low usage spot-up shooter and secondary playmaker
- Below break-even career three-point shooter, True Shooting Percentage fell to below 50% last season
- Really struggled to make spot-up jumpers, shooting percentages have varied throughout his career
- Ineffective as a ball handler, defenders often back away from him to make things tougher for him
- Decent playmaker that makes simple reads, does not always play under control, somewhat turnover prone
- 2022-23 Defensive Degree of Difficulty: 0.386
- 2022-23 Points Prevented: 2.110
- Generally guarded second unit players, solid on-ball defender in the past
- Struggled as an on-ball defender last season, not always able to stay with opposing guards
- Solid pick-and-roll defender, effective at switching, good at fighting over the screen to contain ball handlers
- Gets caught on screens off the ball, good at closing out on spot-up shooters, sometimes takes bad gambles
- More of a stay-at-home defender, Steal Percentage decreased significantly, decent defensive rebounder

Newcomers

Brandon Miller

	Height	Weight	Cap #	Years Left
	6'9"	201	$10.880M	1 + 2 TO

Baseline Basic Stats

MPG	PTS	AST	REB	BLK	STL
22.9	8.9	1.3	3.5	0.4	0.7

Advanced Metrics

USG%	3PTA/FGA	FTA/FGA	TS%	eFG%	3PT%
18.5	0.447	0.248	0.530	0.493	0.342

AST%	TOV%	OREB%	DREB%	STL%	BLK%
9.0	11.4	4.5	12.8	1.5	1.5

PER	ORTG	DRTG	WS/48	BPM	VOL
12.64	103.9	103.9	0.076	-1.09	N/A

- Drafted by Charlotte with the 2nd overall pick in 2023
- Had an up and down performance at the Las Vegas and Sacramento Summer Leagues
- Played better in Las Vegas, mainly used as a high volume scoring wing
- Posted a decent True Shooting Percentage overall, made threes at a below break-even rate at Summer League
- More efficient shooter off the catch, inconsistent when shooting off the dribble, can struggle to score in ball handling situations
- Needs to improve ball handling skills, tends to lose the ball under heavy pressure
- Displayed improved playmaking skills at Summer League, able to make simple reads to find open teammates
- Athletic defender with good length, has potential to defend multiple positions with more development
- More of a team defender right now, had trouble defending on the ball in college
- Struggled to stay with quicker players, can be overpowered by stronger post players
- Solid pick-and-roll defender, good at funneling his man into help, not really asked to switch much in college
- Stays attached to shooters off the ball, will fight through screens and close out in spot-up situations
- Very active help defender at Summer League, posted high steal and block rates, good defensive rebounder

Nick Smith Jr

	Height	Weight	Cap #	Years Left
	6'5"	185	$2.464M	1 + 2 TO

Baseline Basic Stats

MPG	PTS	AST	REB	BLK	STL
17.2	7.1	1.5	1.9	0.2	0.5

Advanced Metrics

USG%	3PTA/FGA	FTA/FGA	TS%	eFG%	3PT%
20.0	0.387	0.175	0.482	0.453	0.310

AST%	TOV%	OREB%	DREB%	STL%	BLK%
14.2	11.5	1.6	8.7	1.4	0.6

PER	ORTG	DRTG	WS/48	BPM	VOL
10.11	95.1	107.9	0.024	-2.61	N/A

- Drafted by Charlotte with the 27th overall pick in 2023
- Uneven performance in the Las Vegas and Sacramento Summer Leagues
- Put up counting numbers at a decently high volume but struggled with his efficiency
- Mainly used as a high volume scoring guard, likely will need to transition to a lower usage role in the NBA
- Posted a True Shooting Percentage below 50%, made threes at a below break-even rate
- Most effective as a stationary spot-up shooter in college
- Inconsistent scorer with the ball in his hands, ineffective as a pick-and-roll ball handler and isolation player
- Good cutter off the ball, does not move off the ball very much
- Scoring minded guard, decent playmaker that makes simple reads, a bit turnover prone
- Defensive performance slowed by a knee injury in college, still may be a capable defender in the NBA
- Hidden in lower leverage assignments, played decent on-ball defense, can stay with opposing guards
- Decent pick-and-roll defender, limited ability to switch, effective at funneling his man into help
- Tends to get caught on screens off the ball, consistently closes out on spot-up shooters
- Got steals at a solid rate in college, did not really get steals at Summer League
- Blocked four shots in six Summer League, solid defensive rebounding guard
- Could use additional seasoning in the G-League to improve his offensive efficiency

DETROIT PISTONS

Last Season: 17 – 65, Missed the Playoffs

Offensive Rating: 110.7, 28th in the NBA

Defensive Rating: 118.9, 28th in the NBA

Primary Executive: Troy Weaver, General Manager

Head Coach: Monty Williams

Key Roster Changes

Subtractions
Alec Burks, free agency
Cory Joseph, free agency
Hamidou Diallo, free agency
Rodney McGruder, free agency
R.J. Hampton, waived
Eugene Omoruyi, waived

Additions
Ausar Thompson, draft
Marcus Sasser, draft
Joe Harris, trade
Monte Morris, trade

Roster

Likely Starting Five
1. Cade Cunningham
2. Jaden Ivey
3. Bojan Bogdanović
4. Isaiah Stewart
5. Jalen Duren

Other Key Rotation Players
Monte Morris
Joe Harris
Ausar Thompson
Alec Burks
Marvin Bagley III

* Italics denotes that a player is likely to be on the floor to close games

Remaining Roster

- James Wiseman
- Isaiah Livers
- Killian Hayes
- Marcus Sasser
- Jared Rhoden, 23, 6'6", 210, Seton Hall (Two-Way)
- Malcolm Cazalon, 21, 6'6", 212, France (Two-Way)
- Tosan Evbuomwan, 22, 6'7", 215, Princeton (Exhibit 10)
- Zavier Simpson, 26, 6'0", 190, Michigan (Exhibit 10)
- Buddy Boeheim, 24, 6'6", 205, Syracuse (Exhibit 10)
- Stanley Umude, 24, 6'6", 210, Arkansas (Exhibit 10)

SCHREMPF Base Rating: 38.2

Season Preview Survey

- *Are the Pistons contending or rebuilding? Where is this team headed?*

The Pistons still in the midst of a full-scale rebuild. Their progress stalled last season because Cade Cunningham was out for most of the year due to a stress fracture in his shin. With him back in the fold, Detroit will look to make some forward progress to show signs that they can compete for a playoff spot in the near future. They have spent the past few seasons accumulating young talent and assets, but now is the point where they have turn them into something resembling a functioning basketball team. If they aren't able to do this, then they may rethink their strategy and possibly start over again to establish a workable direction to build a winner in the future.

- *What are the areas of concern for this team heading into this season?*

The major concern for Detroit is that their rebuilding strategy is already overly dependent on the development of Cade Cunningham to succeed. They drafted him with the hope that he would develop into an elite heliocentric scorer and ball handler to allow others to settle into simplified roles. He's shown his potential in short stretches towards the end of the 2021-22 season. However, he hasn't been able to truly blossom because he's been playing on an over-matched roster, and he had the shin injury that really set him back. That being said, their roster is more talented than it was in his first two years. There's a better chance of him realizing his potential to become the player that they had initially envisioned. If that happens, then everyone else can play their expected roles and the franchise can move forward. If his growth is stunted, then they may need to find some ways to alter their plans to allow their other young players to expand their games to take some of the pressure off him and allow the team to grow in a different direction.

- *List some possible breakout players for this team.*

The Pistons' young players are still in developmental stages, and they haven't really established themselves as finished products, so a lot of them qualify as breakout candidates. Eyes will be on Cunningham and Jaden Ivey because they will need to show that they can thrive as primary scoring options at the NBA level. Both players have the necessary talent to play this kind of role. If they can improve their efficiency, they could make a big leap forward in their development. Additionally, Ausar Thompson showcased a versatile skill set at Summer League because he can attack the rim, make plays for others, and defend. He just needs to improve the consistency of his jump shot to realize his full potential. Then, Jalen Duren is close to being a legitimately impactful center in the league with his rim running and rim protecting skills. At this stage, he has to add more skill to become a bigger threat on offense. Finally, Marcus Sasser might not have a lot of high-end upside, but he could make solid contributions as a pesky defender and a ball control guard that limits mistakes.

- *What should we expect from them this season?*

Most likely, Detroit will remain near the bottom of the standings as a lottery team because they are still in the rebuilding phase. Wins and losses aren't nearly as important as seeing positive development from their primary young players. In particular, they need Cade Cunningham to show that he can effectively handle the responsibilities of being a primary scorer and playmaker because their whole strategy is built around him becoming this sort of player. If he makes strides to tap into his considerable upside, it will be a good sign that the Pistons' plan could work out in the future. Otherwise, they will need to work with their new head coach, Monty Williams to develop a contingency plan to build a future that isn't as dependent on one person to move their franchise forward.

Veterans

Bojan Bogdanović

	Height	Weight	Cap #	Years Left
	6'7"	226	$20.000M	1

Similar at Age 33

		Season	SIMsc
1	Vince Carter	2009-10	925.7
2	Richard Jefferson	2013-14	924.2
3	Michael Finley	2006-07	917.4
4	Glen Rice	2000-01	915.9
5	Jerry Stackhouse	2007-08	910.0
6	Joe Johnson	2014-15	904.3
7	Eddie A. Johnson	1992-93	899.3
8	Rudy Gay	2019-20	897.9
9	Paul Pierce*	2010-11	897.5
10	Mike Miller	2013-14	896.2

Baseline Basic Stats

MPG	PTS	AST	REB	BLK	STL
27.6	12.2	2.1	3.6	0.2	0.6

Advanced Metrics

USG%	3PTA/FGA	FTA/FGA	TS%	eFG%	3PT%
21.6	0.435	0.260	0.571	0.528	0.381

AST%	TOV%	OREB%	DREB%	STL%	BLK%
11.1	11.2	2.3	12.1	1.1	0.5

PER	ORTG	DRTG	WS/48	BPM	VOL
13.94	110.0	113.9	0.092	-0.32	0.208

- Regular starter for Detroit in his first season with the team, missed games due to an Achilles injury
- Greatly increased his effectiveness in his role as Detroit's primary scoring option
- Very reliable three-point shooter throughout his career, most effective when shooting off the catch
- Excellent spot-up shooter, good at shooting off screens, slightly less efficient when shooting off the dribble
- Crafty pick-and-roll ball handler and isolation player that leverages the threat of his shot to create space, willing to absorb contact to draw fouls
- Normally a catch-and-shoot player, improving passer, posted a career high in Assist Percentage
- 2022-23 Defensive Degree of Difficulty: 0.469
- 2022-23 Points Prevented: -1.082
- Hidden in favorable matchups in the past, drew tougher assignments in Detroit
- Average on-ball defender, more effective against stronger post players, has trouble staying with quicker players
- Average pick-and-roll defender, can functionally switch, has lapses when making rotations
- Stays attached to shooters off the ball, fights through screens and closes out in spot-up situations
- Stay-at-home defender, rarely gets steals or blocks, decent defensive rebounder

Cade Cunningham

	Height	Weight	Cap #	Years Left
	6'6"	220	$11.055M	Team Option

Similar at Age 21

		Season	SIMsc
1	Tyreke Evans	2010-11	902.8
2	D'Angelo Russell	2017-18	899.2
3	Devin Booker	2017-18	897.0
4	Emmanuel Mudiay	2017-18	889.4
5	Jerry Stackhouse	1995-96	880.8
6	RJ Barrett	2021-22	879.4
7	Nickeil Alexander-Walker	2019-20	879.0
8	Marcus D. Williams	2006-07	874.9
9	Corey Maggette	2000-01	874.4
10	Kirk Snyder	2004-05	872.9

Baseline Basic Stats

MPG	PTS	AST	REB	BLK	STL
29.3	16.3	3.6	4.3	0.3	0.9

Advanced Metrics

USG%	3PTA/FGA	FTA/FGA	TS%	eFG%	3PT%
25.8	0.224	0.248	0.525	0.485	0.301

AST%	TOV%	OREB%	DREB%	STL%	BLK%
25.7	14.7	3.3	13.7	1.5	1.0

PER	ORTG	DRTG	WS/48	BPM	VOL
14.75	104.4	114.2	0.049	0.13	0.632

- Missed most of last season due to a stress fracture in his left shin
- Production level increased slightly in his role as Detroit's primary scorer and ball handler when healthy
- Dynamic playmaker with excellent court vision to set up teammates, cut his turnover rate significantly
- Good pick-and-roll ball handler that can use the screen to free himself for mid-range pull-up jumpers
- Less effective in isolation situations, not able to explode to the rim due to his shin injury
- Below break-even three-point shooter, struggled to make threes in almost every situation, much more comfortable when shooting from mid-range
- 2022-23 Defensive Degree of Difficulty: 0.492
- 2022-23 Points Prevented: 3.108
- Drew much tougher assignments in limited action in his second season
- Flashed the ability to guard multiple positions as a rookie, less effective when playing on-ball defense last season
- Below average pick-and-roll defender, tended to allow ball handlers to turn the corner or would go too far under screens
- Tends to get caught on screens off the ball, consistently closed out on spot-up shooters
- Steal and Block Percentage decreased due to his shin injury, good defensive rebounder

Isaiah Stewart

	Height	**Weight**	**Cap #**	**Years Left**
	6'8"	250	$5.267M	3 + TO

Similar at Age 21

		Season	SIMsc
1	Thomas Bryant	2018-19	912.7
2	Carlos Boozer	2002-03	902.4
3	Wendell Carter Jr.	2020-21	895.3
4	Omari Spellman	2018-19	895.2
5	J.J. Hickson	2009-10	894.6
6	Al Horford	2007-08	894.6
7	Trendon Watford	2021-22	888.4
8	Patrick Patterson	2010-11	886.0
9	P.J. Washington	2019-20	885.6
10	Zach Collins	2018-19	884.9

Baseline Basic Stats

MPG	PTS	AST	REB	BLK	STL
25.2	10.7	1.5	6.7	0.7	0.6

Advanced Metrics

USG%	3PTA/FGA	FTA/FGA	TS%	eFG%	3PT%
17.3	0.191	0.333	0.565	0.525	0.391

AST%	TOV%	OREB%	DREB%	STL%	BLK%
9.0	13.0	9.4	21.3	1.0	2.2

PER	ORTG	DRTG	WS/48	BPM	VOL
14.73	114.0	112.4	0.102	-0.97	0.312

- Missed games due to injuries to his toe, shoulder, and hip, regular starter for Detroit when healthy
- Moderately effective in a different role as a low volume stretch big
- Below break-even three-point shooter throughout his career
- Mainly a stationary spot-up shooter, occasionally makes threes as a pick-and-pop screener
- High energy rim runner, solid cutter and roll man, solid offensive rebounder, draws fouls
- Rushes shots inside, prone to missing easy shots, below average post player
- Limited passing skills, mainly a catch-and-shoot or catch-and-finish player, good at limiting turnovers
- 2022-23 Defensive Degree of Difficulty: 0.445
- 2022-23 Points Prevented: -1.851
- Below average rim protector, shot blocking rates heavily declined, good defensive rebounder
- Guarded starting level players, below average on-ball defender
- Taller big men can shoot over him, struggles to stay with quicker perimeter players
- Below average pick-and-roll defender, not effective at taking away any specific action
- Tended to sag back into the paint, did not usually come out to contest perimeter shots, tended to get caught on screens off the ball

Jalen Duren

	Height	Weight	Cap #	Years Left
	6'10"	250	$4.331M	2 TO

Similar at Age 19

		Season	SIMsc
1	Derrick Favors	2010-11	920.5
2	Jarrett Allen	2017-18	897.9
3	Isaiah Stewart	2020-21	897.3
4	Enes Freedom	2011-12	893.4
5	Andris Biedrins	2005-06	886.9
6	Dwight Howard	2004-05	882.9
7	Wendell Carter	2018-19	869.9
8	Chris Bosh*	2003-04	865.7
9	Olumide Oyedeji	2000-01	862.3
10	Andre Drummond	2012-13	860.8

Baseline Basic Stats

MPG	PTS	AST	REB	BLK	STL
25.6	10.3	1.5	8.1	1.0	0.7

Advanced Metrics

USG%	3PTA/FGA	FTA/FGA	TS%	eFG%	3PT%
17.0	0.038	0.402	0.647	0.626	0.183

AST%	TOV%	OREB%	DREB%	STL%	BLK%
10.4	15.9	12.8	26.9	1.5	2.9

PER	ORTG	DRTG	WS/48	BPM	VOL
19.88	124.2	111.4	0.163	0.46	0.290

- Named to the All-Rookie 2nd Team, played regular rotational minutes for Detroit
- Highly effective in his role as a low usage rim runner, posted a 65.5% True Shooting Percentage
- Very athletic big man, vertical lob threat with great length, great roll man and cutter, excellent offensive rebounder, great at running the floor in transition
- Offensive skill is limited, below average post player, lacks shooting range outside of ten feet
- Draws fouls but has made less than 65% of his free throws, limited passing skills, a bit turnover prone
- 2022-23 Defensive Degree of Difficulty: 0.403
- 2022-23 Points Prevented: -0.752
- Good shot blocker and defensive rebounder, below average rim protector, undisciplined with his positioning, a bit foul prone
- Guarded second unit big men or lower leverage starters, average on-ball defender
- Lacks strength, can be pushed around by stronger big men inside, good mobility to defend in space
- Decent pick-and-roll defender, good in drop coverages, less effective when switched onto a ball handler
- Tended to get caught on screens off the ball, consistently come out to contest perimeter shots in spot-up situations
- Occasionally can use his length and quick hands to get steals

Jaden Ivey

	Height	Weight	Cap #	Years Left
	6'4"	195	$7.614M	2 TO

Similar at Age 20

		Season	SIMsc
1	Dennis Smith Jr.	2017-18	924.5
2	D'Angelo Russell	2016-17	922.4
3	Brandon Knight	2011-12	922.3
4	Kevin Porter Jr.	2020-21	920.4
5	Emmanuel Mudiay	2016-17	917.5
6	Jalen Suggs	2021-22	916.9
7	Ja Morant	2019-20	911.3
8	Zach LaVine	2015-16	909.3
9	John Wall	2010-11	908.0
10	Coby White	2020-21	907.4

Baseline Basic Stats

MPG	PTS	AST	REB	BLK	STL
31.0	16.5	4.9	3.7	0.3	1.1

Advanced Metrics

USG%	3PTA/FGA	FTA/FGA	TS%	eFG%	3PT%
26.0	0.372	0.313	0.542	0.494	0.360

AST%	TOV%	OREB%	DREB%	STL%	BLK%
25.9	15.1	3.0	10.2	1.5	0.6

PER	ORTG	DRTG	WS/48	BPM	VOL
14.96	106.9	116.0	0.056	-0.83	0.323

- Named to the All-Rookie 2nd Team, regular starting guard for Detroit
- Put up counting numbers in volume, middling efficiency in a role as a high usage ball handler
- Rated by Synergy as average or worse in almost every offensive situation
- Above break-even three-point shooter, most effective as a stand-still spot-up shooter
- Can hit floaters, draws fouls, average scorer in ball handling situations, inconsistent shooter off the dribble
- Explosive finisher in transition, tends to play out of control, does not really move off the ball
- Decent playmaker, can make simple reads, not quite a natural passer, can be a bit turnover prone
- 2022-23 Defensive Degree of Difficulty: 0.423
- 2022-23 Points Prevented: -1.307
- Usually guards starting level players, tends to be hidden in favorable matchups
- Below average on-ball defender, struggled to stay with opposing perimeter players
- Below average pick-and-roll defender, frequently has lapses, not effective at taking away any specific action
- Tends to be out of position off the ball, gets caught on screens, usually is late when closing out
- Mostly a stay-at-home defender, occasionally can get steals or blocks, decent defensive rebounder

Monte Morris

	Height	Weight	Cap #	Years Left
	6'2"	183	$9.801M	UFA

Similar at Age 27

		Season	SIMsc
1	John Paxson	1987-88	932.8
2	George Hill	2013-14	931.4
3	Craig Hodges	1987-88	923.9
4	Howard Eisley	1999-00	912.9
5	Steve Blake	2007-08	912.6
6	Patty Mills	2015-16	912.5
7	Chasson Randle	2020-21	912.1
8	E'Twaun Moore	2016-17	912.1
9	Bryce Drew	2001-02	911.9
10	Mo Williams	2009-10	911.1

Baseline Basic Stats

MPG	PTS	AST	REB	BLK	STL
24.6	9.6	3.3	2.2	0.1	0.8

Advanced Metrics

USG%	3PTA/FGA	FTA/FGA	TS%	eFG%	3PT%
17.2	0.445	0.151	0.568	0.544	0.389

AST%	TOV%	OREB%	DREB%	STL%	BLK%
22.3	10.6	1.5	9.8	1.4	0.5

PER	ORTG	DRTG	WS/48	BPM	VOL
14.31	117.9	113.7	0.113	0.14	0.318

- Regular starting point guard for Washington in his first season with the team, missed games due to an assortment of minor injuries
- Increased his overall effectiveness, mainly used as a low volume, game managing set-up guard
- Great ball control guard, rarely turns the ball over, solid distributor that can effectively read a defense
- Reliable three-point shooter that consistently posts high percentages
- Mostly a stationary spot-up shooter, can make quick pull-up jumpers if defenders go under screens
- Plays with a heavy pass-first mindset, can get to his spots as a pick-and-roll ball handler, better in isolation situations last year
- 2022-23 Defensive Degree of Difficulty: 0.471
- 2022-23 Points Prevented: 0.314
- Took on tougher assignments against higher-end guards, played better on-ball defense last season
- Could effectively defend ones and twos, slight tendency to back off his man to concede jump shots
- Good pick-and-roll defender, effective at funneling his man into help, can functionally switch on a limited basis
- Fights through screens off the ball, sometimes can be late to close out on spot-up shooters
- Stay-at-home defender, does not really get steals or blocks at the same rate that he did in previous seasons, improved to become a decent defensive rebounder

Joe Harris

	Height	Weight	Cap #	Years Left
	6'6"	220	$19.929M	UFA

Similar at Age 31

		Season	SIMsc
1	J.R. Smith	2016-17	948.7
2	Richard Jefferson	2011-12	921.6
3	Quentin Richardson	2011-12	921.1
4	Danny Green	2018-19	920.6
5	Alan Anderson	2013-14	919.9
6	DeShawn Stevenson	2012-13	914.3
7	Kyle Korver	2012-13	909.0
8	Maurice Evans	2009-10	907.3
9	Mike Miller	2011-12	907.0
10	Dennis Scott	1999-00	906.1

Baseline Basic Stats

MPG	PTS	AST	REB	BLK	STL
21.6	6.6	1.3	2.7	0.2	0.6

Advanced Metrics

USG%	3PTA/FGA	FTA/FGA	TS%	eFG%	3PT%
13.5	0.687	0.098	0.589	0.576	0.415

AST%	TOV%	OREB%	DREB%	STL%	BLK%
8.1	10.1	1.9	11.3	1.2	0.8

PER	ORTG	DRTG	WS/48	BPM	VOL
10.00	113.0	114.4	0.070	-1.56	0.430

- Regular rotation player for Brooklyn in his seventh season with the team
- Maintained his usual level of efficiency, used as a low volume shooting specialist off the bench
- Active leader in Three-Point Percentage, currently ranked fourth all-time in Three-Point Percentage
- Excellent shooter off the catch, can spot-up, run off screens, and serve as a pick-and-pop screener
- Can effectively make backdoor cuts if defenders try to crowd him
- Not able to create his own shot, strictly a catch-and-shoot player, limited as a playmaker, rarely turns the ball over
- 2022-23 Defensive Degree of Difficulty: 0.372
- 2022-23 Points Prevented: 0.538
- Took on tougher assignments in the past, mostly guarded lower leverage players last season
- Played effective on-ball defense, could competently defend perimeter players at different positions
- Average pick-and-roll defender, can functionally switch, sometimes is a step slow when making rotations
- Tends to get caught on screens off the ball, consistently closes out on spot-up shooters
- Stay-at-home defender, rarely gets blocks or steals, fairly solid defensive rebounder

Alec Burks

	Height	Weight	Cap #	Years Left
	6'6"	214	$10.490M	UFA

Similar at Age 31

		Season	SIMsc
1	Gordon Hayward	2021-22	924.2
2	Glen Rice	1998-99	918.4
3	Alan Anderson	2013-14	917.4
4	George McCloud	1998-99	914.4
5	DeMarre Carroll	2017-18	914.2
6	Jason Richardson	2011-12	913.2
7	Eric Piatkowski	2001-02	909.9
8	Dan Majerle	1996-97	909.6
9	Marcus Morris	2020-21	909.1
10	Dahntay Jones	2011-12	908.6

Baseline Basic Stats

MPG	PTS	AST	REB	BLK	STL
24.7	10.0	2.0	3.1	0.2	0.7

Advanced Metrics

USG%	3PTA/FGA	FTA/FGA	TS%	eFG%	3PT%
18.8	0.501	0.310	0.568	0.519	0.396

AST%	TOV%	OREB%	DREB%	STL%	BLK%
13.8	9.9	2.2	12.9	1.5	0.7

PER	ORTG	DRTG	WS/48	BPM	VOL
13.83	114.9	112.6	0.107	0.23	0.274

- Missed games due to a foot injury, regular rotation player for Detroit when healthy
- Increased his overall effectiveness in a role as a moderate volume ball handler
- Solid playmaking guard that can make simple reads, good decision-maker, rarely turns the ball over
- Good three-point shooter, has made over 40% of his threes in each of the last three seasons
- Solid spot-up shooter, can effectively make shots if defenders go under screens
- Effective pick-and-roll ball handler and isolation, can use the threat of his shot to get to the rim or hit pull-up jumpers
- 2022-23 Defensive Degree of Difficulty: 0.382
- 2022-23 Points Prevented: -0.288
- Drew tougher assignments in previous seasons, mostly guarded second unit players last season
- Solid on-ball defender in the past, less effective last season, struggled to stay with quicker perimeter players
- Good pick-and-roll defender, can effectively switch to guard ball handlers and screeners
- Fights through screens off the ball, tended to late when closing out on spot-up shooters
- Steal and Block Percentages were consistent with his career averages, good defensive rebounder

Marvin Bagley III

	Height	Weight	Cap #	Years Left
	6'11"	235	$12.500M	1

Similar at Age 23

		Season	SIMsc
1	Mehmet Okur	2002-03	925.3
2	Charlie Villanueva	2007-08	922.6
3	Cherokee Parks	1995-96	919.4
4	Troy Murphy	2003-04	919.3
5	Yi Jianlian	2010-11	918.0
6	Zarko Cabarkapa	2004-05	916.0
7	Alaa Abdelnaby	1991-92	914.3
8	Trey Lyles	2018-19	912.0
9	Bobby Portis	2018-19	911.3
10	Richaun Holmes	2016-17	911.3

Baseline Basic Stats

MPG	PTS	AST	REB	BLK	STL
21.3	9.5	1.0	5.6	0.6	0.5

Advanced Metrics

USG%	3PTA/FGA	FTA/FGA	TS%	eFG%	3PT%
20.4	0.216	0.251	0.559	0.528	0.322

AST%	TOV%	OREB%	DREB%	STL%	BLK%
7.2	9.6	9.0	21.0	1.1	2.2

PER	ORTG	DRTG	WS/48	BPM	VOL
16.51	112.7	112.1	0.106	-1.01	0.368

- Missed games due to a sprained MCL in his right knee and a fractured hand
- Regular rotation player for Detroit when healthy, effective in his role as a moderate usage rim runner and stretch big
- Most effective as a rim runner, athletic big man that can efficiently finish around the rim
- Good cutter and roll man, good offensive rebounder, effective at running the floor in transition
- Has made less than 30% of his career threes, break-even on spot-up threes last season
- Below average post player, can face up and drive by slow big men on occasion
- Limited passing skills, strictly a catch-and-shoot or catch-and-finish player, rarely turns the ball over
- 2022-23 Defensive Degree of Difficulty: 0.437
- 2022-23 Points Prevented: -1.058
- Improved to become a better rim protector, decent shot blocker, fairly good defensive rebounder
- Typically defended starting level big men, played below average on-ball defense
- Could get pushed around inside by stronger big men, better at using his mobility to defend in space
- Below average pick-and-roll defender, ineffective when making rotations, did not look to take away any specific action
- Tended to stay anchored in the paint, did not always come out to contest perimeter shots

James Wiseman

	Height	Weight	Cap #	Years Left
	7'0"	240	$12.119M	RFA

Similar at Age 21

		Season	SIMsc
1	Jason Smith	2007-08	927.7
2	Deyonta Davis	2017-18	918.5
3	Harry Giles	2019-20	910.4
4	Marvin Bagley III	2020-21	908.2
5	Domantas Sabonis	2017-18	904.9
6	Yi Jianlian	2008-09	904.5
7	Spencer Hawes	2009-10	902.2
8	LaMarcus Aldridge	2006-07	901.7
9	Marreese Speights	2008-09	901.4
10	Nikola Vucevic	2011-12	900.9

Baseline Basic Stats

MPG	PTS	AST	REB	BLK	STL
24.1	10.5	1.3	6.4	0.8	0.5

Advanced Metrics

USG%	3PTA/FGA	FTA/FGA	TS%	eFG%	3PT%
21.0	0.044	0.275	0.552	0.524	0.283

AST%	TOV%	OREB%	DREB%	STL%	BLK%
8.0	12.7	8.7	21.8	0.8	2.4

PER	ORTG	DRTG	WS/48	BPM	VOL
14.86	106.5	110.5	0.079	-2.50	0.318

- Played sparingly for Golden State, became a regular starter after he was traded to Detroit
- Used by both teams as a moderate volume rim runner, production level increased last season
- Vertical lob threat, athletic big man with great length, effective roll man and cutter
- Active offensive rebounder that scores on put-backs, runs the floor well in transition
- Offensive skills still unpolished, below average post player, shooting range is not reliable outside of ten feet
- Basically a catch-and-finish player at this stage, limited passing skills, effective at limiting turnovers
- 2022-23 Defensive Degree of Difficulty: 0.414
- 2022-23 Points Prevented: -3.901
- Good shot blocker and defensive rebounder, below average rim protector, undisciplined with his positioning, highly foul prone
- Below average on-ball defender, better at defending post-ups, really struggles to defend quicker players in space
- Below average pick-and-roll defender, frequently has lapses when making rotations
- Usually stays anchored in the paint, does not come out to contest shots in spot-up situations

Isaiah Livers

	Height	Weight	Cap #	Years Left
	6'7"	230	$1.836M	RFA

Similar at Age 24

		Season	SIMsc
1	James Jones	2004-05	930.0
2	Dean Wade	2020-21	926.7
3	Yakhouba Diawara	2006-07	916.3
4	Quincy Pondexter	2012-13	907.6
5	Henry Walker	2011-12	902.9
6	Timothé Luwawu-Cabarrot	2019-20	902.1
7	Semi Ojeleye	2018-19	902.0
8	Shawne Williams	2010-11	902.0
9	Davis Bertans	2016-17	901.7
10	Malcolm Miller	2017-18	899.7

Baseline Basic Stats

MPG	PTS	AST	REB	BLK	STL
19.5	6.9	1.0	2.9	0.3	0.5

Advanced Metrics

USG%	3PTA/FGA	FTA/FGA	TS%	eFG%	3PT%
14.1	0.655	0.164	0.567	0.540	0.370

AST%	TOV%	OREB%	DREB%	STL%	BLK%
7.3	9.4	3.2	12.2	1.2	1.5

PER	ORTG	DRTG	WS/48	BPM	VOL
10.21	113.0	115.7	0.069	-1.33	0.304

- Regular rotation player for Detroit in his second NBA season, missed a month due to a sprained right shoulder
- Decently effective in his role as a very low volume shooting specialist
- Fairly good three-point shooter, has made over 42% of his career corner threes
- Mostly a stationary spot-up shooter, went 22-for-37 (59.5%) on transition threes
- Rarely asked to handle the ball, limited ability to create his own offense
- Strictly a catch-and-shoot player, playmaking skills are limited, rarely turns the ball over
- 2022-23 Defensive Degree of Difficulty: 0.483
- 2022-23 Points Prevented: 0.210
- Drew a lot of tough defensive assignments off the bench, decent on-ball defender
- More effective against bigger players, struggled to stay with quicker players on the perimeter
- Below average pick-and-roll defender, not effective at taking away any specific action
- Stays attached to shooters off the ball, fights through screens and closes out in spot-up situations
- Steal Percentage decreased a bit, effective as a weak side shot blocker, fairly solid defensive rebounder

Killian Hayes

	Height	Weight	Cap #	Years Left
	6'5"	195	$7.414M	RFA

Similar at Age 21

		Season	SIMsc
1	Jay Williams	2002-03	921.0
2	Frank Ntilikina	2019-20	918.3
3	Tyrese Haliburton	2021-22	910.4
4	Smush Parker	2002-03	907.4
5	Emmanuel Mudiay	2017-18	905.3
6	Dennis Smith Jr.	2018-19	905.3
7	Iman Shumpert	2011-12	904.1
8	Markelle Fultz	2019-20	900.9
9	Spencer Dinwiddie	2014-15	898.9
10	Jeremy Lamb	2013-14	898.6

Baseline Basic Stats

MPG	PTS	AST	REB	BLK	STL
26.4	11.7	4.4	3.1	0.4	1.2

Advanced Metrics

USG%	3PTA/FGA	FTA/FGA	TS%	eFG%	3PT%
19.7	0.276	0.185	0.494	0.462	0.315

AST%	TOV%	OREB%	DREB%	STL%	BLK%
28.9	15.9	2.3	10.0	2.2	1.1

PER	ORTG	DRTG	WS/48	BPM	VOL
12.02	103.5	115.0	0.040	-1.64	0.395

- Regular starting point guard for Detroit in his third NBA season
- Largely inefficient but more effective than he was in previous seasons, used as a moderate volume playmaker
- Good playmaker with solid court vision, effectively finds open teammates, still fairly turnover prone
- Rated by Synergy as average or worse in every offensive situation
- Has made less than 30% of his career threes, more comfortable when shooting from mid-range
- Can push the ball in transition, defenders can back off him in a half-court set to limit his effectiveness
- 2022-23 Defensive Degree of Difficulty: 0.460
- 2022-23 Points Prevented: -1.314
- Usually defended starting level guards, matchup difficulty increased a bit, appeared over-matched
- Played below average on-ball defense, struggled to stay with opposing guards on the perimeter
- Below average pick-and-roll defender, tended to go too far under screens, sometimes indecisive when making rotations
- Fights through screens off the ball, usually was late when closing out on spot-up shooters
- Active roaming help defender, gets steals at a high rate, effective weak side shot blocking guard, fairly solid defensive rebounder

Newcomers

Ausar Thompson

	Height	Weight	Cap #	Years Left
	6'7"	215	$7.977M	1 + 2 TO

Baseline Basic Stats

MPG	PTS	AST	REB	BLK	STL
18.9	6.4	1.2	3.8	0.6	0.8

Advanced Metrics

USG%	3PTA/FGA	FTA/FGA	TS%	eFG%	3PT%
16.9	0.304	0.298	0.512	0.480	0.294

AST%	TOV%	OREB%	DREB%	STL%	BLK%
12.4	16.0	6.0	19.2	2.3	3.1

PER	ORTG	DRTG	WS/48	BPM	VOL
12.81	100.6	102.3	0.087	-0.59	0.558

- Drafted by Detroit with the 5th overall pick in 2023
- Spent the past two seasons playing for Overtime Elite
- Had a strong showing in the Las Vegas Summer League
- Effective in his role as a moderate volume secondary playmaker and energy wing
- Athletic slashing wing that can explosively finish above the rim, good quickness to drive by defenders
- Drew fouls at a high rate at Summer League, willing to absorb contact when driving to the basket
- Good court vision, unselfish player that can find open teammates, plays a bit wild, prone to committing turnovers
- Shooting is still a work-in-progress, only went 3-for-11 (27.3%) on threes
- Shooting stroke is still inconsistent, went 11-for-17 (64.7%) on free throws
- Great athlete with a long wingspan, can potentially defend multiple positions in the future
- Showed increased focus against better competition at Summer League, played solid on-ball defense
- Good at pressuring opponents and bothering them with his length, holds his own against stronger players
- Effective pick-and-roll defender, capable of switching and playing in different coverages
- Undisciplined at times when playing for Overtime Elite, tended to take a lot of bad gambles while playing against lesser competition
- Dynamic weak side defender at Summer League, excellent at jumping passing lanes to get steals, great weak side shot blocker, excellent defensive rebounder

Marcus Sasser

	Height	Weight	Cap #	Years Left
	6'2"	195	$2.624M	1 + 2 TO

Baseline Basic Stats

MPG	PTS	AST	REB	BLK	STL
17.4	6.7	1.9	1.9	0.2	0.6

Advanced Metrics

USG%	3PTA/FGA	FTA/FGA	TS%	eFG%	3PT%
18.6	0.499	0.201	0.497	0.464	0.341

AST%	TOV%	OREB%	DREB%	STL%	BLK%
16.0	11.4	1.9	8.8	1.8	0.6

PER	ORTG	DRTG	WS/48	BPM	VOL
11.95	99.5	101.8	0.054	-1.40	N/A

- Drafted by Memphis with the 25th overall pick, traded to Boston, then traded again to Detroit
- Had a strong performance at the Las Vegas Summer League
- Solidly effective in his role as a moderate volume ball handling guard
- Good ball control guard that makes sound decisions, solid playmaker that finds open teammates, rarely turns the ball over
- Struggled with his shooting at Summer League, made less than 30% of his threes and less than 65% of his free throws
- More effective from two-point range, went 21-for-34 (61.8%), effective at making little floaters and using hesitation moves to get to the rim
- Better shooter at the college level last season, most effective at making stand-still spot-up jumpers
- Well-schooled defender with solid athleticism, plays a pesky brand of on-ball defense
- Good at pressuring ball handlers and cutting off penetration, sometimes will commit cheap fouls due to over-aggressiveness
- Solid pick-and-roll defender, limited ability to switch due to lack of size, compensates by making effective rotations in a variety of coverages
- Tends to get caught on screens, good at closing out on spot-up shooters
- Good at using his active hands to get steals, below average defensive rebounder at Summer League
- May benefit from at least a few games of additional seasoning in the G-League to improve his shooting consistency

2023-24 Western Conference Preview

SCHREMPF Rankings
1. Memphis Grizzlies
2. Golden State Warriors
3. New Orleans Pelicans
4. Los Angeles Lakers
5. Dallas Mavericks
6. Los Angeles Clippers
7. Minnesota Timberwolves
8. Denver Nuggets
9. Sacramento Kings
10. Phoenix Suns
11. Oklahoma City Thunder
12. Utah Jazz
13. Houston Rockets
14. San Antonio Spurs
15. Portland Trail Blazers

Rosters are accurate as of August 23, 2023. For my official predictions, turn to page 531.

MEMPHIS GRIZZLIES

Last Season: 51 - 31, Lost 1st Round to Los Angeles Lakers (2 – 4)

Offensive Rating: 115.1, 15th in the NBA		Defensive Rating: 111.2, 2nd in the NBA

Primary Executive: Zach Kleiman, General Manager/Executive Vice President of Basketball Operations

Head Coach: Taylor Jenkins

Key Roster Changes

Subtractions
Tyus Jones, trade
Dillon Brooks, sign-and-trade

Additions
Marcus Smart, trade
Josh Christopher, trade
Isaiah Todd, trade
Derrick Rose, free agency

Roster

Likely Starting Five
1. Ja Morant
2. Marcus Smart
3. Desmond Bane
4. Jaren Jackson Jr.
5. Steven Adams

Other Key Rotation Players
Brandon Clarke
Xavier Tillman Sr.
Santi Aldama
John Konchar
Luke Kennard

* Italics denotes that a player is likely to be on the floor to close games

Remaining Roster

- Derrick Rose
- Ziaire Williams
- David Roddy
- Jake LaRavia
- Kenneth Lofton Jr.
- Josh Christopher
- Isaiah Todd
- Vince Williams Jr., 23, 6'6", 205, VCU (Two-Way)
- Jacob Gilyard, 25, 5'9", 160, Richmond (Two-Way)
- Timmy Allen, 24, 6'6", 210, Texas (Exhibit 10)

SCHREMPF Base Rating: 48.6

Season Preview Survey

- *Are the Grizzlies contending or rebuilding? Where is this team headed?*

The Grizzlies have shown that they can rack up wins in the regular season, but they haven't really been able to turn that into playoff success. Matters are complicated because their best player, Ja Morant has to serve a 25-game suspension to start the season due to his irresponsible brandishing of firearms on his social media feed. They will have to weather the storm without him before they re-integrate him into the fold. From there, they still need to figure out some way to make their team better equipped to counter different opponents and make a deeper playoff run. It will be tough for them to do this with a relatively uncertain day-to-day roster situation. However, they have the talent to keep their place as an upper-tier team in the Western Conference, so they still should win a lot of games this season.

- *What are the areas of concern for this team heading into this season?*

Memphis' main issue is that they are built to win in the regular season, but they lack the versatility and balance to win in the playoffs. On offense, they are overly reliant on the abilities of Ja Morant to penetrate or draw the attention of defenses to generate quality looks. It also doesn't help that they tend to play lineups with multiple big men, and they don't incorporate a lot of off-ball movement into their scheme. Opponents can shift their coverage or matchups to make things more difficult for Morant or choke off their spacing. In the time that Morant is serving his suspension, they will need to find ways to empower their supporting players to diversify their offensive attack. On the other end of the floor, their lineups are a bit inflexible, and they over-emphasize protecting the paint. They are heavily dependent on the rim protection skills of Jaren Jackson Jr. to get stops, but they could be vulnerable to teams that try to spread the floor to attack the other players on the floor. They took a step in right direction to add Marcus Smart, but they still could use some more quality perimeter defenders to improve their ability to defend quicker, five-out lineups in the playoffs.

- *List some possible breakout players for this team.*

The door is open for an unheralded player to emerge as an unexpected contributor because the Grizzlies will need to fill the minutes that are going to be vacated while Morant is serving his suspension. If someone does break out, it will likely be Kenneth Lofton Jr. He's been highly productive in the G-League, and he's had two solid showings at Summer League over the past two seasons. He's a throwback big man that plays a bruising style around the rim to finish from close range efficiently, and he can be a dominant presence on the boards. In addition to this, he's flashed the ability to make threes. If his skills translate to the regular season, then he could be productive bench player that could provide a physical element and some extra scoring.

- *What should we expect from them this season?*

From a talent perspective, the Grizzlies still should be able to maintain their place as a top-tier Western Conference team. They should be able to withstand the absence of Ja Morant while he's suspended to post a good regular season record. The real question is if they made enough moves to improve their ability to counter high-level opponents in the playoffs. On paper, it doesn't seem as they did a whole lot to make themselves better. They will need to creatively work with their roster to find little ways to increase their versatility and diversify their tactics. If they can do that, then they can take the next step to being legitimate title contenders. Otherwise, they could have another early exit in the playoffs this season.

Veterans

Ja Morant

	Height	Weight	Cap #	Years Left
	6'3"	174	$34.005M	4

Similar at Age 23

		Season	SIMsc
1	Derrick Rose	2011-12	919.2
2	De'Aaron Fox	2020-21	918.5
3	Stephon Marbury	2000-01	914.6
4	Zach LaVine	2018-19	900.1
5	Shai Gilgeous-Alexander	2021-22	897.0
6	Kyrie Irving	2015-16	896.6
7	Russell Westbrook	2011-12	894.7
8	Trae Young	2021-22	891.0
9	Dennis Schroder	2016-17	888.1
10	D'Angelo Russell	2019-20	886.0

Baseline Basic Stats

MPG	PTS	AST	REB	BLK	STL
33.7	23.0	6.7	4.3	0.3	1.3

Advanced Metrics

USG%	3PTA/FGA	FTA/FGA	TS%	eFG%	3PT%
32.2	0.277	0.367	0.569	0.516	0.342

AST%	TOV%	OREB%	DREB%	STL%	BLK%
36.2	12.5	3.3	13.2	1.8	0.8

PER	ORTG	DRTG	WS/48	BPM	VOL
23.23	115.2	110.9	0.168	4.06	0.266

- Made his second All-Star team in 2022-23, missed games due to various minor injuries and a suspension for posting a picture of himself with a gun on social media
- Will be suspended for the first 25 games of the 2023-24 season for brandishing a gun on social media
- Thrived as Memphis' primary ball handler, dynamic downhill driver with great speed, draws a lot of fouls
- Excellent playmaker that can really push the ball in transition, good at avoiding turnovers
- Below break-even three-point shooter, better in the corners, has made 38.5% of his career corner threes
- Most effective as a stand-still spot-up shooter, inconsistent shooter off the dribble
- 2022-23 Defensive Degree of Difficulty: 0.404
- 2022-23 Points Prevented: 1.907
- Usually hidden in favorable matchups against lower leverage players, effective on-ball defender in these matchups
- Quick enough to stay with opposing guards, has enough strength to handle taller players
- Solid pick-and-roll defender, good at funneling his man into help, makes sound rotations
- Tends to get caught on screens off the ball, great at closing out on spot-up shooters
- Fairly solid at playing passing lanes to get steals, fairly good defensive rebounding guard

Jaren Jackson Jr.

	Height	Weight	Cap #	Years Left
	6'11"	242	$27.102M	2

Similar at Age 23

		Season	SIMsc
1	Myles Turner	2019-20	899.6
2	Raef LaFrentz	1999-00	867.2
3	Patrick Ewing*	1985-86	860.4
4	Moritz Wagner	2020-21	858.8
5	Derrick Favors	2014-15	858.6
6	Marcus Camby	1997-98	855.4
7	Charlie Villanueva	2007-08	854.6
8	Mo Bamba	2021-22	850.0
9	Richaun Holmes	2016-17	849.6
10	Kelly Olynyk	2014-15	846.3

Baseline Basic Stats

MPG	PTS	AST	REB	BLK	STL
26.9	13.1	1.2	6.5	2.0	0.7

Advanced Metrics

USG%	3PTA/FGA	FTA/FGA	TS%	eFG%	3PT%
23.2	0.358	0.318	0.587	0.546	0.353

AST%	TOV%	OREB%	DREB%	STL%	BLK%
6.3	10.2	6.7	18.7	1.5	7.1

PER	ORTG	DRTG	WS/48	BPM	VOL
19.64	114.7	105.8	0.154	1.31	0.297

- Made his first All-Star team, named Defensive Player of the Year in 2022-23
- Production spiked, highly effective in his role as a moderate volume stretch big and rim runner on offense
- Around a league average three-point shooter, better when shooting threes above the break
- More effective on pick-and-pops, below break-even on spot-up threes
- Athletic rim runner, good roll man and cutter, efficiently scores on put-backs, good at running the floor in transition
- Solid post-up player, can flash to the middle and score on either block, draws fouls at a high rate
- Mostly a catch-and-shoot player, only makes safe passes, rarely turns the ball over
- 2022-23 Defensive Degree of Difficulty: 0.401
- 2022-23 Points Prevented: 0.766
- Great rim protector, led the NBA in Block Percentage for the second straight year, solid defensive rebounder
- Guards starting level big men, used as a roamer, solid on-ball defender against lower leverage starters
- Stout post defender, mobile enough to defend in space, tends to commit unnecessary shooting fouls
- Decent pick-and-roll defender, good in drop coverages, will hedge out on ball handlers, tends to be late to recognize pick-and-pop plays
- Tends to stay anchored in the paint, does not always come out to contest outside shots in spot-up situations

Desmond Bane

	Height	Weight	Cap #	Years Left
	6'5"	215	$3.845M	5

Similar at Age 24

		Season	SIMsc
1	Victor Oladipo	2016-17	942.6
2	Anthony Morrow	2009-10	938.3
3	Shake Milton	2020-21	927.5
4	O.J. Mayo	2011-12	926.5
5	Tim Hardaway Jr.	2016-17	920.6
6	J.R. Smith	2009-10	919.7
7	Malcolm Brogdon	2016-17	916.6
8	Jaylen Brown	2020-21	915.1
9	Denzel Valentine	2017-18	914.0
10	Rodney Hood	2016-17	913.0

Baseline Basic Stats

MPG	PTS	AST	REB	BLK	STL
29.9	15.7	2.8	3.9	0.3	1.0

Advanced Metrics

USG%	3PTA/FGA	FTA/FGA	TS%	eFG%	3PT%
23.9	0.449	0.213	0.589	0.550	0.407

AST%	TOV%	OREB%	DREB%	STL%	BLK%
17.5	10.4	2.3	13.2	1.6	0.9

PER	ORTG	DRTG	WS/48	BPM	VOL
17.64	116.1	111.0	0.140	1.53	0.318

- Missed a month due to a sore right toe, produced at a near All-Star level for Memphis last season
- Thrived in his role as a high volume shooting specialist
- Excellent three-point shooter, has made 42.5% of his career threes
- Outstanding shooter off the catch, knocks down spot-up jumpers, can run off screens
- Can use an on-ball screen to get to the rim on pick-and-rolls and dribble hand-offs
- Not as effective in isolation situations, inconsistent shooter off the dribble, does not create separation without a screen
- Good cutter off the ball, good secondary playmaker, rarely turns the ball over
- 2022-23 Defensive Degree of Difficulty: 0.450
- 2022-23 Points Prevented: 1.364
- Guards starting level players, moved to easier assignments to conserve his energy
- Solid on-ball defender in previous seasons, less effective in one-on-one situations last season
- Good pick-and-roll defender, effectively switches to guard ball handlers and screeners
- Fights through screens off the ball, sometimes can be late to close out on spot-up shooters
- Block Percentage held steady, steal rate declined a bit last season, solid defensive rebounder

Marcus Smart

	Height	Weight	Cap #	Years Left
	6'3"	220	$18.834M	2

Similar at Age 28

		Season	SIMsc
1	Erick Strickland	2001-02	917.1
2	Shelvin Mack	2018-19	916.5
3	Kirk Hinrich	2008-09	912.0
4	Keyon Dooling	2008-09	907.8
5	Jose Calderon	2009-10	906.5
6	Wesley Matthews	2014-15	906.1
7	O.J. Mayo	2015-16	902.1
8	Bobby Phills	1997-98	901.3
9	Mike James	2003-04	901.2
10	Fred Jones	2007-08	900.7

Baseline Basic Stats

MPG	PTS	AST	REB	BLK	STL
28.3	11.0	4.0	2.8	0.2	1.0

Advanced Metrics

USG%	3PTA/FGA	FTA/FGA	TS%	eFG%	3PT%
18.0	0.549	0.204	0.530	0.498	0.351

AST%	TOV%	OREB%	DREB%	STL%	BLK%
23.5	14.8	2.0	9.0	2.0	0.8

PER	ORTG	DRTG	WS/48	BPM	VOL
12.57	108.6	109.8	0.091	-0.50	0.340

- Winner of the NBA Hustle Award for the second consecutive season
- Effectiveness declined slightly, mainly used as a low usage spot-up shooter and playmaker
- Below break-even career three-point shooter, percentages tend to vary from situation-to-situation
- Above break-even three point shooter last season, mostly takes spot-up jumpers, can be pretty streaky
- Inconsistent shooter off the dribble, needs a screen to get downhill or create separation in ball handling situations
- Sometimes can post up smaller guards, good playmaker that finds open teammates, slightly turnover prone
- 2022-23 Defensive Degree of Difficulty: 0.553, had the 19th most difficult set of matchups in the NBA
- 2022-23 Points Prevented: -0.733
- Used as Boston's primary defensive stopper, slightly over-extended in this role
- Good on-ball defender in the past, defends multiple positions, had trouble against elite scorers last season
- Decent pick-and-roll defender, can switch to guard ball handlers and screeners, prone to having lapses when making rotations
- Stays attached to shooters off the ball, fights through screens and closes out in spot-up situations
- Active help defenders, jumps passing lanes to get steals at a high rate, draws charges, decent defensive rebounder

Steven Adams

	Height	Weight	Cap #	Years Left
	6'11"	265	$12.600M	1

Similar at Age 29

		Season	SIMsc
1	Erick Dampier	2004-05	905.9
2	Nene	2011-12	890.6
3	Felton Spencer	1996-97	889.2
4	Kelvin Cato	2003-04	889.1
5	Tristan Thompson	2020-21	884.0
6	Mason Plumlee	2019-20	880.7
7	Miles Plumlee	2017-18	874.6
8	Ian Mahinmi	2015-16	874.4
9	Kosta Koufos	2018-19	874.3
10	Brian Skinner	2005-06	872.8

Baseline Basic Stats

MPG	PTS	AST	REB	BLK	STL
22.3	6.9	1.4	7.0	0.9	0.5

Advanced Metrics

USG%	3PTA/FGA	FTA/FGA	TS%	eFG%	3PT%
13.5	0.002	0.507	0.576	0.572	0.015

AST%	TOV%	OREB%	DREB%	STL%	BLK%
10.9	18.8	15.9	22.4	1.3	3.3

PER	ORTG	DRTG	WS/48	BPM	VOL
15.98	118.8	107.6	0.140	0.37	0.381

- Missed the second half of last due to a knee injury, regular starting center for Memphis when healthy
- Maintained his usual level of effectiveness in a role as a low volume rim runner
- Has been one of the best offensive rebounders in the NBA, draws fouls at a high rate
- High energy rim runner, sets very firm screens, solid cutter and roll man, inconsistent finisher in traffic
- Average post-up player, can occasionally flash to the middle and make hook shots from the left block
- Shooting range does not extend past 16 feet, decent passing big man, fairly turnover prone
- 2022-23 Defensive Degree of Difficulty: 0.497
- 2022-23 Points Prevented: 2.956
- Good rim protector, good shot blocker and defensive rebounder
- Draws a lot of tough assignments against high-end big men, good on-ball defender
- Stout defender in the post, shows good mobility when defending in space
- Solid pick-and-roll defender, good in drop coverages, effective when switched out onto ball handlers
- Consistently will close out on shooters in spot-up situations
- Has active hands, good at getting deflections or playing passes to get steals

Brandon Clarke

	Height	Weight	Cap #	Years Left
	6'8"	215	$12.500M	3

Similar at Age 26

		Season	SIMsc
1	Brandan Wright	2013-14	931.4
2	Khem Birch	2018-19	919.3
3	Daniel Theis	2018-19	914.0
4	Kenny Gattison	1990-91	907.3
5	Amir Johnson	2013-14	903.8
6	Jeremy Evans	2013-14	902.4
7	Pervis Ellison	1993-94	901.7
8	Taj Gibson	2011-12	899.9
9	Willie Reed	2016-17	899.2
10	David Benoit	1994-95	899.1

Baseline Basic Stats

MPG	PTS	AST	REB	BLK	STL
21.3	8.2	1.2	5.2	0.9	0.6

Advanced Metrics

USG%	3PTA/FGA	FTA/FGA	TS%	eFG%	3PT%
16.6	0.067	0.300	0.613	0.590	0.241

AST%	TOV%	OREB%	DREB%	STL%	BLK%
9.0	10.7	8.7	18.3	1.4	3.3

PER	ORTG	DRTG	WS/48	BPM	VOL
17.66	123.3	108.0	0.164	1.35	0.289

- Out of the latter part of last season due to a torn Achilles, likely will miss games in 2023-24 while recovering from this injury
- Highly effective in his regular rotational role as a low usage energy player for Memphis when healthy
- High motor rim runner with great athleticism, explosive finisher before the injury
- Good cutter and roll man, active offensive rebounder, runs hard in transition, draws fouls at a fairly high rate
- Has practically cut the three-point shot out of his game, has made less than 30% of his career threes
- Sticks to shooting spot-up jumpers from mid-range, makes them at an above average rate
- Not really a shot creator, limited as a post-up threat, decent passing big man, rarely turns the ball over
- 2022-23 Defensive Degree of Difficulty: 0.351
- 2022-23 Points Prevented: 0.494
- Solid undersized rim protector, good shot blocker and defensive rebounder, gets steals at a good rate
- Usually guards second unit big men, decent on-ball defender, more effective when defending in space
- Had trouble in the post against taller and stronger big men, tended to commit a lot of shooting fouls inside
- Average pick-and-roll defender, good at switching onto ball handlers, had lapses when rotating onto screeners
- Tends to sag back into the paint, does not always close out on spot-up shooters

Xavier Tillman Sr.

	Height	Weight	Cap #	Years Left
	6'8"	245	$1.931M	UFA

Similar at Age 24

		Season	SIMsc
1	Eduardo Najera	2000-01	917.6
2	Trevor Booker	2011-12	917.0
3	Dante Cunningham	2011-12	916.4
4	Larry Nance Jr.	2016-17	916.2
5	Jabari Parker	2019-20	905.8
6	Drew Eubanks	2021-22	901.3
7	Richaun Holmes	2017-18	895.5
8	Qyntel Woods	2005-06	891.8
9	Renaldo Balkman	2008-09	891.7
10	Lonnie Shelton	1979-80	890.5

Baseline Basic Stats

MPG	PTS	AST	REB	BLK	STL
21.0	7.0	1.0	5.2	0.6	0.8

Advanced Metrics

USG%	3PTA/FGA	FTA/FGA	TS%	eFG%	3PT%
14.9	0.075	0.291	0.570	0.553	0.251

AST%	TOV%	OREB%	DREB%	STL%	BLK%
9.1	11.0	10.1	17.0	2.3	2.3

PER	ORTG	DRTG	WS/48	BPM	VOL
15.95	119.9	107.6	0.144	0.37	0.249

- Regular rotation player for Memphis in his third NBA season
- Continued to improve, had his best season in a role as a low usage rim runner
- Posted a True Shooting Percentage above 62%, high motor rim runner, made over 75% of his shots from three feet and in
- Good cutter, roll man, and offensive rebounder, runs hard in transition
- Has cut the three-point shot out of his game, only shoots from 16 feet and in
- Can occasionally drive by slower big men, decent passer, good at limiting turnovers
- 2022-23 Defensive Degree of Difficulty: 0.458
- 2022-23 Points Prevented: 0.016
- Effective undersized rim protector, solid shot blocker and defensive rebounder, stays vertical to contest shots
- Drew a lot of tough defensive assignments off the bench
- Good on-ball defender that guards big men and taller wings
- Solid pick-and-roll defender, good in drop coverages, effective at switching onto ball handlers
- Tends to sag back into the paint, does not always come out to contest outside shots in spot-up situations
- Great at playing passing lanes, consistently gets steals at a high rate

Santi Aldama

	Height	Weight	Cap #	Years Left
	6'11"	224	$2.194M	TO

Similar at Age 22

		Season	SIMsc
1	Ryan Kelly	2013-14	940.7
2	Donte Greene	2010-11	928.6
3	Donyell Marshall	1995-96	923.6
4	D.J. Wilson	2018-19	923.0
5	Obi Toppin	2020-21	922.2
6	Frank Kaminsky	2015-16	921.3
7	Perry Jones	2013-14	918.2
8	Trey Lyles	2017-18	915.5
9	Austin Daye	2010-11	914.8
10	Omri Casspi	2010-11	913.6

Baseline Basic Stats

MPG	PTS	AST	REB	BLK	STL
19.9	8.3	1.1	4.3	0.5	0.5

Advanced Metrics

USG%	3PTA/FGA	FTA/FGA	TS%	eFG%	3PT%
18.5	0.378	0.245	0.539	0.510	0.320

AST%	TOV%	OREB%	DREB%	STL%	BLK%
8.7	9.9	6.2	17.5	1.2	2.3

PER	ORTG	DRTG	WS/48	BPM	VOL
13.59	110.4	109.9	0.095	-1.25	0.359

- Became a regular rotation player for Memphis in his second NBA season
- Greatly increased his efficiency in his role as a low usage stretch big and rim runner
- Improved to become an above break-even three-point shooter, better in the corners
- Predominantly a stationary spot-up shooter, flashed some ability to make pick-and-pop threes
- Effective rim runner, good at cutting or rolling to the rim, will run the floor in transition, opportunistic offensive rebounder that scores on put-backs
- Below average post player, catch-and-shoot player that makes safe passes, rarely turns the ball over
- 2022-23 Defensive Degree of Difficulty: 0.377
- 2022-23 Points Prevented: 0.546
- Solid defensive rebounder and shot blocker, below average rim protector, undisciplined with his positioning
- Usually guarded second unit big men, average on-ball defender
- Fairly solid post defender that holds position well, has trouble when he's defending in space
- Average pick-and-roll defender, good at hedging out on ball handlers, tends to be a step late when rotating onto screeners
- Consistently comes out to the perimeter to contest outside shots, Steal Percentage increased last season

John Konchar

	Height	Weight	Cap #	Years Left
	6'5"	210	$2.400M	3

Similar at Age 26

		Season	SIMsc
1	Pat Connaughton	2018-19	941.1
2	Cody Martin	2021-22	932.9
3	Davon Reed	2021-22	932.4
4	Caleb Martin	2021-22	925.7
5	Thabo Sefolosha	2010-11	922.4
6	Iman Shumpert	2016-17	916.4
7	Danny Green	2013-14	908.5
8	Kentavious Caldwell-Pope	2019-20	908.3
9	Raja Bell	2002-03	906.9
10	David Nwaba	2018-19	904.7

Baseline Basic Stats

MPG	PTS	AST	REB	BLK	STL
23.7	7.5	1.5	4.0	0.4	0.9

Advanced Metrics

USG%	3PTA/FGA	FTA/FGA	TS%	eFG%	3PT%
12.6	0.536	0.179	0.567	0.544	0.365

AST%	TOV%	OREB%	DREB%	STL%	BLK%
9.3	10.1	4.4	16.6	2.0	1.4

PER	ORTG	DRTG	WS/48	BPM	VOL
12.13	118.4	109.2	0.117	0.52	0.324

- Regular rotation player for Memphis in his fourth NBA season, started some games
- Production level dropped, less effective in a role as a low usage spot-up shooter
- Good three-point shooter throughout his career, Three-Point Percentage fell to around break-even last season
- Primarily a stationary spot-up shooter, not really effective when shooting in other situations
- Lacks the ability to create his own shot, not used as a ball handler on offense
- Good cutter off the ball, showed decent secondary playmaking skills in the past, rarely turns the ball over
- 2022-23 Defensive Degree of Difficulty: 0.438
- 2022-23 Points Prevented: 1.927
- Took on more difficult assignments against starting level players, played fairly effective on-ball defense
- Could effectively stay with opposing perimeter players, struggled against bigger wings inside
- Decent pick-and-roll defender, effective at containing ball handlers, has lapses when rotating onto screeners
- Stays attached to shooters off the ball, fights through screens and closes out in spot-up situations
- Active help defender, can play passing lanes to get steals at a high rate, occasional weak side shot blocker, fairly good defensive rebounder

Luke Kennard

	Height	Weight	Cap #	Years Left
	6'5"	206	$14.764M	TO

Similar at Age 26

		Season	SIMsc
1	Grayson Allen	2021-22	938.0
2	Pat Connaughton	2018-19	924.1
3	Reggie Bullock	2017-18	922.7
4	Troy Daniels	2017-18	921.4
5	Kentavious Caldwell-Pope	2019-20	921.2
6	Allen Crabbe	2018-19	917.0
7	Richie Frahm	2003-04	916.1
8	Damyean Dotson	2020-21	914.6
9	Gary Neal	2010-11	909.7
10	Joe Harris	2017-18	907.0

Baseline Basic Stats

MPG	PTS	AST	REB	BLK	STL
22.4	8.5	1.5	2.7	0.2	0.6

Advanced Metrics

USG%	3PTA/FGA	FTA/FGA	TS%	eFG%	3PT%
15.9	0.626	0.140	0.602	0.577	0.429

AST%	TOV%	OREB%	DREB%	STL%	BLK%
10.6	9.8	1.7	11.6	1.2	0.5

PER	ORTG	DRTG	WS/48	BPM	VOL
11.98	116.9	113.5	0.097	-0.58	0.431

- Traded by the L.A. Clippers to Memphis at the trade deadline, regular rotation player for both teams
- Solidly effective in his role as a low usage shooting specialist, more productive with Memphis
- Led the NBA in Three-Point Percentage for the second straight year, has made almost 44% of his career threes
- Excellent shooter off the catch, good at knocking down spot-up jumpers and running off screens
- Effective pick-and-roll ball handler, not able to create separation to score without a screen
- Makes sharp backdoor cuts if defenders overplay his shot, fairly solid secondary playmaker, rarely turns the ball over
- 2022-23 Defensive Degree of Difficulty: 0.351
- 2022-23 Points Prevented: 1.086
- Usually guarded second unit players or was hidden in favorable matchups
- Played fairly solid on-ball defense, passably guarded multiple positions against lower leverage players
- Average pick-and-roll defender, not really effective at switching, good at funneling ball handlers into help
- Sometimes gets caught on screens off the ball, good at closing out on spot-up shooters
- Stay-at-home defender, does not really get blocks or steals, fairly solid on the defensive glass

Derrick Rose

	Height	Weight	Cap #	Years Left
	6'2"	200	$3.196M	1

Similar at Age 34

		Season	SIMsc
1	Raymond Felton	2018-19	922.0
2	Beno Udrih	2016-17	899.8
3	Goran Dragić	2020-21	889.8
4	John Starks	1999-00	885.8
5	Leandro Barbosa	2016-17	880.8
6	Ron Boone	1980-81	880.6
7	Byron Scott	1995-96	880.3
8	Terry Porter	1997-98	879.1
9	Bobby Jackson	2007-08	875.7
10	Lou Williams	2020-21	874.8

Baseline Basic Stats

MPG	PTS	AST	REB	BLK	STL
22.4	8.1	2.7	2.2	0.1	0.7

Advanced Metrics

USG%	3PTA/FGA	FTA/FGA	TS%	eFG%	3PT%
18.5	0.393	0.170	0.533	0.499	0.362

AST%	TOV%	OREB%	DREB%	STL%	BLK%
19.6	12.5	2.4	10.2	1.5	1.2

PER	ORTG	DRTG	WS/48	BPM	VOL
13.02	109.6	111.0	0.058	-0.47	0.763

- Fell out of New York's rotation, played sparingly in his second full season with the team
- Production heavily declined, used as a low usage spot-up shooter and backup point guard
- True Shooting Percentage fell to below 50%, below break-even career three-point shooter
- Struggled to make spot-up jumpers, better when shooting off the dribble on pick-and-rolls
- Effective at getting to the rim and making little floaters on pick-and-rolls, losing a step due to age, not able to get separation or drive downhill without a screen
- Solid distributor that can still run a team, good at avoiding turnovers
- 2022-23 Defensive Degree of Difficulty: 0.347
- 2022-23 Points Prevented: 2.433
- Mostly guarded second unit players or was hidden in favorable matchups
- Rarely tested on the ball, middling on-ball defender in the past, allowed zero points in five one-on-one possessions last season
- Average pick-and-roll defender, good at funneling his man into help, tends to go too far under screens
- Sometimes gets caught on screens off the ball, fairly good at closing out on spot-up shooters
- Steal and Block Percentages declined last season, fairly decent defensive rebounder

Ziaire Williams

	Height	Weight	Cap #	Years Left
	6'8"	215	$4.810M	TO

Similar at Age 21

		Season	SIMsc
1	Kevin Knox	2020-21	953.3
2	Mario Hezonja	2016-17	944.7
3	Kessler Edwards	2021-22	943.6
4	Troy Brown Jr.	2020-21	931.9
5	Cam Reddish	2020-21	927.9
6	Vit Krejci	2021-22	925.7
7	T.J. Warren	2014-15	924.8
8	Chase Budinger	2009-10	921.7
9	James Anderson	2010-11	921.3
10	OG Anunoby	2018-19	919.3

Baseline Basic Stats

MPG	PTS	AST	REB	BLK	STL
22.5	8.5	1.3	3.3	0.3	0.6

Advanced Metrics

USG%	3PTA/FGA	FTA/FGA	TS%	eFG%	3PT%
16.6	0.358	0.164	0.540	0.513	0.315

AST%	TOV%	OREB%	DREB%	STL%	BLK%
9.0	11.9	3.0	11.5	1.4	0.8

PER	ORTG	DRTG	WS/48	BPM	VOL
10.22	106.8	112.5	0.067	-2.62	0.396

- Fell out of Memphis' rotation in his second NBA season, played limited minutes off the bench
- Efficiency dropped, mainly used as a low usage spot-up shooter and energy player
- Most effective as an energetic rim runner, explosive finisher, good cutter and transition player, has made over 82% of his career shots inside of three feet
- Struggled in almost every half-court situation, lacks the ball handling skills to create his own shot
- Three-Point Percentage fell to below 30% last season, struggled to consistently make spot-up threes
- Catch-and-shoot player, passing slightly improved, turned the ball over at a higher rate last season
- 2022-23 Defensive Degree of Difficulty: 0.378
- 2022-23 Points Prevented: 0.904
- Mostly guarded second unit players or lower leverage starters, rarely tested on the ball
- Thin frame, has trouble guarding stronger players, quick enough to stay with opponents on the perimeter
- Decent pick-and-roll defender, good at containing ball handlers, has some lapses when rotating onto screeners
- Fights through screens off the ball, sometimes will be late to close out on spot-up shooters
- Stay-at-home defender, does not really get steals or blocks, decent defensive rebounder

David Roddy

	Height	Weight	Cap #	Years Left
	6'6"	255	$2.718M	2 TO

Similar at Age 21

		Season	SIMsc
1	OG Anunoby	2018-19	912.5
2	Troy Brown Jr.	2020-21	890.2
3	P.J. Washington	2019-20	888.2
4	Jeremiah Robinson-Earl	2021-22	887.3
5	Stanley Johnson	2017-18	887.2
6	Omari Spellman	2018-19	885.3
7	Kevin Knox	2020-21	880.2
8	Miles Bridges	2019-20	877.6
9	Casey Jacobsen	2002-03	877.1
10	Grant Williams	2019-20	875.9

Baseline Basic Stats

MPG	PTS	AST	REB	BLK	STL
20.8	7.6	1.2	3.6	0.4	0.7

Advanced Metrics

USG%	3PTA/FGA	FTA/FGA	TS%	eFG%	3PT%
15.9	0.362	0.203	0.544	0.518	0.326

AST%	TOV%	OREB%	DREB%	STL%	BLK%
7.4	11.6	4.3	13.3	1.5	1.3

PER	ORTG	DRTG	WS/48	BPM	VOL
10.50	108.0	110.7	0.077	-1.93	0.383

- Regular rotation player for Memphis in his rookie season
- Primarily used in a role as a low volume spot-up shooter
- Below break-even three-point shooter as a rookie, above break-even when shooting corner threes
- Mostly used as a stationary spot-up shooter, flashed some ability to shoot on the move
- Average at best as a rim runner, dives hard to the rim, struggles to finish in traffic, lacks ideal lift
- Not really able to shoot off the dribble, lacks the quickness to get to the rim, struggled as a ball handler
- Catch-and-shoot player right now, only makes safe passes, rarely turns the ball over
- 2022-23 Defensive Degree of Difficulty: 0.370
- 2022-23 Points Prevented: 0.080
- Mainly guarded second unit players, around an average on-ball defender
- Plays angles well on the perimeter, effective at staying with his man, lacking in length, struggled to guard taller players in the post
- Decent pick-and-roll defender, good at containing ball handlers, less effective when switching onto screeners
- Tends to get caught on screens off the ball, not always in position to contest shots in spot-up situations
- Stay-at-home defender, occasionally blocks shots on the weak side, fairly solid defensive rebounder

Jake LaRavia

	Height	Weight	Cap #	Years Left
	6'8"	235	$3.200M	2 TO

Similar at Age 21

		Season	SIMsc
1	OG Anunoby	2018-19	906.5
2	Kevin Knox	2020-21	899.8
3	Kessler Edwards	2021-22	896.6
4	KZ Okpala	2020-21	892.5
5	Rodions Kurucs	2019-20	891.3
6	Jeremiah Robinson-Earl	2021-22	886.7
7	Vit Krejci	2021-22	885.4
8	Juan Hernangomez	2016-17	882.2
9	Grant Williams	2019-20	878.2
10	Troy Brown Jr.	2020-21	877.1

Baseline Basic Stats

MPG	PTS	AST	REB	BLK	STL
20.0	6.6	1.1	3.1	0.4	0.6

Advanced Metrics

USG%	3PTA/FGA	FTA/FGA	TS%	eFG%	3PT%
13.0	0.424	0.186	0.549	0.521	0.345

AST%	TOV%	OREB%	DREB%	STL%	BLK%
7.5	12.6	4.9	11.0	1.5	1.2

PER	ORTG	DRTG	WS/48	BPM	VOL
9.35	110.9	111.9	0.085	-1.85	0.491

- Played limited minutes off the bench for Memphis as a rookie, spent time in the G-League with the Memphis Hustle
- Mainly used in the NBA as a very low volume shooting specialist
- Made threes at a slightly above break-even rate, went 5-for-11 (45.5%) on corner threes
- Good at making stand-still spot-up shooters, really struggled to shoot off screens
- Makes sharp backdoor cuts if defenders try to overplay his shot
- Rarely used in ball handling situations, unproven ability to create his own shot at the NBA level
- Primarily a catch-and-shoot player, only makes safe passes, slightly turnover prone as a rookie
- 2022-23 Defensive Degree of Difficulty: 0.314
- 2022-23 Points Prevented: -0.220
- Generally guarded low leverage second unit players or played in garbage time
- Rarely tested against premium NBA competition, played solid on-ball defense in lower leverage assignments, passably guarded multiple positions
- Decent pick-and-roll defender, funnels ball handlers into help, had lapses when rotating onto screeners
- Tends to get caught on screens, great at closing out on spot-up shooters
- Occasionally gets steals, more of a stay-at-home defender, decent defensive rebounder

Kenneth Lofton Jr.

	Height	Weight	Cap #	Years Left
	6'7"	275	$1.720M	1 + TO

Similar at Age 20

		Season	SIMsc
1	Zach Randolph	2001-02	867.7
2	DeJuan Blair	2009-10	851.3
3	Zion Williamson	2020-21	850.8
4	Caleb Swanigan	2017-18	849.5
5	Jared Sullinger	2012-13	845.8
6	Naz Reid	2019-20	842.7
7	Elton Brand	1999-00	833.0
8	Alton Ford	2001-02	830.0
9	Reggie Perry	2020-21	829.2
10	Jahlil Okafor	2015-16	828.0

Baseline Basic Stats

MPG	PTS	AST	REB	BLK	STL
25.3	12.5	1.7	6.9	0.8	0.8

Advanced Metrics

USG%	3PTA/FGA	FTA/FGA	TS%	eFG%	3PT%
25.1	0.140	0.304	0.570	0.544	0.340

AST%	TOV%	OREB%	DREB%	STL%	BLK%
15.1	11.1	11.0	19.5	1.4	1.6

PER	ORTG	DRTG	WS/48	BPM	VOL
20.32	115.2	108.4	0.159	0.71	0.689

- Spent most of the season on a Two-Way contract with Memphis, played sparingly at the NBA level
- Named G-League Rookie of the Year in 2022-23, effective in limited action as a high usage post-up scorer
- Fairly good post-up player, great at using his strength and girth to bully weaker defenders on the block
- Good passing big man, finds open shooters and hits cutters, good at avoiding turnovers
- Dives hard to the rim as a rim runner, good offensive rebounder, has some trouble finishing in traffic because he's undersized
- Made threes at an above break-even rate in a small sample of shots, struggled to make spot-up threes
- 2022-23 Defensive Degree of Difficulty: 0.199
- 2022-23 Points Prevented: -1.792
- Mostly played in garbage time or guarded lower leverage players, rarely challenged on the ball
- Average on-ball defender in limited action, stout post defender, has some trouble defending in space
- Average pick-and-roll defender, solid in drop coverages, struggled to stop ball handlers from penetrating
- Tended to sag back into the paint, did not always close out on spot-up shooters
- Good rim protector despite low shot blocking rates, stays vertical when contesting shots, fairly good defensive rebounder, highly foul prone

Josh Christopher

	Height	Weight	Cap #	Years Left
	6'5"	215	$2.485M	TO

Similar at Age 21

		Season	SIMsc
1	Lonnie Walker	2019-20	926.8
2	Christian Eyenga	2010-11	922.6
3	Rashad McCants	2005-06	921.3
4	DeShawn Stevenson	2002-03	919.1
5	Jay Scrubb	2021-22	915.1
6	Shannon Brown	2006-07	913.3
7	Jason Richardson	2001-02	912.4
8	Bradley Beal	2014-15	910.5
9	Iman Shumpert	2011-12	910.3
10	Emmanuel Mudiay	2017-18	910.3

Baseline Basic Stats

MPG	PTS	AST	REB	BLK	STL
22.4	9.8	2.0	2.8	0.2	0.7

Advanced Metrics

USG%	3PTA/FGA	FTA/FGA	TS%	eFG%	3PT%
20.8	0.252	0.232	0.520	0.486	0.285

AST%	TOV%	OREB%	DREB%	STL%	BLK%
15.2	14.5	3.3	9.4	1.8	1.0

PER	ORTG	DRTG	WS/48	BPM	VOL
11.62	102.4	115.4	0.034	-2.95	0.358

- Fringe rotation player for Houston in his second NBA season
- Efficiency dropped slightly in a role as a moderate volume scoring guard
- Shot selection is questionable, takes a lot of contested shots, Three-Point Percentage was below 25% last season
- Struggled to make threes in almost every situation last season
- More effective when driving to the rim, capable of getting to the rim or drawing fouls
- Good athlete, explosive finisher in transition, solid cutter but played in a static offense with little movement
- Solid secondary playmaker that makes simple reads, cut his turnover rate last season
- 2022-23 Defensive Degree of Difficulty: 0.337
- 2022-23 Points Prevented: -1.163
- Usually guarded lower leverage second unit players, played around average on-ball defense
- Generally stayed with his man on the perimeter, had trouble in the post against stronger players
- Decent pick-and-roll defender, funnels his man into help, cuts off penetration, goes too far under screens
- Gets caught on screens off the ball, fairly good at closing out on spot-up shooters
- Active help defender, consistently gets steals at a high rate, effective weak side shot blocker, decent defensive rebounder

Isaiah Todd

	Height	Weight	Cap #	Years Left
	6'10"	220	$1.836M	TO

Similar at Age 21

		Season	SIMsc
1	Mario Hezonja	2016-17	889.6
2	Jeremiah Robinson-Earl	2021-22	885.9
3	Trey Lyles	2016-17	880.6
4	Kevin Knox	2020-21	879.8
5	Cam Reddish	2020-21	877.5
6	Santi Aldama	2021-22	875.1
7	Damir Markota	2006-07	874.9
8	Hedo Turkoglu	2000-01	874.2
9	Jumaine Jones	2000-01	874.0
10	Peja Stojakovic	1998-99	873.7

Baseline Basic Stats

MPG	PTS	AST	REB	BLK	STL
20.4	8.7	1.1	3.7	0.4	0.6

Advanced Metrics

USG%	3PTA/FGA	FTA/FGA	TS%	eFG%	3PT%
17.5	0.386	0.220	0.443	0.413	0.276

AST%	TOV%	OREB%	DREB%	STL%	BLK%
8.3	10.1	4.2	15.5	1.5	1.4

PER	ORTG	DRTG	WS/48	BPM	VOL
8.81	93.2	113.9	0.004	-5.70	0.611

- Played sparingly for Washington in his second NBA season, mostly played in the G-League with the Capital City Go-Go
- Struggled to be efficient in a role as a low usage spot-up shooter in both leagues
- Below break-even three-point shooter in the G-League, has made less than 20% of his NBA threes
- Has not really been able to consistently make spot-up jumpers, effective at making corner threes as a rookie
- Not really used as a rim runner or post-up player at the NBA level
- Strictly a catch-and-shoot player, limited as a passer, rarely commits turnovers
- 2022-23 Defensive Degree of Difficulty: 0.291
- 2022-23 Points Prevented: 2.082
- Has only played 135 NBA minutes in two seasons, mostly played in garbage time
- Struggled as an on-ball defender in limited action, can be overpowered in the post, had trouble defending in space
- Effective pick-and-roll defender, decent in drop coverages, mobile enough to switch onto ball handlers
- Consistently closed out on spot-up shooters
- Uncertain ability to protect the rim, decent defensive rebounder, can get steals, middling shot blocker

GOLDEN STATE WARRIORS

Last Season: 44 - 38, Lost 2nd Round to Los Angeles Lakers (2 – 4)

Offensive Rating: 116.1, 8th in the NBA				Defensive Rating: 114.4, 17th in the NBA

Primary Executive: Mike Dunleavy Jr., General Manager

Head Coach: Steve Kerr

Key Roster Changes

Subtractions
Jordan Poole, trade
Patrick Baldwin Jr., trade
Ryan Rollins, trade
Donte DiVincenzo, free agency
JaMychal Green, free agency
Andre Iguodala, free agency
Anthony Lamb, free agency

Additions
Brandin Podziemski, draft
Trayce Jackson-Davis, draft
Chris Paul, trade
Dario Šarić, free agency
Cory Joseph, free agency

Roster

Likely Starting Five
1. Stephen Curry
2. Klay Thompson
3. Andrew Wiggins
4. Draymond Green
5. Kevon Looney

Other Key Rotation Players
Chris Paul
Gary Payton II
Dario Šarić
Jonathan Kuminga
Moses Moody

* Italics denotes that a player is likely to be on the floor to close games

Remaining Roster

- Cory Joseph
- Brandin Podziemski
- Trayce Jackson-Davis
- Lester Quinones, 23, 6'5", 208, Memphis (Two-Way)
- Kendric Davis, 24, 6'0", 180, Memphis (Exhibit 10)
- Javan Johnson, 25, 6'6", 205, DePaul (Exhibit 10)
- Jayce Johnson, 26, 7'0", 235, Marquette (Exhibit 10)

SCHREMPF Base Rating: 46.9

Season Preview Survey

- *Are the Warriors contending or rebuilding? Where is this team headed?*

The Warriors plan to take a two-timeline approach backfired last season because they dealt with chemistry and performance-related issues that caused them slip into being a mid-tier team. They wanted to shake things up to get back to their championship ways. They revamped the front office after Bob Myers elected to leave his post, so they promoted Mike Dunleavy Jr. to serve as the primary decision-maker. Then, in a bold move, they acquired Chris Paul in a trade on draft day. This potentially gives them an injection of efficiency to vault them back to the top. However, they will need to figure out a way to integrate him into their system because the fit isn't exactly clean. If they blend their existing style with Paul's more methodical approach, then they could push for another title this season. Otherwise, they could remain as they are and be a mid-tier playoff team in the West.

- *What are the areas of concern for this team heading into this season?*

The Warriors have several concerns about their team. For starters, their core is aging because their best players are now deep into their 30s. On top of that, they all have some serious injury history, so it's not a guarantee that they will make it out of the regular season unscathed. They run the risk for age-related decline or absence due to possible injury, so they will need some luck on their side to keep their performance at close to peak level. They also need contributions from their bench to help them manage their workloads, but their current second unit group is still unproven right now. This issue will need to be addressed to allow them to move forward. Moreover, the addition of Chris Paul adds another twist because he's used to having the ball in his hands and he plays a methodical style that runs counter to their free flowing, motion-oriented style. They will have to figure out a way to meet him halfway to allow him to play to his strengths while also fitting in with the team. Even so, his smallish stature presents other problems because opponents have a possible weakness to exploit when they are on defense. Overall, the Warriors have to find some creative solutions to resolve these possible pitfalls to maximize their success in this season.

- *List some possible breakout players for this team.*

Golden State's roster is mostly comprised of established veterans, so there aren't many candidates to choose from. That being said, the best breakout candidate on the team is probably Jonathan Kuminga. He quietly has become a plus-level defender in his first two years in the league. With Klay Thompson declining slightly due to his age and previous injuries, the team is in need of another perimeter stopper to go along with Andrew Wiggins. Kuminga could take the leap to become a shutdown defender to boost their defense if he takes advantage of the opportunity. In addition to him, Moses Moody could emerge as another three-and-D wing. Brandin Podziemski could contribute as a scoring guard and playmaker, but he's blocked by their veteran guards. Also, Trayce Jackson-Davis could give them an energetic bruiser to back up Kevon Looney in a limited role.

- *What should we expect from them this season?*

The Warriors will be an interesting team to watch because they are looking to make another big push to win while Stephen Curry is still playing at an elite level. The move to get Chris Paul is intriguing because it potentially boosts their offensive efficiency, but it may force them to adapt their style to adequately fit him in. If they can make this work, then they could be an elite contender once again. Otherwise, if age and the other possible issues work against them, they could wind up in a tight race to earn a guaranteed playoff spot as a lower seed.

Veterans

Stephen Curry

	Height	Weight	Cap #	Years Left
	6'3"	185	$51.916M	2

Similar at Age 34

		Season	SIMsc
1	Goran Dragić	2020-21	897.6
2	Sam Cassell	2003-04	885.0
3	Kyle Lowry	2020-21	880.0
4	Terry Porter	1997-98	872.8
5	Mike Conley	2021-22	872.7
6	Chauncey Billups	2010-11	870.4
7	J.J. Redick	2018-19	868.0
8	Chris Paul	2019-20	867.5
9	Devin Harris	2017-18	865.8
10	Jamal Crawford	2014-15	864.7

Baseline Basic Stats

MPG	PTS	AST	REB	BLK	STL
30.6	17.6	5.3	3.6	0.2	0.9

Advanced Metrics

USG%	3PTA/FGA	FTA/FGA	TS%	eFG%	3PT%
26.7	0.519	0.258	0.611	0.565	0.404

AST%	TOV%	OREB%	DREB%	STL%	BLK%
28.2	12.7	2.0	14.2	1.4	1.0

PER	ORTG	DRTG	WS/48	BPM	VOL
20.66	118.3	111.7	0.164	3.59	0.339

- Named to the All-NBA 2nd Team in 2022-23, missed games due to injuries to his shoulder and left leg
- Played at his usual level of effectiveness, excelled as Golden State's primary scorer and ball handler
- The greater shooter in NBA history, all of his shooting percentages were at or exceeded his career averages
- Excellent all-around shooter, makes spot-up jumpers, runs off screens, good shooter off the dribble
- Efficient three-level scorer, excels as a pick-and-roll ball handler and isolation player
- Outstanding cutter off the ball, excellent playmaker with great court vision, good at avoiding turnovers
- 2022-23 Defensive Degree of Difficulty: 0.418
- 2022-23 Points Prevented: -0.153
- Hidden in lower leverage matchups in previous seasons, drew tougher assignments last season
- Improved to become a fairly solid on-ball defender, competently defends both guard spots, tends to back off his man
- Solid pick-and-roll defender, makes sound rotations, good at funneling his man into help
- Fights through screens off the ball, sometimes will be late to close out on spot-up shooters
- Stay-at-home defender last season, Steal Percentage dropped to a career low, solid defensive rebounder

Klay Thompson

	Height	Weight	Cap #	Years Left
	6'6"	215	$43.219M	UFA

Similar at Age 32

		Season	SIMsc
1	Marcus Morris	2021-22	914.5
2	Caron Butler	2012-13	907.1
3	Michael Finley	2005-06	905.3
4	Bojan Bogdanović	2021-22	902.5
5	Eric Gordon	2020-21	897.9
6	Michael Redd	2011-12	894.8
7	Allan Houston	2003-04	893.9
8	Marco Belinelli	2018-19	893.2
9	Anthony Parker	2007-08	892.6
10	Eric Piatkowski	2002-03	888.1

Baseline Basic Stats

MPG	PTS	AST	REB	BLK	STL
26.6	11.9	2.0	3.3	0.2	0.6

Advanced Metrics

USG%	3PTA/FGA	FTA/FGA	TS%	eFG%	3PT%
22.4	0.544	0.151	0.550	0.524	0.374

AST%	TOV%	OREB%	DREB%	STL%	BLK%
12.4	9.2	1.9	12.2	1.1	1.0

PER	ORTG	DRTG	WS/48	BPM	VOL
13.25	107.5	113.1	0.071	-0.61	0.401

- Played a full starter's workload after being out for almost two and a half seasons due to injuries
- Overall efficiency slightly declined, used as a shooting specialist, usage dropped a bit
- Excellent three-point shooter, made over 41% of his threes last season
- Led the NBA in most points scored off screens, great all-around shooter
- Can hit pull-up threes, getting to the rim less frequently, less efficient when shooting mid-range shots
- Becoming more of a catch-and-shoot specialist instead of a three-level scorer
- Fairly solid secondary playmaker, can make simple reads, rarely turns the ball over
- 2022-23 Defensive Degree of Difficulty: 0.489
- 2022-23 Points Prevented: 0.005
- Ramped up his defensive usage, drew a lot of tough assignments, good on-ball defender in the past
- On-ball defense slipped last season, losing a step, had trouble staying with opposing guards, less effective against bigger players
- Fairly solid pick-and-roll defender, gets around the screen to contain ball handlers, not as effective when switched onto a screener
- Tends to get caught on screens off the ball, not always in position to contest shots in spot-up situations
- Stay-at-home defender, did not really get steals or blocks last season, fairly solid defensive rebounder

Andrew Wiggins

	Height	Weight	Cap #	Years Left
	6'7"	197	$24.330M	2 + PO

Similar at Age 27

		Season	SIMsc
1	Francisco Garcia	2008-09	922.8
2	Wesley Person	1998-99	917.7
3	Dorell Wright	2012-13	913.5
4	Nick Young	2012-13	913.1
5	Terrence Ross	2018-19	912.0
6	Rasual Butler	2006-07	911.7
7	Evan Fournier	2019-20	908.8
8	Chandler Parsons	2015-16	907.7
9	Wesley Johnson	2014-15	907.0
10	Kent Bazemore	2016-17	906.8

Baseline Basic Stats

MPG	PTS	AST	REB	BLK	STL
25.4	11.8	1.7	3.3	0.4	0.8

Advanced Metrics

USG%	3PTA/FGA	FTA/FGA	TS%	eFG%	3PT%
21.2	0.508	0.174	0.557	0.538	0.393

AST%	TOV%	OREB%	DREB%	STL%	BLK%
10.6	8.8	3.7	11.7	1.7	1.7

PER	ORTG	DRTG	WS/48	BPM	VOL
14.19	110.3	111.7	0.091	-0.08	0.280

- Out for most of last season for personal reasons and an adductor injury, regular starter for Golden State when he was in the lineup
- Performed at his usual level of effectiveness in a role as a moderate volume scoring wing
- Around a league average career three-point shooter, made almost 40% of his threes last season
- Slightly above break-even as a spot-up shooter, more effective when shooting on the move
- Good at posting up smaller players, effective cutter, explosive finisher in transition
- Struggled in ball handling situations, inconsistent shooter off the dribble, does not always get to the rim
- Catch-and-shoot player, can make the extra pass, great at avoiding turnovers
- <u>2022-23 Defensive Degree of Difficulty</u>: 0.565, had the 12th toughest set of matchups in the NBA
- <u>2022-23 Points Prevented</u>: -0.650
- Used as Golden State's primary defensive stopper, slightly over-extended in his role
- Solid on-ball defender that guards multiple positions, better as a perimeter defender
- Solid pick-and-roll defender, great at containing ball handlers, had lapses when switched onto screeners
- Sometimes gets caught on screens off the ball, good at closing out on spot-up shooters
- Active help defender, gets steals at a good rate, effective weak side shot blocker, decent defensive rebounder

Draymond Green

	Height	Weight	Cap #	Years Left
	6'6"	230	$22.321M	2 + PO

Similar at Age 32

		Season	SIMsc
1	Rick Fox	2001-02	868.9
2	Sam Lacey	1980-81	859.3
3	Matt Barnes	2012-13	854.0
4	Joe Ingles	2019-20	853.7
5	Andre Iguodala	2015-16	850.8
6	Luke Walton	2012-13	846.5
7	Thaddeus Young	2020-21	845.8
8	Paul Pierce*	2009-10	841.5
9	Damien Wilkins	2011-12	840.5
10	Alan Anderson	2014-15	840.2

Baseline Basic Stats

MPG	PTS	AST	REB	BLK	STL
25.2	7.3	3.6	4.8	0.6	1.0

Advanced Metrics

USG%	3PTA/FGA	FTA/FGA	TS%	eFG%	3PT%
13.2	0.338	0.218	0.557	0.533	0.311

AST%	TOV%	OREB%	DREB%	STL%	BLK%
24.6	24.9	3.6	19.3	1.8	2.2

PER	ORTG	DRTG	WS/48	BPM	VOL
12.00	109.9	107.7	0.096	0.85	0.487

- Named to the All-Defensive 2nd Team in 2022-23
- Solidly effective in his role as a very low usage, pass-first playmaker for Golden State
- Great playmaker with outstanding court vision, finds cutters and open shooters, very highly turnover prone
- Most effective as a roll man, good at leveraging his short roll playmaking skills to get layups
- Rated by Synergy as average or worse in every other situation
- Below break-even three-point shooter, opponents often dare him to shoot by backing way off
- Most reliable when shooting from ten feet and in
- 2022-23 Defensive Degree of Difficulty: 0.473
- 2022-23 Points Prevented: 2.973
- Drew a lot of tough assignments against high-end starters, good on-ball defender
- Has the versatility to defend big men, wing players, and some smaller guards
- Good pick-and-roll defender, can play in many different coverages, great at switching
- Sometimes gets caught on screens off the ball, good at closing out on spot-up shooters
- Still an active help defender, gets steals and blocks at a solid rate, good defensive rebounder and rim protector

Kevon Looney

	Height	Weight	Cap #	Years Left
	6'9"	222	$7.500M	1

Similar at Age 26

		Season	SIMsc
1	Ed Davis	2015-16	924.7
2	Sidney Green	1986-87	909.5
3	Lavoy Allen	2015-16	909.3
4	Tristan Thompson	2017-18	906.4
5	Carl Herrera	1992-93	906.0
6	Larry Smith	1983-84	905.2
7	Kenneth Faried	2015-16	905.2
8	Nazr Mohammed	2003-04	903.6
9	Khem Birch	2018-19	902.4
10	Major Jones	1979-80	902.2

Baseline Basic Stats

MPG	PTS	AST	REB	BLK	STL
22.3	7.1	1.2	7.1	0.6	0.6

Advanced Metrics

USG%	3PTA/FGA	FTA/FGA	TS%	eFG%	3PT%
12.6	0.005	0.390	0.581	0.556	-0.017

AST%	TOV%	OREB%	DREB%	STL%	BLK%
10.6	12.1	13.8	24.1	1.3	2.0

PER	ORTG	DRTG	WS/48	BPM	VOL
15.48	128.4	109.1	0.157	0.05	0.314

- Played in all 82 games for the second straight year, started almost all of his games last season
- Had his best season, highly productive in a role as an extremely low usage rim runner
- Posted a True Shooting Percentage of almost 64%, highly energetic rim runner, dives hard to the rim
- Good roll man and cutter, great offensive rebounder, runs hard down the floor in transition, draws fouls at a good rate
- Limited as a post-up player, shooting range does not extend beyond ten feet
- Fairly good passing big man, effective at hitting cutters or finding open shooters, rarely turns the ball over
- 2022-23 Defensive Degree of Difficulty: 0.486
- 2022-23 Points Prevented: 0.395
- Good defensive rebounder, shot blocking rates declined a bit, less effective as a rim protector
- Generally guarded high-end big men, stout post defender, slight tendency to commit shooting fouls, had trouble when defending in space
- Good pick-and-roll defender, good in drop coverages, can effectively switch onto ball handlers
- Tended to get caught on screens off the ball, consistently closed out on spot-up shooters
- Decent at playing passing lanes, occasionally gets steals

Chris Paul

	Height	Weight	Cap #	Years Left
	6'0"	175	$30.800M	1

Similar at Age 37

		Season	SIMsc
1	John Stockton*	1999-00	906.8
2	Mark Jackson	2002-03	890.2
3	Rod Strickland	2003-04	870.5
4	Terry Porter	2000-01	852.9
5	Derek Harper	1998-99	850.4
6	Rickey Green	1991-92	850.4
7	Jason Terry	2014-15	848.7
8	Gary Payton*	2005-06	845.9
9	Darrell Armstrong	2005-06	845.7
10	Derek Fisher	2011-12	841.0

Baseline Basic Stats

MPG	PTS	AST	REB	BLK	STL
26.5	10.8	6.4	3.0	0.2	1.3

Advanced Metrics

USG%	3PTA/FGA	FTA/FGA	TS%	eFG%	3PT%
20.2	0.325	0.275	0.550	0.502	0.363

AST%	TOV%	OREB%	DREB%	STL%	BLK%
42.8	15.8	1.8	12.2	2.8	0.8

PER	ORTG	DRTG	WS/48	BPM	VOL
18.79	117.4	108.5	0.158	3.69	0.603

- Missed games due to general fatigue, a sore heel, and a sore hip, regular starter for Phoenix when healthy
- Performance declined due to his advanced age, still effective in his role as low usage playmaking guard
- Still an outstanding playmaker that can distribute the ball and run a team, great at limiting turnovers
- Crafty pick-and-roll ball handler and isolation player, can get to his spots to hit pull-up mid-range jumpers
- Solid three-point shooter throughout his career, made 37.5% of his threes last season
- Excellent spot-up shooter, less consistent when shooting threes off the dribble
- Plays a very methodical style, fairly ball dominant, not accustomed to moving off the ball
- 2022-23 Defensive Degree of Difficulty: 0.393
- 2022-23 Points Prevented: 0.012
- Often hidden in favorable matchups against lower leverage players
- Effectively guards ones and twos in lower leverage matchups, can be an exploitable target against better offensive teams
- Decent pick-and-roll defender, limited ability to switch, has to be used in conservative coverages, funnels his man into help
- Tends to get caught on screens off the ball, closes out but taller players can shoot over him
- Still good at playing passing lanes, consistently posts high Steal Percentages, solid defensive rebounder

Gary Payton II

	Height	Weight	Cap #	Years Left
	6'3"	190	$8.715M	PO

Similar at Age 30

		Season	SIMsc
1	Lester Hudson	2014-15	879.6
2	Toney Douglas	2016-17	866.0
3	Gilbert Arenas	2011-12	864.8
4	Alvin Robertson	1992-93	854.7
5	Don Buse	1980-81	854.4
6	Ronnie Price	2013-14	853.5
7	Gary Grant	1995-96	851.3
8	Tony Delk	2003-04	849.9
9	Avery Bradley	2020-21	849.7
10	E'Twaun Moore	2019-20	847.0

Baseline Basic Stats

MPG	PTS	AST	REB	BLK	STL
21.1	6.7	2.1	2.3	0.2	1.0

Advanced Metrics

USG%	3PTA/FGA	FTA/FGA	TS%	eFG%	3PT%
13.3	0.416	0.142	0.634	0.618	0.427

AST%	TOV%	OREB%	DREB%	STL%	BLK%
12.4	12.4	4.8	12.2	2.8	1.0

PER	ORTG	DRTG	WS/48	BPM	VOL
14.37	124.0	109.3	0.145	1.21	0.580

- Out for most of last season due to a core muscle injury, traded from Portland to Golden State
- Fairly effective in a regular rotational role for both teams as a low usage spot-up shooter and energy player
- Above break-even career three-point shooter, made half of his threes last season in limited attempts
- Strictly a stand-still spot-up shooter, took almost 89% of his threes from the corners
- Excellent finisher at the rim, great cutter and roll man, explosive finisher in transition, active offensive rebounder
- Rarely handles the ball, catch-and-shoot player with some passing skills, somewhat turnover prone
- 2022-23 Defensive Degree of Difficulty: 0.444
- 2022-23 Points Prevented: -3.431
- Took on some difficult assignments off the bench, may have been compromised due to injury
- Less effective as an on-ball defender, good at guarding multiple positions in the previous season
- Generally a solid pick-and-roll defender, solid at switching to guard ball handlers and screeners, less effective in Portland
- Can get caught on screens off the ball, sometimes takes bad gambles, tended to be late on his close-outs
- Active help defenders, gets steals at a high rate, can block shots from the weak side, solid defensive rebounder

Dario Šarić

	Height	Weight	Cap #	Years Left
	6'10"	225	$2.020M	UFA

Similar at Age 28

		Season	SIMsc
1	Tim Thomas	2005-06	936.5
2	Marty Conlon	1995-96	930.9
3	Austin Croshere	2003-04	928.2
4	Terry Mills	1995-96	924.9
5	Jonas Jerebko	2015-16	920.1
6	Danny Ferry	1994-95	915.8
7	Walter Herrmann	2007-08	913.0
8	Richard Anderson	1988-89	912.7
9	Vladimir Radmanovic	2008-09	912.6
10	Keith Van Horn	2003-04	911.8

Baseline Basic Stats

MPG	PTS	AST	REB	BLK	STL
22.4	9.3	1.4	4.4	0.3	0.6

Advanced Metrics

USG%	3PTA/FGA	FTA/FGA	TS%	eFG%	3PT%
19.0	0.432	0.259	0.569	0.528	0.376

AST%	TOV%	OREB%	DREB%	STL%	BLK%
10.8	13.1	5.9	18.3	1.4	0.9

PER	ORTG	DRTG	WS/48	BPM	VOL
13.65	110.9	109.7	0.100	-0.87	0.441

- Traded from Phoenix to Oklahoma City at the trade deadline, fringe rotation player for both teams
- Returned from an ACL injury, solidly effective in his role as a low usage stretch big
- Made over 39% of his threes last season, league average career three-point shooter
- Good as a stand-still spot-up shooter and a pick-and-pop screener
- High motor rim runner, solid cutter and roll man, active offensive rebounder, good at running the floor in transition
- Less effective as a post player, solid passing big man, slightly turnover prone
- 2022-23 Defensive Degree of Difficulty: 0.336
- 2022-23 Points Prevented: -0.708
- Middling rim protector, does not really block shots, fairly good defensive rebounder
- Usually guards second unit big men, struggles to handle stronger big men inside, a step slow when defending in space
- Below average pick-and-roll defender, not effective at taking away any specific action
- Willing to close out on spot-up shooters, will give up driving lanes by closing too aggressively

Jonathan Kuminga

	Height	Weight	Cap #	Years Left
	6'8"	210	$6.013M	TO

Similar at Age 20

		Season	SIMsc
1	Gordon Hayward	2010-11	935.1
2	Rodions Kurucs	2018-19	931.3
3	Paul George	2010-11	926.4
4	Jaylen Brown	2016-17	920.9
5	Josh Jackson	2017-18	915.7
6	Tobias Harris	2012-13	915.1
7	Harrison Barnes	2012-13	910.4
8	Cam Reddish	2019-20	909.9
9	Wilson Chandler	2007-08	907.5
10	Maurice Harkless	2013-14	905.1

Baseline Basic Stats

MPG	PTS	AST	REB	BLK	STL
26.7	11.7	1.7	4.5	0.6	0.9

Advanced Metrics

USG%	3PTA/FGA	FTA/FGA	TS%	eFG%	3PT%
21.3	0.362	0.280	0.580	0.550	0.373

AST%	TOV%	OREB%	DREB%	STL%	BLK%
11.0	12.4	4.4	13.6	1.6	1.6

PER	ORTG	DRTG	WS/48	BPM	VOL
14.78	110.8	110.3	0.111	-0.37	0.455

- Regular rotation player for Golden State in his second NBA season
- Decently effective in a role as a lower volume energy player and spot-up shooter off the bench
- Excellent athlete, can explosively finish above the rim in transition, good cutter and roll man
- Improved as a three-point shooter, made threes at an above average rate
- Almost exclusively a stand-still spot-up shooter, made almost 42% of his corner threes last season
- Not really used as a shot creator or ball handler, improving passer, solid at limiting turnovers
- 2022-23 Defensive Degree of Difficulty: 0.480
- 2022-23 Points Prevented: 1.264
- Drew a lot of difficult assignments off the bench, may have the potential to be a stopper in the future
- Fairly good on-ball defender, can guard multiple positions, most effective when guarding perimeter players
- Average pick-and-roll defender, can switch and cut off penetration, tends to go too far under screens
- Stays attached to shooters off the ball, fights through screens and closes out in spot-up situations
- Solid weak side shot blocker, occasionally gets steals, fairly solid defensive rebounder

Moses Moody

	Height	Weight	Cap #	Years Left
	6'6"	205	$3.918M	TO

Similar at Age 20

		Season	SIMsc
1	Ziaire Williams	2021-22	912.9
2	Nassir Little	2020-21	911.4
3	Martell Webster	2006-07	910.3
4	CJ Elleby	2020-21	906.9
5	Patrick Williams	2021-22	901.8
6	Devin Vassell	2020-21	901.6
7	C.J. Miles	2007-08	899.3
8	Kenyon Martin Jr.	2020-21	893.7
9	Gordon Hayward	2010-11	893.2
10	Kevin Knox	2019-20	892.7

Baseline Basic Stats

MPG	PTS	AST	REB	BLK	STL
20.9	7.9	1.3	2.7	0.3	0.6

Advanced Metrics

USG%	3PTA/FGA	FTA/FGA	TS%	eFG%	3PT%
16.6	0.601	0.182	0.579	0.556	0.373

AST%	TOV%	OREB%	DREB%	STL%	BLK%
8.6	10.0	2.9	10.8	1.1	1.0

PER	ORTG	DRTG	WS/48	BPM	VOL
11.31	113.2	114.0	0.086	-1.70	0.397

- Fringe rotation player for Golden State in his second NBA season
- Maintained his effectiveness from last season, mainly used as a low usage shooting specialist
- Has consistently been a league average three-point shooter in his two NBA seasons
- Very good spot-up shooter that can also shoot off screens, good at making threes in transition
- Good at scoring on hand-offs, makes sharp backdoors if defenders try to crowd him
- Lacks ability to create his own shot, catch-and-shoot player that makes safe passes, good at avoiding turnovers
- 2022-23 Defensive Degree of Difficulty: 0.352
- 2022-23 Points Prevented: 1.136
- Usually guarded second unit players, improved to become a decent on-ball defender
- Could effectively stay with opposing perimeter players, stronger players gave him trouble in the post
- Effective pick-and-roll defender, can contain ball handlers and funnel his man into help, had some lapses when switched onto screeners
- Tends to get caught on screens off the ball, good at closing out in spot-up situations
- Stay-at-home defender, rarely gets steals or blocks, decent defensive rebounder

Cory Joseph

	Height	Weight	Cap #	Years Left
	6'3"	200	$2.020M	UFA

Similar at Age 31

		Season	SIMsc
1	Kirk Hinrich	2011-12	942.5
2	Jon Barry	2000-01	939.9
3	Eldridge Recasner	1998-99	927.2
4	Keyon Dooling	2011-12	927.1
5	Willie Green	2012-13	921.7
6	Devin Harris	2014-15	919.8
7	Anthony Johnson	2005-06	918.6
8	Carlos Arroyo	2010-11	918.5
9	Terry Porter	1994-95	916.7
10	Chris Childs	1998-99	916.0

Baseline Basic Stats

MPG	PTS	AST	REB	BLK	STL
22.3	7.5	3.1	2.1	0.2	0.7

Advanced Metrics

USG%	3PTA/FGA	FTA/FGA	TS%	eFG%	3PT%
16.1	0.401	0.222	0.553	0.515	0.390

AST%	TOV%	OREB%	DREB%	STL%	BLK%
23.3	15.0	1.8	8.7	1.5	0.7

PER	ORTG	DRTG	WS/48	BPM	VOL
12.14	111.9	114.2	0.076	-1.50	0.393

- Regular rotation player for Detroit in his second full season with the team
- Solidly effective in his role as a low volume spot-up shooter and ball handler
- Above break-even career three-point shooter, made almost 39% of his threes last season
- Predominantly a stand-still spot-up shooter, was more efficient when shooting off the dribble last season
- Average in ball handling situations, not quite quick enough to get to the rim, good at hitting pull-up jumpers and floaters
- Assist Percentage increased to a career high, makes sound decisions, good at avoiding turnovers
- 2022-23 Defensive Degree of Difficulty: 0.394
- 2022-23 Points Prevented: -1.051
- Usually defended second unit players or lower leverage starters, played below average on-ball defense
- Had trouble staying with opposing guards, struggled when defending taller perimeter players
- Decent pick-and-roll defender, can functionally switch, tends to allow ball handlers to turn the corner
- Stays attached to shooters off the ball, fights through screens and closes out in spot-up situations
- Stay-at-home defender now, only occasionally gets steals, below average defensive rebounder

Newcomers

Brandin Podziemski

	Height	Weight	Cap #	Years Left
	6'5"	205	$3.352M	1 + 2 TO

Baseline Basic Stats

MPG	PTS	AST	REB	BLK	STL
20.4	8.3	1.8	2.8	0.2	0.7

Advanced Metrics

USG%	3PTA/FGA	FTA/FGA	TS%	eFG%	3PT%
18.7	0.376	0.222	0.521	0.492	0.356

AST%	TOV%	OREB%	DREB%	STL%	BLK%
14.0	12.3	3.7	13.0	1.9	0.8

PER	ORTG	DRTG	WS/48	BPM	VOL
12.95	101.4	103.8	0.063	-1.65	N/A

- Drafted by Golden State with the 19th overall pick in 2023
- Had an up-and-down performance at the Las Vegas and Sacramento Summer Leagues
- Used as a moderate volume playmaking guard, played better in Sacramento
- True Shooting Percentage in Summer League action was below 45%, made only 25% of his threes
- Made almost 44% of his threes at Santa Clara, most effective as a shooter off the catch
- Likely will be used as a lower usage shooting specialist, lacks the quickness to create his own shot consistently
- Struggled to create his own offense in ball handling situations at Summer League
- Solid playmaker with good court vision, can find open teammates, tended to play wildly, fairly turnover prone
- Athletically limited, lacks ideal quickness and length, could possibly be a liability at the NBA level
- Usually was hidden in favorable matchups in college, had trouble staying with opposing guards
- Played passable on-ball defense against ones and twos at Summer League
- Below average pick-and-roll defender, tends to allow ball handlers to turn the corner, uncertain ability to switch
- Stays attached to shooters off the ball, fights through screens and closes out in spot-up situations
- Fairly active help defender, plays passing lanes, got steals at a fairly high rate at Summer League, solid defensive rebounder
- Could benefit from some additional seasoning in the G-League to improve his defense and shooting consistency

Trayce Jackson-Davis

	Height	Weight	Cap #	Years Left
	6'9"	245	$1.120M	2 + TO

Baseline Basic Stats

MPG	PTS	AST	REB	BLK	STL
19.3	7.4	0.9	5.0	0.8	0.5

Advanced Metrics

USG%	3PTA/FGA	FTA/FGA	TS%	eFG%	3PT%
18.8	0.014	0.372	0.511	0.476	0.150

AST%	TOV%	OREB%	DREB%	STL%	BLK%
9.8	12.7	9.5	19.7	1.3	3.8

PER	ORTG	DRTG	WS/48	BPM	VOL
16.25	102.3	98.5	0.086	-0.86	N/A

- Drafted by Washington with the 57th overall pick, traded to Golden State
- Had a very strong performance in two games at the Las Vegas Summer League
- Excelled in his role as a moderate volume rim runner and interior scorer
- True Shooting Percentage was almost 68%, good at bullying weaker defenders on post-ups
- Lacks advanced post moves, relies solely on strength, may not be as effective against better post defenders
- Energetic rim runner that dives hard to the rim, good cutter and roll man, excellent offensive rebounder
- Lacks shooting range outside of the paint, made less than 70% of his career free throws
- Fairly solid passing big man that can hit cutters or find open shooters, good at avoiding turnovers
- Undersized center but plays bigger than his actual height
- Solid rim protector at Summer League, great shot blocker, sacrifices position to go for blocks, was a below average defensive rebounder in Vegas
- Middling on-ball defender, taller big men can shoot over him or back him down, mobile enough to defend in space
- Decent pick-and-roll defender, effective at hedging out on ball handlers, a step late when covering screeners
- Consistently comes out to contest perimeter shots in spot-up situations
- Has active hands, good at using length to play passing lanes, got steals at a high rate at Summer League
- Could benefit from some time in the G-League to diversify his skill set and adapt to the modern NBA game

New Orleans Pelicans

Last Season: 42 - 40, Missed the Playoffs

Offensive Rating: 114.4, 21st in the NBA   Defensive Rating: 112.5, 6th in the NBA

Primary Executive: David Griffin, Executive Vice President of Basketball Operations

Head Coach: Willie Green

Key Roster Changes

Subtractions
Josh Richardson, free agency
Jaxson Hayes, free agency
Willy Hernangomez, free agency
Garrett Temple, waived

Additions
Jordan Hawkins, draft
E.J. Liddell, signed 2022 draft pick
Cody Zeller, free agency

Roster

Likely Starting Five
1. C.J. McCollum
2. Herbert Jones
3. Brandon Ingram
4. Zion Williamson
5. Jonas Valančiūnas

Other Key Rotation Players
Trey Murphy III
Larry Nance Jr.
Jose Alvarado
Naji Marshall
Dyson Daniels

* Italics denotes that a player is likely to be on the floor to close games

Remaining Roster

- Cody Zeller
- Kira Lewis Jr.
- Jordan Hawkins
- E.J. Liddell
- Dereon Seabron, 22, 6'7", 180, NC State (Two-Way)
- Landers Nolley II, 23, 6'7", 215, Cincinnati (Exhibit 10)
- Tevian Jones, 23, 6'7", 210, Southern Utah (Exhibit 10)
- Liam Robbins, 24, 7'0", 245, Vanderbilt (Exhibit 10)

SCHREMPF Base Rating: 46.5

Season Preview Survey

- *Are the Pelicans contending or rebuilding? Where is this team headed?*

The Pelicans are trying to become contenders, but their plans are constantly being derailed because they simply have never been at full strength for a whole season. A lot of this is connected to Zion Williamson's injury history because he's missed large portions of his career due to various health issues. Despite these setbacks, they have kept plugging away to build a talented roster that has enough pieces to at least make the playoffs. If they get some luck and find some way to keep Williamson healthy, then they could move forward and test themselves against the top contenders in the league. Otherwise, they may have no choice but to either continue tread water or shake up their roster to effectively move on.

- *What are the areas of concern for this team heading into this season?*

As it was alluded to before, the main concern for New Orleans is Zion Williamson's health. He's missed a lot of games in his career, and it's cost the team some wins. Because of this, he and the organization have had some conflicts over his weight management, recovery preferences, and other issues related to his personal behavior. Overall, the team has been sidetracked in their quest to become contenders. They will have to work with Williamson to either manage his workload or adapt his game to incorporate lower impact elements to find some way to keep him healthy. The reason for this is their roster and strategy are built around him, so if he's absent, then everything falls apart. If he's unable to stay in the lineup, then the Pelicans may have to alter everything to allow them to succeed without him, so they can move forward. Otherwise, they will be stuck in this holding pattern and remain in mediocrity as long as he continues to deal with nagging injuries.

- *List some possible breakout players for this team.*

If there's any kind of silver lining with Williamson's constant injuries, it is that his absence has allowed other young players to develop to become valuable contributors. Herbert Jones has become one of the best perimeter defenders in the league. Trey Murphy III has turned into a reliable complementary shooting specialist while Jose Alvarado has made an impact as pesky defensive guard. There still could be another opportunity for a young player to ascend to a higher role. The best bet to do this is last season's lottery pick, Dyson Daniels. He had his moments in limited action last season because he showed that he could play solid on-ball defense to slow down high-end scorers while providing an extra layer of ball movement as a secondary facilitator. His jump shot still isn't reliable at this stage, but he showed improved scoring ability at Summer League. Specifically, he was effective at posting up smaller guards and slashing to the rim. If these skills translate in this regular season, he could help the team as a change-of-pace guard in the mold of someone like Shaun Livingston.

- *What should we expect from them this season?*

The answer to this question largely depends on the health of Zion Williamson. If he suffers another serious injury, then it will be tough for New Orleans to land a playoff spot because everyone else would have to play at their respective peaks to compensate for this loss. It happened before in the 2021-22 season, but the West has gotten more competitive. They might just wind up staying in their current position as a play-in team if Williamson isn't healthy for the whole year. If he does play for a majority of the time, they could resemble the team that they were in the early part of last season and become a top-tier contender in the Western Conference. They just need some good fortune to go down that path.

Veterans

Brandon Ingram

	Height	Weight	Cap #	Years Left
	6'8"	190	$33.833M	1

Similar at Age 25

		Season	SIMsc
1	Anfernee Hardaway	1996-97	897.1
2	Zach LaVine	2020-21	890.8
3	Willie Anderson	1991-92	885.6
4	Caris LeVert	2019-20	884.6
5	Spencer Dinwiddie	2018-19	883.4
6	Tracy McGrady*	2004-05	882.9
7	Cedric Ceballos	1994-95	881.4
8	Malik Sealy	1995-96	881.0
9	Evan Fournier	2017-18	880.8
10	Reggie Theus	1982-83	879.9

Baseline Basic Stats

MPG	PTS	AST	REB	BLK	STL
32.9	20.9	4.4	4.4	0.5	1.0

Advanced Metrics

USG%	3PTA/FGA	FTA/FGA	TS%	eFG%	3PT%
28.5	0.263	0.321	0.572	0.516	0.360

AST%	TOV%	OREB%	DREB%	STL%	BLK%
24.9	12.0	2.3	13.9	1.2	1.2

PER	ORTG	DRTG	WS/48	BPM	VOL
18.90	112.7	112.6	0.121	1.69	0.359

- Missed half of the season due to a bruised left toe, concussion, and a sprained ankle
- Performed at an All-Star level as a primary perimeter scorer for New Orleans when healthy
- Good pick-and-roll ball handler and isolation player, mainly looks to drive to the rim or pull up for shorter mid-range shots
- League average career three-point shooter, made 39% of his threes last season
- Mostly a stand-still spot-up shooter right now, percentages have varied from year-to-year
- Good at curling off screens to the mid-range area, can post up shorter players, good cutter off the ball
- Great playmaker that finds open shooters or cutters, solid at avoiding turnovers
- 2022-23 Defensive Degree of Difficulty: 0.423
- 2022-23 Points Prevented: 0.301
- Tends to guard lower leverage starters, played average on-ball defense last season
- Struggled to stay with opponents on the perimeter, more effective against power forward types inside
- Average pick-and-roll defender, can switch and cut off penetration, goes too far under screens
- Tends to get caught on screens off the ball, usually was late to close out on spot-up shooters
- Stay-at-home defender, rarely got steals or blocks, solid defensive rebounder

CJ McCollum

	Height	Weight	Cap #	Years Left
	6'3"	190	$35.802M	2

Similar at Age 31

		Season	SIMsc
1	Goran Dragic	2017-18	929.6
2	Joe Dumars*	1994-95	924.0
3	Reggie Jackson	2021-22	921.6
4	Dell Curry	1995-96	916.4
5	Jason Terry	2008-09	911.2
6	Jrue Holiday	2021-22	910.0
7	John Starks	1996-97	907.8
8	Anthony Johnson	2005-06	907.4
9	World B. Free	1984-85	905.8
10	Mike Conley	2018-19	904.7

Baseline Basic Stats

MPG	PTS	AST	REB	BLK	STL
30.3	15.5	4.1	3.1	0.2	1.0

Advanced Metrics

USG%	3PTA/FGA	FTA/FGA	TS%	eFG%	3PT%
24.4	0.387	0.198	0.542	0.510	0.383

AST%	TOV%	OREB%	DREB%	STL%	BLK%
23.4	11.4	2.3	10.3	1.5	0.9

PER	ORTG	DRTG	WS/48	BPM	VOL
15.65	109.7	113.5	0.084	0.53	0.399

- Regular starting guard for New Orleans in his first full season with the team
- Efficiency declined, still effective in his role as his team's primary ball handler
- Reliable three-point shooter, has made 39.5% of his career threes
- Excellent spot-up shooter, around break-even when shooting off screens or off the dribble
- Less effective as a ball handler, better on pick-and-rolls, needs a screen to create separation
- Mid-range efficiency dropped, able to make floaters at the foul line, struggled to make longer pull-up jumpers
- Good playmaker that can run a team and set up teammates, good at avoiding turnovers
- 2022-23 Defensive Degree of Difficulty: 0.431
- 2022-23 Points Prevented: 0.487
- Usually defended starting level players, hidden in previous seasons
- Played good on-ball defense last season, could capably defend ones and twos in one-on-one situations
- Effective pick-and-roll defender, makes sound rotations, funnels his man into help, can functionally switch if necessary
- Stays attached to shooters off the ball, fights through screens and closes out in spot-up situations
- Steal and Block Percentages were consistent with his career averages, decent defensive rebounder

Zion Williamson

	Height	Weight	Cap #	Years Left
	6'6"	284	$34.005M	4

Similar at Age 22

		Season	SIMsc
1	Mark Aguirre	1981-82	850.8
2	Mike Sweetney	2004-05	837.7
3	Eddy Curry	2004-05	835.7
4	Jared Sullinger	2014-15	834.6
5	Clarence Weatherspoon	1992-93	825.4
6	Vitaly Potapenko	1997-98	824.1
7	Gary Trent	1996-97	823.8
8	DeJuan Blair	2011-12	822.8
9	Sean May	2006-07	822.1
10	Elton Brand	2001-02	820.0

Baseline Basic Stats

MPG	PTS	AST	REB	BLK	STL
30.2	16.0	2.3	7.6	0.8	0.8

Advanced Metrics

USG%	3PTA/FGA	FTA/FGA	TS%	eFG%	3PT%
26.7	0.038	0.462	0.610	0.571	0.319

AST%	TOV%	OREB%	DREB%	STL%	BLK%
18.2	12.9	8.8	17.7	1.5	1.8

PER	ORTG	DRTG	WS/48	BPM	VOL
23.46	117.4	109.0	0.181	3.49	0.552

- Made his second All-Star team, missed most of last season due to a strained right hamstring
- Thrived in his role as a high usage interior scorer for New Orleans when healthy
- Excellent at barreling his way to the rim as a pick-and-roll ball handler and isolation player
- Bullies weaker defenders in the post, draws fouls at a high rate, efficient finisher at the rim
- Explosive vertical threat, good cutter, scores off put-backs, dynamic finisher in transition
- Makes spot-up threes at an above break-even rate, percentages have varied from year-to-year
- Good secondary playmaker that makes simple reads, solid at limiting turnovers
- 2022-23 Defensive Degree of Difficulty: 0.385
- 2022-23 Points Prevented: 0.867
- Used as a roamer, usually is hidden in favorable matchups against lower leverage players
- Average on-ball defender, not always engaged on defense, better against perimeter players
- Tended to commit bad shooting fouls, taller big men could shoot over him
- Solid pick-and-roll defender, effective at switching to guard ball handlers or screeners
- Tends to get caught on screens off the ball, good at closing out on spot-up shooters
- Block rate slightly down, less effective as a rim protector, can get steals on occasion, fairly solid defensive rebounder

Jonas Valančiūnas

	Height	Weight	Cap #	Years Left
	6'11"	265	$15.435M	UFA

Similar at Age 30

		Season	SIMsc
1	Mehmet Okur	2009-10	898.8
2	Chris Kaman	2012-13	885.6
3	Emeka Okafor	2012-13	877.0
4	LaMarcus Aldridge	2015-16	876.0
5	Nene	2012-13	873.8
6	Al Jefferson	2014-15	873.1
7	Benoit Benjamin	1994-95	872.0
8	Mason Plumlee	2020-21	870.2
9	Serge Ibaka	2019-20	869.9
10	Marc Jackson	2004-05	869.2

Baseline Basic Stats

MPG	PTS	AST	REB	BLK	STL
26.3	12.6	2.0	8.3	0.8	0.6

Advanced Metrics

USG%	3PTA/FGA	FTA/FGA	TS%	eFG%	3PT%
21.5	0.141	0.275	0.592	0.559	0.406

AST%	TOV%	OREB%	DREB%	STL%	BLK%
12.0	14.0	11.0	28.9	0.9	2.6

PER	ORTG	DRTG	WS/48	BPM	VOL
18.43	115.7	108.6	0.148	0.73	0.474

- Started all but three games at center for New Orleans last season
- Solidly effective in his role as a moderate usage post scorer and stretch big
- Fairly good post-up player, prefers the left block, good at flashing to the middle
- Above break-even career three-point shooter, slightly better when shooting in the corners
- Excellent as a stationary spot-up shooter, less efficient as a pick-and-pop screener
- High motor rim runner, great offensive rebounder, solid cutter and roll man, doesn't get great lift, sometimes misses shots in traffic
- Fairly good passing big man, finds open shooters and cutters inside, good at avoiding turnovers
- 2022-23 Defensive Degree of Difficulty: 0.457
- 2022-23 Points Prevented: -0.880
- Led the NBA in Defensive Rebound Percentage, solid shot blocker
- Below average rim protector, not quick enough to get in position to contest shots, fairly foul prone
- Guards starting level big men, stout post defender, plays angles well to stay with big men on isolations
- Decent pick-and-roll defender, good in drop coverages, has trouble containing ball handlers on the perimeter
- Tends to sag back into the paint, does not always come out to contest outside shots in spot-up situations

Herbert Jones

	Height	Weight	Cap #	Years Left
	6'8"	210	$12.015M	3

Similar at Age 24

		Season	SIMsc
1	James Posey	2000-01	938.7
2	Shane Battier	2002-03	934.7
3	Robert Horry	1994-95	921.8
4	Devean George	2001-02	921.4
5	Chris Morris	1989-90	921.3
6	Jiri Welsch	2003-04	915.9
7	Harold Pressley	1987-88	915.1
8	Maurice Harkless	2017-18	913.6
9	Josh Howard	2004-05	912.5
10	John Salmons	2003-04	909.4

Baseline Basic Stats

MPG	PTS	AST	REB	BLK	STL
29.0	10.8	2.0	4.8	0.6	1.2

Advanced Metrics

USG%	3PTA/FGA	FTA/FGA	TS%	eFG%	3PT%
16.1	0.339	0.287	0.558	0.516	0.345

AST%	TOV%	OREB%	DREB%	STL%	BLK%
11.5	12.6	5.1	11.7	2.3	1.9

PER	ORTG	DRTG	WS/48	BPM	VOL
13.45	112.9	109.4	0.110	0.19	0.279

- Regular starter for New Orleans in his second NBA season
- Consistently effective in his role as a low usage spot-up shooter and energy player
- Has been a break-even three-point shooter in each of his two seasons in the league
- Almost exclusively a stationary spot-up shooter, slightly better when taking threes in transition
- Great athlete, explosive finisher in transition, defenders can back off him to limit his effectiveness around the rim, still made over 65% of his shots inside of three feet last season
- Not really able to create his own shot, fairly solid secondary playmaker, good at avoiding turnovers
- 2022-23 Defensive Degree of Difficulty: 0.606, had the 2nd most difficult set of matchups in the NBA
- 2022-23 Points Prevented: 0.516
- Used as New Orleans' primary defensive stopper, one of the best overall defenders in the league
- Excellent on-ball defender, aggressively pressures his man, guards multiple positions on the floor
- Good pick-and-roll defender, effective at switching onto ball handlers and screeners
- Stays attached to shooters off the ball, fights through screens and closes out in spot-up situations
- Dynamic roamer, gets steals and blocks at a pretty high rate, also gets a lot of deflections, decent defensive rebounder

Trey Murphy III

	Height	Weight	Cap #	Years Left
	6'9"	206	$3.359M	TO

Similar at Age 22

		Season	SIMsc
1	Otto Porter	2015-16	917.6
2	Nicolas Batum	2010-11	916.1
3	Hollis Thompson	2013-14	915.1
4	Corey Kispert	2021-22	914.6
5	Svi Mykhailiuk	2019-20	909.8
6	Furkan Korkmaz	2019-20	908.5
7	Omri Casspi	2010-11	906.3
8	Peja Stojakovic	1999-00	905.0
9	Harrison Barnes	2014-15	903.2
10	Nik Stauskas	2015-16	902.0

Baseline Basic Stats

MPG	PTS	AST	REB	BLK	STL
27.2	11.4	1.5	4.0	0.3	0.8

Advanced Metrics

USG%	3PTA/FGA	FTA/FGA	TS%	eFG%	3PT%
17.6	0.526	0.215	0.598	0.562	0.397

AST%	TOV%	OREB%	DREB%	STL%	BLK%
7.9	7.5	3.4	12.1	1.6	1.2

PER	ORTG	DRTG	WS/48	BPM	VOL
14.45	119.4	112.5	0.126	0.34	0.365

- Became a regular starter for New Orleans in his second NBA season
- Increased his productivity in his role as a low volume shooting specialist
- Has made 40% of his career threes, shoots over 44% on corner threes for his career
- Mainly a stand-still spot-up shooter, occasionally makes shots off screens
- Good at getting to the rim on hand-offs, explosive finisher in transition
- Effective pick-and-roll ball handler, needs a screen to create separation, less effective on isolation plays
- Mostly a catch-and-shoot player, somewhat limited as a playmaker, rarely turns the ball over
- 2022-23 Defensive Degree of Difficulty: 0.425
- 2022-23 Points Prevented: -1.152
- Usually guarded lower leverage starters, average on-ball defender
- Could stay with opposing perimeter players, tends to back off his man too much, has trouble against stronger players inside
- Decent pick-and-roll defender, solid at containing ball handlers, a step late when rotating onto screeners
- Fights through screens off the ball, sometimes can be late to close out on spot-up shooters
- More active as a help defender, got steals and blocks at a much higher rate, decent defensive rebounder

Larry Nance Jr.

	Height	Weight	Cap #	Years Left
	6'7"	245	$10.375M	1

Similar at Age 30

		Season	SIMsc
1	Trevor Booker	2017-18	915.7
2	Matt Barnes	2010-11	906.4
3	Eduardo Najera	2006-07	903.0
4	Ed Nealy	1990-91	899.2
5	Brandon Bass	2015-16	888.8
6	Frank Brickowski	1989-90	885.9
7	Torrey Craig	2020-21	885.7
8	Luc Mbah a Moute	2016-17	882.1
9	James Johnson	2017-18	879.7
10	Grant Long	1996-97	877.4

Baseline Basic Stats

MPG	PTS	AST	REB	BLK	STL
21.0	7.6	1.4	4.7	0.5	0.8

Advanced Metrics

USG%	3PTA/FGA	FTA/FGA	TS%	eFG%	3PT%
14.4	0.260	0.242	0.596	0.575	0.347

AST%	TOV%	OREB%	DREB%	STL%	BLK%
10.6	12.7	7.6	19.0	2.0	2.0

PER	ORTG	DRTG	WS/48	BPM	VOL
14.56	119.9	109.1	0.124	0.64	0.313

- Regular rotation player for New Orleans in his first full season with the team
- Greatly increased his production in a role as a very low usage rim runner and stretch big
- Vertical lob threat with great athleticism, made almost 77% of his shots inside of three feet last season
- Great cutter and roll man, active offensive rebounder, explosive finisher in transition
- Break-even career three-point shooter, percentages have varied from year-to-year
- Good spot-up shooter, less effective when shooting in other situations
- Occasionally can post up smaller players, fairly solid secondary playmaker, good at avoiding turnovers
- 2022-23 Defensive Degree of Difficulty: 0.399
- 2022-23 Points Prevented: -1.360
- Good defensive rebounder, solid shot blocker, below average rim protector, undersized, not always disciplined with his positioning
- Usually guarded second unit players or lower leverage starters, effective on-ball defender in these matchups
- Strong enough to handle taller big men, good quickness to stay with perimeter players
- Decent pick-and-roll defender, good at switching out onto ball handlers, has lapses when covering screeners
- Stays attached to shooters off the ball, fights through screens and closes out in spot-up situations
- Great at using his length and anticipation skills to get steals

Jose Alvarado

	Height	Weight	Cap #	Years Left
	6'0"	179	$1.836M	TO

Similar at Age 24

		Season	SIMsc
1	Cory Alexander	1997-98	929.8
2	Aaron Holiday	2020-21	926.9
3	Tyronn Lue	2001-02	914.4
4	J.J. Barea	2008-09	913.9
5	Jordan McLaughlin	2020-21	912.0
6	David Wesley	1994-95	911.9
7	Brandon Goodwin	2019-20	909.0
8	Lindsey Hunter	1994-95	909.0
9	Shabazz Napier	2015-16	908.6
10	Tony Bennett	1993-94	908.2

Baseline Basic Stats

MPG	PTS	AST	REB	BLK	STL
21.1	8.4	3.3	2.1	0.1	0.9

Advanced Metrics

USG%	3PTA/FGA	FTA/FGA	TS%	eFG%	3PT%
19.7	0.430	0.213	0.529	0.491	0.337

AST%	TOV%	OREB%	DREB%	STL%	BLK%
24.5	12.5	2.3	9.7	2.6	0.6

PER	ORTG	DRTG	WS/48	BPM	VOL
14.47	110.5	110.0	0.101	0.26	0.392

- Regular rotation player for New Orleans in his second NBA season
- Decently effective in his role as a low usage spot-up shooter and secondary ball handler
- Improved to become a break-even three-point shooter, made 38% of his corner threes last season
- Primarily a stationary spot-up shooter, more effective when he was shooting threes in transition
- Below average scorer in ball handling situations, needs a screen to create separation, defenders can back off him to limit his effectiveness if his shot isn't falling
- Fairly solid playmaker that makes sound decisions, good ball control guard that limits turnovers
- 2022-23 Defensive Degree of Difficulty: 0.442
- 2022-23 Points Prevented: 0.997
- Drew a lot of tough assignments off the bench against elite guards, fairly good on-ball defender
- Great at pressuring ball handlers, holds his own against taller players
- Over-aggressive, tends to commit a lot of cheap touch fouls
- Decent pick-and-roll defender, not really able to switch due to size limitations, good at funneling ball handlers into help
- Stays attached to shooters off the ball, fights through screens and closes out in spot-up situations
- Pesky defender that gets steals at a high rate, fairly decent defensive rebounder

Naji Marshall

	Height	Weight	Cap #	Years Left
	6'7"	220	$1.931M	UFA

Similar at Age 25

		Season	SIMsc
1	Omri Casspi	2013-14	942.4
2	Gary Forbes	2010-11	938.1
3	Eric Piatkowski	1995-96	937.4
4	Jarvis Hayes	2006-07	937.2
5	Jiri Welsch	2004-05	935.5
6	Jordan Hamilton	2015-16	934.0
7	Martell Webster	2011-12	932.1
8	J.R. Smith	2010-11	928.8
9	Scott Burrell	1995-96	928.3
10	Sam Mack	1995-96	927.8

Baseline Basic Stats

MPG	PTS	AST	REB	BLK	STL
22.1	8.7	1.5	3.2	0.2	0.7

Advanced Metrics

USG%	3PTA/FGA	FTA/FGA	TS%	eFG%	3PT%
18.4	0.425	0.284	0.543	0.498	0.330

AST%	TOV%	OREB%	DREB%	STL%	BLK%
12.5	12.1	3.3	14.1	1.7	0.8

PER	ORTG	DRTG	WS/48	BPM	VOL
12.52	108.3	110.7	0.085	-1.06	0.343

- Became a regular rotation player for New Orleans in his third NBA season
- Maintained his usual level of effectiveness, used as a low usage spot-up shooter and secondary playmaker
- Has made less than 30% of his career threes, improved to become a solid mid-range shooter
- Predominantly a break-even spot-up shooter, much less efficient when shooting in other situations
- Good at getting to the rim on dribble hand-offs, middling effectiveness in ball handling situations
- Energetic rim runner that scores on hustle plays, solid cutter and roll man, runs hard in transition
- Solid secondary playmaker, makes simple reads to find open shooters or cutters, good at avoiding turnovers
- 2022-23 Defensive Degree of Difficulty: 0.483
- 2022-23 Points Prevented: -0.612
- Drew a lot of tough assignments against elite scorers off the bench, fairly solid on-ball defender
- Effectively guards multiple positions on the perimeter, has some trouble guarding stronger power forwards inside
- Played below average pick-and-roll defense, not effective at taking away any specific action
- Fights through screens off the ball, usually was late when closing out on spot-up shooters
- Steal Percentage dropped but still gets steals at a decent rate, solid defensive rebounder

Dyson Daniels

	Height	Weight	Cap #	Years Left
	6'8"	199	$5.784M	2 TO

Similar at Age 19

		Season	SIMsc
1	Sekou Doumbouya	2019-20	905.6
2	Troy Brown	2018-19	889.2
3	Darius Bazley	2019-20	879.3
4	Giannis Antetokounmpo	2013-14	876.9
5	Joshua Primo	2021-22	874.8
6	Frank Ntilikina	2017-18	871.5
7	Trevor Ariza	2004-05	869.2
8	Justise Winslow	2015-16	869.2
9	Martell Webster	2005-06	867.8
10	Dante Exum	2014-15	867.3

Baseline Basic Stats

MPG	PTS	AST	REB	BLK	STL
22.1	8.2	1.5	3.5	0.3	0.8

Advanced Metrics

USG%	3PTA/FGA	FTA/FGA	TS%	eFG%	3PT%
16.0	0.374	0.244	0.547	0.514	0.354

AST%	TOV%	OREB%	DREB%	STL%	BLK%
16.0	15.9	3.6	16.3	2.1	1.1

PER	ORTG	DRTG	WS/48	BPM	VOL
12.46	110.2	111.7	0.080	-0.70	0.452

- Regular rotation player for New Orleans in his rookie season
- Produced with middling efficiency in a role as a low usage spot-up shooter and secondary facilitator
- True Shooting Percentage was slightly above 50%, below break-even three-point shooter
- Break-even when taking spot-up jumpers, shooting ability is unproven in other situations
- Less effective in ball handling situations, defenders often back off him to make it tougher for him to drive
- Good cutter off the ball, selectively goes to the offensive boards to score on put-backs
- Solid as a secondary playmaker, can push the ball in transition, good at avoiding turnovers
- 2022-23 Defensive Degree of Difficulty: 0.443
- 2022-23 Points Prevented: 2.257
- Drew a lot of tough assignments off the bench, solid on-ball defender, capable of guarding multiple positions
- Still a bit undisciplined, tended to commit shooting fouls in the post, backed off his man too much on the perimeter
- Good pick-and-roll defender, effectively can switch to guard ball handlers and screeners
- Stays attached to shooters off the ball, fights through screens and closes out in spot-up situations
- Fairly active help defender, gets steals at a good rate, occasional weak side shot blocker, solid defensive rebounder

Cody Zeller

	Height	Weight	Cap #	Years Left
	6'11"	240	$2.020M	UFA

Similar at Age 30

		Season	SIMsc
1	Ben Handlogten	2003-04	943.9
2	Mikki Moore	2005-06	898.5
3	Danny Schayes	1989-90	897.9
4	David Andersen	2010-11	895.9
5	Tiago Splitter	2014-15	894.9
6	Dwight Powell	2021-22	891.2
7	Miles Plumlee	2018-19	890.1
8	Mitch Kupchak	1984-85	890.0
9	Clemon Johnson	1986-87	889.2
10	Greg Foster	1998-99	888.3

Baseline Basic Stats

MPG	PTS	AST	REB	BLK	STL
18.2	6.6	0.9	4.9	0.6	0.5

Advanced Metrics

USG%	3PTA/FGA	FTA/FGA	TS%	eFG%	3PT%
16.4	0.026	0.481	0.612	0.574	0.120

AST%	TOV%	OREB%	DREB%	STL%	BLK%
7.9	15.9	11.8	21.7	1.1	2.5

PER	ORTG	DRTG	WS/48	BPM	VOL
15.33	117.7	109.4	0.125	-2.22	0.509

- Signed with Miami late last season, regular rotation player in the playoffs
- Maintained his usual effectiveness in limited regular season action as a low usage rim runner
- Efficient high motor rim runner, made over 72% of his shots from three feet and in
- Good cutter and roll man, runs hard in transition, sometimes will rush his put-back attempts, good offensive rebounder
- Not really a post-up threat, lacks reliable shooting range outside of the paint area
- Decent passing big man that can sometimes hit cutters or find open shooters, slightly turnover prone
- 2022-23 Defensive Degree of Difficulty: 0.370
- 2022-23 Points Prevented: -5.449
- Below average rim protector, not really a shot blocking threat, fairly good defensive rebounder
- Usually guarded second unit big men, struggled to play effective post defender, highly foul prone
- More effective when he was defending opposing big men in space
- Decent pick-and-roll defender, effective in drop coverages, has some trouble stopping ball handlers from penetrating
- Tends to stay anchored in the paint, does not always come out to contest perimeter shots

Kira Lewis Jr.

	Height	Weight	Cap #	Years Left
	6'1"	170	$5.722M	RFA

Similar at Age 21

		Season	SIMsc
1	Rodrigue Beaubois	2009-10	922.5
2	Cory Joseph	2012-13	905.0
3	Tyler Ennis	2015-16	903.8
4	Cameron Payne	2015-16	901.6
5	Delonte West	2004-05	900.7
6	Mo Williams	2003-04	897.8
7	Brandon Jennings	2010-11	891.1
8	Jawun Evans	2017-18	890.3
9	Tyronn Lue	1998-99	888.8
10	Tre Jones	2020-21	888.0

Baseline Basic Stats

MPG	PTS	AST	REB	BLK	STL
19.0	7.5	2.4	2.0	0.2	0.7

Advanced Metrics

USG%	3PTA/FGA	FTA/FGA	TS%	eFG%	3PT%
18.8	0.261	0.196	0.533	0.499	0.343

AST%	TOV%	OREB%	DREB%	STL%	BLK%
18.3	12.7	2.4	9.9	1.8	0.6

PER	ORTG	DRTG	WS/48	BPM	VOL
12.05	108.5	113.1	0.070	-1.53	0.378

- Missed games while recovering from a knee injury, played sparingly for New Orleans in his third NBA season
- Greatly improved, much more effective in his role as a low usage spot-up shooter and ball handler
- Below break-even career three-point shooter, made over 44% of his threes in limited attempts last season
- Mostly a spot-up shooter, efficiently made threes when his body was square to the rim
- Improved shooting made him better as a pick-and-roll ball handler, could get to the rim and hit floaters
- Needs a screen to create separation, not really able to create his own offense in isolation situations
- Solid secondary playmaker that makes simple reads, rarely turns the ball over
- 2022-23 Defensive Degree of Difficulty: 0.270
- 2022-23 Points Prevented: 0.330
- Often hidden in matchups against lower leverage second unit players or played in garbage time
- Rarely tested as an on-ball defender, effectively guarded ones and twos in a small sample of one-on-one possessions
- Decent pick-and-roll defender, limited ability to switch due to his size, good at funneling his man into help
- Sometimes gets caught on screens off the ball, consistently closed out on spot-up shooters
- Can be a pesky defender, good at playing passing lanes to get steals, fairly solid defensive rebounder

Newcomers

Jordan Hawkins

	Height	Weight	Cap #	Years Left
	6'5"	195	$4.310M	1 + 2 TO

Baseline Basic Stats

MPG	PTS	AST	REB	BLK	STL
18.7	7.5	1.4	2.2	0.2	0.6

Advanced Metrics

USG%	3PTA/FGA	FTA/FGA	TS%	eFG%	3PT%
18.5	0.558	0.192	0.526	0.497	0.348

AST%	TOV%	OREB%	DREB%	STL%	BLK%
10.3	10.3	2.3	9.3	1.3	0.9

PER	ORTG	DRTG	WS/48	BPM	VOL
11.33	103.5	105.2	0.057	-1.94	N/A

- Drafted by New Orleans with the 14th overall pick in 2023
- Did not play especially well at the Las Vegas Summer League
- Struggled with his efficiency when used as a high volume scoring guard, will likely play a lower usage role in the NBA
- Posted a True Shooting Percentage below 45%, only made 25% of his threes
- Great shooter off the catch in college, effective at making spot-up jumpers and running off screens
- Needs to improve his ball handling skills, not really able to create space for himself off the dribble
- Willing to absorb contact to draw fouls, still lacks the ability to drive consistently to the rim
- Showed some secondary playmaking skills, played out of control, prone to committing turnovers at Summer League
- Good but not a great athlete, projects to be an average defender in the NBA
- Can passably defend multiple positions, has some trouble defending quicker guards
- Solid pick-and-roll defender, generally makes sound rotations, good at steering his man into help
- Fights through screens off the ball, sometimes would be late when closing out on spot-up shooters
- Good at playing passing lanes to get steals, did not block a shot at Summer League, fairly solid defensive rebounder
- Needs to spend some time in the G-League to adjust to the NBA game and improve his shooting consistency

E.J. Liddell

	Height	Weight	Cap #	Years Left
	6'7"	240	$1.802M	1 + TO

Baseline Basic Stats

MPG	PTS	AST	REB	BLK	STL
14.3	5.3	0.8	3.1	0.4	0.4

Advanced Metrics

USG%	3PTA/FGA	FTA/FGA	TS%	eFG%	3PT%
17.1	0.197	0.313	0.526	0.490	0.316

AST%	TOV%	OREB%	DREB%	STL%	BLK%
8.1	11.1	7.8	15.8	1.3	2.8

PER	ORTG	DRTG	WS/48	BPM	VOL
13.86	105.3	103.1	0.065	-1.78	N/A

- Drafted by New Orleans with the 41st overall pick in 2022
- Missed all of last season due to a torn ACL, spent all of last season on a Two-Way contract
- Had a much stronger performance at the Las Vegas Summer League than he had in 2022
- Highly effective in his role as a low volume energy player
- True Shooting Percentage was just above 69%, drew fouls at a very high rate
- High motor rim runner, good cutter and roll man, runs hard down the floor in transition, opportunistic offensive rebounder that scores on put-backs
- Has great strength, can effectively bully weaker defenders on the block on post-ups
- Not really an established outside shooter, has not really been able to make NBA threes with any consistency
- Limited as a ball handler, likely to be a low usage player in the NBA
- Catch-and-finish player, only makes safe passes, good at avoiding turnovers
- Potentially can defend multiple positions at the NBA level, solid athlete
- Strong enough to push opposing big men off the block, taller big men can shoot over him
- Quick enough to guard perimeter players, takes bad angles when defending in space
- Still learning how to defend pick-and-rolls, better when making rotations at Summer League
- Stays attached to shooters off the ball, fights through screens and closes out in spot-up situations
- Good weak side shot blocker, does not really get steals, fairly solid defensive rebounder
- Needs some additional seasoning in the G-League to improve his skills on both ends

Los Angeles Lakers

Last Season: 43 - 39, Lost Western Conference Finals to Denver (0 – 4)

Offensive Rating: 114.5, 20th in the NBA				Defensive Rating: 113.9, 11th in the NBA

Primary Executive: Rob Pelinka, Vice President of Basketball Operations/General Manager

Head Coach: Darvin Ham

Key Roster Changes

Subtractions
Dennis Schröder, free agency
Troy Brown Jr., free agency
Lonnie Walker IV, free agency
Malik Beasley, free agency
Wenyen Gabriel, free agency
Tristan Thompson, free agency
Shaquille Harrison, free agency
Mo Bamba, waived

Additions
Jalen Hood-Schifino, draft
Maxwell Lewis, draft
Gabe Vincent, free agency
Jaxson Hayes, free agency
Taurean Prince, free agency
Cam Reddish, free agency

Roster

Likely Starting Five
1. D'Angelo Russell
2. Austin Reaves
3. LeBron James
4. Jarred Vanderbilt
5. Anthony Davis

Other Key Rotation Players
Rui Hachimura
Gabe Vincent
Jaxson Hayes
Taurean Prince
Cam Reddish

* Italics denotes that a player is likely to be on the floor to close games

Remaining Roster

- Max Christie
- Jalen Hood-Schifino
- Maxwell Lewis
- Colin Castleton, 23, 6'11", 250, Florida (Two-Way)
- D'Moi Hodge, 25, 6'4", 188, Missouri (Two-Way)
- Alex Fudge, 20, 6'8", 189, Florida (Two-Way)
- Damion Baugh, 22, 6'4", 194, TCU (Exhibit 10)

SCHREMPF Base Rating: 46.1

Season Preview Survey

- *Are the Lakers contending or rebuilding? Where is this team headed?*

After a surprise run to the Conference Finals, the Lakers are looking to build momentum to position themselves to go for a championship. Their offseason was an encouraging sign because they resisted the temptation to make the splashy move. Instead, they mostly kept their rotation intact while they made a few tweaks around the fringes. They should be able to rely on their depth and solid defense to win consistently in the regular season. If LeBron James and Anthony Davis can stay healthy, they should be able to earn a guaranteed playoff berth and make some kind of a run if they get a favorable draw.

- *What are the areas of concern for this team heading into this season?*

The main concern for the Lakers is if they are truly as good as last season's playoff run would suggest. Even though they won two playoff series, they were the beneficiaries of a favorable draw because they were matched up against flawed opponents that played into the Lakers' strengths as a mobile defensive team that forces opponents to grind out every possession. They still don't have the firepower to match up against elite offensive teams, as they have a limited number of reliable shooters and LeBron James is their only consistent shot creator. The latter may be an issue because of his advanced age, so there's always a risk that he could decline at some point. Also, Davis has an extensive injury history, so it's not a guarantee that he'll be able to stay in the lineup for the whole season. A lot of pressure will be on D'Angelo Russell and Austin Reaves to take some of the load off James in the regular season. If they can be more consistent with some increased usage, then the Lakers might be able to generate enough offense to compete with the other contenders. Otherwise, they could be at risk for some kind of regression this season.

- *List some possible breakout players for this team.*

Despite the fact that they have had veteran heavy rosters in the time that they have employed James, the Lakers have been able to develop young players and turn them into useful rotation players. There aren't a lot of breakout candidates on their current roster, but if the conditions are right, a young player or two might emerge this season. Most likely, a breakout could come from Max Christie. He had a productive Summer League and he played well in limited minutes last season. Specifically, he made almost 42% of his threes and he flashed the potential to be a plus-level defender. If he continues his upward trajectory, he could crack the rotation to become a valuable low usage wing that spaces the floor and defends multiple positions. As for the others, Jalen Hood-Schifino and Maxwell Lewis had their moments at Summer League. However, they weren't especially consistent or efficient for the entirety of the event, so they could stand to get some extra developmental time in the G-League to polish their skills.

- *What should we expect from them this season?*

If they don't suffer any setbacks due to injury or age-related decline, the Lakers could build on their performance from the second half of last season and the playoffs to be one of the top six playoff seeds in the Western Conference. They really seem like they found a formula to maximize the output of their roster, so if they can keep that going, they should pull out a good number of wins as a unit that relies on its defense to get stops and fuel their transition game. That being said, they aren't quite a definite contender because they still have holes to fill in their rotation. If they get creative and use their limited assets to make a few strategic upgrades, they could position themselves better to get into the mix for a title. Most likely, they will be a solid playoff team that wins at least one round this season.

Veterans

LeBron James

	Height	Weight	Cap #	Years Left
	6'9"	250	$47.607M	PO

Similar at Age 38

		Season	SIMsc
1	Karl Malone*	2001-02	857.4
2	Grant Hill*	2010-11	815.7
3	Dirk Nowitzki*	2016-17	814.4
4	Sam Perkins	1999-00	814.0
5	Tim Duncan*	2014-15	811.2
6	Michael Jordan*	2001-02	789.3
7	Robert Parish*	1991-92	785.4
8	Clifford Robinson	2004-05	781.9
9	Kareem Abdul-Jabbar*	1985-86	780.9

Baseline Basic Stats

MPG	PTS	AST	REB	BLK	STL
32.9	22.0	5.0	7.6	0.7	1.1

Advanced Metrics

USG%	3PTA/FGA	FTA/FGA	TS%	eFG%	3PT%
31.9	0.205	0.345	0.605	0.562	0.322

AST%	TOV%	OREB%	DREB%	STL%	BLK%
29.6	12.3	3.9	22.8	1.6	1.8

PER	ORTG	DRTG	WS/48	BPM	VOL
25.55	116.1	108.0	0.195	7.13	0.608

- Named to the All-NBA 3rd Team, became the NBA's all-time leader in total points in 2022-23
- Production level declined slightly, still an elite performer as the L.A. Lakers' primary scorer and ball handler
- Outstanding playmaker that makes the game easier for his teammates, good at avoiding turnovers
- Good downhill driver on pick-and-rolls, less effective on isolations, needs a screen to get downhill, inconsistent shooter off the dribble
- Above break-even career three-point shooter, made threes at a below break-even rate last season
- Most effective as a spot-up shooter, better shooter when his feet are set
- 2022-23 Defensive Degree of Difficulty: 0.439
- 2022-23 Points Prevented: 0.316
- Used more as a roamer in the past, took on slightly tougher assignments against starting level players
- Decent on-ball defender, better against power forward types, had some trouble staying with quicker players
- Played average pick-and-roll defense, good in drop coverages, can cut off penetration, tends to go too far under screens
- Can get caught on screens off the ball, good at closing out on spot-up shooters
- More of a stay-at-home defender last season, steal and block rates dropped significantly, good defensive rebounder

Anthony Davis

	Height	Weight	Cap #	Years Left
	6'10"	253	$40.600M	3 + PO

Similar at Age 29

		Season	SIMsc
1	Tim Duncan*	2005-06	906.0
2	Amare Stoudemire	2011-12	891.0
3	Patrick Ewing*	1991-92	884.9
4	Al Jefferson	2013-14	881.5
5	Carlos Boozer	2010-11	880.9
6	Nene	2011-12	880.6
7	Hakeem Olajuwon*	1991-92	880.4
8	Karl Malone*	1992-93	879.7
9	Kevin Love	2017-18	876.7
10	Alonzo Mourning*	1999-00	876.3

Baseline Basic Stats

MPG	PTS	AST	REB	BLK	STL
32.5	18.9	2.7	9.8	1.5	0.9

Advanced Metrics

USG%	3PTA/FGA	FTA/FGA	TS%	eFG%	3PT%
26.9	0.073	0.372	0.573	0.528	0.255

AST%	TOV%	OREB%	DREB%	STL%	BLK%
14.3	10.1	9.2	25.5	1.4	4.1

PER	ORTG	DRTG	WS/48	BPM	VOL
23.51	114.7	104.3	0.184	4.61	0.449

- Missed games due to a foot injury, still able to handle a starter's workload when he was healthy
- Increased his efficiency significantly, highly effective in his role as the L.A. Lakers' primary interior scorer
- Good post-up player, effective at flashing to the middle and using a variety of moves from the left block
- Great rim runner, still a vertical lob threat, excellent roll man and cutter, highly active offensive rebounder, runs the floor hard in transition
- Has mostly cut the three-point shot out of his game, more of a mid-range shooter now, can hit spot-up or pick-and-pop jumpers
- Can drive by slower big men, fairly good passing big man, rarely turns the ball over
- 2022-23 Defensive Degree of Difficulty: 0.462
- 2022-23 Points Prevented: 2.649
- Great rim protector, excellent shot blocker and defensive rebounder
- Usually guards starting level big men, good on-ball defender, holds position well in the post, mobile enough to defend in space
- Good pick-and-roll defender, excellent in drop coverages, effective at switching onto ball handlers
- Fights through screens off the ball, consistently closes out on spot-up shooters
- Has active hands, will use his length to play passing lanes to get deflections and steals

Austin Reaves

	Height	Weight	Cap #	Years Left
	6'5"	206	$12.015M	2 + PO

Similar at Age 24

		Season	SIMsc
1	Luke Kennard	2020-21	930.8
2	Amir Coffey	2021-22	918.5
3	Arron Afflalo	2009-10	916.7
4	Allen Crabbe	2016-17	914.5
5	Anthony Morrow	2009-10	912.6
6	Reggie Williams	2010-11	910.3
7	Terance Mann	2020-21	910.1
8	Caleb Martin	2019-20	902.1
9	Aaron McKie	1996-97	900.6
10	Pat Connaughton	2016-17	900.6

Baseline Basic Stats

MPG	PTS	AST	REB	BLK	STL
25.0	10.0	1.9	3.1	0.3	0.6

Advanced Metrics

USG%	3PTA/FGA	FTA/FGA	TS%	eFG%	3PT%
16.3	0.503	0.350	0.611	0.557	0.362

AST%	TOV%	OREB%	DREB%	STL%	BLK%
13.1	10.7	2.4	10.3	1.1	1.0

PER	ORTG	DRTG	WS/48	BPM	VOL
13.58	120.4	113.9	0.117	-0.13	0.307

- Regular rotation player for the L.A. Lakers in his second NBA season, became a starter late in 2022-23
- Increased his effectiveness in his role as a low usage spot-up shooter and secondary ball handler
- Posted a True Shooting Percentage of almost 69%, made almost 40% of his threes last season
- Mostly a stand-still spot-up shooter, can knock down threes if defenders go under screens on pick-and-rolls
- Good pick-and-roll ball handler and isolation player, great at slashing to the rim, draws fouls at a high rate, good at hitting mid-range pull-up jumpers
- Solid secondary playmaker that makes simple reads, good at avoiding turnovers, rarely moves off the ball
- 2022-23 Defensive Degree of Difficulty: 0.441
- 2022-23 Points Prevented: 1.590
- Mostly guarded starting level players, drew some tough assignments
- Solid on-ball defender, fairly good at defending guards and some wings in one-on-one situation
- Fairly solid pick-and-roll defender, can switch and cut off penetration, tends to go too far under screens
- Fights through screens off the ball, tended to be late when closing out on spot-up shooters
- Stay-at-home defender, does not really get steals or blocks, decent defensive rebounder

D'Angelo Russell

	Height	Weight	Cap #	Years Left
	6'4"	193	$17.308M	PO

Similar at Age 26

		Season	SIMsc
1	Chauncey Billups	2002-03	919.3
2	Kirk Hinrich	2006-07	917.6
3	Willie Green	2007-08	912.6
4	Steve Nash*	2000-01	912.3
5	Vernon Maxwell	1991-92	911.4
6	Jordan Clarkson	2018-19	910.6
7	Jamal Crawford	2006-07	910.0
8	Jarrett Jack	2009-10	909.4
9	Terry Rozier	2020-21	909.1
10	Tyler Johnson	2018-19	908.2

Baseline Basic Stats

MPG	PTS	AST	REB	BLK	STL
30.5	15.5	4.1	3.2	0.3	0.9

Advanced Metrics

USG%	3PTA/FGA	FTA/FGA	TS%	eFG%	3PT%
23.3	0.484	0.232	0.565	0.526	0.367

AST%	TOV%	OREB%	DREB%	STL%	BLK%
25.4	12.7	1.7	9.3	1.5	0.9

PER	ORTG	DRTG	WS/48	BPM	VOL
15.91	112.5	113.8	0.101	0.90	0.306

- Traded from Minnesota to the L.A. Lakers at the trade deadline, regular starter for both teams
- Maintained his usual effectiveness in a role as a moderate usage scorer and ball handler
- Had a True Shooting Percentage above 60%, league average career three-point shooter
- Made almost 40% of his threes last season, great spot-up shooter, less effective when shooting in other situations
- Capable of scoring at all three levels as a pick-and-roll ball handler and isolation player
- Good playmaker that can effectively find open teammates, slightly turnover prone last season
- 2022-23 Defensive Degree of Difficulty: 0.404
- 2022-23 Points Prevented: 0.590
- Often hidden in favorable matchups against lower leverage players
- Below average on-ball defender, struggled to stay with opposing guards, more effective against bigger players inside
- Played solid pick-and-roll defense, good at funneling his man into help, can functionally switch
- Sometimes gets caught on screens off the ball, good at closing out on spot-up shooters
- Steal and Block Percentages held fairly steady, fairly decent defensive rebounder

Jarred Vanderbilt

	Height	Weight	Cap #	Years Left
	6'9"	214	$4.698M	UFA

Similar at Age 23

		Season	SIMsc
1	Al-Farouq Aminu	2013-14	942.4
2	Viktor Khryapa	2005-06	921.5
3	Michael Cage	1984-85	911.3
4	Luc Mbah a Moute	2009-10	906.1
5	Larry Nance Jr.	2015-16	904.6
6	A.C. Green	1986-87	899.8
7	Amir Johnson	2010-11	898.9
8	Chris Wilcox	2005-06	897.9
9	George L. Johnson	1979-80	897.6
10	Cliff Levingston	1983-84	896.1

Baseline Basic Stats

MPG	PTS	AST	REB	BLK	STL
24.2	7.4	1.5	6.7	0.5	1.0

Advanced Metrics

USG%	3PTA/FGA	FTA/FGA	TS%	eFG%	3PT%
13.4	0.125	0.350	0.594	0.565	0.252

AST%	TOV%	OREB%	DREB%	STL%	BLK%
10.2	14.3	10.6	22.5	2.2	1.5

PER	ORTG	DRTG	WS/48	BPM	VOL
15.73	122.6	108.9	0.148	0.66	0.146

- Traded from Utah to the L.A. Lakers at the trade deadline, regular starter for both teams
- Solidly effective in his role as a low usage energy player and occasional spot-up shooter
- High energy rim runner with great athleticism, active offensive rebounder, solid roll man and cutter, runs hard in transition, draws fouls
- Has some trouble finishing shots in traffic, sometimes needs multiple shots to score at the rim
- Expanded his shooting range to the three-point line, still a below break-even spot-up shooter
- Showed improved passing skills in Utah, decent as a secondary playmaker, slightly turnover prone
- 2022-23 Defensive Degree of Difficulty: 0.511
- 2022-23 Points Prevented: -1.333
- Used as a defensive stopper by both teams, over-extended in this role
- Capable of guarding multiple positions, better on the perimeter, had some trouble against big men in the post
- Decent pick-and-roll defender, good in drop coverages, has lapses when switching onto ball handlers
- Sometimes gets caught on screens off the ball, not always in position to close out on spot-up shooters
- Consistently posts high Steal Percentages, Block Percentage went down significantly, good defensive rebounder

Rui Hachimura

	Height	Weight	Cap #	Years Left
	6'8"	230	$15.741M	2

Similar at Age 24

		Season	SIMsc
1	De'Andre Hunter	2021-22	940.6
2	Tobias Harris	2016-17	939.9
3	Kyle Kuzma	2019-20	934.3
4	Marvin Williams	2010-11	928.7
5	Derrick Williams	2015-16	925.2
6	Linas Kleiza	2008-09	921.2
7	Anthony Tolliver	2009-10	920.1
8	Shabazz Muhammad	2016-17	917.5
9	Keita Bates-Diop	2019-20	916.9
10	Jeff Green	2010-11	916.7

Baseline Basic Stats

MPG	PTS	AST	REB	BLK	STL
24.2	10.6	1.4	4.1	0.4	0.6

Advanced Metrics

USG%	3PTA/FGA	FTA/FGA	TS%	eFG%	3PT%
19.4	0.339	0.212	0.563	0.533	0.369

AST%	TOV%	OREB%	DREB%	STL%	BLK%
7.8	8.3	3.9	15.7	1.0	1.2

PER	ORTG	DRTG	WS/48	BPM	VOL
13.80	111.5	113.5	0.082	-0.96	0.308

- Traded from Washington to the L.A. Lakers, regular rotation player for both teams
- Solidly effective in his role as a moderate volume scoring forward off the bench
- Above break-even career three-point shooter, percentages have varied from year-to-year
- Almost exclusively a stationary spot-up shooter, not really able to shoot efficiently in any other situation
- Solid at posting up smaller players, fairly good at driving by slower big men, can hit pull-up jumpers from mid-range
- Good cutter and roll man, catch-and-shoot player, only makes safe passes, rarely turns the ball over
- 2022-23 Defensive Degree of Difficulty: 0.375
- 2022-23 Points Prevented: 2.451
- Usually guarded second unit level players, used as a roaming help defender
- Improved as a weak side shot blocker, does not really get steals, solid defensive rebounder
- Played fairly solid on-ball defense, effective at guarding big men in the post, held his own on the perimeter against wing players
- Fairly solid pick-and-roll defender, decent at switching to guard ball handlers and screeners
- Fights through screens off the ball, sometimes was late to close out on spot-up shooters

Gabe Vincent

	Height	Weight	Cap #	Years Left
	6'3"	200	$10.500M	2

Similar at Age 26

		Season	SIMsc
1	Matt Maloney	1997-98	936.6
2	Charlie Bell	2005-06	935.9
3	Jerryd Bayless	2014-15	923.9
4	Sasha Danilovic	1996-97	921.9
5	Anthony Peeler	1995-96	920.2
6	Royal Ivey	2007-08	919.3
7	Langston Galloway	2017-18	919.2
8	Ben Gordon	2009-10	918.4
9	Troy Daniels	2017-18	917.6
10	Marcus Thornton	2013-14	917.5

Baseline Basic Stats

MPG	PTS	AST	REB	BLK	STL
23.2	8.8	2.2	2.1	0.1	0.7

Advanced Metrics

USG%	3PTA/FGA	FTA/FGA	TS%	eFG%	3PT%
17.5	0.560	0.152	0.539	0.511	0.366

AST%	TOV%	OREB%	DREB%	STL%	BLK%
15.1	12.7	1.6	8.3	1.6	0.5

PER	ORTG	DRTG	WS/48	BPM	VOL
10.38	106.0	113.1	0.054	-2.57	0.337

- Regular rotation player for Miami in his fourth NBA season, started half of his games
- Efficiency dropped slightly, mainly used as a low usage spot-up shooter and secondary ball handler
- Break-even career three-point shooter, made almost 38% of his threes in the playoffs last season
- Most effective as a stand-still spot-up shooter, efficiency dropped when shooting in other situations
- Crafty ball handler that changes speeds well, more effective as a pick-and-roll ball handler and isolation player last season
- Tends to play with a shoot-first mindset, fairly solid secondary playmaker, good at avoiding turnovers
- 2022-23 Defensive Degree of Difficulty: 0.454
- 2022-23 Points Prevented: -0.214
- Drew a much tougher set of matchups against starting level guards, played average on-ball defense
- Struggled to stay with quicker guards on the perimeter, more effective against bigger guards inside
- Solid pick-and-roll defender, good at funneling his man into help, makes sound rotations in different coverages
- Stays attached to shooters off the ball, fights through screens and closes out on spot-up shooters
- Can be a pest, good at getting into passing lanes to get steals, below average defensive rebounder

Jaxson Hayes

	Height	Weight	Cap #	Years Left
	6'11"	220	$2.165M	PO

Similar at Age 22

		Season	SIMsc
1	Thon Maker	2019-20	934.4
2	Nic Claxton	2021-22	919.0
3	Cheick Diallo	2018-19	912.6
4	Skal Labissiere	2018-19	911.7
5	Derrick Alston	1994-95	911.5
6	Hilton Armstrong	2006-07	906.4
7	Nerlens Noel	2016-17	902.8
8	Joakim Noah	2007-08	902.6
9	Chris Wilcox	2004-05	902.5
10	Raef LaFrentz	1998-99	900.8

Baseline Basic Stats

MPG	PTS	AST	REB	BLK	STL
20.7	7.7	0.9	5.2	1.1	0.5

Advanced Metrics

USG%	3PTA/FGA	FTA/FGA	TS%	eFG%	3PT%
15.2	0.122	0.411	0.620	0.589	0.267

AST%	TOV%	OREB%	DREB%	STL%	BLK%
7.2	12.4	8.4	18.5	1.3	3.9

PER	ORTG	DRTG	WS/48	BPM	VOL
16.15	121.9	109.4	0.148	-0.10	0.385

- Fell out of New Orleans' rotation, played limited minutes off the bench
- Effectiveness decreased in a role as a low usage rim runner and occasional stretch big
- Very athletic big man, vertical lob threat, most effective as a high energy rim runner
- Great cutter and roll man, active offensive rebounder, good at running the floor in transition, draws a lot of fouls
- Continued to experiment with shooting threes, shot very poorly last season, made around 10% of his threes
- Limited as a post-up player and passer, fairly solid at avoiding turnovers
- 2022-23 Defensive Degree of Difficulty: 0.343
- 2022-23 Points Prevented: -0.615
- Great rim protector, good shot blocker, solid defensive rebounder
- Generally an average on-ball defender against second unit big men
- Can hold position in the post, has good mobility, tends to bail his man out by committing bad shooting fouls
- Solid pick-and-roll defender, good in drop coverages, effective at switching or hedging out on ball handlers
- Consistently comes out to the perimeter to contest shots in spot-up situations
- Increased his Steal Percentage to a career high, good at using his length to play passing lanes

Taurean Prince

	Height	Weight	Cap #	Years Left
	6'7"	218	$4.516M	UFA

Similar at Age 28

		Season	SIMsc
1	Kyle Korver	2009-10	943.1
2	Jarvis Hayes	2009-10	942.2
3	Mickael Pietrus	2010-11	939.4
4	Sam Mack	1998-99	932.4
5	Cartier Martin	2012-13	931.1
6	Danuel House Jr.	2021-22	930.4
7	Maurice Harkless	2021-22	928.8
8	Tracy Murray	1999-00	928.2
9	James Ennis	2018-19	927.6
10	James Posey	2004-05	924.4

Baseline Basic Stats

MPG	PTS	AST	REB	BLK	STL
20.8	8.2	1.2	2.8	0.2	0.6

Advanced Metrics

USG%	3PTA/FGA	FTA/FGA	TS%	eFG%	3PT%
16.9	0.584	0.183	0.574	0.546	0.385

AST%	TOV%	OREB%	DREB%	STL%	BLK%
8.5	11.7	2.2	12.4	1.4	1.1

PER	ORTG	DRTG	WS/48	BPM	VOL
11.12	109.0	111.8	0.078	-1.84	0.346

- Missed games due to a sprained ankle, regular rotation player for Minnesota when healthy
- Primarily used as a low volume shooting specialist
- Fairly reliable three-point shooter, has made almost 42% of his career corner threes
- Mostly a stand-still spot-up shooter, now fairly solid when shooting off screens
- Good at scoring on dribble hand-offs, effective cutter off the ball
- Rarely used in ball handling situations, not able to create his own offense
- Catch-and-shoot player, willing to make the extra pass, effective at limiting turnovers
- 2022-23 Defensive Degree of Difficulty: 0.395
- 2022-23 Points Prevented: -1.108
- Mostly guarded second unit players, played below average on-ball defense
- Had trouble staying with quicker players on the perimeter, over-matched inside against stronger power forward types
- Below average pick-and-roll defender, not especially effective at taking away any specific action
- Stays attached to shooters off the ball, fights through screens and closes out in spot-up situations
- Now a stay-at-home defender, did not really get steals or blocks last season, fairly solid defensive rebounder

Cam Reddish

	Height	Weight	Cap #	Years Left
	6'8"	218	$2.165M	PO

Similar at Age 23

		Season	SIMsc
1	Jordan Hamilton	2013-14	943.9
2	Sasha Pavlovic	2006-07	939.8
3	Cleanthony Early	2014-15	939.7
4	Jordan Nwora	2021-22	930.6
5	De'Andre Hunter	2020-21	928.2
6	Ed O'Bannon	1995-96	920.5
7	Mario Hezonja	2018-19	919.5
8	Mike Miller	2003-04	917.9
9	James Posey	1999-00	916.2
10	Hollis Thompson	2014-15	915.7

Baseline Basic Stats

MPG	PTS	AST	REB	BLK	STL
22.5	8.9	1.4	3.3	0.3	0.7

Advanced Metrics

USG%	3PTA/FGA	FTA/FGA	TS%	eFG%	3PT%
18.8	0.479	0.221	0.545	0.506	0.340

AST%	TOV%	OREB%	DREB%	STL%	BLK%
8.5	10.7	2.7	11.4	1.7	1.1

PER	ORTG	DRTG	WS/48	BPM	VOL
11.85	106.9	113.6	0.060	-2.07	0.373

- Fell out of New York's rotation, traded to Portland, used as a starter after the trade
- Decently effective in his role as a low volume spot-up shooter for both teams
- Below break-even career three-point shooter, above average when shooting in the corners
- Almost exclusively a stationary spot-up shooter, not really able to shoot efficiently in other situations
- Lacks the ball handling skills to drive consistently and create his own shot off the dribble
- Great athlete, explosive finisher in transition, still learning how to move off the ball
- Strictly a catch-and-shoot player, only makes safe passes, good at avoiding turnovers
- 2022-23 Defensive Degree of Difficulty: 0.462
- 2022-23 Points Prevented: -1.615
- Drew a lot of tough assignments against starting level players, over-extended in these matchups
- Struggled to play effective on-ball defense against guards and wings
- Below average pick-and-roll defender, has lapses when guarding screeners, tends to go too far under screens
- Fights through screens off the ball, sometimes can be late to close out on spot-up shooters
- Steal and Block Percentages are still consistent with his career averages, below average defensive rebounder

Max Christie

	Height	Weight	Cap #	Years Left
	6'6"	190	$1.720M	RFA

Similar at Age 19

		Season	SIMsc
1	Moses Moody	2021-22	924.2
2	Terrance Ferguson	2017-18	908.3
3	Rashad Vaughn	2015-16	901.9
4	Joshua Primo	2021-22	900.7
5	Martell Webster	2005-06	883.4
6	Zhaire Smith	2018-19	878.3
7	Derrick Jones	2016-17	870.4
8	Dante Exum	2014-15	865.3
9	James Young	2014-15	863.8
10	Jahmi'us Ramsey	2020-21	853.5

Baseline Basic Stats

MPG	PTS	AST	REB	BLK	STL
19.1	6.5	1.1	2.2	0.2	0.6

Advanced Metrics

USG%	3PTA/FGA	FTA/FGA	TS%	eFG%	3PT%
13.8	0.506	0.155	0.576	0.553	0.412

AST%	TOV%	OREB%	DREB%	STL%	BLK%
7.9	10.8	1.8	13.1	1.3	0.8

PER	ORTG	DRTG	WS/48	BPM	VOL
9.86	111.0	114.7	0.065	-2.43	0.653

- Played limited minutes off the bench for the L.A. Lakers as a rookie
- Fairly efficient in his role as a very low volume spot-up shooting wing
- Made almost 42% of his threes last season, better when shooting threes above the break
- Predominantly a stand-still spot-up shooter, needs to have his feet set at this stage
- High energy player with great athleticism, explosive finisher in transition, good cutter off the ball
- Rarely used as a ball handler, effective in a small sample of pick-and-rolls, needs a screen to drive to the rim
- Catch-and-shoot player, playmaking skills are limited now, safe player that rarely turns the ball over
- 2022-23 Defensive Degree of Difficulty: 0.438
- 2022-23 Points Prevented: 1.616
- Drew some tough assignments off the bench, decent on-ball defender
- Has good quickness, can stay with perimeter players, thin frame, can be overpowered by stronger players inside
- Below average pick-and-roll defender, struggled to contain ball handlers, goes too far under screens
- Fights through screens off the ball, tends to be late when closing out on spot-up shooters
- Stay-at-home defender, rarely gets steals or blocks, fairly solid defensive rebounder

Newcomers

Jalen Hood-Schifino

	Height	Weight	Cap #	Years Left
	6'6"	215	$3.695M	1 + 2 TO

Baseline Basic Stats

MPG	PTS	AST	REB	BLK	STL
19.4	7.6	1.5	2.5	0.2	0.6

Advanced Metrics

USG%	3PTA/FGA	FTA/FGA	TS%	eFG%	3PT%
18.7	0.321	0.218	0.501	0.467	0.357

AST%	TOV%	OREB%	DREB%	STL%	BLK%
13.2	12.7	2.7	11.3	1.6	0.7

PER	ORTG	DRTG	WS/48	BPM	VOL
11.26	97.7	106.1	0.052	-1.42	N/A

- Drafted by the L.A. Lakers with the 17th overall pick in 2023
- Performed unevenly at the Las Vegas and Sacramento Summer Leagues
- Put up numbers in volume but struggled with his efficiency when used as a high usage scorer, likely will play a lower volume role in the NBA
- True Shooting Percentage was below 40%, made less than 25% of his threes
- Break-even three-point shooter in college, more comfortable when shooting from mid-range
- Less effective at driving to the rim at Summer League, could draw fouls, had trouble finishing around the rim
- Defenders could back off him to limit his effective, took a lot of tough mid-range shots
- Solid secondary playmaker that makes simple reads, good at avoiding turnovers
- Has good physical tools, potentially could be a plus-level defender in the NBA
- Solid on-ball defender, can capably defend guards and wings in one-on-one situations
- Effective pick-and-roll defender, good at containing ball handlers, can functionally switch to cover screeners
- Fights through screens off the ball, sometimes will be late to close out on spot-up shooters
- Active help defender, good at using his anticipation skills to get steals, below average defensive rebounder
- Needs to spend some time in the G-League to become a more consistent three-point threat at the NBA level

Maxwell Lewis

	Height	Weight	Cap #	Years Left
	6'7"	195	$1.120M	2 + TO

Baseline Basic Stats

MPG	PTS	AST	REB	BLK	STL
14.0	4.9	0.9	2.0	0.2	0.5

Advanced Metrics

USG%	3PTA/FGA	FTA/FGA	TS%	eFG%	3PT%
16.4	0.360	0.227	0.497	0.467	0.345

AST%	TOV%	OREB%	DREB%	STL%	BLK%
9.7	11.6	4.0	10.2	1.6	1.2

PER	ORTG	DRTG	WS/48	BPM	VOL
10.84	99.3	104.5	0.046	-2.11	N/A

- Drafted by Denver with the 40th overall pick in 2023, traded to the L.A. Lakers
- Did not really play effectively at either the Las Vegas or Sacramento Summer Leagues
- Struggled with his efficiency in a role as a low usage spot-up shooter
- Posted a True Shooting Percentage below 40%, went 2-for-14 (14.3%) on threes
- Above break-even three-point shooter at the mid-major college level
- Most effective as a stationary spot-up shooter, less effective when shooting in other situations
- Not really able to create his own shot, lacks the necessary ball handling skills, tends to lose the ball when dribbling
- Good cutter off the ball, explosive finisher in transition, prone to missing easy shots due to some wildness
- Catch-and-shoot player, willing to make the extra pass, highly turnover prone at Summer League
- Good athleticism and physical tools, still learning to play effective defense at the NBA level
- Solid on-ball defender, has good quickness and strength, can effectively guard multiple positions
- Fairly good pick-and-roll defender, effective at switching to defend ball handlers and screeners
- Fights through screens off the ball, not always in position to close out on spot-up shooters, will cheat off his man quite a bit
- Did not really get steals at Summer League, fairly effective weak side shot blocker, decent defensive rebounder
- Needs additional seasoning in the G-League to adjust to a higher level of competition and improve his shooting

DALLAS MAVERICKS

Last Season: 38 - 44, Missed the Playoffs

Offensive Rating: 116.8, 6th in the NBA   Defensive Rating: 116.7, 24th in the NBA

Primary Executive: Nico Harrison, President/General Manager

Head Coach: Jason Kidd

Key Roster Changes

Subtractions	Additions
Reggie Bullock, trade	Dereck Lively II, draft
Dāvis Bertāns, trade	Olivier-Maxence Prosper, draft
Christian Wood, free agency	Grant Williams, trade
JaVale McGee, waived*	Richaun Holmes, trade
	Seth Curry, free agency
	Dante Exum, free agency
	Derrick Jones Jr., free agency

* It was reported that McGee was likely to be waived while the book was being finalized.

Roster

Likely Starting Five
1. Kyrie Irving
2. Luka Dončić
3. Tim Hardaway Jr.
4. Grant Williams
5. Dwight Powell

Other Key Rotation Players
Josh Green
Maxi Kleber
Seth Curry
Dereck Lively II
Olivier-Maxence Prosper

* Italics denotes that a player is likely to be on the floor to close games

Remaining Roster

- Derrick Jones Jr.
- Richaun Holmes
- Jaden Hardy
- Dante Exum
- JaVale McGee – expected to be waived-and-stretched
- Markieff Morris (signed while the book was being finalized)
- A.J. Lawson, 23, 6'6", 179, South Carolina (Two-Way)
- Mike Miles Jr., 21, 6"2, 205, TCU (Two-Way)
- Jordan "Jelly" Walker, 23, 5'11", 170, UAB (Exhibit 10)
- Greg Brown III, 22, 6'9", 205, Texas (Exhibit 10)
- Joe Wieskamp, 24, 6'6", 212, Iowa (Exhibit 10)

SCHREMPF Base Rating: 46.1

Season Preview Survey

- *Are the Mavericks contending or rebuilding? Where is this team headed?*

The Mavericks are looking to maximize Luka Doncic's prime years, so they are trying their hardest to build a contending team. The moves from last season blew up in their face because they wound up missing the play-in tournament. This time are around, they are hoping that a full season with Kyrie Irving and a retooled supporting cast will change their fortunes for the better, but it remains to be seen if their new roster construction will work out. If they are able to gel and get back to the brand of basketball that they were playing at the end of the 2021-22 season, then they could make a deep playoff run and possibly be a dark horse to reach the Finals. Otherwise, if they go through some turmoil or things don't go as planned, then they might be looking at a play-in berth this season.

- *What are the areas of concern for this team heading into this season?*

The primary concern for Dallas is if they did enough to rebuild their defense. Two seasons ago, they finished in the top ten in Defensive Efficiency because they had a mobile, switching unit that could apply pressure on the perimeter and force misses. However, their defensive performance slipped last season because they swapped out some of their better defenders for offensive-minded personnel. Therefore, they could not execute their desired strategy as effectively. This offseason, they added a few solid defenders, but they still don't have a reliable perimeter stopper or a proven rim protector. They may have to rely heavily on rookie, Dereck Lively II to perform the latter task, which is a risky bet at the moment. With a defensive unit that is unproven, they will have to lean on their offense to out-score opponents. This would place the burden of responsibility on Doncic and Irving to carry the heavy load to maximize the success of the team. A lot will depend on their ability to figure out a way to coexist with one another. If the Mavericks can establish a strong defensive identity and sort out any potential chemistry issues, then they could bounce back to become contenders in the West. Otherwise, their issues could cause them to fall back to the middling unit that they were last season.

- *List some possible breakout players for this team.*

The most likely breakout candidate for Dallas is their lottery pick, Dereck Lively II. This is mainly because Dallas has a large void to fill at the center slot and he's the only player with upside that can really fill the position. The Mavericks are in need of an athletic shot blocking big man that can also handle the switching responsibilities of a modern defense. Lively has the combination of mobility and vertical athleticism to be an effective defensive center in the NBA. He also could them a vertical lob threat to helps Dallas collapse defenses and open things up for their shooters. He has a chance to step in right away and make an impact if he adjusts quickly to the NBA game. Also, their other first round pick, Olivier-Maxence Prosper could fill the three-and-D role that was vacated when they traded away Dorian Finney-Smith. In addition to these two, Jaden Hardy could take a step forward to give them a scoring guard to boost their bench production and add a little more firepower to their roster.

- *What should we expect from them this season?*

Dallas probably should be a better team than they were last year because they have a lot of talent on paper and their players appear to fit better as well. If they can quickly coalesce and get back to the style of basketball that they were playing two seasons ago, they could rise to the top of the standings and make a deep playoff run. On other hand, if their defense continues to flounder and their chemistry is off, then they may encounter the same issues that they had last season, which would cause them to slide into the play-in range this coming season.

Veterans

Luka Dončić

	Height	Weight	Cap #	Years Left
	6'7"	230	$40.064M	2 + PO

Similar at Age 23

		Season	SIMsc
1	LeBron James	2007-08	876.1
2	Paul Pierce*	2000-01	860.6
3	Tracy McGrady*	2002-03	860.0
4	Jayson Tatum	2021-22	859.4
5	Carmelo Anthony	2007-08	853.4
6	Grant Hill*	1995-96	845.8
7	Jaylen Brown	2019-20	840.8
8	Kevin Durant	2011-12	840.8
9	J.R. Smith	2008-09	836.4
10	James Harden	2012-13	831.7

Baseline Basic Stats

MPG	PTS	AST	REB	BLK	STL
37.5	27.3	5.9	7.3	0.7	1.5

Advanced Metrics

USG%	3PTA/FGA	FTA/FGA	TS%	eFG%	3PT%
35.1	0.366	0.411	0.592	0.540	0.347

AST%	TOV%	OREB%	DREB%	STL%	BLK%
36.9	12.5	3.0	22.1	1.9	1.3

PER	ORTG	DRTG	WS/48	BPM	VOL
26.75	116.2	107.9	0.205	6.54	0.369

- Made the All-Star team and was named to the All-NBA 1st Team for the fourth consecutive season
- Had his best NBA season, excelled as Dallas' primary scorer and ball handler
- Outstanding pick-and-roll ball handler and isolation player, consistently gets to the rim to finish or draw fouls, good at hitting step-back jumpers
- Good at posting up smaller players, can bully weaker defenders in the post or shoot turn-around jumpers
- Dynamic playmaker with excellent court vision, cut his Turnover Percentage last season
- Above break-even three-point shooter, better at shooting off the dribble, inconsistent as a spot-up shooter
- 2022-23 Defensive Degree of Difficulty: 0.399
- 2022-23 Points Prevented: 0.718
- Often hidden in favorable matchups against lower leverage players, played solid on-ball defense in 2022-23
- Capable of defending lower leverage players at different positions
- Below average pick-and-roll defender, not really effective at taking away any specific action
- Gets caught on screens off the ball, good at closing out on spot-up shooters
- Steal Percentage increased to a career high, great defensive rebounder

Kyrie Irving

	Height	Weight	Cap #	Years Left
	6'2"	195	$37.037M	1 + PO

Similar at Age 30

		Season	SIMsc
1	CJ McCollum	2021-22	937.7
2	Stephen Curry	2018-19	916.2
3	Damian Lillard	2020-21	912.2
4	George Hill	2016-17	911.3
5	Derrick Rose	2018-19	909.3
6	Eric Bledsoe	2019-20	907.6
7	Lou Williams	2016-17	902.7
8	Kemba Walker	2020-21	902.3
9	Terry Porter	1993-94	901.3
10	Mike James	2005-06	899.7

Baseline Basic Stats

MPG	PTS	AST	REB	BLK	STL
32.0	19.5	5.2	3.5	0.3	0.9

Advanced Metrics

USG%	3PTA/FGA	FTA/FGA	TS%	eFG%	3PT%
26.8	0.415	0.232	0.588	0.546	0.383

AST%	TOV%	OREB%	DREB%	STL%	BLK%
26.0	11.0	2.3	10.9	1.4	1.3

PER	ORTG	DRTG	WS/48	BPM	VOL
19.53	116.3	116.3	0.124	2.60	0.514

- Suspended for several weeks for a refusal to renounce antisemitic beliefs, traded from Brooklyn to Dallas
- Made his 8th All-Star team, thrived as a high usage scoring point guard for both teams
- Excellent one-on-one scorer, efficient in all three levels as a pick-and-roll ball handler and isolation player
- Reliable three-point shooter throughout his career
- Good spot-up shooter, very good at knocking down pull-up jumpers, very ball dominant, rarely moves off the ball
- Great playmaker with excellent court vision to find open teammates, rarely turns the ball over
- 2022-23 Defensive Degree of Difficulty: 0.454
- 2022-23 Points Prevented: 0.785
- Generally defends starting level players, fairly solid defender if he's engaged
- Decent on-ball defender, can stay with opposing guards, has some trouble against taller players
- More effective pick-and-roll defender in Brooklyn, could funnel his man into help, struggled to make rotations without a reliable rim protector behind him
- Stays attached to shooters off the ball, fights through screens, solid at closing out in spot-up situations
- Gets steals at a solid rate, better at blocking shots from the weak side, fairly solid defensive rebounder

Tim Hardaway Jr.

	Height	Weight	Cap #	Years Left
	6'5"	205	$17.898M	1

Similar at Age 30

		Season	SIMsc
1	Marco Belinelli	2016-17	930.5
2	Raja Bell	2006-07	926.4
3	Jodie Meeks	2017-18	925.9
4	Voshon Lenard	2003-04	925.0
5	Terrence Ross	2021-22	924.4
6	Wesley Matthews	2016-17	924.3
7	Anthony Morrow	2015-16	923.3
8	Reggie Bullock	2021-22	921.5
9	Nick Young	2015-16	921.1
10	C.J. Miles	2017-18	920.7

Baseline Basic Stats

MPG	PTS	AST	REB	BLK	STL
25.7	10.4	1.8	2.6	0.2	0.7

Advanced Metrics

USG%	3PTA/FGA	FTA/FGA	TS%	eFG%	3PT%
18.8	0.601	0.176	0.550	0.523	0.376

AST%	TOV%	OREB%	DREB%	STL%	BLK%
9.9	7.6	1.3	11.5	1.3	0.6

PER	ORTG	DRTG	WS/48	BPM	VOL
11.72	109.8	114.2	0.069	-1.33	0.338

- Regular starter for Dallas in his fourth full season with the team
- Production declined slightly in a role as a moderate usage shooting specialist
- League average career three-point shooter, made 38.5% of his threes last season, percentages vary quite a bit
- Good spot-up shooter that can also run off screens, inconsistent shooter off the dribble
- Lacks ideal ball handling skills, below average as a pick-and-roll ball handler and isolation player
- Catch-and-shoot player, can make the extra pass, rarely turns the ball over
- 2022-23 Defensive Degree of Difficulty: 0.479
- 2022-23 Points Prevented: 0.380
- Guarded starting level players, drew some tough assignments against top scorers
- Fairly solid on-ball defender, capably defends multiple positions, has some trouble against quicker guards
- Played below average pick-and-roll defense, indecisive, not effective when making rotations without a reliable rim protection presence
- Tends to get caught on screens off the ball, good at closing out on spot-up shooters
- Stay-at-home defender last season, did not really get steals or blocks, fairly solid defensive rebounder

Grant Williams

	Height	Weight	Cap #	Years Left
	6'6"	236	$12.405M	3

Similar at Age 24

		Season	SIMsc
1	Stanley Johnson	2020-21	913.8
2	Quincy Pondexter	2012-13	912.8
3	Jared Dudley	2009-10	912.6
4	Mickael Pietrus	2006-07	907.5
5	James Jones	2004-05	907.1
6	Arron Afflalo	2009-10	899.9
7	Danny Green	2011-12	898.2
8	Admiral Schofield	2021-22	896.4
9	Josh Hart	2019-20	895.6
10	Lamar Stevens	2021-22	894.9

Baseline Basic Stats

MPG	PTS	AST	REB	BLK	STL
24.2	9.0	1.4	3.9	0.4	0.7

Advanced Metrics

USG%	3PTA/FGA	FTA/FGA	TS%	eFG%	3PT%
15.1	0.552	0.239	0.595	0.562	0.394

AST%	TOV%	OREB%	DREB%	STL%	BLK%
8.3	10.6	4.1	13.7	1.2	1.5

PER	ORTG	DRTG	WS/48	BPM	VOL
12.02	117.9	112.1	0.112	-0.53	0.341

- Played starter level minutes off the bench for Boston in his fourth NBA season
- Solidly effective in his role as a low volume spot-up shooter
- Made 39.5% of his threes last season, career Three-Point Percentages in the corner is almost 43%
- Almost exclusively a stationary spot-up shooter, flashes some ability to make pick-and-pop threes
- Less effective as a rim runner, lacks ideal vertical lift, struggles to finish in traffic
- Selectively will hit the offensive boards, effective transition player, runs out for layups and hits trail threes
- Catch-and-shoot player, makes safe passes, good at avoiding turnovers
- <u>2022-23 Defensive Degree of Difficulty</u>: 0.470
- <u>2022-23 Points Prevented</u>: -1.100
- Drew a lot of difficult assignments off the bench, had success in specific situations when guarding Giannis Antetokounmpo
- Over-extended in other matchups against elite players, too undersized to guard big men, a step slow when defending perimeter players
- Decent pick-and-roll defender, solid in drop coverages, has some trouble containing quicker ball handlers
- Fights through screens off the ball, tends to late when closing out on spot-up shooters
- Stay-at-home defender last season, Block Percentage dropped significantly, solid defensive rebounder

Dwight Powell

	Height	Weight	Cap #	Years Left
	6'10"	240	$4.000M	1 + PO

Similar at Age 31

		Season	SIMsc
1	Mark West	1991-92	907.3
2	Fabricio Oberto	2006-07	898.5
3	Mikki Moore	2006-07	894.9
4	Nick Collison	2011-12	891.6
5	Rick Mahorn	1989-90	889.7
6	Danny Schayes	1990-91	889.3
7	Vin Baker	2002-03	889.0
8	Sean Rooks	2000-01	888.4
9	Jeff Foster	2007-08	885.6
10	Mark Bryant	1996-97	885.3

Baseline Basic Stats

MPG	PTS	AST	REB	BLK	STL
21.1	6.4	1.0	5.1	0.6	0.5

Advanced Metrics

USG%	3PTA/FGA	FTA/FGA	TS%	eFG%	3PT%
13.2	0.050	0.482	0.653	0.622	0.224

AST%	TOV%	OREB%	DREB%	STL%	BLK%
7.6	14.9	10.1	15.5	1.3	1.8

PER	ORTG	DRTG	WS/48	BPM	VOL
14.65	128.3	110.6	0.153	-0.82	0.424

- Played regular rotation level minutes for Dallas, started most of his games last season
- Boosted his efficiency in his role as a very low volume rim runner
- True Shooting Percentage was almost 74% last season, excellent finisher around the rim, draws fouls at a high rate
- High energy big man, great cutter and roll man, good offensive rebounder, runs hard in transition
- Shot some threes in previous seasons, no longer takes outside jumpers, only shoots from ten feet and in
- Catch-and-finish player, limited as a passer, slightly turnover prone
- 2022-23 Defensive Degree of Difficulty: 0.476
- 2022-23 Points Prevented: 0.146
- Average rim protector, will challenge shots but not really a shot blocking threat, below average defensive rebounder
- Will draw some tough assignments against top big men, fairly solid on-ball defender
- Good post defender despite being slightly undersized, has some trouble defending in space, highly foul prone
- Played below average pick-and-roll defense, not especially effective at taking away any specific action
- Consistently comes out to contest perimeter shots in spot-up situations

Josh Green

	Height	Weight	Cap #	Years Left
	6'5"	200	$4.765M	RFA

Similar at Age 22

		Season	SIMsc
1	Ben McLemore	2015-16	946.9
2	Josh Richardson	2015-16	946.5
3	Ayo Dosunmu	2021-22	938.7
4	Josh Hart	2017-18	932.5
5	Kyle Weaver	2008-09	927.9
6	Chris Carr	1996-97	926.1
7	Bruce Brown	2018-19	920.3
8	Iman Shumpert	2012-13	919.8
9	Chris Robinson	1996-97	917.5
10	Caris LeVert	2016-17	916.0

Baseline Basic Stats

MPG	PTS	AST	REB	BLK	STL
24.1	9.5	2.0	3.0	0.3	0.8

Advanced Metrics

USG%	3PTA/FGA	FTA/FGA	TS%	eFG%	3PT%
17.1	0.380	0.202	0.573	0.549	0.369

AST%	TOV%	OREB%	DREB%	STL%	BLK%
12.6	12.8	3.6	10.7	1.7	0.8

PER	ORTG	DRTG	WS/48	BPM	VOL
12.17	111.4	113.3	0.080	-1.47	0.288

- Regular rotation player for Dallas in his third NBA season, missed games due to an elbow injury
- Highly efficient in his role as a low volume spot-up shooter
- Above average career three-point shooter, made over 40% of his threes last season
- Strictly a stand-still spot-up shooter, does not really take outside shots in other situations
- Improved as a pick-and-roll ball handler, could get to the rim and make pull-up mid-range jumpers, not able to drive by defenders without a screen
- Catch-and-shoot player, shows some ability to make simple reads, good at avoiding turnovers
- 2022-23 Defensive Degree of Difficulty: 0.427
- 2022-23 Points Prevented: -0.698
- Usually guards lower-end starters or upper-tier bench players, improved as an on-ball defender
- Capably could guard multiple positions against lower leverage players
- Solid pick-and-roll defender, effective at switching to guard ball handlers or screeners
- Fights through screens off the ball, tended to be late when closing out on spot-up shooters
- More of a stay-at-home defender, Steal and Block Percentages decreased significantly, fairly decent defensive rebounder

Maxi Kleber

	Height	Weight	Cap #	Years Left
	6'10"	240	$11.000M	2

Similar at Age 31

		Season	SIMsc
1	Anthony Tolliver	2016-17	921.7
2	Matt Bonner	2011-12	917.9
3	Jonas Jerebko	2018-19	909.8
4	Troy Murphy	2011-12	909.1
5	Markieff Morris	2020-21	905.2
6	Vladimir Radmanovic	2011-12	905.0
7	Wilson Chandler	2018-19	900.5
8	Channing Frye	2014-15	895.1
9	Patrick Patterson	2020-21	891.5
10	Brad Lohaus	1995-96	891.4

Baseline Basic Stats

MPG	PTS	AST	REB	BLK	STL
17.9	5.8	0.8	3.2	0.4	0.3

Advanced Metrics

USG%	3PTA/FGA	FTA/FGA	TS%	eFG%	3PT%
12.5	0.675	0.184	0.584	0.561	0.377

AST%	TOV%	OREB%	DREB%	STL%	BLK%
6.6	10.1	3.8	15.5	0.8	2.3

PER	ORTG	DRTG	WS/48	BPM	VOL
10.60	116.3	111.9	0.097	-0.90	0.370

- Missed most of last season due to a hamstring injury, regular rotation player for Dallas when healthy
- Usage dropped when he was in the lineup, still used as a stretch big that spaces the floor
- Around a league average three-point shooter for his career, percentages tend to vary from year-to-year
- More reliable as a stationary spot-up shooter, less effective on pick-and-pops
- Can be an effective rim runner, plays with a high motor, good cutter and roll man
- Strictly a catch-and-shoot player, only makes safe passes, good at avoiding turnovers
- 2022-23 Defensive Degree of Difficulty: 0.420
- 2022-23 Points Prevented: 2.132
- Solid rim protector, fairly good shot blocker, usually a solid defensive rebounder
- Guards starting level big men and some wing players, effective on-ball defender
- Strong enough to play effective post defender, good mobility allows him to defend in space
- Average pick-and-roll defender, good in drop coverages, has trouble containing ball handlers on switches
- Consistently comes out to the perimeter to contest outside shots

Seth Curry

	Height	Weight	Cap #	Years Left
	6'2"	185	$4.516M	1

Similar at Age 32

		Season	SIMsc
1	Patty Mills	2020-21	937.3
2	George Hill	2018-19	931.1
3	Eddie House	2010-11	930.9
4	Steve Kerr	1997-98	920.6
5	J.J. Redick	2016-17	917.4
6	Mike James	2007-08	911.9
7	Marco Belinelli	2018-19	909.3
8	Rex Chapman	1999-00	906.9
9	Mike Bibby	2010-11	906.2
10	Dell Curry	1996-97	904.6

Baseline Basic Stats

MPG	PTS	AST	REB	BLK	STL
22.7	9.4	2.5	2.1	0.1	0.7

Advanced Metrics

USG%	3PTA/FGA	FTA/FGA	TS%	eFG%	3PT%
18.2	0.549	0.145	0.572	0.546	0.388

AST%	TOV%	OREB%	DREB%	STL%	BLK%
15.5	11.1	1.3	8.7	1.4	0.4

PER	ORTG	DRTG	WS/48	BPM	VOL
12.31	111.4	113.9	0.080	-1.47	0.337

- Regular rotation player for Brooklyn, missed a few games due to an assortment of minor injuries
- Maintained his usual effectiveness in a role as a lower usage shooting specialist off the bench
- Excellent three-point shooter, ranked 6th in Career Three-Point Percentage
- Great all-around three-point shooter, makes spot-up and pull-up jumpers, good at running off screens
- Crafty player, effective at scoring as a pick-and-roll ball handler, lacks quickness to drive by defenders on isolations
- Catch-and-shoot player, has some secondary playmaking skills, rarely turns the ball over
- 2022-23 Defensive Degree of Difficulty: 0.350
- 2022-23 Points Prevented: -0.669
- Tended to guard second unit players or was hidden in favorable matchups
- Played effective on-ball defense against lower leverage players, could competently defend both guard spots
- Fairly solid pick-and-roll defender, could funnel ball handlers in to help, limited ability to switch, struggled when switched onto the roll man
- Gets caught on screens off the ball, good at closing out on spot-up shooters
- More active as a help defender, Steal Percentage increased a bit, below average defensive rebounder

Derrick Jones Jr.

	Height	Weight	Cap #	Years Left
	6'5"	210	$2.020M	UFA

Similar at Age 25

		Season	SIMsc
1	Greg Buckner	2001-02	909.1
2	Martell Webster	2011-12	897.5
3	Quincy Acy	2015-16	897.3
4	Maurice Harkless	2018-19	896.9
5	Wesley Iwundu	2019-20	895.5
6	Bruce Brown	2021-22	894.0
7	Mickael Pietrus	2007-08	893.7
8	Brandon Rush	2010-11	888.1
9	Cody Martin	2020-21	887.5
10	Kent Bazemore	2014-15	887.4

Baseline Basic Stats

MPG	PTS	AST	REB	BLK	STL
20.6	7.0	1.2	3.3	0.4	0.7

Advanced Metrics

USG%	3PTA/FGA	FTA/FGA	TS%	eFG%	3PT%
14.3	0.407	0.300	0.584	0.548	0.335

AST%	TOV%	OREB%	DREB%	STL%	BLK%
7.5	10.3	5.7	12.6	1.5	2.6

PER	ORTG	DRTG	WS/48	BPM	VOL
12.58	117.7	111.6	0.110	-0.66	0.355

- Fringe rotation player for Chicago in his second season with the team
- Slightly more effective in his role as a low usage energy player and spot-up shooter
- Highly explosive athlete, finishes with emphatic dunks, sometimes rushes his attempts in transition
- Solid cutter and roll man, active offensive rebounder that keeps possessions alive, draws fouls at a solid rate
- Below break-even career three-point shooter, made threes at a break-even rate last season
- Almost exclusively a stationary spot-up shooter, better at shooting in the corners with Chicago
- Not really able to create his own shot, catch-and-shoot player, only makes safe passes, rarely turns the ball over
- 2022-23 Defensive Degree of Difficulty: 0.358
- 2022-23 Points Prevented: 2.664
- Used as a stopper in the past, mainly was used as a roamer against second unit players last season
- Excellent weak side shot blocker, can use his length to get steals, decent defensive rebounder
- Fairly solid on-ball defender that guards multiple positions, tended to commit a lot of unnecessary shooting fouls
- Solid pick-and-roll defender, can effectively switch to guard ball handlers and screeners
- Fights through screens off the ball, sometimes will be late to close out on spot-up shooters

Richaun Holmes

	Height	Weight	Cap #	Years Left
	6'10"	235	$12.046M	PO

Similar at Age 29

		Season	SIMsc
1	Melvin Turpin	1989-90	927.0
2	Scott Williams	1997-98	915.6
3	Dwight Powell	2020-21	911.2
4	Jon Leuer	2018-19	909.8
5	Enes Freedom	2021-22	908.0
6	Ben Poquette	1984-85	905.5
7	Clemon Johnson	1985-86	904.4
8	Chris Wilcox	2011-12	904.1
9	Kurt Nimphius	1987-88	901.9
10	John Lambert	1981-82	901.6

Baseline Basic Stats

MPG	PTS	AST	REB	BLK	STL
16.5	5.2	0.8	4.1	0.5	0.5

Advanced Metrics

USG%	3PTA/FGA	FTA/FGA	TS%	eFG%	3PT%
13.8	0.042	0.285	0.624	0.594	0.433

AST%	TOV%	OREB%	DREB%	STL%	BLK%
5.2	12.5	9.4	18.5	1.0	2.5

PER	ORTG	DRTG	WS/48	BPM	VOL
13.97	122.6	111.6	0.127	-1.14	0.484

- Fell out of Sacramento's rotation, played sparingly last season
- Productivity declined slightly in a role as a low volume rim runner
- Energetic rim runner, career True Shooting Percentage is over 64%
- Solid roll man and cutter, active offensive rebounder, great at running the floor in transition, sometimes will rush his attempts at the rim
- Solid mid-range shooter in previous seasons, flashes some ability to make spot-up threes
- Catch-and-finish player, limited passing skills, fairly good at avoiding turnovers
- 2022-23 Defensive Degree of Difficulty: 0.301
- 2022-23 Points Prevented: -2.615
- Solid shot blocker and defensive rebounder, below average rim protector, undisciplined with his positioning, highly foul prone
- Tended to guard second unit big men or played in garbage time
- Solid on-ball defender in lower leverage matchups, effective post defender, mobile enough to defend in space
- Below average pick-and-roll defender, not particularly effective at taking away any specific action
- Tends to sag back into the paint, does not always come out to contest perimeter shots

Jaden Hardy

	Height	Weight	Cap #	Years Left
	6'4"	198	$1.720M	1

Similar at Age 20

		Season	SIMsc
1	Malik Monk	2018-19	930.8
2	Kevin Porter Jr.	2020-21	927.4
3	Jordan Poole	2019-20	922.8
4	Tyler Herro	2019-20	920.5
5	Cam Thomas	2021-22	914.4
6	Tyrese Maxey	2020-21	904.6
7	Jamal Murray	2017-18	900.6
8	D'Angelo Russell	2016-17	898.8
9	Emmanuel Mudiay	2016-17	895.6
10	Daequan Cook	2007-08	895.6

Baseline Basic Stats

MPG	PTS	AST	REB	BLK	STL
25.5	13.8	3.0	3.1	0.2	0.7

Advanced Metrics

USG%	3PTA/FGA	FTA/FGA	TS%	eFG%	3PT%
25.6	0.492	0.215	0.582	0.545	0.411

AST%	TOV%	OREB%	DREB%	STL%	BLK%
17.5	11.5	1.8	11.7	1.2	0.8

PER	ORTG	DRTG	WS/48	BPM	VOL
15.24	111.3	116.3	0.076	-0.96	0.416

- Fringe rotation player for Dallas as a rookie, spent some time in the G-League with the Texas Legends
- Had a production rookie season in a role as a high usage scoring guard off the bench
- Good pick-and-roll ball handler, can use the screen to get to the rim or hit pull-up jumpers
- Less effective in isolation situations, fairly heavy tendency to go left
- Made over 40% of his threes, most effective when shooting off the catch
- Hits spot-up threes, can occasionally shoot off screens, a bit streaky when shooting off the dribble
- Plays with a score-first mindset, decent secondary playmaker, good at avoiding turnovers
- 2022-23 Defensive Degree of Difficulty: 0.305
- 2022-23 Points Prevented: -0.188
- Usually hidden in favorable matchups against lower leverage second unit players
- Average on-ball defender, quick enough to stay with opposing guards, struggles to defend taller players
- Fairly decent pick-and-roll defender, limited ability to switch, effective at funneling ball handlers into help
- Tends to get caught on screens off the ball, good at closing out on spot-up shooters
- Stay-at-home defender in the NBA, rarely got steals or blocks, better at getting steals in the G-League, solid defensive rebounder

JaVale McGee

	Height	Weight	Cap #	Years Left
	7'0"	270	$5.734M	PO

Similar at Age 35

		Season	SIMsc
1	Brendan Haywood	2014-15	893.3
2	Dwight Howard	2020-21	841.7
3	Patrick Ewing*	1997-98	839.1
4	James Donaldson	1992-93	835.0
5	Erick Dampier	2010-11	834.4
6	Nene	2017-18	832.7
7	Hakeem Olajuwon*	1997-98	825.5
8	Emeka Okafor	2017-18	821.1
9	Arvydas Sabonis*	1999-00	818.3
10	Danny Schayes	1994-95	810.3

Baseline Basic Stats

MPG	PTS	AST	REB	BLK	STL
17.1	6.7	0.7	5.6	1.0	0.4

Advanced Metrics

USG%	3PTA/FGA	FTA/FGA	TS%	eFG%	3PT%
19.3	0.030	0.386	0.610	0.587	0.272

AST%	TOV%	OREB%	DREB%	STL%	BLK%
5.1	17.9	12.1	25.9	0.9	5.3

PER	ORTG	DRTG	WS/48	BPM	VOL
16.94	111.4	106.1	0.128	-1.59	0.607

- Not really able to crack Dallas' rotation, played sparingly in his second stint with the team
- Still effective in limited action in his typical role as a lower usage rim runner
- True Shooting Percentage was at 65% last season, still a vertical lob threat despite his age
- Good roll man and cutter, active offensive rebounder, declining foot speed, does not run the floor as much as he did in the past
- Experimenting with shooting but still not a reliable shooter, not really a post-up threat, limited passing skills, fairly turnover prone
- 2022-23 Defensive Degree of Difficulty: 0.396
- 2022-23 Points Prevented: -2.620
- Great shot blocker and defensive rebounder, struggled to effectively protect the rim due to mobility limitations
- Mainly guarded second unit big men, stout post defender, tended to commit shooting fouls in the post, has trouble defending in space
- Average pick-and-roll defender, good in drop coverages, struggles to contain ball handlers on switches
- Willing to come out to the perimeter to contest outside shots in spot-up situations
- Was reported while the book was being finalized that he is expected to be waived

Returning to the NBA

Dante Exum

	Height	Weight	Cap #	Years Left
	6'5"	214	$3.000M	1

Baseline Basic Stats

MPG	PTS	AST	REB	BLK	STL
23.9	9.1	2.4	3.4	0.3	0.9

Advanced Metrics

USG%	3PTA/FGA	FTA/FGA	TS%	eFG%	3PT%
18.7	0.443	0.334	0.597	0.548	0.361

AST%	TOV%	OREB%	DREB%	STL%	BLK%
16.7	15.1	4.0	11.5	2.1	0.8

PER	ORTG	DRTG	WS/48	BPM	VOL
13.16	118.9	122.2	0.081	-0.34	0.817

- Has been out of the NBA since the 2020-21 season, played for KK Partizan in the Adriatic League last season
- Projection is based on his translated EuroLeague stats from the 2022-23 season
- Highly effective in his role as a high usage ball handler
- True Shooting Percentage has been above 66% over his past two seasons in Europe
- Has made over 42% of his threes over the past two seasons, great spot-up shooter, can knock down pull-up threes if defenders back off him
- Can slash to the rim and draw fouls as a pick-and-roll ball handler, less effective on isolations
- Fairly good playmaker with solid court vision, somewhat turnover prone
- Generally guarded second unit players when he was in the NBA
- Fairly solid on-ball defender, can defend smaller guards and taller wing players
- Generally a solid pick-and-roll defender, good at fighting over screens and containing ball handlers, has some lapses when switching onto screeners
- Tends to gamble too much, can be caught out of position, sometimes is late on his close-outs, good at fighting through screens off the ball
- Active help defender in Europe, gets steals at a fairly high rate, solid rebounding guard
Slowed by injuries in the past, has remained healthy for the past two seasons

Newcomers

Dereck Lively II

	Height	Weight	Cap #	Years Left
	7'1"	230	$4.776M	1 + 2 TO

Baseline Basic Stats

MPG	PTS	AST	REB	BLK	STL
18.2	6.6	0.7	4.8	1.4	0.5

Advanced Metrics

USG%	3PTA/FGA	FTA/FGA	TS%	eFG%	3PT%
15.0	0.086	0.305	0.556	0.537	0.262

AST%	TOV%	OREB%	DREB%	STL%	BLK%
7.2	13.6	8.9	18.4	1.2	5.7

PER	ORTG	DRTG	WS/48	BPM	VOL
15.16	109.4	99.8	0.101	-0.91	N/A

- Drafted by Oklahoma City with the 12th overall pick in 2023, traded to Dallas
- Had a strong performance at the Las Vegas Summer League
- Effective in his role as a very low usage rim runner
- Posted a True Shooting Percentage above 66%, very athletic big man that plays with high energy
- Vertical lob threat, great roll man and cutter, very good offensive rebounder, runs hard in transition
- Limited offensive skill, not really a post-up threat, rarely shoots jump shots in games
- Shooting stroke needs improvement, made less than 60% of his free throws at Summer League
- Not really a passer, highly turnover prone
- Has great defensive potential, very long big men with great quickness and leaping ability
- Good rim protector, solid shot blocker, good defensive rebounder, plays a bit out of control, can be foul prone
- Struggled to play effective post defense due to his thin frame, can be pushed around inside
- Much better when defending in space, mobility allows him to stay with perimeter players on switch
- Good pick-and-roll defender, very good in drop coverages, effective at switching or hedging out handlers
- Consistently comes out to contest perimeter shots in spot-up situations
- Could potentially be Dallas' starting center as soon as this coming season

	Height	Weight	Cap #	Years Left
Olivier-Maxence Prosper	6'8"	230	$2.734M	1 + 2 TO

Baseline Basic Stats

MPG	PTS	AST	REB	BLK	STL
18.2	6.9	1.1	3.0	0.3	0.6

Advanced Metrics

USG%	3PTA/FGA	FTA/FGA	TS%	eFG%	3PT%
17.0	0.354	0.275	0.520	0.488	0.332

AST%	TOV%	OREB%	DREB%	STL%	BLK%
7.8	10.9	5.4	12.0	1.5	1.1

PER	ORTG	DRTG	WS/48	BPM	VOL
12.00	103.5	104.6	0.065	-1.52	N/A

- Drafted by Sacramento with the 24th overall pick in 2023, traded to Dallas
- Played very well at the Las Vegas Summer League
- Highly effective in his role as a low usage spot-up shooter and energy player, will likely play a similar role in the NBA
- Much more effective as a rim running energy player, drew fouls at an extremely high rate
- Explosive finisher in transition, great cutter off the ball, selectively crashed the offensive boards to score on put-backs
- Not especially efficient as an outside shooter, made less than 25% of his threes
- Shooting still needs improvement, below break-even three-point shooter in college, strictly a stationary spot-up shooter
- Not really used in ball handling situations, not likely to be able to create his own offense in the NBA
- Catch-and-shoot player, only makes safe passes, good at avoiding turnovers
- Good athlete, can potentially develop into a plus-level defender
- Great on-ball defender in college, can guard multiple positions
- Solid pick-and-roll defender, shows good versatility to switch, can guard ball handlers or screeners
- Stays attached to shooters off the ball, fights through screens and closes out in spot-up situations
- Used as a roaming free safety type in college, played more as a stay-at-home defender at Summer League
- Fairly good at playing passing lanes to get steals, solid defensive rebounder
- May benefit from some additional seasoning in the G-League to improve his outside shooting

Los Angeles Clippers

Last Season: 44 - 38, Lost 1st Round to Phoenix (1 – 4)

Offensive Rating: 115.0, 16th in the NBA   Defensive Rating: 114.5, 18th in the NBA

Primary Executive: Lawrence Frank, President of Basketball Operations

Head Coach: Tyronn Lue

Key Roster Changes

Subtractions
Eric Gordon, waived

Additions
Kobe Brown, draft
Kenyon Martin Jr., trade

Roster

Likely Starting Five
1. Russell Westbrook
2. *Kawhi Leonard*
3. *Paul George*
4. Marcus Morris
5. Ivica Zubac

Other Key Rotation Players
Mason Plumlee
Terance Mann
Norman Powell
Nicolas Batum
Bones Hyland

* Italics denotes that a player is likely to be on the floor to close games

Remaining Roster

- Kenyon Martin Jr.
- Robert Covington
- Amir Coffey
- Brandon Boston Jr.
- Jason Preston
- Kobe Brown
- Mousse Diabaté, 22, 6'11", 210, Michigan (Two-Way)
- Jordan Miller, 24, 6'7", 195, Miami (FL) (Two-Way)
- Xavier Castaneda, 23, 6'1", 188, Akron (Exhibit 10)

SCHREMPF Base Rating: 44.7

Season Preview Survey

- *Are the Clippers contending or rebuilding? Where is this team headed?*

The Clippers are trying to compete for a championship, but they just can't sustain any kind of positive momentum for an entire season. Their lineup is always in flux because their stars have trouble staying healthy and the effects of these issues almost always forces them to be short-handed in some way. On top of this, their roster is also aging, which means that their window is either closing or it has already slammed shut. They will need to figure out some way to stay healthy to realize the potential that they show on paper. Otherwise, it's likely that their talent will take them to the playoffs, but they will fall short once again and make an exit in one of the first two rounds.

- *What are the areas of concern for this team heading into this season?*

The primary concern for the Clippers is the same as it has been for the past few years and that is that they have been unable to play at full strength for an entire playoff run. Some of this is due to bad luck and timing because both Paul George and Kawhi Leonard have suffered serious injuries in the middle of the playoffs. It's understandable as to why they have implemented their load management strategies, but even that hasn't really worked to keep them in the lineup on a regular basis. They may need to shake up their rotation or roster to add a durable presence to allow them to maintain some kind of momentum through the long season. The rumored trade for James Harden could help in that regards, but that doesn't quite resolve the other issue, which is that they have an aging roster. Almost all of their expected rotation players are in their 30s, so they do run the risk of having their performance drop due to an age-related decline. To counter this, they might need to go in the other direction and find younger contributors to offset the age of their core group.

- *List some possible breakout players for this team.*

As it mentioned earlier, the Clippers have a pretty old team, so they don't have a lot of young, breakout candidates on their roster. Normally, the amount of the depth that the Clippers have would mean that any young player would be blocked for playing time. However, the combination of load management, injuries, and constant shuffling of the lineup strangely provides opportunities for younger players to emerge as key contributors. In particular, younger veterans like Kenyon Martin Jr. and Bones Hyland could take leaps forward in their development to become more impactful players. Martin could emerge as an athletic three-and-D wing that can come in to spell either of the two stars while Hyland could give them a boost with his scoring abilities if he increases his consistency. From there, rookie Kobe Brown could help out by being a floor spacing and playmaking four that can occasionally slide down to be a small-ball five, if they need him to do so.

- *What should we expect from them this season?*

Unless they get a good stroke of luck and they can play at full strength for a whole season, it's likely that the Clippers will be a tantalizing unit that flashes the potential to be a title contender but doesn't stay healthy enough to play to their highest capability. If they are in their usual short-handed situation, they still will have enough talent to make the playoffs and be a tough out because they can defend and use their deep array of shooters to generate effective offense. On the other hand, if they are lucky and their two elite stars stay healthy, then they could amplify their strengths to be a dark horse candidate to reach the Finals and make a title run in that optimistic scenario.

Veterans

Kawhi Leonard

	Height	Weight	Cap #	Years Left
	6'7"	225	$45.640M	PO

Similar at Age 31

		Season	SIMsc
1	Gordon Hayward	2021-22	915.7
2	Carmelo Anthony	2015-16	912.0
3	Glenn Robinson	2003-04	904.3
4	Jimmy Butler	2020-21	903.1
5	Stephen Jackson	2009-10	901.3
6	Clyde Drexler*	1993-94	900.9
7	Larry Bird*	1987-88	899.2
8	Vince Carter	2007-08	899.1
9	Manu Ginobili*	2008-09	895.3
10	Chris Bosh*	2015-16	893.8

Baseline Basic Stats

MPG	PTS	AST	REB	BLK	STL
33.3	20.4	4.2	5.6	0.4	1.3

Advanced Metrics

USG%	3PTA/FGA	FTA/FGA	TS%	eFG%	3PT%
26.9	0.295	0.321	0.600	0.545	0.399

AST%	TOV%	OREB%	DREB%	STL%	BLK%
21.0	10.2	3.5	15.5	1.9	1.1

PER	ORTG	DRTG	WS/48	BPM	VOL
21.95	120.0	111.6	0.176	4.75	0.431

- Missed many games due to a knee injury, played at his usual All-Star level when healthy
- Excelled as the L.A. Clippers primary scorer, thrived in every offensive situation
- Efficient three-level scorer, great isolation player and pick-and-roll ball handler
- Can drive to the rim, draw fouls, make pull-up jumpers, and post up smaller players
- Great three-point shooter throughout his career, made almost 42% of his threes last season
- Efficient shooter in all situations, makes spot-up jumpers, runs off screens, and shoots off the dribble
- Moves well without the ball, good playmaker, rarely turns the ball over
- 2022-23 Defensive Degree of Difficulty: 0.498
- 2022-23 Points Prevented: 1.409
- Drew a lot of tough assignments against elite perimeter scorers
- Excellent on-ball defender that guards multiple positions on the floor
- Good pick-and-roll defender, effectively switches to defend ball handlers and screeners
- Sometimes gets caught on screens, good at closing out on spot-up shooters
- Still an active help defender, good at using his length to get steals, occasional weak side shot blocker, fairly good defensive rebounder

Paul George

	Height	Weight	Cap #	Years Left
	6'8"	220	$45.640M	PO

Similar at Age 32

		Season	SIMsc
1	Stephen Jackson	2010-11	920.9
2	Scottie Pippen*	1997-98	908.9
3	Manu Ginobili*	2009-10	898.1
4	Marcus Morris	2021-22	897.9
5	Carmelo Anthony	2016-17	897.9
6	Clyde Drexler*	1994-95	888.8
7	Vince Carter	2008-09	888.3
8	Grant Hill*	2004-05	883.5
9	Jerry Stackhouse	2006-07	881.2
10	DeMar DeRozan	2021-22	878.1

Baseline Basic Stats

MPG	PTS	AST	REB	BLK	STL
31.3	17.0	3.8	5.1	0.4	1.1

Advanced Metrics

USG%	3PTA/FGA	FTA/FGA	TS%	eFG%	3PT%
26.7	0.421	0.263	0.553	0.507	0.350

AST%	TOV%	OREB%	DREB%	STL%	BLK%
21.9	13.7	2.4	16.9	2.0	1.0

PER	ORTG	DRTG	WS/48	BPM	VOL
17.02	107.2	108.7	0.097	2.17	0.511

- Missed games due to a sore knee and a hamstring injury, named to his 8th All-Star team in 2022-23
- Highly productive as a high usage scoring wing for the L.A. Clippers last season
- Efficient scorer at all three-levels, slightly more effective as a pick-and-roll ball handler, good post-up wing
- Slightly inconsistent when shooting off the dribble, better at making pull-up jumpers from mid-range, average in isolation situations
- Reliable three-point shooter, great stand-still spot-up shooter, inefficient when shooting on the move
- Good playmaking wing, sometimes struggles to handle the ball under pressure, good at avoiding turnovers
- 2022-23 Defensive Degree of Difficulty: 0.520
- 2022-23 Points Prevented: 0.088
- Used as the Clippers' primary defensive stopper, good on-ball defender throughout his career
- Effectively guards multiple positions, had a little bit of trouble staying with quicker guards
- Good pick-and-roll defender that can switch to guard ball handlers or screeners
- Sometimes gets caught on screens off the ball, good at closing out on spot-up shooters
- Consistently gets steals at a high rate despite his injury history, fairly good defensive rebounder

Russell Westbrook

	Height	Weight	Cap #	Years Left
	6'3"	200	$3.836M	PO

Similar at Age 34

		Season	SIMsc
1	Sam Cassell	2003-04	895.5
2	Andre Miller	2010-11	885.7
3	Dwyane Wade*	2015-16	881.5
4	Goran Dragić	2020-21	876.5
5	Kobe Bryant*	2012-13	876.3
6	Steve Nash*	2008-09	876.1
7	Chauncey Billups	2010-11	875.4
8	Vinnie Johnson	1990-91	870.1
9	Byron Scott	1995-96	868.1
10	Gary Payton*	2002-03	864.3

Baseline Basic Stats

MPG	PTS	AST	REB	BLK	STL
30.4	14.9	6.5	4.4	0.2	1.0

Advanced Metrics

USG%	3PTA/FGA	FTA/FGA	TS%	eFG%	3PT%
24.7	0.257	0.309	0.526	0.485	0.332

AST%	TOV%	OREB%	DREB%	STL%	BLK%
35.5	17.6	4.0	16.2	1.5	1.0

PER	ORTG	DRTG	WS/48	BPM	VOL
16.61	106.4	111.2	0.074	0.32	0.520

- Traded from the L.A. Lakers to Utah, signed with the L.A. Clippers after he was bought out
- Played starter level minutes last season, used as a high usage scorer and playmaker
- Excellent playmaker, consistently posts high Assist Percentages, fairly turnover prone
- Great at pushing the ball in transition, aggressively drives to the rim, better as a pick-and-roll ball handler
- Below break-even three-point shooter, more effective at making pull-up jumpers from 10 to 16 feet
- Less effective in isolation situations, defenders back off him to limit his effectiveness
- More efficient with better spacing with the Clippers
- 2022-23 Defensive Degree of Difficulty: 0.456
- 2022-23 Points Prevented: 1.347
- Usually guards starting level players, draws some tough assignments
- Played average on-ball defense, can competently defend ones and twos, over-aggressive, tends to commit unnecessary shooting fouls
- Average pick-and-roll defender, can funnel his man into help, prone to taking bad angles
- Stays attached to shooters off the ball, fights through screens and closes out in spot-up situations
- More active as a help defender, steal and blocks rate increased, good defensive rebounder
- Does not cheat off his man to go for rebounds as much as he did in the past

Ivica Zubac

	Height	Weight	Cap #	Years Left
	7'0"	240	$10.933M	1

Similar at Age 25

		Season	SIMsc
1	Alton Lister	1983-84	930.9
2	Tyson Chandler	2007-08	926.7
3	Dave Corzine	1981-82	922.5
4	Will Perdue	1990-91	921.8
5	Dale Davis	1994-95	918.7
6	Joakim Noah	2010-11	916.4
7	Cody Zeller	2017-18	916.3
8	Benoit Benjamin	1989-90	914.2
9	Gorgui Dieng	2014-15	914.2
10	Samuel Dalembert	2006-07	910.2

Baseline Basic Stats

MPG	PTS	AST	REB	BLK	STL
26.5	10.0	1.3	8.2	1.3	0.6

Advanced Metrics

USG%	3PTA/FGA	FTA/FGA	TS%	eFG%	3PT%
16.2	0.013	0.427	0.624	0.594	0.172

AST%	TOV%	OREB%	DREB%	STL%	BLK%
7.4	15.7	11.7	24.2	1.0	3.5

PER	ORTG	DRTG	WS/48	BPM	VOL
17.24	120.1	107.5	0.149	0.02	0.307

- Regular starting center for the L.A. Clippers in his fourth full season with the team
- Solidly effective in a role as a low volume rim runner
- True Shooting Percentage has been above 65% for each of the last four seasons
- High motor rim runner, good offensive rebounder, solid roll man and cutter, runs hard in transition
- Effective on post-ups, good at flashing to the middle, scores off drop-steps from the right block
- Improving as a mid-range shooter, catch-and-finish player that makes safe passes, slightly turnover prone
- 2022-23 Defensive Degree of Difficulty: 0.472
- 2022-23 Points Prevented: 2.040
- Good rim protector, provide strong resistance around the basket, good defensive rebounder and shot blocker
- Guards starting level centers, stout post defender, limited mobility, has trouble defending in space
- Average pick-and-roll defender, good in drop coverages, not really able to switch or hedge out on ball handlers
- Tends to stay anchored in the paint, does not always come out to contest outside shots in spot-up situations

Marcus Morris

	Height	Weight	Cap #	Years Left
	6'8"	218	$17.116M	UFA

Similar at Age 33

		Season	SIMsc
1	Michael Finley	2006-07	950.2
2	Caron Butler	2013-14	949.9
3	Mike Miller	2013-14	931.8
4	Glen Rice	2000-01	929.3
5	Chuck Person	1997-98	928.1
6	Richard Jefferson	2013-14	927.2
7	Mike Dunleavy Jr.	2013-14	926.5
8	Kiki Vandeweghe	1991-92	921.1
9	Joe Johnson	2014-15	920.0
10	Gerald Green	2018-19	918.2

Baseline Basic Stats

MPG	PTS	AST	REB	BLK	STL
23.6	9.0	1.5	3.3	0.2	0.5

Advanced Metrics

USG%	3PTA/FGA	FTA/FGA	TS%	eFG%	3PT%
17.8	0.464	0.173	0.534	0.506	0.368

AST%	TOV%	OREB%	DREB%	STL%	BLK%
9.2	9.1	2.2	13.5	1.2	0.9

PER	ORTG	DRTG	WS/48	BPM	VOL
11.30	106.4	110.4	0.076	-1.23	0.415

- Regular starter for the L.A. Clippers in his third full season with the team
- Production level declined in a new role as a lower volume spot-up shooter
- Solid three-point shooter in his career, has made over 39% of his threes in his years with the Clippers
- Primarily a stationary spot-up shooter, has some ability to make threes off screens
- Rated by Synergy as being average or worse in most offensive situations
- Losing a step, not able to consistently drive by defenders, post-up effectiveness declined
- Strictly a catch-and-shoot player, only makes safe passes, rarely turns the ball over
- 2022-23 Defensive Degree of Difficulty: 0.503
- 2022-23 Points Prevented: -0.311
- Drew a lot of difficult assignments while the stars were out of the lineups, over-extended in these matchups
- Average on-ball defender, has trouble against quicker players, decent when guarding bigger players
- Solid pick-and-roll defender, effective at switching, good at making rotations in different coverages
- Gets caught on screens off the ball, sometimes is late to close out on spot-up shooters
- Stay-at-home defender, rarely gets steals or blocks, fairly solid defensive rebounder

Mason Plumlee

	Height	Weight	Cap #	Years Left
	6'11"	254	$5.000M	UFA

Similar at Age 32

		Season	SIMsc
1	Erick Dampier	2007-08	896.6
2	Jeff Foster	2008-09	892.6
3	Samuel Dalembert	2013-14	892.5
4	Will Perdue	1997-98	890.9
5	Brad Miller	2008-09	888.3
6	Marcin Gortat	2016-17	884.2
7	Zaza Pachulia	2016-17	881.9
8	DeAndre Jordan	2020-21	878.6
9	Bob Lanier*	1980-81	878.5
10	Fabricio Oberto	2007-08	878.2

Baseline Basic Stats

MPG	PTS	AST	REB	BLK	STL
22.6	7.3	1.5	7.3	0.9	0.5

Advanced Metrics

USG%	3PTA/FGA	FTA/FGA	TS%	eFG%	3PT%
13.8	0.018	0.495	0.627	0.617	0.110

AST%	TOV%	OREB%	DREB%	STL%	BLK%
13.8	18.7	10.3	24.7	1.2	2.7

PER	ORTG	DRTG	WS/48	BPM	VOL
15.91	121.7	109.7	0.142	0.64	0.427

- Traded from Charlotte to the L.A. Clippers at the trade deadline, played starter level minutes last season
- Had his most productive season in a role as a low usage rim runner
- High motor big man, made almost 77% of his shots inside of three feet
- Good offensive rebounder, great cutter and roll man, consistently runs the floor in transition
- Switched his shooting hand, improved as a free throw shooter, able to make a few mid-range jumpers
- Great passing big man that finds open shooters and hits cutters, slightly turnover prone
- 2022-23 Defensive Degree of Difficulty: 0.461
- 2022-23 Points Prevented: -0.698
- Below average rim protector, shot blocking rates are declining, good defensive rebounder
- Guarded starting level big men, below average on-ball defender, gets pushed around in the post, has trouble defending in space
- Middling pick-and-roll defender, willing to hedge out on ball handlers, tends to late when rotating to cover screeners
- Fairly good at closing out on spot-up shooters, tended to sag back into the paint in Charlotte
- Steal Percentage declined, good in previous seasons at playing passing lanes to get steals

Terance Mann

	Height	Weight	Cap #	Years Left
	6'5"	215	$10.577M	1

Similar at Age 26

		Season	SIMsc
1	Malcolm Brogdon	2018-19	947.9
2	Glenn Robinson III	2019-20	935.4
3	Kentavious Caldwell-Pope	2019-20	933.8
4	Iman Shumpert	2016-17	932.7
5	Josh Hart	2021-22	931.3
6	Arron Afflalo	2011-12	927.6
7	Cody Martin	2021-22	925.0
8	Joe Harris	2017-18	922.9
9	Martell Webster	2012-13	921.0
10	Caleb Martin	2021-22	920.0

Baseline Basic Stats

MPG	PTS	AST	REB	BLK	STL
26.3	10.6	2.2	3.6	0.3	0.8

Advanced Metrics

USG%	3PTA/FGA	FTA/FGA	TS%	eFG%	3PT%
17.1	0.364	0.241	0.581	0.545	0.384

AST%	TOV%	OREB%	DREB%	STL%	BLK%
13.7	11.4	3.8	12.5	1.3	0.9

PER	ORTG	DRTG	WS/48	BPM	VOL
13.60	116.6	113.1	0.107	-0.19	0.436

- Played in all but one game for the Clippers, shifted back and forth from the bench to the starting lineup
- Increased his efficiency in his role as a low usage spot-up shooter and energy guard
- Good three-point shooter, more efficient when shooting threes above the break
- Predominantly a stationary spot-up shooter, can occasionally make pull-up threes on pick-and-rolls
- Good cutter off the ball, excellent finisher in transition, selectively goes to the offensive boards to score on put-backs
- Crafty pick-and-roll ball handler that changes speeds well, lacks the ball handling skills to drive on isolations
- Solid secondary playmaker that makes simple reads, good at avoiding turnovers
- 2022-23 Defensive Degree of Difficulty: 0.492
- 2022-23 Points Prevented: 0.898
- Drew a lot of difficult matchups against elite scoring guards, solid on-ball defender
- Fairly effective at defending both guard spots, a bit too aggressive, tended to commit shooting fouls
- Solid pick-and-roll defender, good at containing ball handlers, can functionally switch, has lapses when rotating onto screeners
- Sometimes gets caught on screens off the ball, good at closing out on spot-up shooters
- Stay-at-home defender, rarely gets blocks or steals, fairly solid defensive rebounder

Norman Powell

	Height	Weight	Cap #	Years Left
	6'3"	215	$18.000M	2

Similar at Age 29

		Season	SIMsc
1	Eric Gordon	2017-18	929.3
2	Voshon Lenard	2002-03	922.4
3	Gerald Henderson	2016-17	914.3
4	Terrence Ross	2020-21	910.9
5	Ben Gordon	2012-13	907.6
6	Michael Redd	2008-09	904.4
7	Gary Neal	2013-14	903.5
8	Alec Burks	2020-21	901.1
9	Randy Foye	2012-13	898.7
10	Erick Strickland	2002-03	896.8

Baseline Basic Stats

MPG	PTS	AST	REB	BLK	STL
26.8	13.1	2.1	2.8	0.3	0.8

Advanced Metrics

USG%	3PTA/FGA	FTA/FGA	TS%	eFG%	3PT%
22.8	0.439	0.309	0.568	0.521	0.383

AST%	TOV%	OREB%	DREB%	STL%	BLK%
11.5	10.2	1.7	10.0	1.5	0.9

PER	ORTG	DRTG	WS/48	BPM	VOL
14.33	110.6	115.1	0.082	-0.78	0.449

- Missed games due to strained groin and a partial shoulder dislocation
- Effective in his role as a high volume scorer off the bench for the L.A. Clippers
- Pretty reliable three-point shooter, has made almost 44% of his career corner threes
- Great shooter off the catch, less effective when shooting off the dribble, good cutter if defenders crowd him
- Solid pick-and-roll ball handler and isolation players, changes speeds to get to the rim, can make short mid-range pull-up jumpers and floaters
- Mostly scoring focused, not a true playmaker but can make the extra pass, good at avoiding turnovers
- 2022-23 Defensive Degree of Difficulty: 0.373
- 2022-23 Points Prevented: -0.486
- Mostly guarded second unit players, drew tougher assignments in the past
- Fairly solid on-ball defender, can capably guard taller wings, has some trouble staying with quicker guards
- Played below average pick-and-roll defense, can functionally switch, tended to have lapses when making rotations last season
- Fights through screens off the ball, tended to be a step late when closing out on spot-up shooters
- Gets steals at a moderate rate, occasionally blocks shots from the weak side, decent defensive rebounder

Nicolas Batum

	Height	Weight	Cap #	Years Left
	6'8"	230	$11.711M	UFA

Similar at Age 34

		Season	SIMsc
1	Shane Battier	2012-13	928.0
2	Trevor Ariza	2019-20	914.8
3	Matt Barnes	2014-15	909.2
4	Anthony Tolliver	2019-20	907.8
5	Danny Green	2021-22	900.0
6	Danny Ferry	2000-01	898.3
7	Mike Dunleavy Jr.	2014-15	896.9
8	Joe Ingles	2021-22	896.0
9	Jeff Green	2020-21	895.1
10	Chuck Person	1998-99	894.7

Baseline Basic Stats

MPG	PTS	AST	REB	BLK	STL
22.5	6.2	1.3	3.3	0.6	0.7

Advanced Metrics

USG%	3PTA/FGA	FTA/FGA	TS%	eFG%	3PT%
12.0	0.777	0.134	0.568	0.553	0.373

AST%	TOV%	OREB%	DREB%	STL%	BLK%
8.9	10.2	3.8	15.0	1.6	2.6

PER	ORTG	DRTG	WS/48	BPM	VOL
10.95	115.2	110.7	0.108	0.19	0.355

- Regular rotation player for the L.A. Clippers in his third season with the team
- Production level declined a bit, mainly used as a very low usage spot-up shooter
- Has made almost 40% of his threes with the Clippers, more than 83% of his shots were threes last season
- Almost exclusively a stationary spot-up shooter, occasionally can make pick-and-pop threes
- Makes sharp backdoor cuts if defenders try to crowd him, good at running the break in transition
- Very rarely used in ball handling situations, strictly a catch-and-shoot player now
- Good secondary playmaker in the past, can make the extra pass now, rarely turns the ball over
- 2022-23 Defensive Degree of Difficulty: 0.480
- 2022-23 Points Prevented: -0.127
- Drew a lot of difficult assignments off the bench, over-matched against top scorers, a step slower due to age
- Played below average on-ball defense, struggled to stay with perimeter players, less effective against big men
- Below average pick-and-roll defender, not especially effective at taking away any specific action
- Tends to get caught on screens, good at closing out on spot-up shooters
- Steal Percentage declined slightly, solid weak side shot blocker and defensive rebounder

Bones Hyland

	Height	Weight	Cap #	Years Left
	6'3"	173	$2.306M	TO

Similar at Age 22

		Season	SIMsc
1	Anfernee Simons	2021-22	921.6
2	Immanuel Quickley	2021-22	913.5
3	Malachi Flynn	2020-21	907.0
4	Aaron Holiday	2018-19	901.6
5	Leandro Barbosa	2004-05	901.0
6	Jordan Poole	2021-22	897.6
7	Damon Jones	1998-99	897.1
8	Malik Monk	2020-21	896.9
9	Ian Clark	2013-14	888.8
10	Rodrigue Beaubois	2010-11	887.8

Baseline Basic Stats

MPG	PTS	AST	REB	BLK	STL
24.4	12.4	3.0	2.7	0.2	0.8

Advanced Metrics

USG%	3PTA/FGA	FTA/FGA	TS%	eFG%	3PT%
24.4	0.488	0.209	0.548	0.514	0.371

AST%	TOV%	OREB%	DREB%	STL%	BLK%
21.2	11.0	1.9	11.2	1.7	0.9

PER	ORTG	DRTG	WS/48	BPM	VOL
14.89	110.0	114.1	0.079	-0.50	0.275

- Traded from Denver to the L.A. Clippers at the trade deadline, regular rotational player for both teams
- Improved a bit in his role as a high volume scoring guard off the bench for both teams
- Solid three-point shooter, made over 44% of his corner threes last season
- Good spot-up shooter, knocks down pull-up threes if defenders go under screens, rarely moves off the ball
- Better as a pick-and-roll ball handler, shifty driver that can change speeds, needs a screen to get to the rim
- Fairly good playmaker that makes simple reads, Assist Percentage increased with the Clippers, good at avoiding turnovers
- 2022-23 Defensive Degree of Difficulty: 0.313
- 2022-23 Points Prevented: -0.831
- Usually was hidden in favorable matchups against lower leverage second unit players
- Below average on-ball defender, struggles to stay with guards on the perimeter, can be overpowered by bigger players due to his slight frame
- Decent pick-and-roll defender, limited ability to switch, effective at funneling his man into help
- Takes bad gambles, not always in good position, gets caught on screens off the ball, does not always close out on spot-up shooters
- Active when roaming on the weak side, gets steals at a solid rate, fairly solid defensive rebounder

Kenyon Martin Jr.

	Height	Weight	Cap #	Years Left
	6'6"	215	$1.931M	UFA

Similar at Age 22

		Season	SIMsc
1	Harrison Barnes	2014-15	920.5
2	Miles Bridges	2020-21	917.6
3	Derrick Jones Jr.	2019-20	909.2
4	Desmond Bane	2020-21	909.0
5	Maurice Harkless	2015-16	907.8
6	Josh Hart	2017-18	907.6
7	Jumaine Jones	2001-02	907.2
8	Jaylen Brown	2018-19	905.5
9	Dillon Brooks	2017-18	903.3
10	Keldon Johnson	2021-22	903.1

Baseline Basic Stats

MPG	PTS	AST	REB	BLK	STL
28.1	12.0	1.8	4.4	0.5	0.8

Advanced Metrics

USG%	3PTA/FGA	FTA/FGA	TS%	eFG%	3PT%
17.9	0.342	0.254	0.603	0.579	0.361

AST%	TOV%	OREB%	DREB%	STL%	BLK%
9.6	10.1	4.5	13.7	1.2	1.5

PER	ORTG	DRTG	WS/48	BPM	VOL
14.95	118.5	115.7	0.103	-0.29	0.351

- Regular starter for Houston in his third NBA season, played in all 82 games
- Had his best season in a role as a low usage spot-up shooter and energy player
- Above break-even career three-point shooter, Three-Point Percentage fell to below break-even last season
- Predominantly a stand-still spot-up shooter, 87.5% of his threes were spot-up jumpers
- Explosive athlete, better as an energy player, made over 80% of his shots from three feet and in last season
- Great cutter and roll man, athletic finisher in transition, good at scoring off put-backs after an offensive rebound
- Mainly a catch-and-shoot player, only makes safe passes, rarely turns the ball over
- <u>2022-23 Defensive Degree of Difficulty</u>: 0.377
- <u>2022-23 Points Prevented</u>: -0.729
- Usually guarded second unit players, on-ball defense was around average
- Solid against perimeter players, showed good quickness to stay with his man, had trouble against stronger players inside
- Middling pick-and-roll defender, can functionally switch and cut off penetration, goes too far under screens
- Tends to get caught on screens off the ball, usually a step late when closing out on spot-up shooters
- More of a stay-at-home defender, steal and block rates dropped a bit, fairly good on the defensive boards

Robert Covington

	Height	Weight	Cap #	Years Left
	6'7"	209	$11.692M	UFA

Similar at Age 32

		Season	SIMsc
1	Danny Green	2019-20	907.2
2	Walt Williams	2002-03	889.6
3	James Posey	2008-09	886.8
4	Devean George	2009-10	886.5
5	Dan Majerle	1997-98	886.0
6	Francisco Garcia	2013-14	882.9
7	Matt Barnes	2012-13	882.6
8	Bryon Russell	2002-03	881.3
9	Kyle Korver	2013-14	874.5
10	Thabo Sefolosha	2016-17	872.5

Baseline Basic Stats

MPG	PTS	AST	REB	BLK	STL
24.8	7.7	1.5	4.1	0.6	0.9

Advanced Metrics

USG%	3PTA/FGA	FTA/FGA	TS%	eFG%	3PT%
13.5	0.697	0.139	0.571	0.552	0.380

AST%	TOV%	OREB%	DREB%	STL%	BLK%
9.2	12.4	3.3	17.7	1.9	2.8

PER	ORTG	DRTG	WS/48	BPM	VOL
11.70	111.5	109.7	0.093	0.40	0.424

- Fringe rotation player for the L.A. Clippers in his first full season with the team
- Efficiency increased in a limited role as a low volume spot-up shooter
- League average career three-point shooter, has made 42% of his threes with the Clippers
- Mostly a stationary spot-up shooter, can make threes in transition and some pick-and-pop jumpers
- Rated by Synergy as being average or worse in every other situation
- Athleticism declining, less effective when finishing as a rim runner, not able to create his own shot
- Assist Percentage increased to a career high, strictly a catch-and-shoot player now, rarely turns the ball over
- 2022-23 Defensive Degree of Difficulty: 0.371
- 2022-23 Points Prevented: -0.011
- Used as a defensive stopper in the past, mostly guards second unit level players
- Fairly solid on-ball defender, better at guarding big men as a small-ball five, struggles to stay with quicker perimeter players
- Good pick-and-roll ball handler, effectively switches to defend ball handlers and screeners
- Fights through screens off the ball, tends to be late when closing out on spot-up shooters
- Very active help defender, great at getting steals, very good weak side shot blocker, good defensive rebounder

Amir Coffey

	Height	Weight	Cap #	Years Left
	6'7"	210	$3.667M	1

Similar at Age 25

		Season	SIMsc
1	Martell Webster	2011-12	937.8
2	Glenn Robinson III	2018-19	937.3
3	Oscar Torres	2001-02	934.5
4	Antoine Wright	2009-10	934.0
5	Wesley Iwundu	2019-20	927.1
6	Von Wafer	2010-11	925.0
7	Chase Budinger	2013-14	924.8
8	Eric Piatkowski	1995-96	922.8
9	Sam Mack	1995-96	921.7
10	Tim Breaux	1995-96	921.6

Baseline Basic Stats

MPG	PTS	AST	REB	BLK	STL
21.2	7.5	1.3	2.7	0.3	0.6

Advanced Metrics

USG%	3PTA/FGA	FTA/FGA	TS%	eFG%	3PT%
15.2	0.441	0.281	0.553	0.507	0.362

AST%	TOV%	OREB%	DREB%	STL%	BLK%
10.4	10.5	2.8	9.7	1.1	0.8

PER	ORTG	DRTG	WS/48	BPM	VOL
10.67	111.5	114.6	0.073	-1.94	0.453

- Played limited minutes for the L.A. Clippers in his fourth NBA season
- Effectiveness significantly declined, mainly used as a low usage spot-up shooter and energy player
- True Shooting Percentage dropped to below 50% last season, made less than 30% of his threes last season
- League average career three-point shooter, primarily a stationary spot-up shooter
- Most effective at crashing to the rim on pick-and-rolls and transition plays, drew a lot of fouls
- Not really able to drive by defenders on isolations, needs a screen to get to the rim
- Catch-and-shoot player, decent secondary playmaker, good at avoiding turnovers
- 2022-23 Defensive Degree of Difficulty: 0.411
- 2022-23 Points Prevented: -0.909
- Usually guarded second unit players, drew a few tough assignments off the bench
- Played below average on-ball defense, struggled in one-on-one situations, better defender in previous seasons
- Fairly solid pick-and-roll defender, can switch and cut off penetration, tends to go too far under screens
- Tends to get caught on screens off the ball, not always in position to contest shots in spot-up situations
- Stay-at-home defender, rarely gets steals or blocks, below average defensive rebounder
- Was arrested on a firearms misdemeanor in the offseason

Brandon Boston Jr.

	Height	Weight	Cap #	Years Left
	6'7"	185	$1.836M	RFA

Similar at Age 21

		Season	SIMsc
1	Richard Hamilton	1999-00	915.4
2	Furkan Korkmaz	2018-19	915.3
3	James Bouknight	2021-22	912.5
4	Manny Harris	2010-11	911.8
5	Alec Burks	2012-13	907.4
6	Antonio Blakeney	2017-18	904.6
7	Ricky Ledo	2013-14	903.6
8	Kevin Martin	2004-05	902.3
9	Jamal Crawford	2001-02	900.7
10	Malachi Richardson	2016-17	895.3

Baseline Basic Stats

MPG	PTS	AST	REB	BLK	STL
24.0	11.9	2.0	2.7	0.2	0.7

Advanced Metrics

USG%	3PTA/FGA	FTA/FGA	TS%	eFG%	3PT%
23.7	0.214	0.288	0.527	0.479	0.358

AST%	TOV%	OREB%	DREB%	STL%	BLK%
14.4	10.4	2.5	10.4	1.5	0.6

PER	ORTG	DRTG	WS/48	BPM	VOL
13.58	104.7	113.8	0.054	-1.45	0.508

- Played sparingly for the L.A. Clippers in his second NBA season, missed games due to a tailbone injury
- Increased his effectiveness in limited action as a high usage scoring guard off the bench
- Below break-even career three-point shooter, made over 41% of his threes in a small sample of attempts
- Shooting stroke may still be inconsistent, struggled to make jumpers on spot-ups and pick-and-rolls, most effective in transition or on broken plays
- Athletic finisher in transition, willing to draw fouls, inconsistent when trying to score off the dribble
- Improving as a secondary playmaker, rarely turns the ball over
- 2022-23 Defensive Degree of Difficulty: 0.313
- 2022-23 Points Prevented: 0.209
- Mostly guarded lower leverage second unit players or played in garbage time
- Rarely tested on the ball, decent on-ball defender in limited action, can stay with perimeter players, struggled against stronger players due to his thin frame
- Played solid pick-and-roll defense, funnels his man into help, effective at containing ball handlers
- Takes bad gambles, gets caught on screens, usually was late to close out on spot-up shooters
- Can use his length to play passing lanes to get steals, did not block a shot last season, fairly solid defensive rebounder

Jason Preston

	Height	Weight	Cap #	Years Left
	6'4"	187	$1.836M	RFA

Similar at Age 23

		Season	SIMsc
1	Jamison Brewer	2003-04	885.5
2	Quinn Cook	2016-17	882.4
3	Daryl Macon	2018-19	876.6
4	Darius Morris	2013-14	868.5
5	Damon Jones	1999-00	868.0
6	Jordan Bone	2020-21	866.3
7	Cameron Payne	2017-18	860.8
8	Alex Acker	2005-06	857.6
9	Kendall Marshall	2014-15	852.5
10	Bryn Forbes	2016-17	850.6

Baseline Basic Stats

MPG	PTS	AST	REB	BLK	STL
17.0	5.8	2.4	1.9	0.1	0.5

Advanced Metrics

USG%	3PTA/FGA	FTA/FGA	TS%	eFG%	3PT%
17.5	0.429	0.106	0.501	0.497	0.305

AST%	TOV%	OREB%	DREB%	STL%	BLK%
25.6	15.3	2.0	14.3	1.3	0.2

PER	ORTG	DRTG	WS/48	BPM	VOL
11.31	104.2	114.1	0.043	-1.94	0.231

- Split time between the L.A. Clippers and the Ontario Clippers in the G-League, played very sparingly for the L.A. Clippers
- Mainly used as a pass-first playmaker in both leagues, played a lower usage role in the NBA
- Unselfish playmaker that can distribute the ball to open teammates, somewhat turnover prone
- Made over 38% of his threes in the G-League, struggled to shoot efficiently in the NBA
- Primarily a stand-still spot-up shooter at this stage, not really able to shoot off screens or off the dribble
- Limited ability to score in ball handling situations, struggles to drive all the way to the rim
- 2022-23 Defensive Degree of Difficulty: 0.238
- 2022-23 Points Prevented: -3.756
- Mainly played in garbage time, very rarely tested on the ball in games
- Struggled in a very small sample of one-on-one possessions at the NBA level
- Effective in limited action as a pick-and-roll defender, not really able to switch, good at funneling his man into help
- Tended to get caught on screens off the ball, good at closing out on spot-up shooters
- Generally a stay-at-home defender, occasionally can get steals, solid defensive rebounder

Newcomers

Kobe Brown

	Height	Weight	Cap #	Years Left
	6'7"	250	$2.413M	1 + 2 TO

Baseline Basic Stats

MPG	PTS	AST	REB	BLK	STL
18.0	6.7	1.2	3.0	0.3	0.7

Advanced Metrics

USG%	3PTA/FGA	FTA/FGA	TS%	eFG%	3PT%
17.8	0.317	0.261	0.522	0.487	0.332

AST%	TOV%	OREB%	DREB%	STL%	BLK%
10.5	12.0	5.6	13.6	1.9	1.2

PER	ORTG	DRTG	WS/48	BPM	VOL
12.98	104.1	103.9	0.066	-1.68	N/A

- Drafted by the L.A. Clippers with the 30th overall pick in 2023
- Had a strong showing at the Las Vegas Summer League
- Highly effective in his role as a moderate volume scoring combo forward, likely will play a lower usage role in the NBA
- Had a True Shooting Percentage of almost 58%, went 13-for-30 (43.3%) on threes
- Good spot-up shooter, also effective as a pick-and-pop screener
- Good at using his strength to bully weaker defenders on post-ups, lacks ideal quickness to consistently create his own shot on isolations
- Energetic rim runner, good roll man and cutter, willing to crash the offensive boards to score on put-backs, runs hard in transition, draws fouls at a solid rate
- Flashes solid secondary playmaking skills, can make reads in the short roll game, rarely turns the ball over
- Has good quickness and length to compensate for his lack vertical pop, fairly effective defender in college
- Can potentially guard multiple positions, quick enough to stay with perimeter players, stout post defender, lacks ideal height to effectively contest shots inside
- More effective at defending pick-and-rolls at Summer League, could functionally switch, made fairly sound rotations
- Consistently will close out on spot-up shooters, willing to fight through screens
- Very active weak side defender, posted high steal and block rates at Summer League, good defensive rebounder
- May be polished enough to push for a rotation spot as soon as this coming season

MINNESOTA TIMBERWOLVES

Last Season: 42 - 40, Lost 1st Round to Denver (1 – 4)

Offensive Rating: 113.7, 23rd in the NBA   Defensive Rating: 113.8, 10th in the NBA

Primary Executive: Tim Connelly, President of Basketball Operations/General Manager

Head Coach: Chris Finch

Key Roster Changes

Subtractions
Taurean Prince, waived
Jaylen Nowell, free agency
Austin Rivers, free agency
Nathan Knight, free agency

Additions
Leonard Miller, draft
Shake Milton, free agency
Troy Brown Jr., free agency

Roster

Likely Starting Five
1. *Mike Conley*
2. *Anthony Edwards*
3. *Jaden McDaniels*
4. *Karl-Anthony Towns*
5. *Rudy Gobert*

Other Key Rotation Players
Kyle Anderson
Naz Reid
Nickeil Alexander-Walker
Shake Milton
Troy Brown Jr.

* Italics denotes that a player is likely to be on the floor to close games

Remaining Roster

- Jordan McLaughlin
- Leonard Miller
- Wendell Moore Jr.
- Josh Minott
- Luka Garza, 25, 6'11", 235, Iowa (Two-Way)
- Jaylen Clark, 22, 6'5", 205, UCLA (Two-Way)

SCHREMPF Base Rating: 44.7

Season Preview Survey

- *Are the Timberwolves contending or rebuilding? Where is this team headed?*

The Timberwolves are trying to win and advance deep into the playoffs, but the vision to get to that point is unclear at best. They committed a significant number of resources to land Rudy Gobert last offseason, but they didn't really get the opportunity to fully integrate him into the complete version of their team. This was mainly due to the complications that arose from Karl-Anthony Towns' calf strain, which caused him to miss four months of last season. It's still uncertain as to what direction they will trend in if they go through this season at full strength. If things work out as they had initially planned, then they could earn a guaranteed playoff berth. Otherwise, they might wind up in the same place as a back-end playoff seed or a play-in berth this season.

- *What are the areas of concern for this team heading into this season?*

The biggest concern for Minnesota is simply how they will fit together. Gobert and Towns have played as centers for the bulk of their careers, so this presents a number of challenges to get them coexist on both ends. They were only effective to a slightly above average degree in the limited number of minutes that they played together. They had issues with incompatibility on both ends, and they tended to play better when they were separated. They will need to figure out some sort of scheme to allow both players to maximize their production. Even so, there's another question about which player is the optimal player to build around because Anthony Edwards is arguably their most valuable player. After all, he's much younger than Gobert and Towns, so he's in the upswing phase of his career. Rather than try to keep fitting these square pegs into round holes, they may need to step back and assess their situation to see if there is a better way to build a team that puts the best talent around Edwards to amplify his abilities.

- *List some possible breakout players for this team.*

The back-end players on Minnesota's roster are still pretty raw, and they are in need of some extra seasoning to improve their games. Leonard Miller played well at Summer League because he showed that he could utilize his athleticism to make plays on both ends. However, his outside shot is still a work-in-progress. He might not be able to effectively fit in with their main lineups right away, so he will need to spend a little bit of time back in the G-League to improve this skill. Along those lines, Wendell Moore Jr. and Josh Minott could also use extra seasoning to polish up their games. If they get a breakthrough from their rotation, it will be because either Edwards or Jaden McDaniels improved to reach another level. It's possible because both players are still young and have room to grow. If they increase their efficiency or add some new skills, they could give their team a bigger boost to help them win more games.

- *What should we expect from them this season?*

In all probability, Minnesota is going to be in the mix to earn a guaranteed playoff spot. At this stage, it's unclear as to how high their ceiling is because their primary starting unit hasn't been together for very long and they are still working out the details on how to make their unique roster construction work. On the flip side, their floor is pretty high because they have a good enough base of talent to consistently win regular season games, even if their team has moments where they appear disjointed. At worst, they should be a play-in team that winds up coming away with a lower playoff seed. The key for them is to sort out the schematic issues that are involved with making their team fit together. If they can iron out those issues, they could raise their ceiling to become a contending team in the future. Otherwise, they will remain as they are and be maxed out as a mid-tier playoff team in the West.

Veterans

Anthony Edwards

	Height	Weight	Cap #	Years Left
	6'4"	225	$13.535M	5

Similar at Age 21

		Season	SIMsc
1	Donovan Mitchell	2017-18	934.4
2	Jamal Murray	2018-19	903.3
3	O.J. Mayo	2008-09	898.7
4	Dion Waiters	2012-13	897.3
5	Quentin Richardson	2001-02	893.6
6	Paul Pierce*	1998-99	893.2
7	Eric Gordon	2009-10	892.3
8	Jayson Tatum	2019-20	891.4
9	Jerry Stackhouse	1995-96	889.4
10	Talen Horton-Tucker	2021-22	889.3

Baseline Basic Stats

MPG	PTS	AST	REB	BLK	STL
33.9	19.4	3.5	4.4	0.4	1.2

Advanced Metrics

USG%	3PTA/FGA	FTA/FGA	TS%	eFG%	3PT%
26.1	0.279	0.266	0.547	0.509	0.345

AST%	TOV%	OREB%	DREB%	STL%	BLK%
18.0	12.6	2.4	12.5	1.9	1.1

PER	ORTG	DRTG	WS/48	BPM	VOL
15.69	106.6	112.3	0.075	0.84	0.244

- Named to his first All-Star team in his third season in the NBA
- Excelled as Minnesota's primary scoring option
- Good pick-and-roll ball handler and isolation player, good at driving downhill to attack the rim
- Effectively makes enough threes off the dribble to keep defenders honest, solid overall three-point shooter
- Excellent at making spot-up threes, still inefficient when shooting off screens
- Explosive athlete, finishes way above the rim in transition, sometimes drives out of control when he's at full speed
- Fairly good secondary playmaker that makes simple reads, solid at avoiding turnovers
- 2022-23 Defensive Degree of Difficulty: 0.475
- 2022-23 Points Prevented: 0.618
- Took on more difficult assignments against starters, played average on-ball defense
- Had some trouble against taller wings, tended to back off his man on the perimeter
- Decent on-ball defender, can switch and contain ball handlers, has some lapses when rotating onto screeners
- Stays attached to shooters off the ball, fights through screens and closes out in spot-up situations
- Active help defender, consistently gets steals, solid weak side shot blocker, solid defensive rebounder

Rudy Gobert

	Height	Weight	Cap #	Years Left
	7'1"	258	$41.000M	1 + PO

Similar at Age 30

		Season	SIMsc
1	Tyson Chandler	2012-13	904.5
2	DeAndre Jordan	2018-19	896.5
3	Dwight Howard	2015-16	892.9
4	Brendan Haywood	2009-10	892.9
5	Dikembe Mutombo*	1996-97	875.9
6	Mason Plumlee	2020-21	866.8
7	Samuel Dalembert	2011-12	866.3
8	Ervin Johnson	1997-98	866.2
9	Joel Przybilla	2009-10	863.1
10	Erick Dampier	2005-06	862.0

Baseline Basic Stats

MPG	PTS	AST	REB	BLK	STL
27.9	10.5	1.1	10.2	1.4	0.5

Advanced Metrics

USG%	3PTA/FGA	FTA/FGA	TS%	eFG%	3PT%
15.9	0.005	0.632	0.659	0.640	0.072

AST%	TOV%	OREB%	DREB%	STL%	BLK%
5.9	16.1	12.0	30.7	1.0	4.3

PER	ORTG	DRTG	WS/48	BPM	VOL
19.19	124.1	104.5	0.180	1.85	0.360

- Regular starting center for Minnesota in his first season with the team
- Production level declined a bit, still effective as a low usage rim runner
- Vertical lob threat, has posted a True Shooting Percentage above 65% in each of the last seven seasons
- Great roll man and cutter, good offensive rebounder, runs hard in transition, draws fouls at a very high rate
- Great at flashing to the middle on post-ups, less effective with his back to the basket on either block
- Lacks reliable shooting range outside of three feet, has made less than 65% of his career free throws
- Catch-and-finish player, limited as a passer, decent ability to avoid turnovers
- 2022-23 Defensive Degree of Difficulty: 0.457
- 2022-23 Points Prevented: 2.161
- Great rim protector, great shot blocker but block rate was down, excellent defensive rebounder
- Usually guarded starting level centers, stout post defender, has trouble when defending in space
- Decent pick-and-roll defender, great in drop coverages, can struggle to contain ball handlers on the perimeter
- Consistently would come out to the perimeter to contest spot-up jumpers

Karl-Anthony Towns

	Height	Weight	Cap #	Years Left
	6'11"	248	$36.016M	4

Similar at Age 27

		Season	SIMsc
1	Troy Murphy	2007-08	908.2
2	Nikola Vucevic	2017-18	900.2
3	Spencer Hawes	2015-16	899.4
4	Mehmet Okur	2006-07	894.1
5	Blake Griffin	2016-17	890.5
6	Andray Blatche	2013-14	888.8
7	Greg Monroe	2017-18	885.7
8	Julius Randle	2021-22	881.4
9	Cody Zeller	2019-20	881.3
10	Marreese Speights	2014-15	880.9

Baseline Basic Stats

MPG	PTS	AST	REB	BLK	STL
28.6	15.6	2.6	7.4	0.6	0.7

Advanced Metrics

USG%	3PTA/FGA	FTA/FGA	TS%	eFG%	3PT%
24.5	0.392	0.323	0.610	0.562	0.387

AST%	TOV%	OREB%	DREB%	STL%	BLK%
17.3	13.0	6.5	23.0	1.2	1.8

PER	ORTG	DRTG	WS/48	BPM	VOL
19.63	118.1	111.3	0.153	2.20	0.492

- Missed most of last season due to a strained right calf
- Effectiveness as Minnesota's main interior scoring option declined a bit
- Reliable three-point shooter, has made 39.5% of his career threes
- Normally a good spot-up shooter, still very effective when shooting off screens or pick-and-pops
- Effective rim runner, good roll man and cutter, draws fouls at a solid rate
- High volume scorer in the post, good at making hook shots on the left block
- Less effective when driving on isolation plays, may have been slowed by the injury
- Great passing big man that finds open shooters and cutters, slightly turnover prone
- 2022-23 Defensive Degree of Difficulty: 0.375
- 2022-23 Points Prevented: 0.874
- Used as a roaming help defender, moved to lower leverage matchups
- Solid rim protector despite a diminished block rate, stays vertical to contest shots, good defensive rebounder
- Better on-ball defender against lower leverage players, solid in the post, mobile enough to defend in space
- Average pick-and-roll defender, good in drop coverages, has trouble containing ball handlers on the perimeter
- Consistently comes out to the perimeter to contest spot-up jumpers

Mike Conley

	Height	Weight	Cap #	Years Left
	6'1"	175	$24.360M	UFA

Similar at Age 35

		Season	SIMsc
1	Jason Terry	2012-13	938.7
2	Tim Hardaway*	2001-02	936.7
3	Darrell Armstrong	2003-04	920.3
4	Kyle Lowry	2021-22	913.3
5	Danny Ainge	1994-95	911.1
6	Bobby Jackson	2008-09	910.0
7	Lou Williams	2021-22	901.6
8	Joe Dumars*	1998-99	899.4
9	Terry Porter	1998-99	897.0
10	Chris Paul	2020-21	896.9

Baseline Basic Stats

MPG	PTS	AST	REB	BLK	STL
22.6	9.4	4.4	2.3	0.2	0.9

Advanced Metrics

USG%	3PTA/FGA	FTA/FGA	TS%	eFG%	3PT%
18.3	0.458	0.242	0.556	0.518	0.381

AST%	TOV%	OREB%	DREB%	STL%	BLK%
27.0	14.5	2.1	8.8	1.9	0.7

PER	ORTG	DRTG	WS/48	BPM	VOL
14.38	116.4	112.7	0.122	1.28	0.465

- Traded from Utah to Minnesota at the trade deadline, regular starting point guard for both teams
- Maintained his usual efficiency level, adapted to a new role as a low usage pass-first point guard
- Steady veteran distributor, good playmaker that can run a team, good ball control guard that limits turnovers
- Reliable three-point shooter throughout his career, excellent shooter in the corners
- Most effective when shooting off the catch, makes spot-up jumpers, good at running off screens
- A step slower due to his age, needs a screen to create separation or drive downhill in ball handling situations
- Inconsistent shooter off the dribble, less effective as an isolation player, better on pick-and-rolls
- 2022-23 Defensive Degree of Difficulty: 0.493
- 2022-23 Points Prevented: -0.141
- Drew a lot of tough assignments against elite guards, fairly solid on-ball defender despite size limitations
- Still quick enough to stay with opposing guards, taller perimeter players could shoot over him
- Decent pick-and-roll defender, generally makes sound rotations, had lapses while adjusting to different coverages in Minnesota
- Sometimes gets caught on screens off the ball, good at closing out on spot-up shooters
- Still posts solid a Steal Percentage, below average defensive rebounder

Jaden McDaniels

	Height	Weight	Cap #	Years Left
	6'9"	185	$3.901M	RFA

Similar at Age 22

		Season	SIMsc
1	Otto Porter	2015-16	915.1
2	Nicolas Batum	2010-11	904.9
3	Kevin Martin	2005-06	891.9
4	Hollis Thompson	2013-14	891.5
5	Reggie Miller*	1987-88	887.8
6	Furkan Korkmaz	2019-20	886.1
7	Harrison Barnes	2014-15	883.6
8	Austin Daye	2010-11	883.2
9	Terrence Ross	2013-14	882.9
10	Maurice Harkless	2015-16	882.8

Baseline Basic Stats

MPG	PTS	AST	REB	BLK	STL
28.4	11.7	1.9	4.2	0.5	0.9

Advanced Metrics

USG%	3PTA/FGA	FTA/FGA	TS%	eFG%	3PT%
16.8	0.424	0.205	0.590	0.562	0.385

AST%	TOV%	OREB%	DREB%	STL%	BLK%
9.8	11.3	3.5	12.1	1.6	2.1

PER	ORTG	DRTG	WS/48	BPM	VOL
13.25	113.6	112.4	0.103	-0.38	0.446

- Started all but three games for Minnesota in his third NBA season
- Continued to improve in his role as a low volume spot-up shooter and energy player
- Made almost 40% of his threes, around a league average three-point shooter for his career
- Primarily a stand-still shooter that makes spot-up jumpers and threes in transition, occasionally shoots off screens
- Athletic finisher, great at running the floor in transition, good cutter and roll man
- Needs a screen to create separation in ball handling situations, solid scorer on pick-and-rolls
- Catch-and-shoot player, only makes safe passes, rarely turns the ball over
- 2022-23 Defensive Degree of Difficulty: 0.583, had the 8th most difficult set of matchups in the NBA
- 2022-23 Points Prevented: 0.556
- Became Minnesota's primary defensive stopper last season, fairly good on-ball defender
- Long and active defender that can pressure opposing perimeter players, has trouble with stronger players inside due to his thin frame
- Played below average pick-and-roll defense, not effective at taking away any specific action
- Fights through screens off the ball, sometimes will be late when closing out on spot-up shooters
- Steal Percentage increased slightly, good weak side shot blocker, decent defensive rebounder

Kyle Anderson

	Height	Weight	Cap #	Years Left
	6'9"	230	$9.220M	UFA

Similar at Age 29

		Season	SIMsc
1	Andrei Kirilenko	2010-11	919.6
2	James Johnson	2016-17	916.7
3	Pete Chilcutt	1997-98	916.0
4	Robert Horry	1999-00	903.6
5	Jorge Garbajosa	2006-07	900.6
6	Marvin Williams	2015-16	898.6
7	Rudy Gay	2015-16	897.7
8	Matt Barnes	2009-10	897.4
9	Jeff Green	2015-16	897.0
10	Josh Smith	2014-15	896.7

Baseline Basic Stats

MPG	PTS	AST	REB	BLK	STL
24.9	8.8	2.4	5.2	0.7	0.9

Advanced Metrics

USG%	3PTA/FGA	FTA/FGA	TS%	eFG%	3PT%
15.8	0.258	0.263	0.545	0.515	0.375

AST%	TOV%	OREB%	DREB%	STL%	BLK%
17.2	13.7	4.9	18.1	1.8	2.5

PER	ORTG	DRTG	WS/48	BPM	VOL
14.23	113.2	109.4	0.102	1.39	0.334

- Played starter level minutes for Minnesota in his first season with the team
- Increased his effectiveness in a role as a low usage secondary playmaker
- Very good playmaking forward, good set-up man in the hand-off game, finds open shooters and cutters, slightly turnover prone
- Above break-even career three-point shooter, made 41% of his threes last season
- Strictly a stationary spot-up shooter, needs an extra split second to get a clean shot away
- Energetic rim runner, good cutter and roll man, selectively goes to the glass to score on put-backs
- Can change speeds to drive to the rim as a ball handler, not really able to make jumpers off the dribble
- 2022-23 Defensive Degree of Difficulty: 0.462
- 2022-23 Points Prevented: -0.411
- Drew some tough assignments against starting level players, average on-ball defender
- Can capably guard multiple positions, has some trouble against stronger or quicker players
- Good pick-and-roll defender, can effectively switch to guard ball handlers or screeners
- Stays attached to shooters off the ball, fights through screens and closes out in spot-up situations
- Active help defender, gets steals at a solid rate, effective weak side shot blocker, solid defensive rebounder

Naz Reid

	Height	Weight	Cap #	Years Left
	6'9"	264	$12.950M	1 + PO

Similar at Age 23

		Season	SIMsc
1	Richaun Holmes	2016-17	903.9
2	Victor Alexander	1992-93	891.4
3	Kevin Seraphin	2012-13	886.1
4	Mfiondu Kabengele	2020-21	880.2
5	Terrence Jones	2014-15	878.3
6	Andrew Nicholson	2012-13	877.6
7	John Collins	2020-21	874.0
8	Derrick Favors	2014-15	874.0
9	Jahlil Okafor	2018-19	871.4
10	Chimezie Metu	2020-21	870.8

Baseline Basic Stats

MPG	PTS	AST	REB	BLK	STL
21.8	10.3	1.2	5.5	0.8	0.6

Advanced Metrics

USG%	3PTA/FGA	FTA/FGA	TS%	eFG%	3PT%
22.7	0.267	0.245	0.576	0.551	0.344

AST%	TOV%	OREB%	DREB%	STL%	BLK%
9.6	11.6	7.5	20.9	1.4	3.4

PER	ORTG	DRTG	WS/48	BPM	VOL
17.39	110.5	108.6	0.117	-0.05	0.473

- Regular rotation player for Minnesota in his fourth NBA season
- Had his most productive season in a role as a moderate volume stretch big and rim runner off the bench
- Consistently an above break-even three-point shooter for his career
- Mainly a stationary spot-up shooter, occasionally makes pick-and-pop jumpers, can make threes in transition
- High motor rim runner, good roll man and cutter, selectively goes to the glass to score on put-backs, good at running the floor in transition
- Not really a post-up threat, passing skills have improved, good at avoiding turnovers
- 2022-23 Defensive Degree of Difficulty: 0.401
- 2022-23 Points Prevented: 0.011
- Good rim protector, good at blocking shots and grabbing defensive rebounds
- Usually guards second unit big men or lower leverage starters, average on-ball defender
- Can be overpowered by stronger big men, tends to commit shooting fouls inside, better at using his mobility to defend in space
- Solid pick-and-roll defender, good in drop coverage, effective at hedging out on ball handlers
- Tends to sag back into the paint, does not always come out to contest outside shots
- Has active hands, can use his length to play passing lanes and get steals

Nickeil Alexander-Walker

	Height	Weight	Cap #	Years Left
	6'6"	205	$4.688M	1

Similar at Age 24

		Season	SIMsc
1	PJ Dozier	2020-21	941.7
2	Rodney Carney	2008-09	935.3
3	George McCloud	1991-92	927.7
4	Ben McLemore	2017-18	922.0
5	Marko Guduric	2019-20	920.2
6	Norman Powell	2017-18	919.6
7	Damyean Dotson	2018-19	918.6
8	Danny Green	2011-12	918.5
9	Josh Jackson	2021-22	916.5
10	Caris LeVert	2018-19	916.5

Baseline Basic Stats

MPG	PTS	AST	REB	BLK	STL
22.2	9.5	2.0	2.8	0.3	0.7

Advanced Metrics

USG%	3PTA/FGA	FTA/FGA	TS%	eFG%	3PT%
20.3	0.514	0.198	0.535	0.505	0.354

AST%	TOV%	OREB%	DREB%	STL%	BLK%
15.5	12.2	2.3	11.4	1.6	1.5

PER	ORTG	DRTG	WS/48	BPM	VOL
12.15	106.3	113.3	0.057	-1.06	0.326

- Traded from Utah to Minnesota, fringe rotation player for both teams, started in the playoffs
- Increased his effectiveness in a role as a low volume spot-up shooter
- Made over 38% of his threes last season, around a break-even career three-point shooter
- Mainly a stationary spot-up shooter, flashed some ability to make pull-up threes on pick-and-rolls
- Inconsistent shooter off the dribble, needs a screen to create space for himself, better at scoring off pick-and-rolls
- Fairly solid secondary playmaker that makes simple reads, solid at avoiding turnovers
- 2022-23 Defensive Degree of Difficulty: 0.465
- 2022-23 Points Prevented: 1.642
- Drew some tough assignments off the bench, usually guarded starting level players
- Improved to become a solid on-ball defender, guards multiple positions, can struggle against stronger wings
- Middling pick-and-roll defender, indecisive, had trouble containing ball handler, tended to have lapses when rotating onto screeners
- Fights through screens off the ball, sometimes would be late to close out on spot-up shooters
- Active weak side defender, gets steals and blocks at a good rate, decent defensive rebounder

Shake Milton

	Height	Weight	Cap #	Years Left
	6'5"	205	$5.000M	1

Similar at Age 26

		Season	SIMsc
1	Randy Foye	2009-10	940.6
2	Josh Richardson	2019-20	937.9
3	Voshon Lenard	1999-00	937.3
4	Rodney Stuckey	2012-13	932.4
5	Bryant Stith	1996-97	930.9
6	Malcolm Brogdon	2018-19	930.6
7	O.J. Mayo	2013-14	928.6
8	Bogdan Bogdanovic	2018-19	928.3
9	Fred Jones	2005-06	925.1
10	Sasha Danilovic	1996-97	924.7

Baseline Basic Stats

MPG	PTS	AST	REB	BLK	STL
25.5	10.6	2.5	2.8	0.2	0.8

Advanced Metrics

USG%	3PTA/FGA	FTA/FGA	TS%	eFG%	3PT%
19.2	0.348	0.208	0.541	0.503	0.358

AST%	TOV%	OREB%	DREB%	STL%	BLK%
17.8	12.2	2.5	10.5	1.3	0.8

PER	ORTG	DRTG	WS/48	BPM	VOL
12.44	109.1	112.5	0.082	-1.77	0.230

- Regular rotation player for Philadelphia in his fifth NBA season
- Raised his efficiency in a role as a low usage spot-up shooter and secondary ball handler
- Above average career three-point shooter, percentages have varied from year-to-year
- Predominantly a stand-still spot-up shooter, less effective when shooting in other situations
- More effective at driving to the rim when his shot is falling, average scorer in ball handling situations
- Solid cutter but played in a static offense, fairly good secondary playmaker, good at avoiding turnovers
- 2022-23 Defensive Degree of Difficulty: 0.354
- 2022-23 Points Prevented: -1.158
- Usually guarded second unit players, played fairly solid on-ball defense
- Effectively stays with opposing guards, has trouble defending stronger players inside
- Solid pick-and-roll defender, can switch to guard ball handlers and screeners, makes sound rotations
- Fights through screens off the ball, sometimes is late to close out on spot-up shooters
- Stay-at-home defender, rarely gets steals or blocks, decent defensive rebounder

Troy Brown Jr.

	Height	Weight	Cap #	Years Left
	6'6"	215	$4.000M	1

Similar at Age 23

		Season	SIMsc
1	Tony Snell	2014-15	932.0
2	Denzel Valentine	2016-17	929.3
3	Glenn Robinson III	2016-17	927.6
4	Allen Crabbe	2015-16	924.3
5	Chase Budinger	2011-12	924.2
6	Dorian Finney-Smith	2016-17	924.2
7	Josh Hart	2018-19	924.1
8	Austin Reaves	2021-22	921.3
9	Chris Johnson	2013-14	919.4
10	Henry Walker	2010-11	917.3

Baseline Basic Stats

MPG	PTS	AST	REB	BLK	STL
23.8	8.7	1.7	3.5	0.3	0.7

Advanced Metrics

USG%	3PTA/FGA	FTA/FGA	TS%	eFG%	3PT%
15.0	0.577	0.149	0.558	0.535	0.376

AST%	TOV%	OREB%	DREB%	STL%	BLK%
9.8	9.9	3.2	14.6	1.4	0.7

PER	ORTG	DRTG	WS/48	BPM	VOL
11.25	112.3	113.2	0.084	-0.86	0.440

- Regular rotation player for the L.A. Lakers in his first season with the team, started most of his games
- Solidly effective in his role as a very low volume spot-up shooter
- Above break-even career three-point shooter, made over 38% of his threes last season
- Predominantly a stand-still spot-up shooter, around break-even when shooting in other situations
- Athletic finisher, will run the break in transition, good cutter off the ball
- Limited ability to create his own shot, occasionally could drive to the rim on a small sample of isolations
- Mainly a catch-and-shoot player, only makes safe passes, rarely turns the ball over
- 2022-23 Defensive Degree of Difficulty: 0.477
- 2022-23 Points Prevented: 0.056
- Guarded starting level players, drew a lot of tough assignments against higher-end wing players
- Played fairly solid on-ball defense, guards multiple positions, has some trouble staying with quicker players
- Solid pick-and-roll defender, can effectively switch to guard ball handlers and screeners
- Fights through screens off the ball, sometimes will be late when closing out on spot-up shooters
- Slightly less active as a help defender, gets steals at a moderate rate, fairly solid defensive rebounder

Jordan McLaughlin

	Height	Weight	Cap #	Years Left
	5'11"	185	$2.320M	UFA

Similar at Age 26

		Season	SIMsc
1	Brandon Goodwin	2021-22	904.1
2	Travis Diener	2008-09	897.7
3	Isaiah Canaan	2017-18	892.6
4	Yogi Ferrell	2019-20	891.6
5	Scott Brooks	1991-92	891.5
6	Patty Mills	2014-15	890.9
7	Chris Quinn	2009-10	890.0
8	Jerian Grant	2018-19	887.4
9	A.J. Price	2012-13	887.2
10	Travis Best	1998-99	886.9

Baseline Basic Stats

MPG	PTS	AST	REB	BLK	STL
20.0	7.2	3.5	1.8	0.1	0.8

Advanced Metrics

USG%	3PTA/FGA	FTA/FGA	TS%	eFG%	3PT%
15.0	0.442	0.219	0.544	0.510	0.357

AST%	TOV%	OREB%	DREB%	STL%	BLK%
27.2	15.4	2.3	8.2	2.1	0.6

PER	ORTG	DRTG	WS/48	BPM	VOL
13.69	116.3	112.9	0.097	0.05	0.622

- Minutes decreased in his fourth season with Minnesota, playing time was limited last season
- Less effective in his role as a very low usage, game managing backup point guard
- Good distributor that can run a team, usually makes sound decision, somewhat turnover prone last season
- Below break-even three-point shooter last season, has made almost 42% of his career corner threes
- Struggled to make stand-still spot-up jumpers, rarely took shots in other situations
- Rated by Synergy as being average or worse in almost every offensive situation
- Defenders could back off him to limit his effectiveness as a pick-and-roll ball handler or isolation player
- 2022-23 Defensive Degree of Difficulty: 0.345
- 2022-23 Points Prevented: -0.865
- Usually guards second unit players, rarely tested on the ball
- Played solid on-ball defense in a small sample of possessions, passably guards ones and twos in lower leverage matchups
- Decent pick-and-roll defender, limited ability to switch due to size limitations, funnels his man into help
- Tends to get caught on screens off the ball, usually a step late when closing out on spot-up shooters
- Pesky defender, can pressure ball handlers and play passing lanes, gets steals at a high rate, below average defensive rebounder

Wendell Moore Jr.

	Height	Weight	Cap #	Years Left
	6'5"	213	$2.422M	2 TO

Similar at Age 21

		Season	SIMsc
1	Christian Eyenga	2010-11	913.8
2	Lance Stephenson	2011-12	906.8
3	Jay Scrubb	2021-22	906.6
4	Vincent Yarbrough	2002-03	894.7
5	Allen Crabbe	2013-14	894.5
6	Willie Warren	2010-11	891.6
7	Nate Hinton	2020-21	891.1
8	Malcolm Lee	2011-12	890.8
9	Shannon Brown	2006-07	890.3
10	Sergey Karasev	2014-15	890.2

Baseline Basic Stats

MPG	PTS	AST	REB	BLK	STL
17.8	6.0	1.5	2.4	0.2	0.7

Advanced Metrics

USG%	3PTA/FGA	FTA/FGA	TS%	eFG%	3PT%
15.1	0.321	0.175	0.507	0.482	0.229

AST%	TOV%	OREB%	DREB%	STL%	BLK%
14.5	14.4	3.0	10.9	2.1	1.4

PER	ORTG	DRTG	WS/48	BPM	VOL
10.05	103.9	111.1	0.072	-1.78	0.401

- Split time between Minnesota and Iowa in the G-League, played sparingly in the NBA as a rookie
- Used as a moderate volume spot-up shooter and secondary playmaker in the G-League, played a lower usage role in the NBA
- Struggled to shoot efficiently at the NBA level, solid three-point shooter in the G-League
- Mainly a stand-still spot-up shooter, percentages tended to vary with Iowa
- Not really used in ball handling situations, unproven ability to create his own shot
- Solid secondary playmaker in the G-League, showed good passing skills in limited NBA minutes, slightly turnover prone
- 2022-23 Defensive Degree of Difficulty: 0.337
- 2022-23 Points Prevented: -4.632
- Usually guarded second unit players or played in garbage time at the NBA level
- Had some trouble guarding perimeter players in one-on-one situations, committed untimely shooting fouls, better in a very small sample of possessions when defending in the post
- Decent pick-and-roll defender, could contain ball handlers, had lapses when rotating onto screeners
- Tends to get caught on screens, not always in position to contest shots in spot-up situations
- Posted high steal and block rates in limited NBA minutes, decent defensive rebounder

Josh Minott

	Height	Weight	Cap #	Years Left
	6'8"	205	$1.720M	1 + TO

Similar at Age 20

		Season	SIMsc
1	Travis Outlaw	2004-05	884.3
2	Greg Brown III	2021-22	882.2
3	Brandan Wright	2007-08	871.4
4	Gerald Green	2005-06	870.7
5	Anthony Randolph	2009-10	865.3
6	Wilson Chandler	2007-08	861.0
7	Alen Smailagić	2020-21	857.3
8	Paul George	2010-11	856.7
9	Antonis Fotsis	2001-02	853.8
10	Tobias Harris	2012-13	850.1

Baseline Basic Stats

MPG	PTS	AST	REB	BLK	STL
22.5	9.5	1.2	4.9	0.8	0.8

Advanced Metrics

USG%	3PTA/FGA	FTA/FGA	TS%	eFG%	3PT%
20.1	0.198	0.240	0.566	0.518	0.350

AST%	TOV%	OREB%	DREB%	STL%	BLK%
8.7	8.6	5.8	20.2	1.9	3.6

PER	ORTG	DRTG	WS/48	BPM	VOL
17.70	115.0	106.8	0.143	0.12	0.674

- Split time between Minnesota and Iowa in the G-League, played sparingly in the NBA as a rookie
- Mainly used by both teams as a rim running energy player, played a lower usage role in the NBA
- Good athlete that plays with high energy, made over 71% of his shots inside of three feet in the NBA
- Good cutter, selectively goes to the offensive glass to score on put-backs, plays out of control, can miss some easy shots in transition
- Average three-point shooter in the G-League, percentages tended to vary, could be rather streaky
- Mainly a stationary spot-up shooter at this stage, not really able to create his own offense
- Catch-and-shoot player, showed some passing skills in the G-League, rarely turns the ball over
- 2022-23 Defensive Degree of Difficulty: 0.250
- 2022-23 Points Prevented: 3.274
- Did not really play meaningful minutes in the NBA, mainly played in garbage time
- True defensive ability is still uncertain, struggled in a handful of possessions as an on-ball defender
- Played solid pick-and-roll defense, could effectively switch to defend ball handlers and screeners
- Fights through screens off the ball, tended to be late when closing out on spot-up shooters
- Active help defender, great weak side shot blocker, good at getting steals, good defensive rebounder

Newcomers

Leonard Miller

	Height	Weight	Cap #	Years Left
	6'10"	210	$1.800M	2 + TO

Baseline Basic Stats

MPG	PTS	AST	REB	BLK	STL
18.8	7.2	1.0	4.7	0.6	0.5

Advanced Metrics

USG%	3PTA/FGA	FTA/FGA	TS%	eFG%	3PT%
18.3	0.161	0.547	0.551	0.525	0.288

AST%	TOV%	OREB%	DREB%	STL%	BLK%
8.8	12.5	9.2	23.2	1.7	2.1

PER	ORTG	DRTG	WS/48	BPM	VOL
14.77	108.8	113.4	0.076	-0.31	0.650

- Drafted by San Antonio with the 33rd overall pick in 2023, traded to Minnesota
- Played well at the Las Vegas Summer League
- Highly effective in his role as a high usage scoring wing, likely will play a lower volume role in the NBA
- Shooting improved, posted a True Shooting Percentage above 54%, made almost 37% of his threes
- Mostly a stationary spot-up shooter at this stage, less effective when shooting in other situations
- Great athlete, has good quickness to attack the rim, willing to absorb contact to draw fouls
- Inconsistent shooter off dribble, may have some trouble creating his own offense at the NBA level
- Explosive finisher, good rim runner that can cut or roll to the rim, active offensive rebounder
- Fairly solid secondary playmaker, unselfish, willing to make the extra pass
- Not polished as a ball handler, tends to lose the ball a lot, somewhat turnover prone
- Great physical tools on the defensive end, potentially could be a plus-level defender with versatility
- Solidly defends multiple positions on the ball when he's fully engaged, lost focus in the G-League with the Ignite team due to their lack of competitiveness
- Decent pick-and-roll defender, capable of switching to guard ball handlers and screeners, has minor lapses when making rotations
- Tends to make bad gambles, gets caught out of position a lot, not always in a good spot to get around off-ball screens or close out on shooters
- Very active help defender, posted high steal and block rates at Summer League, good defensive rebounder

DENVER NUGGETS

Last Season: 53 - 29, 2022-23 NBA Champions

Offensive Rating: 117.6, 5th in the NBADefensive Rating: 114.2, 15th in the NBA

Primary Executive: Calvin Booth, General Manager

Head Coach: Michael Malone

Key Roster Changes

Subtractions
Bruce Brown, free agency
Jeff Green, free agency
Thomas Bryant, free agency
Ish Smith, free agency

Additions
Hunter Tyson, draft
Julian Strawther, draft
Jalen Pickett, draft
Justin Holiday, free agency

Roster

Likely Starting Five
1. Jamal Murray
2. Kentavious Caldwell-Pope
3. Michael Porter Jr.
4. Aaron Gordon
5. Nikola Jokić

Other Key Rotation Players
Christian Braun
Reggie Jackson
Vlatko Čančar (I) – torn ACL
Zeke Nnaji
DeAndre Jordan

* Italics denotes that a player is likely to be on the floor to close games

Remaining Roster

- Peyton Watson
- Justin Holiday
- Julian Strawther
- Jalen Pickett
- Hunter Tyson
- Braxton Key, 26, 6'8", 230, Virginia (Two-Way)
- Collin Gillespie, 24, 6'3", 195, Villanova (Two-Way)
- Jay Huff, 25, 7'1", 240, Virginia (Two-Way)
- Armaan Franklin, 22, 6'4", 195, Virginia (Exhibit 10)
- Andrew Funk, 24, 6'5", 200, Penn State (Exhibit 10)
- Souley Boom, 25, 6'3", 175, Xavier (Exhibit 10)

SCHREMPF Base Rating: 43.6

Season Preview Survey

- *Are the Nuggets contending or rebuilding? Where is this team headed?*

After winning the franchise's first championship last season, the Nuggets are looking to get back to the Finals and repeat. Things could be more difficult this time around because they will be going through this season with a less experienced bench. The future penalties in the newest version of the CBA caused them to let valuable reserves like Bruce Brown and Jeff Green sign with other teams. The Nuggets will need to depend on their internal development system to build up their young talent and make up for these departures. They also will have to lean more on their starters in the short-term to keep themselves in contention. If they can pull off the delicate balancing act of trying to win games now while developing young talent for the future, then they could make a push for second championship. Otherwise, they could be vulnerable, which could open the door for another team to get past them to win the West.

- *What are the areas of concern for this team heading into this season?*

The Nuggets have their entire starting five from last season's championship returning, so it would seem as if they don't have many issues. However, their unproven bench could be a concern for them this season. This could be true for a couple of reasons. On a micro level, it could be tougher for them to manage games because they don't know what they are getting from their second unit, as Christian Braun is the only holdover from last year's playoff bench rotation. They may have some stretches where they are outplayed by a better bench, which could force them to lean more heavily on their starters. This could pose another problem because Michael Porter Jr. has had serious injury history related to his multiple back surgeries. They are now highly dependent on him staying healthy for an entire season, which hasn't been something that he hasn't proved that he can do on a consistent basis. If he or some other starter gets injured, then they might suffer a drop-off that would seriously hurt their title chances. They will need to find ways to add another experienced role player or two to give them a better chance to defend their title.

- *List some possible breakout players for this team.*

On the flip side, the lack of experience of their bench provides a number of pathways for a young player to break out and become a greater contributor. Most notably, Christian Braun could step up his game to develop into a highly valuable sixth man that provides an impact similar to Bruce Brown in the sense that he would be able to defend, space the floor, move the ball, and inject some additional energy into the team. From there, Zeke Nnaji could take advantage of the additional playing time to play a role as additional three-point shooting threat at the five spot. On top of this, they might get a boost from one of their three rookies. They purposely chose polished players to make more of an immediate contribution. Julian Strawther and Hunter Tyson might step in to give them some more shooting on the wing while Jalen Pickett could be an extra ball handler on the floor. As it stands now, they have some young players that could surprise and play key roles if things work out for the Nuggets.

- *What should we expect from them this season?*

Overall, Denver still should be a leading contender to come out of the West because Nikola Jokic is still operating at the peak of his powers, and they have all of their top players in the fold. This should offset a lot of the concerns about their bench unit and its inexperience, so they should post another high regular season win total. However, the playoffs could be a different story because they don't have the same number of reliable options to counter opponents that they had last season, so it could be tougher to pull out a tight playoff series if things get close. If they can build up their bench either internally or with another move, they could solidify their chances of a repeat title this season.

Veterans

Nikola Jokić

	Height	Weight	Cap #	Years Left
	6'11"	284	$47.607M	4

Similar at Age 27

		Season	SIMsc
1	Jusuf Nurkić	2021-22	870.2
2	Joel Embiid	2021-22	854.0
3	DeMarcus Cousins	2017-18	852.3
4	Blake Griffin	2016-17	823.3
5	Giannis Antetokounmpo	2021-22	819.1
6	Andre Drummond	2020-21	817.9
7	Jonas Valančiūnas	2019-20	817.1
8	Chris Kaman	2009-10	814.6
9	Kevin Love	2015-16	810.2
10	Greg Monroe	2017-18	808.8

Baseline Basic Stats

MPG	PTS	AST	REB	BLK	STL
31.6	21.6	4.5	10.8	0.9	1.0

Advanced Metrics

USG%	3PTA/FGA	FTA/FGA	TS%	eFG%	3PT%
28.4	0.212	0.374	0.644	0.603	0.357

AST%	TOV%	OREB%	DREB%	STL%	BLK%
35.4	14.9	8.5	31.1	1.7	2.1

PER	ORTG	DRTG	WS/48	BPM	VOL
28.01	124.6	108.4	0.249	6.70	0.381

- 2022-23 NBA Finals MVP, named to the All-NBA 2nd Team
- Has the led the NBA in PER and Win Shares for three straight seasons, excels as Denver's primary scorer and playmaker
- Arguably the greatest passing center of all-time, extraordinary distributor with outstanding court vision
- Dominant post player that can bully weaker defenders and score with a variety of moves
- Great rim runner, very good as a roll man and cutter, active offensive rebounder
- Above break-even three-point shooter, good spot-up shooter and pick-and-pop screener
- Great at pushing the ball in transition, draws at a fairly high rate
- <u>2022-23 Defensive Degree of Difficulty</u>: 0.433
- <u>2022-23 Points Prevented</u>: -0.236
- Mild shot blocking threat, average rim protector, excellent defensive rebounder
- Defends starting big men, stout post defender, has trouble defending in space due to lumbering foot speed
- Decent pick-and-roll defender, willing to hedge out on ball handlers, a step slow when covering screeners
- Consistently comes out to contest shots in spot-up situations
- Has active hands, can play passing lanes to get steals at a high rate

Jamal Murray

	Height	Weight	Cap #	Years Left
	6'3"	215	$33.833M	1

Similar at Age 25

		Season	SIMsc
1	Eric Gordon	2013-14	933.2
2	Buddy Hield	2017-18	932.0
3	Bradley Beal	2018-19	924.5
4	Dion Waiters	2016-17	923.5
5	Beno Udrih	2007-08	918.2
6	Chauncey Billups	2001-02	917.7
7	Donovan Mitchell	2021-22	917.3
8	Randy Foye	2008-09	917.0
9	Shelvin Mack	2015-16	912.7
10	Jordan Crawford	2013-14	912.1

Baseline Basic Stats

MPG	PTS	AST	REB	BLK	STL
30.6	17.2	3.9	3.4	0.3	1.0

Advanced Metrics

USG%	3PTA/FGA	FTA/FGA	TS%	eFG%	3PT%
25.4	0.415	0.232	0.573	0.533	0.385

AST%	TOV%	OREB%	DREB%	STL%	BLK%
23.0	11.7	2.4	10.3	1.6	0.8

PER	ORTG	DRTG	WS/48	BPM	VOL
17.65	113.2	113.9	0.098	1.13	0.399

- Returned to regular starting duties after missing all of the 2021-22 season with a torn ACL
- Performed at a near All-Star level as a high usage scoring guard for Denver
- Fairly reliable three-point shooter, made almost 40% of his threes last season
- Great spot-up shooter, good at shooting off screens, fairly good when shooting off the dribble
- Good pick-and-roll ball handler and isolation player, can effectively score at all three levels
- Shows excellent chemistry with Nikola Jokic in the hand-off game, solid cutter
- Good playmaker that makes the right read, effectively limits turnovers
- 2022-23 Defensive Degree of Difficulty: 0.451
- 2022-23 Points Prevented: -0.766
- Drew tougher assignments before the ACL injury, eased into less difficult matchups last season
- Less effective as an on-ball defender, had trouble staying with opposing guards, struggled against taller players
- Decent pick-and-roll defender, can fight over the screen to contain ball handlers, had lapses when switched onto a screener
- Sometimes gets caught on screens off the ball, good at closing out on spot-up shooters
- Steal Percentage decreased slightly, fairly solid defensive rebounder

Aaron Gordon

	Height	Weight	Cap #	Years Left
	6'8"	235	$22.266M	1 + PO

Similar at Age 27

		Season	SIMsc
1	Kenny Gattison	1991-92	914.5
2	Tobias Harris	2019-20	911.1
3	Ken Norman	1991-92	909.3
4	Trevor Booker	2014-15	905.4
5	LaPhonso Ellis	1997-98	904.0
6	Montrezl Harrell	2020-21	902.7
7	Antoine Walker	2003-04	902.5
8	Sam Perkins	1988-89	901.6
9	Ersan Ilyasova	2014-15	900.4
10	Kenyon Martin	2004-05	899.4

Baseline Basic Stats

MPG	PTS	AST	REB	BLK	STL
27.6	12.6	2.0	5.6	0.6	0.7

Advanced Metrics

USG%	3PTA/FGA	FTA/FGA	TS%	eFG%	3PT%
20.5	0.269	0.328	0.572	0.543	0.338

AST%	TOV%	OREB%	DREB%	STL%	BLK%
13.2	11.4	7.1	16.0	1.3	1.7

PER	ORTG	DRTG	WS/48	BPM	VOL
16.16	114.1	112.1	0.102	0.19	0.294

- Regular starting forward for Denver in his second full season with the team
- Had a near All-Star level season in a role as a moderate volume energy player
- Excels as a rim runner, explosive finisher, vertical lob threat, good offensive rebounder, great cutter and roll man, excellent transition player
- Effective at posting up smaller players or driving by slower big men on isolation plays
- Above break-even three-point shooter last season, typically a below break-even career three-point shooter
- Mainly a spot-up shooter, showed some ability to make pick-and-pop threes
- Good secondary playmaker, finds open teammates in the short roll game, rarely turns the ball over
- 2022-23 Defensive Degree of Difficulty: 0.531
- 2022-23 Points Prevented: 0.740
- Used as Denver's primary defensive stopper, solid on-ball defender
- More effective when guarding big men inside, has a little bit of trouble staying with quicker perimeter players
- Fairly solid pick-and-roll defender, good in drop coverages, sometimes allows ball handlers to get penetration
- Tends to get caught on screens, good at closing out on spot-up shooters
- Good weak side shot blocker, does not really get steals, solid defensive rebounder

Michael Porter Jr.

	Height	Weight	Cap #	Years Left
	6'10"	218	$33.387M	3

Similar at Age 24

		Season	SIMsc
1	Vladimir Radmanovic	2004-05	931.5
2	Nikola Mirotic	2015-16	931.3
3	Matt Bullard	1991-92	926.8
4	Kyle Kuzma	2019-20	919.5
5	Rodney Hood	2016-17	916.3
6	Jake Layman	2018-19	915.8
7	Dean Wade	2020-21	914.3
8	Juan Hernangómez	2019-20	912.3
9	Dario Saric	2018-19	911.0
10	Taurean Prince	2018-19	909.7

Baseline Basic Stats

MPG	PTS	AST	REB	BLK	STL
23.5	10.5	1.4	4.5	0.4	0.6

Advanced Metrics

USG%	3PTA/FGA	FTA/FGA	TS%	eFG%	3PT%
20.9	0.490	0.185	0.560	0.532	0.357

AST%	TOV%	OREB%	DREB%	STL%	BLK%
8.5	9.0	4.4	18.1	1.3	1.3

PER	ORTG	DRTG	WS/48	BPM	VOL
14.60	110.5	112.3	0.088	-0.38	0.401

- Missed a month due to a bruised heel, regular starter for Denver when healthy
- Returned from a back injury, solidly effective as a moderate volume, off-ball scorer
- Almost a 42% career three-point shooter, has made almost 48% of his career corner threes
- Excellent spot-up shooter, able to make shots off screens, inconsistent shooter off the dribble
- Doesn't get to the rim regularly when he drives, better at pulling up from mid-range
- Good cutter, strictly a catch-and-shoot player, limited passing ability, rarely turns the ball over
- 2022-23 Defensive Degree of Difficulty: 0.408
- 2022-23 Points Prevented: 0.188
- Often hidden in favorable matchups against lower leverage players, played decent on-ball defense
- Can passably defend multiple positions, better when guarding interior players, has trouble staying with quicker perimeter players
- Solid pick-and-roll defender last season, can effectively switch or steer opponents into the inefficient areas of the court
- Tends to get caught on screens, usually is late to close out on spot-up shooters
- Generally a stay-at-home defender, did not really get steals or blocks, fairly good defensive rebounder
- Injury risk, has had multiple back surgeries since November 2017

Kentavious Caldwell-Pope

	Height	Weight	Cap #	Years Left
	6'5"	204	$14.705M	PO

Similar at Age 29

		Season	SIMsc
1	Courtney Lee	2014-15	954.8
2	Raja Bell	2005-06	943.6
3	Anthony Morrow	2014-15	930.9
4	Trent Tucker	1988-89	930.5
5	Randy Foye	2012-13	929.2
6	Damion Lee	2021-22	922.3
7	Wesley Matthews	2015-16	921.3
8	Justin Holiday	2018-19	921.0
9	Ime Udoka	2006-07	916.1
10	Greg Buckner	2005-06	915.5

Baseline Basic Stats

MPG	PTS	AST	REB	BLK	STL
25.7	9.2	1.9	2.8	0.3	0.8

Advanced Metrics

USG%	3PTA/FGA	FTA/FGA	TS%	eFG%	3PT%
15.7	0.483	0.184	0.558	0.525	0.388

AST%	TOV%	OREB%	DREB%	STL%	BLK%
10.4	10.6	1.9	9.7	1.8	1.0

PER	ORTG	DRTG	WS/48	BPM	VOL
11.15	110.3	112.7	0.076	-1.22	0.304

- Regular starter for Denver in his first season with the team
- Consistently effective in his role as a very low usage spot-up shooter
- Solid three-point shooter in his career, made over 42% of his threes last season
- Excels as a stand-still spot-up shooter, can effectively shoot off screens
- Lacks the ball handling skills to create his own shot, more effective with a screen
- Can make pull-up jumpers and occasionally get to the rim as a pick-and-roll ball handler
- Good cutter off the ball, catch-and-shoot player, willing to make the extra pass, rarely turns the ball over
- 2022-23 Defensive Degree of Difficulty: 0.517
- 2022-23 Points Prevented: -0.787
- Used as a defensive stopper in previous seasons, drew a lot of tough assignments against elite scorers
- Can capably guard multiple positions, slightly over-extended against top players last season
- Played below average pick-and-roll defense, not effective at taking away any specific action
- Tends to get caught on screens, sometimes was late to close out on spot-up shooters
- Active help defender, consistently gets steals at a high rate, can block shots on the weak side, below average defensive rebounder

Christian Braun

	Height	Weight	Cap #	Years Left
	6'7"	218	$2.949M	2 TO

Similar at Age 21

		Season	SIMsc
1	Kelly Oubre	2016-17	922.9
2	Kenyon Martin Jr.	2021-22	921.9
3	OG Anunoby	2018-19	921.4
4	Jumaine Jones	2000-01	920.0
5	Khris Middleton	2012-13	918.3
6	Justise Winslow	2017-18	918.3
7	Kawhi Leonard	2012-13	917.7
8	Kevin Knox	2020-21	912.3
9	Kessler Edwards	2021-22	911.1
10	Jaylen Brown	2017-18	910.6

Baseline Basic Stats

MPG	PTS	AST	REB	BLK	STL
24.6	9.1	1.4	3.8	0.4	0.8

Advanced Metrics

USG%	3PTA/FGA	FTA/FGA	TS%	eFG%	3PT%
14.8	0.279	0.220	0.555	0.532	0.344

AST%	TOV%	OREB%	DREB%	STL%	BLK%
8.2	10.7	4.4	11.8	1.7	1.2

PER	ORTG	DRTG	WS/48	BPM	VOL
10.89	111.5	113.3	0.076	-1.66	0.328

- Regular rotation player for Denver as a rookie
- Fairly effective in his role as a low usage spot-up shooter and energy player
- Above break-even three-point shooter, made 40% of his corner threes
- Almost exclusively a stand-still spot-up shooter, more effective when shooting threes in transition
- Energetic player that plays very hard, great cutter, excellent at running the break, can explosively finish above the rim
- Very rarely used as a ball handler, catch-and-shoot player, only makes safe passes, rarely turns the ball over
- 2022-23 Defensive Degree of Difficulty: 0.386
- 2022-23 Points Prevented: 1.342
- Usually guarded second unit players, played average on-ball defense
- Stays with opposing guards and holds his own in the post against taller players, tends to commit cheap fouls
- Fairly solid pick-and-roll defender, good at getting around the screen to contain ball handlers, has lapses when switched onto a screeners
- Stays attached to shooters off the ball, fights through screens and closes out in spot-up situations
- Active help defender, can play passing lanes to get steals, occasional weak side shot blocker, fairly solid defensive rebounder

Reggie Jackson

	Height	Weight	Cap #	Years Left
	6'2"	208	$5.000M	PO

Similar at Age 32

		Season	SIMsc
1	Deron Williams	2016-17	928.3
2	Beno Udrih	2014-15	923.6
3	Anthony Peeler	2001-02	921.8
4	Jose Calderon	2013-14	910.1
5	Mike Conley	2019-20	909.8
6	Chauncey Billups	2008-09	903.6
7	Ray Allen*	2007-08	902.1
8	Derrick Rose	2020-21	902.1
9	Bobby Jackson	2005-06	901.4
10	Randy Foye	2015-16	901.2

Baseline Basic Stats

MPG	PTS	AST	REB	BLK	STL
25.3	10.6	3.5	2.6	0.1	0.8

Advanced Metrics

USG%	3PTA/FGA	FTA/FGA	TS%	eFG%	3PT%
20.5	0.460	0.167	0.527	0.494	0.351

AST%	TOV%	OREB%	DREB%	STL%	BLK%
21.4	14.1	1.7	9.7	1.4	0.4

PER	ORTG	DRTG	WS/48	BPM	VOL
11.85	105.5	113.3	0.058	-2.05	0.470

- Traded from the L.A. Clippers to Charlotte, signed with Denver after he was waived
- Production declined, used as a moderate usage ball handler and spot-up shooter
- Above break-even career three-point shooter, percentages tend to vary from year-to-year
- Not really consistent at shooting in any specific situation, most effective as a spot-up shooter with the Clippers
- Below average in ball handling situations, now a step slower, defenders back off him to limit his effectiveness
- Decent playmaker that can make simple reads, good at avoiding turnovers
- 2022-23 Defensive Degree of Difficulty: 0.427
- 2022-23 Points Prevented: -0.312
- Normally guards starting level guards, around an average on-ball defender
- Plays angles well, can stay with opposing guards, had some trouble against taller players
- Fairly good pick-and-roll defender, funnels his man into help, can functionally switch onto screeners
- Tends to get caught on screens, sometimes can be late to close out on spot-up shooters
- Stay-at-home defender, Steal Percentage was consistent with his career average, decent defensive rebounder

Vlatko Čančar

	Height	Weight	Cap #	Years Left
	6'8"	236	$2.234M	Team Option

Similar at Age 25

		Season	SIMsc
1	Georges Niang	2018-19	931.5
2	Anthony Tolliver	2010-11	921.7
3	Sasha Pavlovic	2008-09	915.0
4	Abdel Nader	2018-19	911.7
5	Glenn Robinson III	2018-19	909.9
6	Derrick Williams	2016-17	908.9
7	Kyle Singler	2013-14	908.8
8	Brian Scalabrine	2003-04	908.4
9	Victor Claver	2013-14	906.8
10	Stanley Johnson	2021-22	905.9

Baseline Basic Stats

MPG	PTS	AST	REB	BLK	STL
18.6	6.1	1.2	3.0	0.3	0.5

Advanced Metrics

USG%	3PTA/FGA	FTA/FGA	TS%	eFG%	3PT%
14.5	0.506	0.186	0.582	0.556	0.405

AST%	TOV%	OREB%	DREB%	STL%	BLK%
10.9	11.6	3.8	13.3	1.2	1.2

PER	ORTG	DRTG	WS/48	BPM	VOL
11.51	114.7	112.8	0.093	-1.13	0.303

- Fringe rotation player for Denver in his fourth NBA season
- Solidly effective in his role as a low usage spot-up shooter and energy player
- Posted a True Shooting Percentage above 60%, made over 37% of his threes last season
- Predominantly a stationary spot-up shooter, limited ability to shoot on the move or off the dribble
- Energetic rim runner, plays with a high motor, made almost 72% of his shots from three feet and in
- Good cutter and roll man, selectively goes to offensive boards to score on put-backs
- Not really able to create his own offense, has decent passing skills, cut his turnover rate last season
- 2022-23 Defensive Degree of Difficulty: 0.325
- 2022-23 Points Prevented: -1.005
- Usually guarded second unit players, below average on-ball defender
- Lacks the quickness to stay with opposing perimeter players, not strong enough to effectively guard big men
- Below average pick-and-roll defender, not effective at taking away any specific action
- Stays attached to shooters off the ball, fights through screens and closes out in spot-up situations
- Stay-at-home defender, does not really get steals, occasional weak side shot blocker, fairly solid defensive rebounder
- Tore the ACL in his left knee in August 2023, will likely miss the entire 2023-24 season

Zeke Nnaji

	Height	Weight	Cap #	Years Left
	6'9"	240	$4.306M	RFA

Similar at Age 22

		Season	SIMsc
1	Sandro Mamukelashvili	2021-22	926.6
2	Richaun Holmes	2015-16	911.1
3	Josh McRoberts	2009-10	910.3
4	Perry Jones	2013-14	910.0
5	DaJuan Summers	2009-10	907.1
6	Montrezl Harrell	2015-16	906.1
7	Noah Vonleh	2017-18	905.1
8	Obi Toppin	2020-21	902.0
9	Pat Garrity	1998-99	901.6
10	D.J. Wilson	2018-19	900.3

Baseline Basic Stats

MPG	PTS	AST	REB	BLK	STL
17.0	6.9	1.0	3.9	0.5	0.4

Advanced Metrics

USG%	3PTA/FGA	FTA/FGA	TS%	eFG%	3PT%
17.0	0.325	0.299	0.607	0.579	0.348

AST%	TOV%	OREB%	DREB%	STL%	BLK%
7.1	12.6	7.7	15.4	1.2	2.3

PER	ORTG	DRTG	WS/48	BPM	VOL
14.27	117.3	112.0	0.122	-1.48	0.476

- Missed over month with a sprained shoulder, fringe rotation player for Denver when healthy
- Effectiveness declined slightly in a role as a low usage stretch big and rim runner
- Made over 43% of his threes in his first two seasons, Three-Point Percentage crashed to below 30% last season
- Struggled to make spot-up jumpers, better at shooting as a pick-and-pop screener
- Energetic rim runner, effective cutter and rim runner, good offensive rebounder, great at running the floor in transition
- Not really a post-up threat, limited passing skills, good at avoiding turnovers
- 2022-23 Defensive Degree of Difficulty: 0.332
- 2022-23 Points Prevented: 0.334
- Improved to become a solid rim protector, blocked more shots last season, sacrifices position to go for blocks, below average defensive rebounder
- Guards second unit big men, can be overpowered in the post, tends to commit shooting fouls, better at using his mobility to defend in space
- Below average pick-and-roll defender, not effective at taking away any specific action
- Consistently comes out to contest outside shots in spot-up situations

DeAndre Jordan

	Height	Weight	Cap #	Years Left
	6'11"	265	$2.020M	UFA

Similar at Age 34

		Season	SIMsc
1	Erick Dampier	2009-10	920.7
2	Dwight Howard	2019-20	892.6
3	Marcin Gortat	2018-19	865.3
4	Stojko Vrankovic	1997-98	858.0
5	JaVale McGee	2021-22	857.9
6	Ervin Johnson	2001-02	848.9
7	Nene	2016-17	846.8
8	Joel Anthony	2016-17	843.3
9	Elton Brand	2013-14	840.1
10	Mark West	1994-95	834.1

Baseline Basic Stats

MPG	PTS	AST	REB	BLK	STL
17.2	4.6	0.7	5.5	0.9	0.3

Advanced Metrics

USG%	3PTA/FGA	FTA/FGA	TS%	eFG%	3PT%
12.7	0.023	0.419	0.642	0.649	0.491

AST%	TOV%	OREB%	DREB%	STL%	BLK%
6.7	21.8	12.5	26.9	0.9	4.8

PER	ORTG	DRTG	WS/48	BPM	VOL
14.14	114.8	109.4	0.104	-1.67	0.710

- Played limited minutes for Denver in his first season with the team
- Production level declined, mainly used as a very low volume rim runner
- Still an efficient despite his advancing age, posted a True Shooting Percentage above 73%
- Good roll man and cutter, active offensive rebounder, diminishing speed, does run as well as he did in the past
- Not a post-up threat, lacks reliable shooting range outside of ten feet, has made less than 50% of his career free throws
- Strictly a catch-and-finish player, very limited passing skills, fairly turnover prone
- 2022-23 Defensive Degree of Difficulty: 0.363
- 2022-23 Points Prevented: 0.031
- Good defensive rebounder and shot blocker, less effective as a rim protector due to declining mobility
- Guards second unit big men, average on-ball defender, holds position on the block, prone to biting on fakes
- Somewhat able to play angles to compensate for lack of quickness when defending in space
- Average pick-and-roll defense, solid in drop coverages, struggles to stop ball handlers from penetrating
- Consistently will come out to the perimeter to contest outside jumpers

Peyton Watson

	Height	Weight	Cap #	Years Left
	6'8"	200	$2.304M	2 TO

Similar at Age 20

		Season	SIMsc
1	Brandan Wright	2007-08	906.0
2	Greg Brown III	2021-22	886.1
3	Derrick Jones	2017-18	872.0
4	Jalen Smith	2020-21	869.6
5	Nicolas Claxton	2019-20	867.3
6	Patrick Williams	2021-22	866.6
7	Gordon Hayward	2010-11	866.3
8	Travis Outlaw	2004-05	866.1
9	Alen Smailagić	2020-21	863.9
10	Kenyon Martin Jr.	2020-21	863.8

Baseline Basic Stats

MPG	PTS	AST	REB	BLK	STL
20.2	7.9	0.9	3.5	0.7	0.6

Advanced Metrics

USG%	3PTA/FGA	FTA/FGA	TS%	eFG%	3PT%
17.8	0.322	0.259	0.569	0.550	0.409

AST%	TOV%	OREB%	DREB%	STL%	BLK%
7.5	9.9	4.7	14.6	1.0	3.4

PER	ORTG	DRTG	WS/48	BPM	VOL
13.62	112.2	112.3	0.093	-1.07	0.553

- Split time between Denver and Grand Rapids in the G-League during his rookie season
- Fairly effective in limited minutes as a low volume spot-up shooter and energy player
- Went 6-for-14 (42.9%) on threes in the NBA, made less than 25% of his threes in the G-League
- Mainly a stand-still spot-up shooter, shooting stroke is still inconsistent, Free Throw Percentage varied quite a bit
- High energy wing with great athleticism, explosive finisher around the rim
- Good cutter, can run the floor to get dunks in transition, plays rather wildly, can miss easy shots at the rim
- Not really able to create his own shot right now, only makes safe passes, good at avoiding turnovers
- <u>2022-23 Defensive Degree of Difficulty</u>: 0.339
- <u>2022-23 Points Prevented</u>: 2.153
- Usually guards second unit players or plays in garbage time, rarely tested on the ball
- Quick enough to stay with perimeter players, has some trouble against stronger players inside
- Fairly solid pick-and-roll defender, good at fighting over the screen to contain ball handlers
- Stays attached to shooters off the ball, fights through screens and closes out in spot-up situations
- Very good weak side shot blocker overall, got steals at a solid rate in the G-League, solid defensive rebounder

Justin Holiday

	Height	Weight	Cap #	Years Left
	6'6"	180	$2.020M	UFA

Similar at Age 33

		Season	SIMsc
1	Brent Barry	2004-05	909.2
2	Garrett Temple	2019-20	905.1
3	Ron Harper	1996-97	902.4
4	Bruce Bowen	2004-05	888.1
5	Trent Tucker	1992-93	888.0
6	Gerald Green	2018-19	887.0
7	Roger Mason	2013-14	885.2
8	Wesley Person	2004-05	884.4
9	Eddie Jones	2004-05	875.5
10	Craig Ehlo	1994-95	874.7

Baseline Basic Stats

MPG	PTS	AST	REB	BLK	STL
22.4	7.0	1.6	2.5	0.4	0.7

Advanced Metrics

USG%	3PTA/FGA	FTA/FGA	TS%	eFG%	3PT%
14.3	0.656	0.108	0.519	0.505	0.339

AST%	TOV%	OREB%	DREB%	STL%	BLK%
8.6	9.9	1.7	9.6	1.5	1.6

PER	ORTG	DRTG	WS/48	BPM	VOL
8.79	103.6	112.5	0.051	-1.94	0.646

- Traded from Atlanta to Houston at the trade deadline, signed with Dallas after he was waived
- Fringe rotation player for both teams, production declined, used as a low usage spot-up shooter
- League average career three-point shooter, Three-Point Percentage fell to below break-even last season
- Strictly a stationary spot-up shooter, percentages were much higher in Atlanta before he was traded
- Rarely used in ball handling situations, good cutter but played in very static offenses with little movement
- Catch-and-shoot player, not really much of a playmaker, rarely turns the ball over
- 2022-23 Defensive Degree of Difficulty: 0.349
- 2022-23 Points Prevented: -0.474
- Used as a defensive stopper in previous seasons, mostly guarded second unit players this season
- On-ball defense declined, not really effective at guards or wings in one-on-one situations
- Fairly solid pick-and-roll defender, can functionally switch and cut off penetration, tended to go too far under screens
- Can get caught on screens off the ball, tended to be late when closing out on spot-up shooters
- Does not really get steals, improved his ability to block shots on the weak side, now a below average defensive rebounder

Newcomers

Julian Strawther

	Height	Weight	Cap #	Years Left
	6'7"	205	$2.431M	1 + 2 TO

Baseline Basic Stats

MPG	PTS	AST	REB	BLK	STL
18.8	7.3	1.1	2.5	0.2	0.5

Advanced Metrics

USG%	3PTA/FGA	FTA/FGA	TS%	eFG%	3PT%
17.3	0.452	0.234	0.513	0.481	0.342

AST%	TOV%	OREB%	DREB%	STL%	BLK%
8.8	10.2	3.4	11.7	1.4	0.9

PER	ORTG	DRTG	WS/48	BPM	VOL
11.58	101.5	103.6	0.070	-0.95	N/A

- Drafted by Indiana with the 29th overall pick in 2023, traded to Denver
- Played very well at the Las Vegas Summer League
- Highly effective in a role as a moderate usage scoring wing, will likely be used in a lower volume role in the NBA
- Posted a True Shooting Percentage above 56%, made threes at an above break-even rate
- Good shooter off the catch, makes spot-up jumpers and shots off screens, inconsistent shooter off the dribble
- Very effective energy player that scores on hustle plays around the rim, great cutter, athletic finisher in transition
- Can slash to the rim as a pick-and-roll ball handler, not really able to drive by defenders on isolations
- Catch-and-shoot player, willing to make the extra pass, rarely turns the ball over
- Average defensive player in college with less than ideal tools, gave better defensive effort at Summer League
- Struggled in one-on-one situations in college, played passable on-ball defense in Vegas
- Average pick-and-roll defender, good at containing ball handlers, less effective when switched onto a screener
- Tends to get caught on screens off the ball, good at closing out on spot-up situations
- Stay-at-home defender, does not really get steals or blocks, solid defensive rebounder

Jalen Pickett

	Height	Weight	Cap #	Years Left
	6'4"	209	$1.708M	2 + TO

Baseline Basic Stats

MPG	PTS	AST	REB	BLK	STL
18.8	6.7	2.3	2.5	0.2	0.6

Advanced Metrics

USG%	3PTA/FGA	FTA/FGA	TS%	eFG%	3PT%
17.6	0.334	0.186	0.506	0.479	0.345

AST%	TOV%	OREB%	DREB%	STL%	BLK%
19.8	12.8	3.0	12.5	1.6	0.9

PER	ORTG	DRTG	WS/48	BPM	VOL
12.87	102.2	104.5	0.061	-1.06	N/A

- Drafted by Indiana with the 32nd overall pick in 2023, traded to Indiana
- Put up a solid performance at the Las Vegas Summer League
- Highly productive in his role as a low usage, pass-first point guard
- Great distributor that can run a team and find open teammates, slightly turnover prone at Summer League
- True Shooting Percentage was almost 60%, showed good shot selection, went 6-for-14 (42.9%) on threes
- Needs space to get his shot away, better as a spot-up shooter, can hit some threes as a pick-and-roll ball handler
- Good at posting up smaller guards, crafty ball handler, effectively got to his spots on pick-and-rolls and isolations
- Not explosively quick, may have trouble creating his own offense against elite defenders
- Lacks ideal length and quickness, around an average defender in college
- High effort defender at Summer League, could passably defend lower leverage players, may have trouble against higher-end players
- Good pick-and-roll defender, funnels his man into help, generally makes sound rotations
- Stays attached to shooters off the ball, fights through screens and closes out in spot-up situations
- Active help defender, plays passing lanes to get steals, good weak side shot blocking guard, solid defensive rebounder

Hunter Tyson

	Height	Weight	Cap #	Years Left
	6'8"	215	$1.120M	2 + TO

Baseline Basic Stats

MPG	PTS	AST	REB	BLK	STL
16.5	6.0	0.9	2.5	0.2	0.5

Advanced Metrics

USG%	3PTA/FGA	FTA/FGA	TS%	eFG%	3PT%
15.7	0.511	0.178	0.544	0.517	0.358

AST%	TOV%	OREB%	DREB%	STL%	BLK%
7.3	9.1	3.4	14.9	1.4	0.9

PER	ORTG	DRTG	WS/48	BPM	VOL
11.49	106.4	105.9	0.045	-2.16	N/A

- Drafted by Oklahoma City with the 37th overall pick in 2023, traded to Denver
- Named to the All-Summer League 1st Team at the Las Vegas Summer League
- Had an excellent performance in his role as a high usage scoring wing, likely will play a lower volume role as a rookie
- Shot very efficiently, True Shooting Percentage was above 73%, made half of his threes, displayed excellent shot selection
- Great movement shooter that can run off screens and make spot-up jumpers
- Makes sharp backdoor cuts if defenders overplay his shot, willing to absorb contact and draw fouls
- Can post up smaller players, showed better ball handling skills at Summer League, not really quick enough to create his own shot at the NBA level
- Catch-and-shoot player, flashed some passing skills, rarely turned the ball over
- Lacks ideal physical tools, compensates for his limitations by playing angles and exerting a high effort level
- Effective on-ball defender that can competently guard multiple positions, has some trouble staying with quicker players
- Solid pick-and-roll defender, can functionally switch, makes sound rotations
- Sometimes gets caught on screens off the ball, consistently closes out on spot-up shooters
- Only got steals at a moderate rate, fairly effective weak side shot blocker at Summer League, fairly good defensive rebounder

SACRAMENTO KINGS

Last Season: 48 - 34, Lost 1st Round to Golden State (3 – 4)

Offensive Rating: 119.4, 1st in the NBA   Defensive Rating: 116.8, 25th in the NBA

Primary Executive: Monte McNair, President of Basketball Operations/General Manager

Head Coach: Mike Brown

Key Roster Changes

Subtractions
Richard Holmes, trade
Terence Davis, free agency
Chimezie Metu, free agency
Matthew Dellavedova, free agency
P.J. Dozier, waived

Additions
Colby Jones, draft
Chris Duarte, trade
Sasha Vezenkov, signed/rights held
Nerlens Noel, free agency

Roster

Likely Starting Five
1. *De'Aaron Fox*
2. Kevin Huerter
3. Keegan Murray
4. Harrison Barnes
5. *Domantas Sabonis*

Other Key Rotation Players
Malik Monk
Davion Mitchell
Trey Lyles
Sasha Vezenkov
Chris Duarte

* Italics denotes that a player is likely to be on the floor to close games

Remaining Roster

- Kessler Edwards
- Alex Len
- Nerlens Noel
- Neemias Queta
- Colby Jones
- Keon Ellis, 24, 6'6", 175, Alabama (Two-Way)
- Jalen Slawson, 24, 6'7", 215, Furman (Two-Way)
- Jake Stephens, 24, 6'11", 270, Chattanooga (Exhibit 10)
- Skal Labissiere, 27, 6'10", 235, Kentucky (Exhibit 10)

SCHREMPF Base Rating: 43.6

Season Preview Survey

- *Are the Kings contending or rebuilding? Where is this team headed?*

The Kings are trending upwards after they suddenly improved to go from the lottery to a top seed in the West last season. They mostly relied on a newly installed motion offense that amplified the skills of everyone in the system. They got highly productive seasons out of De'Aaron Fox and Domantas Sabonis as well as their primary rotation players. Even though they couldn't quite pull out a win against Golden State in Game 7 of their first round playoff series, they are primed to have another great regular season and possibly make a deep playoff run due to the fact that they kept their roster intact. If they can prove that their success from last year was legitimate, then they could build on their chemistry to reach another level in the coming season.

- *What are the areas of concern for this team heading into this season?*

The Kings have a couple of areas of concern heading into this year. The main one is if they can continue to be as effective on offense as they were a season ago. Everything broke perfectly for the Kings last season because they were able to sneak up opponents because they weren't initially expected to be contenders. They were able to bank some wins and surprise opponents with their offensive tactics. However, this year, it's likely that teams will catch on to their bread and butter actions to limit their effectiveness. The Kings will have to work in some new wrinkles to maintain their offensive success. Otherwise, they could be headed for a regression. Also, they need to shore up their defense because they ranked near the bottom of the league last year. They didn't make significant changes with their personnel, so they will need to adjust their tactics to get more stops and make them a more well-rounded team.

- *List some possible breakout players for this team.*

Most of the Kings' rotation is locked in place and every one of their key players have settled into clear roles, so there's not a lot of room for someone to have great individual breakthrough. If someone is able to level up their game, it would Keegan Murray. He had a very solid year as a complementary option. With another year of experience, he could improve his efficiency and take on a larger role to increase his production. In addition to him, Sasha Vezenkov could be another player to watch. He has earned numerous accolades in Europe, including the EuroLeague's MVP award last season. He's an excellent shooter that thrives in virtually every catch-and-shoot situation. His ability to run off screens and knock down threes should fit very well into the Kings' system. He could wind up becoming a highly productive scorer off the bench if he's able to adjust to the NBA game.

- *What should we expect from them this season?*

If they are able to sustain their success from last season, the Kings should be a solid playoff team this year. It will be tougher for them this time around because opponents will have a better idea of what to expect from them. They will need to add some new elements to their offense to prevent their system from getting stale. They also could stand to shore up their weak areas on defense to hedge against any possible offensive regression. This could be an important season where they get a good idea of where they stand in the Western Conference. If they can maintain their position near the top of the West, then they could look to take the step towards contention by making smaller tweaks to maximize their system. Otherwise, if they fall back towards the pack, they may need to look into adding more impactful pieces to improve their chances of competing against the elite contenders in the league.

Veterans

Domantas Sabonis

	Height	Weight	Cap #	Years Left
	6'11"	240	$30.600M	4

Similar at Age 26

		Season	SIMsc
1	Brad Daugherty	1991-92	903.1
2	Christian Laettner	1995-96	900.5
3	Brad Miller	2002-03	894.0
4	Jack Sikma*	1981-82	890.7
5	Dave Corzine	1982-83	887.8
6	Giannis Antetokounmpo	2020-21	886.3
7	Jeff Ruland	1984-85	885.7
8	Karl-Anthony Towns	2021-22	883.0
9	Tyrone Hill	1994-95	882.6
10	Mehmet Okur	2005-06	882.3

Baseline Basic Stats

MPG	PTS	AST	REB	BLK	STL
35.0	18.3	3.9	10.0	0.9	0.9

Advanced Metrics

USG%	3PTA/FGA	FTA/FGA	TS%	eFG%	3PT%
22.2	0.113	0.440	0.622	0.574	0.349

AST%	TOV%	OREB%	DREB%	STL%	BLK%
23.7	15.4	8.9	26.4	1.2	1.5

PER	ORTG	DRTG	WS/48	BPM	VOL
21.53	122.3	109.8	0.186	4.75	0.379

- Made his third All-Star team, named to the All-NBA 3rd Team in 2022-23
- Excelled as a playmaking center and moderate usage interior scorer for Sacramento
- Dynamic passing center, great at hitting cutters out, good in the hand-off game, slightly turnover prone
- Scores in volume as a post-up player, good at flashing to the middle, can get pushed off his spots a bit
- Effective as a high energy rim runner, solid cutter and roll man, good offensive rebounder
- Made threes at an above average rate last season, below break-even career three-point shooter
- Solid spot-up shooter, also effective as a screener on pick-and-pop plays
- <u>2022-23 Defensive Degree of Difficulty</u>: 0.427
- <u>2022-23 Points Prevented</u>: -1.702
- Led the NBA in Rebounds per Game, average rim protector, not really a shot blocking threat
- Below average on-ball defender, can be overpowered by stronger big men in the post, struggles to defend in space
- Average pick-and-roll defender, willing to hedge out on ball handlers, less effective in drop coverages
- Tends to sag back into the paint, does not always come out to contest outside shots in spot-up situations

De'Aaron Fox

	Height	Weight	Cap #	Years Left
	6'3"	185	$32.600M	2

Similar at Age 25

		Season	SIMsc
1	Kyrie Irving	2017-18	934.1
2	Jrue Holiday	2015-16	926.9
3	Damian Lillard	2015-16	926.3
4	Tony Parker*	2007-08	922.9
5	Devin Harris	2008-09	922.6
6	Andrew Toney	1982-83	921.2
7	Gilbert Arenas	2006-07	918.0
8	Kirk Hinrich	2005-06	917.3
9	Lou Williams	2011-12	915.8
10	Stephen Curry	2013-14	914.6

Baseline Basic Stats

MPG	PTS	AST	REB	BLK	STL
34.1	20.6	6.1	3.7	0.3	1.3

Advanced Metrics

USG%	3PTA/FGA	FTA/FGA	TS%	eFG%	3PT%
28.2	0.284	0.319	0.573	0.525	0.337

AST%	TOV%	OREB%	DREB%	STL%	BLK%
30.1	12.3	1.9	10.7	1.8	0.8

PER	ORTG	DRTG	WS/48	BPM	VOL
20.24	113.8	112.6	0.132	2.09	0.310

- Made his first All-Star team, named to the All-NBA 3rd Team in 2022-23
- Had a breakout season, thrived in his role as Sacramento's primary ball handler and scorer
- Excellent playmaker with great court vision, makes sound decisions, good at avoiding turnovers
- Quick penetrating guard, uses great speed to push the ball in transition to create efficient early offense
- Good at slashing to the rim as an isolation player and pick-and-roll ball handler, draws fouls at a solid rate
- Below break-even career three-point shooter, made spot-up threes at an above break-even rate
- Inconsistent when taking threes off the dribble, better at making pull-up jumpers from mid-range
- 2022-23 Defensive Degree of Difficulty: 0.466
- 2022-23 Points Prevented: -0.834
- Drew some tough assignments against elite guards, solid on-ball defender
- Uses his great quickness to stay with opposing guards, has trouble against taller players due to thin frame
- Decent pick-and-roll defender, good at steering his man into help, tended to go too far under screens
- Stays attached to shooters off the ball, fights through screens and closes out in spot-up situations
- Can be a pesky defender, plays passing lanes, gets steals at a solid rate, fairly solid defensive rebounder

Kevin Huerter

	Height	Weight	Cap #	Years Left
	6'7"	190	$15.670M	2

Similar at Age 24

		Season	SIMsc
1	Terrence Ross	2015-16	934.4
2	Kyle Korver	2005-06	924.6
3	Cedi Osman	2019-20	921.6
4	Damyean Dotson	2018-19	917.7
5	Evan Fournier	2016-17	915.4
6	Marco Belinelli	2010-11	914.8
7	Furkan Korkmaz	2021-22	914.7
8	Brent Barry	1995-96	913.3
9	Hollis Thompson	2015-16	912.8
10	Chris Duarte	2021-22	912.8

Baseline Basic Stats

MPG	PTS	AST	REB	BLK	STL
27.2	11.9	2.3	3.1	0.3	0.9

Advanced Metrics

USG%	3PTA/FGA	FTA/FGA	TS%	eFG%	3PT%
19.6	0.527	0.168	0.570	0.543	0.385

AST%	TOV%	OREB%	DREB%	STL%	BLK%
14.3	9.8	2.0	10.9	1.6	1.0

PER	ORTG	DRTG	WS/48	BPM	VOL
13.97	113.0	113.3	0.096	0.07	0.308

- Regular starting guard for Sacramento in his first season with the team
- Effectively improved in a role as a lower volume shooting specialist
- Reliable three-point shooter throughout his career, has made almost 43% of his career corner threes
- Excellent shooter off the catch, very efficient at making spot-up jumpers, can run off screens and make threes on hand-off plays
- Moves well without the ball, great cutter, good at slipping on pick-and-rolls
- Inconsistent shooter off the drive, can occasionally drive to the rim if defenders try to crowd him
- Good secondary playmaker, can find open teammates to relieve pressure, rarely turns the ball over
- 2022-23 Defensive Degree of Difficulty: 0.411
- 2022-23 Points Prevented: -1.244
- Tended to be hidden in favorable matchups against lower leverage starter, average on-ball defender
- Plays angles well, can stay with opposing perimeter players, has trouble against stronger players inside
- Played below average pick-and-roll defense, not especially effective at taking away any specific action
- Tended to get caught on screens off the ball, usually was a step late when closing out on spot-up shooters
- Steal Percentage increased, better at getting deflections or playing passing lanes, decent defensive rebounder

Harrison Barnes

	Height	Weight	Cap #	Years Left
	6'8"	225	$17.000M	2

Similar at Age 30

		Season	SIMsc
1	Luol Deng	2015-16	927.1
2	Eric Piatkowski	2000-01	925.0
3	Richard Jefferson	2010-11	923.7
4	Wilson Chandler	2017-18	919.9
5	Peja Stojakovic	2007-08	917.8
6	Bryon Russell	2000-01	916.0
7	Joe Johnson	2011-12	909.3
8	Marcus Morris	2019-20	908.1
9	Danilo Gallinari	2018-19	907.2
10	Bojan Bogdanović	2019-20	905.8

Baseline Basic Stats

MPG	PTS	AST	REB	BLK	STL
30.3	13.7	1.9	4.5	0.2	0.7

Advanced Metrics

USG%	3PTA/FGA	FTA/FGA	TS%	eFG%	3PT%
18.2	0.451	0.362	0.595	0.540	0.384

AST%	TOV%	OREB%	DREB%	STL%	BLK%
8.7	9.6	3.4	14.1	1.1	0.5

PER	ORTG	DRTG	WS/48	BPM	VOL
13.99	117.6	114.5	0.103	-0.50	0.323

- Started all 82 games for Sacramento in his fourth full season with the team
- Efficient in his role as a low usage complementary shooting combo forward
- Reliably efficient career three-point shooter, career corner Three-Point Percentage is almost 42%
- Primarily a stationary spot-up shooter, knocks down threes in transition, rarely shoots in other situations
- Great cutter off the ball, good at scoring on hand-offs, can post up smaller players
- Effective at attacking switches as a ball handler, makes hard straight-line drives to the rim, draws a lot of fouls
- Largely a catch-and-shoot player, sticks to making safe passes, rarely turns the ball over
- 2022-23 Defensive Degree of Difficulty: 0.508
- 2022-23 Points Prevented: 0.491
- Used as Sacramento's primary defensive stopper, good on-ball defender
- Effective at guarding multiple positions, solid perimeter defender, can guard bigger player for short stretches
- Average pick-and-roll defender, good at switching onto screeners, had trouble defending ball handlers
- Sometimes gets caught on screens off the ball, good at closing out on spot-up shooters
- Stay-at-home defender, rarely gets steals or blocks, fairly solid defensive rebounder

Keegan Murray

	Height	Weight	Cap #	Years Left
	6'8"	215	$8.409M	2 TO

Similar at Age 22

		Season	SIMsc
1	Corey Kispert	2021-22	929.8
2	Harrison Barnes	2014-15	927.2
3	Nicolas Batum	2010-11	916.9
4	Desmond Bane	2020-21	912.9
5	Wilson Chandler	2009-10	903.4
6	Obi Toppin	2020-21	902.9
7	Jumaine Jones	2001-02	901.9
8	Saddiq Bey	2021-22	901.8
9	Justin Jackson	2017-18	900.0
10	Otto Porter Jr.	2015-16	899.2

Baseline Basic Stats

MPG	PTS	AST	REB	BLK	STL
27.2	11.9	1.6	4.0	0.4	0.7

Advanced Metrics

USG%	3PTA/FGA	FTA/FGA	TS%	eFG%	3PT%
18.3	0.525	0.164	0.584	0.559	0.406

AST%	TOV%	OREB%	DREB%	STL%	BLK%
7.5	8.0	3.7	12.7	1.3	1.2

PER	ORTG	DRTG	WS/48	BPM	VOL
13.55	115.3	114.7	0.094	-0.45	0.451

- Named to the All-Rookie 1st Team in 2022-23, regular starting forward for Sacramento
- Highly efficient in his role as a low volume spot-up shooter
- Made over 41% of his threes last season, Three-Point Percentage in the corners was over 43%
- Mostly a stand-still spot-up shooter, more efficient when he had time and his feet were set
- Good at scoring at the rim on hand-offs, good cutter, efficient scorer on put-backs
- Rarely used as a ball handler, lacks ideal quickness, only average as a pick-and-roll ball handler
- Strictly a catch-and-shoot player at this stage, only makes safe passes, rarely turns the ball over
- 2022-23 Defensive Degree of Difficulty: 0.421
- 2022-23 Points Prevented: -1.095
- Usually guards lower leverage starters, played decent on-ball defense in these matchups
- More effective when guarding bigger players inside, had trouble staying with quicker perimeter players
- Below average pick-and-roll defender, indecisive, not effective at taking away any specific action
- Tends to get caught on screens, usually late when closing out on spot-up shooters
- Did not really get steals, occasionally blocked shots from the weak side, fairly solid defensive rebounder

Malik Monk

	Height	Weight	Cap #	Years Left
	6'3"	200	$9.946M	UFA

Similar at Age 24

		Season	SIMsc
1	Brandon Knight	2015-16	939.6
2	Jerryd Bayless	2012-13	937.8
3	Chauncey Billups	2000-01	930.7
4	Ben Gordon	2007-08	930.5
5	Jordan Crawford	2012-13	930.4
6	Kendrick Nunn	2019-20	929.4
7	Shake Milton	2020-21	924.7
8	Daniel Gibson	2010-11	922.6
9	Malik Beasley	2020-21	918.8
10	Bradley Beal	2017-18	918.3

Baseline Basic Stats

MPG	PTS	AST	REB	BLK	STL
29.5	15.1	3.7	3.1	0.2	0.9

Advanced Metrics

USG%	3PTA/FGA	FTA/FGA	TS%	eFG%	3PT%
23.4	0.477	0.243	0.579	0.535	0.375

AST%	TOV%	OREB%	DREB%	STL%	BLK%
21.4	12.7	2.1	10.6	1.4	0.9

PER	ORTG	DRTG	WS/48	BPM	VOL
16.00	112.7	115.0	0.081	0.04	0.431

- Regular rotation player for Sacramento in his first season with the team
- Production level improved, effective in a sixth man role as a high usage scoring guard
- League average career three-point shooter, percentages vary a bit from year-to-year
- Great spot-up shooter, makes pull-up threes on pick-and-rolls, less effective when shooting off screens
- Good pick-and-roll ball handler, less effective on isolation plays, needs a screen to create proper separation
- Improved to become a very good playmaker, Assist Percentage increased to a career high, consistently good at limiting turnovers
- 2022-23 Defensive Degree of Difficulty: 0.322
- 2022-23 Points Prevented: -0.230
- Tended to be hidden in favorable matchups against lower leverage bench players
- Played below average on-ball defense, struggled to stay with opposing guards, had trouble defending taller wings
- Decent pick-and-roll defender, can functionally switch, cuts off penetration, goes too far under screens
- Gets caught on screens off the ball, usually a step late when closing out on spot-up shooters
- Stay-at-home defender, rarely gets steals or blocks, decent defensive rebounder

Davion Mitchell

	Height	Weight	Cap #	Years Left
	6'2"	205	$5.064M	TO

Similar at Age 24

		Season	SIMsc
1	Daniel Gibson	2010-11	931.7
2	Langston Galloway	2015-16	929.9
3	Rex Walters	1994-95	926.7
4	Fred VanVleet	2018-19	923.6
5	Kendrick Nunn	2019-20	923.0
6	Terry Rozier	2018-19	921.5
7	Chauncey Billups	2000-01	919.0
8	Khalid Reeves	1996-97	919.0
9	Chris Quinn	2007-08	915.6
10	Shannon Brown	2009-10	912.6

Baseline Basic Stats

MPG	PTS	AST	REB	BLK	STL
23.1	9.1	2.8	2.2	0.2	0.7

Advanced Metrics

USG%	3PTA/FGA	FTA/FGA	TS%	eFG%	3PT%
17.7	0.468	0.147	0.534	0.507	0.345

AST%	TOV%	OREB%	DREB%	STL%	BLK%
19.6	12.4	1.6	8.1	1.5	0.7

PER	ORTG	DRTG	WS/48	BPM	VOL
11.45	108.3	115.6	0.054	-1.54	0.322

- Regular rotation player for Sacramento in his second NBA season, played in all but two games in 2022-23
- Efficiency increased in a new role as a low usage spot-up shooter and backup point guard
- Below break-even three-point shooter, shot selection improved, took fewer inefficient long twos
- Mostly a spot-up shooter, less effective in half-court situations, better at making threes in transition
- More efficient at driving to the rim as an isolation player and pick-and-roll ball handler
- Improved his ability to finish at the rim and make short floaters in the paint, good scorer on hand-offs
- Solid secondary playmaker that makes simple reads, good at avoiding turnovers
- <u>2022-23 Defensive Degree of Difficulty</u>: 0.472
- <u>2022-23 Points Prevented</u>: -0.027
- Drew a lot of tough defensive assignments off the bench, improved to become a good on-ball defender
- Actively pressures opposing guards on the perimeter, effectively can guard taller perimeter players
- Solid pick-and-roll defender, can functionally switch to guard ball handlers and screeners
- Stays attached to shooters off the ball, fights through screens and closes out in spot-up situations
- Generally a stay-at-home defender, Steal Percentage increased a bit, below average defensive rebounder

Trey Lyles

	Height	Weight	Cap #	Years Left
	6'9"	234	$8.000M	1

Similar at Age 27

		Season	SIMsc
1	Austin Croshere	2002-03	929.7
2	Mike Scott	2015-16	929.0
3	Marvin Williams	2013-14	925.3
4	Nikola Mirotic	2018-19	920.2
5	Omri Casspi	2015-16	919.9
6	Scott Padgett	2003-04	918.5
7	Matt Bonner	2007-08	915.2
8	Ersan Ilyasova	2014-15	913.4
9	Patrick Patterson	2016-17	909.0
10	Walter Herrmann	2006-07	908.4

Baseline Basic Stats

MPG	PTS	AST	REB	BLK	STL
19.7	7.6	1.1	4.3	0.3	0.5

Advanced Metrics

USG%	3PTA/FGA	FTA/FGA	TS%	eFG%	3PT%
17.2	0.519	0.278	0.572	0.530	0.352

AST%	TOV%	OREB%	DREB%	STL%	BLK%
8.0	11.2	5.3	20.1	1.2	1.5

PER	ORTG	DRTG	WS/48	BPM	VOL
13.18	113.0	112.1	0.098	-0.78	0.327

- Regular rotation player for Sacramento in his first full season with the team
- Solidly effective in his role as a low usage stretch big and rim runner
- League average three-point shooter last season, percentages tend to vary from year-to-year
- Primarily a stand-still spot-up shooter, flashed some ability to make pick-and-pop jumpers
- Fairly solid rim runner that plays with a high motor, solid cutter and roll man, good at running the floor in transition
- Not really a post-up threat or a ball handler, lacks the ability to take on additional usage
- Catch-and-shoot player, only makes safe passes, good at avoiding turnovers
- 2022-23 Defensive Degree of Difficulty: 0.309
- 2022-23 Points Prevented: -1.294
- Decent rim protector, stays vertical when contesting shots, Block Percentage increased a bit, good defensive rebounder
- Usually guarded second unit big men, below average on-ball defender
- Can be overpowered by stronger centers in the post, struggles to defend in space
- Solid pick-and-roll defender, effective in drop coverages, willing to switch out on ball handlers
- Tends to sag back into the paint, does not always come out to contest shots in spot-up situations

Chris Duarte

	Height	Weight	Cap #	Years Left
	6'6"	190	$4.124M	TO

Similar at Age 25

		Season	SIMsc
1	Lucious Harris	1995-96	938.9
2	Evan Fournier	2017-18	936.6
3	Justin Holiday	2014-15	932.6
4	Nik Stauskas	2018-19	932.3
5	Brent Barry	1996-97	929.2
6	Tim Hardaway Jr.	2017-18	928.8
7	Alec Burks	2016-17	926.7
8	Wesley Iwundu	2019-20	925.7
9	Reggie Williams	2011-12	925.4
10	Wesley Person	1996-97	924.6

Baseline Basic Stats

MPG	PTS	AST	REB	BLK	STL
23.6	10.0	1.8	2.7	0.2	0.8

Advanced Metrics

USG%	3PTA/FGA	FTA/FGA	TS%	eFG%	3PT%
19.6	0.486	0.212	0.530	0.491	0.356

AST%	TOV%	OREB%	DREB%	STL%	BLK%
11.6	10.9	2.1	11.6	1.6	0.8

PER	ORTG	DRTG	WS/48	BPM	VOL
11.46	104.6	114.4	0.052	-1.85	0.399

- Missed games due to ankle injuries, fringe rotation player for Indiana in his second NBA season
- Effectiveness declined sharply, mainly used as a low usage spot-up shooter
- Three-Point Percentage fell to below break-even last season, mainly a spot-up shooter
- Career Three-Point Percentage is still above break-even
- Not really effective as a ball handler, defenders could back off him to negate his effectiveness
- Good at scoring on hustle plays around the rim, solid cutter and roll man
- Catch-and-shoot player, willing to make the extra pass, good at limiting turnovers
- 2022-23 Defensive Degree of Difficulty: 0.346
- 2022-23 Points Prevented: 0.318
- Usually guarded second unit players, good on-ball defender in these lower leverage matchups
- Capably could defend multiple positions, less effective when guarding starting level players
- Solid pick-and-roll defender, effective at switching to defend ball handlers or screeners
- Gambles a bit too much, gets caught out of position, does not always get around screens or close out on spot-up shooters
- More of a stay-at-home defender, did not really get steals or blocks last season, fairly solid defensive rebounder

Kessler Edwards

	Height	Weight	Cap #	Years Left
	6'8"	215	$1.928M	RFA

Similar at Age 22

		Season	SIMsc
1	Paul Zipser	2016-17	946.5
2	Jason Kapono	2003-04	931.5
3	Allen Crabbe	2014-15	929.0
4	KZ Okpala	2021-22	923.4
5	Sergei Monia	2005-06	918.0
6	Obi Toppin	2020-21	914.9
7	Troy Brown Jr.	2021-22	914.6
8	Sasha Pavlovic	2005-06	914.5
9	Rodney Hood	2014-15	914.2
10	Juancho Hernangomez	2017-18	914.2

Baseline Basic Stats

MPG	PTS	AST	REB	BLK	STL
21.9	7.8	1.2	3.4	0.3	0.7

Advanced Metrics

USG%	3PTA/FGA	FTA/FGA	TS%	eFG%	3PT%
14.8	0.486	0.163	0.543	0.517	0.358

AST%	TOV%	OREB%	DREB%	STL%	BLK%
8.0	10.6	4.6	12.8	1.6	1.5

PER	ORTG	DRTG	WS/48	BPM	VOL
11.08	110.1	113.2	0.080	-1.88	0.420

- Traded from Brooklyn to Sacramento, played sparingly for both teams in his second NBA season
- Production level held steady, mainly used as a very low usage spot-up shooter
- Three-Point Percentage fell to below break-even in limited action last season
- Strictly a stationary spot-up shooter, shot more efficiently in Sacramento
- Flashed an ability to move effectively without the ball, good cutter
- Not really able to create his own shot, rarely used in situations other than spot-up shooting
- Catch-and-shoot player that only makes safe passes, good at avoiding turnovers
- 2022-23 Defensive Degree of Difficulty: 0.423
- 2022-23 Points Prevented: 1.863
- Drew a lot of tougher assignments off the bench in limited minutes, played fairly good on-ball defense
- Flashed the potential to guard multiple positions in a smaller role
- Played below average pick-and-roll defense, indecisive when making rotations, struggled to effectively contain ball handlers
- Tended to get caught on screens off the ball, usually was a step late when closing out on spot-up shooters
- Steal Percentage increased, occasionally blocks shots from the weak side, fairly solid defensive rebounder

Alex Len

	Height	Weight	Cap #	Years Left
	7'0"	250	$2.020M	UFA

Similar at Age 29

		Season	SIMsc
1	Jason Thompson	2015-16	908.7
2	Duane Causwell	1997-98	900.2
3	Cody Zeller	2021-22	897.9
4	Zan Tabak	1999-00	895.9
5	Salah Mejri	2015-16	894.9
6	Zeljko Rebraca	2001-02	886.7
7	Will Perdue	1994-95	882.5
8	Melvin Turpin	1989-90	881.2
9	Bismack Biyombo	2021-22	880.6
10	Alton Lister	1987-88	878.5

Baseline Basic Stats

MPG	PTS	AST	REB	BLK	STL
16.4	4.6	0.5	5.3	1.0	0.4

Advanced Metrics

USG%	3PTA/FGA	FTA/FGA	TS%	eFG%	3PT%
13.4	0.046	0.427	0.579	0.546	0.076

AST%	TOV%	OREB%	DREB%	STL%	BLK%
6.9	21.5	12.6	25.5	1.1	4.4

PER	ORTG	DRTG	WS/48	BPM	VOL
13.24	110.5	109.4	0.095	-2.74	0.558

- Played sparingly for Sacramento in his second season with the team
- Used in very limited action as a low usage rim runner, has not been a rotational player since 2018-19
- Efficient finisher around the rim, made almost 74% of his shots inside of three feet
- Draws fouls at a high rate, has made less than 70% of his free throws, has some trouble finishing in traffic
- Solid cutter and roll man, active offensive rebounder, willing to run the floor in transition
- Shot threes in 2018-19, below break-even career three-point shooter, no longer takes shots beyond 16 feet
- Not really a post-up threat, decent passing big man, fairly turnover prone
- 2022-23 Defensive Degree of Difficulty: 0.276
- 2022-23 Points Prevented: 3.374
- Effective rim protector in limited minutes, good defensive rebounder and shot blocker
- Usually played in garbage time, played below average on-ball defense
- Struggled to guard opposing big men, had trouble defending in space, highly foul prone
- Middling pick-and-roll defender, decent in drop coverages, struggled to contain ball handlers on switches
- Tended to stay anchored in the paint, did not really come out to contest shots in spot-up situations

Nerlens Noel

	Height	Weight	Cap #	Years Left
	6'11"	220	$2.020M	UFA

Similar at Age 28

		Season	SIMsc
1	Calvin Booth	2004-05	890.6
2	Brett Szabo	1996-97	887.7
3	Joe Meriweather	1981-82	876.3
4	Cole Aldrich	2016-17	873.5
5	Tellis Frank	1993-94	873.4
6	Kim Hughes	1980-81	871.8
7	Charles Jones	1985-86	871.6
8	Jim McIlvaine	2000-01	865.7
9	Robert Horry	1998-99	864.7
10	Francisco Elson	2004-05	863.6

Baseline Basic Stats

MPG	PTS	AST	REB	BLK	STL
18.1	4.6	0.8	4.3	1.1	0.6

Advanced Metrics

USG%	3PTA/FGA	FTA/FGA	TS%	eFG%	3PT%
11.5	0.039	0.296	0.510	0.474	0.285

AST%	TOV%	OREB%	DREB%	STL%	BLK%
6.0	20.0	8.3	18.9	2.5	4.5

PER	ORTG	DRTG	WS/48	BPM	VOL
10.83	101.4	104.5	0.076	-1.73	0.708

- Waived by Detroit, later signed to a ten-day contract with Brooklyn, played sparingly for both teams
- Production has continued to decline, mainly used as a low usage rim runner
- True Shooting Percentage was below 45%, extensive injury history has sapped his athleticism
- Struggled to finish around the rim as a rim runner, lacks the lift to effectively score around the basket
- Has difficulty running the floor, less effective as a transition player
- Limited skill, not a post-up or shooting threat, limited passing ability, fairly turnover prone
- <u>2022-23 Defensive Degree of Difficulty</u>: 0.529
- <u>2022-23 Points Prevented</u>: -1.305
- Good shot blocker and defensive rebounder, still gets steals at a high rate
- Average rim protector, sacrifices positioning to go for blocks
- Spent a lot of his possessions guarding Joel Embiid and other starting centers
- Struggled to play effective post defense, better when defending in space
- Average pick-and-roll defender, could hedge out on ball handlers on pick-and-rolls, mixed results in drop coverages
- Tends to stay anchored in the paint, does not always come out to contest outside shots

Neemias Queta

	Height	Weight	Cap #	Years Left
	7'0"	245	$2.020M	1

Similar at Age 23

		Season	SIMsc
1	Scott Haskin	1993-94	880.1
2	Alton Lister	1981-82	872.3
3	Dan McClintock	2000-01	870.6
4	Walter Tavares	2015-16	870.2
5	Mike Smrek	1985-86	868.2
6	Jakob Poeltl	2018-19	866.4
7	Darko Milicic	2008-09	866.2
8	Robert Swift	2008-09	860.4
9	Paul Mokeski	1979-80	855.0
10	Eric Riley	1993-94	854.6

Baseline Basic Stats

MPG	PTS	AST	REB	BLK	STL
14.0	5.1	0.6	4.0	0.9	0.3

Advanced Metrics

USG%	3PTA/FGA	FTA/FGA	TS%	eFG%	3PT%
17.2	0.003	0.361	0.573	0.567	0.048

AST%	TOV%	OREB%	DREB%	STL%	BLK%
6.2	12.1	13.4	20.8	0.8	5.2

PER	ORTG	DRTG	WS/48	BPM	VOL
16.36	115.8	109.0	0.125	-2.00	0.485

- Has only played 149 NBA minutes in two seasons, played mostly in the G-League with Stockton
- Named to the All-G League 1st Team in 2022-23, mainly used as a rim runner in both leagues
- High motor rim runner, plays physical, draws a lot of fouls, True Shooting Percentage in the G-League was almost 76% last season
- Good offensive rebounder, good cutter, lacks ideal lift and quickness, less effective on rolls to the rim
- Can bully weaker defenders in the post at the G-League, not really used on post-ups in the NBA
- Showed solid passing skills in the G-League, slightly turnover prone
- 2022-23 Defensive Degree of Difficulty: 0.317
- 2022-23 Points Prevented: -4.657
- Great shot blocker and defensive rebounder in the G-League, less effective as a rim protector due to mobility limitations
- Mostly guarded second unit centers or played in garbage time, below average on-ball defender
- Foul prone in the post, undisciplined with his positioning, struggles to defend in space
- Middling pick-and-roll defender, has lapses when guarding screeners, willing to hedge out on ball handlers
- Tended to sag back into the paint, did not always come out to contest perimeter shots in spot-up situations

Newcomers

Colby Jones

	Height	Weight	Cap #	Years Left
	6'6"	205	$2.020M	2 + TO

Baseline Basic Stats

MPG	PTS	AST	REB	BLK	STL
14.3	4.4	1.3	2.0	0.2	0.5

Advanced Metrics

USG%	3PTA/FGA	FTA/FGA	TS%	eFG%	3PT%
15.5	0.328	0.238	0.508	0.478	0.329

AST%	TOV%	OREB%	DREB%	STL%	BLK%
14.9	14.7	3.5	11.1	1.7	1.2

PER	ORTG	DRTG	WS/48	BPM	VOL
10.69	100.5	105.3	0.047	-1.92	N/A

- Drafted by Charlotte with the 34th overall pick in 2023, traded to Boston, then traded to Sacramento
- Played well at the Sacramento Summer League, was less effective in Las Vegas
- Struggled with his consistency in a role as a moderate volume scoring guard, likely will be a lower usage player in the NBA
- True Shooting Percentage was just below 50% in Summer League action, made less than 30% of his threes
- Above break-even career three-point shooter in college, most effective when taking threes in transition
- Percentages in half-court situation varied quite a bit
- Solid at attacking the rim on hand-offs or as a pick-and-roll ball handler
- Needs to improve his ball handling, not really used as an isolation player in college
- Good cutter, can sometimes post up smaller guards
- Showed decent secondary playmaking skills at Summer League, played somewhat out of control, committed turnovers at a fairly high rate
- Above average athlete, has good defensive instincts, could be a solid defender in the future
- Solid on-ball defender in college, strong enough to handle bigger wings, good quickness to stay with opposing guards, tends to back off his man too much
- Decent pick-and-roll defender, good at containing ball handlers, had lapses when switched onto screeners
- Fights through screens off the ball, tends to be late when closing out on spot-up shooters
- Very active help defender at Summer League, great at playing passing lanes to get steals, effective weak side shot blocker, solid defensive rebounder

Sasha Vezenkov

	Height	Weight	Cap #	Years Left
	6'9"	225	$6.341M	1 + TO

Baseline Basic Stats

MPG	PTS	AST	REB	BLK	STL
20.0	7.9	1.1	4.1	0.3	0.6

Advanced Metrics

USG%	3PTA/FGA	FTA/FGA	TS%	eFG%	3PT%
19.0	0.517	0.244	0.593	0.554	0.357

AST%	TOV%	OREB%	DREB%	STL%	BLK%
9.9	10.1	6.6	20.2	1.7	1.2

PER	ORTG	DRTG	WS/48	BPM	VOL
14.47	118.0	112.4	0.101	-0.10	0.583

- Drafted by Brooklyn with the 57th overall pick in 2017, rights traded to Cleveland in 2021, then traded again to Sacramento in 2022
- Played last season with Olympiakos in the Greek A1 league, projection uses translated EuroLeague stats
- Named EuroLeague MVP in 2022-23, also earned the Alphonso Ford EuroLeague Top Scorer trophy
- Thrives at the EuroLeague level as a high usage shooting specialist
- Reliable three-point shooter, has made over 40% of his threes over the last four seasons
- Excellent movement shooter, great at running off screens and knocking down spot-up jumpers
- Very rarely dribbles the ball in games, lacks ideal quickness, not likely to be used as a ball handler at the NBA level
- Makes sharp backdoor cuts if defenders overplay his shot
- Good secondary playmaker that can find open teammates to relieve pressure, rarely turns the ball over
- Not really an explosive athlete, lacks ideal length, possibly could be a liability on defense
- Often hidden in favorable matchups or in zones at the EuroLeague level
- Struggles to stay with quicker players, may have enough strength to hold position in the post against bigger players
- Middling pick-and-roll defender, funnels his man into help, limited ability to aggressively switch
- High effort defender, will fight through screens and close out in spot-up situations
- Can effectively play passing lanes to get steals, good defensive rebounder
- Likely will be a rotational shooting specialist for Sacramento as a rookie
- 2023-24 will be his age-28 season

PHOENIX SUNS

Last Season: 45 - 37, Lost 2nd Round to Denver (2 – 4)

Offensive Rating: 115.1, 14th in the NBA   Defensive Rating: 113.0, 7th in the NBA

Primary Executive: James Jones, President of Basketball Operations

Head Coach: Frank Vogel

Key Roster Changes

<u>Subtractions</u>
Chris Paul, trade
Landry Shamet, trade
Cameron Payne, trade
Torrey Craig, free agency
Darius Bazley, free agency
Jock Landale, free agency
Terrence Ross, free agency
T.J. Warren, free agency
Bismack Biyombo, free agency

<u>Additions</u>
Bradley Beal, trade
Jordan Goodwin, trade
Toumani Camara, draft
Eric Gordon, free agency
Yuta Watanabe, free agency
Bol Bol, free agency
Drew Eubanks, free agency
Keita Bates-Diop, free agency
Chimezie Metu, free agency

Roster

<u>Likely Starting Five</u>
1. *Bradley Beal*
2. *Devin Booker*
3. Eric Gordon
4. *Kevin Durant*
5. Deandre Ayton

Other Key Rotation Players
Josh Okogie
Damion Lee
Jordan Goodwin
Yuta Watanabe
Drew Eubanks

* Italics denotes that a player is likely to be on the floor to close games

Remaining Roster

- Bol Bol
- Chimezie Metu
- Keita Bates-Diop
- Ish Wainwright
- Toumani Camara
- Saben Lee, 24, 6'2", 183, Vanderbilt (Two-Way)
- Udoka Azubuike, 24, 6'10", 280, Kansas (Two-Way)

SCHREMPF Base Rating: 43.4

Season Preview Survey

- *Are the Suns contending or rebuilding? Where is this team headed?*

The Suns pushed all of their chips into the middle by expending the rest of their limited resources to add former All-Star Bradley Beal to a team that already has Devin Booker and Kevin Durant. It was a bold move that signified that they were going into championship or bust mode because it left them with very little maneuverability to build a balanced roster. They are really leaning on their star power to carry them through the regular season and playoffs because their back-end is all comprised of minimum salary players. If things break right, they could be prime contenders to win the title this season. Otherwise, if they have to deal with chemistry or injury issues, they might fall short and be a middle of the pack playoff team this season.

- *What are the areas of concern for this team heading into this season?*

Even though the Suns have considerable star power, they aren't a flawless unit. In particular, they are extremely top heavy because they didn't have a lot of space to build out a capable bench. They could have some trouble putting together lineups to stay effective when their stars aren't in the game, so they run the risk of going through significant droughts for stretches of time. They also don't have a lot of margin for error because they will need their stars to stay healthy for the entire season, which has been an issue for all three of their stars at various points of their respective careers. If someone winds up being out for a long time, then they may not have enough supporting talent withstand that loss. That being said, their team is not very balanced, even if it is at full strength. Specifically, their roster largely skews towards the offensive side, so there aren't a lot of reliable defenders on the roster, which could make it hard for them to get key stops. Additionally, they don't have a pure distributor on the team. Their offense could also become disjointed as they try to distribute usage between three players that are accustomed to a high volume.

- *List some possible breakout players for this team.*

The Suns' roster is almost exclusively comprised of established veterans, so there are very few candidates that qualify as one that could be unexpected breakout players. Of the players that are expected to get regular minutes, Jordan Goodwin and Josh Okogie best fit the bill as players that could improve significantly to make an impact for Phoenix this year. The Suns don't really have a lot of high-end defenders or a distributing point guard, so Goodwin could step up to fill this void in their lineup if he builds on his solid performance in Washington last season. Also, Okogie could fill the vacant defensive specialist role because he's shown that he can handle tough assignments against elite scorers. He just needs to continue to improve as an offensive threat. Then, the only rookie on their roster, Toumani Camara has a chance to crack the rotation as a low volume energy wing if he gets a shot to play.

- *What should we expect from them this season?*

The Suns are going to be a fascinating team to watch this season because their talent gives them the upside to push for a title, but they have several issues that they have to resolve. They first have to figure out how their stars are going to fit together because there's one ball and a lot of high usage players to account for. Also, they aren't really a balanced team, so they still may have weaknesses that they will need to account for. They also will have to cobble together a working rotation that allows them to manage the long schedule, but that will be tough because their depth isn't proven at this point. With so many question marks, it's unlikely that everything will fall into place right away. They could have some good and bad points, so they are likely to be a solid playoff team this coming season.

Veterans

Kevin Durant

	Height	Weight	Cap #	Years Left
	6'10"	240	$47.649M	2

Similar at Age 34

		Season	SIMsc
1	LeBron James	2018-19	897.1
2	Dirk Nowitzki*	2012-13	873.6
3	David West	2014-15	856.6
4	Al Horford	2020-21	853.0
5	Paul Pierce*	2011-12	845.0
6	Brad Miller	2010-11	844.4
7	Derrick Coleman	2001-02	843.9
8	Larry Bird*	1990-91	841.6
9	LaMarcus Aldridge	2019-20	841.5
10	Dan Issel*	1982-83	840.6

Baseline Basic Stats

MPG	PTS	AST	REB	BLK	STL
32.4	20.8	4.8	7.2	0.9	0.8

Advanced Metrics

USG%	3PTA/FGA	FTA/FGA	TS%	eFG%	3PT%
27.5	0.292	0.341	0.633	0.580	0.384

AST%	TOV%	OREB%	DREB%	STL%	BLK%
24.6	12.2	2.7	20.7	1.1	3.1

PER	ORTG	DRTG	WS/48	BPM	VOL
24.03	120.9	110.5	0.186	4.83	0.506

- Traded from Brooklyn to Phoenix, missed games due to knee and ankle sprains
- Made his 13th All-Star team, thrived as a primary scorer for Brooklyn and Phoenix
- Outstanding three-level scorer, great one-on-one player, efficient on isolations and post-ups
- Reliable three-point shooter, made over 40% of his threes last season, excellent shooter off the catch
- Less effective when shooting threes on isolations, better with an on-ball screen on pick-and-rolls
- Good pick-and-roll ball handler, excellent on hand-offs, explosive finisher in transition
- Very good playmaker that makes the right pass out of double teams, good at avoiding turnovers
- 2022-23 Defensive Degree of Difficulty: 0.471
- 2022-23 Points Prevented: 2.121
- Drew tougher assignments against higher-end starters, fairly solid on-ball defender
- Capable of guarding multiple positions, had some lapses when guarding perimeter players in Brooklyn, less effective against bigger players in Phoenix
- Average pick-and-roll defender, can functionally switch, does not always make sound rotations
- Tends to get caught on screens, good at closing out on spot-up shooters
- Fairly good roamer, good defensive rebounder and weak side shot blocker

Devin Booker

	Height	Weight	Cap #	Years Left
	6'5"	206	$36.016M	4

Similar at Age 26

		Season	SIMsc
1	Zach LaVine	2021-22	936.8
2	Bradley Beal	2019-20	933.8
3	Caris LeVert	2020-21	928.4
4	Ray Allen*	2001-02	914.8
5	Kobe Bryant*	2004-05	914.4
6	Spencer Dinwiddie	2019-20	913.6
7	Damian Lillard	2016-17	913.5
8	Jordan Clarkson	2018-19	907.9
9	Gordon Hayward	2016-17	905.9
10	Bogdan Bogdanovic	2018-19	904.7

Baseline Basic Stats

MPG	PTS	AST	REB	BLK	STL
33.3	21.2	4.3	4.1	0.3	1.0

Advanced Metrics

USG%	3PTA/FGA	FTA/FGA	TS%	eFG%	3PT%
29.8	0.328	0.291	0.578	0.526	0.359

AST%	TOV%	OREB%	DREB%	STL%	BLK%
22.9	10.6	2.3	11.7	1.5	0.8

PER	ORTG	DRTG	WS/48	BPM	VOL
20.03	114.1	112.1	0.140	3.08	0.354

- Missed games due to injuries to his groin and hamstring, All-Star level performer for Phoenix when healthy
- Productivity increased when he was in the lineup, thrived in his role as a primary scoring option
- Efficient scorer at all three levels, good isolation player and pick-and-roll ball handler
- Most effective when driving to the rim or pulling up for mid-range jumpers, can post up smaller guards
- Around a league average three-point shooter, capable of making a lot of difficult shots
- Elite shooter off the catch, below break-even three-point shooter off the dribble
- Good playmaker that usually makes sound decisions, rarely turns the ball over, good cutter off the ball
- 2022-23 Defensive Degree of Difficulty: 0.424
- 2022-23 Points Prevented: 0.580
- Usually guards lower leverage starters, played average on-ball defense
- More effective against stronger players inside, had trouble staying with quicker guards
- Solid pick-and-roll defender, effective on switches, good at steering ball handlers into help
- Fights through screens off the ball, sometimes will be late when closing out on spot-up shooters
- Mostly a stay-at-home defender, occasionally gets steals, fairly solid defensive rebounder

Bradley Beal

	Height	Weight	Cap #	Years Left
	6'3"	207	$46.742M	2 + PO

Similar at Age 29

		Season	SIMsc
1	Ben Gordon	2012-13	922.8
2	Jarrett Jack	2012-13	914.7
3	Kyrie Irving	2021-22	914.1
4	Jrue Holiday	2019-20	911.9
5	CJ McCollum	2020-21	910.0
6	Reggie Jackson	2019-20	905.8
7	Voshon Lenard	2002-03	901.8
8	Deron Williams	2013-14	895.2
9	Cory Joseph	2020-21	894.1
10	Erick Strickland	2002-03	892.7

Baseline Basic Stats

MPG	PTS	AST	REB	BLK	STL
30.5	18.2	4.4	3.4	0.3	0.9

Advanced Metrics

USG%	3PTA/FGA	FTA/FGA	TS%	eFG%	3PT%
27.4	0.305	0.253	0.567	0.523	0.358

AST%	TOV%	OREB%	DREB%	STL%	BLK%
24.3	11.9	2.6	10.1	1.3	1.1

PER	ORTG	DRTG	WS/48	BPM	VOL
17.97	111.8	115.5	0.095	1.36	0.380

- Missed 32 games last season due to an assortment of minor injuries
- Still an All-Star caliber player, excelled as Washington's primary scorer and ball handler
- Very good three-level scorer, does not get to the rim as frequently as he did in the past
- Solid three-point shooter, most reliable as a stationary spot-up shooter, good mid-range shooter
- Can hit no dribble threes on isolations, less effective when running off screens
- Good scorer on hand-offs and pick-and-rolls, may need a screen to create proper separation
- Has developed into a good playmaker that makes sound decisions, good at avoiding turnovers
- 2022-23 Defensive Degree of Difficulty: 0.470
- 2022-23 Points Prevented: 1.152
- Drew tougher matchups against higher-end starters, fairly solid on-ball defender
- Good perimeter defender that stays with opposing guards, has trouble defending taller wings in the post
- Decent pick-and-roll defender, funnels ball handlers into help, tends to late when recognizing pick-and-pop plays
- Tends to get caught on screens off the ball, usually a step late when closing out on spot-up shooters
- Does not really get steals, Block Percentage increased to a career high last season, decent defensive rebounder

Deandre Ayton

	Height	Weight	Cap #	Years Left
	6'11"	250	$32.459M	2

Similar at Age 24

		Season	SIMsc
1	Dave Corzine	1980-81	942.0
2	Mehmet Okur	2003-04	922.3
3	Jonas Valanciunas	2016-17	922.0
4	Channing Frye	2007-08	919.9
5	Marreese Speights	2011-12	917.6
6	Melvin Turpin	1984-85	917.2
7	Al Horford	2010-11	916.6
8	Jason Thompson	2010-11	915.9
9	Darryl Dawkins	1980-81	915.3
10	Nikola Vucevic	2014-15	914.5

Baseline Basic Stats

MPG	PTS	AST	REB	BLK	STL
26.6	12.7	1.5	7.6	0.9	0.6

Advanced Metrics

USG%	3PTA/FGA	FTA/FGA	TS%	eFG%	3PT%
21.6	0.055	0.253	0.601	0.568	0.325

AST%	TOV%	OREB%	DREB%	STL%	BLK%
9.6	11.3	9.0	25.2	1.0	2.3

PER	ORTG	DRTG	WS/48	BPM	VOL
19.47	117.3	107.8	0.158	0.69	0.351

- Regular starting center for Phoenix in his fifth NBA season
- Efficiency dropped slightly, still effective in his role as a moderate volume post scorer and rim runner
- Solid post-up player, good at flashing to the middle, less effective with his back to the basket on either block
- Made almost 81% of his shots inside of three feet, athletic rim runner, can be a vertical lob threat
- Good cutter and roll man, active offensive rebounder, solid at running the floor in transition
- Solid mid-range spot-up shooter, experimenting with shooting threes, has made less than 30% of his career threes
- Mainly a catch-and-finish player, able to make simple passes, good at avoiding turnovers
- 2022-23 Defensive Degree of Difficulty: 0.461
- 2022-23 Points Prevented: 0.252
- Good rim protector, decent shot blocker, stays vertical when challenging shots, very good defensive rebounder
- Takes on tough assignments against top big men, played average on-ball defense
- Usually a good post defender, had trouble against elite scoring big men, has trouble defending in space
- Average pick-and-roll defender, solid in drop coverages, tends to back away from ball handlers
- Tends to stay anchored in the paint, does not always come out to contest shots in spot-up situations

Eric Gordon

	Height	Weight	Cap #	Years Left
	6'3"	215	$3.196M	PO

Similar at Age 34

		Season	SIMsc
1	Joe Dumars*	1997-98	911.2
2	Terry Porter	1997-98	904.8
3	Jose Calderon	2015-16	895.1
4	Ray Allen*	2009-10	894.9
5	J.J. Redick	2018-19	894.1
6	Anthony Parker	2009-10	893.0
7	Jim Jackson	2004-05	888.1
8	Anthony Peeler	2003-04	888.1
9	Byron Scott	1995-96	886.6
10	Michael Finley	2007-08	881.6

Baseline Basic Stats

MPG	PTS	AST	REB	BLK	STL
26.3	10.9	2.4	2.4	0.2	0.6

Advanced Metrics

USG%	3PTA/FGA	FTA/FGA	TS%	eFG%	3PT%
17.8	0.557	0.238	0.578	0.542	0.382

AST%	TOV%	OREB%	DREB%	STL%	BLK%
13.8	12.6	1.4	8.2	1.1	1.0

PER	ORTG	DRTG	WS/48	BPM	VOL
12.22	111.3	116.8	0.062	-1.33	0.422

- Traded from Houston to the L.A. Clippers at the trade deadline, played starter level minutes for both teams
- Solidly effective in his role as a low usage spot-up shooter and secondary ball handler
- Fairly good three-point shooter, percentages have varied from year-to-year
- Great spot-up shooter, can make pull-up threes on pick-and-rolls, struggled to shoot off screens last season
- Crafty ball handler that can leverage the threat of his shot to score on pick-and-rolls and isolation plays, still able to drive to the rim and draw fouls
- Solid secondary playmaker that makes simple reads, good at limiting turnovers
- 2022-23 Defensive Degree of Difficulty: 0.480
- 2022-23 Points Prevented: -0.012
- Usually guarded starting level players, drew a lot of tough assignments against elite perimeter scorers
- Solid on-ball defender, effective when guarding taller wings, plays angles well to stay with opposing guards
- Played below average pick-and-roll defense, not especially effective at taking away any specific action
- Fights through screens off the ball, sometimes was late to close out on spot-up shooters
- Stay-at-home defender, Steal and Block Percentages increased slightly, below average defensive rebounder

Josh Okogie

	Height	Weight	Cap #	Years Left
	6'4"	213	$2.816M	PO

Similar at Age 24

		Season	SIMsc
1	Greg Buckner	2000-01	912.6
2	Fred Hoiberg	1996-97	911.1
3	Tony Allen	2005-06	910.3
4	Norman Powell	2017-18	909.5
5	Fred Jones	2003-04	904.5
6	James Ennis	2014-15	903.8
7	Cody Martin	2019-20	903.0
8	Caleb Martin	2019-20	902.7
9	Rashad McCants	2008-09	901.4
10	Mitchell Butler	1994-95	899.7

Baseline Basic Stats

MPG	PTS	AST	REB	BLK	STL
19.3	6.4	1.3	2.9	0.3	0.8

Advanced Metrics

USG%	3PTA/FGA	FTA/FGA	TS%	eFG%	3PT%
15.8	0.449	0.372	0.549	0.499	0.341

AST%	TOV%	OREB%	DREB%	STL%	BLK%
9.0	11.8	6.3	11.5	2.0	1.8

PER	ORTG	DRTG	WS/48	BPM	VOL
12.39	112.6	112.4	0.092	-0.68	0.301

- Regular rotation player for Phoenix in his first season with the team
- Had his most production season, mainly used as a low usage spot-up shooter and energy player
- Made threes at a break-even rate last season, career Three-Point Percentage is below 30%
- Predominantly a stand-still spot-up shooter, slightly better at making threes in transition
- Good at making backdoor cuts, aggressive player that seeks out contact, draws fouls at a high rate
- Limited ability to create his own shot, defenders can back off him to negate his effectiveness
- Mainly a catch-and-shoot player, improved as a passer, good at avoiding turnovers
- 2022-23 Defensive Degree of Difficulty: 0.504
- 2022-23 Points Prevented: 1.173
- Used as one of Phoenix's main defensive stoppers, good on-ball defender
- Solid at defending guards and wings, good at pressuring ball handlers and taking away air space
- Good pick-and-roll defender, effective at switching to guard ball handlers and screeners
- Tends to get caught on screens off the ball, sometimes can be late to close out on spot-up shooters
- Very active as a roaming help defender, consistently gets steals and blocks at a high rate, fairly solid defensive rebounder

Damion Lee

	Height	Weight	Cap #	Years Left
	6'5"	210	$2.528M	PO

Similar at Age 30

		Season	SIMsc
1	Kyle Korver	2011-12	931.0
2	Jodie Meeks	2017-18	928.4
3	James Ennis	2020-21	927.5
4	Anthony Morrow	2015-16	926.2
5	Maurice Evans	2008-09	924.8
6	Kevin Gamble	1995-96	924.7
7	Keith Bogans	2010-11	922.5
8	Rodney McGruder	2021-22	920.9
9	Morris Peterson	2007-08	918.3
10	Brandon Rush	2015-16	916.8

Baseline Basic Stats

MPG	PTS	AST	REB	BLK	STL
21.3	7.4	1.4	2.5	0.2	0.6

Advanced Metrics

USG%	3PTA/FGA	FTA/FGA	TS%	eFG%	3PT%
15.0	0.547	0.194	0.575	0.542	0.391

AST%	TOV%	OREB%	DREB%	STL%	BLK%
9.2	11.2	2.4	12.8	1.3	0.6

PER	ORTG	DRTG	WS/48	BPM	VOL
10.64	112.6	112.0	0.091	-1.63	0.317

- Regular rotation player for Phoenix in his first season with the team
- Production held steady, mainly utilized as a low usage shooting specialist
- Made 44.5% of his threes last season, percentages tend to vary from year-to-year
- Primarily effective as a stationary spot-up shooter, much less effective when shooting off screens
- Makes sharp backdoor cuts if defenders overplay his shot, good at making trail threes in transition
- Limited ability to create his own shot, not really used in ball handling situations
- Strictly a catch-and-shoot player, only makes safe passes, good at avoiding turnovers
- 2022-23 Defensive Degree of Difficulty: 0.346
- 2022-23 Points Prevented: 0.028
- Usually guarded second unit players, played below average on-ball defense
- Struggled to stay with quicker perimeter players, not effective against stronger players inside
- Average pick-and-roll defender, good at steering ball handlers into help, has lapses when switching onto screeners
- Stays attached to shooters off the ball, fights through screens and closes out in spot-up situations
- Stay-at-home defender, Steal Percentage declined significantly, solid defensive rebounder

Jordan Goodwin

	Height	Weight	Cap #	Years Left
	6'3"	200	$1.928M	TO

Similar at Age 24

		Season	SIMsc
1	Milton Doyle	2017-18	902.2
2	Tyrone Wallace	2018-19	896.6
3	Markel Brown	2015-16	896.1
4	Gabe Vincent	2020-21	893.5
5	Jeff Trepagnier	2003-04	893.4
6	Royal Ivey	2005-06	888.8
7	LaBradford Smith	1993-94	887.4
8	Ray McCallum	2015-16	886.9
9	Darius Morris	2014-15	882.6
10	Beno Udrih	2006-07	882.4

Baseline Basic Stats

MPG	PTS	AST	REB	BLK	STL
22.9	8.9	2.6	2.4	0.1	0.8

Advanced Metrics

USG%	3PTA/FGA	FTA/FGA	TS%	eFG%	3PT%
19.4	0.349	0.174	0.444	0.415	0.306

AST%	TOV%	OREB%	DREB%	STL%	BLK%
17.2	11.3	2.7	12.9	1.7	0.8

PER	ORTG	DRTG	WS/48	BPM	VOL
7.64	89.6	113.4	-0.040	-4.52	0.857

- Became a regular rotation player for Washington in his second NBA season, projection undershot due to a bad six minutes in his rookie season
- Effective in his role as a low usage table setter and spot-up shooter
- Solid playmaker that can run a team and make sound decisions, good at limiting turnovers
- Below break-even three-point shooter, went 13-for-25 (52.0%) on corner threes last season
- Had trouble making spot-up jumpers and shots off the dribble, most effective when taking threes in transition
- Not really effective in ball handling situations, defenders back off him to limit his effectiveness
- Good at pushing the ball in transition, did not really move off the ball in Washington
- 2022-23 Defensive Degree of Difficulty: 0.401
- 2022-23 Points Prevented: -0.873
- Usually guarded second unit players, drew a few tough assignments off the bench
- Effective on-ball defender against lower leverage ones and twos
- Middling pick-and-roll defender, effective at cutting off penetration, goes too far under screens
- Fights through screens off the ball, tends to be late when closing out on spot-up shooters
- Active help defender, posted high steal and block rates last season, solid defensive rebounder

Yuta Watanabe

	Height	Weight	Cap #	Years Left
	6'9"	215	$2.347M	PO

Similar at Age 28

		Season	SIMsc
1	Shawne Williams	2014-15	929.7
2	Darrell Arthur	2016-17	925.1
3	Robert Covington	2018-19	922.8
4	Maurice Harkless	2021-22	918.1
5	Danuel House Jr.	2021-22	917.9
6	James Ennis	2018-19	913.7
7	Luke Babbitt	2017-18	913.6
8	James Jones	2008-09	910.2
9	Torrey Craig	2018-19	907.6
10	Jason Kapono	2009-10	907.3

Baseline Basic Stats

MPG	PTS	AST	REB	BLK	STL
18.8	6.2	1.0	3.4	0.4	0.6

Advanced Metrics

USG%	3PTA/FGA	FTA/FGA	TS%	eFG%	3PT%
14.3	0.603	0.198	0.567	0.543	0.375

AST%	TOV%	OREB%	DREB%	STL%	BLK%
7.2	9.9	4.1	15.6	1.4	2.1

PER	ORTG	DRTG	WS/48	BPM	VOL
11.28	113.1	111.8	0.080	-1.58	0.415

- Fringe rotation player for Brooklyn in his first season with the team
- Greatly improved his efficiency in his role as a low volume spot-up shooter
- Made 44.4% of his threes last season, good career three-point shooter, percentages vary from year-to-year
- Almost exclusively a stationary spot-up shooter, needs time and space to get his shot away
- Can get to the rim on dribble hand-offs, solid cutter off the ball, selectively crashes the offensive glass to score on put-backs
- Rarely used in ball handling situations, not really able to create his own offense
- Strictly a catch-and-shoot player, only makes safe passes, rarely turns the ball over
- <u>2022-23 Defensive Degree of Difficulty</u>: 0.357
- <u>2022-23 Points Prevented</u>: -0.126
- Usually guarded second unit players, below average on-ball defender
- Has trouble staying with quicker players, can be overpowered in the post by stronger wings
- Average pick-and-roll defender, solid at containing ball handlers, has lapses when rotating onto screeners
- Gets caught on screens off the ball, tends to be late when closing out on spot-up shooters
- Steal and Block Percentages were down from his career averages, solid defensive rebounder

Drew Eubanks

	Height	Weight	Cap #	Years Left
	6'9"	245	$2.347M	PO

Similar at Age 25

		Season	SIMsc
1	Samaki Walker	2001-02	927.4
2	Bismack Biyombo	2017-18	926.0
3	Clint Capela	2019-20	919.7
4	Richaun Holmes	2018-19	916.3
5	Marcin Gortat	2009-10	910.9
6	Etan Thomas	2003-04	910.6
7	Brian Skinner	2001-02	908.5
8	Gorgui Dieng	2014-15	907.6
9	Ronny Turiaf	2007-08	904.8
10	Andrew Lang	1991-92	904.7

Baseline Basic Stats

MPG	PTS	AST	REB	BLK	STL
20.8	7.2	1.0	5.9	1.1	0.5

Advanced Metrics

USG%	3PTA/FGA	FTA/FGA	TS%	eFG%	3PT%
14.7	0.041	0.365	0.617	0.591	0.362

AST%	TOV%	OREB%	DREB%	STL%	BLK%
8.4	15.2	9.9	21.7	1.3	4.1

PER	ORTG	DRTG	WS/48	BPM	VOL
16.04	119.7	110.9	0.115	-0.52	0.361

- Regular rotation player for Portland in his first full season with the team, started some games
- Solidly effective in his role as a low usage rim runner
- Made almost 76% of his shots inside of three feet last season, plays with a high motor
- Solid cutter and roll man, active offensive rebounder, runs hard down the floor in transition
- Effective at flashing to the middle on post-ups, occasionally can bully weaker defenders on the right block
- Can make shorter mid-range spot-up jumpers, went 5-for-11 (45.5%) on spot-up threes last season
- Decent passer, can hit cutters and find open shooters, cut his turnover rate last season
- 2022-23 Defensive Degree of Difficulty: 0.436
- 2022-23 Points Prevented: 0.191
- Good defensive rebounder and shot blocker, below average rim protector, limited mobility, not always in position to contest shots
- Guards starting level big men, average on-ball defender
- Struggles to guard elite big men, has trouble defending in space, fairly foul prone
- Below average pick-and-roll defender, not effective at taking away any specific action
- Tends to sag back into the paint, does not always come out to contest outside shots in spot-up situations

Bol Bol

	Height	Weight	Cap #	Years Left
	7'2"	220	$2.020M	UFA

Similar at Age 23

		Season	SIMsc
1	Donatas Motiejunas	2013-14	879.1
2	Keith Closs	1999-00	868.8
3	Granville Waiters	1983-84	868.7
4	John Henson	2013-14	867.4
5	Carlos Rogers	1994-95	866.5
6	Donte Greene	2011-12	865.9
7	Mo Bamba	2021-22	865.7
8	William Bedford	1986-87	864.7
9	Chimezie Metu	2020-21	859.8
10	Skal Labissière	2019-20	859.6

Baseline Basic Stats

MPG	PTS	AST	REB	BLK	STL
17.9	7.0	0.9	4.5	1.0	0.4

Advanced Metrics

USG%	3PTA/FGA	FTA/FGA	TS%	eFG%	3PT%
18.4	0.223	0.270	0.575	0.553	0.315

AST%	TOV%	OREB%	DREB%	STL%	BLK%
7.9	14.6	6.7	21.6	1.2	4.7

PER	ORTG	DRTG	WS/48	BPM	VOL
15.22	107.8	107.7	0.098	-0.37	0.530

- Became a regular rotation player in his first healthy season with Orlando
- Had his most effective season, mainly used as a spot-up shooter and energy player
- Has made less than 30% of his career threes, shooting range is more reliable from 16 feet and in
- Very efficient finisher at the rim, has made almost 87% of his shots inside of three feet for his career
- Good cutter and roll man, efficiently scores on put-backs, solid rim runner
- Likes to push the ball in transition and operate as a pick-and-roll ball handler, tends to play wild, not efficient in those situations
- Not really an effective shot creator, passing ability is limited, somewhat turnover prone
- 2022-23 Defensive Degree of Difficulty: 0.368
- 2022-23 Points Prevented: 0.084
- Good shot blocker and defensive rebounder, below average rim protector, undisciplined with his positioning
- Does not provide enough resistance at the rim due to his thin frame
- Guards second unit players, great length made him somewhat effective as a post defender, struggled to defend in space
- Below average pick-and-roll defender, opponents can exploit his lack of quickness when he makes rotations
- Stays attached to shooters off the ball, fights through screens and closes out in spot-up situations

Chimezie Metu

	Height	Weight	Cap #	Years Left
	6'9"	225	$2.020M	UFA

Similar at Age 25

		Season	SIMsc
1	Earl Clark	2012-13	920.8
2	Michael Beasley	2013-14	918.8
3	Darrell Arthur	2013-14	918.3
4	Omri Casspi	2013-14	916.4
5	Daniel Theis	2017-18	913.7
6	JaMychal Green	2015-16	911.6
7	Jon Leuer	2014-15	910.7
8	Brian Cook	2005-06	909.8
9	Quincy Acy	2015-16	907.9
10	Scott Padgett	2001-02	905.9

Baseline Basic Stats

MPG	PTS	AST	REB	BLK	STL
19.5	7.7	1.0	4.2	0.4	0.6

Advanced Metrics

USG%	3PTA/FGA	FTA/FGA	TS%	eFG%	3PT%
17.4	0.317	0.263	0.580	0.549	0.279

AST%	TOV%	OREB%	DREB%	STL%	BLK%
8.0	11.2	5.7	20.9	1.4	2.0

PER	ORTG	DRTG	WS/48	BPM	VOL
14.24	114.1	111.3	0.102	-0.82	0.293

- Fell out of Sacramento's rotation, played limited minutes last season
- Increased his efficiency in a reduced role as a low usage rim runner and occasional stretch big
- Fairly solid rim runner, lacks the lift to finish in traffic, more efficient finisher in Sacramento's motion offense
- Solid cutter and roll man, fairly active offensive rebounder, good at running the floor in transition
- Has made less than 30% of his career threes, inconsistent spot-up shooter from beyond ten feet
- Occasionally can score on the right block on post-ups or drive by slower big men, not a consistent shot creator
- Catch-and-shoot or catch-and-finish player that makes safe passes, good at limiting turnovers
- 2022-23 Defensive Degree of Difficulty: 0.348
- 2022-23 Points Prevented: -1.352
- Good defensive rebounder, solid shot blocker, below average rim protector, undisciplined with his positioning
- Below average on-ball defender against second unit big men, struggles to guard stronger or quicker players
- Below average pick-and-roll defender, not especially effective at taking away any specific action
- Tends to stay anchored in the paint, does not come out to the perimeter to contest shots in spot-up situations
- Effective at using his length to play passing lanes, gets steals at a solid rate

Keita Bates-Diop

	Height	Weight	Cap #	Years Left
	6'8"	229	$2.347M	PO

Similar at Age 27

		Season	SIMsc
1	Mike Scott	2015-16	937.4
2	Lance Thomas	2015-16	927.3
3	Marvin Williams	2013-14	924.5
4	Al Thornton	2010-11	920.1
5	Jonas Jerebko	2014-15	919.7
6	JaMychal Green	2017-18	919.5
7	David Benoit	1995-96	919.4
8	Luc Mbah a Moute	2013-14	916.8
9	Larry Nance Jr.	2019-20	916.7
10	Chase Budinger	2015-16	915.5

Baseline Basic Stats

MPG	PTS	AST	REB	BLK	STL
22.0	7.7	1.3	4.1	0.3	0.6

Advanced Metrics

USG%	3PTA/FGA	FTA/FGA	TS%	eFG%	3PT%
15.6	0.353	0.253	0.566	0.534	0.375

AST%	TOV%	OREB%	DREB%	STL%	BLK%
8.9	11.4	5.1	16.0	1.5	1.1

PER	ORTG	DRTG	WS/48	BPM	VOL
12.85	112.3	113.0	0.086	-0.97	0.335

- Played rotational minutes for San Antonio in his third season with the team, started most of his games
- Continued to improve, more effective in his role as a low usage spot-up shooter and energy player
- Break-even career three-point shooter, made over 39% of his threes last season
- Almost exclusively a stationary spot-up shooter, not really able to shoot on the move or off the dribble
- High motor rim runner, scores in volume around the rim, solid cutter and roll man
- Occasionally can post up smaller players, sometimes can curl off screens to hit short mid-range jumpers
- Can use an on-ball screen to get to the rim, not able to create proper separation to score on isolations
- Catch-and-shoot player, improved slightly as a passer, rarely turns the ball over
- 2022-23 Defensive Degree of Difficulty: 0.448
- 2022-23 Points Prevented: 0.692
- Typically guarded starting level players, average on-ball defender
- More effective when guarding bigger players inside, had trouble staying with quicker perimeter players
- Played below average pick-and-roll defense, not effective at taking away any specific action
- Tends to get caught on screens off the ball, a step late when closing out on spot-up shooters
- Stay-at-home defender now, occasionally gets steal, did not really block shots, fairly solid defensive rebounder

Ish Wainright

	Height	Weight	Cap #	Years Left
	6'6"	250	$1.928M	RFA

Similar at Age 28

		Season	SIMsc
1	Scott Padgett	2004-05	889.2
2	Solomon Hill	2019-20	884.7
3	Ryan Gomes	2010-11	882.5
4	Anthony Gill	2020-21	879.1
5	James Jones	2008-09	876.7
6	Danuel House Jr.	2021-22	874.6
7	Justin Anderson	2021-22	874.1
8	Brian Scalabrine	2006-07	873.3
9	Torrey Craig	2018-19	870.0
10	Mickael Pietrus	2010-11	868.5

Baseline Basic Stats

MPG	PTS	AST	REB	BLK	STL
15.9	4.4	0.9	2.6	0.3	0.5

Advanced Metrics

USG%	3PTA/FGA	FTA/FGA	TS%	eFG%	3PT%
12.4	0.653	0.172	0.524	0.503	0.324

AST%	TOV%	OREB%	DREB%	STL%	BLK%
6.7	9.9	5.6	12.3	1.7	1.8

PER	ORTG	DRTG	WS/48	BPM	VOL
9.00	110.0	110.5	0.081	-2.35	0.433

- Began the season on a Two-Way contract with Phoenix, later signed to a standard contract
- Fringe rotation player, primarily used as a low usage spot-up shooter
- Below break-even career three-point shooter, around league average when shooting corner threes
- Strictly a stand-still spot-up shooter, ineffective when shooting in other situations
- Less effective as a rim runner, played in a static offense, lacks the ideal lift to finish in traffic, only effective as a cutter
- Not able to create his own offense, catch-and-shoot player that makes safe passes, rarely turns the ball over
- 2022-23 Defensive Degree of Difficulty: 0.383
- 2022-23 Points Prevented: 0.212
- Usually guarded second unit level players, around an average on-ball defender
- More effective when guarding taller wings in the post, had trouble staying with quicker perimeter players
- Below average pick-and-roll defender, struggled to contain ball handlers, had lapses when rotating onto screener
- Stay attached to shooters off the ball, fights through screens and closes out in spot-up situations
- Very active help defender, gets steals and blocks at a pretty high rate, decent defensive rebounder

Newcomers

Toumani Camara

	Height	Weight	Cap #	Years Left
	6'8"	220	$1.120M	2 + TO

Baseline Basic Stats

MPG	PTS	AST	REB	BLK	STL
17.8	5.8	0.9	3.3	0.4	0.6

Advanced Metrics

USG%	3PTA/FGA	FTA/FGA	TS%	eFG%	3PT%
15.5	0.222	0.316	0.503	0.471	0.312

AST%	TOV%	OREB%	DREB%	STL%	BLK%
8.1	12.7	6.8	14.6	1.8	1.7

PER	ORTG	DRTG	WS/48	BPM	VOL
12.08	100.2	98.7	0.061	-1.38	N/A

- Drafted by Phoenix with the 52nd overall pick in 2023
- Played pretty well at the Las Vegas Summer League
- Highly productive in his role as a high usage scoring wing, will likely play a lower volume role in the NBA
- Effective at attacking the rim, drew fouls at a very high rate, good at bullying smaller perimeter players in the post
- Drives hard to the rim, still needs to improve his ball handling, tended to lose the ball while dribbling, fairly turnover prone
- Energetic rim runner, great cutter and roll man, good offensive rebounder, runs the floor and explosively finishes in transition
- Made less than 25% of his threes at Summer League, below break-even three-point shooter in college
- Showed decent secondary playmaking skills, could effectively make simple reads
- Long and athletic defender, has the potential to become a plus-level defender with versatility
- Solid on-ball defender that guards multiple position, can defend on the perimeter and in the post, backs off a bit too much on the perimeter
- Good pick-and-roll defender, effectively switches to guard ball handlers and screeners
- Stays attached to shooters off the ball, fights through screens and closes out in spot-up situations
- More of a stay-at-home defender at Summer League, did not really get steals, occasional weak side shot blocker, fairly solid defensive rebounder
- May benefit from some additional seasoning in the G-League to improve his shooting if he plays on the wing
- Might push for regular rotational minutes if deployed as a small-ball center

OKLAHOMA CITY THUNDER

Last Season: 40 - 42, Missed the Playoffs

Offensive Rating: 115.2, 13th in the NBA   Defensive Rating: 114.2, 14th in the NBA

Primary Executive: Sam Presti, Executive Vice President/General Manager

Head Coach: Mark Daigneault

Key Roster Changes

Subtractions
Dario Šarić, free agency
Lindy Waters III, free agency*

Additions
Cason Wallace, draft
Dāvis Bertāns, trade
Victor Oladipo, trade
Vasilije Micic, signed/rights held

* Oklahoma City let Waters go, then re-signed him to a Two-Way contract

Roster

Likely Starting Five
1. Shai Gilgeous-Alexander
2. Josh Giddey
3. Luguentz Dort
4. Jalen Williams
5. Chet Holmgren

Other Key Rotation Players
Isaiah Joe
Kenrich Williams
Aaron Wiggins
Aleksej Pokusevski
Vasilije Micic

* Italics denotes that a player is likely to be on the floor to close games

Remaining Roster

- Jaylin Williams
- Jeremiah Robinson-Earl
- Tre Mann
- Cason Wallace
- Ousmane Dieng
- Usman Garuba (waived while the book was being finalized)
- Dāvis Bertāns
- Victor Oladipo
- Jack White
- Keyontae Johnson, 23, 6'5", 230, Kansas State (Two-Way)
- Lindy Waters III, 26, 6'6", 215, Oklahoma State (Two-Way)
- Olivier Sarr, 24, 7'0", 237, Kentucky (Two-Way)
- KJ Williams, 24, 6'10", 250, LSU (Exhibit 10)
- Adam Flagler, 24, 6'2", 190, Baylor (Exhibit 10)
- Caleb McConnell, 24, 6'7", 200, Rutgers (Exhibit 10)

SCHREMPF Base Rating: 41.9

Season Preview Survey

- *Are the Thunder contending or rebuilding? Where is this team headed?*

The Thunder is a team on the upswing because they were able to make the play-in tournament after spending a few years in a rebuilding mode. They are looking to make a full transition into being a true playoff contender, but they have taken a more cautious approach because they are mostly going to depend on their internal growth to reach the next level. The one notable addition that they will be getting will come in the form of Chet Holmgren, as he's set to recover from the broken foot that he suffered last offseason. He should fill a sizeable hole on the interior, so the team is set to improve this season. If they build up their chemistry and coalesce as a unit, they could exceed expectations again and get into the playoffs. Otherwise, they could wind up back in the play-in tournament, but they would be in an improved position to pull out some wins to give them a chance to land a lower playoff seed this year.

- *What are the areas of concern for this team heading into this season?*

Oklahoma City has a young team with minimal expectations because they have been rebuilding for a while. There aren't too many pressing concerns that they have to address immediately. However, they have some issues that they may need to resolve to give them the chances at the best possible future. In particular, they have to find a way to be less reliant on Shai Gilgeous-Alexander to generate offense. Their offensive system veered towards a heliocentric approach because almost everything revolved around him. They were able to be an above average offensive team because they really pushed the pace, but their offense tended to stall in half-court situations if Gilgeous-Alexander was having an off night. They didn't incorporate a lot of movement and they didn't have many reliable secondary sources of offense. They will have to work to diversify their attack to make themselves more effective against better defensive teams. The addition of Holmgren will help to a degree because it will give them another threat to attack the rim and space the floor, but they will need to adjust their tactics to allow different types of players to thrive in their system.

- *List some possible breakout players for this team.*

Oklahoma City's active roster is almost entirely filled with young players that are still in the developmental phases of their career. Basically, the whole team has a chance to break out and take their game to another level. A lot will depend on who exactly winds up in the team's regular rotation. Of the players that are expected to receive consistent playing time, the ones are set to level up and improve significantly are Jalen Williams and Aleksej Pokusevski. Williams really came on in the second half of last season to emerge as an intriguing talent that could provide secondary scoring to support Gilgeous-Alexander and active off-ball defense. Pokusevski was on his way to career best season, but he ended up missing time due to a leg injury. If he recovers from his latest injury, he could wind up becoming an x-factor off their bench by being a seven-footer that can knock down threes, handle the ball, and block shots from the weak side.

- *What should we expect from them this season?*

Oklahoma City is going to be a wild card in the Western Conference because they have enormous potential that is still unrealized. They have a lot of developing young players around Shai Gilgeous-Alexander, so if they can channel their abilities in a way that makes them a cohesive team, then they could be a surprising unit that makes a strong playoff push this season. However, in all likelihood, they will be a team that has its ups and downs because their inexperience will show up. Even so, they are still talented enough to earn a berth in the play-in tournament this year.

Veterans

Shai Gilgeous-Alexander

	Height	Weight	Cap #	Years Left
	6'6"	180	$33.387M	3

Similar at Age 24

		Season	SIMsc
1	Zach LaVine	2019-20	934.9
2	Richard Hamilton	2002-03	902.0
3	De'Aaron Fox	2021-22	896.8
4	Kobe Bryant*	2002-03	889.4
5	Brandon Ingram	2021-22	888.0
6	Kevin Martin	2007-08	881.5
7	Kyrie Irving	2016-17	880.1
8	Michael Jordan*	1987-88	880.0
9	Andrew Wiggins	2019-20	880.0
10	Rodney Stuckey	2010-11	874.3

Baseline Basic Stats

MPG	PTS	AST	REB	BLK	STL
36.1	24.3	4.9	4.8	0.5	1.4

Advanced Metrics

USG%	3PTA/FGA	FTA/FGA	TS%	eFG%	3PT%
30.6	0.229	0.431	0.596	0.522	0.361

AST%	TOV%	OREB%	DREB%	STL%	BLK%
27.2	11.0	2.5	12.7	2.0	1.6

PER	ORTG	DRTG	WS/48	BPM	VOL
23.85	118.3	111.2	0.187	3.48	0.359

- Made his first All-Star team, named to the All-NBA 1st Team in 2022-23
- Had a breakout season, thrived as Oklahoma City's primary scorer and ball handler
- Great downhill driver on pick-and-rolls and isolation plays, slashes to the rim and draws a lot of fouls, good at making pull-up jumpers and floaters from mid-range
- Above break-even career three-point shooter, has made almost 40% of his career threes
- Most effective as a stationary spot-up shooter, needs space to shoot efficiently
- Good cutter, great playmaker that can also push the ball in transition, rarely turns the ball over
- 2022-23 Defensive Degree of Difficulty: 0.414
- 2022-23 Points Prevented: 0.795
- Usually guards lower leverage starters to conserve energy, effective on-ball defender in these matchups
- Can capably defend multiple positions, solid on the perimeter, effective when guarding taller wings
- Solid pick-and-roll defender, good at switching to guard ball handlers and screeners, makes sound rotations
- Sometimes gets caught on screens off the ball, good at closing out on spot-up shooters
- More active as a help defender, Steal and Block Percentages increased to career highs, fairly solid defensive rebounder

Josh Giddey

	Height	Weight	Cap #	Years Left
	6'8"	210	$6.587M	TO

Similar at Age 20

		Season	SIMsc
1	Darius Bazley	2020-21	905.7
2	Harrison Barnes	2012-13	895.8
3	Jayson Tatum	2018-19	893.0
4	Cade Cunningham	2021-22	888.2
5	Josh Jackson	2017-18	886.7
6	RJ Barrett	2020-21	882.6
7	Luol Deng	2005-06	880.0
8	Franz Wagner	2021-22	876.1
9	Joe Johnson	2001-02	874.5
10	Tobias Harris	2012-13	873.3

Baseline Basic Stats

MPG	PTS	AST	REB	BLK	STL
31.9	16.0	3.1	5.7	0.4	1.0

Advanced Metrics

USG%	3PTA/FGA	FTA/FGA	TS%	eFG%	3PT%
24.3	0.281	0.200	0.539	0.509	0.331

AST%	TOV%	OREB%	DREB%	STL%	BLK%
24.1	14.0	5.0	17.4	1.5	1.0

PER	ORTG	DRTG	WS/48	BPM	VOL
16.98	108.0	110.7	0.096	1.14	0.316

- Regular starter for Oklahoma City in his second NBA season
- Greatly improved, highly effective in his role as a moderate volume playmaker
- Outstanding playmaker that has excellent court vision, able to see angles that others don't, somewhat turnover prone
- Made spot-up threes at a break-even rate, still inefficient when shooting in other situations
- Can push the ball in transition, solid cutter, got to the rim a bit more last season
- Inconsistent in ball handling situations, defenders back off him to limit his effectiveness when driving
- 2022-23 Defensive Degree of Difficulty: 0.367
- 2022-23 Points Prevented: -0.932
- Often hidden in favorable matchups against lower leverage players, average on-ball defender
- Tends to back off his man on the perimeter, prone to committing shooting fouls in the post
- Average pick-and-roll defender, has lapses when rotating onto screeners, good at funneling his man into help
- Gets caught on screens off the ball, consistently closes out on spot-up shooters
- Stay-at-home defender last season, did not really get steals or blocks, good defensive rebounder

Jalen Williams

	Height	Weight	Cap #	Years Left
	6'6"	195	$4.559M	2 TO

Similar at Age 21

		Season	SIMsc
1	Alec Burks	2012-13	915.5
2	Ray Allen*	1996-97	914.0
3	Kobe Bryant*	1999-00	911.1
4	Ben McLemore	2014-15	911.0
5	Kevin Huerter	2019-20	910.2
6	Andre Iguodala	2004-05	908.5
7	Luke Kennard	2017-18	907.4
8	Devin Vassell	2021-22	907.3
9	Gordon Hayward	2011-12	904.2
10	C.J. Miles	2008-09	903.0

Baseline Basic Stats

MPG	PTS	AST	REB	BLK	STL
31.0	14.3	2.9	3.7	0.4	1.1

Advanced Metrics

USG%	3PTA/FGA	FTA/FGA	TS%	eFG%	3PT%
19.5	0.221	0.287	0.571	0.526	0.354

AST%	TOV%	OREB%	DREB%	STL%	BLK%
16.0	12.6	3.3	10.9	2.0	0.9

PER	ORTG	DRTG	WS/48	BPM	VOL
14.72	113.5	112.9	0.107	0.62	0.417

- Named to the All-Rookie 1st Team, runner-up Rookie of the Year voting
- Highly effective in his role as a low usage complementary wing for Oklahoma City
- Around a league average three-point shooter, almost exclusively a spot-up shooter at this stage
- Good isolation player and pick-and-roll ball handler, slashes downhill to get to the rim, effective enough at shooting off the dribble to keep defenders honest
- Good cutter off the ball, great athlete that explosively finishes in transition
- Solid secondary playmaker that makes simple reads, good at avoiding turnovers
- 2022-23 Defensive Degree of Difficulty: 0.433
- 2022-23 Points Prevented: -1.166
- Typically guarded starting level players as a rookie, decent on-ball defender
- Quick enough to stay with opposing perimeter players, had trouble when guarding stronger players inside
- Decent pick-and-roll defender, can functionally switch, has some lapses when defending ball handlers
- Gambles a bit too much, gets caught on screens off the ball, not always in position to contest spot-up jumpers
- Active help defender, gets steals at a fairly high rate, occasionally blocks shots on the weak side, fairly solid defensive rebounder

Luguentz Dort

	Height	Weight	Cap #	Years Left
	6'3"	215	$15.278M	2 + PO

Similar at Age 23

		Season	SIMsc
1	Norman Powell	2016-17	938.6
2	Buddy Hield	2016-17	924.8
3	O.J. Mayo	2010-11	923.7
4	Frank Jackson	2021-22	920.1
5	Randy Foye	2006-07	919.1
6	Lonnie Walker IV	2021-22	918.5
7	Malik Monk	2021-22	915.8
8	Jamal Murray	2020-21	915.0
9	Gerald Henderson	2010-11	911.9
10	Desmond Bane	2021-22	909.4

Baseline Basic Stats

MPG	PTS	AST	REB	BLK	STL
27.5	13.3	2.4	3.1	0.3	0.9

Advanced Metrics

USG%	3PTA/FGA	FTA/FGA	TS%	eFG%	3PT%
21.9	0.483	0.263	0.543	0.500	0.361

AST%	TOV%	OREB%	DREB%	STL%	BLK%
12.2	9.8	3.3	10.5	1.7	0.9

PER	ORTG	DRTG	WS/48	BPM	VOL
13.72	109.1	113.5	0.077	-1.15	0.280

- Regular starter for Oklahoma City in his fourth NBA season
- Efficiency declined in a new role as a low volume spot-up shooter and energy player
- Around a break-even career three-point shooter, has made over 40% of his career threes
- Slightly above break-even as a spot-up shooter, inconsistent shooter off the dribble
- Average in ball handling situations, willing to absorb contact to draw fouls
- Lacks the ball handling skills to consistently get to the rim, drives wildly, prone to missing easy shots inside
- Mainly a catch-and-shoot player, only makes safe passes, rarely turns the ball over
- 2022-23 Defensive Degree of Difficulty: 0.592, had the 6th most difficult set of matchups in the NBA
- 2022-23 Points Prevented: 0.623
- Has been Oklahoma City's main defensive stopper for several years
- Great on-ball defender that can effectively defend guards and wings across multiple positions
- Played below average pick-and-roll defense, took bad angles, not effective at taking away any specific action
- Fights through screens off the ball, usually was a step late when closing out on spot-up shooters
- Got steals at a moderately high rate, decent defensive rebounder

Isaiah Joe

	Height	Weight	Cap #	Years Left
	6'4"	165	$1.997M	TO

Similar at Age 23

		Season	SIMsc
1	Landry Shamet	2020-21	926.8
2	Alex Abrines	2016-17	902.3
3	Armoni Brooks	2021-22	893.8
4	Travis Diener	2005-06	888.8
5	Tyler Johnson	2015-16	888.1
6	Malik Beasley	2019-20	887.0
7	Sasha Vujacic	2007-08	883.3
8	Rudy Fernandez	2008-09	882.9
9	Leandro Barbosa	2005-06	881.5
10	Daniel Gibson	2009-10	881.2

Baseline Basic Stats

MPG	PTS	AST	REB	BLK	STL
22.8	10.0	1.8	2.3	0.2	0.6

Advanced Metrics

USG%	3PTA/FGA	FTA/FGA	TS%	eFG%	3PT%
18.3	0.739	0.184	0.576	0.543	0.383

AST%	TOV%	OREB%	DREB%	STL%	BLK%
11.3	7.5	1.5	10.2	1.5	0.6

PER	ORTG	DRTG	WS/48	BPM	VOL
13.05	116.4	114.1	0.105	-0.41	0.358

- Became a regular rotation player for Oklahoma City after he was waived by Philadelphia
- Highly effective in his role as a low usage shooting specialist
- Above break-even three-point shooter in two years with Philadelphia, made almost 41% of his threes last season
- Great shooter off the catch, makes spot-up jumpers, runs off screens, good on pick-and-pops
- Good at scoring on dribble hand-offs, solid at running the break to get layups in transition
- Lacks the ball handling skills to create his own shot off the dribble
- Catch-and-shoot player that makes safe passes, rarely turns the ball over
- 2022-23 Defensive Degree of Difficulty: 0.313
- 2022-23 Points Prevented: -0.144
- Usually was hidden in matchups against low leverage second unit players
- Effective defender in these assignments, could passably defend ones and twos on the ball
- Solid pick-and-roll defender, can functionally switch, good at steering his man into help
- Stays attached to shooters off the ball, fights through screens and closes out in spot-up situations
- Active help defender, plays passing lanes to get steals at a solid rate, fairly solid defensive rebounder

Kenrich Williams

	Height	Weight	Cap #	Years Left
	6'6"	210	$6.175M	2 + TO

Similar at Age 28

		Season	SIMsc
1	Kyle Korver	2009-10	921.1
2	Juan Toscano-Anderson	2021-22	919.4
3	Bobby Simmons	2008-09	914.9
4	Shandon Anderson	2001-02	910.2
5	James Ennis	2018-19	907.6
6	Solomon Hill	2019-20	907.2
7	Iman Shumpert	2018-19	905.3
8	Jud Buechler	1996-97	904.1
9	Damion Lee	2020-21	902.5
10	Chris Morris	1993-94	902.2

Baseline Basic Stats

MPG	PTS	AST	REB	BLK	STL
19.1	6.5	1.1	3.1	0.2	0.6

Advanced Metrics

USG%	3PTA/FGA	FTA/FGA	TS%	eFG%	3PT%
15.0	0.457	0.168	0.553	0.539	0.364

AST%	TOV%	OREB%	DREB%	STL%	BLK%
10.5	9.9	6.3	13.9	1.7	1.0

PER	ORTG	DRTG	WS/48	BPM	VOL
12.67	115.2	111.1	0.102	-0.41	0.349

- Missed games due to a wrist injury that required surgery, regular rotation player for Oklahoma City when healthy
- Had a career best season, mainly utilized as a low usage spot-up shooter
- Above break-even three-point shooter, has made over 39% of his career corner threes
- Almost exclusively a stand-still spot-up shooter, not efficient when shooting in other situations
- Effective energy player that scores on hustle plays, active offensive rebounder, good cutter and roll man, great at running the break to finish in transition
- Limited as a shot creator, solid secondary playmaker, rarely turns the ball over
- 2022-23 Defensive Degree of Difficulty: 0.447
- 2022-23 Points Prevented: -1.540
- Draws some tough assignments off the bench, average on-ball defender
- Decent multiple position defender in the past, better against bigger players inside, had trouble staying with quicker perimeter players
- Good pick-and-roll defender, solid at switching to cover ball handlers and screeners
- Tends to get caught on screens off the ball, usually was a step late when closing out on spot-up shooters
- Fairly good at playing passing lanes to deflect passes or get steals, solid defensive rebounder

Aaron Wiggins

	Height	Weight	Cap #	Years Left
	6'6"	200	$1.836M	TO

Similar at Age 24

		Season	SIMsc
1	Dorell Wright	2009-10	936.1
2	Martell Webster	2010-11	933.1
3	PJ Dozier	2020-21	932.7
4	James Ennis	2014-15	929.5
5	Terance Mann	2020-21	924.1
6	Wayne Ellington	2011-12	923.7
7	DerMarr Johnson	2004-05	923.4
8	Quincy Pondexter	2012-13	923.3
9	Reggie Williams	2010-11	923.1
10	Allen Crabbe	2016-17	923.0

Baseline Basic Stats

MPG	PTS	AST	REB	BLK	STL
23.8	9.0	1.7	3.0	0.3	0.7

Advanced Metrics

USG%	3PTA/FGA	FTA/FGA	TS%	eFG%	3PT%
16.4	0.447	0.197	0.571	0.541	0.364

AST%	TOV%	OREB%	DREB%	STL%	BLK%
10.5	11.2	3.7	11.6	1.4	1.0

PER	ORTG	DRTG	WS/48	BPM	VOL
12.40	112.2	113.6	0.082	-1.17	0.404

- Regular rotation player for Oklahoma City in his second NBA season
- Efficiency improved, effective in his role as a low usage spot-up shooter
- Made over 39% of his threes last season, more effective when shooting threes above the break
- Almost exclusively a stationary spot-up shooter, more efficient when shooting threes in transition
- Makes sharp backdoor cuts if defenders try to crowd him, good at rolling to the rim for layups
- Sometimes can drive to the rim on pick-and-rolls, lacks the ball handling skills to create his own shot on isolation plays
- Mainly a catch-and-shoot player that makes safe passes, good at avoiding turnovers
- 2022-23 Defensive Degree of Difficulty: 0.415
- 2022-23 Points Prevented: -1.897
- Drew some tougher assignments off the bench, more effective as an on-ball defender
- Could solidly guard multiple positions on the ball in lower leverage assignments
- Played below average pick-and-roll defense, not especially effective at taking away specific action
- Gets caught on screens off the ball, usually was late when closing out on spot-up shooters
- Stay-at-home defender, steal and block rates increased slightly, fairly solid defensive rebounder

Aleksej Pokusevski

	Height	Weight	Cap #	Years Left
	7'0"	190	$5.010M	RFA

Similar at Age 21

		Season	SIMsc
1	Austin Daye	2009-10	895.4
2	Thon Maker	2018-19	870.3
3	Quincy Miller	2013-14	869.1
4	Jonathan Isaac	2018-19	869.0
5	Jaden McDaniels	2021-22	856.6
6	DerMarr Johnson	2001-02	856.1
7	Chris McCullough	2016-17	852.1
8	Darius Bazley	2021-22	848.7
9	Donte Greene	2009-10	847.6
10	Jonathan Bender	2001-02	847.2

Baseline Basic Stats

MPG	PTS	AST	REB	BLK	STL
18.8	7.4	1.2	3.8	0.8	0.5

Advanced Metrics

USG%	3PTA/FGA	FTA/FGA	TS%	eFG%	3PT%
18.0	0.261	0.213	0.529	0.507	0.329

AST%	TOV%	OREB%	DREB%	STL%	BLK%
12.3	14.5	6.8	16.7	1.5	3.7

PER	ORTG	DRTG	WS/48	BPM	VOL
13.01	105.9	110.8	0.072	-0.45	0.579

- Missed most of last season due to a leg injury, regular starter for Oklahoma City when healthy
- Had his most efficient season when healthy, used as a low usage spot-up shooter and secondary playmaker
- Made less than 30% of his threes before this season, became an above average three-point shooter
- Better as a stand-still spot-up shooter, below break as a pick-and-pop screener
- Struggles to finish shots in traffic due to his thin frame, less effective as a rim runner
- Rarely used in ball handling situations, still learning shot selection, can take some questionable shots
- Solid secondary playmaker that flashes ball handling skills, cut his turnover rate last season
- 2022-23 Defensive Degree of Difficulty: 0.413
- 2022-23 Points Prevented: 2.690
- Used as a roamer, hidden a bit in favorable matchups against lower leverage starters
- Excellent weak side shot blocker, occasionally gets steals, fairly good defensive rebounder
- Decent on-ball defender, good at staying with perimeter players, lacks strength, struggles against bigger players on the interior
- Solid pick-and-roll defender, effective at switching to cover screeners and ball handlers
- Fights through screens off the ball, good at closing out on spot-up shooters

Jaylin Williams

	Height	Weight	Cap #	Years Left
	6'10"	240	$2.000M	1 + TO

Similar at Age 20

		Season	SIMsc
1	Ryan Anderson	2008-09	925.2
2	Noah Vonleh	2015-16	915.8
3	Trey Lyles	2015-16	914.2
4	Domantas Sabonis	2016-17	904.5
5	Sekou Doumbouya	2020-21	899.2
6	Zeke Nnaji	2020-21	894.9
7	Marquese Chriss	2017-18	894.3
8	Danilo Gallinari	2008-09	888.1
9	Zach Collins	2017-18	886.4
10	OG Anunoby	2017-18	882.3

Baseline Basic Stats

MPG	PTS	AST	REB	BLK	STL
17.9	7.2	1.1	4.7	0.4	0.5

Advanced Metrics

USG%	3PTA/FGA	FTA/FGA	TS%	eFG%	3PT%
17.5	0.418	0.271	0.581	0.548	0.398

AST%	TOV%	OREB%	DREB%	STL%	BLK%
10.9	13.0	7.0	21.9	1.4	1.4

PER	ORTG	DRTG	WS/48	BPM	VOL
14.58	116.1	111.4	0.111	-0.80	0.400

- Started most of his games, played fringe rotational minutes for Oklahoma City as a rookie
- Solidly effective in his role as a low volume stretch big
- Made almost 41% of his threes, went 10-for-18 (55.6%) on corner threes
- Excellent spot-up shooter, also knocks down threes in transition, less effective when shooting on the move
- Lacks strength, had trouble finishing in traffic, not really effective in rim running situations
- Not really a post-up threat, fairly solid passing big man that finds open shooters and cutters, good at avoiding turnovers
- 2022-23 Defensive Degree of Difficulty: 0.426
- 2022-23 Points Prevented: -3.379
- Solid rim protector despite low shot blocking rates, good defensive rebounder
- Takes a lot of charges, also prone to committing blocking fouls if a charge attempt is unsuccessful
- Usually guarded starting level centers, stout post defender, has trouble defending in space
- Solid pick-and-roll defender, good in drop coverages, effective at hedging out on ball handlers
- Tends to stay anchored in the paint, does not always come out to contest shots in spot-up situations
- Has fairly active hands, can use his length to get steals at a fairly solid rate

Jeremiah Robinson-Earl

	Height	Weight	Cap #	Years Left
	6'9"	230	$1.900M	TO

Similar at Age 22

		Season	SIMsc
1	Sam Dekker	2016-17	957.2
2	Juan Hernangomez	2017-18	942.7
3	Obi Toppin	2020-21	936.6
4	Omri Casspi	2010-11	933.3
5	D.J. Wilson	2018-19	930.2
6	Luke Babbitt	2011-12	923.1
7	Paul Zipser	2016-17	913.7
8	Jon Leuer	2011-12	912.9
9	Donyell Marshall	1995-96	911.2
10	Marvin Williams	2008-09	910.0

Baseline Basic Stats

MPG	PTS	AST	REB	BLK	STL
19.4	7.1	1.0	3.9	0.4	0.6

Advanced Metrics

USG%	3PTA/FGA	FTA/FGA	TS%	eFG%	3PT%
15.6	0.403	0.198	0.553	0.525	0.365

AST%	TOV%	OREB%	DREB%	STL%	BLK%
7.6	9.1	6.7	16.4	1.5	1.5

PER	ORTG	DRTG	WS/48	BPM	VOL
13.21	114.6	111.8	0.102	-1.09	0.367

- Missed over a month with a sprained ankle, regular rotation player for Oklahoma City when healthy
- Efficiency increased in his role as a low usage stretch big
- Above break-even three-point shooter in his two-year career, predominantly a stationary spot-up shooter
- Less effective when shooting in other situations, not really a post-up threat or ball handler
- Lacks the ideal vertical lift, has trouble finishing in heavy traffic, middling effectiveness as a rim runner
- Plays with a high motor, will dive hard to the rim, solid as a cutter off the ball
- Strictly a catch-and-shoot player, only makes safe passes, rarely turns the ball over
- 2022-23 Defensive Degree of Difficulty: 0.448
- 2022-23 Points Prevented: -1.611
- Solid rim protector despite low shot blocking rates, stays vertical when challenging shots
- Fairly solid defensive rebounder, can sometimes play passing lanes to get steals
- Guards starting level big men, struggles against bigger centers in the post, better when defending in space
- Average pick-and-roll defender, effective at switching onto ball handlers, has trouble when guarding rolling big men
- Tends to sag back into the paint, does not always come out to contest outside shots in spot-up situations

Tre Mann

	Height	Weight	Cap #	Years Left
	6'3"	178	$3.191M	TO

Similar at Age 21

		Season	SIMsc
1	Jeremy Lamb	2013-14	937.3
2	Anfernee Simons	2020-21	929.0
3	Tyler Dorsey	2017-18	924.4
4	Bones Hyland	2021-22	920.2
5	Zach LaVine	2016-17	919.8
6	Cameron Payne	2015-16	919.5
7	Elie Okobo	2018-19	918.2
8	Immanuel Quickley	2020-21	917.7
9	Malik Monk	2019-20	917.2
10	Jaylen Nowell	2020-21	915.3

Baseline Basic Stats

MPG	PTS	AST	REB	BLK	STL
22.1	10.3	2.4	2.5	0.2	0.7

Advanced Metrics

USG%	3PTA/FGA	FTA/FGA	TS%	eFG%	3PT%
20.8	0.341	0.174	0.519	0.491	0.340

AST%	TOV%	OREB%	DREB%	STL%	BLK%
16.1	11.5	2.2	10.4	1.7	0.7

PER	ORTG	DRTG	WS/48	BPM	VOL
11.69	104.5	114.1	0.047	-2.31	0.311

- Regular rotation player for Oklahoma City in his second NBA season
- Efficiency dropped slightly, mainly used as a moderate volume scoring guard off the bench
- Three-Point Percentage fell to below break-even last season, has made over 44% of his career corner threes
- Struggled to make spot-up jumpers and shots off the dribble, most effective when taking threes in transition
- Decent at driving by defenders on isolations, can make mid-range pull-up jumpers or floaters
- Shot selection is still questionable, improved to become a decent secondary playmaker, rarely turns the ball over
- 2022-23 Defensive Degree of Difficulty: 0.271
- 2022-23 Points Prevented: -0.169
- Often hidden in favorable matchups against lower leverage second unit players
- Played solid on-ball defense against lower-end players, passably can guard ones and twos
- Solid pick-and-roll defender, limited ability to switch, funnels his man into help, makes sound rotations
- Stays attached to shooters off the ball, fights through screens and closes out in spot-up situations
- Effective at using his anticipation skills to play passing lanes and get steals, decent defensive rebounder

Ousmane Dieng

	Height	Weight	Cap #	Years Left
	6'10"	216	$4.798M	2 TO

Similar at Age 19

		Season	SIMsc
1	Sekou Doumbouya	2019-20	914.9
2	Troy Brown	2018-19	911.0
3	Martell Webster	2005-06	896.4
4	Aaron Gordon	2014-15	894.1
5	Darius Bazley	2019-20	888.5
6	JT Thor	2021-22	887.9
7	James Young	2014-15	881.7
8	Kevin Knox	2018-19	878.8
9	Alen Smailagić	2019-20	873.7
10	Nikoloz Tskitishvili	2002-03	872.9

Baseline Basic Stats

MPG	PTS	AST	REB	BLK	STL
19.4	7.5	1.2	3.7	0.4	0.6

Advanced Metrics

USG%	3PTA/FGA	FTA/FGA	TS%	eFG%	3PT%
17.9	0.418	0.215	0.543	0.520	0.316

AST%	TOV%	OREB%	DREB%	STL%	BLK%
12.2	11.4	4.5	18.4	1.6	1.4

PER	ORTG	DRTG	WS/48	BPM	VOL
13.24	109.3	112.4	0.066	-1.49	0.423

- Played limited minutes for Oklahoma City, spent time in the G-League with the Oklahoma City Blue
- Mainly used as a low volume spot-up shooter in his rookie season
- Shooting is still a work-in-progress, made less than 30% of his threes, strictly a spot-up shooter
- Stroke is still inconsistent, made less than two-thirds of his free throws last season
- Great athlete, better as a rim runner, made almost 79% of his shots inside of three feet
- Great cutter, explosive finisher in transition, lacks the ball handling skills to create his own shot
- Mostly a catch-and-shoot player, flashes some passing skills, good at avoiding turnovers
- <u>2022-23 Defensive Degree of Difficulty</u>: 0.229
- <u>2022-23 Points Prevented</u>: 0.295
- Mostly played in garbage time, also used as a roamer, guarded lower leverage bench players
- Rarely tested as an on-ball defender, effective when guarding perimeter players, can be overpowered by stronger players in the post
- Solid pick-and-roll defender, fairly good at switching to defend ball handlers and screeners
- Fights through screens off the ball, tends to be a step late when closing out on spot-up shooters
- Stay-at-home defender last season, did not really get steals or blocks, solid defensive rebounder

Usman Garuba

	Height	Weight	Cap #	Years Left
	6'8"	220	$2.588M	TO

Similar at Age 20

		Season	SIMsc
1	Kevon Looney	2016-17	907.2
2	Greg Brown III	2021-22	885.4
3	Julian Wright	2007-08	876.0
4	Ivan Rabb	2017-18	869.8
5	Kenyon Martin Jr.	2020-21	865.1
6	Paul George	2010-11	864.8
7	Wilson Chandler	2007-08	863.9
8	Onyeka Okongwu	2020-21	862.6
9	Marquese Chriss	2017-18	862.6
10	Nicolas Batum	2008-09	858.4

Baseline Basic Stats

MPG	PTS	AST	REB	BLK	STL
20.2	7.0	1.3	4.7	0.6	0.8

Advanced Metrics

USG%	3PTA/FGA	FTA/FGA	TS%	eFG%	3PT%
13.9	0.345	0.231	0.551	0.528	0.353

AST%	TOV%	OREB%	DREB%	STL%	BLK%
10.3	14.6	9.2	20.2	1.9	2.3

PER	ORTG	DRTG	WS/48	BPM	VOL
13.70	115.5	111.4	0.095	-0.61	0.481

- Fringe rotation player for Houston in his second NBA season
- Increased his efficiency in a role as a low usage stretch big and rim runner
- Made almost 41% of his threes last season, slightly more efficient when shooting threes above the break
- Mainly a stand-still spot-up shooter, effective pick-and-pop screener in a small sample of attempts
- Good athlete, energetic rim runner that dives hard to the rim, undersized big man, struggles to finish shots in traffic
- Not really a post-up or ball handling threat, passing skills are limited, fairly turnover prone
- 2022-23 Defensive Degree of Difficulty: 0.346
- 2022-23 Points Prevented: -1.589
- Average rim protector, shot blocking rates were down, fairly good defensive rebounder
- Guards second unit big men, effective post defender despite being undersized, good mobility allows him to defend in space
- Below average pick-and-roll defender, better in drop coverages, tends to go way under screens
- Consistently will close out on shooters in spot-up situations
- Good at using his length to play passing lanes and get steals at a fairly high rate
- Waived while the book was being finalized

Dāvis Bertāns

	Height	Weight	Cap #	Years Left
	6'10"	225	$17.000M	ETO

Similar at Age 30

		Season	SIMsc
1	Steve Novak	2013-14	935.4
2	Matt Bullard	1997-98	922.4
3	Jonas Jerebko	2017-18	914.2
4	James Jones	2010-11	913.3
5	Brad Lohaus	1994-95	909.8
6	Walter McCarty	2004-05	903.1
7	Matt Bonner	2010-11	896.8
8	Patrick Patterson	2019-20	896.3
9	Brian Scalabrine	2008-09	888.2
10	Mike Dunleavy Jr.	2010-11	885.1

Baseline Basic Stats

MPG	PTS	AST	REB	BLK	STL
14.5	5.4	0.6	1.9	0.2	0.3

Advanced Metrics

USG%	3PTA/FGA	FTA/FGA	TS%	eFG%	3PT%
15.5	0.799	0.130	0.582	0.560	0.376

AST%	TOV%	OREB%	DREB%	STL%	BLK%
5.9	5.9	2.3	11.9	1.1	1.3

PER	ORTG	DRTG	WS/48	BPM	VOL
11.00	116.4	113.4	0.090	-1.24	0.335

- Missed two months due to knee and calf injuries, fringe rotation player for Dallas when healthy
- Increased his efficiency, mostly used as a low usage shooting specialist
- Almost a 40% career three-point shooter, has made 50% of his career corner threes
- Great shooter off the catch, consistently makes spot-up threes, good at running off screens
- Almost exclusively plays away from the basket, rarely used as a rim runner
- Strictly a catch-and-shoot player, limited as a passer, rarely turns the ball over
- 2022-23 Defensive Degree of Difficulty: 0.288
- 2022-23 Points Prevented: 0.583
- Often hidden in favorable matchups against lower leverage bench players
- Below average on-ball defender, struggles to guard stronger or quicker players
- Middling pick-and-roll defender, decent in drop coverages, has trouble staying with ball handlers on the perimeter
- Gets caught on screens off the ball, tends to be late when closing out on spot-up shooters
- Usually a stay-at-home defender, rarely gets steals, occasional weak side shot blocker, decent defensive rebounder

Victor Oladipo

	Height	Weight	Cap #	Years Left
	6'4"	213	$9.450M	UFA

Similar at Age 30

		Season	SIMsc
1	Bobby Phills	1999-00	928.2
2	Erick Strickland	2003-04	917.3
3	Devin Brown	2008-09	903.5
4	Jeremy Lin	2018-19	900.5
5	Randy Foye	2013-14	897.7
6	Gary Neal	2014-15	897.4
7	Jodie Meeks	2017-18	893.2
8	Mario Elie	1993-94	892.3
9	George McCloud	1997-98	891.1
10	Ime Udoka	2007-08	891.1

Baseline Basic Stats

MPG	PTS	AST	REB	BLK	STL
21.4	8.1	2.4	2.6	0.2	0.8

Advanced Metrics

USG%	3PTA/FGA	FTA/FGA	TS%	eFG%	3PT%
19.3	0.439	0.203	0.515	0.481	0.332

AST%	TOV%	OREB%	DREB%	STL%	BLK%
17.7	14.7	1.9	12.5	2.1	0.8

PER	ORTG	DRTG	WS/48	BPM	VOL
11.02	101.9	111.2	0.048	-2.00	0.441

- Missed most of last season due to knee and ankle injuries, regular rotation player for Miami when healthy
- Production declined, used as a moderate usage spot-up shooter and ball handler off the bench
- Above break-even three-point shooter, percentages tend to vary from year-to-year
- Around a break-even spot-up shooter, efficient shooter on pick-and-rolls in a small sample of shots
- Rated by Synergy as being average or worse in most situations
- Athleticism sapped by past injuries, effectiveness on drives has diminished, less effective as a shot creator
- Solid playmaker that makes simple reads, slightly turnover prone
- 2022-23 Defensive Degree of Difficulty: 0.427
- 2022-23 Points Prevented: -0.840
- Drew some tough assignments off the bench, usually guarded starting level players
- Struggled to play effective on-ball defense, had trouble handling his assignment on the perimeter and in the post
- Solid pick-and-roll defender, effective at switching onto ball handlers and screeners
- Stays attached to shooters off the ball, fights through screens, closes out in spot-up situations
- Active help defender, still gets steals at a very high rate, fairly solid defensive rebounder

Jack White

	Height	Weight	Cap #	Years Left
	6'7"	225	$1.802M	1

Similar at Age 25

		Season	SIMsc
1	Justin Anderson	2018-19	921.7
2	Jalen Jones	2018-19	915.5
3	Damien Wilkins	2004-05	905.8
4	Keita Bates-Diop	2020-21	903.2
5	Mickael Pietrus	2007-08	903.1
6	Paul Watson	2019-20	898.6
7	Kostas Papanikolaou	2015-16	896.7
8	Abdel Nader	2018-19	896.0
9	Alex Poythress	2018-19	895.1
10	Jaron Blossomgame	2018-19	890.8

Baseline Basic Stats

MPG	PTS	AST	REB	BLK	STL
17.2	5.7	0.8	2.9	0.3	0.5

Advanced Metrics

USG%	3PTA/FGA	FTA/FGA	TS%	eFG%	3PT%
14.8	0.513	0.187	0.541	0.516	0.362

AST%	TOV%	OREB%	DREB%	STL%	BLK%
7.6	10.9	7.5	16.1	1.6	1.7

PER	ORTG	DRTG	WS/48	BPM	VOL
11.61	112.2	111.7	0.089	-1.67	0.469

- Played on a Two-Way contract with Denver, spent most of last season in the G-League with Grand Rapids
- Played sparingly in the NBA, used as a low volume spot-up shooter, usage was higher in the G-League
- Made almost 44% of his threes in the G-League, went 3-for-9 (33.3%) at the NBA level
- Only used as a spot-up shooter at the NBA, good shooter off the catch in the G-League
- Effective at running the floor in transition to get layups, active offensive rebounder
- Not really used in ball handling situations in the NBA, lacks the ability to create his own shot
- Catch-and-shoot player, playmaking skills are limited, rarely turns the ball over
- 2022-23 Defensive Degree of Difficulty: 0.155
- 2022-23 Points Prevented: -0.413
- Only played 66 minutes in the NBA, usually played in garbage time, true defensive ability is uncertain
- Struggled in a small sample of one-on-one possessions, lacks quickness to stay with perimeter players, not quite strong enough to guard interior players
- Played below average pick-and-roll defense, not able to contain ball handlers, tended to commit cheap fouls
- Fights through off-ball screens, was a step late when closing out on spot-up shooters
- Active help defender in limited action, effective weak side shot blocker, gets steals at a solid rate, fairly good defensive rebounder

Newcomers

Chet Holmgren

	Height	Weight	Cap #	Years Left
	7'0"	195	$10.386M	2 TO

Baseline Basic Stats

MPG	PTS	AST	REB	BLK	STL
23.1	8.6	1.2	5.4	1.1	0.7

Advanced Metrics

USG%	3PTA/FGA	FTA/FGA	TS%	eFG%	3PT%
17.2	0.241	0.294	0.519	0.493	0.314

AST%	TOV%	OREB%	DREB%	STL%	BLK%
8.2	12.7	7.4	18.6	1.4	4.6

PER	ORTG	DRTG	WS/48	BPM	VOL
14.77	100.8	95.0	0.092	-0.54	N/A

- Drafted by Oklahoma City with the 2nd overall pick in 2022
- Missed all of last season due to a Lisfranc injury in his right foot
- Has played well in Summer League action over the past two summers in Las Vegas and Utah
- Efficiency decreased with increased usage, effective in his role as a stretch big and interior scorer
- True Shooting Percentage is almost 60% over two summers, struggled with his outside shot this summer
- Has made 30% of his threes over two summers, had trouble finding his rhythm after returning from injury
- Mainly a spot-up shooter, less effective when shooting on the move
- Athletic rim runner, vertical lob threat if healthy, much more physical this summer, drew fouls at a higher rate
- Good cutter and roll man, pushes the ball in transition, also will finish with explosive dunks
- Good post-up player that can shoot over shorter players, better at holding position on the block
- Solid passing big man with good court vision, fairly turnover prone
- Has excellent defensive potential due to his length, athleticism, and rim protection skills
- Great rim protector at Summer League, blocks shots at a very high rate, fairly solid defensive rebounder
- Solid on-ball defender, frame is still thin but provides better resistance when playing post defense, good mobility to defend on the perimeter
- Fairly good pick-and-roll defender, good in drop coverages, effectively switches onto ball handlers
- Good at using his length to play passing lanes to post high steal rates
- One of the early Rookie of the Year contenders for this coming season

Cason Wallace

	Height	Weight	Cap #	Years Left
	6'4"	193	$5.291M	1 + 2 TO

Baseline Basic Stats

MPG	PTS	AST	REB	BLK	STL
20.5	8.1	2.9	2.4	0.2	0.9

Advanced Metrics

USG%	3PTA/FGA	FTA/FGA	TS%	eFG%	3PT%
19.2	0.335	0.219	0.515	0.482	0.335

AST%	TOV%	OREB%	DREB%	STL%	BLK%
22.9	15.2	2.8	10.3	2.4	0.8

PER	ORTG	DRTG	WS/48	BPM	VOL
13.36	102.3	105.0	0.059	-1.20	N/A

- Drafted by Dallas with the 10th overall pick in 2023, traded to Oklahoma City
- Had an uneven performance at the Las Vegas Summer League
- Scored in volume, inefficient in a role as higher usage scoring guard, likely will play a lower volume role in the NBA
- True Shooting Percentage was below 50%, made almost 39% of his threes
- Solid spot-up shooter at Summer League, ability to shoot on the move or off the dribble is still a work-in-progress
- Really struggled to score from two-point range, went 6-for-21 (28.6%) on two-pointers
- Had trouble driving by defenders, lacks elite ball handling skills, struggles to go right when he drives
- Decent secondary playmaker that makes simple reads, played a bit out of control, slightly turnover prone
- Good defensive potential, has excellent length and athleticism to defend both guard spots
- Fairly good on-ball defender, actively pressures ball handlers, capable of defending taller guards
- Plays too aggressively, can get caught out position, sometimes commits cheap touch fouls on the perimeter
- Needs to improve pick-and-roll defense, effective at switching, sometimes takes bad angles when guarding ball handlers
- Fights through screens off the ball, gambles too much, not always in position to contest shots in spot-up situations
- Active help defender, great at jumping passing lanes to get steals, below average defensive rebounder
- Needs some additional seasoning in the G-League to improve his overall shooting efficiency

Vasilije Micic

	Height	Weight	Cap #	Years Left
	6'5"	200	$7.723M	1 + TO

Baseline Basic Stats

MPG	PTS	AST	REB	BLK	STL
21.5	8.8	2.4	2.1	0.1	0.6

Advanced Metrics

USG%	3PTA/FGA	FTA/FGA	TS%	eFG%	3PT%
19.6	0.559	0.239	0.574	0.529	0.351

AST%	TOV%	OREB%	DREB%	STL%	BLK%
20.6	15.6	1.6	10.5	1.5	0.4

PER	ORTG	DRTG	WS/48	BPM	VOL
11.60	111.7	120.9	0.065	-0.50	0.721

- Drafted by Philadelphia with the 52nd overall pick in 2014
- Rights were acquired by Oklahoma City in 2020, played last season with Anadolu Efes in the Turkish BSL
- Projection is based on his translated EuroLeague stats, EuroLeague MVP in 2020-21
- Highly productive player at the EuroLeague level, excels in a role as a high usage playmaker
- Great playmaker with outstanding court vision to find open teammates
- Somewhat turnover prone, tends to over-dribble and make errant passes
- Reliable three-point shooter at the EuroLeague level, made almost 40% of his three last season
- Good spot-up shooter, can make pull-up jumpers and sometimes shoot off screens
- Shifty ball handler that leverages the threat of shot to get to the rim
- Lacks ideal quickness and explosion, gets his shot blocked frequently, may be less successful as a ball handler in the NBA
- Possible liability on defense, lacks ideal length and lateral quickness
- Had trouble defending EuroLeague players on the ball, struggled to keep up with quicker guards
- Below average pick-and-roll defender, has lapses when making rotations, only able to steer his man into help
- Plays with a high effort level, will fight through screens and close out on spot-up shooters
- Effective at jumping passing lanes to get steals, below average defensive rebounder
- Will play in his age-30 season as a rookie in 2023-24

UTAH JAZZ

Last Season: 37 - 45, Missed the Playoffs

Offensive Rating: 115.8, 10th in the NBA   Defensive Rating: 116.7, 23rd in the NBA

Primary Executive: Danny Ainge, CEO of Basketball Operations/Alternate Governor

Head Coach: Will Hardy

Key Roster Changes

Subtractions
Rudy Gay, trade
Juan Toscano-Anderson, free agency
Damian Jones, free agency
Udoka Azubuike, free agency

Additions
Taylor Hendricks, draft
Keyonte George, draft
Brice Sensabaugh, draft
John Collins, trade
Omer Yurtseven, free agency

Roster

Likely Starting Five
1. *Jordan Clarkson*
2. Ochai Agbaji
3. *Lauri Markkanen*
4. John Collins
5. *Walker Kessler*

Other Key Rotation Players
Collin Sexton
Kelly Olynyk
Talen Horton-Tucker
Kris Dunn
Taylor Hendricks

* Italics denotes that a player is likely to be on the floor to close games

Remaining Roster

- Keyonte George
- Brice Sensabaugh
- Omer Yurtseven
- Simone Fontecchio
- Luka Šamanić
- Micah Potter, 25, 6'10", 248, Wisconsin (Two-Way)
- Johnny Juzang, 22, 6'7", 215, UCLA (Two-Way)
- Joey Hauser, 24, 6'9", 220, Michigan State (Two-Way)
- Taevion Kinsey, 23, 6'5", 190, Marshall (Exhibit 10)

SCHREMPF Base Rating: 41.3

Season Preview Survey

- *Are the Jazz contending or rebuilding? Where is this team headed?*

The Jazz are in an interesting position because they are trying to rebuild their franchise while still remaining competitive. After the trades to deal away Donovan Mitchell and Rudy Gobert, it was thought that they would be one of the worst teams in the league. However, they ended up being much more competitive than expected due to some creative lineups and tactics from head coach, Will Hardy. They will be doing the balancing act of trying to win while also developing their young players. The team was able to find some core pieces last season, so they could build on what they did last season to find more promising players to help their franchise move forward.

- *What are the areas of concern for this team heading into this season?*

It's a strange thing to be concerned about, but there's a possibility that the Jazz played a little bit too well last season to allow them to create a pathway to a future title. By ending up within range of a play-in berth, they were unable to position themselves for a high enough draft pick to land a potential star. This combined with their ability to punch above their weight and their status as a team in a very small market means that they could be locked out from landing an elite talent in the future. There's a chance that they could top out as a good but not great team in the future. On the flip side, this is a good situation to be in because their floor is going to be high, so they should eventually be in a position to consistently make the playoffs in the future with the talent and coaching staff that they have in place. In order to raise their ceiling, they will have to continue to make sound decisions and hope that they land someone that over-achieves. If that happens, then they could level up to become future contenders someday.

- *List some possible breakout players for this team.*

The door is open for someone to break out because Hardy has been willing to play young players and they have a fairly deep rotation, so someone could step up to become an impact player similar to how Walker Kessler did last season. Of their young players, the best candidate to emerge could be Keyonte George, one of their first round picks from this past draft. He had an impressive Summer League where he displayed more explosive athleticism as a result of losing 25 pounds, and he flashed the potential to be a three-level scorer in the future. The Jazz are in need of a dynamic ball handling threat, so George could fill that role if his performance from Summer League translates. In addition to him, Ochai Agbaji could improve to become a plus-level defensive stopper while their current lottery pick, Taylor Hendricks could make solid contributions as a floor spacing wing that also defends multiple positions.

- *What should we expect from them this season?*

More or less, Utah is likely to finish around the same range that they did last season. They have an interesting mix of young players and veterans to count on. They also have some positive chemistry to fall back on because they kept a lot of the important parts of their team intact. They should be able to play the same sort of style that allowed them to be competitive on a night-to-night basis. Specifically, they will look to be a team that pushes the pace and shoots threes at a high volume. This style should help them to outscore opponents on hot shooting night, but they will also be vulnerable to having some bad losses if their shots don't fall. Overall, Utah is still a developing team that is working to become a more consistent playoff contender. In the meantime, they will field an entertaining, up-tempo unit that will put up a lot of points and get close to a playoff spot, but they might not have the defense or front-end talent to keep pace with the top teams in the league. This will mean that they will end up being a lottery team again this season.

Veterans

Lauri Markkanen

	Height	Weight	Cap #	Years Left
	7'0"	240	$17.260M	1

Similar at Age 25

		Season	SIMsc
1	Frank Kaminsky	2018-19	923.0
2	Charlie Villanueva	2009-10	917.0
3	Dirk Nowitzki*	2003-04	905.4
4	Kelly Olynyk	2016-17	902.8
5	Andrea Bargnani	2010-11	895.9
6	Mike Scott	2013-14	886.8
7	Austin Croshere	2000-01	886.0
8	Dario Šarić	2019-20	885.4
9	Kyle Kuzma	2020-21	884.7
10	Troy Murphy	2005-06	884.1

Baseline Basic Stats

MPG	PTS	AST	REB	BLK	STL
25.9	14.0	1.6	5.4	0.5	0.6

Advanced Metrics

USG%	3PTA/FGA	FTA/FGA	TS%	eFG%	3PT%
23.0	0.478	0.316	0.614	0.563	0.393

AST%	TOV%	OREB%	DREB%	STL%	BLK%
8.6	8.6	5.0	18.7	1.1	1.4

PER	ORTG	DRTG	WS/48	BPM	VOL
18.91	120.8	112.2	0.159	2.09	0.376

- Made his first All-Star team, won the Most Improved Player Award in 2022-23
- Excelled in his new role as Utah's primary scoring option
- Reliable three-point shooter throughout his career, has made 42.5% of his career threes
- Outstanding shooter off the catch, knocks down spot-up jumpers, great movement shooter
- Makes sharp backdoor cuts if defenders try to crowd him
- Rarely used as a ball handler, effectively attacks switches as a change-of-pace
- Catch-and-shoot player, only makes safe passes, rarely turns the ball over
- 2022-23 Defensive Degree of Difficulty: 0.469
- 2022-23 Points Prevented: 1.518
- Drew some tough assignments against starting level players, decent on-ball defender
- Capable of guarding big men and wing players, better against bigger players, has some trouble staying with quicker wings
- Decent pick-and-roll defender, solid in drop coverages, sometimes allows ball handlers to turn the corner
- Stays attached to shooters off the ball, fights through screens and closes out in spot-up situations
- Stay-at-home defender, rarely gets steals or blocks, good defensive rebounder

Walker Kessler

	Height	Weight	Cap #	Years Left
	7'1"	245	$2.831M	2 TO

Similar at Age 21

		Season	SIMsc
1	Mitchell Robinson	2019-20	893.8
2	Alex Len	2014-15	864.8
3	Steven Adams	2014-15	860.5
4	Jarrett Allen	2019-20	860.2
5	Daniel Gafford	2019-20	859.8
6	Andris Biedrins	2007-08	858.7
7	Moses Brown	2020-21	855.8
8	Clint Capela	2015-16	848.8
9	Mo Bamba	2019-20	846.6
10	Darko Milicic	2006-07	845.2

Baseline Basic Stats

MPG	PTS	AST	REB	BLK	STL
24.6	9.1	1.0	7.7	1.5	0.6

Advanced Metrics

USG%	3PTA/FGA	FTA/FGA	TS%	eFG%	3PT%
14.2	0.004	0.400	0.648	0.652	0.291

AST%	TOV%	OREB%	DREB%	STL%	BLK%
6.4	13.2	14.3	22.1	1.1	5.7

PER	ORTG	DRTG	WS/48	BPM	VOL
18.84	129.5	109.3	0.171	1.91	0.208

- Named to the All-Rookie 1st Team in 2022-23, became a full-time starter for Utah late in the season
- Highly efficient in his role as a very low usage rim runner
- High motor big man, plays physical, made over 81% of his shots inside of three feet
- Very cutter and roll man, dives hard to the rim, great offensive rebounder, runs hard in transition
- Very rarely posted up, mainly looks to flash to the middle, lacks reliable shooting range outside of ten feet
- Strictly a catch-and-finish player, limited passing skills, good at avoiding turnovers
- 2022-23 Defensive Degree of Difficulty: 0.393
- 2022-23 Points Prevented: 1.539
- Great rim protector, excellent shot blocker, very good defensive rebounder
- Effective on-ball defender against mostly lower leverage players, stout post defender, mobile enough to defend in space
- Decent pick-and-roll defender, willing to hedge out on ball handlers, good on drop coverages, tends to late to recognize pick-and-pop plays
- Consistently comes out to the perimeter to contest spot-up jumpers

Jordan Clarkson

	Height	Weight	Cap #	Years Left
	6'4"	194	$23.488M	2

Similar at Age 30

		Season	SIMsc
1	Dell Curry	1994-95	934.2
2	CJ McCollum	2021-22	925.8
3	Derrick Rose	2018-19	917.9
4	Flip Murray	2009-10	916.5
5	Rex Chapman	1997-98	916.0
6	Marco Belinelli	2016-17	914.0
7	Ray Allen*	2005-06	911.9
8	J.J. Redick	2014-15	909.0
9	Jaren Jackson	1997-98	908.8
10	Joe Dumars*	1993-94	908.7

Baseline Basic Stats

MPG	PTS	AST	REB	BLK	STL
28.7	15.0	2.9	2.9	0.2	0.9

Advanced Metrics

USG%	3PTA/FGA	FTA/FGA	TS%	eFG%	3PT%
25.3	0.441	0.198	0.540	0.505	0.345

AST%	TOV%	OREB%	DREB%	STL%	BLK%
17.3	11.6	2.9	9.7	1.3	0.6

PER	ORTG	DRTG	WS/48	BPM	VOL
14.42	107.4	113.2	0.070	-0.75	0.290

- Played as a regular starting guard for Utah in his third full season with the team
- Efficiency increased in a role as the team's primary ball handler
- Solid pick-and-roll ball handler and isolation player, can get to the rim, good at hitting floaters and pull-up jumpers from mid-range
- Break-even career three-point shooter, percentages tend to vary from year-to-year
- Consistency varies situation-to-situations, most effective when taking threes in transition, streaky shooter off the dribble
- Fairly solid playmaker, able to make simple reads, fairly good at avoiding turnovers
- 2022-23 Defensive Degree of Difficulty: 0.448
- 2022-23 Points Prevented: 0.984
- Drew more difficult assignments than he did in the past, played decent on-ball defense last season
- Fairly effective at staying with opposing guards, taller wings gave him some trouble
- Below average pick-and-roll defender, struggled to contain ball handler, not really effective on switches
- Stays attached to shooters off the ball, fights through off-ball screens and closes out in spot-up situations
- Stay-at-home defender, did not really get steals or blocks last season, fairly decent defensive rebounder

John Collins

	Height	Weight	Cap #	Years Left
	6'9"	235	$25.340M	1 + PO

Similar at Age 25

		Season	SIMsc
1	Ersan Ilyasova	2012-13	935.1
2	Brian Cook	2005-06	924.4
3	Marvin Williams	2011-12	918.1
4	Marcus Morris	2014-15	917.2
5	Austin Croshere	2000-01	916.2
6	Dario Šarić	2019-20	910.9
7	Jerami Grant	2019-20	909.3
8	Charlie Villanueva	2009-10	908.4
9	Brad Lohaus	1989-90	906.8
10	Kris Humphries	2010-11	906.5

Baseline Basic Stats

MPG	PTS	AST	REB	BLK	STL
26.1	11.3	1.6	5.4	0.6	0.7

Advanced Metrics

USG%	3PTA/FGA	FTA/FGA	TS%	eFG%	3PT%
19.1	0.332	0.249	0.569	0.532	0.347

AST%	TOV%	OREB%	DREB%	STL%	BLK%
8.3	9.5	5.2	18.5	1.1	2.2

PER	ORTG	DRTG	WS/48	BPM	VOL
14.97	114.2	111.5	0.108	-0.20	0.194

- Regular starter for Atlanta in his sixth NBA season
- Production declined significantly, used as a low usage spot-up shooter and rim runner
- League average career three-point shooter, percentages plummeted because he was playing with an injured finger on his shooting hand
- Normally a solid stationary spot-up shooter, can also make pick-and-pop jumpers
- Better as a rim runner, good cutter and roll man, explosive finisher in transition, vertical lob threat
- Can flash to the middle on post-ups, catch-and-shoot player, limited as a passer, rarely turns the ball over
- 2022-23 Defensive Degree of Difficulty: 0.459
- 2022-23 Points Prevented: -1.028
- Good rim protector despite being undersized, solid shot blocker, good defensive rebounder
- Average on-ball defender against starting level players, taller big men can shoot over him, has some trouble staying with quicker players
- Middling pick-and-roll defender, good in drop coverages, struggled when switched onto ball handlers
- Tends to sag back into the paint, does not always close out on spot-up shooters

Ochai Agbaji

	Height	Weight	Cap #	Years Left
	6'5"	215	$4.114M	2 TO

Similar at Age 22

		Season	SIMsc
1	Desmond Bane	2020-21	939.8
2	Doron Lamb	2013-14	924.3
3	Timothe Luwawu-Cabarrot	2017-18	922.5
4	Josh Hart	2017-18	920.6
5	Corey Kispert	2021-22	920.0
6	Aaron Nesmith	2021-22	917.2
7	Iman Shumpert	2012-13	916.8
8	Luke Kennard	2018-19	914.4
9	Miye Oni	2019-20	911.2
10	Troy Brown Jr.	2021-22	909.1

Baseline Basic Stats

MPG	PTS	AST	REB	BLK	STL
22.9	8.8	1.5	3.0	0.2	0.6

Advanced Metrics

USG%	3PTA/FGA	FTA/FGA	TS%	eFG%	3PT%
16.6	0.540	0.192	0.571	0.540	0.376

AST%	TOV%	OREB%	DREB%	STL%	BLK%
9.2	9.6	3.2	9.4	1.0	0.9

PER	ORTG	DRTG	WS/48	BPM	VOL
11.26	114.6	116.8	0.073	-1.61	0.464

- Regular rotation player for Utah in his rookie season, started some games
- Fairly effective in his role as a low volume spot-up shooter
- Around a league average three-point shooter, made almost 46% of his corner threes last season
- Predominantly a stand-still spot-up shooter at this stage, less effective when shooting on the move
- Moves well without the ball, good cutter, can make mid-range jumpers off screens
- Needs to improve his ball handling, not really able to create his own offense
- Strictly a catch-and-shoot player, passing skills are limited, rarely turns the ball over
- 2022-23 Defensive Degree of Difficulty: 0.471
- 2022-23 Points Prevented: 1.756
- Drew a lot of tough assignments against elite scorers late in the season, played decent on-ball defense
- Can stay with perimeter players, tends to give his man too much space, has some trouble against stronger players inside
- Decent pick-and-roll defender, can functionally switch and cut off penetration, goes too far under screens
- Stays attached to shooters off the ball, fights through screens and closes out in spot-up situations
- Stay-at-home defender, rarely gets steals or blocks, below average defensive rebounder

Collin Sexton

	Height	Weight	Cap #	Years Left
	6'1"	190	$17.325M	2

Similar at Age 24

		Season	SIMsc
1	Travis Mays	1992-93	928.6
2	Eric Bledsoe	2013-14	918.8
3	Mike Bibby	2002-03	915.6
4	Salim Stoudamire	2006-07	915.2
5	Nolan Smith	2012-13	914.4
6	Trey Burke	2016-17	910.7
7	Tony Delk	1997-98	908.5
8	Jacque Vaughn	1999-00	906.3
9	Jalen Brunson	2020-21	904.6
10	Shammond Williams	1999-00	901.6

Baseline Basic Stats

MPG	PTS	AST	REB	BLK	STL
23.6	11.0	3.3	2.4	0.1	0.8

Advanced Metrics

USG%	3PTA/FGA	FTA/FGA	TS%	eFG%	3PT%
23.2	0.308	0.333	0.573	0.522	0.361

AST%	TOV%	OREB%	DREB%	STL%	BLK%
21.1	13.5	3.1	8.5	1.4	0.3

PER	ORTG	DRTG	WS/48	BPM	VOL
15.62	112.4	114.8	0.097	-0.60	0.472

- Missed most of last season due to hamstring injuries, regular rotation player for Utah when healthy
- Greatly increased his efficiency in a new role as a scoring sixth man off the bench
- Good pick-and-roll ball handler and isolation player, aggressively attacks the rim, draws fouls at a high rate, efficiently makes floaters or mid-range pull-up jumpers
- Reliable three-point shooter, great stationary spot-up shooter, credible threat when shooting off the dribble
- Good at scoring on hand-offs, great at pushing the ball in transition
- Fairly solid playmaker that makes simple reads, effectively avoids turnovers
- 2022-23 Defensive Degree of Difficulty: 0.449
- 2022-23 Points Prevented: -0.214
- Generally defended starting level guards, played solid on-ball defense
- Effectively can guard ones and twos in moderate to lower leverage matchups
- Played below average pick-and-roll defense, limited ability to switch, struggled to contain ball handlers
- Stays attached to shooters off the ball, fights through screens and closes out in spot-up situations
- Stay-at-home defender last season, did not really get steals or blocks, below average defensive rebounder

Kelly Olynyk

	Height	Weight	Cap #	Years Left
	6'11"	240	$12.195M	UFA

Similar at Age 31

		Season	SIMsc
1	Christian Laettner	2000-01	913.9
2	Nemanja Bjelica	2019-20	913.1
3	Blake Griffin	2020-21	906.9
4	Brad Miller	2007-08	900.7
5	James Johnson	2018-19	893.9
6	Bob Lanier*	1979-80	893.2
7	Tim Thomas	2008-09	891.7
8	Gorgui Dieng	2020-21	888.8
9	Frank Brickowski	1990-91	888.4
10	Jonas Jerebko	2018-19	886.4

Baseline Basic Stats

MPG	PTS	AST	REB	BLK	STL
24.1	9.7	2.5	5.3	0.4	0.7

Advanced Metrics

USG%	3PTA/FGA	FTA/FGA	TS%	eFG%	3PT%
17.8	0.415	0.337	0.595	0.544	0.361

AST%	TOV%	OREB%	DREB%	STL%	BLK%
17.0	16.6	5.0	18.1	1.5	1.6

PER	ORTG	DRTG	WS/48	BPM	VOL
14.28	114.5	112.5	0.101	0.24	0.429

- Regular starter for Utah in his first season with the team
- Increased his offensive efficiency in a role as a low usage stretch big
- Made over 39% of his threes last season, percentages tend to vary from year-to-year
- Mainly a stand-still spot-up shooter, occasionally effective as a pick-and-pop screener
- High motor rim runner, drew fouls at a high rate, dives hard to the rim
- Good cutter and roll man, efficiently finishes on put-backs, high effort player that runs hard in transition
- Not really a post player or ball handler, good passer that finds open teammates, somewhat turnover prone
- 2022-23 Defensive Degree of Difficulty: 0.466
- 2022-23 Points Prevented: -1.185
- Effective rim protector despite limited shot blocking abilities, takes charges, stays vertical when challenging shots, fairly solid defensive rebounder
- Average on-ball defender against starting centers, fairly foul prone, struggles against stronger or quicker players
- Average pick-and-roll defender, can passably switches, has lapses when making rotations
- Slight tendency to stay anchored in the paint, tended to be late when closing out on spot-up shooters
- Has active hands, good at playing passing lanes to get steals

Talen Horton-Tucker

	Height	Weight	Cap #	Years Left
	6'4"	234	$11.020M	UFA

Similar at Age 22

		Season	SIMsc
1	Kirk Snyder	2005-06	904.5
2	Justise Winslow	2018-19	895.7
3	Emmanuel Mudiay	2018-19	892.8
4	Eric Gordon	2010-11	892.4
5	Rodney White	2002-03	890.6
6	Dion Waiters	2013-14	890.4
7	Tyreke Evans	2011-12	888.7
8	Beno Udrih	2004-05	887.7
9	Marcus Smart	2016-17	887.7
10	Jaylen Brown	2018-19	887.5

Baseline Basic Stats

MPG	PTS	AST	REB	BLK	STL
24.4	11.1	2.5	3.1	0.3	0.9

Advanced Metrics

USG%	3PTA/FGA	FTA/FGA	TS%	eFG%	3PT%
21.9	0.328	0.241	0.522	0.486	0.324

AST%	TOV%	OREB%	DREB%	STL%	BLK%
19.3	13.5	2.7	12.1	1.8	1.3

PER	ORTG	DRTG	WS/48	BPM	VOL
12.92	104.1	112.8	0.050	-1.64	0.490

- Regular rotation player for Utah in his first season with the team
- Slightly increased his effectiveness in a role as a high usage ball hander off the bench
- Has become a very good playmaker, Assist Percentage increased to a career high, a bit turnover prone
- Career Three-Point Percentage is below 30%, lacks reliable shooting range from beyond ten feet
- Break-even spot-up shooter, less effective when shooting in other situations
- Drives aggressively to the rim, defenders can back off him to limit his effectiveness
- Has some trouble finishing in traffic, undersized, also does not always play under control
- 2022-23 Defensive Degree of Difficulty: 0.443
- 2022-23 Points Prevented: 0.370
- Drew a lot of tough assignments off the bench, solid on-ball defender, can guard multiple positions
- Effective when guarding taller players, has some trouble staying with quicker guards
- Below average pick-and-roll defender, not especially effective at taking away any specific action
- Fights through screens off the ball, tends to be a step late when closing out on spot-up shooters
- Fairly active help defender, gets steals and blocks at a solid rate, fairly solid defensive rebounder

Kris Dunn

	Height	Weight	Cap #	Years Left
	6'3"	205	$2.587M	UFA

Similar at Age 28

		Season	SIMsc
1	Rusty LaRue	2001-02	909.9
2	Laron Profit	2005-06	906.5
3	Jeremy Lin	2016-17	902.6
4	Donald Sloan	2015-16	896.5
5	Kirk Hinrich	2008-09	895.5
6	Anthony Johnson	2002-03	894.6
7	Marcus Banks	2009-10	893.4
8	Jason Hart	2006-07	890.7
9	Mateen Cleaves	2005-06	889.7
10	Dwight Buycks	2017-18	888.2

Baseline Basic Stats

MPG	PTS	AST	REB	BLK	STL
19.1	6.5	2.7	2.0	0.1	0.8

Advanced Metrics

USG%	3PTA/FGA	FTA/FGA	TS%	eFG%	3PT%
17.5	0.270	0.227	0.519	0.479	0.322

AST%	TOV%	OREB%	DREB%	STL%	BLK%
24.7	14.6	1.6	12.7	2.1	1.0

PER	ORTG	DRTG	WS/48	BPM	VOL
12.78	106.9	110.1	0.082	-1.67	0.669

- Signed with Utah in the second half of last season, became a regular rotation player
- Highly effective in his minutes as a moderate usage playmaker
- Very good distributor that can run a team and set up his teammates, effectively limits turnovers
- Below break-even career three-point shooter, went 17-for-36 (47.2%) on threes last season
- Primarily a stand-still spot-up shooter, occasionally made pull-up threes on pick-and-rolls
- Much more effective in ball handling situations as a pick-and-roll ball handler and isolation player
- Defenders had to guard him honestly, more efficient when driving to the rim and taking pull-up mid-range jumpers
- 2022-23 Defensive Degree of Difficulty: 0.463
- 2022-23 Points Prevented: 0.118
- Used as a stopper in the past, drew a lot of tough assignments off the bench
- Solid on-ball defender, can defend both guard spots, had trouble when guarding elite scorers
- Fairly solid pick-and-roll defender, good at containing ball handlers, less effective when switched onto screeners
- Tends to get caught on screens off the ball, good at closing out on spot-up shooters
- Very active help defender, gets steals at a high rate, solid weak side shot blocker, fairly good defensive rebounder

Omer Yurtseven

	Height	Weight	Cap #	Years Left
	7'0"	264	$2.800M	1

Similar at Age 24

		Season	SIMsc
1	Kosta Koufos	2013-14	903.3
2	Johan Petro	2009-10	899.6
3	Erick Dampier	1999-00	896.9
4	Chris Mihm	2003-04	894.5
5	Robert Sacre	2013-14	894.3
6	Andrew Bogut	2008-09	891.0
7	Nathan Knight	2021-22	890.9
8	Tyler Zeller	2013-14	889.8
9	Noah Vonleh	2019-20	888.9
10	Justin Hamilton	2014-15	887.2

Baseline Basic Stats

MPG	PTS	AST	REB	BLK	STL
17.4	7.0	0.7	4.7	0.8	0.3

Advanced Metrics

USG%	3PTA/FGA	FTA/FGA	TS%	eFG%	3PT%
19.1	0.102	0.260	0.582	0.555	0.306

AST%	TOV%	OREB%	DREB%	STL%	BLK%
7.4	11.5	10.4	22.3	1.0	3.4

PER	ORTG	DRTG	WS/48	BPM	VOL
16.71	115.1	106.7	0.139	-1.24	0.583

- Missed most of last season due to a stress reaction in his left ankle, played sparingly for Miami in his second NBA season
- Mainly used as a low usage rim runner when he was healthy
- Effectiveness was limited due to the injury, high energy rim runner when he is at full strength
- Good offensive rebounder, solid cutter and roll man, lacks lift, has some trouble finishing in traffic
- Occasionally can score on post-ups, experimenting with shooting threes, went 3-for-7 (42.9%) on threes last season
- Decent passing big man that can find open shooters and hit cutters, good at avoiding turnovers
- 2022-23 Defensive Degree of Difficulty: 0.217
- 2022-23 Points Prevented: -5.545
- Good defensive rebounder, solid shot blocker, below average rim protector, struggles with his positioning due to limited mobility
- Stout post defender, tends to commit a lot of shooting fouls, plays angles well enough to defend in space
- Middling pick-and-roll defender, good at hedging out onto ball handlers, a step late when defending screeners
- Tends to stay anchored in the paint, does not always come out to contest outside shots in spot-up situations

Simone Fontecchio

	Height	Weight	Cap #	Years Left
	6'8"	209	$3.045M	RFA

Similar at Age 27

		Season	SIMsc
1	Gerald Green	2012-13	938.8
2	Mindaugas Kuzminskas	2016-17	935.4
3	Lloyd Daniels	1994-95	929.4
4	Devean George	2004-05	925.5
5	Sean Higgins	1995-96	921.3
6	Sam Mack	1997-98	917.0
7	Rodney Hood	2019-20	916.1
8	Jake Layman	2021-22	909.3
9	Otto Porter	2020-21	909.2
10	Jason Kapono	2008-09	909.1

Baseline Basic Stats

MPG	PTS	AST	REB	BLK	STL
21.0	7.8	1.1	2.8	0.3	0.6

Advanced Metrics

USG%	3PTA/FGA	FTA/FGA	TS%	eFG%	3PT%
17.8	0.613	0.150	0.533	0.509	0.367

AST%	TOV%	OREB%	DREB%	STL%	BLK%
8.1	10.1	3.5	10.5	1.3	1.1

PER	ORTG	DRTG	WS/48	BPM	VOL
10.47	106.7	115.6	0.045	-1.87	0.457

- Fringe rotation player for Utah in his rookie season
- Struggled to play efficiently, mainly used as a moderate volume shooting specialist off the bench
- True Shooting Percentage was below 50%, below break-even three-point shooter
- Made over 39% of his spot-up threes, had a lot of difficulty making threes off screens
- Good scorer on dribble hand-offs, could curl off screens to hit short mid-range jumpers
- Rated by Synergy as being below average or worse in almost every other offensive situation
- Strictly a catch-and-shoot player, only makes safe passes, rarely turns the ball over
- 2022-23 Defensive Degree of Difficulty: 0.330
- 2022-23 Points Prevented: -1.458
- Usually guarded second unit level players, below average on-ball defender
- Has trouble staying with quicker players, struggles against stronger players inside
- Below average pick-and-roll defender, not especially effective at taking away any specific action
- Tends to get caught on screens, usually is late when closing out on spot-up shooters
- Stay-at-home defender, rarely gets steals or blocks, below average defensive rebounder

Luka Šamanić

	Height	Weight	Cap #	Years Left
	6'10"	227	$2.067M	UFA

Similar at Age 23

		Season	SIMsc
1	D.J. Wilson	2019-20	926.4
2	Bostjan Nachbar	2003-04	921.4
3	Michael Porter Jr.	2021-22	913.9
4	Trey Lyles	2018-19	913.1
5	Chimezie Metu	2020-21	911.5
6	Vladimir Radmanovic	2003-04	908.5
7	Marcus Morris	2012-13	903.7
8	Omri Casspi	2011-12	902.5
9	Scott Padgett	1999-00	902.3
10	De'Andre Hunter	2020-21	902.1

Baseline Basic Stats

MPG	PTS	AST	REB	BLK	STL
20.5	8.4	1.1	3.8	0.3	0.6

Advanced Metrics

USG%	3PTA/FGA	FTA/FGA	TS%	eFG%	3PT%
19.0	0.533	0.227	0.563	0.537	0.335

AST%	TOV%	OREB%	DREB%	STL%	BLK%
9.2	12.2	3.0	18.4	1.5	1.3

PER	ORTG	DRTG	WS/48	BPM	VOL
12.58	107.8	111.5	0.067	-1.58	0.458

- Waived by Boston, signed a ten-day contract with Utah, later signed to a standard contract
- Mainly used as a low usage stretch big in the NBA, played most of the season in the G-League with the Maine Celtics
- Below break-even three-point shooter in the G-League, strictly a spot-up shooter if his shot is falling
- More effective as an energetic rim runner, made over 70% of his shots from ten feet and in
- Good cutter off the ball, dives hard to the rim, effective scorer on hand-offs
- Not really a post-up player or ball handler, limited to being a low usage player
- Flashed solid passing skills in limited minutes, good at avoiding turnovers
- 2022-23 Defensive Degree of Difficulty: 0.472
- 2022-23 Points Prevented: -2.087
- Effective rim protector in very limited action, stays vertical when challenging shots, shot blocking rate was down, fairly solid defensive rebounder
- Over-matched in a difficult set of assignment, spent a lot of possessions guarding LeBron James
- Played decent on-ball defense, effective post defender, has trouble defending quicker players in space
- Solid pick-and-roll defender, capable of switching to guard ball handlers and screeners
- Tended to sag into the paint, not always in position to contest outside shots in spot-up situations

Newcomers

Taylor Hendricks

	Height	Weight	Cap #	Years Left
	6'9"	210	$5.570M	1 + 2 TO

Baseline Basic Stats

MPG	PTS	AST	REB	BLK	STL
21.7	8.2	1.3	3.8	0.6	0.6

Advanced Metrics

USG%	3PTA/FGA	FTA/FGA	TS%	eFG%	3PT%
17.4	0.334	0.266	0.509	0.474	0.317

AST%	TOV%	OREB%	DREB%	STL%	BLK%
8.9	10.7	5.4	13.9	1.4	2.4

PER	ORTG	DRTG	WS/48	BPM	VOL
12.74	101.4	101.8	0.069	-1.40	N/A

- Drafted by Utah with the 9th overall pick in 2023
- Did not participate in Summer League play in either Utah or Las Vegas due to a hamstring injury
- Effective in college as a moderate volume stretch four and energy player, projects to play a similar role in the NBA
- Solid three-point shooter in college, made over 39% of his threes in his only season at UCF
- Good spot-up shooter, effective as a pick-and-pop screener, can knock down threes in transition
- Energetic rim runner with good athleticism, explosive finisher in transition, effective roll man and cutter
- Effective at posting up smaller players, can hit turn-around jumpers or bully weaker defenders on the block
- Ball handling needs improvement, not really able to consistently create his own shot
- Great defensive potential due to his length and athleticism, potentially can be a plus-level defender
- Good on-ball defender in college, effectively guards multiple positions on the floor
- Good pick-and-roll defender, good at switching to defend ball handlers and screeners
- Stays attached to shooters off the ball, fights through screens and closes out on spot-up shooters
- Very active help defender, excellent weak side shot blocker, good at using his length to deflect passes or get steals, solid defensive rebounder
- Likely will be at least a rotational player for Utah as a rookie

Keyonte George

	Height	Weight	Cap #	Years Left
	6'4"	185	$3.890M	1 + 2 TO

Baseline Basic Stats

MPG	PTS	AST	REB	BLK	STL
22.1	9.8	2.5	2.6	0.2	0.7

Advanced Metrics

USG%	3PTA/FGA	FTA/FGA	TS%	eFG%	3PT%
21.7	0.405	0.247	0.503	0.466	0.331

AST%	TOV%	OREB%	DREB%	STL%	BLK%
18.4	13.9	2.7	10.7	1.8	0.7

PER	ORTG	DRTG	WS/48	BPM	VOL
12.26	96.9	106.9	0.040	-1.88	N/A

- Drafted by Utah with the 16th overall pick in 2023
- Named to the All-Summer League 1st Team in Las Vegas
- Thrived in a role as a primary scorer and ball handler at Summer League, may have to adapt to playing with less usage
- True Shooting Percentage was 60%, made almost 39% of his threes at Summer League
- More consistent as a spot-up shooter, capable of making shots off the dribble and off screens
- Lost 25 pounds over the summer, appeared to be more explosive, increased efficiency as a ball handler
- Better at slashing to the rim and making pull-up jumpers, drew fouls at a high rate
- Improved as a playmaker, made good reads, effectively could set up teammates for scoring opportunities, good at controlling the ball to limit turnovers
- Has good length and athleticism, hidden in favorable matchups in college, more effective defender at Summer League
- Decent on-ball defender, can competently guard ones and twos
- Solid pick-and-roll defender, makes sound rotations, good at funneling his man into help
- Stays attached to shooters off the ball, fights through screens and closes out in spot-up situations
- Active on the weak side, good at using his length to play passing lanes to get steals, decent defensive rebounder
- Likely will be at least a rotational player for Utah, has the potential to ascend to a greater role in the near future

Brice Sensabaugh

	Height	Weight	Cap #	Years Left
	6'6"	235	$2.449M	1 + 2 TO

Baseline Basic Stats

MPG	PTS	AST	REB	BLK	STL
19.6	8.0	1.2	3.2	0.3	0.6

Advanced Metrics

USG%	3PTA/FGA	FTA/FGA	TS%	eFG%	3PT%
20.5	0.338	0.216	0.506	0.478	0.340

AST%	TOV%	OREB%	DREB%	STL%	BLK%
10.1	11.5	4.8	14.2	1.5	1.1

PER	ORTG	DRTG	WS/48	BPM	VOL
13.48	99.7	103.8	0.061	-1.43	N/A

- Drafted by Utah with the 28th overall pick in 2023
- Did not participate in Summer League action due to a knee injury
- Highly productive in college as a high usage stretch four, likely will need to adapt to a lower volume role in the NBA
- Very good three-point shooter at Ohio State, made 40.5% of his threes last season
- Predominantly a stationary spot-up shooter, rarely shot threes in other situations
- Lacks the ball handling skills and quickness to consistently create separation against NBA caliber wings, may only be able to attack switches when he has the ball
- Effective at bullying weaker players in the post, capable of driving by slower big men
- Not really able to get a lot of lift when he jumps, has trouble finishing inside against length
- High motor player that dives hard to the rim, good at scoring on backdoor cuts
- Showed decent secondary playmaking skills, can find open shooters to relieve pressure, good at avoiding turnovers
- Lacks ideal physical tools on defense, plays angles well, positioning is usually sound
- Solid on-ball defender that can guard multiple positions
- Quick enough to stay with perimeter players, holds position well when defending in the post
- Fairly solid pick-and-roll defender, can functionally switch, has some trouble when rotating onto screeners
- Stays attached to shooters off the ball, fights through screens and closes out in spot-up situations
- Does not really get steals, occasionally blocks shots from the weak side, fairly good defensive rebounder
- May need to spend some time in the G-League to adapt to the pro level and polish his skills on both ends

HOUSTON ROCKETS

Last Season: 22 - 60, Missed the Playoffs

Offensive Rating: 111.4, 27th in the NBA

Defensive Rating: 119.3, 29th in the NBA

Primary Executive: Rafael Stone, General Manager

Head Coach: Ime Udoka

Key Roster Changes

Subtractions
Kenyon Martin Jr., trade
Josh Christopher, trade
Usman Garuba, trade
TyTy Washington, trade
Boban Marjanović, free agency
Frank Kaminsky, free agency
D.J. Augustin, free agency
Daishen Nix, waived

Additions
Amen Thompson, draft
Cam Whitmore, draft
Dillon Brooks, sign-and-trade
Fred VanVleet, free agency
Jeff Green, free agency
Jock Landale, free agency
Aaron Holiday, free agency

Roster

Likely Starting Five
1. *Fred VanVleet*
2. *Jalen Green*
3. *Dillon Brooks*
4. *Jabari Smith, Jr.*
5. *Alperen Sengun*

Other Key Rotation Players
Kevin Porter, Jr.
Tari Eason
Amen Thompson
Jeff Green
Jock Landale

* Italics denotes that a player is likely to be on the floor to close games

Remaining Roster

- Jae'Sean Tate
- Cam Whitmore
- Aaron Holiday
- Darius Days, 24, 6'7", 245, LSU (Two-Way)
- Trevor Hudgins, 24, 6'0", 180, Northwest Missouri State (Two-Way)
- Jermaine Samuels, 25, 6'7", 230, Villanova (Two-Way)
- Nate Hinton, 24, 6'5", 210, Houston (Exhibit 10)
- Jeenathan Williams, 24, 6'5", 205, Buffalo (Exhibit 10)
- Matthew Mayer, 24, 6'9", 225, Illinois (Exhibit 10)
- Joshua Obiesie, 23, 6'6", 190, Germany (Exhibit 10)

SCHREMPF Base Rating: 37.8

Season Preview Survey

- *Are the Rockets contending or rebuilding? Where is this team headed?*

The Rockets have been rebuilding for the past few seasons. Based on their active summer, they are looking to make a push to become more competitive because they added several veterans including former All-Star Fred VanVleet along with Jeff Green, Jock Landale, and Dillon Brooks. They also made an upgrade in the coaching department by hiring Ime Udoka to serve as head coach. These additions could work to speed up their development process to make them a more respectable team, but they still might not have enough to be a playoff team. Even so, they seem to be trending upwards and they could be an exciting unit to watch out for in the coming seasons.

- *What are the areas of concern for this team heading into this season?*

The main issue for the Rockets is that they don't have a clear identity to lean on to get wins. They have mostly been focused on accumulating young talent and building up their skills from an individual perspective. This emphasis has caused their team to be disjointed at both ends of the floor. Even though their free agent additions give them more experience and a talent boost, they still don't give them a clear strength on offense or defense. They will have to depend on Udoka to implement a structure to allow everyone to settle into definitive roles and turn them into a competitive unit. Udoka doesn't have the same kind of talent in Houston that he had in Boston, so they won't immediately become a winner. However, they could make positive strides to have more accountability on defense and exert more effort on a regular basis.

- *List some possible breakout players for this team.*

Houston had excellent performances from its representatives at this year's Summer League, as they all showed that they could emerge as valuable players this season. Namely, Jabari Smith Jr. showcased the scoring prowess and potential that made him a high draft pick in 2022. He displayed the range to knock down shots from outside and he could use his height to shoot over defenders or score around the rim. He also did a better job of reading defenses to identify mismatches and get himself higher quality looks, so he could be primed to deliver on his considerable upside this season. In addition to him, Tari Eason was effective as an off-ball defender and a complementary energy wing, so he could help in those areas in his second year. Even though his Summer League was cut short due to an ankle injury, Amen Thompson flashed the athleticism, slashing ability, and court vision that made him the fourth pick in this year's draft. Last but definitely not least, Cam Whitmore was named MVP of the Las Vegas Summer League due to his ability to defend, knock down spot-up jumpers, and create offense for himself. If he translates this performance to the regular season, he could wind up being the steal of this year's draft, which would help the Rockets tremendously.

- *What should we expect from them this season?*

In all likelihood, the Rockets will still be a team that finishes on the outside of the playoff picture because they just don't have a proven front-end player to carry them through the regular season. However, they do have an interesting collection of young talent and now, they have some veterans and a more accomplished coaching staff in place to help guide them in the right direction. This improved support system should allow their top young players to grow into better versions of themselves and as a whole, they should be a much more competitive unit. The goal for Houston this season is to show signs of positive growth to help them become a more consistent winner in the future.

Veterans

Fred VanVleet

	Height	Weight	Cap #	Years Left
	6'1"	197	$40.806M	1 + TO

Similar at Age 28

		Season	SIMsc
1	Raymond Felton	2012-13	926.8
2	Mike Bibby	2006-07	916.9
3	Eric Bledsoe	2017-18	916.4
4	Kyrie Irving	2020-21	906.6
5	Mike James	2003-04	905.6
6	Jason Williams	2003-04	903.5
7	Terry Porter	1991-92	899.5
8	Mike Conley	2015-16	897.3
9	Reggie Jackson	2018-19	895.6
10	Bobby Jackson	2001-02	895.0

Baseline Basic Stats

MPG	PTS	AST	REB	BLK	STL
30.8	14.5	5.5	3.3	0.3	1.2

Advanced Metrics

USG%	3PTA/FGA	FTA/FGA	TS%	eFG%	3PT%
22.2	0.520	0.214	0.533	0.491	0.350

AST%	TOV%	OREB%	DREB%	STL%	BLK%
27.9	11.8	1.7	10.9	2.0	1.2

PER	ORTG	DRTG	WS/48	BPM	VOL
15.82	112.5	112.3	0.099	1.73	0.172

- Made the All-Star team in 2021-22, has played at the same level for the past three seasons
- Highly productive as Toronto's primary playmaker and ball handler
- Great distributor and ball control guard, makes good decisions, rarely turns the ball over
- Reliable three-point shooter throughout his career, great shooter off the catch
- Three-Point Percentage fell to just above break-even, had to take tougher shots off the dribble
- Crafty ball handler, draws some fouls, makes pull-up jumpers, better with a screen as a pick-and-roll ball handler
- 2022-23 Defensive Degree of Difficulty: 0.496
- 2022-23 Points Prevented: -0.438
- Drew a lot of tough assignments against elite scoring guards, solid on-ball defender
- Fairly effective at defending both guard spots, better against taller two-guards, had trouble against quicker guards
- Fairly solid pick-and-roll defender, can switch and cut off penetration, tends to go too far under screens
- Gets caught on screens off the ball, good at closing out on spot-up shooters
- Good at playing passing lanes to get steals, occasional weak side shot blocker, solid defensive rebounder

Alperen Şengün

	Height	Weight	Cap #	Years Left
	6'9"	235	$3.536M	TO

Similar at Age 20

		Season	SIMsc
1	John Collins	2017-18	923.7
2	Chris Webber*	1993-94	910.1
3	Nikola Jokic	2015-16	904.5
4	Derrick Favors	2011-12	902.8
5	Lamar Odom	1999-00	895.6
6	Aaron Gordon	2015-16	894.4
7	Shawn Kemp	1989-90	892.1
8	Marquese Chriss	2017-18	890.1
9	Al Harrington	2000-01	888.3
10	Rudy Gay	2006-07	887.8

Baseline Basic Stats

MPG	PTS	AST	REB	BLK	STL
28.4	14.6	2.6	7.5	1.1	0.9

Advanced Metrics

USG%	3PTA/FGA	FTA/FGA	TS%	eFG%	3PT%
24.0	0.144	0.353	0.590	0.552	0.330

AST%	TOV%	OREB%	DREB%	STL%	BLK%
19.0	15.6	9.8	20.1	1.6	2.7

PER	ORTG	DRTG	WS/48	BPM	VOL
20.15	114.5	111.5	0.140	1.81	0.445

- Became Houston's regular starting center in his second NBA season
- Effectiveness increased in a role as a moderate volume post-up player and rim runner
- Good post player, uses crafty moves and subtle fakes to score, better from the right block
- Good passing big man, can hit cutters out of the high post, fairly turnover prone
- High motor rim runner, lacks ideal vertical lift, has some trouble finishing in traffic, good offensive rebounder, solid roll man and cutter
- Taking fewer outside shots, mainly shoots from 16 feet and in
- 2022-23 Defensive Degree of Difficulty: 0.449
- 2022-23 Points Prevented: -0.683
- Good shot blocker and defensive rebounder, lacks ideal length to contest shots, below average rim protector
- Guards starting level big men, longer big men can shoot over him in the post, mobile enough to defend in space
- Below average pick-and-roll defender, not effective at taking away any specific action
- Consistently comes out to contest perimeter shots in spot-up situations
- Has active hands, can get into passing lanes to get steals

Jalen Green

	Height	Weight	Cap #	Years Left
	6'4"	178	$9.891M	TO

Similar at Age 20

#	Player	Season	SIMsc
1	Zach LaVine	2015-16	932.6
2	Ja Morant	2019-20	915.0
3	Tre Mann	2021-22	907.8
4	Brandon Knight	2011-12	906.7
5	Collin Sexton	2018-19	906.6
6	Trae Young	2018-19	903.5
7	R.J. Hampton	2021-22	903.3
8	Jamal Murray	2017-18	902.9
9	Bradley Beal	2013-14	900.2
10	Coby White	2020-21	898.6

Baseline Basic Stats

MPG	PTS	AST	REB	BLK	STL
30.2	17.3	4.3	3.6	0.2	0.9

Advanced Metrics

USG%	3PTA/FGA	FTA/FGA	TS%	eFG%	3PT%
27.4	0.435	0.289	0.553	0.505	0.356

AST%	TOV%	OREB%	DREB%	STL%	BLK%
20.3	11.8	2.0	10.3	1.3	0.6

PER	ORTG	DRTG	WS/48	BPM	VOL
15.61	109.4	117.9	0.062	-0.83	0.366

- Regular starting guard for Houston in his second NBA season
- Led the team in scoring, increased his effectiveness in a role as a high usage ball handler
- Scored in volume as a ball handler, efficiency was average, inconsistent when shooting threes off the dribble
- Drew more fouls, better at making pull-up mid-range shots as a pick-and-roll ball handler and isolation player
- Above break-even three-point shooter, similar effectiveness when shooting in every situation
- Explosive finisher in transition, rarely moves off the ball, shot selection can be questionable at times
- Improved to be a fairly good secondary playmaker, makes simple reads, good at avoiding turnovers
- 2022-23 Defensive Degree of Difficulty: 0.460
- 2022-23 Points Prevented: 0.059
- Drew tougher assignments than he did last season, above average on-ball defender
- Quick enough to stay with opposing guards on the perimeter, struggles against stronger players inside
- Decent pick-and-roll defender, can functionally switch and cut off penetration, tends to go too far under screens
- Tends to get caught on screens off the ball, good at closing out on spot-up shooters
- Stay-at-home defender, does not really get steals or blocks, decent defensive rebounder

Jabari Smith Jr.

	Height	Weight	Cap #	Years Left
	6'10"	220	$9.327M	2 TO

Similar at Age 19

		Season	SIMsc
1	Eddie Griffin	2001-02	927.0
2	Chris Bosh*	2003-04	913.8
3	Kevin Knox	2018-19	907.1
4	Marquese Chriss	2016-17	895.2
5	Darius Bazley	2019-20	892.8
6	Kevin Garnett*	1995-96	888.2
7	Aaron Gordon	2014-15	881.5
8	Jayson Tatum	2017-18	878.2
9	Patrick Williams	2020-21	869.7
10	Michael Kidd-Gilchrist	2012-13	869.2

Baseline Basic Stats

MPG	PTS	AST	REB	BLK	STL
30.0	13.6	1.9	6.1	0.8	0.8

Advanced Metrics

USG%	3PTA/FGA	FTA/FGA	TS%	eFG%	3PT%
21.2	0.321	0.275	0.542	0.500	0.323

AST%	TOV%	OREB%	DREB%	STL%	BLK%
10.3	10.8	5.4	20.0	1.3	2.2

PER	ORTG	DRTG	WS/48	BPM	VOL
14.76	109.9	115.2	0.069	-1.88	0.446

- Named to the All-Rookie 2nd Team in 2022-23, started all but three games for Houston as a rookie
- Decently effective in his role as a lower usage spot-up shooter
- Below break-even three-point shooter, more efficient when shooting in the corners
- Almost exclusively used as a stand-still spot-up shooter, better when shooting threes in transition
- Not really used as a ball handler, decent post-up player that can face up or shoot over smaller players
- Somewhat effective as a rim runner, good slipping screens on pick-and-rolls, has trouble finishing in traffic
- Catch-and-shoot player right now, not really an advanced playmaker, rarely turns the ball over
- 2022-23 Defensive Degree of Difficulty: 0.481
- 2022-23 Points Prevented: -1.224
- Drew a lot of difficult assignments against high-end starting wings as a rookie, tended to be over-matched
- Uses his length well to contest shots, takes bad angles when guarding quicker players, not quite strong enough to handle interior players
- Average pick-and-roll defender, good in drop coverages, can cut off penetration against ball handlers, tends to go too far under screens
- Fights through off-ball screens, tends to be late when closing out on spot-up shooters
- Very good weak side shot blocker, does not really get steals, good defensive rebounder

Dillon Brooks

	Height	Weight	Cap #	Years Left
	6'7"	225	$22.628M	3

Similar at Age 27

		Season	SIMsc
1	Sam Mack	1997-98	942.5
2	Tracy Murray	1998-99	937.5
3	Morris Peterson	2004-05	921.6
4	C.J. Miles	2014-15	920.0
5	Jared Dudley	2012-13	919.9
6	Andres Nocioni	2006-07	919.2
7	Bostjan Nachbar	2007-08	917.8
8	J.R. Smith	2012-13	917.0
9	Bogdan Bogdanović	2019-20	916.9
10	Walt Williams	1997-98	916.2

Baseline Basic Stats

MPG	PTS	AST	REB	BLK	STL
26.2	12.3	1.8	3.5	0.3	0.8

Advanced Metrics

USG%	3PTA/FGA	FTA/FGA	TS%	eFG%	3PT%
22.4	0.437	0.186	0.525	0.494	0.364

AST%	TOV%	OREB%	DREB%	STL%	BLK%
11.9	9.3	2.6	10.7	1.5	0.8

PER	ORTG	DRTG	WS/48	BPM	VOL
12.63	106.4	111.4	0.071	-1.21	0.324

- Named to the All-Defensive 2nd Team in 2022-23
- Production level sharply declined, used as a moderate volume spot-up shooter
- Below break-even three-point shooter last season, posted a True Shooting Percentage below 50%
- Takes a lot of questionable shots that hurt his percentages, historically better as a spot-up shooter
- Rated by Synergy as average or worse in every offensive situation, best used as a cutter off the ball
- Defenders can back off him to limit his effectiveness as a ball handler, inconsistent shooter off the dribble
- Shows solid secondary playmaking skills, rarely turns the ball over
- 2022-23 Defensive Degree of Difficulty: 0.594, had the 4th most difficult set of matchups in the NBA
- 2022-23 Points Prevented: 1.089
- Used as Memphis' primary defensive stopper, tries too hard to be an irritant, antics can be disruptive to his team
- Good on-ball defender that can effectively guard multiple positions on the floor
- Average pick-and-roll defender, good at containing ball handlers, has lapses when switched onto a screener
- Tends to get caught on screens off the ball, good at closing out on spot-up shooters
- More of a stay-at-home defender, Steal Percentage declined, below average defensive rebounder

Kevin Porter Jr.

	Height	Weight	Cap #	Years Left
	6'4"	203	$15.860M	2 + TO

Similar at Age 22

		Season	SIMsc
1	Jamal Murray	2019-20	943.5
2	Emmanuel Mudiay	2018-19	928.0
3	Marcus Thornton	2009-10	919.8
4	Bradley Beal	2015-16	919.5
5	Beno Udrih	2004-05	916.9
6	Jordan Poole	2021-22	916.2
7	Dion Waiters	2013-14	915.9
8	Jordan Clarkson	2014-15	912.6
9	Jerryd Bayless	2010-11	911.4
10	Dwyane Wade*	2003-04	910.7

Baseline Basic Stats

MPG	PTS	AST	REB	BLK	STL
28.3	14.6	3.7	3.4	0.3	1.0

Advanced Metrics

USG%	3PTA/FGA	FTA/FGA	TS%	eFG%	3PT%
24.2	0.397	0.269	0.554	0.515	0.366

AST%	TOV%	OREB%	DREB%	STL%	BLK%
24.6	14.0	3.1	11.4	1.9	0.8

PER	ORTG	DRTG	WS/48	BPM	VOL
16.19	110.0	115.2	0.078	0.26	0.400

- Missed games due to a bruised left foot, regular starting guard for Houston when healthy
- Had his most production NBA season in a role as a higher usage scorer and ball handler
- Good playmaker that finds open shooters and makes interior passes, fairly turnover prone
- Solid three-point shooter for the past two seasons, has made over 44% of his career corner threes
- Very good shooter off the catch, makes spot-up jumpers and can run off screens
- Above average scorer in ball handling situations, draws fouls, doesn't always get to the rim, makes pull-up jumpers from mid-range, inconsistent shooter from long range
- 2022-23 Defensive Degree of Difficulty: 0.511
- 2022-23 Points Prevented: -0.997
- Used as Houston's primary perimeter stopper, over-extended in that role
- Average on-ball defender, better against taller wings, had trouble staying with quicker guards
- Average pick-and-roll defender, can switch, good at cutting off penetration, goes too far under screens
- Takes bad gambles, gets caught on screens off the ball, tends to be late when closing out on spot-up shooters
- Active help defender, plays passing lanes, gets steals at a fairly high rate, fairly solid defensive rebounder

Tari Eason

	Height	Weight	Cap #	Years Left
	6'8"	216	$3.527M	2 TO

Similar at Age 21

		Season	SIMsc
1	Jumaine Jones	2000-01	917.8
2	Al-Farouq Aminu	2011-12	912.3
3	Paul George	2011-12	910.9
4	Thaddeus Young	2009-10	905.6
5	Shawn Marion	1999-00	905.5
6	Darius Bazley	2021-22	900.5
7	Wilson Chandler	2008-09	899.9
8	Josh Jackson	2018-19	899.8
9	Kawhi Leonard	2012-13	897.5
10	Justise Winslow	2017-18	896.0

Baseline Basic Stats

MPG	PTS	AST	REB	BLK	STL
27.3	11.3	1.6	5.9	0.6	1.1

Advanced Metrics

USG%	3PTA/FGA	FTA/FGA	TS%	eFG%	3PT%
19.0	0.198	0.249	0.537	0.501	0.341

AST%	TOV%	OREB%	DREB%	STL%	BLK%
9.1	12.8	8.8	18.2	2.4	1.7

PER	ORTG	DRTG	WS/48	BPM	VOL
14.99	109.2	110.0	0.094	-0.10	0.428

- Named to the All-Rookie 2nd Team, regular rotation player for Houston, played in all 82 games
- Solidly effective in his role as a low usage spot-up shooter and energy player
- Above break-even three-point shooter, above average when shooting in the corners
- Good spot-up shooter in the half-court, fairly slow release, needs time to get his shot off
- Great athlete, explosive finisher at the rim, draws fouls at a solid rate, plays somewhat wildly, tends to rush his attempts around the basket
- Not really used as a ball handler, catch-and-shoot player that makes safe passes, good at avoiding turnovers
- 2022-23 Defensive Degree of Difficulty: 0.403
- 2022-23 Points Prevented: -1.952
- Usually guarded second unit players or lower leverage starters, average on-ball defender
- Has good quickness to stay with perimeter players, struggled against stronger players in the post
- Average pick-and-roll defender, can switch and cut off penetration, usually goes too far under screens
- Tends to get caught on screens off the ball, good at closing out on spot-up shooters
- Very active help defender, gets steals and blocks at a very high rate, fairly good defensive rebounder

Jeff Green

	Height	Weight	Cap #	Years Left
	6'8"	235	$9.600M	TO

Similar at Age 36

		Season	SIMsc
1	Sam Perkins	1997-98	927.4
2	Antawn Jamison	2012-13	917.7
3	Richard Jefferson	2016-17	909.1
4	Joe Johnson	2017-18	908.6
5	Frank Brickowski	1995-96	905.6
6	Grant Hill*	2008-09	898.0
7	Mike Dunleavy	2016-17	896.6
8	Carmelo Anthony	2020-21	893.7
9	Matt Barnes	2016-17	889.9
10	Dan Issel*	1984-85	879.7

Baseline Basic Stats

MPG	PTS	AST	REB	BLK	STL
20.2	7.5	1.1	3.0	0.3	0.5

Advanced Metrics

USG%	3PTA/FGA	FTA/FGA	TS%	eFG%	3PT%
16.6	0.386	0.287	0.557	0.514	0.308

AST%	TOV%	OREB%	DREB%	STL%	BLK%
7.8	10.2	2.9	12.6	0.9	1.3

PER	ORTG	DRTG	WS/48	BPM	VOL
10.63	109.0	113.2	0.077	-3.28	0.362

- Missed games due to injuries to his hand and knee, regular rotation player for Denver when healthy
- Slightly less effective in his role as a low usage stretch big off the bench
- Break-even career three-point shooter, Three-Point Percentage fell to below 30% last season
- Almost exclusively a stand-still spot-up shooter at this stage, less effective when shooting in other situations
- Solid rim runner despite his advancing age, good at running in transition and cutting off the ball
- Not really used in ball handling situations, below average as a post-up player
- Catch-and-shoot player that makes safe passes, consistently avoids turnovers
- 2022-23 Defensive Degree of Difficulty: 0.393
- 2022-23 Points Prevented: -1.063
- Below average rim protector, does not really block shots, below average defensive rebounder
- Usually guards second unit level players, played solid on-ball defense last season
- Good at holding position in the post against big men, mobile enough to guard wing players
- Played below average pick-and-roll defense, not especially effective at taking away any specific action
- Gets caught on screens off the ball, tended to be late when closing out on spot-up shooters
- Stay-at-home defender, has not historically gotten steals throughout his career

Jock Landale

	Height	Weight	Cap #	Years Left
	6'11"	256	$8.000M	2 + TO

Similar at Age 27

		Season	SIMsc
1	Raef LaFrentz	2003-04	904.8
2	Spencer Hawes	2015-16	901.5
3	Malik Allen	2005-06	899.3
4	Frank Kaminsky	2020-21	899.2
5	Willy Hernangómez	2021-22	898.5
6	Scott Padgett	2003-04	896.4
7	Tyler Zeller	2016-17	895.4
8	Dwight Powell	2018-19	895.0
9	Melvin Ely	2005-06	894.4
10	Matt Bonner	2007-08	894.0

Baseline Basic Stats

MPG	PTS	AST	REB	BLK	STL
18.1	7.4	1.0	4.8	0.6	0.5

Advanced Metrics

USG%	3PTA/FGA	FTA/FGA	TS%	eFG%	3PT%
18.2	0.276	0.298	0.591	0.551	0.331

AST%	TOV%	OREB%	DREB%	STL%	BLK%
9.3	12.4	10.5	18.8	1.2	2.4

PER	ORTG	DRTG	WS/48	BPM	VOL
16.42	118.1	109.7	0.138	-0.03	0.467

- Fringe rotation player for Phoenix in his first season with the team
- Production was consistent with his career averages, solid as a low usage rim runner and stretch big
- Most effective as a high motor rim runner, does most of his damage from ten feet and in
- Great cutter and roll man, good offensive rebounder, runs hard down the floor in transition, draws fouls at a solid rate
- Effective at flashing to the middle on post-ups, less effective when using normal post moves on the block
- Struggled to make outside shots, below break-even career three-point shooter
- Solid passing big man that can hit cutters or find open shooters, good at avoiding turnovers
- 2022-23 Defensive Degree of Difficulty: 0.351
- 2022-23 Points Prevented: 0.598
- Fairly good rim protector, decent shot blocker, solid defensive rebounder, stays vertical to challenge shots
- Usually guards second unit big men, highly foul prone, can be overpowered by stronger big men inside, has trouble defending in space
- Middling pick-and-roll defender, effective at hedging out on ball handlers, usually a step late when covering the roll man
- Consistently comes out to contest outside shots in spot-up situations

Jae'Sean Tate

	Height	Weight	Cap #	Years Left
	6'4"	230	$6.500M	1

Similar at Age 27

		Season	SIMsc
1	Rodney Rogers	1998-99	904.7
2	Maurice Evans	2005-06	899.5
3	Devin Brown	2005-06	898.5
4	Matt Barnes	2007-08	896.4
5	P.J. Tucker	2012-13	889.8
6	Fred Jones	2006-07	889.6
7	Randy Foye	2010-11	889.5
8	Ruben Patterson	2002-03	889.3
9	Joey Graham	2009-10	889.1
10	Stephen Graham	2009-10	888.6

Baseline Basic Stats

MPG	PTS	AST	REB	BLK	STL
22.3	8.2	1.9	3.5	0.3	0.8

Advanced Metrics

USG%	3PTA/FGA	FTA/FGA	TS%	eFG%	3PT%
18.4	0.315	0.261	0.540	0.508	0.335

AST%	TOV%	OREB%	DREB%	STL%	BLK%
15.8	14.3	5.8	13.5	1.6	1.1

PER	ORTG	DRTG	WS/48	BPM	VOL
12.70	108.7	113.4	0.070	-1.28	0.268

- Missed games due to an ankle injury, fell out of Houston's rotation in his third NBA season
- Effectiveness slightly dropped in a role as a low usage spot-up shooter and secondary playmaker
- Below break-even career three-point shooter, struggles to make stand-still spot-up jumpers
- More reliable when shooting from ten feet and in, energetic rim runner, decent cutter and roll man, has some trouble finishing in traffic
- Has become a solid secondary playmaker, slightly turnover prone
- Effective when used as a pick-and-roll ball handler and isolation player in a small sample of possessions
- 2022-23 Defensive Degree of Difficulty: 0.509
- 2022-23 Points Prevented: 0.581
- Generally has been used as a defensive stopper that draws tough assignments
- Fairly solid on-ball defender, good against perimeter players, has trouble against taller wings in the post
- Decent pick-and-roll defender, can functionally switch, tended to allow ball handlers to turn the corner
- Fights through screens off the ball, not always in position to contest shots in spot-up situations
- More of a stay-at-home defender, steal and block rates decreased, fairly solid defensive rebounder

Aaron Holiday

	Height	Weight	Cap #	Years Left
	6'0"	185	$2.020M	UFA

Similar at Age 26

		Season	SIMsc
1	Yogi Ferrell	2019-20	933.5
2	Patty Mills	2014-15	926.8
3	Tony Smith	1994-95	923.2
4	Luther Head	2008-09	917.7
5	Shabazz Napier	2017-18	916.9
6	Patrick Beverley	2014-15	915.5
7	Eddie Gill	2004-05	913.5
8	Eddie House	2004-05	912.4
9	Shammond Williams	2001-02	911.4
10	Craig Hodges	1986-87	908.9

Baseline Basic Stats

MPG	PTS	AST	REB	BLK	STL
20.1	7.8	2.6	1.9	0.1	0.7

Advanced Metrics

USG%	3PTA/FGA	FTA/FGA	TS%	eFG%	3PT%
17.3	0.401	0.157	0.525	0.496	0.380

AST%	TOV%	OREB%	DREB%	STL%	BLK%
18.0	13.3	2.2	8.1	1.9	0.8

PER	ORTG	DRTG	WS/48	BPM	VOL
11.21	106.3	113.1	0.052	-1.92	0.396

- Fringe rotation player for Atlanta in his first season with the team
- Production level dropped in a role as a very low usage spot-up shooter and backup point guard
- Reliable three-point shooter, made almost 41% of his threes last season
- Mostly a stationary spot-up shooter, could occasionally knock down pull-up threes off pick-and-rolls
- Occasionally drives to the rim as a change-of-pace, lacks the quickness to regularly create his own offense
- Solid ball control guard that avoids turnovers, fairly good distributor
- Largely was used off the ball, played mostly in a static offense with limited movement
- 2022-23 Defensive Degree of Difficulty: 0.390
- 2022-23 Points Prevented: -0.488
- Usually guarded second unit level guards, rarely was asked to guard higher-end starters
- Played solid on-ball defense, can effectively defend ones and twos in lower leverage matchups
- Solid pick-and-roll defender, limited ability to switch, funnels his man into help, makes sound rotations
- Fights through screens off the ball, usually closes out but opponents can shoot over due to his smallish size
- Pesky defender, pressures ball handlers and plays passing lanes to get steals, Block Percentage increased, below average defensive rebounder

Newcomers

Amen Thompson

	Height	Weight	Cap #	Years Left
	6'7"	209	$8.809M	1 + 2 TO

Baseline Basic Stats

MPG	PTS	AST	REB	BLK	STL
19.5	7.5	1.6	3.6	0.6	0.8

Advanced Metrics

USG%	3PTA/FGA	FTA/FGA	TS%	eFG%	3PT%
17.6	0.130	0.249	0.515	0.478	0.556

AST%	TOV%	OREB%	DREB%	STL%	BLK%
18.5	12.5	6.1	9.4	2.7	5.1

PER	ORTG	DRTG	WS/48	BPM	VOL
14.98	106.4	104.2	0.098	-0.46	0.691

- Drafted by Houston with the 4th overall pick in 2023
- Spent the past two seasons playing for Overtime Elite
- Played very well in one Summer League game in Las Vegas, shut down due to a sprained ankle
- Mainly used as a moderate volume playmaker and scoring wing
- Displayed great playmaking skills, can read defenses while driving downhill, made sound decisions, solid at avoiding turnovers
- Excellent athlete, uses his great quickness to slash to the rim, will absorb contact to draw fouls
- Great at pushing the ball in transition, explosive finisher
- Shot the ball more efficiently in Vegas, played with a greater level of control, posted a True Shooting Percentage above 54%
- Shooting is still a work-in-progress, made less than 30% of his threes with Overtime Elite
- Inconsistent stroke due to mechanical flaws, made less than 65% of his free throws
- Has ideal physical tools on defense, can potentially develop into a plus-level defender
- Gambled frequently and took bad angles with Overtime Elite, played with more discipline at Summer League
- Defended with a high effort level at Summer League, could capably defend multiple positions
- Flashed the potential to switch on pick-and-rolls, still learning NBA level rotation schemes at this stage
- Better at fighting through screens and closing out on spot-up shooters
- Extremely active help defender, excellent weak side shot blocker, disruptive roamer that gets steals at a very high rate, below average defensive rebounder at Summer League

Cam Whitmore

	Height	Weight	Cap #	Years Left
	6'7"	232	$3.218M	1 + 2 TO

Baseline Basic Stats

MPG	PTS	AST	REB	BLK	STL
19.8	7.3	1.2	3.2	0.3	0.8

Advanced Metrics

USG%	3PTA/FGA	FTA/FGA	TS%	eFG%	3PT%
18.4	0.331	0.195	0.498	0.470	0.294

AST%	TOV%	OREB%	DREB%	STL%	BLK%
9.1	11.4	3.9	13.7	1.9	0.9

PER	ORTG	DRTG	WS/48	BPM	VOL
12.05	97.1	102.4	0.060	-1.11	N/A

- Drafted by Houston with the 20th overall pick in 2023
- Named MVP of the Las Vegas Summer League
- Highly productive in his role as a high usage scoring wing, likely will be used off the bench or in a lower usage role as a rookie in the NBA
- More of a volume scorer, three-point shot was inconsistent and streaky
- Better at making spot-up jumpers, inconsistent when shooting off the dribble
- More effective when attacking the rim, explosive finisher in transition, great cutter, opportunistic offensive rebounder that scores off put-backs
- Can drive by defenders on straight-line drives, needs to improve his ball handling, does not change direction very well
- Generally a catch-and-shoot player, only makes safe passes, good at avoiding turnovers
- Good athlete, has the potential to be solid defender that guards multiple positions
- Played with a greater level of control, solid on-ball defender at Summer League, could capably defend wings and guards
- Solid as a pick-and-roll defender, could effectively switch to guard ball handlers and screeners
- Tended to get caught on screens off the ball, good at closing out on spot-up shooters
- Very active help defender, great at using his anticipation skills to get steals, decent weak side shot blocker, solid defensive rebounder

SAN ANTONIO SPURS

Last Season: 22 - 60, Missed the Playoffs

Offensive Rating: 110.2, 29th in the NBA

Defensive Rating: 120.0, 30th in the NBA

Primary Executive: R.C. Buford, Chief Executive Officer

Head Coach: Gregg Popovich

Key Roster Changes

Subtractions
Romeo Langford, free agency
Keita Bates-Diop, free agency
Gorgui Dieng, free agency

Additions
Victor Wembanyama, draft
Sidy Cissoko, draft
Reggie Bullock, trade
Cedi Osman, trade
Cameron Payne, trade

Roster

Likely Starting Five
1. Tre Jones
2. Keldon Johnson
3. Jeremy Sochan
4. Victor Wembanyama
5. Zach Collins

Other Key Rotation Players
Devin Vassell
Malaki Branham
Charles Bassey
Doug McDermott
Devonte' Graham

* Italics denotes that a player is likely to be on the floor to close games

Remaining Roster

- Reggie Bullock
- Cedi Osman
- Cameron Payne
- Blake Wesley
- Julian Champagnie
- Sandro Mamukelashvili
- Khem Birch
- Sidy Cissoko
- Dominick Barlow, 20, 6'9", 221, Overtime Elite (USA – Dumont, NJ) (Two-Way)
- Sir'Jabari Rice, 25, 6'4", 180, Texas (Two-Way)
- Charles Bediako, 21, 6'11", 220, Alabama (Exhibit 10)
- Seth Millner, 23, 6'6", 200, Toledo (Exhibit 10)

SCHREMPF Base Rating: 37.6

Season Preview Survey

- *Are the Spurs contending or rebuilding? Where is this team headed?*

The Spurs are still in the rebuilding phase, but their plan to move towards contention has become clearer because they were fortunate enough to win the lottery and take Victor Wembanyama in the draft. He gives them a foundational core piece to build around, so the main goal for the Spurs this season will be ensure that he stays on the path to realizing his vast potential. It will be important for them to build up the support system to allow him to succeed in the league. The individual growth of him and their other young players take a higher priority for them, so they may sacrifice some short-term wins to ensure that they will have the best possible long-term future.

- *What are the areas of concern for this team heading into this season?*

The primary concern for the Spurs is if they have the sort of support system that is needed to allow Wembanyama to play to his strengths and maximize his production. After all, they are coming off a season where they finished as one of the worst teams in the league. They were over-matched on both ends of the floor, so Wembanyama is being thrown into an adverse situation where his team will be at a disadvantage. He will really have to work to get efficient looks, and he'll be the focal point of the opponent's game plan, so he'll have a lot of responsibility right away. If he shows that he can handle this burden while the team tries to build up the players around him, then the Spurs should be in good shape moving forward. Otherwise, they may need to find some way to break him in slowly to allow him to make the proper adjustment to the league.

- *List some possible breakout players for this team.*

San Antonio is fielding a very young roster, so there are ample opportunities for someone to break out and become a higher impact player. The focus will be on Wembanyama because he's one of the most talented prospect to enter the league in a while, so he will be the favorite to win Rookie of the Year. Aside from him, the Spurs have some interesting young talent on their team. Last year's lottery pick, Jeremy Sochan flashed the potential to be a versatile shutdown defender and a useful ball moving complementary player. With another year under his belt, he could refine his skills to become a valuable connector on offense and a stopper on defense. Keldon Johnson and Devin Vassell were over-extended as higher usage scorers last year, but they could boost their efficiency this season because the presence of Wembanyama would allow them to shift to secondary scoring roles that better fit their skill sets. Then, Charles Bassey could emerge as a valuable center for the Spurs because they are in need of a bigger bodied player to absorb physical contact to reduce the punishment that Wembanyama could take as a rookie. Bassey fits the description of the type of player that could fit this role, so he could also take a leap forward and make an impact this year.

- *What should we expect from them this season?*

Most likely, the Spurs will finish as a lottery team this season. Though they have an incredible young talent in Wembanyama, they don't have a good enough roster from top to bottom to really push for a playoff spot right now. The key for them will be to utilize their existing talent in a way that maximizes Wembanyama and all their other young players, so they can lay the foundation for a better future. If Wembanyama puts together a strong rookie season, then the season will be considered a success and they can work on finding the right mix of players to complement him. Otherwise, things don't go as planned, they will need to make some tweaks or adjust their development plans to allow him to better reach his potential in the future.

Veterans

Keldon Johnson

	Height	Weight	Cap #	Years Left
	6'5"	220	$20.000M	3

Similar at Age 23

		Season	SIMsc
1	Jaylen Brown	2019-20	948.3
2	J.R. Smith	2008-09	938.0
3	Quentin Richardson	2003-04	936.9
4	Kyle Kuzma	2018-19	925.2
5	Von Wafer	2008-09	923.9
6	Michael Redd	2002-03	923.8
7	Jason Richardson	2003-04	922.6
8	Marcus Thornton	2010-11	921.5
9	Corey Maggette	2002-03	920.8
10	Desmond Bane	2021-22	920.6

Baseline Basic Stats

MPG	PTS	AST	REB	BLK	STL
31.3	16.9	2.6	4.4	0.3	1.0

Advanced Metrics

USG%	3PTA/FGA	FTA/FGA	TS%	eFG%	3PT%
25.4	0.375	0.273	0.557	0.517	0.358

AST%	TOV%	OREB%	DREB%	STL%	BLK%
13.8	9.5	3.3	14.0	1.4	0.6

PER	ORTG	DRTG	WS/48	BPM	VOL
16.64	110.8	114.5	0.085	-0.19	0.335

- Regular starting wing for San Antonio in his fourth NBA season
- Maintained his usual level off efficiency in a new role as a primary scoring option
- Solid pick-and-roll ball handler and isolation player, good at slashing to the rim, hits floaters
- Good cutter, great at running the break in transition, effectively gets to the rim on hand-offs
- League average career three-point shooter, Three-Point Percentage fell to below break-even with increased attention
- Primarily a stationary spot-up shooter, occasionally can shoot off screens, struggles to shoot off the dribble
- Improved to become a solid secondary playmaker, can make simple reads, rarely turns the ball over
- <u>2022-23 Defensive Degree of Difficulty</u>: 0.463
- <u>2022-23 Points Prevented</u>: -1.228
- Usually guarded starting level players, solid on-ball defender in previous seasons
- Struggled to defend in one-on-one situations with limited surrounding talent
- Played below average pick-and-roll defense, not especially effective at taking away any specific action
- Gets caught on screens off the ball, usually was late to close out on spot-up shooters
- Stay-at-home defender, does not really get steals or blocks, fairly solid defensive rebounder

Jeremy Sochan

	Height	Weight	Cap #	Years Left
	6'9"	230	$5.317M	2 TO

Similar at Age 19

		Season	SIMsc
1	Luol Deng	2004-05	934.0
2	Ersan Ilyasova	2006-07	930.7
3	Aaron Gordon	2014-15	927.3
4	Tobias Harris	2011-12	927.0
5	Al Harrington	1999-00	925.1
6	Marvin Williams	2005-06	916.2
7	Jabari Parker	2014-15	907.6
8	Marquese Chriss	2016-17	905.3
9	Cliff Robinson	1979-80	903.9
10	Stanley Johnson	2015-16	901.1

Baseline Basic Stats

MPG	PTS	AST	REB	BLK	STL
26.5	11.6	1.6	5.2	0.5	0.8

Advanced Metrics

USG%	3PTA/FGA	FTA/FGA	TS%	eFG%	3PT%
21.0	0.219	0.259	0.546	0.515	0.331

AST%	TOV%	OREB%	DREB%	STL%	BLK%
13.7	12.6	6.1	17.2	1.7	1.3

PER	ORTG	DRTG	WS/48	BPM	VOL
14.87	108.5	114.5	0.058	-1.81	0.349

- Named to the All-Rookie 2nd Team in 2022-23, regular starter for San Antonio last season
- Mainly used as a lower volume energy player and spot-up shooter
- Great athlete, plays with high energy, dives hard to the rim on cuts off the ball, active offensive rebounder
- Made less than 25% of his threes, more effective when taking short mid-range jumpers
- Strictly a stand-still spot-up shooter, shooting still needs considerable improvement
- Below average in ball handler situations, defenders back off him to negate his effectiveness
- Solid secondary playmaker, hits cutters and finds open shooters, good at avoiding turnovers
- 2022-23 Defensive Degree of Difficulty: 0.512
- 2022-23 Points Prevented: -1.084
- Used as San Antonio's primary defensive stopper as a rookie, slightly overmatched in this role
- Could competently guard multiple positions, had difficulty when guarding elite scorers
- Good pick-and-roll defender, effective at switching to guard ball handlers and screeners
- Gambles a bit too much, tends to get caught out of position, does not always get around screens or close out on spot-up shooters
- More of a stay-at-home defender, occasionally gets steals or blocks, solid defensive rebounder

Tre Jones

	Height	Weight	Cap #	Years Left
	6'1"	185	$9.896M	1

Similar at Age 23

		Season	SIMsc
1	Mo Williams	2005-06	942.6
2	Mike Bibby	2001-02	928.8
3	Bimbo Coles	1991-92	927.5
4	Jalen Brunson	2019-20	926.8
5	Frank Johnson	1981-82	925.6
6	Aaron Holiday	2019-20	925.6
7	B.J. Armstrong	1990-91	925.5
8	Lorenzo Romar	1981-82	925.4
9	Chris Duhon	2005-06	925.1
10	Mike Conley	2010-11	922.3

Baseline Basic Stats

MPG	PTS	AST	REB	BLK	STL
26.3	10.2	4.7	2.6	0.1	1.0

Advanced Metrics

USG%	3PTA/FGA	FTA/FGA	TS%	eFG%	3PT%
18.4	0.229	0.245	0.539	0.494	0.322

AST%	TOV%	OREB%	DREB%	STL%	BLK%
28.3	12.9	2.5	9.8	2.0	0.4

PER	ORTG	DRTG	WS/48	BPM	VOL
15.49	114.7	113.7	0.102	-0.40	0.320

- Regular starting point guard for San Antonio in his third NBA season
- Increased his productivity in his role as a low volume, table setting point guard
- Very good playmaker, makes sound decisions, can run a team, good at limiting turnovers
- Has made less than 30% of his threes, more effective when shooting mid-range shots
- Most effective when shooting pull-up jumpers on pick-and-rolls, struggles to make spot-up jumpers
- Good on hand-offs and pick-and-rolls, needs a screen to create separation or get downhill
- Good cutter, effective at pushing the ball in transition
- 2022-23 Defensive Degree of Difficulty: 0.472
- 2022-23 Points Prevented: -0.559
- Typically defending starting level guards, drew some tough assignments, decent on-ball defender
- Good quickness allows him to stay with opposing guards, taller players can shoot over him
- Average pick-and-roll defender, good at containing ball handlers, limited ability to switch, struggles when rotated onto a screener
- Fights through screens off the ball, tends to late when closing out on spot-up shooters
- Very good at playing passing lanes, gets steals at a fairly high rate, decent defensive rebounder

Zach Collins

	Height	Weight	Cap #	Years Left
	6'11"	250	$7.700M	UFA

Similar at Age 25

		Season	SIMsc
1	Darryl Dawkins	1981-82	925.0
2	Tarik Black	2016-17	911.2
3	Kyle O'Quinn	2015-16	904.0
4	Vitor Faverani	2013-14	901.7
5	Jelani McCoy	2002-03	901.6
6	Karl-Anthony Towns	2020-21	901.5
7	Spencer Hawes	2013-14	898.0
8	Chris Anstey	1999-00	897.7
9	Tyler Zeller	2014-15	897.2
10	Kelly Olynyk	2016-17	897.1

Baseline Basic Stats

MPG	PTS	AST	REB	BLK	STL
20.8	9.9	1.6	5.5	0.9	0.5

Advanced Metrics

USG%	3PTA/FGA	FTA/FGA	TS%	eFG%	3PT%
20.6	0.227	0.333	0.593	0.549	0.339

AST%	TOV%	OREB%	DREB%	STL%	BLK%
14.4	16.7	8.5	21.1	1.2	3.2

PER	ORTG	DRTG	WS/48	BPM	VOL
16.70	111.6	111.2	0.107	0.09	0.399

- Regular rotation player for San Antonio in his second season with the team
- Maintained his effectiveness in a role as a low usage stretch big and rim runner
- Made over 37% of his threes last season, above break-even career three-point shooter
- Solid as a stand-still spot-up shooter, below break-even shooter on pick-and-pop plays
- Fairly good rim runner, active offensive rebounder, solid roll man and cutter, runs the floor in transition
- Improving post player, good at flashing to the middle, effective at making hook shots on the left block
- Good passing big man, hits cutters, finds open shooters, somewhat turnover prone
- 2022-23 Defensive Degree of Difficulty: 0.401
- 2022-23 Points Prevented: 0.093
- Below average rim protector, undisciplined with his positioning, shot blocking rates decreased, good defensive rebounder
- Below average on-ball defender against lower leverage starting centers
- Can be overpowered in the post, highly foul prone, more effective when he defends in space
- Average pick-and-roll defender, good in drop coverages, takes bad angles against ball handlers
- Tends to stay anchored in the paint, does not always come out to contest perimeter shots

Devin Vassell

	Height	Weight	Cap #	Years Left
	6'5"	200	$5.888M	RFA

Similar at Age 22

		Season	SIMsc
1	Nickeil Alexander-Walker	2020-21	934.2
2	Jaylen Nowell	2021-22	929.8
3	Lonnie Walker	2020-21	926.2
4	Luke Kennard	2018-19	924.2
5	Gary Trent Jr.	2020-21	920.8
6	Daequan Cook	2009-10	919.8
7	Malik Beasley	2018-19	917.2
8	Marco Belinelli	2008-09	916.3
9	Terence Davis	2019-20	916.2
10	Malik Monk	2020-21	916.1

Baseline Basic Stats

MPG	PTS	AST	REB	BLK	STL
25.3	12.4	2.2	3.1	0.3	0.8

Advanced Metrics

USG%	3PTA/FGA	FTA/FGA	TS%	eFG%	3PT%
22.1	0.449	0.181	0.559	0.529	0.385

AST%	TOV%	OREB%	DREB%	STL%	BLK%
14.7	9.1	1.6	12.8	1.7	1.1

PER	ORTG	DRTG	WS/48	BPM	VOL
14.91	110.3	113.8	0.073	0.19	0.299

- Missed most of last season due to a knee injury, regular starting guard for San Antonio when healthy
- Increased his efficiency in a new role as a higher volume scoring guard
- Made almost 39% of his threes last season, corner Three-Point Percentage was almost 48% in 2022-23
- Mainly a spot-up shooter, good at making pull-up threes on pick-and-rolls, less effective when shooting off screens
- Good scorer on hand-offs, needs a screen to create space, inefficient as an isolation player
- Passing improved, good secondary playmaker, rarely turns the ball over, good cutter off the ball
- 2022-23 Defensive Degree of Difficulty: 0.427
- 2022-23 Points Prevented: -0.691
- Generally guarded starting level players, appeared to be over-matched in these assignments
- Played below average on-ball defense, struggled to defend quicker or stronger players in one-on-one situations
- Below average pick-and-roll defender, not effective at taking away any specific action
- Fights through screens off the ball, usually was late when closing out on spot-up shooters
- Block Percentage decreased, gets steals at a solid rate, fairly solid defensive rebounder

Malaki Branham

	Height	Weight	Cap #	Years Left
	6'5"	180	$3.072M	2 TO

Similar at Age 19

		Season	SIMsc
1	Jalen Green	2021-22	925.5
2	Coby White	2019-20	922.0
3	Théo Maledon	2020-21	913.6
4	Zach LaVine	2014-15	911.5
5	R.J. Hampton	2020-21	902.3
6	Jamal Murray	2016-17	899.1
7	Frank Ntilikina	2017-18	890.6
8	Keon Johnson	2021-22	890.5
9	Joshua Primo	2021-22	889.2
10	Jrue Holiday	2009-10	884.0

Baseline Basic Stats

MPG	PTS	AST	REB	BLK	STL
24.8	11.6	2.4	2.9	0.2	0.7

Advanced Metrics

USG%	3PTA/FGA	FTA/FGA	TS%	eFG%	3PT%
20.8	0.404	0.171	0.563	0.537	0.361

AST%	TOV%	OREB%	DREB%	STL%	BLK%
15.6	10.9	1.8	11.7	1.4	0.5

PER	ORTG	DRTG	WS/48	BPM	VOL
12.95	109.6	118.8	0.048	-2.69	0.283

- Regular rotation player for San Antonio in his rookie season, started some games
- Decently effective in his role as a low usage spot-up shooter and secondary ball handler
- Below break-even three-point shooter, efficient mid-range shooter last season
- Good at making pull-up jumpers from mid-range, mainly a stationary spot-up when he takes threes
- Moves well without the ball, good cutter, can curl off screens to make a few outside shots
- Decent pick-and-roll ball handler, inefficient isolation player, needs a screen to create separation
- Fairly solid secondary playmaker that can make simple reads, good at avoiding turnovers
- 2022-23 Defensive Degree of Difficulty: 0.377
- 2022-23 Points Prevented: -1.107
- Usually defended second unit level players, played below average on-ball defense
- Struggled to stay with opposing guards, stronger players could overpower him in the post
- Decent pick-and-roll defender, can functionally switch, takes bad angles, allows ball handlers to turn the corner
- Tends to get caught on screens off the ball, usually was late when closing out on spot-up shooters
- Stay-at-home defender, rarely gets steals or blocks, decent defensive rebounder

Charles Bassey

	Height	Weight	Cap #	Years Left
	6'11"	235	$2.600M	2

Similar at Age 22

		Season	SIMsc
1	Nick Fazekas	2007-08	901.9
2	Daniel Gafford	2020-21	896.5
3	Isaiah Hartenstein	2020-21	896.3
4	Drew Eubanks	2019-20	891.0
5	Greg Oden	2009-10	890.4
6	Tony Bradley	2019-20	889.3
7	Harry Giles	2020-21	881.9
8	Sean Williams	2008-09	878.7
9	Scott Williams	1990-91	877.9
10	Jakob Poeltl	2017-18	876.5

Baseline Basic Stats

MPG	PTS	AST	REB	BLK	STL
16.8	6.1	1.0	4.8	1.0	0.5

Advanced Metrics

USG%	3PTA/FGA	FTA/FGA	TS%	eFG%	3PT%
16.0	0.048	0.295	0.622	0.602	0.201

AST%	TOV%	OREB%	DREB%	STL%	BLK%
10.8	16.0	12.7	22.6	1.6	5.6

PER	ORTG	DRTG	WS/48	BPM	VOL
18.63	120.6	108.2	0.155	0.66	0.407

- Waived by Philadelphia, signed to a Two-Way contract with San Antonio, later was signed to a standard contract
- Effective in limited minutes, primarily used as a low volume rim runner
- Efficient rim runner, made almost 76% of his shots inside of three feet, high motor, plays physical
- Great offensive rebounder that scores on put-backs, solid roll man and cutter, does not always run the floor in transition
- Can flash to the middle on post-ups, occasionally can score with a limited set of moves from the right block
- Flashed the ability to make pick-and-pop jumpers, went 3-for-8 (37.5%) on threes, decent mid-range shooter
- Improved to become a solid passing big man, hits cutters and finds open shooters, fairly turnover prone
- 2022-23 Defensive Degree of Difficulty: 0.352
- 2022-23 Points Prevented: 1.690
- Great defensive rebounder and shot blocker, average rim protector, undisciplined with his positioning, highly foul prone
- Guarded second unit centers, stout post defender, has some trouble defending in space
- Decent pick-and-roll defender, has lapses when covering screeners, solid at switching out on ball handlers
- Consistently comes out to the perimeter to contest spot-up jumpers

Doug McDermott

	Height	Weight	Cap #	Years Left
	6'7"	225	$13.750M	UFA

Similar at Age 31

		Season	SIMsc
1	Walt Williams	2001-02	931.2
2	Henry James	1996-97	930.5
3	Marcus Morris	2020-21	927.7
4	Richard Jefferson	2011-12	925.9
5	Dennis Scott	1999-00	924.7
6	Mirza Teletovic	2016-17	919.1
7	Mike Scott	2019-20	918.4
8	Eric Piatkowski	2001-02	917.5
9	Andres Nocioni	2010-11	915.8
10	Alan Anderson	2013-14	914.0

Baseline Basic Stats

MPG	PTS	AST	REB	BLK	STL
22.1	9.1	1.3	2.9	0.2	0.5

Advanced Metrics

USG%	3PTA/FGA	FTA/FGA	TS%	eFG%	3PT%
18.0	0.526	0.168	0.585	0.560	0.412

AST%	TOV%	OREB%	DREB%	STL%	BLK%
9.2	9.6	2.3	11.2	0.9	0.6

PER	ORTG	DRTG	WS/48	BPM	VOL
12.21	112.8	115.5	0.075	-1.66	0.453

- Regular rotation player for San Antonio in his second season with the team
- Maintained his production level in a role as a lower usage shooting specialist
- Excellent three-point shooter, career Three-Point Percentage is 41%
- Made over 51% of his spot-up threes, around break-even when shooting on the move
- Makes sharp backdoor cuts if defenders try to crowd him
- Rarely is used as a ball handler, was not used on any isolation plays, not able to create his own shot
- Strictly a catch-and-shoot player, Assist Percentage increased to a career high, rarely turns the ball over
- 2022-23 Defensive Degree of Difficulty: 0.313
- 2022-23 Points Prevented: -1.426
- Usually was hidden in favorable matchups against lower leverage second unit players
- Played average on-ball defense, struggled to stay with perimeter players, more effective when defending in the post
- Decent pick-and-roll defender, good at funneling his man into help, less effective when guarding screeners
- Fights through screens off the ball, tends to be late when closing out on spot-up shooters

Devonte' Graham

	Height	Weight	Cap #	Years Left
	6'1"	195	$12.100M	1

Similar at Age 27

		Season	SIMsc
1	Derek Fisher	2001-02	930.1
2	Patty Mills	2015-16	922.9
3	Jerryd Bayless	2015-16	917.2
4	Shammond Williams	2002-03	915.2
5	Ben McLemore	2020-21	906.4
6	Terry Rozier	2021-22	905.5
7	Raul Neto	2019-20	903.1
8	Austin Rivers	2019-20	903.0
9	Langston Galloway	2018-19	902.5
10	Chris Duhon	2009-10	901.4

Baseline Basic Stats

MPG	PTS	AST	REB	BLK	STL
24.8	10.1	3.4	2.3	0.2	0.9

Advanced Metrics

USG%	3PTA/FGA	FTA/FGA	TS%	eFG%	3PT%
18.4	0.652	0.225	0.534	0.497	0.355

AST%	TOV%	OREB%	DREB%	STL%	BLK%
22.0	11.4	1.6	8.4	1.7	0.6

PER	ORTG	DRTG	WS/48	BPM	VOL
12.63	111.4	114.9	0.069	-0.58	0.360

- Traded from New Orleans to San Antonio, regular rotation player for both teams
- Production level held steady in a role as a low usage shooter and ball handler
- Around a league average career three-point shooter, career corner Three-Point Percentage is over 41%
- Great stand-still spot-up shooter, less effective when shooting off screens or off the dribble
- Average scorer in ball handling situations, can leverage the threat of his shot to occasionally drive, needs a screen to create space or get downhill
- Does not really move off the ball, tends to stand idly on the perimeter
- Solid playmaker, makes sound decisions, rarely turns the ball over
- 2022-23 Defensive Degree of Difficulty: 0.353
- 2022-23 Points Prevented: -0.554
- Typically guarded second unit level guards, played solid on-ball defense in these matchups
- Passably could defend lower leverage ones and twos, less effective against starting level players
- Average pick-and-roll defender, funnels his man into help, limited ability to switch, struggled in San Antonio with limited surrounding talent
- Sometimes gets caught on screens off the ball, tended to be late when closing out on spot-up shooters
- Steal Percentage stayed constant, Block Percentage increased, below average defensive rebounder

Reggie Bullock

	Height	Weight	Cap #	Years Left
	6'6"	205	$11.014M	UFA

Similar at Age 31

		Season	SIMsc
1	DeShawn Stevenson	2012-13	926.5
2	Danny Green	2018-19	926.0
3	Raja Bell	2007-08	922.1
4	Kyle Korver	2012-13	915.7
5	Justin Holiday	2020-21	912.6
6	Nick Young	2016-17	912.1
7	Richard Jefferson	2011-12	909.4
8	J.R. Smith	2016-17	902.3
9	Wesley Person	2002-03	901.1
10	Brandon Rush	2016-17	900.7

Baseline Basic Stats

MPG	PTS	AST	REB	BLK	STL
26.1	8.4	1.8	3.3	0.2	0.8

Advanced Metrics

USG%	3PTA/FGA	FTA/FGA	TS%	eFG%	3PT%
12.6	0.717	0.122	0.567	0.549	0.383

AST%	TOV%	OREB%	DREB%	STL%	BLK%
8.8	9.5	1.8	12.1	1.3	0.6

PER	ORTG	DRTG	WS/48	BPM	VOL
9.38	112.2	114.3	0.065	-1.85	0.409

- Regular starter for Dallas in his second season with the team
- Decently efficient in his role as an extremely low usage shooting specialist
- Reliable three-point shooter that has made over 38% of his career threes
- Solid spot-up shooter, occasionally can make threes off screens, career corner Three-Point Percentage is over 43%
- Better at moving off the ball, can make pick-and-pop jumpers, good cutter
- Lacks the ability to create his own offense, very seldomly is used in ball handling situations
- Strictly a catch-and-shoot player, only makes safe passes, rarely turns the ball over
- 2022-23 Defensive Degree of Difficulty: 0.518
- 2022-23 Points Prevented: -0.193
- Became Dallas' primary defensive stopper at the end of last season, solid on-ball defender
- Can guard multiple positions, had some trouble staying with quicker players, slightly over-matched against bigger power forwards
- Solid pick-and-roll defender, effectively switches to guard ball handlers and screeners
- Fights through screens off the ball, sometimes is a step late when closing out on spot-up shooters
- Stay-at-home defender, does not really get steals or blocks, fairly solid defensive rebounder

Cedi Osman

	Height	Weight	Cap #	Years Left
	6'7"	230	$6.719M	UFA

Similar at Age 27

		Season	SIMsc
1	Sam Mack	1997-98	940.3
2	Dennis Scott	1995-96	929.7
3	Eric Piatkowski	1997-98	928.2
4	Jae Crowder	2017-18	927.4
5	Georges Niang	2020-21	925.5
6	Mickael Pietrus	2009-10	925.5
7	Kareem Rush	2007-08	924.4
8	Bogdan Bogdanović	2019-20	922.3
9	Tracy Murray	1998-99	921.3
10	Taurean Prince	2021-22	920.2

Baseline Basic Stats

MPG	PTS	AST	REB	BLK	STL
23.9	9.4	1.5	3.2	0.2	0.7

Advanced Metrics

USG%	3PTA/FGA	FTA/FGA	TS%	eFG%	3PT%
17.9	0.618	0.177	0.560	0.539	0.374

AST%	TOV%	OREB%	DREB%	STL%	BLK%
11.0	9.8	2.4	11.7	1.4	0.7

PER	ORTG	DRTG	WS/48	BPM	VOL
11.99	110.7	111.1	0.092	-0.42	0.309

- Regular rotation player for Cleveland in his sixth NBA season
- Fairly effective in his role as a low usage shooting specialist off the bench
- Made over 37% of his threes last season, percentages tend to vary from year-to-year
- Mostly a stationary spot-up shooter, improved his ability to make shots on the move and off the dribble
- Improved his ability to move off the ball, solid at scoring off screens, good cutter, can run the break to get layups in transition
- Better as a ball handler in a limited capacity, can use the threat of his shot to drive to the rim
- Solid secondary playmaker that makes simple reads, rarely turns the ball over
- <u>2022-23 Defensive Degree of Difficulty</u>: 0.340
- <u>2022-23 Points Prevented</u>: 0.939
- Usually guarded second unit level players, played effective on-ball defense in these matchups
- Could competently guard multiple wing positions, less effective when guarding starting level players
- Played below average pick-and-roll defense, not especially effective at taking away any specific action
- Stays attached to shooters off the ball, fights through screens and closes out in spot-up situations
- Stay-at-home defender, rarely gets steals or blocks, decent defensive rebounder

Cameron Payne

	Height	Weight	Cap #	Years Left
	6'1"	183	$6.500M	UFA

Similar at Age 28

		Season	SIMsc
1	George Hill	2014-15	947.3
2	Mo Williams	2010-11	935.0
3	J.J. Barea	2012-13	926.4
4	Mike Conley	2015-16	925.2
5	Jannero Pargo	2007-08	923.9
6	Eddie House	2006-07	919.3
7	Luke Ridnour	2009-10	913.0
8	Tony Delk	2001-02	912.9
9	Brian Roberts	2013-14	912.4
10	Jameer Nelson	2010-11	912.3

Baseline Basic Stats

MPG	PTS	AST	REB	BLK	STL
25.8	11.4	4.1	2.6	0.1	0.9

Advanced Metrics

USG%	3PTA/FGA	FTA/FGA	TS%	eFG%	3PT%
21.7	0.423	0.181	0.529	0.497	0.374

AST%	TOV%	OREB%	DREB%	STL%	BLK%
28.0	14.1	1.7	10.6	1.7	0.7

PER	ORTG	DRTG	WS/48	BPM	VOL
14.02	107.6	111.0	0.078	-0.12	0.394

- Missed games due to injuries to his back and both feet, regular rotational guard for Phoenix when healthy
- Production held fairly steady, used as a moderate usage ball handler off the bench
- Very good playmaker, finds open teammates and make solid decisions, good at avoiding turnovers
- Around a league average career three-point shooter, percentages tend to vary from year-to-year
- Solid spot-up shooter, less effective off the dribble, shot can be streaky
- Average as a pick-and-roll ball handler and isolation player, effectiveness limited due to injury, not quite able to consistently drive to the rim
- Good at scoring on hand-offs, rarely moves off the ball, tends to stand idly on the perimeter
- 2022-23 Defensive Degree of Difficulty: 0.358
- 2022-23 Points Prevented: -0.637
- Typically guarded second unit guards, played better on-ball defense than he has in the past
- Played angles well to stay with opposing guards, taller players could shoot over due to his smallish size
- Middling pick-and-roll defender, limited ability to switch, tends to go too far under screens when guarding ball handlers
- Fights through screens off the ball, usually is a step late when closing out on spot-up shooters
- Steal Percentage was consistent with his career average, decent defensive rebounder

Blake Wesley

	Height	Weight	Cap #	Years Left
	6'5"	185	$2.505M	2 TO

Similar at Age 19

		Season	SIMsc
1	Frank Ntilikina	2017-18	925.2
2	Keon Johnson	2021-22	920.9
3	Marquis Teague	2012-13	907.6
4	Killian Hayes	2020-21	905.5
5	Zach LaVine	2014-15	901.1
6	Archie Goodwin	2013-14	900.4
7	Shaun Livingston	2004-05	898.6
8	C.J. Miles	2006-07	893.2
9	DeShawn Stevenson	2000-01	889.4
10	R.J. Hampton	2020-21	885.6

Baseline Basic Stats

MPG	PTS	AST	REB	BLK	STL
20.3	7.7	2.7	2.5	0.2	0.8

Advanced Metrics

USG%	3PTA/FGA	FTA/FGA	TS%	eFG%	3PT%
19.2	0.228	0.237	0.493	0.462	0.397

AST%	TOV%	OREB%	DREB%	STL%	BLK%
22.2	17.4	2.1	12.4	2.2	0.7

PER	ORTG	DRTG	WS/48	BPM	VOL
10.32	98.1	114.6	0.003	-4.30	0.534

- Rarely played in the first half of 2022-23, became a regular rotation player for San Antonio in the second half
- Struggled with his effectiveness as a rookie, used as a low usage spot-up shooter and ball handler
- Made 38.5% of his overall threes and half of his corner threes last season
- Almost exclusively a spot-up shooter at this stage, did hit a few pull-up threes on pick-and-rolls
- Rated by Synergy as being below average or worse in every offensive situation
- Tends to play wildly, highly turnover prone, shows decent playmaking skills when he's under control
- Shot selection is very questionable, can be baited into taking a lot of inefficient mid-range shots that hurt his percentages
- 2022-23 Defensive Degree of Difficulty: 0.331
- 2022-23 Points Prevented: -1.087
- Usually guarded lower leverage bench players, below average on-ball defender
- Takes bad angles when defending on the perimeter, struggles to guard taller wing players inside
- Below average pick-and-roll defender, not effective at taking away any specific action
- Tends to get caught on screens off the ball, good at closing out on spot-up shooters
- Good at jumping passing lanes, gets steals at a fairly good rate, decent defensive rebounder

Julian Champagnie

	Height	Weight	Cap #	Years Left
	6'8"	220	$3.000M	2 + TO

Similar at Age 21

		Season	SIMsc
1	Kevin Knox	2020-21	929.8
2	Mario Hezonja	2016-17	903.7
3	Chase Budinger	2009-10	903.6
4	Troy Brown Jr.	2020-21	900.1
5	Cam Reddish	2020-21	899.0
6	Aaron Nesmith	2020-21	897.5
7	Saddiq Bey	2020-21	897.2
8	Kessler Edwards	2021-22	896.6
9	Nicolas Batum	2009-10	894.9
10	Trey Murphy III	2021-22	893.9

Baseline Basic Stats

MPG	PTS	AST	REB	BLK	STL
16.3	6.7	1.0	3.0	0.2	0.5

Advanced Metrics

USG%	3PTA/FGA	FTA/FGA	TS%	eFG%	3PT%
17.6	0.421	0.165	0.586	0.563	0.373

AST%	TOV%	OREB%	DREB%	STL%	BLK%
7.4	9.0	3.7	16.4	1.3	1.1

PER	ORTG	DRTG	WS/48	BPM	VOL
13.03	114.7	117.3	0.079	-2.32	0.234

- Started last season on a Two-Way contract with Philadelphia, waived then claimed by San Antonio
- Played limited minutes at the NBA level, spent most of the year in the G-League with Austin and Delaware, used as low usage spot-up shooter
- Made over 40% of his NBA threes in limited attempts, break-even three-point shooter in the G-League
- Fairly explosive finisher in transition, good cutter off the ball, can score on hand-offs
- Not really used in ball handling situations, limited ability to create his own shot
- Strictly a catch-and-shoot player, only makes safe passes, rarely turns the ball over
- 2022-23 Defensive Degree of Difficulty: 0.279
- 2022-23 Points Prevented: -0.692
- Mostly guarded lower leverage bench players or played in garbage time
- Played decent on-ball defense in limited minutes, capable of staying with perimeter players, had trouble against stronger players inside
- Decent pick-and-roll defender, can functionally switch, prone to taking bad angles when making rotations
- Fights through screens off the ball, tended to be late when closing out on spot-up shooters
- Stay-at-home defender in the NBA, effective weak side shot blocker in the G-League, fairly good defensive rebounder

Sandro Mamukelashvili

	Height	Weight	Cap #	Years Left
	6'11"	240	$2.020M	UFA

Similar at Age 23

		Season	SIMsc
1	Mike Muscala	2014-15	918.2
2	Mehmet Okur	2002-03	912.1
3	Moritz Wagner	2020-21	911.5
4	Tyler Cavanaugh	2017-18	909.4
5	Donte Greene	2011-12	909.0
6	Zarko Cabarkapa	2004-05	909.0
7	Perry Jones	2014-15	908.4
8	Trey Lyles	2018-19	904.5
9	Luka Garza	2021-22	902.6
10	Greg Foster	1991-92	900.4

Baseline Basic Stats

MPG	PTS	AST	REB	BLK	STL
18.3	7.7	1.1	4.4	0.5	0.4

Advanced Metrics

USG%	3PTA/FGA	FTA/FGA	TS%	eFG%	3PT%
18.2	0.432	0.235	0.557	0.526	0.341

AST%	TOV%	OREB%	DREB%	STL%	BLK%
10.8	11.4	8.8	18.0	1.0	1.9

PER	ORTG	DRTG	WS/48	BPM	VOL
14.68	114.3	112.4	0.106	-1.01	0.391

- Played on a Two-Way contract with Milwaukee, waived then claimed by San Antonio, later was signed to a standard contract
- More effective in limited minutes as a low usage stretch big and rim runner with San Antonio
- Above break-even career three-point shooter, made threes at a below break-even rate last season
- Generally a spot-up shooter and pick-and-pop screener when his shot is falling
- High energy rim runner, lacks ideal vertical lift, had some trouble finishing in traffic
- Good offensive rebounder, fairly solid cutter and rim runner, tends to rush his shots in transition
- Not really a post-up threat, improving as a passing big man, good at avoiding turnovers
- 2022-23 Defensive Degree of Difficulty: 0.319
- 2022-23 Points Prevented: -2.050
- Below average rim protector, not really a shot blocking threat, undisciplined with his positioning, solid defensive rebounder
- Guards second unit big men, effective on-ball defender against lower leverage players
- Fairly stout post defender, has enough mobility to defend in space
- Below average pick-and-roll defender, not effective at taking away any specific action
- Gets caught on screens off the ball, does not always close out on spot-up shooters

Khem Birch

	Height	Weight	Cap #	Years Left
	6'9"	233	$6.985M	UFA

Similar at Age 30

		Season	SIMsc
1	Sam Pellom	1981-82	922.7
2	Amal McCaskill	2003-04	921.4
3	Major Jones	1983-84	918.0
4	Adam Keefe	2000-01	916.5
5	Ben Poquette	1985-86	914.7
6	Kent Benson	1984-85	912.7
7	Cherokee Parks	2002-03	909.8
8	Nick Collison	2010-11	905.2
9	Kevin Restani	1981-82	903.1
10	Taj Gibson	2015-16	898.0

Baseline Basic Stats

MPG	PTS	AST	REB	BLK	STL
15.5	4.4	0.8	3.9	0.5	0.4

Advanced Metrics

USG%	3PTA/FGA	FTA/FGA	TS%	eFG%	3PT%
12.2	0.047	0.298	0.560	0.521	0.231

AST%	TOV%	OREB%	DREB%	STL%	BLK%
6.7	15.7	9.8	16.1	1.4	2.4

PER	ORTG	DRTG	WS/48	BPM	VOL
11.78	113.6	109.1	0.098	-2.32	0.291

- Traded from Toronto to San Antonio, missed most of last season due to a knee injury
- Mildly effective in limited action as an extremely low volume rim runner
- Energetic rim runner when healthy, most effective as a cutter and roll man, runs hard in transition
- Less active on the offensive boards due to the knee injury, has some trouble finishing in traffic due to being undersized
- Lacks reliable shooting range outside of three feet, not really a threat to post up
- Strictly a catch-and-finish player, limited passing skills, somewhat turnover prone
- 2022-23 Defensive Degree of Difficulty: 0.473
- 2022-23 Points Prevented: -1.210
- Effective rim protector that blocks shots, sacrifices positioning to go for blocks, middling defensive rebounder
- Spent of a lot of his limited minutes guarding Joel Embiid, solid post defender, had trouble when defending in space
- Decent pick-and-roll defender, effective when switched onto ball handlers, had lapses when guarding screeners
- Consistently will close out on spot-up shooters on the perimeter

Newcomers

Victor Wembanyama

	Height	Weight	Cap #	Years Left
	7'4"	209	$12.161M	1 + 2 TO

Baseline Basic Stats

MPG	PTS	AST	REB	BLK	STL
19.5	7.9	1.0	4.8	1.1	0.4

Advanced Metrics

USG%	3PTA/FGA	FTA/FGA	TS%	eFG%	3PT%
19.1	0.310	0.300	0.525	0.490	0.306

AST%	TOV%	OREB%	DREB%	STL%	BLK%
9.7	12.0	7.1	23.1	1.2	5.9

PER	ORTG	DRTG	WS/48	BPM	VOL
15.69	102.8	99.2	0.118	0.31	0.521

- Drafted by San Antonio with the 1st overall pick in 2023
- Played last season with Metropolitans 92 in the French LNB, projection uses translated LNB stats
- Had a strong showing at the Las Vegas Summer League, played two games then was shut down for rest purposes
- Mostly excelled in his role as a primary scoring option, will likely be featured in a similar role in the NBA
- Most effective as a rim runner and post-up option, outstanding vertical threat due to his extreme length and athleticism
- Dives hard to the rim, great cutter and roll man, runs hard in transition, willing to go to the offensive boards
- Can be pushed off the block due to his thin frame, effectively can shoot over most defenders inside, draws fouls at a high rate
- Handles the ball fairly well, can drive by slower big men, tended to lose the ball when he was pressured
- Jump shot is still a work-in-progress, made 30% of his threes at Summer League
- Excellent defensive potential due to his length, athleticism, and mobility
- Excellent rim protector, has outstanding to cover a lot of ground, great shot blocker and defensive rebounder
- Fairly solid on-ball defender, quick enough to stay with perimeter players, lacks strength, can be out-muscled inside by stronger big men
- Solid pick-and-roll defender, good in drop coverages, mobile enough to switch onto ball handlers
- Great at closing out on spot-up shooters, consistent threat to block three-point shots with his length
- Likely will be the odds-on favorite to win Rookie of the Year in the 2023-24 season

Sidy Cissoko

	Height	Weight	Cap #	Years Left
	6'8"	220	$1.120M	2

Baseline Basic Stats

MPG	PTS	AST	REB	BLK	STL
19.0	6.8	1.1	3.4	0.5	0.5

Advanced Metrics

USG%	3PTA/FGA	FTA/FGA	TS%	eFG%	3PT%
16.6	0.401	0.221	0.526	0.499	0.286

AST%	TOV%	OREB%	DREB%	STL%	BLK%
14.5	14.4	3.3	11.3	1.4	1.7

PER	ORTG	DRTG	WS/48	BPM	VOL
10.64	101.6	117.7	0.050	-0.12	0.460

- Drafted by San Antonio with the 44th overall pick in 2023
- Played last season in the G-League with G-League Ignite, projection uses translated G-League stats
- Did not play especially well in Summer League action in Las Vegas and Sacramento
- Struggled with his efficiency in a role as a very low usage energy player
- True Shooting Percentage was 40%, made less than 20% of his threes in Summer League action
- Below break-even three-point shooter in the G-League, shooting is still a work-in-progress
- Ball handling skills need improvement, tends to lose the ball when he dribbles
- Most effective as an energetic rim runner, great athlete, explosive finisher in transition, good cutter and roll man
- Flashes decent passing skills, can hit cutters and find open shooters, plays a bit wildly, highly turnover prone
- Very long and athletic defender, potentially could be a plus-level defender
- Played great on-ball defense at Summer League, could effectively guard multiple positions on the floor
- Generally an effective pick-and-roll defender, good at switching, sometimes takes bad angles
- Gambles quite a bit, gets caught out of position, does not always get around screens, sometimes will be late to close out on spot-up shooters
- Great weak side shot blocker, occasionally got steals at Summer League, fairly good defensive rebounder
- Needs to spend some additional time in the G-League to polish his skills on both ends

PORTLAND TRAIL BLAZERS

Last Season: 33 - 49, Missed the Playoffs

Offensive Rating: 114.8, 18th in the NBA

Defensive Rating: 118.8, 27th in the NBA

Primary Executive: Joe Cronin, General Manager

Head Coach: Chauncey Billups

Key Roster Changes

Subtractions
Cam Reddish, free agency
Drew Eubanks, free agency
Justise Winslow, free agency
Kevin Knox, free agency
Trendon Watford, waived
Jeenathan Williams, waived

Additions
Scoot Henderson, draft
Kris Murray, draft
Rayan Rupert, draft
Moses Brown, free agency

Roster

Likely Starting Five
1. Damian Lillard
2. Anfernee Simons
3. Matisse Thybulle
4. Jerami Grant
5. Jusuf Nurkić

Other Key Rotation Players
Scoot Henderson
Shaedon Sharpe
Nassir Little
Jabari Walker
Kris Murray

* Italics denotes that a player is likely to be on the floor to close games

Remaining Roster

- Keon Johnson
- Rayan Rupert
- Moses Brown (signed while the book was being finalized)
- John Butler Jr., 21, 7'1", 175, Florida State (Two-Way)
- Ibou Badji, 21, 7'1", 240, Senegal (Two-Way)
- Antoine Davis, 25, 6'1", 165, Detroit-Mercy (Exhibit 10)
- Malachi Smith, 24, 6'4", 210, Gonzaga (Exhibit 10)
- Ashton Hagans, 24, 6'3", 190, Kentucky (Exhibit 10)

SCHREMPF Base Rating: 36.2

Season Preview Survey

- *Are the Blazers contending or rebuilding? Where is this team headed?*

The Blazers should be rebuilding, but they just don't seem to want to commit to a specific direction. They have been trying to develop young talent and remain competitive at the same time, but it hasn't worked out. It has gotten to a point where their superstar, Damian Lillard has grown frustrated and requested a trade. It has put the team in a difficult position, but the longer that this issue hangs over the franchise's head, the worse it will get because it could lead to the stunted growth of their promising young backcourt of Scoot Henderson and Shaedon Sharpe. Most likely, they will want to prevent this from happening, so Lillard will be dealt at some point to signify that they are headed for a complete rebuild for the next few years.

- *What are the areas of concern for this team heading into this season?*

If Lillard is traded, then the Blazers' biggest concern is somewhat alleviated because the major question is whether or not the organization has a clear understanding of their current situation. The Blazers have been marred by suspect decision-making during Lillard's time with the team, and failing to get an accurate read on their situation would be another poor decision to add to the list. If they continue to delay in making a move or don't come away with a satisfactory return, then it wouldn't inspire confidence that Joe Cronin's front office regime can turn things around once the rebuilding process actually starts. Based on the most recent history with this team, the Blazers probably should look to find a different voice to usher them into a new future.

- *List some possible breakout players for this team.*

An impeding Lillard trade is going to create a lot of opportunities for Portland's younger players to get significant playing time and gain developmental experience. This could be the type of environment that allows last year's lottery pick, Shaedon Sharpe to make a major leap forward in his development. He flashed the potential to be a dynamic scorer in the future because he can knock down threes and use his athleticism to finish plays way above the rim. He's better suited to being an off-ball player because his playmaking skills are still a work-in-progress, so he's not able to be a lead ball handler right now. Fortunately for him, they drafted Scoot Henderson with the third overall pick to fill that role. If his performance from the G-League translates, he could contribute immediately as a penetrating scorer that can also set up others and inject some additional intensity to boost the team. In addition to these two, Kris Murray could contribute as a complementary shooting wing to give these two some additional space to operate.

- *What should we expect from them this season?*

No matter what happens with Lillard, it's expected that Portland will be headed for the lottery once again this season. Most likely, they will finish with one of the NBA's worst records because they just don't have the level of polished talent to consistently beat teams in the league on a regular basis. The question is if they will embrace their situation and make more deals to accelerate the rebuilding process. If they can sell off a few of their veterans after a possible Lillard trade, then they could acquire more young talent and increase their optionality to make bigger moves in the future. Otherwise, if they stay inactive and continue on their current path, it could take them a while to get back into playoff contention and they could be in this rebuilding phase for the foreseeable future.

Veterans

Damian Lillard

	Height	Weight	Cap #	Years Left
	6'2"	195	$45.640M	3

Similar at Age 32

		Season	SIMsc
1	Lou Williams	2018-19	918.9
2	Stephen Curry	2020-21	900.6
3	Mo Williams	2014-15	883.8
4	Derrick Rose	2020-21	881.0
5	Chauncey Billups	2008-09	868.0
6	Sam Cassell	2001-02	867.2
7	Joe Dumars*	1995-96	865.1
8	Terry Porter	1995-96	862.4
9	Deron Williams	2016-17	859.6
10	Tony Parker*	2014-15	857.2

Baseline Basic Stats

MPG	PTS	AST	REB	BLK	STL
31.8	21.2	5.8	3.9	0.3	1.0

Advanced Metrics

USG%	3PTA/FGA	FTA/FGA	TS%	eFG%	3PT%
28.7	0.532	0.338	0.600	0.536	0.365

AST%	TOV%	OREB%	DREB%	STL%	BLK%
31.7	12.6	2.0	12.0	1.2	0.8

PER	ORTG	DRTG	WS/48	BPM	VOL
21.18	118.7	117.3	0.151	4.52	0.495

- Made his 7th All-Star team, named to the All-NBA 3rd Team in 2022-23
- Had a career best season, excelled as Portland's primary scorer and ball handler
- Outstanding pick-and-roll ball handler and isolation player, efficient three-level scorer
- Can pull up to make jumpers from anywhere, great at slashing to the rim, drew more fouls last season
- Reliable three-point shooter with very deep range, slightly more efficient when shooting corner threes
- Great shooter in all situations, excellent when taking catch-and-shoot threes, good shooter off the dribble
- Great cutter off the ball, excellent playmaker with outstanding court vision, consistently avoids turnovers
- 2022-23 Defensive Degree of Difficulty: 0.418
- 2022-23 Points Prevented: -0.739
- Tends to be hidden in favorable matchups against lower leverage starters, middling on-ball defender
- Had trouble staying with opposing guards, slightly more effective against taller perimeter players in the post
- Decent pick-and-roll defender, good at steering his man into help, limited ability to switch, struggles when rotating onto screeners
- Tends to get caught on screens, usually is a step late when closing out on spot-up shooters
- Stay-at-home defender, does not really get steals or blocks, fairly solid defensive rebounder

Jerami Grant

	Height	Weight	Cap #	Years Left
	6'8"	210	$27.586M	3 + PO

Similar at Age 28

		Season	SIMsc
1	Gerald Green	2013-14	923.2
2	Gordon Hayward	2018-19	922.1
3	Danny Granger	2011-12	920.4
4	Walt Williams	1998-99	919.3
5	Alec Burks	2019-20	919.2
6	Sean Elliott	1996-97	913.4
7	Josh Howard	2008-09	913.3
8	Tobias Harris	2020-21	913.2
9	Glen Rice	1995-96	911.7
10	Andres Nocioni	2007-08	911.0

Baseline Basic Stats

MPG	PTS	AST	REB	BLK	STL
31.2	15.5	2.4	4.3	0.4	0.8

Advanced Metrics

USG%	3PTA/FGA	FTA/FGA	TS%	eFG%	3PT%
22.4	0.415	0.314	0.569	0.519	0.382

AST%	TOV%	OREB%	DREB%	STL%	BLK%
11.7	10.2	2.7	12.2	1.2	1.7

PER	ORTG	DRTG	WS/48	BPM	VOL
15.00	111.3	113.6	0.087	0.07	0.361

- Missed a month due to a bruised quad, regular starter for Portland in his first season with the team
- Solidly effective in his role as a moderate volume scoring wing
- Made just over 40% of his threes last season, league average career three-point shooter
- Primarily a stand-still spot-up shooter, rarely shoots off screens, does not look to shoot threes off the dribble
- Improved his ability to drive as a pick-and-roll ball handler and isolation player, draws fouls at a solid rate
- Can post up smaller players, good cutter off the ball, explosive finisher in transition
- Mainly a catch-and-shoot player, fairly solid secondary playmaker, rarely turns the ball over
- 2022-23 Defensive Degree of Difficulty: 0.534
- 2022-23 Points Prevented: -0.617
- Used as one of Portland's main defensive stoppers, very good on-ball defender
- Effectively guards multiple positions on the floor
- Decent pick-and-roll defender, good at containing ball handlers, can functionally switch, tends to commit shooting fouls when rotating onto screeners
- Fights through screens off the ball, tended to be late when closing out on spot-up shooters
- Does not really get steals, fairly effective weak side shot blocker, fairly solid defensive rebounder

Anfernee Simons

	Height	Weight	Cap #	Years Left
	6'3"	181	$24.107M	2

Similar at Age 23

		Season	SIMsc
1	Damian Lillard	2013-14	912.3
2	Malik Monk	2021-22	911.8
3	Leandro Barbosa	2005-06	911.6
4	A.J. Price	2009-10	906.8
5	Jordan Farmar	2009-10	906.5
6	Rex Chapman	1990-91	905.0
7	Avery Bradley	2013-14	904.1
8	Monte Morris	2018-19	903.6
9	Landry Shamet	2020-21	903.3
10	Jamal Murray	2020-21	902.3

Baseline Basic Stats

MPG	PTS	AST	REB	BLK	STL
26.0	13.1	3.0	2.7	0.2	0.8

Advanced Metrics

USG%	3PTA/FGA	FTA/FGA	TS%	eFG%	3PT%
23.5	0.555	0.184	0.573	0.539	0.376

AST%	TOV%	OREB%	DREB%	STL%	BLK%
19.3	10.5	1.4	9.0	1.2	0.5

PER	ORTG	DRTG	WS/48	BPM	VOL
15.17	113.0	117.7	0.076	-0.53	0.340

- Regular starting guard for Portland in his fifth NBA season
- Maintained his productivity in a role as a high usage scorer and playmaker
- Effectively scores at all three levels as a pick-and-roll ball handler
- Less efficient in isolation situations, needs a screen to create separation or drive downhill
- Reliable three-point shooter, excellent in the corners, career corner Three-Point Percentage in 42.5%
- Great spot-up shooter, can make pull-up threes if there's an on-ball screen, below break-even when shooting off screens
- Solid playmaker that can make simple reads, consistently avoids turnovers
- 2022-23 Defensive Degree of Difficulty: 0.458
- 2022-23 Points Prevented: 0.727
- Drew tougher matchups than he did in previous seasons against starting guards
- Below average on-ball defender, has trouble staying with opposing guards, struggles against taller wings
- Decent pick-and-roll defender, limited ability to switch due to his thin frame, good at funneling his man into help
- Stays attached to shooters off the ball, fights through screens and closes out in spot-up situations
- Stay-at-home defender, does not really get steals or blocks, below average offensive rebounder

Jusuf Nurkić

	Height	Weight	Cap #	Years Left
	6'11"	290	$16.875M	2

Similar at Age 28

		Season	SIMsc
1	Andre Drummond	2021-22	872.9
2	Jonas Valančiūnas	2020-21	871.7
3	DeMarcus Cousins	2018-19	861.7
4	Glen Davis	2013-14	854.0
5	Marc Jackson	2002-03	847.3
6	Gorgui Dieng	2017-18	846.6
7	Dewayne Dedmon	2017-18	846.0
8	Kosta Koufos	2017-18	845.9
9	Vitaly Potapenko	2003-04	845.6
10	Cody Zeller	2020-21	844.4

Baseline Basic Stats

MPG	PTS	AST	REB	BLK	STL
23.3	11.5	2.0	7.8	0.8	0.7

Advanced Metrics

USG%	3PTA/FGA	FTA/FGA	TS%	eFG%	3PT%
21.9	0.152	0.394	0.573	0.540	0.310

AST%	TOV%	OREB%	DREB%	STL%	BLK%
15.0	16.0	9.9	28.4	1.6	2.7

PER	ORTG	DRTG	WS/48	BPM	VOL
17.82	111.1	109.0	0.114	0.24	0.577

- Missed 30 games due to various injuries, regular starting center for Portland when healthy
- Consistently effective in his role as a moderate usage interior scorer and stretch big
- Can bully weaker defenders with drop steps on the right block when he posts up
- High motor rim runner, does have great lift, sometimes has trouble finishing in traffic
- Good roll man, solid cutter, willing to run the floor in transition, active offensive rebounder
- Improved to become a league average three-point shooter last season
- Most effective as a stand-still spot-up shooter, much less efficient as a pick-and-pop screener
- Good passing center, effective in the short roll game, somewhat turnover prone
- 2022-23 Defensive Degree of Difficulty: 0.512
- 2022-23 Points Prevented: 0.569
- Solid rim protector, provides good resistance at the rim, great defensive rebounder, solid shot blocker
- Guards elite scoring centers, stout post defender, has trouble defending in space due to mobility limitations
- Fairly solid pick-and-roll defender, solid in drop coverages, willing to hedge out onto ball handlers, tends to late to recognize pick-and-pop plays
- Consistently comes out to the perimeter to contest shots in spot-up situations
- Has active hands, good at using his length to play passing lanes and get steals

Matisse Thybulle

	Height	Weight	Cap #	Years Left
	6'5"	201	$10.500M	1 + PO

Similar at Age 25

		Season	SIMsc
1	Pat Connaughton	2017-18	891.4
2	Kent Bazemore	2014-15	878.8
3	Mickael Pietrus	2007-08	877.5
4	Iman Shumpert	2015-16	877.2
5	John Konchar	2021-22	876.2
6	Maurice Harkless	2018-19	875.9
7	Alex Caruso	2019-20	874.2
8	Chris Johnson	2015-16	872.8
9	Myke Henry	2017-18	871.1
10	Damyean Dotson	2019-20	870.4

Baseline Basic Stats

MPG	PTS	AST	REB	BLK	STL
21.2	6.6	1.3	3.4	0.5	0.9

Advanced Metrics

USG%	3PTA/FGA	FTA/FGA	TS%	eFG%	3PT%
12.8	0.532	0.160	0.553	0.530	0.335

AST%	TOV%	OREB%	DREB%	STL%	BLK%
8.0	10.8	3.5	12.0	2.6	2.3

PER	ORTG	DRTG	WS/48	BPM	VOL
10.95	111.2	109.7	0.088	-0.30	0.362

- Fell out of Philadelphia's rotation, became a regular starter after he was traded to Portland
- Maintained his usual effective in a role as a very low volume spot-up shooter for both teams
- Made threes at just above the league average last season, break-even career three-point shooter
- Strictly a stand-still spot-up shooter, almost half of his threes come from the corners
- Great athlete, effective as an energetic rim runner, good cutter, explosive finisher in transition
- Not used at all as a ball handler, lacks the ability to create his own shot
- Catch-and-shoot player that only makes safe passes, rarely turns the ball over
- 2022-23 Defensive Degree of Difficulty: 0.556, had the 18th toughest set of matchups in the NBA
- 2022-23 Points Prevented: 0.227
- One of the top defensive stoppers in the league, good on-ball defender that guards multiple positions
- Plays a unique scrambling style while he's playing on-ball defense, positioning on isolation is not always sound
- Fairly solid pick-and-roll defender, can effectively switch, slight tendency to go too far under screens
- Sometimes gets caught on screens off the ball, good at closing out on spot-up shooters
- Dynamic roaming help defender, excellent at jumping passing lane to get steals, solid weak side shot blocker, fairly decent defensive rebounder

Shaedon Sharpe

	Height	Weight	Cap #	Years Left
	6'6"	200	$6.314M	2 TO

Similar at Age 19

		Season	SIMsc
1	Martell Webster	2005-06	922.4
2	Jamal Murray	2016-17	913.5
3	Moses Moody	2021-22	910.1
4	Joshua Primo	2021-22	905.3
5	Devin Booker	2015-16	901.3
6	RJ Barrett	2019-20	901.2
7	Bradley Beal	2012-13	896.1
8	Zhaire Smith	2018-19	894.3
9	Jayson Tatum	2017-18	893.9
10	J.R. Smith	2004-05	893.2

Baseline Basic Stats

MPG	PTS	AST	REB	BLK	STL
26.5	11.6	1.9	3.2	0.3	0.7

Advanced Metrics

USG%	3PTA/FGA	FTA/FGA	TS%	eFG%	3PT%
20.1	0.402	0.193	0.581	0.557	0.396

AST%	TOV%	OREB%	DREB%	STL%	BLK%
11.7	10.6	2.9	12.1	1.3	0.9

PER	ORTG	DRTG	WS/48	BPM	VOL
13.56	111.6	116.7	0.067	-1.80	0.300

- Regular rotational guard for Portland in his rookie season
- Solidly efficient in his role as a lower usage spot-up shooter
- Made threes at a league average rate, shot almost 41% on corner threes
- Excellent stationary spot-up shooter, still needs improvement when shooting on the move
- Below average in ball handling situations, inconsistent shooter off the dribble, defenders back off him to limit his effectiveness
- Excellent athlete, explosive finisher in transition, good cutter off the ball
- Catch-and-shoot player, only makes safe passes, rarely turns the ball over
- 2022-23 Defensive Degree of Difficulty: 0.377
- 2022-23 Points Prevented: -1.640
- Tended to guard higher-end second unit players or lower leverage starters
- Played solid on-ball defense in these matchups, capable of guarding multiple positions on the floor
- Decent pick-and-roll defender, can functionally switch and cut off penetration, tends to go too far under screens
- Fights through screens off the ball, usually is a step late when closing out on spot-up shooters
- Stay-at-home defender, rarely gets steals or blocks, decent defensive rebounder

Nassir Little

	Height	Weight	Cap #	Years Left
	6'5"	220	$6.250M	3

Similar at Age 22

		Season	SIMsc
1	Josh Hart	2017-18	928.1
2	Obi Toppin	2020-21	922.6
3	Romeo Langford	2021-22	919.8
4	Desmond Bane	2020-21	919.5
5	Justin Anderson	2015-16	918.0
6	Henry Walker	2009-10	917.6
7	Ignas Brazdeikis	2020-21	915.6
8	Sterling Brown	2017-18	914.9
9	Iman Shumpert	2012-13	914.8
10	Troy Brown Jr.	2021-22	913.4

Baseline Basic Stats

MPG	PTS	AST	REB	BLK	STL
22.0	9.1	1.4	3.6	0.3	0.6

Advanced Metrics

USG%	3PTA/FGA	FTA/FGA	TS%	eFG%	3PT%
17.1	0.476	0.217	0.574	0.546	0.363

AST%	TOV%	OREB%	DREB%	STL%	BLK%
9.1	10.2	3.8	14.4	1.2	1.6

PER	ORTG	DRTG	WS/48	BPM	VOL
12.56	112.9	116.6	0.072	-1.38	0.443

- Missed over a month due to a strained hip, regular rotation player for Portland when healthy
- Efficiency dropped slightly, mainly used as a low volume spot-up shooter
- Made threes at above the league average last season, break-even career three-point shooter
- Predominantly a stand-still spot-up shooter, percentages tend to vary from year-to-year
- Flashed some ability to curl off screens to make mid-range shots, athletic finisher, tended to rush his shots in rim running situations
- Inefficient in ball handling situations, strictly a catch-and-shoot player that makes safe passes, good at avoiding turnovers
- 2022-23 Defensive Degree of Difficulty: 0.399
- 2022-23 Points Prevented: -1.169
- Generally guarded higher-end bench players or low leverage starters, played below average on-ball defense
- Struggled to stay with opposing perimeter players, had trouble against stronger wings inside
- Below average as a pick-and-roll defender, not effective at taking away any specific action
- Gets caught on screens off the ball, usually was late when closing out on spot-up shooters
- Rarely gets steals, fairly solid weak side shot blocker, solid defensive rebounder

Jabari Walker

	Height	Weight	Cap #	Years Left
	6'9"	215	$1.720M	1

Similar at Age 20

		Season	SIMsc
1	Wilson Chandler	2007-08	935.8
2	Antonis Fotsis	2001-02	927.2
3	Rodions Kurucs	2018-19	924.5
4	Jalen Smith	2020-21	920.7
5	Shawne Williams	2006-07	919.3
6	Al-Farouq Aminu	2010-11	918.1
7	Rashard Lewis	1999-00	914.0
8	Chris Wilcox	2002-03	911.2
9	Greg Brown III	2021-22	910.7
10	DerMarr Johnson	2000-01	907.9

Baseline Basic Stats

MPG	PTS	AST	REB	BLK	STL
21.2	8.3	1.1	4.2	0.5	0.7

Advanced Metrics

USG%	3PTA/FGA	FTA/FGA	TS%	eFG%	3PT%
18.5	0.322	0.220	0.530	0.494	0.335

AST%	TOV%	OREB%	DREB%	STL%	BLK%
8.5	11.5	7.0	15.7	1.3	1.8

PER	ORTG	DRTG	WS/48	BPM	VOL
12.52	107.5	114.3	0.059	-2.57	0.456

- Played sparingly for Portland early last season, became a regular rotation player late in the year
- Uneven performance in his rookie season, used as a low usage spot-up shooter and energy player
- Posted a True Shooting Percentage below 50%, made less than 30% of his threes
- Struggled to shoot efficiently on spot-up jumpers, more efficient when taking threes in transition or on pick-and-pop play
- Explosive finisher in transition, willing to absorb contact to draw fouls
- Tends to play out of control, has some trouble finishing in traffic, prone to missing easy shots on rim runs
- Limited shot creation skills, catch-and-shoot player that makes safe passes, good at avoiding turnovers
- 2022-23 Defensive Degree of Difficulty: 0.305
- 2022-23 Points Prevented: 0.523
- Mainly guarded lower leverage second unit players or played in garbage time, decent on-ball defender
- Good against perimeter players, has quickness to stay with his man, struggled against bigger players inside
- Middling pick-and-roll defender, some ability to switch, good at cutting off penetration, tends to go too far under screens
- Stays attached to shooters off the ball, fights through screens and closes out in spot-up situations
- Does not really get steals, solid weak side shot blocker and defensive rebounder

Keon Johnson

	Height	Weight	Cap #	Years Left
	6'5"	186	$2.809M	TO

Similar at Age 20

		Season	SIMsc
1	Frank Ntilikina	2018-19	925.5
2	Archie Goodwin	2014-15	925.2
3	Théo Maledon	2021-22	910.9
4	Dejounte Murray	2016-17	908.7
5	Jamal Crawford	2000-01	908.3
6	Evan Fournier	2012-13	907.7
7	Brandon Boston Jr.	2021-22	906.9
8	Malik Beasley	2016-17	902.5
9	Emmanuel Mudiay	2016-17	902.1
10	D'Angelo Russell	2016-17	901.5

Baseline Basic Stats

MPG	PTS	AST	REB	BLK	STL
19.7	8.1	2.5	2.6	0.3	0.8

Advanced Metrics

USG%	3PTA/FGA	FTA/FGA	TS%	eFG%	3PT%
22.2	0.415	0.207	0.502	0.472	0.348

AST%	TOV%	OREB%	DREB%	STL%	BLK%
20.0	15.0	3.0	11.0	2.0	1.2

PER	ORTG	DRTG	WS/48	BPM	VOL
11.38	99.9	114.2	0.014	-2.77	0.262

- Played limited minutes for Portland in his first full season with the team
- Raised his production level slightly, still inefficient in his role as a higher usage scoring guard off the bench
- Career True Shooting Percentage is below 50%, above break-even career three-point shooter
- Struggles to efficiently make spot-up jumpers, better when shooting off the dribble
- Effective at driving to the rim as a pick-and-roll ball handler and isolation player, shot selection is suspect, tends to settle for a lot of contested mid-range shots
- Does not really move off the ball, wildly rushes his shots in transition
- Unselfish player with solid secondary playmaking skills, fairly turnover prone
- 2022-23 Defensive Degree of Difficulty: 0.335
- 2022-23 Points Prevented: -2.199
- Usually guards lower leverage second unit players, rarely tested in one-on-one situations
- Decent perimeter defender in a small sample of possessions, had troubled against stronger wings inside
- Played below average pick-and-roll defense, not especially effective at taking away any specific action
- Tended to get caught on screens off the ball, good at closing out on spot-up shooters
- Active help defender, good at jumping passing lanes to get steals, effective weak side shot blocker, below average defensive rebounder

Newcomers

Scoot Henderson

	Height	Weight	Cap #	Years Left
	6'2"	195	$9.771M	1 + 2 TO

Baseline Basic Stats

MPG	PTS	AST	REB	BLK	STL
17.4	7.3	2.5	1.8	0.2	0.6

Advanced Metrics

USG%	3PTA/FGA	FTA/FGA	TS%	eFG%	3PT%
21.4	0.264	0.233	0.503	0.465	0.282

AST%	TOV%	OREB%	DREB%	STL%	BLK%
30.4	16.1	2.0	12.1	1.5	0.8

PER	ORTG	DRTG	WS/48	BPM	VOL
12.29	100.3	120.0	0.036	-0.04	0.590

- Drafted by Portland with the 3rd overall pick in 2023
- Played the past two years in the G-League with G-League Ignite, projection uses translated G-League stats
- Played well in his only game at the Las Vegas Summer League, shut down due to a shoulder injury
- Highly effective in his role as high usage scorer and playmaker at Summer League
- Displayed great playmaking skills, could find open shooters and cutters, effectively limited turnovers
- Very athletic guard with great quickness, good at driving downhill on pick-and-rolls and isolations, will seek out contact, draws fouls at a good rate
- Jump shot is still a work-in-progress, below break-even three-point shooter in the G-League, went 1-for-3 (33.3%) on threes at Summer League
- Needs to clean up his mechanics when shooting from long range, better as a mid-range shooter
- Great at pushing the ball in transition, explosive finisher on the break
- Has great athleticism and length, potentially can be a good defensive guard, not always engaged at this end
- Average on-ball defender, good at pressuring opposing guards, taller players give him trouble
- Decent pick-and-roll defender, solid at containing ball handlers, sometimes takes bad angles when making rotations
- Gambles a bit too much off the ball, gets caught out of position, does not always get around screens or close out on spot-up shooters
- Actively plays passing lanes to get steals, did not block a shot at Summer League, good defensive rebounding guard

Kris Murray

	Height	Weight	Cap #	Years Left
	6'8"	220	$2.847M	1 + 2 TO

Baseline Basic Stats

MPG	PTS	AST	REB	BLK	STL
21.6	8.0	1.2	3.6	0.4	0.6

Advanced Metrics

USG%	3PTA/FGA	FTA/FGA	TS%	eFG%	3PT%
17.4	0.395	0.205	0.517	0.490	0.332

AST%	TOV%	OREB%	DREB%	STL%	BLK%
9.1	9.5	5.5	13.0	1.5	1.6

PER	ORTG	DRTG	WS/48	BPM	VOL
13.12	104.7	104.6	0.073	-1.11	N/A

- Drafted by Portland with the 23rd overall pick in 2023
- Had a solid performance at the Las Vegas Summer League
- Effective in his role as a low usage complementary shooter
- Below break-even three-point shooter at Summer League, above break-even three-point shooter in college
- Needs to be wide open to shoot efficiently, most effective when taking threes in transition
- Struggles to create separation against opposing wings, better at attacking mismatches
- Effective at posting up smaller players, occasionally can drive by slower big men
- Energetic rim runner that scores on hustle plays, good cutter, selectively goes to the offensive boards to score on put-backs
- Mainly a catch-and-shoot player, only makes safe passes, solid at limiting turnovers
- Has solid athleticism, fundamentally sound defender that makes good rotations
- Solid on-ball defender, plays angles well, can stay with opposing perimeter players, can handle bigger players for short stretches
- Solid pick-and-roll defender, effective on switches, good at containing ball handlers
- Stays attached to shooters off the ball, fights through screens and closes out in spot-up situations
- Active as a help defender, great at playing passing lanes to get steals, did not block a shot at Summer League, decent defensive rebounder
- Twin brother of Sacramento Kings' forward Keegan Murray, will play in his age-23 season as a rookie

Rayan Rupert

	Height	Weight	Cap #	Years Left
	6'6"	205	$1.120M	1 + TO

Baseline Basic Stats

MPG	PTS	AST	REB	BLK	STL
15.1	4.9	0.9	2.1	0.2	0.5

Advanced Metrics

USG%	3PTA/FGA	FTA/FGA	TS%	eFG%	3PT%
14.4	0.438	0.227	0.480	0.446	0.258

AST%	TOV%	OREB%	DREB%	STL%	BLK%
10.0	11.6	2.5	10.1	1.7	0.8

PER	ORTG	DRTG	WS/48	BPM	VOL
9.02	95.3	103.7	0.065	-0.11	0.316

- Drafted by Portland with the 43rd overall pick in 2023
- Played for the New Zealand in the Australian NBL last season, projection uses translated NBL stats
- Did not play particularly well at the Las Vegas Summer League
- Really struggled with his efficiency in a role as a low volume energy player
- True Percentage was below 35%, made only 25% of his field goals, did not make a three at Summer League
- Still very raw, has not been able to shoot efficiently in the NBL and his early years in France
- Defenders were really able to back off him to limit his effectiveness when driving
- Decent ball handler with good quickness, drives aggressively to the rim, draws fouls at a high rate
- Great athlete that can explosively finish with emphatic dunks in transition
- Catch-and-shoot player at Summer League, flashes some passing ability, plays out of control, somewhat turnover prone
- Long and athletic defender with good potential, still undisciplined at this stage
- Unpolished as an on-ball defender, tends to bite on fakes and take bad angles
- Below average pick-and-roll defender, indecisive, not especially effective at taking away any specific action
- Gambles a bit too much, gets caught out of position, does not always get around screens or close out on spot-up shooters
- Solid at playing passing lanes to get steals, solid defensive rebounder
- Needs to spend at least a season in the G-League to improve his overall skill level and basketball IQ

Unsigned Players

P.J. Washington

	Height	Weight	Cap #	Years Left
	6'7"	230	RFA	X

Similar at Age 24

		Season	SIMsc
1	OG Anunoby	2021-22	940.5
2	Cedi Osman	2019-20	923.4
3	Draymond Green	2014-15	922.3
4	Scott Burrell	1994-95	919.3
5	Tracy Murray	1995-96	911.6
6	Vladimir Radmanovic	2004-05	910.6
7	Kyle Singler	2012-13	910.6
8	Taurean Prince	2018-19	909.8
9	Danny Green	2011-12	909.8
10	Mike Miller	2004-05	909.7

Baseline Basic Stats

MPG	PTS	AST	REB	BLK	STL
27.8	12.5	2.1	4.5	0.5	0.9

Advanced Metrics

USG%	3PTA/FGA	FTA/FGA	TS%	eFG%	3PT%
19.7	0.481	0.212	0.560	0.529	0.365

AST%	TOV%	OREB%	DREB%	STL%	BLK%
12.3	10.9	3.6	14.5	1.5	2.3

PER	ORTG	DRTG	WS/48	BPM	VOL
14.17	110.5	112.3	0.079	-0.03	0.359

- RFA rights are held by Charlotte
- Regular starter for Charlotte in his fourth NBA season
- Efficiency dropped slightly in a role as a moderate volume stretch four
- Above average career three-point shooter, Three-Point Percentage dropped slightly with higher usage
- Predominantly a stand-still spot-up shooter, can make pick-and-pop jumpers and threes in transition
- Energetic rim runner, good roll man and cutter, undersized has some trouble finishing in traffic
- Can post up smaller players, not really a ball handler, solid secondary playmaker, rarely turns the ball over
- 2022-23 Defensive Degree of Difficulty: 0.464
- 2022-23 Points Prevented: 0.957
- Usually guarded starting level players, played fairly effective on-ball defense
- Can hold position inside against bigger players, has some trouble staying with quicker perimeter players
- Average pick-and-roll defender, solid in drop coverages, struggled to contain ball handlers
- Stays attached to shooters off the ball, fights through screens and closes out in spot-up situations
- Better as a rim protector, fairly solid shot blocker, decent on the defensive boards

Christian Wood

	Height	Weight	Cap #	Years Left
	6'10"	214	UFA	X

Similar at Age 27

		Season	SIMsc
1	Rashard Lewis	2006-07	905.2
2	Jerami Grant	2021-22	894.1
3	Serge Ibaka	2016-17	891.2
4	Nikola Mirotic	2018-19	887.7
5	Nikola Vucevic	2017-18	887.7
6	Lamar Odom	2006-07	887.7
7	Donyell Marshall	2000-01	884.8
8	Dino Radja*	1994-95	884.2
9	Derrick Coleman	1994-95	884.2
10	Larry Nance	1986-87	883.0

Baseline Basic Stats

MPG	PTS	AST	REB	BLK	STL
32.9	18.0	2.4	8.0	1.2	0.8

Advanced Metrics

USG%	3PTA/FGA	FTA/FGA	TS%	eFG%	3PT%
24.2	0.333	0.319	0.595	0.562	0.390

AST%	TOV%	OREB%	DREB%	STL%	BLK%
11.8	11.6	6.2	24.5	1.1	2.9

PER	ORTG	DRTG	WS/48	BPM	VOL
19.20	113.6	110.3	0.129	1.16	0.357

- UFA rights are held by Dallas
- Regular rotational player for Dallas in his first season with the team
- Maintained his usual level of effectiveness in a sixth man as a scoring stretch big and rim runner
- Fairly good three-point shooter, career Three-Point Percentage is almost 38%
- Made over 43% of his spot-up and pick-and-pop threes last season
- Athletic rim runner, effective as a cutter and roll man, efficiently scores off put-backs
- Decent post player, can face up big men or shoot over smaller players
- Fairly solid passing big man that can kick the ball out to open shooters, good at limiting turnovers
- 2022-23 Defensive Degree of Difficulty: 0.376
- 2022-23 Points Prevented: -0.900
- Good defensive rebounder, solid shot blocker, average rim protector at best, undisciplined with his positioning
- Usually hidden in matchups against second unit level players, middling on-ball defender
- Can be overpowered in the post against bigger centers, more effective when defending in space
- Below average pick-and-roll defender, indecisive, not especially effective when making rotations
- Tends to stay anchored in the paint, does not always come out to contest perimeter shots

Kelly Oubre Jr.

	Height	Weight	Cap #	Years Left
	6'7"	203	UFA	X

Similar at Age 27

		Season	SIMsc
1	C.J. Miles	2014-15	935.3
2	Evan Fournier	2019-20	921.7
3	Dorell Wright	2012-13	918.8
4	Caris LeVert	2021-22	917.6
5	Terrence Ross	2018-19	911.7
6	Eric Piatkowski	1997-98	911.7
7	Kyle Korver	2008-09	909.3
8	Bobby Simmons	2007-08	909.2
9	Nick Young	2012-13	908.8
10	Rasual Butler	2006-07	906.9

Baseline Basic Stats

MPG	PTS	AST	REB	BLK	STL
26.3	12.8	1.6	3.4	0.4	0.8

Advanced Metrics

USG%	3PTA/FGA	FTA/FGA	TS%	eFG%	3PT%
22.7	0.514	0.214	0.545	0.515	0.360

AST%	TOV%	OREB%	DREB%	STL%	BLK%
7.9	7.6	3.4	12.4	1.7	1.1

PER	ORTG	DRTG	WS/48	BPM	VOL
14.04	108.3	113.0	0.073	-0.63	0.285

- UFA rights are held by Charlotte
- Missed games due to injuries to his hand, back, and shoulder, regular starter for Charlotte when healthy
- Production held fairly steady in a role as a high usage scoring wing
- Below break-even career three-point shooter, made 41% of his corner threes last season
- Mainly a break-even spot-up shooter, efficiency in other situations tends to vary
- Streaky shooter off the dribble, better at attacking the rim and hitting pull-up mid-range jumpers if his threes are falling, decent cutter and transition player
- Good at scoring on hand-offs, catch-and-shoot player, passing skills are limited, rarely turns the ball over
- 2022-23 Defensive Degree of Difficulty: 0.469
- 2022-23 Points Prevented: -1.574
- Used as a defensive stopper in the past, drew a lot of tougher assignments against higher-end starters
- Fairly decent on-ball defender, competently guards multiple positions, tends to back off his man too much on the perimeter
- Played below average pick-and-roll defense, not especially effective at taking away any specific action
- Prone to making bad gambles, does not always get around screens or close out on spot-up shooters
- Good at playing passing lanes to get steals, occasional weak side shot blocker, solid defensive rebounder

Blake Griffin

	Height	Weight	Cap #	Years Left
	6'10"	250	UFA	X

Similar at Age 33

		Season	SIMsc
1	Aron Baynes	2019-20	907.8
2	Nemanja Bjelica	2021-22	904.6
3	Matt Bonner	2013-14	903.8
4	Drew Gooden	2014-15	890.1
5	Sean Marks	2008-09	886.0
6	Eduardo Najera	2009-10	884.8
7	David Lee	2016-17	882.2
8	Danny Ferry	1999-00	881.7
9	Rashard Lewis	2012-13	881.5
10	Channing Frye	2016-17	881.1

Baseline Basic Stats

MPG	PTS	AST	REB	BLK	STL
14.0	4.9	1.0	3.2	0.3	0.3

Advanced Metrics

USG%	3PTA/FGA	FTA/FGA	TS%	eFG%	3PT%
15.0	0.486	0.230	0.536	0.509	0.298

AST%	TOV%	OREB%	DREB%	STL%	BLK%
11.5	12.4	7.5	19.2	1.2	1.6

PER	ORTG	DRTG	WS/48	BPM	VOL
11.80	113.7	110.1	0.108	-1.24	0.355

- UFA rights are held by Boston
- Played limited minutes off the bench in his first season with Boston
- Production held steady in a role as a low usage stretch big and rim runner
- Below break-even career three-point shooter, made threes at an above break-even rate last season
- Most effective as a stand-still spot-up shooter, not quite as efficient on pick-and-pops
- Effective rim runner, not as explosive as he used to be, solid roll man and cutter, active offensive rebounder
- Occasionally can bully smaller defenders on post-ups, lacks the quickness to drive by defenders right now
- Good passing big man, effective playmaker in the short roll game, good at avoiding turnovers
- 2022-23 Defensive Degree of Difficulty: 0.407
- 2022-23 Points Prevented: -1.066
- Below average rim protector, not really a shot blocking threat, good defensive rebounder
- Drew a few tough matchups off the bench, usually guarded high-end bench players or lower-tier starters
- Played solid on-ball defenses in these matchups, effective post defender, good at defending in space
- Average pick-and-roll defender, can functionally switch, tended to have lapses when making rotations
- Usually was anchored in the paint, did not always come out to contest outside shots in spot-up situations

Terence Davis

	Height	Weight	Cap #	Years Left
	6'4"	201	UFA	X

Similar at Age 25

		Season	SIMsc
1	Donte DiVincenzo	2021-22	917.3
2	Shannon Brown	2010-11	906.9
3	C.J. Miles	2012-13	906.3
4	Buddy Hield	2017-18	905.9
5	Troy Daniels	2016-17	903.2
6	Grayson Allen	2020-21	901.6
7	Marcus Thornton	2012-13	900.7
8	Gabe Vincent	2021-22	899.7
9	Norman Powell	2018-19	899.4
10	Caleb Martin	2020-21	897.4

Baseline Basic Stats

MPG	PTS	AST	REB	BLK	STL
24.1	11.8	1.9	3.0	0.2	0.8

Advanced Metrics

USG%	3PTA/FGA	FTA/FGA	TS%	eFG%	3PT%
22.0	0.602	0.132	0.564	0.542	0.377

AST%	TOV%	OREB%	DREB%	STL%	BLK%
12.3	10.7	2.6	13.4	1.8	1.1

PER	ORTG	DRTG	WS/48	BPM	VOL
13.93	109.0	113.2	0.064	-0.27	0.225

- UFA rights were renounced by Sacramento
- Fringe rotation player for Sacramento in his second full season with the team
- Decently efficient in his role as a moderate volume scoring guard off the bench
- Above average career three-point shooter, career corner Three-Point Percentage is above 42%
- Excellent spot-up shooter, solid at making threes in transition, not consistently effective when shooting in other situations
- Solid scorer as a pick-and-roll ball handler, needs a screen to create separation, average isolation player
- Fairly solid secondary playmaker that can make simple reads, good at avoiding turnovers
- 2022-23 Defensive Degree of Difficulty: 0.388
- 2022-23 Points Prevented: -1.803
- Generally guarded second unit players, struggled to play effective on-ball defense
- Had trouble staying with opposing guards, struggled against taller wing players
- Below average pick-and-roll defender, not effective at taking away any specific action
- Gets caught on screens off the ball, tended to be late when closing out on spot-up shooters
- Active help defender, consistently posts high Steal Percentages, fairly good defensive rebounder

My 2023-24 NBA Predictions

If you have reached this point, then you have seen how my SCHREMPF projection model has projected the performance of every team in the NBA as well as every player that is listed on their active roster. If you just skipped ahead to this part, that's okay too. The following is my adjustment to the overall forecast of how I expect the upcoming 2023-24 season to play out. Most of the time, my evaluations are pretty close to the forecasting system. In other cases, I do have some disagreements. In order to account for these differences, I made some adjustments based on all of the available information and my general best estimates. Here are my predictions for the Eastern Conference.

Eastern Conference

	SCHREMPF Rankings		**My Rankings**
1	Boston	1	Boston
2	Milwaukee	2	Milwaukee
3	Philadelphia	3	**Cleveland**
4	Cleveland	4	**Philadelphia**
5	New York	5	**Miami**
6	Miami	6	**New York**
7	Atlanta	7	Atlanta
8	Toronto	8	**Brooklyn**
9	Brooklyn	9	**Chicago**
10	Chicago	10	**Toronto**
11	Washington	11	**Orlando**
12	Orlando	12	**Indiana**
13	Indiana	13	**Washington**
14	Charlotte	14	Charlotte
15	Detroit	15	Detroit

I mostly agree with how the system rated the teams in the East. I just would make some minor tweaks to the order. Boston and Milwaukee appear to be the top two teams, and both of them don't really have glaring holes that would knock them down, so I left them alone. The latest James Harden trade holdout will probably hurt Philadelphia's regular season win total a little bit, as they would be going through a chunk of the season short-handed. For that reason, I would drop them a bit and bump Cleveland up. Cleveland is likely to post a high regular season win total because they are younger, and their roster has a better track record of staying healthy. Therefore, they should be able to effectively manage the full 82-game schedule better. I also moved Miami up because their projection is largely based on their down regular season from last year. When accounting for their performance in the playoffs and the possible addition of Damian Lillard, I conservatively bumped them up to the fifth spot. As a result, New York moved down a spot to sixth. From there, I moved Brooklyn and Chicago each up one slot because both teams are high effort, defensive outfits that could be competitive all season and pull off some close wins to boost their win total slightly. Toronto doesn't have a clear identity right now, and they are adjusting to a new system under a new coach. There could be a slight adjustment period that knocks them down. After this, I moved Washington down to the 13th spot because they are expected to be a rebuilding team that will sell off some its veterans as they approach the trade deadline. It's likely that they will get gradually worse as the season progress. They might not be able to fully bottom out because they do have some talent on their roster, so they might be able to pull off some wins against some of the lower-tier teams in the league. Even so, the Wizards will probably finish towards the bottom, which would elevate Orlando and Indiana up a notch. Of these two teams, Orlando could be a dark horse to sneak into the play-in tournament with their collection of young talent. As a final note, Charlotte and Detroit will remain near the bottom of the standings because they are in rebuilding situations, and they didn't really add much to their teams to suggest that their fortunes will change for the better.

Western Conference

	SCHREMPF Rankings		**My Rankings**
1	Memphis	1	Memphis
2	Golden State	2	**Denver**
3	New Orleans	3	**L.A. Lakers**
4	L.A. Lakers	4	**Golden State**
5	Dallas	5	Dallas
6	L.A. Clippers	6	**Sacramento**
7	Minnesota	7	**Phoenix**
8	Denver	8	**L.A. Clippers**
9	Sacramento	9	**Minnesota**
10	Phoenix	10	**New Orleans**
11	Oklahoma City	11	Oklahoma City
12	Utah	12	Utah
13	Houston	13	Houston
14	San Antonio	14	San Antonio
15	Portland	15	Portland

Just like last season, I disagreed with my system on how it rated the teams in the West. For starters, Denver's projection was undershot in a significant way. Some of this is based on the fact that it assumes that everyone will play in a neutral environment, which isn't the case for the Nuggets because they play half of their games in elevation. The elevation has been an advantage for them, especially during this era with Nikola Jokic. However, the exact effect of this elevation is very difficult to quantify, so my system can't really account for it. I bumped them up to the second spot because their starting five and their ability to win at home should allow them to post a high win total. That being said, they are much more vulnerable than they were last season. In particular, their bench is highly unproven, which would place a higher workload on their starters. This could be problematic because they would have less flexibility to mix and match lineups against other teams, and they would be at a high risk to decline if they were hit with any kind of injury. They might need to fortify their depth at the trade deadline to boost their chances of repeating.

From there, I dropped New Orleans and the L.A. Clippers due to injury concerns because both of them have just not been able to keep their stars healthy. Based on their recent history, they are not likely to be at full strength for the entire season, so I dropped them accordingly. On the flip side, if either of those teams gets a full season from their stars, they could rack up regular season wins and possibly make some noise in the playoffs. Out of the teams that I moved to the third and fourth slots, I rated the Lakers higher because their chemistry is a little more established because they are more or less running back the team that made the Conference Finals last season. Golden State is a wild card because they added a high-end piece in Chris Paul that should boost their offensive efficiency. However, it will be interesting to see how this addition works out because the fit isn't perfect. After all, the Warriors employ a fast-paced, motion offense while Paul has historically played a methodical style. If they can assimilate him into the offense, they could vault back into contention. Otherwise, they could fall further down the standings. I moved Sacramento and Phoenix up because their projection was slightly undershot. There are warning signs for both teams. Sacramento had something of a magical season where everything broke perfectly, and they took a lot of people by surprise. Teams have a better idea of what to expect from the Kings this time around. They could drop down a bit, but it likely will not be as much as my system says because they have too much talent for that. Phoenix has excellent front-end talent, so that should make them a better team than the system projects them to be, but there are some red flags about. Namely, they simply don't have much depth after their stars and Deandre Ayton. They don't really have a clear fifth starter on their roster, so they may have to mix and match with a bunch of players that were signed for the league minimum. Also, their stars have had some injury history. It's not a certainty that they will be at full strength for the entire season, so their record could take a hit as a result. On top of this, they are trying to take several very high usage players and turn them into cohesive unit. This process normally takes months or even years to accomplish, so there's a chance that they could stumble out of the gates while they try to figure out their chemistry. Even with all being said, their talent gives them considerable upside and if everything gels properly, then they could be title contenders, but a lot has to fall into place to make that happen. From this point, the bottom third of the West should be the same as it was for the projection system. Out of the five teams that were listed near the bottom, Oklahoma City has the best chance to be a surprise team because they have an excellent collection of young talent that is still ascending. They also are getting an addition without needing to make a move because Chet Holmgren is returning from his foot injury. He fills a major role by giving them a much needed rim protector and interior presence. If they continue to grow and develop, they could leapfrog a few teams to get a playoff spot or another berth in the play-in tournament. Utah will be a competitive team, but they might not have enough to push for the playoffs this season. As a final note, it's expected that Houston, San Antonio, and Portland will finish near the bottom because they don't quite have enough polished talent to win on a regular basis.

Projections for the 2023 NBA In-Season Tournament

Group Stage (Group winners in **Bold**, Wild Card teams in *Italics*, seed in parentheses)

East A	East B	East C	West A	West B	West C
Cleveland (3)	**Milwaukee (2)**	**Boston (1)**	**L.A. Lakers (4)**	**Denver (5)**	**Golden State (6)**
Philadelphia	*Miami (8)*	Chicago	*Phoenix (7)*	Dallas	Sacramento
Atlanta	New York	Orlando	Memphis	New Orleans	Minnesota
Indiana	Washington	Brooklyn	Utah	L.A. Clippers	Oklahoma City
Detroit	Charlotte	Toronto	Portland	Houston	San Antonio

Quarterfinals
- 1. Boston over 8. Miami
- 4. L.A. Lakers over 5. Denver
- 2. Milwaukee over 7. Phoenix
- 6. Golden State over 3. Cleveland

Semi-Finals (in Las Vegas)
- 4. L.A. Lakers over 1. Boston
- 2. Milwaukee over 6. Golden State

Finals (in Las Vegas)
- 2. Milwaukee over 4. L.A. Lakers (Milwaukee wins the NBA Cup)

Playoffs

Play-In Tournament
- (E) 7/8 Matchup: Brooklyn beats Atlanta (Brooklyn gets the 7th seed)
- (E) 9/10 Matchup: Chicago beats Toronto
- (E) 7/8 Loser v. 9/10 Winner: Atlanta beats Chicago (Atlanta gets the 8th seed)
- (W) 7/8 Matchup: Phoenix beats L.A. Clippers (Phoenix gets the 7th seed)
- (W) 9/10 Matchup: Minnesota beats New Orleans
- (W) 7/8 Loser v. 9/10 Winner: L.A. Clippers beat Minnesota (L.A. Clippers get the 8th seed)

First Round
- (E) 1. Boston over 8. Atlanta (4 – 1)
- (E) 2. Milwaukee over 7. Brooklyn (4 – 1)
- (E) 6. New York over 3. Cleveland (4 – 3)
- (E) 5. Miami over 4. Philadelphia (4 – 2)
- (W) 1. Memphis over 8. L.A. Clippers (4 – 3)
- (W) 2. Denver over 7. Phoenix (4 – 3)
- (W) 3. L.A. Lakers over 6. Sacramento (4 – 2)
- (W) 4. Golden State over 5. Dallas (4 – 2)

Second Round
- (E) 1. Boston over 5. Miami (4 – 3)
- (E) 2. Milwaukee over 6. New York (4 – 2)
- (W) 4. Golden State over 1. Memphis (4 – 2)
- (W) 2. Denver over 3. L.A. Lakers (4 – 3)

Conference Finals
- (E) 1. Boston over 2. Milwaukee (4 – 2)
- (W) 4. Golden State over 2. Denver (4 – 3)

NBA Finals
- E1. Boston over W4. Golden State (4 – 3)

THANK YOU

A very big thanks goes out to everybody that made this book possible. I really appreciate the support that all of you have given me. It helps a lot to push me through to the finish and the feedback I get makes the writing process much more satisfying. I hope you all enjoyed reading the new edition of the preview almanac, and I once again thank you for your support. If you liked this book and want to read past editions of any of the previous titles, then please follow me on my Amazon author page, which is listed below:

www.amazon.com/author/rvlhoops

If you have any additional questions or comments, please feel free to contact me by email at lurv82@gmail.com. For further updates on any new content releases, you can also follow me on the application formerly known as Twitter under the username @rvlhoops. Once again, thank you to all of my readers for supporting my work. Please be on the lookout for my annual draft almanac that is set to be released in June 2024, and enjoy the 2023-24 NBA season.

Alphabetical Player Index

Precious Achiuwa, Toronto	144
Steven Adams, Memphis	277
Bam Adebayo, Miami	106
Ochai Agbaji, Utah	465
Santi Aldama, Memphis	280
Nickeil Alexander-Walker, Minnesota	380
Grayson Allen, Milwaukee	45
Jarrett Allen, Cleveland	76
Jose Alvarado, New Orleans	314
Kyle Anderson, Minnesota	378
Giannis Antetokounmpo, Milwaukee	41
Thanasis Antetokounmpo, Milwaukee	52
Cole Anthony, Orlando	210
OG Anunoby, Toronto	138
Deni Avdija, Washington	191
Deandre Ayton, Phoenix	426
Marvin Bagley III, Detroit	264
Patrick Baldwin Jr., Washington	198
LaMelo Ball, Charlotte	239
Lonzo Ball, Chicago	183
Mo Bamba, Philadelphia	66
Paolo Banchero, Orlando	205
Desmond Bane, Memphis	275
Dalano Banton, Boston	36
Harrison Barnes, Sacramento	409
Scottie Barnes, Toronto	139
R.J. Barrett, New York	91
Charles Bassey, San Antonio	499
Keita Bates-Diop, Phoenix	435
Nicolas Batum, L.A. Clippers	363
Darius Bazley, Brooklyn	163
Bradley Beal, Phoenix	425
Malik Beasley, Milwaukee	49
MarJon Beauchamp, Milwaukee	51
Davis Bertans, Oklahoma City	453
Patrick Beverley, Philadelphia	64
Saddiq Bey, Atlanta	124
Khem Birch, San Antonio	508
Goga Bitadze, Orlando	216
Anthony Black, Orlando	218
Bogdan Bogdanovic, Atlanta	125
Bojan Bogdanovic, Detroit	256
Bol Bol, Phoenix	433
Devin Booker, Phoenix	424
Brandon Boston Jr., L.A. Clippers	368
Chris Boucher, Toronto	143
James Bouknight, Charlotte	249
Malaki Branham, San Antonio	498
Christian Braun, Denver	394
Mikal Bridges, Brooklyn	153
Miles Bridges, Charlotte	242
Oshae Brissett, Boston	34
Malcolm Brogdon, Boston	31
Dillon Brooks, Houston	482
Bruce Brown, Indiana	224
Jaylen Brown, Boston	27
Kobe Brown, L.A. Clippers	370
Troy Brown Jr., Minnesota	382
Jalen Brunson, New York	90
Thomas Bryant, Miami	113
Kobe Bufkin, Atlanta	133
Reggie Bullock, San Antonio	502
Alec Burks, Detroit	263

Jimmy Butler, Miami	105
Kentavious Caldwell-Pope, Denver	393
Toumani Camara, Phoenix	437
Vlatko Cancar, Denver	396
Clint Capela, Atlanta	122
Jevon Carter, Chicago	174
Wendell Carter Jr., Orlando	207
Alex Caruso, Chicago	175
Julian Champagnie, San Antonio	506
Max Christie, L.A. Lakers	333
Josh Christopher, Memphis	288
Sidy Cissoko, San Antonio	510
Brandon Clarke, Memphis	278
Jordan Clarkson, Utah	463
Nic Claxton, Brooklyn	155
Noah Clowney, Brooklyn	166
Amir Coffey, L.A. Clippers	367
John Collins, Utah	464
Zach Collins, San Antonio	496
Mike Conley, Minnesota	376
Pat Connaughton, Milwaukee	47
Xavier Cooks, Washington	201
Bilal Coulibaly, Washington	202
Robert Covington, L.A. Clippers	366
Torrey Craig, Chicago	178
Jae Crowder, Milwaukee	48
Cade Cunningham, Detroit	257
Seth Curry, Dallas	345
Stephen Curry, Golden State	292
Dyson Daniels, New Orleans	316
Anthony Davis, L.A. Lakers	324
Johnny Davis, Washington	199
Terence Davis, Unsigned	530
DeMar DeRozan, Chicago	171
Gradey Dick, Toronto	150
Ousmane Dieng, Oklahoma City	451
Spencer Dinwiddie, Brooklyn	156
Donte DiVincenzo, New York	96
Luka Doncic, Dallas	338
Luguentz Dort, Oklahoma City	443
Ayo Dosunmu, Chicago	177
Andre Drummond, Chicago	179
Chris Duarte, Sacramento	414
Kris Dunn, Utah	469
Kevin Durant, Phoenix	423
Jalen Duren, Detroit	259
Tari Eason, Houston	484
Anthony Edwards, Minnesota	373
Kessler Edwards, Sacramento	415
Joel Embiid, Philadelphia	58
Drew Eubanks, Phoenix	432
Dante Exum, Dallas	350
Bruno Fernando, Atlanta	131
Dorian Finney-Smith, Brooklyn	157
Malachi Flynn, Toronto	149
Simone Fontecchio, Utah	471
Evan Fournier, New York	100
De'Aaron Fox, Sacramento	407
Markelle Fultz, Orlando	208
Daniel Gafford, Washington	190
Danilo Gallinari, Washington	194
Darius Garland, Cleveland	75
Usman Garuba, Oklahoma City	452
Keyonte George, Utah	474
Paul George, L.A. Clippers	356
Josh Giddey, Oklahoma City	441

Shai Gilgeous-Alexander, Oklahoma City	440
Anthony Gill, Washington	197
Rudy Gobert, Minnesota	374
Jordan Goodwin, Phoenix	430
Aaron Gordon, Denver	391
Eric Gordon, Phoenix	427
Devonte' Graham, San Antonio	501
Jerami Grant, Portland	514
A.J. Green, Milwaukee	53
Draymond Green, Golden State	295
Jalen Green, Houston	480
Jeff Green, Houston	485
Josh Green, Dallas	343
A.J. Griffin, Atlanta	127
Blake Griffin, Unsigned	529
Quentin Grimes, New York	93
Mouhamed Gueye, Atlanta	134
Rui Hachimura, L.A. Lakers	328
Tyrese Haliburton, Indiana	222
Tim Hardaway Jr., Dallas	340
James Harden, Philadelphia	59
Jaden Hardy, Dallas	348
Montrezl Harrell, Philadelphia	68
Gary Harris, Orlando	209
Joe Harris, Detroit	262
Tobias Harris, Philadelphia	61
Josh Hart, New York	95
Isaiah Hartenstein, New York	97
Sam Hauser, Boston	33
Jordan Hawkins, New Orleans	319
Jaxson Hayes, L.A. Lakers	330
Killian Hayes, Detroit	267
Gordon Hayward, Charlotte	240
Scoot Henderson, Portland	522
Taylor Hendricks, Utah	473
Tyler Herro, Miami	107
Buddy Hield, Indiana	225
Haywood Highsmith, Miami	114
Aaron Holiday, Houston	488
Jrue Holiday, Milwaukee	42
Justin Holiday, Denver	400
Richaun Holmes, Dallas	347
Chet Holmgren, Oklahoma City	456
Jalen Hood-Schifino, L.A. Lakers	334
Al Horford, Boston	30
Talen Horton-Tucker, Utah	468
Danuel House Jr., Philadelphia	67
Caleb Houstan, Orlando	214
Jett Howard, Orlando	219
Kevin Huerter, Sacramento	408
De'Andre Hunter, Atlanta	123
Bones Hyland, L.A. Clippers	364
Joe Ingles, Orlando	213
Brandon Ingram, New Orleans	307
Kyrie Irving, Dallas	339
Jonathan Isaac, Orlando	217
Jaden Ivey, Detroit	260
Isaiah Jackson, Indiana	231
Reggie Jackson, Denver	395
Andre Jackson Jr., Milwaukee	54
Jaren Jackson Jr., Memphis	274
Trayce Jackson-Davis, Golden State	304
LeBron James, L.A. Lakers	323
Jaime Jaquez Jr., Miami	117
DaQuan Jeffries, New York	102
Ty Jerome, Cleveland	85

Isaiah Joe, Oklahoma City	444
Cameron Johnson, Brooklyn	154
Jalen Johnson, Atlanta	128
Keldon Johnson, San Antonio	493
Keon Johnson, Portland	521
Nikola Jokic, Denver	389
Carlik Jones, Chicago	181
Colby Jones, Sacramento	419
Damian Jones, Cleveland	84
Herbert Jones, New Orleans	311
Kai Jones, Charlotte	248
Tre Jones, San Antonio	495
Tyus Jones, Washington	189
Derrick Jones Jr., Dallas	346
DeAndre Jordan, Denver	398
Cory Joseph, Golden State	302
Nikola Jovic, Miami	116
Luke Kennard, Memphis	282
Walker Kessler, Utah	462
Corey Kispert, Washington	192
Maxi Kleber, Dallas	344
Christian Koloko, Toronto	148
John Konchar, Memphis	281
Furkan Korkmaz, Philadelphia	69
Luke Kornet, Boston	37
Jonathan Kuminga, Golden State	300
Kyle Kuzma, Washington	187
Jock Landale, Houston	486
Jake LaRavia, Memphis	286
Zach LaVine, Chicago	170
Damion Lee, Phoenix	429
Alex Len, Sacramento	416
Kawhi Leonard, L.A. Clippers	355
Caris LeVert, Cleveland	78
Maxwell Lewis, L.A. Lakers	335
Kira Lewis Jr., New Orleans	318
E.J. Liddell, New Orleans	320
Damian Lillard, Portland	513
Nassir Little, Portland	519
Dereck Lively II, Dallas	351
Isaiah Livers, Detroit	266
Chris Livingston, Milwaukee	55
Kenneth Lofton Jr., Memphis	287
Kevon Looney, Golden State	296
Brook Lopez, Milwaukee	44
Robin Lopez, Milwaukee	50
Kevin Love, Miami	111
Kyle Lowry, Miami	108
Trey Lyles, Sacramento	413
Sandro Mamukelashvili, San Antonio	507
Terance Mann, L.A. Clippers	361
Tre Mann, Oklahoma City	450
Lauri Markkanen, Utah	461
Naji Marshall, New Orleans	315
Caleb Martin, Miami	109
Cody Martin, Charlotte	245
Kenyon Martin Jr., L.A. Clippers	365
Garrison Mathews, Atlanta	132
Bennedict Mathurin, Indiana	227
Wesley Matthews, Atlanta	130
Tyrese Maxey, Philadelphia	60
Miles McBride, New York	99
C.J. McCollum, New Orleans	308
T.J. McConnell, Indiana	232
Jaden McDaniels, Minnesota	377
Jalen McDaniels, Toronto	145

Doug McDermott, San Antonio	500
JaVale McGee, Dallas	349
Bryce McGowens, Charlotte	247
Jordan McLaughlin, Minnesota	383
De'Anthony Melton, Philadelphia	63
Sam Merrill, Cleveland	86
Chimezie Metu, Phoenix	434
Vasilije Micic, Oklahoma City	458
Khris Middleton, Milwaukee	43
Brandon Miller, Charlotte	252
Leonard Miller, Minnesota	386
Patty Mills, Atlanta	129
Shake Milton, Minnesota	381
Josh Minott, Minnesota	385
Davion Mitchell, Sacramento	412
Donovan Mitchell, Cleveland	74
Evan Mobley, Cleveland	77
Malik Monk, Sacramento	411
Moses Moody, Golden State	301
Wendell Moore Jr., Minnesota	384
Ja Morant, Memphis	273
Marcus Morris, L.A. Clippers	359
Monte Morris, Detroit	261
Trey Murphy III, New Orleans	312
Dejounte Murray, Atlanta	121
Jamal Murray, Denver	390
Keegan Murray, Sacramento	410
Kris Murray, Portland	523
Mike Muscala, Washington	196
Larry Nance Jr., New Orleans	313
Andrew Nembhard, Indiana	226
Aaron Nesmith, Indiana	229
Georges Niang, Cleveland	81
Zeke Nnaji, Denver	397
Nerlens Noel, Sacramento	417
Frank Ntilikina, Charlotte	251
Jusuf Nurkic, Portland	516
Jordan Nwora, Indiana	233
Royce O'Neale, Brooklyn	158
Chuma Okeke, Orlando	215
Josh Okogie, Phoenix	428
Onyeka Okongwu, Atlanta	126
Isaac Okoro, Cleveland	80
Victor Oladipo, Oklahoma City	454
Kelly Olynyk, Utah	467
Cedi Osman, San Antonio	503
Kelly Oubre Jr., Unsigned	528
Chris Paul, Golden State	297
Cameron Payne, San Antonio	504
Gary Payton II, Golden State	298
Filip Petrusev, Philadelphia	71
Julian Phillips, Chicago	184
Jalen Pickett, Denver	402
Mason Plumlee, L.A. Clippers	360
Brandin Podziemski, Golden State	303
Jakob Poeltl, Toronto	140
Aleksej Pokusevski, Oklahoma City	447
Jordan Poole, Washington	188
Kevin Porter Jr., Houston	483
Michael Porter Jr., Denver	392
Otto Porter Jr., Toronto	146
Bobby Portis, Milwaukee	46
Kristaps Porzingis, Boston	28
Dwight Powell, Dallas	342
Norman Powell, L.A. Clippers	362
Jason Preston, L.A. Clippers	369

Taurean Prince, L.A. Lakers	331
Payton Pritchard, Boston	35
Olivier-Maxence Prosper, Dallas	352
Neemias Queta, Sacramento	418
Immanuel Quickley, New York	94
Julius Randle, New York	89
Austin Reaves, L.A. Lakers	325
Cam Reddish, L.A. Lakers	332
Paul Reed, Philadelphia	65
Naz Reid, Minnesota	379
Nick Richards, Charlotte	244
Josh Richardson, Miami	112
Duncan Robinson, Miami	110
Mitchell Robinson, New York	92
Orlando Robinson, Miami	115
Jeremiah Robinson-Earl, Oklahoma City	449
Isaiah Roby, New York	101
David Roddy, Memphis	285
Ryan Rollins, Washington	200
Derrick Rose, Memphis	283
Terry Rozier, Charlotte	241
Ricky Rubio, Cleveland	83
Rayan Rupert, Portland	524
D'Angelo Russell, L.A. Lakers	326
Domantas Sabonis, Sacramento	406
Luka Samanic, Utah	472
Dario Saric, Golden State	299
Marcus Sasser, Detroit	269
Dennis Schroder, Toronto	141
Alperen Sengun, Houston	479
Brice Sensabaugh, Utah	475
Collin Sexton, Utah	466
Landry Shamet, Washington	193
Day'Ron Sharpe, Brooklyn	164
Shaedon Sharpe, Portland	518
Ben Sheppard, Indiana	236
Pascal Siakam, Toronto	137
Ben Simmons, Brooklyn	159
Kobi Simmons, Charlotte	250
Anfernee Simons, Portland	515
Jericho Sims, New York	98
Marcus Smart, Memphis	276
Jalen Smith, Indiana	230
Dennis Smith Jr., Brooklyn	162
Jabari Smith Jr., Houston	481
Nick Smith Jr., Charlotte	253
Jeremy Sochan, San Antonio	494
Jaden Springer, Philadelphia	70
Isaiah Stewart, Detroit	258
Julian Strawther, Denver	401
Max Strus, Cleveland	79
Jalen Suggs, Orlando	211
Jae'Sean Tate, Houston	487
Jayson Tatum, Boston	26
Terry Taylor, Chicago	182
Dalen Terry, Chicago	180
Daniel Theis, Indiana	234
Cam Thomas, Brooklyn	161
Amen Thompson, Houston	489
Ausar Thompson, Detroit	268
Klay Thompson, Golden State	293
J.T. Thor, Charlotte	246
Matisse Thybulle, Portland	517
Xavier Tillman Sr., Memphis	279
Isaiah Todd, Memphis	289
Obi Toppin, Indiana	228

Karl-Anthony Towns, Minnesota	375
Gary Trent Jr., Toronto	142
P.J. Tucker, Philadelphia	62
Myles Turner, Indiana	223
Hunter Tyson, Denver	403
Jonas Valanciunas, New Orleans	310
Jarred Vanderbilt, L.A. Lakers	327
Fred VanVleet, Houston	478
Devin Vassell, San Antonio	497
Sasha Vezenkov, Sacramento	420
Gabe Vincent, L.A. Lakers	329
Nikola Vucevic, Chicago	172
Dean Wade, Cleveland	822
Franz Wagner, Orlando	206
Moritz Wagner, Orlando	212
Ish Wainright, Phoenix	436
Jabari Walker, Portland	520
Jarace Walker, Indiana	235
Lonnie Walker IV, Brooklyn	160
Cason Wallace, Oklahoma City	457
Jordan Walsh, Boston	38
P.J. Washington, Unsigned	526
Yuta Watanabe, Phoenix	431
Trendon Watford, Brooklyn	165
Peyton Watson, Denver	399
Victor Wembanyama, San Antonio	509
Blake Wesley, San Antonio	505
Russell Westbrook, L.A. Clippers	357
Coby White, Chicago	176
Derrick White, Boston	29
Jack White, Oklahoma City	455
Dariq Whitehead, Brooklyn	167
Cam Whitmore, Houston	490
Aaron Wiggins, Oklahoma City	446
Andrew Wiggins Golden State	294
Grant Williams, Dallas	341
Jalen Williams, Oklahoma City	442
Jaylin Williams, Oklahoma City	448
Kenrich Williams, Oklahoma City	445
Mark Williams, Charlotte	243
Patrick Williams, Chicago	173
Robert Williams, Boston	32
Ziaire Williams, Memphis	284
Zion Williamson, New Orleans	309
James Wiseman, Detroit	265
Christian Wood, Unsigned	527
Delon Wright, Washington	195
Thaddeus Young, Toronto	147
Trae Young, Atlanta	120
Omer Yurtseven, Utah	470
Cody Zeller, New Orleans	317
Ivica Zubac, L.A. Clippers	358

Made in United States
North Haven, CT
28 August 2023